Time Out

Prague

timeout.com/prague

Published by Time Out Guides Ltd, a wholly owned subsidiary of Time Out Group Ltd.
Time Out and the Time Out logo are trademarks of Time Out Group Ltd.

Previous editions 1995, 1997, 1998, 2000, 2002

10 9 8 7 6 5 4 3 2 1

This edition first published in Great Britain in 2004 by Ebury
Ebury is a division of The Random House Group Ltd,
20 Vauxhall Bridge Road, London SW1V 2SA

Random House Australia Pty Limited, 20 Alfred Street, Milsons Point, Sydney, New South Wales 2061, Australia
Random House New Zealand Limited, 18 Poland Road, Glenfield, Auckland 10, New Zealand
Random House South Africa (Pty) Limited, Endulini, 5A Jubilee Road, Parktown 2193, South Africa

Random House UK Limited Reg. No. 954009

Distributed in USA by Publishers Group West
1700 Fourth Street, Berkeley, California 94710

Distributed in Canada by Penguin Canada Ltd
10 Alcorn Avenue, Toronto, Ontario, Canada M4V 3B2

For further distribution details, see www.timeout.com

ISBN 1-904978-13-4

A CIP catalogue record for this book is available from the British Library

Colour reprographics by Icon, Crowne House, 56-58 Southwark Street, London SE1 1UN

Printed and bound by Cayfosa-Quebecor, Ctra. De Caldes, KM 3 08 130 Sta, Perpètua de Mogoda, Barcelona, Spain

Edited and designed by
Time Out Guides Limited
Universal House
251 Tottenham Court Road
London W1T 7AB
Tel + 44 (0)20 7813 3000
Fax + 44 (0)20 7813 6001
Email guides@timeout.com
www.timeout.com

Editorial
Editor Will Tizard
Deputy Editor Jessica Eveleigh
Listings Editors Jana Mlcochová, Radka Slabá, Nina Valvodová
Proofreader Terri McCargar
Indexer Jonathan Cox

Editorial/Managing Director Peter Fiennes
Series Editor Ruth Jarvis
Deputy Series Editor Lesley McCave
Guides Co-ordinator Anna Norman
Accountant Sarah Bostock

Design
Art Director Mandy Martin
Acting Art Director Scott Moore
Acting Art Editor Tracey Ridgewell
Acting Senior Designer Astrid Kogler
Designer Sam Lands
Junior Designer Oliver Knight
Digital Imaging Dan Conway
Ad Make-up Charlotte Blythe

Picture Desk
Picture Editor Jael Marschner
Deputy Picture Editor Kit Burnet
Picture Researcher Ivy Lahon, Kate Duncan

Advertising
Sales Director Mark Phillips
International Sales Manager Ross Canadé
International Sales Executive James Tuson
Advertising Sales (Prague) ARBOMedia.net Praha
Advertising Assistant Lucy Butler

Marketing
Marketing Manager Mandy Martinez
US Publicity & Marketing Associate Rosella Albanese

Production
Guides Production Director Mark Lamond
Production Controller Samantha Furniss

Time Out Group
Chairman Tony Elliott
Managing Director Mike Hardwick
Group Financial Director Richard Waterlow
Group Commercial Director Lesley Gill
Group Marketing Director Christine Cort
Group General Manager Nichola Coulthard
Group Art Director John Oakey
Online Managing Director David Pepper
Group Production Director Steve Proctor
Group IT Director Simon Chappell

Contributors
Introduction Will Tizard. **History** Jonathan Cox, Paul Lewis (*Great indulgers, The rudeness thing* Will Tizard). **Prague Today** Scott MacMillan. **Architecture** Barbara Frye, Andy Markowitz (*Outside the box* Andy Markowitz). **Literary Prague** Will Tizard. **Bad Bohemia** Will Tizard. **Where to Stay** Theodore Schwinke, Mark Nessmith, Dinah Spritzer. **Sightseeing** Carole Cadwalladr, Jonathan Cox, Frank Kuznik, Will Tizard, Emma Young (*You can ring my bell* Jana Mlcochová). **Museums** Mark Nessmith, Mimi Rogers. **Restaurants** Will Tizard. **Cafés, Pubs & Bars** Will Tizard (*All smashed up* Pavla Kozáková). **Shops & Services** Jennifer Sokolowsky, Theodore Schwinke (*Bad Bohemia: Salon Joshua, Bad Bohemia: Faux pas* Jennifer Sokolowsky; *Meat market* Theodore Schwinke). **Festivals & Events** Will Tizard. **Children** Mark Nessmith, Alena Živnůstková. **Film** Raymond Johnston. **Galleries** Mimi Rogers. **Gay & Lesbian** Wendy Wrangham. **Music: Classical & Opera** Frank Kuznik. **Music: Rock, Roots & Jazz** Will Tizard. **Nightlife** Will Tizard. **Sport & Fitness** Sam Beckwith. **Theatre & Dance** Lizzie Lequesne. **Trips Out of Town** Jonathan Cox, Pavla Kozáková, Will Tizard (*Ready for Moravavíno, Jacques?* Jana Mlcochová). **Directory** Mark Baker, Jana Mlcochová, Dave Rimmer, Will Tizard (*Girls' war* Emma Young).

Maps by JS Graphics (john@jsgraphics.co.uk).

Photography Rene Jakl, except: pages 6, 14 Corbis; pages 7, 8 AKG; page 11 Hulton Archive; page 192 Czech TV; page 232 Jifii Volek 2003; page 203 Alexander Hackenscmied/Courtesy Joseph Sudek Studio; page 217 Havelka & His Melody Makers; pages 237, 238 Švandovo Divadlo; pages 247, 262 Alamy Pictures; page 258 Czech Tourism; pages 222, 261 Julie Denesha. The following images were provided by the featured establishments/artist: pages 29, 31, 107, 167, 177, 198, 210, 214, 219, 220, 227, 239, 242, 249, 253, 275.

The Editor would like to thank Krzyszstof Dabrowski; Adam Havlín and the adept members of the Blue Moon Quartet; Hotel Josef for accommodation assistance; Luboš Košťak; Scott MacMillan; Sasha Štěpan; Julie, Barbara and Bill Tizard; the Statní Opera; Stillking Productions; and especially Martina Lišková. Transport graciously provided by Hertz Czech Republic.

Contents

Introduction

In early 2004 the Czech Tourist Authority launched a major television campaign featuring chest-swelling classical music and aerial shots of its finest castles caught in splendid morning light. After cataloguing all the stresses that are part of daily life in the West – traffic jams, rising prices, tough competition in the marketplace – a velvet-smooth voice pauses before revealing what's different about the Czech Republic from all that: 'Come to slow down?' he says finally.

The mixed message of the slogan, aired just weeks before Czechs became full members of the European Union, is interesting. As people who are still new to the free-market democracy – with all its demands for efficiency, customer service, reliability, transparency and a modernised legal system – Czechs are indeed pegged well by a phrase that suggests a more laissez-faire, idyllic approach to life.

But could it also be seen as a disclaimer? We're ready for luxury goods and tourist cash, Praguers might be saying, and are even developing a taste for haute cuisine and high fashion. But don't expect us to jump to our feet and smile the minute you walk into a shop, sir.

Another tagline circulating at the same time is equally insightful. Banks in Prague, disappointed at the low level of household debt, are actively encouraging Czechs to borrow and spend like there's no tomorrow. One such lending institution was displaying huge posters of luscious-looking snails in garlic butter, the words 'No more fast food' floating in the foreground.

Czechs, of course, have had to swallow a lot of slogans over the years. A small country, ever on the edge of great powers, it's been a province of one superpower or another for half a millennium – each with their own sophisticated propaganda departments.

And most of them were drawn by the same things that are likely to capture the visitor's heart today: affordability, a surfeit of desirable goods, stunning architecture, geographic convenience... and something else, which is difficult to define. Call it a mysterious, borderline sinister quality, as Kafka had it. Or a decadent, sexy feel. Or Praguer citizens' love for the good times, music, theatre and beer.

Put another way, Czechs are used to seeing great forces and civilizations pass through without getting that bothered about it.

Take a walk down Dlouhá in Staré Mêsto and you'll discover a street with everything that the Velvet Revolution promised in 1989: nightclubs, smart cafês, full shops. But it also features businesses that were here two centuries ago, with their signs marked *zlatnictvi*, *zelezarstvi* and *obuv*. Come what may, Prague still need its goldsmith, ironmonger and cobbler.

If that means you may not get your order in 15 minutes, well, it doesn't seem to be costing Prague many devotees. In fact, there's something bittersweet about seeing the speed at which Czech westernise, as author Karel Čapek once noted while observing a group of very slow local bricklayers.

ABOUT THE TIME OUT CITY GUIDES

Time Out Prague is one of an expanding series of Time Out City Guides, now numbering more than 45, produced by the people behind London and New York's successful listings magazines. Our guides are all written and updated by resident experts who have striven to provide you with all the most up-to-date information you'll need to explore the city or read up on its background, whether you're a local or a first-time visitor. The guide contains detailed practical information, plus features that focus on unique aspects of the city.

THE LOWDOWN ON THE LISTINGS

Above all, we have tried to make this book as useful as possible. Addresses, telephone numbers, websites, transport information, opening times, admission prices and credit card details are included in our listings. And, as far as possible, we've given details of facilities, services and events, all checked and correct at the time we went to press. However, owners and managers can change their arrangements at any time. Many small shops and businesses do not keep precise opening hours and may close earlier or later than stated here. Although arts and entertainment listings are generally reliable in Prague, we would similarly advise you whenever possible to phone ahead and check opening times, ticket prices and other particulars. While every effort has been made to ensure the accuracy of this guide, the publishers cannot accept responsibility for any errors that it may contain.

PRICES AND PAYMENT

While the Czech Republic is a new member of the European Union, there were no plans to join the euro at press time. However, some hotels do accept payment in euros. The prices given in this guide should be treated as guidelines, not gospel. If they vary wildly from those we've quoted, please write and let us know. We aim to give the best and most up-to-date advice, so we always want to know when you've been badly treated or overcharged.

We have listed prices in *koruna česká* or Czech crown (Kč) throughout, and we have noted whether venues take credit cards, but have only listed the major cards – American Express (**AmEx**), Diners Club (**DC**), MasterCard (**MC**), Visa (**V**). Many businesses will also accept other cards, including **JCB**. Some shops, restaurants and attractions take travellers' cheques.

THE LIE OF THE LAND

We have divided the city into areas and the relevant area name is given with each venue listed in this guide. Wherever possible, a map reference is provided for venues, indicating the page and grid reference for where it can be found in the street maps at the back of the book.

TELEPHONE NUMBERS

To dial Prague from outside the Czech Republic, first dial the international code, then 420 (for the Czech Republic and Prague) and finally the local number (always nine digits in Prague). To dial a mobile phone number from outside the Czech Republic, just call the international code, then 420, then the mobile number. For more information on telephones and codes, *see p289*.

ESSENTIAL INFORMATION

For all the practical information you might need for visiting Prague, including emergency phone numbers and details of local transport, turn to the **Directory** chapter at the back of the guide. It starts on page 269.

LANGUAGE

Most Czechs living in Prague speak at least a little English, and while street signs are in Czech, most tourist information and menus are available in English. The majority of places are referred to by their Czech names but we have also included the English name where useful.

Advertisers

We would like to stress that no establishment has been included in this guide because it has advertised in any of our publications and no payment of any kind has influenced any review. The opinions given in this book are those of *Time Out* writers and entirely independent.

MAPS

At the back of this guide (and within the **Sightseeing** chapter) you'll find a series of maps providing overviews of the greater Prague area and its neighbourhoods, along with detailed street maps of Hradčany, Malá Strana and other districts, including Staré Mêsto, the Old Town. There's also a comprehensive street index, a map of the region for planning trips out of town and a map of the Metro.

LET US KNOW WHAT YOU THINK

We hope you enjoy *Time Out Prague*, and we'd like to know what you think of it. We welcome tips for places that you consider we should include in future editions and take note of your criticism of our choices. You can email your comments to us at guides@timeout.com.

There is an online version of this guide, and guides to over 45 international cities, at **www.timeout.com**.

In Context

Features

Crowds on Wenceslas Square. *See p15.*

History

Situated on the fringe of great powers, Prague has had to learn to lie low during its bloody past.

In around 400 BC a Celtic tribe called the Boii occupied the region where the Czech Republic now lies and gave it the name Bohemia. The Boii successfully repelled attacking armies for the best part of 1,000 years, but they were eventually driven out by the Germanic Marcomanni and the Quadi tribes who, in turn, were wiped out by Attila the Hun in AD 451. Slavic tribes moved into the area sometime during the seventh century, ruled over by the Avars whose harsh regime provoked a successful Slavic rebellion.

PŘEMYSLID ROOTS

Czechs had to wait until the eighth century and the founding of the Přemyslid dynasty for real independence. One of the dynasty's origin myths relates that, in the absence of a male heir, Čech tribe leader Krok was succeeded by his soothsaying daughter Libuše. When the indignant men of the tribe told her to find a husband, she went into a trance and sent her white horse over the hills to find a ploughman with two spotted oxen. His name was Přemysl.

Prague's own origin myth holds that, standing atop Vyšehrad, Libuše foretold the birth of 'a city whose splendour will reach to the stars'. This time a craftsman making a door sill (*práh*), was found, for, as Libuše said, 'mighty Lords bend before a low door'. His workshop was promptly declared the site of the Praha.

In the ninth century Charlemagne briefly occupied the region, a Slavic state was created in Moravia and in AD 860 he appealed to the Pope for Slavic-speaking Christian apostles to help end the worship of sun gods. The Byzantine emperor sent Greek monks Cyril and Methodius (designers of the Cyrillic alphabet), but the Slavonic liturgy they established was made illegal after Methodius's death in AD 885.

Slav leader Svatopluk (AD 871-94) sided with the Germans and seized power, building an empire that encompassed Moravia, Bohemia and Slovakia. After his death the Magyars took a piece of Slovakia and held on to it until the early 20th century, disrupting all attempts to unite Slovaks and Czechs.

EARLY SKIRMISHES

Over the next four centuries Bohemia rode a roller coaster from chaos to political supremacy in central Europe. Although there are Christmas carols that still sing his praises, many Czech nobles felt that 'Good King' Wenceslas (actually Prince Václav or Wenceslas, AD 921-29) sold out to the Germans. They backed Wenceslas's brother, Boleslav the Cruel (AD 935-67), who had Wenceslas murdered in AD 929 in present-day town of Olomouc. Prague was made a bishopric in 973, thus completing the Christianisation of Bohemia, but internal bickering soon broke down order.

National prestige reached new heights with Přemysl Otakar II (1253-78) grabbing Cheb from the Germans and briefly controlling an empire that stretched from Florence to Poland. An invasion by Holy Roman Emperor Rudolf of Habsburg in 1276 soon supplanted the Přemysls when the last one, Václav III, was assassinated in 1306.

German emigration to the Czech lands flourished, and the new arrivals assumed great influence over the Church and the trades, dividing Prague into three autonomous areas: Malá Strana, Hradčany and Staré Město (Old Town). Malá Strana's Jewish community was forced into a ghetto in Staré Město.

By the 14th century, Czech and German nobles were in conflict, as they would be from that time on. In 1310 John of Luxembourg, the 14-year-old son of the Holy Roman Emperor, was elected King of Bohemia, but his contribution was limited to attempting to re-create the Knights of the Round Table by inviting all the great knights of Europe to the city. Unfortunately, none turned up, though Prague did gain a town hall, became the dominant centre of Bohemia and scored an archbishopric in 1344.

THE SALAD DAYS

After John died in a kamikaze charge against Welsh archers at the Battle of Crécy, his son Charles IV was elected Holy Roman Emperor in 1346, which made his position as king of Bohemia unassailable. With that force behind him, Charles (1346-78) launched a golden age and Prague even managed to escaped the Black Death in 1348. Laying claim to Přemyslid lineage through his mother, the 'Father of his Country' brought the 23-year-old Swabian architect Peter Parler to Prague to build the Charles Bridge and to work on St Vitus's Cathedral. In 1348 he established Central Europe's first university, then founded the Nové Město (New Town) along modern grid principles, unlike the warren of workshops that was Staré Město.

Charles declared the union of Bohemia, Moravia, Silesia and Upper Lusatia indissoluble and grafted bits of Germany on to Bohemia. As a devout Christian, he refused to accept papal dictates north of the Alps and stood against Church corruption but granted clergy half the land.

NOT-SO-GOOD KING WENCESLAS

His incorrigible son, Wenceslas IV (1378-1419), was at least champion of the common man. He would go out shopping dressed in commoners' clothing and execute any swindlers; soon Prague was crime-free.

He also railed against the Church, however, and at his christening he was alleged to have urinated into the holy water. He is said to have spent his last years in a drunken stupor and barely escaped imprisonment by the nobles.

In 1403 the rector of Prague University, Jan Hus, took up the campaign against Church corruption. Germans academics left for Leipzig to found their own university and the Church deemed Hus's arguments heretical.

In November 1414 Hus was summoned by Wenceslas's brother, Sigismund, King of Hungary, to appear before the General Council at Constance. Hus went in good faith but on arrival was arrested and ordered to recant. He refused and on his 46th birthday was burnt at the stake.

Up in flames: **Jan Hus** is burnt at the stake.

Royal reveller **Rudolf II.**

Hus became a martyr to two vital Czech hopes: reform of the Church and independence from German dominance. His motto 'truth will prevail', still chanted during the Velvet Revolution of 1989, became a rallying cry for his followers. And the chalice became a symbol of participation in the Sacrament.

HUSSITES GIVE 'EM HELL

An angry mob of several hundred Czech nobles stormed the Nové Město town hall on 30 July 1419 and threw the mayor and his councillors through the window to their deaths, minting the quintessentially Czech form of protest, defenestration.

When Wenceslas died in an apoplectic fit a few days later, Hussite mobs marked the occasion by rioting and sacking the monasteries. Sigismund elbowed his way on to the Bohemian throne, but radical preachers such as Jan Želivský furiously denounced him and Rome. The Pope called for a holy crusade against Bohemia, and radical Hussites burnt alive nine monks in Prague. Rome's call to arms against the heretic nation was taken up all over Europe and the Czechs were soon surrounded. They were united, however, behind a powerful moral cause and their brilliant one-eyed general, Jan Žižka. He not only repelled the enemies from Vítkov hill in what is now Žižkov in Prague, but, by 1432, he and his Warriors of God were pillaging all the way up to the Baltic coast. Women fought and died alongside men.

Most Hussites, known as Praguers, were moderate and middle class and their leaders were based at Prague University. The more extreme group, known as Táborites, were based on a fortified hillside. They banned all class divisions, shared their property and held religious services only in Czech.

Unable to win a holy war, the Pope invited the Czechs to discuss a peace settlement, but that proved unnecessary when, in 1434, the Praguers marched their army down to wipe out 13,000 Táborites at the Battle of Lipany.

THE FIRST BOHEMIAN KING

During the Hussite wars, the Church's power was devastated and the vacuum filled by the nobles, who seized church property and ruled mercilessly over the peasants. The new Czech king, George of Poděbrady (Jiří z Poděbrad), tried to restore order by choosing successors from the Polish Jagellon dynasty. But after George's death in 1471, Vladislav II, then Ludvík, ruled ineffectually in absentia. After Ludvík's death, the Estates of Bohemia elected the Habsburg Duke Ferdinand I king of Bohemia. This foreign Catholic monarch sent troops into Prague to suppress Protestant dissidents, while inviting the Jesuit Order to Bohemia to spearhead the Counter-Reformation.

'Rudolfine Prague was a dazzling confluence of art, science and mysticism, host to scores of brilliant or mad creatives.'

EMPEROR RUDOLF'S PARTY PALACE

In 1583 the Habsburg Rudolf II (1576-1611) moved his court from Vienna to Prague and, for the first time in 200 years, the city became the centre of an empire. But the Empire badly needed a man of action, vision and direction to deal with Turkish invaders raging to the south and the demands of Bohemia's Protestants. What it got was a dour, eccentric monarch engrossed in alchemy, who tended to ignore everyone except Otakar, his pet lion. While Europe headed towards the Thirty Years' War, Prague became a surreal fantasy world.

Yet Rudolfine Prague was a dazzling confluence of art, science and mysticism, host to scores of brilliant or mad creatives. As word of Rudolf's sponsorships spread, the flood began. One recipient was Tycho Brahe, the Danish astronomer who first shattered Aristotle's theories, had a metal nose and died of an intestinal implosion after overeating. As Turkish armies thrust northwards, however, and an attack on Vienna loomed, a coterie of archdukes concluded that Rudolf had to go. His brother Matthias picked up the reins.

LOOK OUT BELOW

Neither Matthias nor his successor, Ferdinand II, both strong Counter-Reformation Catholics, did much to win over Protestants. In Prague, on 23 May 1618, an assembly of Protestants marched to the Old Royal Palace at Prague Castle. They were met by the emperor's die-hard Roman Catholic councillors, Slavata and Martinic, who were then thrown out the window but landed in a dung heap and survived.

Prague's most famous defenestration turned out to be the first violent act of the Thirty Years' War. Then Frederick of the Palatinate, son-in-law of James I of England and Scotland, was elected to the Bohemian throne and failed spectacularly to rally the Protestant princes of Europe to defend Bohemia. On 8 November 1620 the Protestants were trounced at the Battle of White Mountain (Bílá Hora) on the outskirts of Prague.

On the first anniversary of the defenestration, 27 Protestant leaders were beheaded on Old Town Square, their heads then skewered on the towers of Charles Bridge.

Ferdinand maintained that it was 'better to have no population than a population of heretics'. Soon Bohemia lost three-quarters of its native nobility, along with its eminent scholars and any remaining vestige of national independence. War further reduced its population from three million to 900,000. Three-quarters of the land in Bohemia was seized to pay war expenses. All Protestants who refused to abandon their faith were driven from the country and the depopulated towns and villages filled with German immigrants. Jesuits swarmed in to 're-educate', and the peasants were forced to stay and work the land.

General Wallenstein (or Valdštejn), a Bohemian-born convert from Protestantism, became leader of the Imperial Catholic armies of Europe and scored spectacular victories, but the emperor's Jesuit advisors conspired to have him dismissed. Wallenstein, whose palace still covers much of Malá Strana and who had been secretly negotiating with the Swedish enemy, then joined the Protestants.

After he entered Bohemia in 1634 Czech hopes for a Wallenstein victory were dashed when a band of Irish mercenaries jumped him in Cheb, stabbed him and dragged him down the stairs to his death. The Thirty Years' War petered out on Charles Bridge in 1648, as Swedish Protestants scuffled with newly Catholicised students and Jews.

OPPRESSIVELY BAROQUE

By the mid 17th century, German had replaced Czech as the official language of government. The lifeline of Czech heritage now rested entirely with the enslaved and illiterate peasantry. Meanwhile the oppression resulted in the construction of Prague's most stunning baroque palaces and churches.

During the 18th century, Empress Maria Theresa centralised Bohemia with a new wave of Germanisation in schools and government. Maria Theresa's successor, the enlightened despot Joseph II, had little patience with the Church, though, and kicked out the Jesuits. He nationalised the education system, freed Jews from the ghetto and expanded the Empire's bureaucracy. As the industrial revolution began, this was all good news for the Czechs.

Though the Czech language had gone underground, a revival gradually took root. By the end of the 18th century, suppressed works were published, notably Balbín's *Defence of the Czech Language*; the Bohemian Diet began to whisper in Czech; the Church, seeing rows of empty pews, started to preach in Czech; and Emperor Leopold II even established a chair in Czech Language at Prague University.

The cultural revival continued under Ferdinand V (1835-48), with Josef Dobrovský's *Detailed Textbook of the Czech Language* and František Palacký's *History of the Czech Nation*, while Prague's theatres staged patriotic dramas.

1848: AN EMPIRE SHAKEN

Finally, the Czechs demanded equal rights for their language in government and schools. As the 1848 revolutions swept through Europe, the shaken Emperor Ferdinand V tossed promises in Prague's direction.

But Prince Windischgrätz fired on a peaceful gathering in Wenceslas Square, provoking a riot to give himself an excuse for wholesale suppression. The new emperor, Franz Josef (1848-1916), came to the throne on 2 December 1848 on a tidal wave of terror, then declared all Habsburg territories one entity.

A group known as the Young Czechs attacked the more moderate Prague establishment for pursuing a 'policy of crumbs'. Adopting Jan Hus as their hero and supported by Realist Party leader Professor Tomáš Garrigue Masaryk, they swept the 1891 elections to the Diet.

Czechs finally began to forge the political, social and economic infrastructure of a nation. Rapid industrialisation transformed the region, and an efficient rail network linked the Czech lands to the European economy. Industrialisation gave rise to working-class political movements and Czech arts flourished. The era produced composers Smetana, Dvořák and Janáček, and painters such as Mucha. The Czech Academy of Sciences and Arts also achieved renown.

'An underground society known as the "Mafia" waged a campaign of agitation against the imperial regime.'

WORLD WAR I

The Czechs assumed during World War I that they could win concessions on a federal constitution in return for support for the war. The Empire didn't agree, and the Czechs soon realised that their hopes lay in the downfall of the Empire itself. Czechs deserted to the other side and in Prague an underground society, which was known as the 'Mafia' waged, a campaign of agitation against the imperial regime.

Masaryk and Edvard Beneš drummed up Allied support for an independent state. Europe's elite hardly signed up to that, but the United States took the lead, and granted de jure recognition to a provisional Czechoslovak government under Masaryk.

On 28 October 1918 a National Committee member, Antonín Švehla, marched into the Corn Institute and announced that the Committee was going to take over food production. Later that day the Habsburg government sent a note to the American President Woodrow Wilson acquiescing to Czechoslovak independence.

INDEPENDENCE AND ETHNIC TENSIONS

With little damage from the war, developed industry, coal and iron, an efficient communications infrastructure and a well-trained and educated workforce, the new Republic of Czechoslovakia bloomed into a liberal democracy.

Great indulgers

Bohemia is synonymous with indulgence. Wenceslas IV, son of the great Charles IV, was not, alas, destined to lead a Golden Age like his father. A serious boozer, it's said that he may have only remained free from prison in the early 1400s because the League of Lords failed to catch him at a bathhouse, where he was recovering from a mighty hangover. Wily Wenceslas instead persuaded a beautiful female attendant to rescue him.

Emperor Rudolf II, the only Habsburg to move his court to Prague, had partying in mind. Orgies, fooling around with chemicals, art, wine and song all flowed with abandon through Prague Castle during his rule, even as the invading Turks were encircling Vienna.

One of his pet projects, the Danish astronomer Tycho Brahe, set the standard of the day – eating, drinking and making merry to such an extent that his stomach finally imploded. Admittedly, the metal-nosed Brahe was particularly prone to medical oddities. He owed his lost nose solely to indulging in pride. It was apparently lopped off by a superior swordsman in a duel. Rudolf's modern sucessors have kept up the tradition and done him proud.

Prime minister Miloš Zeman was known throughout the nation as a major 'fan' of the West Bohemian herbal liqueur known as *Becherovka*. And, although staff openly worried this may have been behind some of his remarkable diplomatic gaffes (comparing Israeli security forces to Nazis on a state visit? ouch), his appetite for booze was seen as essentially patriotic.

Even the stolid (to say the least) Klement Gottwald, known in Czech history as the First Working Class President, ended up hosting bacchanalias in the end. It's unclear how big a partier he was during his lifetime, but after being entombed in the memorial atop the hill known as Vítkov, his final resting place became the sight of much boozing and whoring. Senior party officials used to wryly say to one another: 'Let's go up to Gottwald's place.' Then they'd head for the crypt, bottles and girls in tow.

Václav Havel, himself, though considered a bit ostentatious in his own country, can nevertheless hold his own with any beer drinker. He invariably took foreign heads of state for a beer and was (secretly) a two cigarette packs a day kind of president.

The Nazis parade through the streets of Prague.

Slovaks, however, were largely an agricultural people long ruled by Hungarians rather than Habsburgs, and they looked upon the Catholic Church as a symbol of freedom.

The Jews, who comprised only 2.5 per cent of the population, formed a significant part of the intelligentsia, but spoke German, which created Czech resentment. The Germans, who formed 23 per cent of the population, presented the biggest obstacle to a united nation. Still powerful, though now resentful of being minorities, they were spread throughout the Czech lands but concentrated in Prague and the Sudeten area near the German border.

Konrad Henlein, head of the pro-Hitler Sudeten German Fatherland Front, cashed in on all these tensions. By 1935 the Sudeten Party was the second largest parliamentary bloc. In 1938 the Sudeten Nazis demanded union with Germany. British Prime Minister Neville Chamberlain, for whom the Sudeten crisis was a 'quarrel in a faraway country between people of whom we know nothing', went to Munich with the French premier to meet both Mussolini and Hitler. All of the parties involved (except Czechoslovakia, which wasn't invited) agreed that Germany should take the Sudetenland in exchange for Hitler's promise of peace.

With Poland and Hungary also eyeing its borders, Czechoslovakia found itself encircled, and abandoned by its allies. Six months later Hitler took the rest of the country, with Poland snatching Těšín and Hungary grabbing parts of southern Slovakia. On 14 March 1939, a day before Hitler rode into Prague, the Slovaks declared independence and established a Nazi puppet government.

DARKNESS DESCENDS

In Czechoslovakia, now the Reich Protectorate of Bohemia and Moravia, everybody except for Jews and Gypsies fared better under occupation than did people in most other European countries. A National Government of Czechs was set up to follow Reich orders. Hitler had often expressed his hatred of 'Hussite Bolshevism', but he needed Czech industrial resources and skilled manpower for his war machine.

Hitler made fierce examples of resisters; 1,200 students were sent to concentration camps for demonstrating, and all Czech universities were closed. Reinhard Heydrich, later to chair the infamous Wannsee Conference on the Final Solution, was appointed Reichsprotektor and began rounds of calculated terror, while enticing workers and peasants to collaborate.

Beneš fled to London where he joined Jan Masaryk (son of Tomáš) to form a provisional Czechoslovak government in exile. There they were joined by thousands of Czech soldiers and airmen, who fought alongside the British forces. Czech intelligence agents passed approximately 20,000 messages on to London, including the details of Germany's ambitious plans for the invasion of the Soviet Union.

Beneš, with the help of British Special Operations Executive, hatched a plan for the assassination of Heydrich using British-trained Czech parachutists. Jan Kubiš and Josef Gabčik were dropped into Bohemia and, on 27 May 1942, successfully ambushed Heydrich's open-top Mercedes, fatally injuring the hated Reichsprotektor.

'Men were murdered, women were sent to concentration camps and the children were "re-educated" or killed.'

The assassins and their accomplices were hunted down to the crypt of the Orthodox Cathedral of Sts Cyril and Methodius. Anyone with any connection to the paratroopers was murdered. The villages of Lidice and Ležáky were mistakenly picked out for aiding the assassins and razed to the ground; the men were murdered, the women were sent to concentration camps (in Ležáky they were shot) and the children were 're-educated', placed with German families or killed. The transportation of Jews to concentration camps was stepped up.

Occasional acts of sabotage continued, but the main resistance took place in the Slovak puppet state, where an uprising that began on 30 August 1944 lasted four months. The Czechs' act of defiance came in the last week of the war. In May 1945 5,000 died during a four-day uprising in Prague. The US forces that had just liberated Pilsen (Plzeň) to the west were only a few miles from Prague. But Allied leaders at Yalta had promised the Soviets the honour of liberating Prague, so General Eisenhower ordered his troops to pull back. General Patton was willing to ignore the order and sent a delegation to the leaders of the Prague uprising, asking for an official request for the American troops to liberate the capital. The communist leaders refused. Although communist power was not consolidated until 1948, the country already found itself inside the Soviet sphere of influence.

More than 300,000 Czechoslovaks perished in the war, the majority of them Jews. The Jewish population of Czechoslovakia was destroyed. Most Jews were rounded up and sent to the supposedly 'model' Theresienstadt (Terezín) ghetto. Many died there, but the remainder were transported to Auschwitz and other concentration camps. In fact, around 90 per cent of Prague's ancient Jewish community had been murdered.

For at least 1,000 years the community had been walled into a ghetto in Staré Město, where life was characterised by pogroms, poverty and mysticism. Between the late 18th century, when they left the ghetto, and the arrival of the Nazis, Jews had dominated much of Prague's cultural life. Now the rich literary culture that had produced Franz Kafka had been wiped out. Indeed, Kafka's family perished in Auschwitz. The only thing that saved some of Prague's synagogues and communal Jewish buildings from destruction was the Germans' morbid intention to use them after the war to house 'exotic exhibits of an extinct race'.

The Czech government under the Reich Protectorate actively supported the extermination of its Romany citizens and helped to run dozens of concentration camps for Gypsies all over Bohemia and Moravia. An estimated 90 per cent of the region's Czech Romany died in Nazi concentration camps, mostly in Germany and Poland. Beneš's faith in liberalism had been dented by the way the Western powers had ditched his country. He began to perceive the political future of Czechoslovakia as a bridge between capitalism and communism. His foreign minister Jan Masaryk, was less idealistic, stating that 'cows like to stop on a bridge and shit on it'.

Beneš needed a big power protector and believed that, if he could win Stalin's trust, he could handle the popular Communist Party of Czechoslovakia, while keeping the country independent and democratic. During the war he signed a friendship and mutual assistance treaty with the Soviet Union, and later on he established a coalition government comprising principally communists and socialists. In 1945 Stalin knew that a straightforward takeover of a formerly democratic state was not politically expedient. He needed Beneš as an acceptable front in order to buy time. For all his tightrope diplomacy, Beneš was effectively shuffling his country into Soviet clutches.

THE BIG PUTSCH

The Soviets and Czech communists were widely regarded as war heroes and won a handsome victory in the 1946 elections. Klement Gottwald became prime minister of a communist-led coalition. Beneš, still hoping that Stalinist communism could co-exist in a pluralistic democracy, remained president. The communists made political hay, setting up workers' militias in the factories, installing communist loyalists in the police force and infiltrating the army and rival socialist parties.

One of the first acts of the government, approved by the Allies, was to expel more than 2.5 million Germans from Bohemia. It was a popular move and, as Klement Gottwald remarked, 'an extremely sharp weapon with which we can reach to the very roots of the bourgeoisie'. Thousands were executed or given life sentences and many more were killed in a wave of self-righteous revenge.

In 1947 Czechoslovakia was forced to turn down the American economic aid promised by the Marshall Plan. Stalin knew that aid came with strings, and he was determined to be the only puppetmaster. In February 1948, with elections looming and communist popularity declining, Gottwald sent the workers' militias on to the streets of Prague. The police occupied crucial party headquarters and offices, and the country was incapacitated by a general strike. Beneš's diplomatic skill was no match for the brutal tactics of Moscow-trained revolutionaries. With the Czech army neutralised by communist infiltration and the Soviet army casting a long shadow over Prague, Beneš capitulated and consented to an all-communist government. Gottwald now became Czechoslovakia's first 'Working Class President'.

The rudeness thing

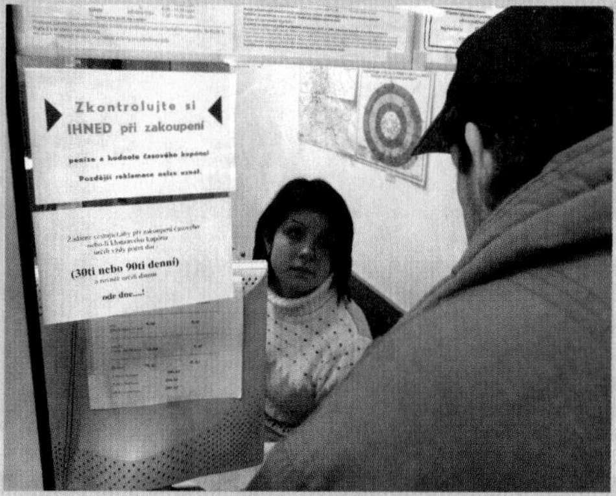

The Tourist Authority doesn't talk about it. It isn't in any of the guides to the Czech Republic and resident foreigners here just try to laugh about it. They don't always succeed. Czechs just get embarrassed about it.

The great taboo? Manners. But if, by some wild chance, while eating out in Prague, your waiter should bring you the wrong order, stone cold, after 45 minutes, and you point it out nicely, try not to be discomfited by the icy stare you're likely to receive. Instead, try to consider it as a historical hangover.

'Of course, sometimes we can recognise some types of ignorance or the inability to understand needs of the customer,' says Charles University historian Jiří Buriánek. 'Mostly it's a relic of the past.' Something about the half-millennium of foreign occupation seems to have affected Czech politeness towards foreigners.

Once the ice is broken, however, Czechs are famous for inviting near strangers into their houses, their liquor cabinets and even their beds.

But customers? Let's just say you had best watch your step. There are still small grocery shops all around Prague where bored-looking clerks suddenly take interest when customers walk in – so that they can follow them around the shop to be sure they're not stealing or messing up the displays. 'Hey,' points out Buriánek, 'it's better than in Eastern countries.'

Still, the historian acknowledges, there may be 'issues' with Czechs in the service sector: 'Most of this dark side of our behaviour towards customers is some kind of residue of the previous regime. In the period between the two wars there was a good tradition of communication and service to clients and customer service.'

Indeed – as in much of the West – Czech films of the 1930s show people exchanging courtesies with strangers that are practically unheard of today.

Resentment towards Westerners, who are perceived as having lived a privileged life, may be a factor too. Buriánek says: 'Among Slavic people, it's a special feature.' An old joke in many Slavic countries tells how one farmer at the gates of heaven is offered anything he likes, as long as his old neighbour back on earth gets it double. 'Pluck out one of my eyes,' says the farmer with glee.

Just a little something to bear in mind, should it come up. But, whatever you do, don't send your order back, says Jana, a student in Prague. The reason? 'They'll spit in it.'

People confront Warsaw Pact soldiers, protesting against the occupation of Prague Castle.

Shortly after the coup Jan Masaryk fell to his death from his office window. The communists said it was suicide. But, when his body was found, the window above was tightly fastened. The defenestration had a distinctly Czech flavour, but the purges that followed had the stamp of Moscow. They were directed against resistance fighters, Spanish Civil War volunteers, Jews (often survivors of concentration camps) and anyone in the party hierarchy who might have posed a threat to Moscow. The most infamous trial was that of Rudolf Slánský, a loyal sidekick of Gottwald who had orchestrated his fair share of purges. After being showered with honours, he was arrested just a few days later. In March 1951 Slánský and ten senior communists (mostly Jews) were found guilty of being Trotskyite, Titoist or Zionist traitors in the service of US imperialists. They 'confessed' under torture, and eight were sentenced to death.

PRAGUE SPRING

Gottwald dutifully followed his master, Stalin, to the grave in 1953 and the paranoia that had gripped Prague took a long time to ease. By the 1960s communist student leaders and approved writers on the fringes of the party hierarchy began tentatively to suggest that, just possibly, Gottwald and Stalin might have taken the wrong route to socialism. Slowly, the drizzle of criticism turned into a shower of anger and awkward questions. Then, on 5 January 1968, an alliance of disaffected Slovak communists and reformists within the party replaced Antonín Novotný in a political move with a reformist Slovak communist named Alexander Dubček.

For the next eight months the whole world watched the developments in Prague as Dubček rehabilitated political prisoners and virtually abandoned press censorship. Understandably, Moscow was alarmed and tried to intimidate Dubček by holding full-scale military manoeuvres in Czechoslovakia, but still the reforms continued. On 27 June 70 leading writers signed the widely published *Two Thousand Word Manifesto* supporting the reformist government. Suppressed literature was published or performed on stage and Prague was infused with the air of freedom. Dubček called it 'socialism with a human face'.

Soviet leader Leonid Brezhnev failed to influence the Czechoslovak leader. On the night of 20 August 1968 nearly half a million Warsaw Pact troops entered the country, took over Prague Castle and abducted Dubček and his closest supporters. The leaders fully expected to be shot, but Brezhnev needed some sort of a front for his policy of repression with a human face.

Meanwhile, on the streets of Prague, crowds of thousands of people confronted the tanks. Free radio stations using army transmitters continued to broadcast, and newspapers went underground and encouraged Czechs to refuse any assistance to the occupiers. Street signs and house numbers were removed, and the previously Stalinist workers' militia found a way to defend a clandestine meeting of the national party conference.

The resistance prevented nothing. Dubček stayed in power for eight more months and watched his collaborators being replaced by pro-Moscow ministers. In April 1969 Dubček too was removed in favour of Gustav Husák who was eager to push for more of Moscow's 'normalisation'. Husák purged the party and state machinery, the army and the police, the unions, the media, every company and every other organ of the country that might have a voice in the nation's affairs. Anyone who was not for Husák was assumed to be against him. Within a short time every aspect of daily Czechoslovak life was dictated by Husák's many mediocre yes-men. Without firing a shot, Husák was able to subdue the nation back into apathy by permitting an influx of consumer goods.

UP IN SMOKE

On 16 January 1969, a 21-year-old philosophy student called Jan Palach stood at the top of Wenceslas Square, poured a can of petrol over himself and set himself alight. He died four days later. A group of his friends had agreed to burn themselves to death one by one until the restrictions were lifted. On his deathbed Palach begged his friends not to go through with it, though some did.

Palach's death symbolised, with malicious irony, the extinguishing of the flame of hope. As Václav Havel wrote: 'People withdrew into themselves and stopped taking an interest in public affairs. An era of apathy and widespread demoralisation began, an era of grey, everyday totalitarian consumerism'.

Instead of mass arrests, tortures and show trials, the communists now bound up the nation in an endless tissue of lies and fabrications and psychologically bludgeoned all critical thought by rewarding people for not asking awkward questions and punishing them for refusing to spy on their neighbours. Punishment could mean spells in prison and severe beatings, but for most it meant losing a good job and being forced into menial work. During this time, Prague had an abnormally high percentage of window cleaners with PhDs.

There were some, however, who refused to be bowed. A diverse alternative culture emerged in which underground (*samizdat*) literature was circulated around a small group of dissidents. In December 1976 a group led by Václav Havel issued a statement demanding that leading Czechoslovak authorities should observe human rights obligations, and Charter 77 became a small voice of conscience inside the country, spawning a number of smaller groups trying to defend civil liberties. In 1989 it had 1,500 signatories. But there seemed hope for real change unless events from outside took a new turn. Then, in the mid 1980s, Mikhail Gorbachev came to power in the Soviet Union and initiated his policy of *perestroika*.

'In 1989 the Berlin Wall came down and the communist regimes began to falter.'

THE VELVET REVOLUTION

The Soviet leader came to Prague in 1988. When his spokesman was asked what he thought the difference was between the Prague Spring and *glasnost*, he replied '20 years'. In the autumn of 1989 the Berlin Wall came down and then the communist regimes of Eastern Europe began to falter. The Czechoslovak government, one of the most hardline regimes in Eastern Europe, seemed firmly entrenched until 17 November, when police violently broke up a demonstration on Národní třída commemorating the 50th anniversary of the closure of Czech universities by the Nazis. A rumour, picked up by Reuters news agency, said that a demonstrator had been killed. Another demonstration was called to protest against police brutality.

On 20 November, 200,000 people gathered in Prague to demand the resignation of the government. The police behaved with restraint and the demonstrations were broadcast on television. The government announced that the man who had allegedly been killed on the 17th was alive, but many were sceptical. Some months after the revolution it emerged that the KGB had probably been behind the rumour as part of a plan to replace the government with something in line with Soviet *glasnost*.

That there had not been a death made little difference ultimately. A committee of opposition groups formed itself into the Civic Forum (Občanské fórum), led by Václav Havel, who addressed the masses in Wenceslas Square. On 24 November 300,000 people assembled there to see him, joined by Dubček. The government had lost control of the media and millions watched the scenes on television. Students from Prague raced out to factories and farms to galvanise the workers into supporting a general strike on the 27th. Workers' militias had put the communists into power in 1948; it was crucial that they chose not to stand by communism in its final hour.

The acting communist Prime Minister Adamec also appealed to the crowds and further purges within the Communist Party followed. The party then declared that it felt that the 1968 Soviet invasion had been wrong after all, promising free elections and a multi-party coalition. It was all too late. A new government of reform communists was proposed, but rejected by Civic Forum. Negotiations continued between the communists and Civic Forum for weeks until 27 December, when a coalition of strongly reformist communists and a majority of non-communists – mainly from Civic Forum – took power with Havel as president. Not a single person died. Havel's co-revolutionary Rita Klímová called it the Velvet Revolution. But in some ways, given the KGB's involvement in the handover of power, it might as well have been called the Velvet Putsch.

THE WILD FREE-MARKET RIDE

For months after the revolution Prague floated in a dream world and the playwright-president captured the world's imagination, but the serious issues of economic transformation were put off. In the summer of 1992 the right of centre Civic Democratic Party (ODS), led by Václav Klaus, a no-nonsense free-marketeer, was voted into power. But, just as Klaus got down to the business of privatisation and decentralisation, calls for Slovak independence were taken up by Vladimír Mečiar's Slovak separatist HZDS party.

Slovaks had always resented what they had felt was a benign neglect by Prague, and Havel had never been popular among them. One of his first acts as president was to abandon the arms trade, dealing a big blow to the Slovak economy. Slovaks complained that economic reforms were going too fast. But Klaus would not compromise and had a mandate from Czech voters to press on. Mečiar upped his separatist threats until, with Machiavellian manoeuvring, Klaus called Mečiar's bluff and announced that he would back Slovak independence.

The two leaders divided up the assets of the state, and the countries peacefully parted ways on 1 January 1993 without so much as a referendum. Havel was elected president of the new Czech Republic, but Klaus had also outmanoeuvred him, forcing Havel into a predominantly ceremonial role.

Klaus indicated that he had little time for a policy of flushing out communists from responsible positions (known as 'lustration'). Thus communists successfully dodged the spotlight amid a blizzard of accusations and counter-accusations. A significant number of Czechs seemed to have skeletons in their cupboards, and it became nearly impossible to untangle the good from the bad. Dissidents watched helplessly, while communists remained in charge of the country's largest factories.

The first four years of the Czech Republic under Klaus's leadership produced massive economic changes, which helped make the Czechs the envy of the East and the pride of the West. Foreign investors and businesses quickly capitalised on the massive opportunities for profit and development. The Czech Republic moved to the head of the queue for accession into the European Union.

THE PARTY'S OVER

Economic differences between the haves and have-nots have increased drastically since 1992. Klaus's Pragocentric policies and the decision to prioritise macroeconomic issues backfired in the 1996 elections, when his ODS party barely managed to keep power. A year later, with the boom days of foreign investment clearly over and headlines alleging secret ODS campaign funding from interested parties, Klaus shocked the nation by stepping down. Miloš Zeman and his Czech Social Democratic Party gained the most votes, but not an absolute majority. Zeman agreed to become prime minister with Klaus and his party in charge of Parliament. This pact of opposites was called absurd by everyone, including Havel, who was alarmed by the proposal to limit the power of smaller parties.

Czech membership in NATO, announced in 1999, has been followed by the next step towards full European citizenship, membership in the European Union, formalised in early 2004. As if on cue, moral leader Havel has finally been replaced by none other than Klaus as president. Where once the hot issues were civic questions, now attention is focused on foreign investment, the streamlining of old socialist benefits and cleaning up endemic corruption. Meanwhile, pensioners, industrial workers, doctors, labourers and teachers have watched their incomes dwindle. Others, of course, have prospered tremendously since 1989: hundreds of bold, honest entrepreneurs, but also scores of sleazy developers, speculators, media barons and sex kings.

EU requirements for worker safety, transparency in government and consumer protection will surely end some of the fun of life in Bohemia – But, by and large, even if it is arguably another foreign influence, a higher bar for the marketplace and civic society are mostly acknowledged to be just in time.

Half a millennium of occupation does affect one's confidence, but Czechs of the 21st century is looking hardly less able to manage their own destiny than any European sovereign state.

Key events

c400 BC Celtic Boii tribe occupies Bohemia.
AD 600s Slavic tribes settle in region.
c700 The Přemyslid dynasty begins.
863 Cyril and Methodius bring writing and Christianity to Great Moravia.
929 'Good King' Wenceslas is killed by his brother and becomes a martyr and the Czech patron saint.
973 Prague is made a bishopric.
1235 Staré Město gets a Royal Charter; Jews forced into the ghetto.
1253 Otakar II becomes king.
1306 Přemyslid dynasty ends with the murder of Václav III.
1346 Charles IV becomes Holy Roman Emperor and King of Bohemia; founds Central Europe's first university in Prague.
1352 Swabian architect Peter Parler begins work on St Vitus's Cathedral.
1357 Foundations laid for Charles Bridge.
1378 King Wenceslas IV crowned.
1389 3,000 Jews killed in pogrom.
1403 Jan Hus, rector of Prague University, begins preaching against Church corruption.
1415 Hus, having been excommunicated and declared a heretic, is burned at the stake.
1419 Hussite mob throws the mayor out of new town hall window; Hussite wars begin.
1420s-30s Hussites repel all attacks.
1434 Moderate Hussites wipe out the radicals and the Pope agrees to allow them considerable religious freedom.
1458 Czech noble George of Poděbrady becomes the 'People's king', but is soon excommunicated by the pope.
1471-1526 Jagellon dynasty rules Bohemia.
1526 Habsburg rule begins with Ferdinand I.
1556 Ferdinand invites the Jesuits to Prague to counter fierce anti-Catholicism in Bohemia.
1583 Habsburg Emperor Rudolf II moves the court to Prague for next 20 years.
1609 Tycho Brahe's work leads to his *Laws of Planetary Motion*; Rudolf concedes some religious rights to Bohemia's Protestants.
1618 Protestants throw two Catholic councillors from a window in the castle, thus starting the Thirty Years' War.
1620 Protestants lose the Battle of White Mountain.
1621 27 Protestant leaders executed in Old Town Square.
1648 The Thirty Years' War ends on Charles Bridge as the citizens of Prague repel the invading Swedes.
1740 Maria Theresa becomes Empress.
1743 French attack Prague.
1757 Prussians attack Prague.
1781 Emperor Joseph II abolishes the Jesuits and closes monasteries.
1848 Revolutions in Europe; unsuccessful uprisings in Prague against Austrian troops.
1893 Clearing of the Jewish ghetto begins.
1914 Outbreak of World War I; Habsburgs refuse concessions on federalism and Czech soldiers desert to the Allies.
1918 Czechoslovak Republic founded with Tomáš Masaryk as its first president.
1938 Chamberlain agrees to let Hitler take over the Sudetenland.
1939 Hitler takes all Czechoslovakia.
1942 Czech paratroopers assassinate Reichsprotektor Reinhard Heydrich. Nazis destroy villages Lidice and Ležáky in revenge.
1945 Prague uprising; the Red Army arrives.
1948 The Communist Party assumes power under Klement Gottwald.
1951 The Slánský show trials and mass purges take place.
1968 Reformist communist Dubček becomes first secretary and promotes 'socialism with a human face', but the Prague Spring is crushed by Warsaw Pact troops.
1969 Philosophy student Jan Palach immolates himself in protest.
1977 The underground movement Charter 77 is established to monitor human rights abuses.
1989 Student demos turn into full-scale revolution and the communist regime falls.
1990 Poet, writer and anti-communist activist Václav Havel elected president of Czechoslovakia.
1993 The Slovak Republic and the Czech Republic divide and become separate, independent states.
1996 Michael Jackson's statue briefly takes up the spot vacated by Stalin's in Letná Park, as part of his History tour.
1998 The largest demonstrations since the Velvet Revolution sweep the city to celebrate the Czech hockey team winning an Olympic gold.
2000 The largest demonstrations since the Olympics fill Wenceslas Square to demand the ousting of Prime Minister Miloš Zeman and ODS head Václav Klaus.
2004 Havel steps down and the Czech Republic is admitted to the European Union.

Palác Flora. *See p19.*

Prague Today

New money, same old corruption.

A decade and a half after the Velvet Revolution inaugurated a new democratic age, Prague's persistent, crusty patina is being scrubbed clean, gradually giving way to the burnished façades of shopping malls, chain pubs and hired Audis driven by Czech middle managers. For years the city has still had the unmistakable whiff of a society in transition. Too often, though, it was the smell of stale cigarette smoke – and of cabbage steaming in a workers' canteen (still a feature of any Czech firm with more than ten employees, it seems).

But, today, the surfaces are cleaner and the air fresher than ever, if less enthralling to naïve romantics questing for a mythic Prague.

WHAT'S NORMAL?

One way to put it: Prague is undergoing a process of normalisation. Be careful with that word, though. It's the term the Soviet occupiers used to describe the pacification of Czechoslovakia following the Warsaw Pact invasion of 1968, the intervention that quashed the popular movement towards freedom of expression. Yes, Czech flower children did briefly blare out the Velvet Underground, write provocative poems and folk rock songs, and lay daisies at the feet of cops. That's difficult to imagine as you survey the kids of today, however, lounging jadedly in bars while happy house reverberates, each sucking on a Marlboro, the guys in Quiksilver club gear, the girls in obligatory low-slung jeans, thong prominently on display.

All part of the new normalisation, it would seem. As hypermarkets, multiplexes and chain restaurants proliferate and the Czech Republic moves into the EU proper, Prague is looking more and more like just another safe, world-weary, medium-sized European metropolis – a wise place to invest, with a healthy growth in consumer demand and disposable income, the Ministry of Trade and Economics would hasten to add. (Never mind those 17,000 recently laid off from the army, the threat of the country's first railroad strikes since 1948, the ongoing corruption troubles, the well-entrenched history of stripping shareholders' assets and taking off for Bermuda.)

And the euro? Czechs are showing no sign of wanting to extend their commitment to the EU by joining the single currency as yet – no referendum had been scheduled or was being debated at press time. Still, there are signs of warming to it, if only to ease the economics of tourism, with many high-end hotels and restaurants already accepting euros.

SELL OUT

We've all read much of *Magic Prague*, Angelo Maria Ripellino's dream vision of the city in the mist, where mad Emperor Rudolf II's influence still pervades and people live their lives according to a tragically beautiful poetry only Slavs seem to understand. You might catch a flavour of that Prague if you pick up one of the newly minted expat literary journals (try the online one www.instigator.cz, if it's still around next week; *see also p30*) or a film adaptation of a Milan Kundera book like *The Unbearable Lightness of Being* (perhaps tellingly, Kundera hadn't lived in Prague for years when he wrote the novel that inspired the film).

But you'd have more trouble finding that spirit in real-life Prague. Every great city is mythologised in films and novels, of course, but the gulf between the spiritual pull of Prague and the genuine article is, well, significant. The place to catch the real zeitgeist is, without question, the Palác Flora shopping centre (*see p158*) on any Tuesday night. While most of us are lucky enough to grow up surrounded by countless breakfast cereal varieties and home electronics (sold with a guarantee they'll replace a faulty item or offer you your money back), even the young Czechs of today still remember places that fixed the same pair of shoes every year and rude clerks who let you know in no uncertain terms that any problem you had with their goods – or their attitude – was your problem. In fact, these things are far from extinct even now, just much less in your face.

It's hardly surprising, then, that a bright, gleaming, well-stocked mall with designer cafés and live salsa music played by Ukrainians and Cubans (who are also appreciating Prague's improved commercial offerings) should captivate young Czechs. Yet, the sight of them lingering here for entire evenings, clearly having decided this is the best option going for a night out, does seem a tad, well, creepy. Sure, everyone appreciates least the place they grow up in. But can there really be so little interest in skulking among the medieval warrens of Staré Město, the Old Town? Where you find, mainly, Prague Piss-up tours (www.praguepissup.com) and a shrinking number of expats annoyed by them?

For a laugh, try telling that to a Czech thirtysomething. Negative side effects to capitalism? What is this, a riff on the 'What have the Romans ever done for us?' sketch from *The Life of Brian*? Apart from a stable democracy, open borders, freedom of expression, an exponentially greater selection of goods and services, a modern infrastructure and generally improved life as we know it, the West hasn't really done a thing for Prague, has it?

SLEAZE NATION

Dirty dealing and a laissez-faire approach Adam Smith could only dream of are very much still part of Prague. Look a bit beyond the recessed lighting and marble floors of the shopping meccas and you'll soon see the signs. To say anything goes in the Czech capital is putting it mildly (*see also p33*). For better and for worse, you can still get away with far more here than you could even imagine further west: booze is cheap and ubiquitous, the nights are long and every vice going is at your fingertips, from pot to prostitution, but now it's accompanied by sushi and new BMWs. It's not for nothing that Prague has earned the moniker 'the Amsterdam of the East', packing in British stag parties to the extent that locals, long tolerant of invaders and hesitant to knock anything that brings in hard currency, are actually starting to wonder if there may be limits. Discreet signs have begun popping up on the windows of Staré Město's more dignified clubs: 'No Stag Parties'.

And, of course, the days of the so-called Velvet Hangover are hardly over. The heady post-revolution free-for-all of the early 1990s gave way to a pounding pain in the temples, economically and politically. The decade following the 1989 collapse of the old regime was a period of breathtaking change that culminated in the devaluation of the Czech currency in 1997, the collapse of the centre-right government of Václav Klaus that same year, and an ensuing three-year recession. During the 1998 election to replace Klaus, the Czech chattering classes spoke as though the very future of the young Republic rested on the outcome. For a time it almost looked as if the 2002 general elections would be a humdrum affair – as elections tend to be in stable, affluent democracies. Klaus's Social Democrat foes trounced him again, even though party in-fighting has taken a severe toll on the ruling party's numbers in the polls. Prague was almost starting to look like a run-of-the-mill Western system.

Then it hit. In February 2002, the best-recognised Czech icon after Kafka, the playwright president Václav Havel, stepped down from the presidency before Parliament could agree on a replacement and, for a month, Prague Castle stood tenantless. The solution reached sent the nation into shock. Klaus, the man voters had turned down as potential prime minister just eight months earlier, became head of the Czech state. By late 2003 not only were Klaus's Civic Democrats (ODS) back on top of the polls, but the Social Democrats themselves had suffered near breakdown after an embarrassing split over the presidential succession.

RED ALL OVER

As if that wasn't enough, a more sinister spectre was becoming apparent: the Communist Party. Yes, that Communist Party. Some 14 years after the return of free elections, Czech Reds, who resemble a sclerotic pensioners' club more than stormy young idealists, are now ODS coalition partners, the ruling Social Democrats

Prague by numbers

On the ground

1.2 million population of Prague
10.3 million population of the Czech Republic
78,866sq km (30,450sq miles) area of Czech Republic
1,600sq km (618sq miles) amount of Czech land confiscated in 1918 that the Lichtenstein royal family claims

Ethnic divisions

94.4 per cent Czech
3 per cent Slovak
0.6 per cent Polish
0.5 per cent German
0.3 per cent Romany
0.2 per cent Hungarian
1 per cent other

Religions

39.8 per cent Atheist
39.2 per cent Roman Catholic
4.6 per cent Protestant
3 per cent Orthodox
13.4 per cent other

Lifestyle

72 average life expectancy for a Czech male
79 average life expectancy for a Czech female
20 per cent decline in Czech population predicted in 50 years due to low birth rate
£8,472 ($15,300) GDP per capita
9.8 per cent unemployment rate
15,000 Kč average monthly wage in the Czech Republic
1st ranking of taxes and insurance in expenses of an average Czech family
150,000 number of bank loans Czechs are unable to pay back
56 billion amount in Kč that Czechs owe in consumer loans
7.7 million hectolitres (169,376,321 gallons) amount of Pilsner Urquell drunk in 2003
2.69 million number of internet users

Housing

10 per cent predicted rise in regulated rents for Czechs in 2004
6,000 number of homeless in Prague
500 number of beds available for homeless in Prague

Foreigners

6 million number of visitors to the Czech Republic in 2003
10-12 per cent increase in tourism anticipated for 2004
14,200 number of foreigners checked for papers in a police sting in November 2003
34 per cent increase in asylum seekers applying to the Czech Republic in 2003
1 rank of Russians among them

Sex

6 number of crude comments from high-ranking male MPs published in the Czech press about the breast reduction surgery of Education Minister Petra Buzková
850 number of brothels in the Czech Republic
3,000-6,000 estimated number or street prostitutes in Prague
0.1 per cent HIV/AIDS infection rate

Road kill

5 average number of people killed daily on Czech roads in July 2003
20,000 number of 'Do Only Idiots Crash' videos given out by Czech police to drivers
80 per cent amount of Škoda cars exported in 2003
70 per cent amount of Škoda cars sold domestically in 1991
5 number in euros that a Czech auto worker makes per hour
40 number of euros a German auto worker makes per hour

Beer-guzzlers cop an eyeful at one of Prague's topless pub nights.

pushed to the position of second most popular party in the land. In Prague itself, where you'd be hard pressed to find a local who doesn't regard the communists with scorn, it's easy to forget that more than one in ten Czechs support the unreformed communists.

Perhaps communism is just one of many curious traditions Czechs cling to with what you'd almost call increasing desperation. The fly-specked smoke-filled Czech pub is as packed as ever, giving any state-of-the-art shopping mall a run for its money. Fried food, dumplings, gristly goulash and alcohol remain the mainstays of Czech culinary couture. Bad haircuts and pot bellies worthy of the old regime are still the fashion in most parts of town. The only difference is that these days *Nahoře bez*, or topless, nights are held in mainstream pubs all over town and jaded locals barely seem to register the difference. The crowd at **Pod Smetankou** (Mánesova 7, Vinohrady, Prague 2, no phone) on Friday nights is indistinguishable from the beer guzzlers and goulash eaters of any other night. Prostitution, though nominally illegal, is rampant, and brothels advertise openly. And, at the darker edges of the night, you'll find the all-hours *herna* bar, where night owls and taxi drivers gather to drink beer and gamble long into the night. On the more quotidian side, the unfriendly and poorly stocked neighbourhood grocery shop, or *potraviny*, so typical of moribund daily life under communism, is still hanging on – though it may finally have to be placed on the endangered species list as the big chains roll into town.

SPEAK NO EVIL, SEE NO EVIL

But modernising isn't just needed in grocery shops. In 2002 Prague mayor Jan Kasl, an architect and city socialite, resigned in part because he said he couldn't reel in the low-level corruption at City Hall. That same year a senior official at the Ministry of Foreign Affairs was charged with attempting to engineer the murder of a journalist who had been investigating corruption for the leading daily *Mlada fronta Dnes*. The only reason the plot fell through was that the hit man balked at killing a woman and squealed, sending the official, Karel Srba, up the river for eight years. Did someone say free expression?

Perhaps even more alarmingly, there's increasing evidence that the Czech-German border region has become a discount market for child molesters. In 2002 two reporters for the BBC's *Today* programme posed as German visitors to the western Bohemian town of Cheb and were offered girls of nine and 11 for sex. The pimp assured the journalists there would be 'no problem' with the police. In 2003 a UNICEF report alleged that about 100,000 Germans regularly travel to the Czech Republic to engage in sex tourism, and that half of them are paedophiles. Czech officials say the reports are greatly exaggerated.

Karel Srba, jailed for eight years following an attempt on the life of a journalist. *See p21.*

Tales of graft and sleaze have become so common in Czech society that it's often difficult to tell where reality ends and where paranoia begins. Czechs may be notoriously fond of conspiracy theories, but it's a fact that the police anti-corruption squads have recently investigated major government transactions, including the construction of a major highway in the Ostrava area and the privatisation of a coal mine to a group connected with former US Secretary of State Lawrence Eagleburger. Few are ever charged. The promise of 'clean hands', the anti-corruption catchphrase that brought the Social Democrats to power in 1998, has become a sad joke.

WHAT REVOLUTION?

Most Czechs today are too busy trying to get ahead – or just keep up – to worry much about the as yet unfinished transformation of their society. Though doubts linger about some EU issues, they overwhelmingly voted to join in 2003. As membership formally takes place at time of going to press, growing middle-class families and cheap mortgages have fuelled a residential construction boom. Perhaps Czechs have become too caught up with living average European lives – and, perhaps, too accustomed to dishonest officials – to bother about politics.

Though the country as a whole is ageing, the birth rate is down and youth culture looms large, with many young Czechs proving more cosmopolitan than their parents could ever have imagined. Many have lived, worked and studied in Western Europe and the United States. A gulf of understanding separates those who began their adult lives before and after 1989. Think of the generation gap between Western baby boomers and their parents after rock 'n' roll and the 1960s drove a wedge between them. Now multiply that by five. A generation is coming of age for which communism was but a dim childhood memory – if a memory at all. On the 14th anniversary of the Velvet Revolution *Mlada fronta Dnes* ran a series of kid-on-the-street interviews with 14-year-olds. Said one: 'I don't know what happened on 17 November 1989. The Velvet Revolution? That doesn't say anything to me.'

The new generation is probably past the point of questioning what capitalism has brought. You won't find these kids protesting against greedy developers of the latest hypermarket that's slated to replace a shabby park; they're too busy enjoying the Dolby effects at multiplexes and shopping for Nikes to raise so much as a peep. They've found a peace – or at least a stand-off – with Prague's deep contradictions, a capital simultaneously vibrant and dodgy.

But have courage, seekers of gritty film-noir versions of Bohemia: long after the shopping malls have closed, the hidden artery-clogged heart of the city still beats away, guzzling beer and pumping coins into a slot machine at a nicotine-stained *herna* bar.

Municipal House. *See p26.*

Architecture

History carved in stone – Prague's architectural treasures, unique in Europe, have tales of woe and rejoicing to tell.

Prague is a compelling architectural fairytale – written in cycles of repression and strife yet ultimately resolving in happy endings. Indeed the current state of the art might be most aptly likened to *Sleeping Beauty*.

Communism's spell left Prague's city centre crammed with monstrosities like the former **Federal Assembly** (*see p95*), which is now the headquarters of Radio Free Europe. Reconstructed in the late 1960s from the former Stock Exchange building, it's a block of black steel and smoked glass with a protruding two-storey addition plopped on top. Glowering down on Wenceslas Square from between the splendid **State Opera** (*see p214*) and the grand **National Museum** (*see p94*), it's a building so ugly it seems like an act of spite.

Now that the spell has been lifted, thoughtful architects working here today say their greatest challenge is to create something new, while not desecrating a virtually sacred cityscape. It's a daunting quest. Little wonder, then, that one of the most notable recent developments in the centre is **Slovanský dům** (*see p158*), an award-winning reconstruction of an existing building on ritzy Na příkopě. It's a significant achievement – workers had to lift the original building in order to replace the foundation – but one more akin to a careful restoration of a masterful painting.

Harmonising the old with something genuinely new is a more elusive, if not impossible, task. Many architects think the swaying **Dancing Building** (*see p101*) comes close; it's certainly the one recent structure to achieve iconic status, its playful post-'89 exuberance representing its time in the same way that the landmarks highlighted below sum up theirs. Modern, market-driven Prague may not develop an epoch-defining

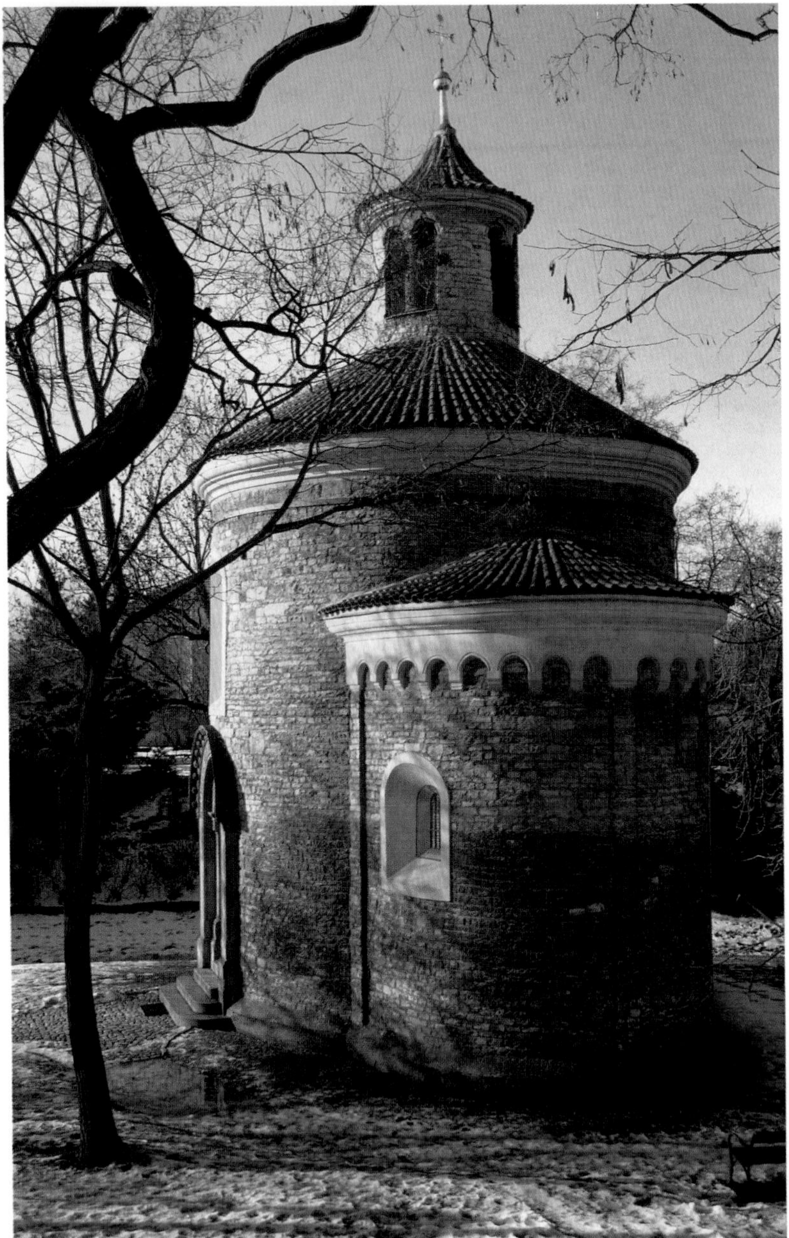

Perfectly formed – **St Martin's Rotunda**. *See p25.*

signature style, but the city's architecture has a way of roaring back after periods of war and foreign occupation. There's no reason why the post-communist period can't hold the same promise eventually. Maybe the roar is just too faint to hear yet.

BEGINNINGS

Property development in Prague dates from the seventh century, when Slavic tribes began building settlements along the Vltava river. A couple of hundred years later the prototype of **Prague Castle** (*see p61*) was built on an outcrop above the river, and the race was on. The city proper began taking shape around the castle, Vyšehrad and Staré Město (Old Town) in the 11th and 12th centuries; the most extensive surviving structure from the era is **St George's Basilica** (*see p66*) in the castle complex. Behind the creamy baroque façade thrown up in 1671 are the heavy arches, sly windows and thick pillars of the basilica's Romanesque roots. Walk around back for a look at the round towers, built in 1142 by some of the first of the Italian craftsmen who would have a major hand in shaping the city for centuries to come.

The early Romanesque period also meant rotundas, and two survive more or less intact: **St Martin's Rotunda** at Vyšehrad (*see p106*), and Staré Město's **Rotunda of the Holy Cross** (*see p90*), both mutely evocative links to a dim and distant past.

GOTHIC

The French-reared Gothic style appeared in Bohemia around 1230, adding ribbed vaults, flying buttresses, pointed arches and lacy trefoils to the architect's quiver. The **Old-New Synagogue** (*see p92*), built around 1280 and one of the best-preserved medieval buildings in Europe, offers a concentrated dose. Two octagonal columns support its ribbed, nine-metre-high (30-foot) vaulting; above the portal is a tympanum with a gorgeous carving of a vine-covered tree of life. Little natural light penetrates the two oriel windows and 12 narrow stained-glass windows, which match the still-used synagogue's modest dimensions – building size was severely limited in the densely packed Jewish ghetto.

Other examples of the period include: **St Agnes's Convent** (*see p93*), the city's earliest Gothic structure; the **House at the Stone Bell** (*see p85*) on Old Town Square and the **Church of Our Lady Before Týn** (*see p82*) towering imposingly above it; the austere **Powder Tower** (*see p67*) and east tower of the **New Town Hall** (*see p102*); and, of course, the incomparable **Charles Bridge** (*see p88*).

RENAISSANCE

Bloodied by the Hussite Reformation in the first half of the 15th century, Prague entered the 16th century in relative calm. The city's architects began looking to the burgeoning Italian style for inspiration, creating buildings that celebrated humanity instead of reaching towards heaven. The soaring vertical spaces of Gothic cathedrals gave way to airy, horizontal palaces. The Renaissance arrived with the **Belvedere** (*see p70*) in Prague Castle gardens, one of the first summer palaces built outside Italy. Paolo della Stella's arcaded exterior and Ionic columns, which were interspersed with reliefs of mythological scenes, make it a perfect Renaissance specimen, but its roof, shaped like an inverted ship's keel, makes it like no other building in Prague. Sadly, it's a grimy specimen, and the metal bars inserted between the columns to help it carry the load of the upstairs gallery mar its grandeur.

Further examples of the Renaissance period are the **Schwarzenberg Palace** (*see p70*), a riot of gables and sgraffito (unfortunately closed for reconstruction until 2007, but you can still stand in front and gawk) and the neighbouring **Martinic Palace** (Hradcanske náměstí 67, Hradčany, Prague 1), its symmetrical coupled windows and biblical etchings combining the simplicity of the early Renaissance with the flourish of the latter part of the period.

'Back with a vengeance, the Catholics created Prague's baroque magnum opus, the Church of St Nicholas.'

BAROQUE

When the smoke cleared from the Thirty Years' War the Catholics were back in charge with a vengeance. The Counter-Reformation wasn't the only force behind the building wave that remade Prague in the 17th and 18th centuries, but it's hard to miss the message in the city's baroque magnum opus, the **Church of St Nicholas** (*see p74*). The crowning achievement of father-and-son architects Kristof and Kilián Dientzenhofer, St Nicholas's may be history's most sumptuously sheathed iron fist. The enormous verdigris dome lords it over Malostranské náměstí; and beneath it, the elaborate curves and decoration testify not so much to the majesty and mystery of the Church as to its power. The locals converted in short order.

The Gothic **Old-New Synagogue**. *See p25.*

Elswhere you'll find the formidable **Clementinum** (*see p86*), Prague's other major signifier of Jesuit ascendancy; the **Wallenstein Palace** (*see p75*), Renaissance style carried into baroque spectacle by dint of its patron's ego; Old Town Square's **Kinský Palace** (*see p85*) and **Villa Amerika** (*see p102*) in Nové Město (New Town), among other splendid chocolate boxes; and the gloriously over-the-top **Loreto** (*see p71*), the triumphant Church's potent cocktail of blood-soaked mysticism and gratuitous wealth.

NEO-CLASSICAL

The enlightened absolutist Joseph II was having none of that rococo nonsense when he took the throne in 1780, and the Premonstratensians of Strahov Abbey saw the rationalist handwriting on the wall. The result is the **Strahov Monastery Library** (*see p71*), a politically adroit flanking manoeuvre (the wily monks brought in books by the ton to convince the monastery-closing monarch they ran an educational institution). Architecturally the bridge is a bridge into the classically minded Age of Reason, its baroque frills tempered by a soaring façade of capital-topped pilasters. Inside the breathtaking Philosophical Hall the bookcases and balustrades rise to a frescoed ceiling, science meeting art in religious drag.

To seek out further neo-classical style head to Anton Haffenecker's imposing, Corinthian-fronted **Estates Theatre** (*see p89*), home to the premiere of *Don Giovanni* – and don't you forget it – and **U Hybernů** (Na poříčí 3, Nové Město, Prague 1), with its Doric columns and cornices showing off the high Empire style of the Napoleonic era.

REVIVALISM

Few 'national' buildings are as worthy of the name as the **National Theatre** (*see p99*), dreamt up by the cream of the Czech revival movement and paid for entirely with public contributions. In May 1868, 50,000 people marched in a procession behind the foundation stone. The theatre opened 13 years later to the strains of Smetana's patriotic opera *Libuše*, then promptly burned down. The public dug deep again and the whole thing was rebuilt in two years, with Josef Schulz adapting mentor Josef Zítek's original plan and the 'National Theatre generation' of artists contributing the painting and statuary, which strikes a fittingly heroic note atop the lofty arched portico. The gold-crowned oblong dome is one of the icons of the Czech nation; the bucking horses atop the balustrade are pretty dramatic too.

Zítek and Schulz also lent their neo-Renaissance stylings to the monumental **Rudolfinum** (*see p93*) and Schulz did the honours for the grandiose **National Museum** (*see p94*), an impressive if not bombastic shrine to civic pride but breathtaking by night.

'Prague's flamboyant art nouveau Municpal House is festooned with decorative filigree.'

ART NOUVEAU

Erected just as the Austro-Hungarian Empire melted down, the gaudy, glitzy **Municipal House** (*see p97*) dazzles like a gilt-trimmed butterfly emerging from a chrysalis. The 'ding-dong, the witch is dead' vibe is unmistakable, but it took more than incipient independence to create the jewel of Prague's flamboyant art nouveau, festooned with stained glass, floral motifs and other decorative filigree. Production and population were booming, fuelling a business fund with a taste for symbolism and style. Architects Antonín Balšánek and Osvald Polívka, aided by the leading artistic lights of

Outside the box

The fractured perspective of cubist painting thrilled Prague's early 20th-century demi-monde – and not just those wielding brushes. Picasso and Braque made a deep impression on a group of radical sculptors and architects, who consequently banded together in 1911 as Skupina výtvarných umělců (SVU), the Group of Fine Artists. Rejecting the methodical logic of modernism and embracing the baroque legacy of rippling, rhythmic surfaces, the SVU architects aimed to reproduce in real space the multiple planes and dramatic shadow play of cubist canvases. The results are unique in the world of architecture.

The first cubist building, Josef Gočár's angular **House of the Black Madonna** (pictured; *see p109*), is named for the ebony icon mounted in a gilded cage at one corner (the one you see is a replica; the original is inside for safekeeping) and was first opened in 1912 as a department store. With its recessed bay windows and repeated rectangular motifs, the house was altogether modern but managed to mesh surprisingly well with its Staré Město (Old Town) surroundings. However, the purest expressions of the form are Josef Chocol's remarkable **residential buildings** below Vyšehrad (Neklanova 30 and Libušina 3, Nové Město, Prague 2), which are kaleidoscopic in their profusion of radiating lines and prismatic broken surfaces. The Libušina street villa even extends the cubist concept to the garden and gate.

Czech artists reinterpreted cubism as sculpture, furniture, even glasswork (all are on display at the House of the Black Madonna, reopened under the auspices of the National Gallery in late 2003 after a three-year renovation); tucked away in a corner of Jungmannovo náměstí is the world's one and only **cubist lamp post**. But World War I and a trend towards more realistic representation in cubism sapped the movement. In the post-war days of the First Republic SVU stalwarts envisaged a new 'national style', later dubbed 'Rondocubism', which grafted an eye-boggling array of circular forms and folk symbols on to a cubist base. Dense with decorative frippery, Gočár's **Bank of the Czechoslovak Legions** (Na Poříčí 24, Nové Město, Prague 1) and Pavel Janák's **Adria Palace** (Národní 40, Nové Město, Prague 1) are fascinating but not widely reproducible, and Prague gave in to a flat-fronted future of constructivism and functionalism. Strikingly new as it was, cubism was in many ways the last gasp of pre-modernism.

'Prague is a conservatory of Europe's past,' says Tomáš Vlček, the National Gallery's director of contemporary art. 'That is why [architectural] cubism was possible only in Prague.'

the day, harnessed the new energies into an extraordinary catalogue of patriotic pomp (stately Smetana Hall) and swirling, swinging optimism (the Alfons Mucha-designed Mayor's Hall), oozing aspiration from every floor.

Other examples of art nouveau worth seeking out are Polívka's colourfully ornamental Prague **Insurance Building** and **Topic Building** (Národní 7 and 9, Nové Město, Prague 1); the **Grand Hotel Evropa** (*see p97*) on Wenceslas Square, with its gleaming façade undimmed by years of communist neglect inside; the grand row of apartment houses running down **Masaryk Embankment**; and Josef Fanta's original **Hlavní nádraží** (Main Train Station, Wilsonova, Nové Město, Prague 2; *see p270*) – tatty yet still carrying a whiff of opulence.

MODERNISM

Cubism (*see p27* **Outside the box**), functionalism and constructivism all stamped themselves onto the cityscape in the first decades of the 20th century, but the city's most striking modern building is none of the above. Following no one's uncompromising theoretical blueprint, the **Church of the Sacred Heart** (*see p106*) sprung whole from the febrile imagination of Slovene architect Josip Plečnik, who also gave Prague Castle a between-the-wars touch-up. With its enormous clock-face rose window beaming over the great brick block of a church down on a Vinohrady square, Plečnik's creation mixes and matches with abandon, bathing the chilly geometry of modernism in a warm, Gothic-tinted glow.

Modernist architecture is also represented by the constructivist mass of Holešovice's **Veletržní palác** (Trade Fair Palace; *see p103*); circa-1911 **Koruna Palace**'s (Wenceslas Square and Na příkopě, Nové Město, Prague 1) futurism is pulled off with a Babylonian twist; the clean lines and practical spaces of 1930s housing estate **Baba** (above Podbabská 15-39, Dejvice, Prague 6); and functionalist landmark **Mánes** gallery (*see p224*), its river-spanning rectilinear slab outfitted with modern art and somehow blending in with the 15th-century water tower next door.

COMMUNISM

Prague architecture circa 1948-89 suggests the communists' puzzling inability to recognise that even workers like to be surrounded by beauty. Most relics of the period are blocky and grim, but the communist-era building Praguers most love to hate is the streamlined **Žižkov Tower** (*see p108*), a fusillade of television antennas built atop an old Jewish cemetery. At 216 metres (709 feet), it's the tallest structure in Prague – you might have stood in line for bread but, by God, you were going to have good reception. Completed just before the revolution, it does manage to muster a sort of charm on misty evenings, with artist/provocateur David Černý's climbing black babies silhouetted in the twilight.

Ringing the city, the ubiquitous prefab **panelák housing estates** (Metro Zličín or Háje) still house much of the population, while local governments try to break up their grey monotony with two-tone paint jobs. **Kotva** department store (*see p158*), with its odd angles and brown panelling, and the **Česká Typografie** building (Na Poříčí and Na Florenci streets, Nové Město, Prague 1) – formerly the office of the communist newspaper *Rude právo* – which the party made sure was the tallest building in Prague 1 when it opened in 1989, still ring out their communist-era foundations.

> **'In gritty Karlin, Danube House won kudos from the *Architectural Review* even before it opened in 2003.'**

POST-COMMUNISM

Architects no longer labour under communist overlords, but they work under the watchful eyes of preservationists and impatient investors. In gritty Karlin, the riverside **Danube House** (River City Prague, Rohanské Nábřeží, Karlín, Prague 6) office building won kudos from the esteemed *Architectural Review* even before it opened in the autumn of 2003. Its ship's-prow shape is unquestionably contemporary, but its architects chose materials that resemble the soft sandstone of many neighbouring buildings and the magazine's judges likened its large atrium to crystals set in 'solid stone volumes', with a nod to traditional Czech glass-making skills.

Other post-communist treats include the eye-catching **Dancing Building** (*see p101*), nicknamed 'Fred and Ginger' by its designers, US superstar Frank Gehry and Croatian Vlado Milunic, and the **Euro Palace** (Václavské náměstí 2, Nové Město, Prague 1), which was designed as a 21st-century counterpart to **Koruna Palace** (*see p97*) on the other side of Wenceslas Square. Judge for yourself if this glass-sheathed construction is worthy of its situation right at the nexus of Prague's flourishing high-street shopping district.

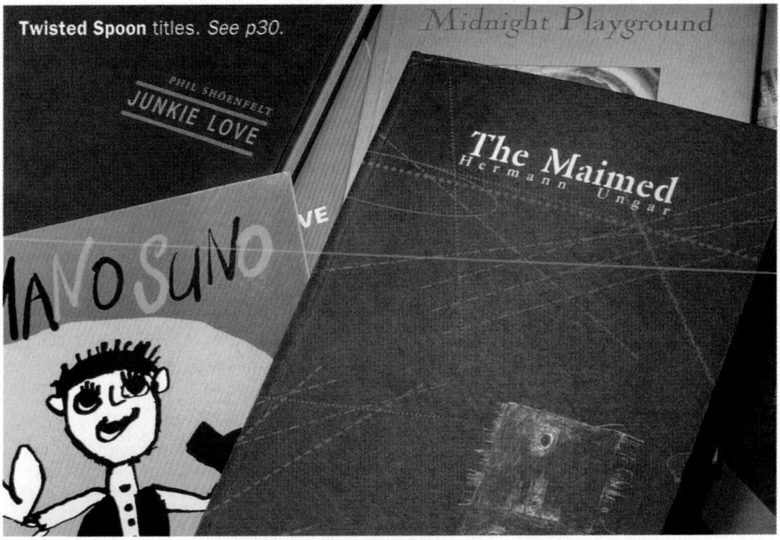

Twisted Spoon titles. *See p30.*

Literary Prague

The same muses who inspired Franz Kafka and Václav Havel are seducing a new generation of Prague writers.

Inspired by a medieval tract called *Rules for the Practising Alchemist*, a band of writers, poets and musicians has been meeting each week in Prague for longer than anyone can remember, seeking literary gold. The Monday night readings, known as **Alchemy** (www.alchemyprague.com) and most recently held at **Výletna** (*see p143*), have little more than a mission statement as structure – to 'provide a forum that supports and nurtures creative literary, art and performance work being produced in the Czech Republic', 'to introduce exciting new voices', 'to assist… a cooperative, supportive creative community' and 'to encourage experiments, exploration, collaboration in any creative realm'.

The inclusive approach is something that, for better or worse, has predominated the Prague literary scene, at least for English speakers, since not long after the Velvet Revolution. Before that the canon belonged to the likes of Václav Havel, whose absurdist parodies of life under communism (*The Memorandum*, *The Garden Party* and *Audience*) landed him in jail, and a host of contemporary writers and artists such as Ivan Klíma, Ludvík Vaculík and Jiří Kolář.

Their forerunners can be traced to the first of the Czech-language publishing successes (always risky in Habsburg-occupied Prague), during the city's literary National Revival of the mid 19th century. Božena Němcová, known for *Babička*, or Grandmother, inaugurated a new era for writing in colloquial Czech with morbid, tender fairytales still read to children today.

Jaroslav Hašek, author of *The Good Soldier Švejk*, is credited with personifying Czech political dissent in his main character, who never misses an opportunity to get an order wrong, a strategy that helps him to make it through World War I intact while driving his supposed superiors out of their heads. Kafka himself, of course, ranks as Prague's most famous son (*see p83* **Bad Bohemia: Franz Kafka**). Prague's German-speaking Jewish community of the early 20th century couldn't have known a more troubled cauldron, but the period produced luminary work by Kafka's contemporaries, particularly the poet Max Brod, who was instructed to burn Kafka's manuscripts upon his death. Novelists like Paul Leppin (*Severin's Journey into the Dark*) and Gustav Meyrink (*The Golem*) also wrote an enthralling account of the last days of the Empire, while two Holocaust survivors, Jiří Weil and Arnošt Lustig, greatly enriched Czech literature – all have been translated into English.

The poet Vítězslav Nezval, who founded the Czech Surrealists in the 1930s, was part of a wave that encompassed much Bohemian art in every medium. Nezval was a member of the seminal *Devětsil* avant-garde movement, as was Nobel laureate poet Jaroslav Seifert.

After the communists seized power in 1948, independent-minded writers were forced underground. Other writers continued working secretly, publishing *samizdat* manuscripts, illicitly distributing individually typewritten pages among themselves. Aside from Havel, Zdeněk Urbánek (*On the Sky's Clayey Bottom*) and the scientist-poet Miroslav Holub (*Vanishing Lung Syndrome*) were part of that network. The novels of Bohumil Hrabal (*Closely Observed Trains, I Served the King of England*) are too fantastical to fit the label dissident, though he was clearly suspect for his quirky tales of paper recyclers, scrap metal gatherers and railroad clerks who somehow transcend their drab worlds. Hrabal died in 1997 after a fall from a fifth-floor window while feeding pigeons – just as a character in one of his books did.

The post-Velvet Revolution Czech writers are difficult to categorise, but a good survey of their work in translation can be found in the imprints of Twisted Spoon (www.twistedspoon.com). These lush books, on good paper, with original illustrations and fresh translations of both new and classic Czech writing, are a gold mine for readers.

One Czech writer early out of the gates, the poet and novelist Jáchym Topol, cast Prague as a sleazy, noirish place of jackals in *City, Sister, Silver*, but in a town changing as fast as this one, his depiction, barely five years old, already seems to have little in common with Prague. Lukáš Tomin's introspective *Ashtrays*, *The Doll* and *Kye* are open-ended poetic collections, which are true to the perpetually tangled life of a Prague intellectual.

Titles from all of the above are available at Prague's two literary oases, **The Globe Bookstore & Coffeehouse** (*see p163*) and **Shakespeare & Sons** (*see p156*). **Big Ben Bookshop** (*see p163*) is also an excellent source of indie titles and collections of short stories by international writers, such as *This Side of Reality* (Serpent's Tail).

JOURNALS

The Globe and Shakespeare & Sons are where you'll find the state of central European commentary, poetry and art under magazine titles like *Jejune* and *Umělec* (www.divus.cz) and the *Prague Literary Review* (www.shakes.cz).

Other periodic literary journals come and go, but some once vital ones like *Optimism*, *Trafika* and the *Prague Revue* have been quiet for some time. However, they're worth asking about at the Globe.

'Writers love to schmooze and no city's finer for it than Prague, with its dens of wine-soaked debate.'

FESTIVALS

Aside from some titles crowding the shelves of the Globe and Shakespeare & Sons, the literary scene in Prague is most evident at the city's many literary festivals. Writers do love to schmooze and, indeed, no city's finer for it than Prague, with its countless cafés and dens of wine-soaked debate. In summer, not a month goes by without an important writers' gathering.

A brand new one, the first **Prague International Poetry Festival** (www.geocities.com/praguepoetryfestival), launches in May 2004, jointly co-ordinated by the *Prague Literary Review*, Shakespeare & Sons, Twisted Spoon Press and the InterCultural Studies Programme at Charles University. A few of the talents attending, Charles Bernstein from the US, Franz Josef Czernin of Austria, Trevor Joyce of Ireland, John Kinsella of Australia, Allen Fisher of the UK and Anselm Hollo of Finland, provide an indication of the scope.

The more established **Prague Writers' Festival** (*see p183*) in March has been a star-studded series in the past, with writers like Martin Amis, Margaret Atwood and William Styron, but seems a bit more muted these days, with less commercial talents on the roster.

READINGS

The favoured venue of expat scribblers, Alchemy, which was based at press time at Výletna (*see p29*) but slated to move, is the only regular event at which to catch new talent. The Globe hosts an increasing number of author visits, both local and international, and is on the international circuit. Amy Tan or Ian McEwan or a local beat poet may take over any evening.

But Shakespeare & Sons (*see above*) is the up-and-coming place to catch literary events, which may include slams, signings or a jazz jam, but always an eclectic crowd of miscreants.

Prague distractions

Christopher Cook (pictured), author of the novel *Robbers* and the collection *Screen Door Jesus & Other Stories*, discusses Prague and his stand-up writing career.

Q Why are so many writers drawn to Prague?
A It's a charming city. And affordable. For writers struggling to conserve their time (and money) for writing, that's important. Praguers are open-minded and tolerant, which provides a liberating ambience for creativity.
Q Are there energies or inspirations conducive to good storytelling or art-making in Prague?
A Inspiration is a critical part of creative work, but it is a common human experience and happens everywhere. Interesting ideas occur and we notice them. But following through by expressing the inspiration in a structured creative medium is what some folks do – while others simply don't. It's hard work.
Q Doesn't Prague attract a lot of inhabitants who never produce – and distract you with nights of drunkenness and decadence? Or is there also a useful support network?
A Writers learning to write often attend open mic readings and there are several groups in Prague. I personally find them neither a help nor a hindrance. But I support writing as an activity, so I occasionally attend them.
Q Why do you think the widely anticipated 'great Prague novel' from a new Hemingway or Fitzgerald never turned up? Or has it?
A The novel probably has been written, and it was written by a Czech. But Czech writers receive little literary attention globally.
Q Is much of the publishing in English in Prague really just vanity publishing?
A I think publishing in English in Prague is a terrific idea. I support publishing books in any language anywhere. And it's the only way some books will get published, given the business these days.
Q Weren't you working on a book set in Prague when you were here?
A I don't talk about work-in-progress. But I will say the inspiration was sensuality and lust. Prague is a very sexy place.
Q Best bar in Prague for writers? Best activity here to stir the creative juices?
A I'm not a bar person, so I can't answer that. I can't write when I'm drinking, or the day after. Writers who think they can are usually deluding themselves. In my experience, the best activity for stirring the creative juices is a good day's work.
Q Influenced by Czech writers at all?
A Not much, no. I like reading Czech writers, but my own writing reflects my own American cultural experience and background, which is working class and southern. Writing about anything else results in inauthentic writing.
Q Does it help an American writer's work to get out of America?
A My novel *Robbers*, though set in Texas, was entirely written in San Miguel de Allende, Mexico. And yes, living outside the USA is very important for my work. It gives me the distance and isolation I need to maintain a creative bubble.
Q You write standing up at your podium. Is it a bit like conducting a symphony?
A Well, I try to be a stand-up guy, you know. But a good novel does seem as complicated as a symphony to me, and I do think and feel in musical forms as I write. Sometimes I listen to music while working, if it pertains to what I'm writing. While writing *Robbers*, I listened to blues and Dwight Yoakam.
Q It's fair to say there is a dark sensibility in most of your work?
A My work is full of irony and humour (often black). It's the only way to stay honest and sane. Czechs have that humour too.
Cook, a former journalist and editor and native of East Texas, has lived in France, Mexico and the Czech Republic. His books have been published in the USA and have been printed in many languages.

... Let´s become friends !
ALCOHOL
BAR
Enjoy each moment of your life.
• 250 cocktails
• 200 single malt whisky
• 75 brands of rum
• world finest cigars
• live music 5 days a week
• each Friday and Saturday best radio DJ's
• friendly atmosphere
Alcohol Bar • Dušní 6, Praha 1 • Staré město
www.alcoholbar.cz

Absinth. *See p35.*

Bad Bohemia

Yes, it's about excess, and no, nobody's watching the clock. Welcome to party-heaven Praha.

There could scarcely be a better name for living in Prague than bohemian. Long before the name of the province of which Prague is capital became synonymous with decadence and excess, Praguers were widely renowned for the good life.

Certainly, even here, most of those trapped in the usual orbits of life, the people who bake the bread before dawn, clean the streets and reconstruct apartments for the more privileged, can ill afford a life of drinking and idleness.

But even so, as the beloved Czech writer Karel Čapek once observed (while contemplating whether a young Czechoslovakia ever would, or should, keep pace with industrious Westerners) the habits of the men repairing his house probably were an insight as to the inevitable answer. In the end it was with affection that he described their long breaks for beer and cigarettes, loose work schedule and tendency to spend as much time philosophising as laying bricks.

Foreign travellers to this day in the Czech lands will notice a remarkable patience among Czechs with railroad clerks, who take time to finish their gossiping with colleagues before troubling to tell you which platform to catch your train from.

It's almost as if Bohemians are suspicious of working fast and conscientiously. After all, anyone who did that under the old regime (about which was said: 'we pretended to work and they pretended to pay us') would have been a fool. Right?

VICE PRESIDENCY

But it's fair to say there's a bit more going on here than a conditioned response to communist inefficiencies. Čapek penned his observations during the 1930s and the meaning of small-b bohemian clearly dates back to well before that time – Puccini borrowed it in 1895 for an inspiration he ended up titling *La Boheme*.

Good old Emperor Rudolf II, the only Habsburg to move his court to Prague, must have heard the news. This was the place, away from uptight Vienna, to push the boat well and truly out (*see p10* **Great indulgers**).

And the libations continue to flow in Prague today. Despite all the red tape required for everything imaginable in the Czech Republic – someone recently estimated there are some 40 approval stamps required from various state offices in order to open most brick-and-mortar businesses and it's illegal to actually sell over the internet here – liquor licenses are still unheard of in Bohemia. If you want to booze your way through days and nights spent in Prague, you can buy beer, vodka or absinth at any café or newsstand at any hour of any day of the week.

Indeed, heads of state in modern times, while trying to demonstrate that the new Czech Republic is indeed a viable competitor – and a good place for investment, never mind those tales of rampant insider stealing – have nevertheless found time for boozing, smoking and carousing.

'The state of health among Czechs is far behind other nations and the mortality rate far higher.'

Even the moral high ground occupied by the playwright president Václav Havel was never seen to be compromised – far from it – by his habit of taking foreign heads of state for a beer after official business was done. Perhaps he was on to something the West could benefit from. 'I always saw a sparkle in their eye,' Havel said about his guests' reactions.

Neither could he have been called a prude. It was acknowledged throughout the country that after Havel's wife Olga, who had seen him through his days from prison to the presidency, died, it was only out of propriety that he didn't immediately move in her replacement, the much younger actress Dagmar Veškrnová. (An uncharitable press nevertheless often referred to her as Dašenka, the name of Čapek's dog.)

Perhaps less inspired was his nicotine habit. Havel smoked like a chimney but, wary of promoting the habit, he forbade the press from filming him while puffing.

FAT OF THE LAND

The state of health among Czechs – heart disease in particular – though it's been improving, is far behind other nations and the mortality rate far higher (*see p20* **Prague by numbers**), thanks to the local passion for frying, salting and slathering cream sauce on beef. Pork is considered the other white meat, and vegetarian offerings on menus are still often limited to fried cheese or a few soggy cabbage leaves.

But anyone can pig out, surely. And smoking too much? Even young American actors do that. Where are the bohemians who live for art, music, laughter? One look at a typical Prague shop clerk and you'd be forgiven for assuming smiles have been outlawed. Easygoing? Ever seen a Praguer without four kinds of ID, their exact change counted out – down to the heller, a hundredth of a crown – and an unswerving dedication to using the formal term of address? Employees may work in a firm of six people for ten years, but the boss will always be addressed as *'Vy'*, most likely with *'Pan Doctor Inženýr'* tacked on before his name.

Hence an essential irony: Czechs have had to tread lightly, learn the correct formalities and become adroit at foreign nuances to get by. The multiple titles thing is down to the Austro-Hungarians – one of whom was Rudolf II.

THE REAL BOHEMIANS?

It's more likely that you'll find the *La Boheme* kind of bohemian, then, at **The Globe Bookstore & Coffeehouse** (*see p163*) or at the **U Malého Glena** jazz club (*see p221*). Or at the aptly named **Marquis de Sade** (*see p150*) – could there possibly have been a better name for a dilapidated, hedonistic mecca in Prague? – downing absinth (*see p35* **The absinth drinker**). He'll be the one with the cap on backwards who doesn't speak Czech.

Real Bohemians, it seems, are still willing to sin. Indeed, based on the talent on display at the city's countless sex clubs – who said Czechs don't apply themselves at work? – they are more than willing (*see p230* **Sin City**). But only if there's a decent percentage in it. And if it's all about commerce, well, where's the fun in that?

There are, of course, many young Czechs and Europeans from further east who manage to scrape out creative lives Puccini would recognise. Students, if they can get past brutal entrance exams and crusty professors, are entitled to small state subsidies, and usually no attendance is taken at lecture halls. State apartments obtained by parents under the old regime are often passed on to kids. Some are willing to squat in abandoned factories – or work part-time in the lucrative film or sex biz. Many such characters manage to mount photo exhibitions of their trip to Tunisia at **Velryba** (*see p153*) or **Gallery Art Factory** (*see p197*), where anyone can exhibit for 1,000 Kč a day. Others join the minions of club kids, DJ-ing at **Akropolis** (*see p215*) and some live for performance art at the **Alfred ve Dveře Theatre** (*see p233*).

Another apparent contradiction: don't bohemians love indulging all the senses? Why, then, this inveterate refusal to budge on stodgy food? Duck with sauerkraut, while delicious, is about as exotic as it gets.

Perhaps the answer to this one lies in perspective. Real Bohemians seem genuinely rapturous about their pork, beer and dumplings and are happy to be loyal to these alone until their dying day. Which won't be far off, by the look of it.

BETTER THE DEVIL YOU KNOW

A recent programme to inspire commuters, called 'Poetry on the Metro', has resulted in odes to things dear to the Czech soul, which now appear on cheery posters inside crammed Metro carriages. The words for potato and soup – and matches – pop up with regularity in these poems.

Ultimately, then, Prague is not so different from anywhere else. Everyone indulges in the sin of their choice, to the extent they can afford. It just so happens that for a time, rents were cheap, the dollar was strong and any visitor who could impart a bit of English was welcome.

These days, for better or worse, Prague has grown up a bit. The pot-smoking skate punks of yesteryear are leasing responsible cars, working in banks and look… well, you'd almost say… stressed. Just like the rest of us.

If it was all just a dream that had to end, perhaps Diana Krall, the smoky jazz singer who would be as fine a patron saint of Bohemians as anyone – even her name is a corruption of the Czech for king – summed it up best in one of her more swinging hits: 'Let come tomorrow what may… That's how I live and I die, devil may care.'

The absinth drinker

With a recipe notoriously difficult to even define, it's no wonder absinth captivated the likes of Hemingway and Fitzgerald and has been depicted as a green fairy and/or seductress in paintings by Picasso and Degas.

It's generally agreed that the favourite tipple so associated with Bohemian artists and literati of the Jazz Age – and first produced by Henri Louis Pernod in 1805 – has at least these three qualities: it's distilled from wormwood, flavoured with anise, and tinged an ominous aqua green.

Even this last property is just a general description, since a delicate dance of effects has to be carried out by each distiller of absinth. Wormwood is a bitter flavour, hence the anise to add sweetness. Too much anise, however, and you dominate the other, more delicate herbal flavours. Not enough, and you lose the louching, or clouding, effect when water is added, *à la Pastis*, which some drinkers consider the hallmark of a fine absinth.

Oh, yes, and the effect. Aside from typically containing up to 70 per cent alcohol, some absinths contain thujone and other sedative herbs and terpenes, which cause 'mind affecting reactions', according to one respected distiller. In short, you're in for a knock-out punch.

This, and the effect of the sedative herbs, probably explains why so many myths have sprung up surrounding absinth. Everyone's heard it was once banned because it was causing madness and mayhem. Indeed, it is still illegal in some parts of Europe, and one manufacturer cautions that in the US: 'we believe that it is legal to possess, drink and import absinth for personal consumption.'

Absinth is certainly legal in the UK, France, Spain, Portugal, Switzerland, Germany and the Czech Republic, at any rate. Cognoscenti maintain that Spanish and French absinth distillers have a far better feel for the herbal bouquet ideal for the concoction, and one French firm, La Fée Absinthe, claims to have recreated the exact recipe that so inspired – and so pickled – the bohemians of Paris before the war, according to a 19th century formula approved by the French Absinthe Museum.

Czech absinth, though once the toast of libertines from Prague to Paris, is not what it once was. Local brands tend to taste either too bitter – one drops pieces of wormwood into the bottle – or too strongly of anise or exactly like cleaning fluid. That said, critics have praised Sebor for its refined blend of flavours, if limited louching.

Hill's, meanwhile, doesn't get much respect, but is cheap and available everywhere. Other brands sold in the Czech Republic, many of which ship to the UK, are Schulz Absinth, Staroplzeňsky (or L'OR) Absinth, Absinth King, Prague Absinth, Absinthe Orginal and Logan Fils.

If you want to fuel your curiosity further, www.feeverte.net is an authoritative online guide to the potent green stuff.

Where to Stay

Features

Where to Stay

The suites are sharper and the moderate to budget stays cushier than ever, while boutiques are beginning to bloom.

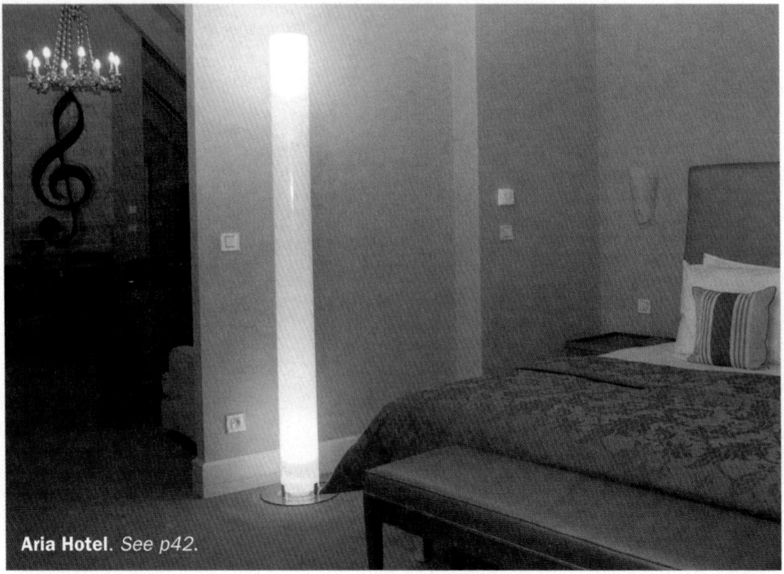

Aria Hotel. *See p42.*

Recent developments in Prague hospitality mean you no longer detect the stale funk of socialism that formerly plagued even the city's most luxurious lodgings. Every day brings more hotel rooms on the market, and joining the *crème de la crème* recently are the **Carlo IV** (*see p51*), preservationist masterpieces like the **Iron Gate** (*see p47*) and **Le Palais** (*see p52*), the boutique stunner **Aria** (*see p42*) and the über-cool **Hotel Josef** (*see p47*).

Good news also for those who like their mattresses well-worn: the Czech capital still offers outstanding value in terms of cheap food and drink, entertainment and the most basic accommodation. Dozens of hostels and hundreds of spare rooms sprout like dandelions every summer only to wither with the autumn.

Finding a room somewhere between opulence and austerity has finally become an enjoyable pursuit too, after years of lagging in this sector. Travelling families have tempting options all over town, from hotels like **The Julian** (*see p56*), **Hotel U Žluté boty** (*see p42*), **Hotel Anna** (*see p54*) or the lovely **Hotel Černy Slon** (*see p47*) just off Old Town Square, to small, family-owned inns, such as **Residence Řetězová** (*see p49*) or **Pension Vyšehrad** (*see p56*), none of which is more than ten minutes by tram from the centre.

INFORMATION AND BOOKING

Prague has a diverse profusion of renovated or brand-new hotels, from inns with medieval foundations to giant multi-star hotels. An absence of perfect weather and business conferences make October to March and a few weeks in later summer the most competitive times of the year among the best hotels. Hostels stay full from May through September.

Many of Prague's hotels give discounts to groups and for longer stays (around ten days or more); rooms are generally about 20 to 40 per cent cheaper off-season, and many deluxe hotels give 10 to 20 per cent discounts in July and August. Smaller places may offer a significant reduction for cash payment. Establish this, preferably with printed or written confirmation, before you arrive.

Service at higher-end hotels is comparable to that in any European capital. But that's not the case at some of the more moderate hotels, where the staff can give the impression that it's your privilege to stay with them. As with luxury hotels worldwide, you can get hit with ludicrous charges for both local and international phone calls. Watch out also for the taxis that cluster around the hotel entrances: for these hustlers, a taxi meter is a jackpot that always pays out. If the hotel has its own fleet, it's a better option, although charges may still be double those set for regular city taxis. Hotels are also infamous for refusing to call honest taxi services for guests (such as **AAA** or **Profi**; *see p271*), as they're in on the game.

Availability varies hugely with seasons too. Even with all the new stock, rooms in Prague still haven't caught up with summer demand. If you come to the city in peak months without a reservation, expect to pound the pavement for hours before you find a decent place. Whatever the season, it's always wise to book ahead. All deluxe hotels have English-speaking staff; those at cheaper establishments may struggle. Many hotels can arrange airport pick-ups for a fixed price, saving you time, money and hassle.

PRICES AND CLASSIFICATION

Hotels are classified below according to their cheapest double room; prices include breakfast, unless stated otherwise. These prices are usually only available off-season and some of the more upmarket hotels fix their room rates in euros or US dollars. For ease of use we've converted all prices into Czech crowns, but exchange-rate fluctuations may affect these.

Hotels are listed by area and the price categories work as follows: a deluxe hotel is one in which the cheapest double room costs 8,000 Kč-plus per night; an expensive hotel costs 6,000 to 8,000 Kč; moderate is 3,000 to 6,000 Kč; budget hotels cost under 3,000 Kč; and hostels are grouped together. All rooms in the 'deluxe' and 'expensive' categories have an en suite bathroom. This also applies to the 'moderate' category, unless otherwise stated. Facilities in other categories vary – check exactly what you'll be getting when you book. For a selection of hotels that are particularly welcoming to gay guests, *see p205*.

Accommodation agencies

Agentura Kirke

Moskevská 25, Vršovice, Prague 10 (271 720 399). Metro Náměstí Míru/tram 4, 22. **Open** 8.30am-5pm Mon-Fri. **No credit cards**.

Run by British expat Nicholas Kirke, this respected agency offers long- and short-term rentals on flats (minimum lease one year). All flats are unfurnished.

Prague Accommodations

Petřínská 4, Prague 5 (608 228 999/251 512 502/ www.pragueaccommodations.com).

It makes no sense to visit this apartment and pension company in person – either book by phone or online before you come. The agency's properties include some of the most centrally located and elegant historic buildings you could possibly stay in.

Stop City

Vinohradská 24, Prague 5 (222 521 252/ www.stopcity.com). Metro Muzeum/tram 11. **Open** *Jan-Apr, Oct-Dec* 10am-9pm; *Mar-Sept* 11am-8pm daily. **Credit** AmEx, MC, V. **Map** p311 M6.

The helpful, incredibly patient staff at Stop City will book you into a pension, private room or hotel starting at less than 500 Kč per person, with a 10% discount offered for online bookings. They don't handle hostel bookings though.

Hradčany

Staying within the shadow of Prague Castle in Hradčany (*see p61*) does limit your options, but a number of surprisingly affordable, enchanting options lie in the back streets, away from the tourist throng.

Deluxe

Hotel Savoy

Keplerova 6, Prague 1 (224 302 430/fax 224 302 128/www.hotel-savoy.cz). Tram 22, 23. **Rates** 7,260-10,560 single/double. **Credit** AmEx, MC, V. **Map** p306 A3.

Neat and modern, with brass and green accents, the Hotel Savoy is a welcoming space from the outset with a reading room and fireplace in the lobby. Yet it's also a haven for prima donna celebs such as King Crimson and Princess Caroline of Monaco. Outstanding service and a quiet atmosphere go along with tasteful, modern rooms. Standard rooms are spacious, and the deluxes amount almost to a suite. Concierge service is top-notch.

Hotel services *Beauty salon. Business conference rooms. Disabled: adapted room. Gym. Hot tub. Interpreting services. No-smoking rooms. Solarium.* **Room services** *Dataport. Fax. Room service (24hrs). TV: pay movies/satellite. VCR.*

Expensive

Hotel Neruda

Nerudova 44, Prague 1 (257 535 556/fax 257 531 492/www.hotelneruda-praha.cz). Metro Malostranská/tram 12, 20, 22, 23. **Rates** 5,775-6,600 Kč single; 6,435-7,260 Kč double. **Credit** AmEx, MC, V. **Map** p306 C3.

This three-storey building, which has only served as a hotel for the past three years, dates back to 1348. The designers were careful to gracefully mesh old-world charm with the open, airy feel of a modern inn. Rooms are comfortable but plain, so be sure to ask for one with a view of Nerudova street. Attentive, friendly service. Children six and under stay free.
Hotel services *Air-conditioning. Bar. Café. No-smoking rooms. Laundry. Parking (call ahead to reserve). Restaurant. Terrace.* **Room services** *Minibar. Room service (until 11pm). TV: satellite. Safe.*

Hotel Questenberk

Úvoz 15, Prague 1 (220 407 600/fax 220 407 601/www.questenberk.cz). Tram 22, 23. **Rates** 6,600-7,920 Kč double; 9,240-11,550 Kč junior suite. **Credit** AmEx, MC, V. **Map** p306 A3.
This baroque building, located just metres from Prague Castle, was established in the 1660s. Keep the address handy when you're looking for it – you may walk right by, thinking it's a cathedral, which is perhaps something to do with the dramatic stone crucifix at the entrance. Despite the hotel's grand exterior, however, the rooms inside are standard fare for this price category and location, which is what you're really paying for.
Hotel services *No-smoking rooms. Parking. Solarium.* **Room services** *Fax. Internet. Minibar. Safe. TV: satellite.*

Moderate

Dům U velké boty

Vlašská 30, Prague 1 (257 532 088/fax 257 533 234/www.dumuvelkeboty.cz). Metro Malostranská/12, 20, 22, 23 tram. **Rates** 1,800 Kč single; 3,000-3,760 Kč double; 4,100 Kč suite. **No credit cards**. **Map** p306 C3.
As homely as it gets, this eight-room house dates back to 1470 and has been saved from neglect by the Rippl couple – press the buzzer with their name on it to get in. They look after guests like family and are avid collectors of gorgeous period furniture. A favourite of visiting writers and actors, the House at the Big Boot is also good for families. Some rooms can be joined to form suites with a kitchen. Breakfast is an extra 200 Kc.
Hotel services *Fax. Gym. Laundry. Safe.* **Room services** *TV: cable.*

Romantik Hotel U raka

Černínská 10, Prague 1 (220 511 100/fax 233 358 041/www.romantikhotels.com). Tram 12, 22, 23. **Rates** 4,500-6,900 Kč single; 5,900-7,900 Kč double. **Credit** AmEx, MC, V. **Map** p304 A2.
Aptly named, this charmer presents visitors with what looks to be an old-fashioned, timbered country inn that somehow got overlooked by developers. Built in 1739, this six-room pension with four standalone cabins is ideal for couples and is located streets from the castle. Surprising polish and service go with the rustic feel. The main house features a cosy breakfast/reading room with brick hearth. Book well in advance. No children under 12. No bar.
Hotel services *Air-conditioning. Limousine service. Parking. Safe.* **Room services** *Room service (6am-8pm).*

U Červeného Lva

Nerudova 41, Prague 1 (257 533 832/fax 257 532 746/www.starshotelsprague.com). Metro Malostranská/tram 12, 22. **Rates** 3,828-6,930 Kč single; 4290-7590 Kč double. **Credit** AmEx, MC, V. **Map** p306 D3.
An incredible find for the location, in the middle of Nerudova, normally thought of as a tourist thoroughfare on the Royal Route from Staré Město to Prague Castle. Dappled walls and hand-painted vaulted ceilings fill out the authentic 17th-century decor. Fully reconstructed with modern amenities, it still offers plenty of heart and a sense of life during the Renaissance. Service is adequate, though can be a bit lethargic. If full, staff will book you into the equally lovely sister hotel across the street.
Hotel services *Bar. Parking (off-site). Restaurants (3).* **Room services** *Hairdryer. Minibar. Safe. TV: satellite.*

U krále Karla

Úvoz 4, Prague 1 (257 532 869/fax 257 533 591/ www.romantichotels.cz). Metro Malostranská/tram 12, 22. **Rates** 4,000-6,500 Kč single; 5,000-6,900 Kč double; 7,000-7,900 Kč suite. **Credit** AmEx, MC, V. **Map** p304 C3.
A seasoned traveller's secret for years, this small hotel, formerly owned by the Benedictine Order, seduces with oak furnishings, vaulted ceilings, stained-glass windows and antique detail. Service lives up to the appearance, which is saying a lot: it's a baroque treasure that will leave you feeling like an aristocrat in your country house. Discounts for cash payment are sometimes available.
Hotel services *Babysitting. Bar. Laundry. Parking (call ahead to reserve). Restaurant. Solarium.* **Room services** *Minibar. Room service (until 10pm). Safe.*

Zlatá Hvězda

Nerudova 48, Prague 1 (257 532 867/fax 257 533 624/www.starshotelsprague.com). Metro Malostranská/tram 12, 22. **Rates** 3,828-6930 Kč single; 4,290-7,590 Kč double. **Credit** AmEx, MC, V. **Map** p306 C3.
Known in English as the Golden Star, the building dates to 1372. A reconstruction in 2000 didn't tamper with the five-storey house's original architectural elements, including vaulted ceilings and a spiral staircase. Period furniture makes guests feel they're staying in a museum, but lifts and contemporary bathrooms are nods to modern amenities. Rooms ending with a five are spacious and feature huge, luxurious bathrooms. Tip: discounts for extended stays can sometimes be negotiated via the website.
Hotel services *Internet. Laundry. Parking (off-site). Restaurant.* **Room services** *Minibar. Safe. TV: satellite.*

Budget

Golden Horse House

Úvoz 8, Prague 1 (tel/fax257 532 700/ www.goldhorse.cz). Metro Malostranská/tram 12, 20, 22, 23. **Rates** 1,000-2,200 Kč double. **No credit cards. Map** p306 C3.

A fortuitous find for any district, the Golden Horse is all the more unexpected so close to Prague Castle. You could easily pay five times the price for similar rooms on a par with a good hostel, though here you also get your own private bath. Amiable service. Breakfast is 100 Kč and it's right next door to one of the hippest cafés in the city: U zavěšenýho kafe (*see p145*).

Hotel services *Cooking facilities. Safe (in reception).* **Room services** *TV: satellite.*

Hotel U Žluté boty

Jánský vršek 11, Prague 1 (257 532 269/fax 257 534 134/www.zlutabota.cz). Tram 12, 20, 22, 23. **Rates** 2,800-4,200 Kč single/double; 3,900-5,600 Kč apartment. **Credit** AmEx, MC, V. **Map** p306 C3.

Located on a quiet alley, this hotel offers visitors all the rustic delights – and some of the drawbacks – of old Prague. This historic baroque house was renovated in 2001. Some guests, however, complain of connecting doors between some rooms that are so thin you can hear all your neighbours' sightseeing that day. Still, there's a certain antique charm to a gorgeous wood-lined building that dates back to the 1630s. Breakfasts highly recommended.

Hotel services *Fax. Pet-friendly. Terrace.* **Room services** *Internet. Radio. TV.*

Pension Corto II

Nerudova 27, Prague 1 (257 534 281/fax 257 534 282/www.corto.cz). Metro Malostranská/tram 12, 20, 22, 23. **Rates** 1,500-2,400 Kč single; 1,800-2,800 Kč double; 3,000-4,200 Kč apartment. **Credit** AmEx, DC, MC, V. **Map** p307 C3.

Rooms are neat, clean and quite large – if a bit plain. Never mind, though, as the Corto II offers some of the best value in this part of the city. A gem for budget travellers intent on staying near the castle.

Hotel services *Safe (in reception).* **Room services** *TV: cable/satellite.*

Malá Strana

The Lesser Quarter (*see p73*) feels like a small town in its own right. Stay on peaceful old lanes next to embassies, Parliament or an odd palace, and amble into busy Staré Město, crossing the Charles Bridge whenever you like.

Deluxe

Aria Hotel

Tržiště 9, Prague 1 (225 334 111/fax 257 535 357/ www.ariahotel.net). Metro Malostranská/tram 12, 20, 22, 23. **Rates** 10,725 Kč single; 10,725-11,385 Kč double; 12,375-32,175 Kč suite. **Credit** AmEx, MC, V. **Map** 307 D3.

First, let's dispel any notion that the music-themed Aria Hotel is mere theme hotel. The amenities, the service and the location are all tremendous. Comfortable rooms are jammed with features, including DVD players, fresh orchids and fruit, and custom-designed furniture from Spatium. Now for (drum roll, please!) the music: the floors are divided by genre – classical, opera, contemporary, jazz – and each room is dedicated to an artist. Computers in every room feature a custom site with bio and songs from its namesake. There's a music-lending library in the lobby, where the Aria's musical director, the knowledgeable Dr Ivana Stehlíková, holds court. The roof terrace may just have the best view anywhere in the city. Request a room that faces the baroque gardens.

Hotel services *Airport transfers (free). Bar. Business services. Concierge. Garden. Gym. Massage. Music library. No-smoking rooms. Parking. Private screening room. Restaurant. Sauna.* **Room services** *Bathrobe. Computer with high-speed internet and music bank. DVD player. Minibar. Room service (24hrs). Safe. TV: satellite.*

Expensive

Hotel Hoffmeister

Pod Bruskou 7, Prague 1 (251 017 111/ fax 251 017 112/www.hoffmeister.cz). Metro Malostranská/tram 12, 18, 22. **Rates** 3,960-5,445 Kč single; 6,270-9,570 Kč double; 9,075-14,190 Kč suite. **Credit** AmEx, MC, V. **Map** p307 F1.

A storied place where the literati of the inter-war First Republic once hung out, the luxurious Hoffmeister is also very handy for Malá Strana and Prague Castle. It's on a street with busy traffic, but the soundproofed windows are effective. Rooms are spacious and tastefully done, and the halls are filled with original works by artist Adolf Hoffmeister. Amenities and service have improved of late.

Hotel services *Air-conditioning. Babysitting. Bar. Café. Disabled: adapted room. Parking. Restaurant. Terrace.* **Room services** *Dataport. Minibar. Room service (7-1am). Safe. TV: pay movies/satellite.*

Rezidence Lundborg

U Lužického semináře 3, Prague 1 (257 011 911/ fax 257 011 966/www.lundborg.se/gb/index_english. html). Metro Malostranská/tram 12, 20, 22, 23. **Rates** 5,610-6,000 Kč single/double. **Credit** AmEx, DC, MC, V. **Map** 305 F3.

With a prime view of Charles Bridge, and built on the site of the older Judith Bridge, this Scandinavian-owned hotel exudes luxury. A prime example of the executive residence/hotel hybrid, Rezidence Lundborg pampers guests with 13 suites, each a distinct and tasteful blend of reconstructed Renaissance decor and modern business amenities. It's a major splurge, but every conceivable need has been anticipated, from wine cellar to internet-connected computers in every room. The desk will efficiently arrange anything else you can think of asking for.

Four Seasons Hotel Prague. *See p46.*

The best Hotels

For breakfasting with Hollywood heartthrobs
Hotel Savoy (*see p39*): top-notch discreet service and spacious rooms.

For business travellers
Go for Scandinavian-style luxury at **Rezidence Lundborg** (*see p42*), all the mod-cons at the **Diplomat Hotel Praha** (*see p53*) or executive touches, with executive views to match at the **Mövenpick Hotel** (*see p53*).

For cool aesthetes
Enjoy minimal chic at **Hotel Josef** (*see p47*) or go luxe-deluxe with a stay **Andel's Hotel Prague** (*see p52*).

For flat-out gorgeous interiors
Enjoy Kampa-Island life at **Residence Nosticova** (*see p45*), experience a Renaissance at **Residence Řetězová** (*see p49*), revel in the 16th-century decadence of **U Zlaté studny** (*see p49*) or the seamless blend of old and new at the **Hotel Elite** (*see p51*).

For a Kafkaesque experience
Get stuck in time at **Grand Hotel Evropa** (*see p51*).

For quintessential quaint Malá Strana
Turn on the romance at **Dům U velké boty** (*see p41*), soak up the atmosphere while you soak in a tub at **Hotel U Zlaté Studně** (*see p45*) or combine curiosities with modern amenities at **Zlatá Hvězda** (*see p41*).

For saying you stayed 'at Prague Castle'
If your stay is all about location, location, location try the excellent-value **Golden Horse House** (*see p42*) or the sturdy grandeur of **U krále Karla** (*see p41*).

For an unforgettable honeymoon
Hide away in a cottage at **Romantik Hotel U raka** (*see p41*) or get intimate in the serene setting of **Hotel U páva** (*see p45*).

For the state of boutique hotellery
Try themed antiquity at **Bohemia Plaza** (*see p54*) or authenic burgher decor **U Červeného Lva** (*see p41*).

For a thorough workout
Sweat off your *pivo* gut in the gym at the convenient **Marriott** (*see p51*).

Hotel Josef. *See p47.*

Hotel services *Air-conditioning. Bar. Conference room. Internet. Parking.* **Room services** *Computer. DVD player (2 rooms). Internet (free). Jacuzzi. Kitchenette. Minibar. Room service (until 10pm). Safe. Stereo. TV: satellite.*

Moderate

Blue Key

Letenská 14, Prague 1 (257 534 361/fax 257 534 372/www.bluekey.cz). Metro Malostranská/tram 12, 22, 23. **Rates** 3,630-4,620 Kč single; 4,290-5,610 Kč double; 6,369-9,075 Kč suite; under-14s free with 2 adults. **Credit** AmEx, MC, V. **Map** p307 E3.

This 14th-century townhouse is a hop away from Malostranské náměstí. Ask for a room facing the courtyard. Double rooms are quite spacious and are equipped with kitchenettes. Some rooms are only accessible by stairs. Repeat guests get discounts.

Hotel services *Internet. No-smoking rooms. Sauna. Two whirlpools.* **Room services** *Kitchenettes (non-suites only). Minibar. Refrigerator. Safe. TV: satellite.*

Hotel U páva

U Lužického semináře 32, Prague 1 (257 533 573/fax 257 530 919/www.romantichotels.cz). Metro Malostranská/tram 12, 20, 22, 23. **Rates** 4,300-6,400 Kč single; 4,500-6,900 Kč double; 6,900-7,900 Kč suite. **Credit** AmEx, DC, MC, V. **Map** p307 F3.

With a fantastic location in a lovely corner of Malá Strana near the river, At the Peacock also offers dark timbered ceilings and crystal chandeliers. Although their sister hotel, U krále Karla (*see p41*) is preferred by some, there's a much better chance of finding one of the 54 rooms here free, some of which have their own fireplace. Suite No.s 201, 301, 401 and 402 look on to Prague Castle. Some rooms are not accessible by lift.

Hotel services *Café. Laundry. Limousine service. Massage. No-smoking rooms. Parking. Restaurant. Sauna. Solarium. Whirlpool.* **Room services** *Minibar. Room service (7.30am-10pm). TV: satellite.*

Hotel U Zlaté Studně

U Zlaté studně 4, Prague 1 (257 011 213/fax 257 533 320/www.zlatastudna.cz). Metro Malostranská/tram 12, 22, 23. **Rates** 5,150-7,900 Kč single; 5,150-9,200 Kč double; 6,950-9,900 Kč suite. **Credit** AmEx, DC, MC, V. **Map** p307 D2.

Hotel U Zlaté Studně is nestled on a secluded street. Rooms in this tasteful, high-end hideaway feature wood floors and ceilings, and stylish furniture. Ask for a room with a huge bath. You can eat breakfast on a terrace that boasts a fine view of the city, while the view from the indoor dining area is also tremendous.

Hotel services *Garden. Internet. Parking.* **Room services** *Bathrobe. Fax (suites only). Minibar. Safe. TV: satellite.*

Hotel Waldstein

Valdštejnské Náměstí 6, Prague 1 (257 533 938/fax 257 531 143/www.avetravel.cz). Metro Malostranská/tram 12, 18, 22, 23. **Rates** 2,640-6,600 Kč single; 3,630-7,920 Kč double. **Credit** AmEx, MC, V. **Map** p307 E2.

The newly reconstructed Hotel Waldstein features a Renaissance vault where hearty buffet breakfasts are served every morning. The lobby is all stone tile floors and vaulted ceilings, and rooms have antique furniture and 17th-century ceiling frescoes, if no lifts. Budget travellers can opt for the Waldstein annexe. These 11 apartments and one suite are a little plainer, but still classy.

Hotel services *Atrium. Laundry. No-smoking hotel. Parking.* **Room services** *Kitchenette (in some annexe rooms). Minibar. Safe. TV: satellite.*

Pension Dientzenhofer

Nosticova 2, Prague 1 (257 311 319/fax 257 320 888/www.dientzenhofer.cz). Metro Malostranská/tram 12, 20, 22, 23. **Rates** 3,200-3,300 Kč single; 4,000-4,350 Kč double; 3,300-6,900 Kč suite. **Credit** AmEx, DC, MC, V. **Map** p307 E4.

The quiet courtyard and back garden offer a lovely respite in the midst of Malá Strana. Rooms aren't tremendously posh but are bright, and the staff friendly. The 16th-century house is the birthplace of baroque architect Kilian Ignaz Dientzenhofer, whose work fills this quarter of the city. Book well ahead.

Hotel services *Airport/railway station transfers (for fee). Bar. Disabled: adapted rooms. Internet. Laundry. Parking. Pet-friendly.* **Room services** *Minibar. TV: satellite.*

Residence Nosticova

Nosticova 1, Prague 1 (257 312 513/257 312 516/fax 257 312 517/www.nosticova.com). Metro Malostranská/tram 12, 22. **Rates** 5,346-7,260 Kč suite; 7,920-16,500 Kč large suite; 396 Kč daily for maid service. **Credit** AmEx, MC, V. **Map** p307 E4.

Hotels with apartments are known as residences in Prague but, like this one, they offer better value than many, plus the comforts of home. That is, if your home happens to be a modernised baroque building on a quiet lane just off Kampa Island. The suites range from ample to capacious and come with antique furniture, well-designed, roomy bathrooms and, best of all, fully equipped kitchenettes. Two have working fireplaces and one a rooftop terrace. Continental breakfast is served for around 300 Kč.

Hotel services *Internet (in lobby). Parking. Restaurant.* **Room services** *Dataport. Kitchenette. Minibar. Safe. TV: satellite.*

U Karlova mostu

Na Kampě 15, Prague 1 (257 531 430/ fax 257 533 168/www.archibald.cz). Metro Malostranská/tram 12, 20, 22, 23. **Rates** 3,200-4,600 Kč single; 3,400-5,600 Kč double; 4,200-7,200 Kč apartment. **Credit** AmEx, DC, MC, V. **Map** p307 F4.

Formerly named Na Kampě 15, At the Charles Bridge affords some fine views of the bridge and Staré Město, but you'd never guess you're this close to a tourist thoroughfare. With rooms over a rustic, riverfront pub, you'll feel like you've stepped into the 19th century. A sensitive restoration of this tavern dating from the 1400s means homely rooms with wood floors, exposed beams and garret windows

U Žluté boty looks pretty in pink. *See p42.*

alongside modern furnishings. The two cellar pubs and the beer garden offer a traditional menu and a nice collection of Czech and French wines, plus stellar Czech beer on tap. Check their website for last-minute bargains. Friendly service.
Hotel services *Air-conditioning. Bar. Garden. Laundry. No-smoking rooms. Restaurants (2).*
Room services *Minibar. Safe. TV: satellite.*

Budget

Hotel U Kříže

Újezd 20, Prague 1 (257 312 451/fax 257 312 542/www.ukrize.com). Tram 6, 9, 12, 20, 22, 23. **Rates** 2,400-3,700 Kč single; 2,800-3,900 Kč double; 3,300-5,600 Kč suite. **Credit** MC, V. **Map** p307 E5.

This hotel is a great bargain in this price category, with pleasant rooms and a strategic location: it's across the street from Petřín hill, a quick walk to Kampa Island, two stops to Malostranská náměstí, and just a few steps away from the popular Bohemia Bagel (*see p119*)! Ask for a room facing the atrium. Other rooms look out to Petřín hill (great!), but also the tram tracks (not so great). Other boons include free coffee and cake, which are served in the lobby noon-6 pm.
Hotel services *Bar. Garden. Internet. No-smoking rooms. Parking (covered). Pet friendly. Restaurant.*
Room services *Minibar. Safe. TV: satellite.*

Hotel William

Hellichova 5, Prague 1 (257 310 629/fax 257 310 927/www.euroagentur.cz). Tram 12, 20, 22, 23. **Rates** 2,640-4,785 Kč single; 2,970-5,115 Kč double. **Credit** AmEx, MC, V. **Map** p307 D4.

Opened in 2001, this inconspicuous hotel sits on a great location a quick walk to the funicular up Petřín hill and just one tram stop from Malostranské náměstí. The interior decorators went a wee bit overboard trying for a 'castle feel'. The rooms, however, are comfortable and good-value. Ask for one at the back of the hotel, away from the noise of the trams.
Hotel services *No-smoking rooms. Parking.*
Room services *Minibar. Safe. TV: satellite.*

Hostels

Hostel Sokol

Nosticova 2, Prague 1 (257 007 397/fax 257 007 340/hostelsocool@seznam.cz). Metro Malostranská/tram 12, 20, 22, 23. **Rates** 300-350 Kč per person, dorm; 660-900 Kč double. **No credit cards**. **Map** p307 E5.

The entrance to this place is via the yard behind the Sokol sports centre. Find Hostel Sokol and you've found the student travel nerve centre of Prague, located not far from Prague Castle and Charles Bridge. The hostel has a great terrace for beer-sipping with a view, but many bunks are in a large gymnasium. Breakfast not included. Book ahead.
Hostel services *Bedding. Kitchen. Lockers. No-smoking hostel. Parking. Terrace.*

Staré Město

Prague's Old Town, Staré Město (*see p81*), remains a haunting, mostly pedestrianised knot of ancient streets and Gothic shadows. The trade-off for being in the heart of everything is higher prices, but small, impossibly pretty inns constantly open, with competition providing an edge on standards.

Deluxe

Four Seasons Hotel Prague

Veleslavínova 2A, Prague 1 (221 427 000/fax 221 426 000/www.fourseasons.com/prague). Metro Staroměstská/tram 17. **Rates** 8,880-18,240 Kč single; 9,440-18,240 Kč double; 22,240-31,840 Kč suite. **Credit** AmEx, MC, V. **Map** p308 G3.

The only fault of the Four Seasons hotel is that it is perhaps too perfect. While the hotel is a seamless melding of restored Gothic, baroque, Renaissance and neo-classical buildings, guests

will be hard-pressed to catch even a whiff of musty history. Of course, there's no shortage of that just outside the walls, so you might as well enjoy the pampered surroundings and service. The top-flight rooms have sweeping views of Prague Castle and Charles Bridge.
Hotel services *Babysitting. Disabled: adapted rooms. Gym. Parking. Sauna. Translation service.* **Room services** *CD player. Dataport. Laundry. Minibar. Room service (24hrs). Safe. TV: pay movies/satellite.*

Iron Gate

Michalská 19, Prague 1 (225 777 777/fax 225 777 778/www.irongate.cz). Metro Staroměstská or Národní třída/6, 9, 18, 21, 22, 23, 26 tram. **Rates** 9,280 single/double; 21,220 Kč suites. **Credit** AmEx, MC, V. **Map** p308 H4.
Antiquarians take note: the Prague Municipality recognised the Iron Gate as the best historic reconstruction in 2003. The two buildings date from the 14th and 16th centuries and preserve the original painted ceiling beams and frescoes. To maintain the Gothic look, the suites' kitchenettes are discreetly tucked inside antique armoires. The Tower Suite is over the top in more ways than one – stashed away on three floors of the building, it features a heart-shaped bed, hot tub for two, and a study with views of the Old Town Hall and Prague Castle.
Hotel services *Air-conditioning. Babysitting. Bar. Concierge. Gym. Restaurant.* **Room services** *Bathrobe. Hairdryer. Kitchenette. Minibar. Newspaper. Room service. TV: satellite.*

Expensive

Hotel Josef

Rybná 20, Prague 1 (221 700 111/fax 221 700 999/ www.hoteljosef.com). Metro Náměstí Republiky/tram 5, 8, 9, 14. **Rates** 6,600-8,200 Kč single; 7,900-9,500 Kč double. **Credit** AmEx, MC, V. **Map** p309 K2.
Definitely the hippest, if not the only, designer hotel in Staré Město, the Josef opened in 2002. The flash interiors, unique fabrics and glass bathrooms (superior rooms only) are the work of London-based designer Eva Jiřičná. The hotel is in the thick of the historic centre, with the top-floor rooms in the 'Pink House' having the best views.
Hotel services *Air-conditioning. Bar. Concierge. Conference rooms. Garden. Gym. Internet point. Laundry. No-smoking floors. Parking (520 Kč per night).* **Room services** *Bathrobe. Dataport. DVD player. Hairdryer. Minibar. Room service. Safe. TV: satellite.*

Moderate

Cloister Inn

Konviktská 14, Prague 1 (224 211 020/fax 224 210 800/www.cloister-inn.com). Metro Národní třída/tram 6, 9, 18, 22, 23. **Rates** 3,100-4,300 Kč single; 3,300-4,500 Kč double. **Credit** AmEx, DC, MC, V. **Map** p308 G5.
No austere nunnery here, just a well-tended basic hotel. The customer care, great location and price make this worth considering even if you're a sinner – in which case the nearby house of nuns is ready to offer redemption. The 73 rooms are bright and cheery, and the lobby offers free internet access, plus free coffee and tea, and a lending library. Keep your eye on their website for special deals.
Hotel services *Concierge. Internet. Laundry. No-smoking rooms. Parking.* **Room services** *Fax (executive rooms only). Minibar (executive rooms only). Safe. TV: satellite.*

Hotel Černy Slon

Tynská 1, Prague 1 (222 321 521/fax 222 310 351/www.hotelcernyslon.cz). Metro Staroměstská/ tram 17, 18. **Rates** 1,950-3,150 Kč single; 3,100-5,400 Kč double. **Credit** AmEx, MC, V. **Map** p308 J3.
Amazingly, this old townhouse sitting in the shadow of the Týn church is an affordable, warm, 16-room inn ensconced in a 14th-century building on the UNESCO World Heritage list. Gothic stone arches lead to smallish, but comfortable, rooms with wooden floors and basic amenities. Windows look out on cobbled mews, with a constant parade of characters. Fortunately, the lanes are some of the district's quieter ones.
Hotel services *Bar. Café. Parking (off-site). Restaurant.* **Room services** *Minibar. Safe. TV: satellite.*

Hotel Liberty

28 října 11, Prague 1 (224 239 598/fax 224 237 694/www.hotelliberty.cz). Metro Můstek/tram 6, 9, 11 18, 21, 23. **Rates** 4,950-8,745 Kč double. **Credit** AmEx, DC, MC, V. **Map** p308 J5.
Its slogan ('Where the rooms have not only a number – but also a soul') may be a bit much, but the stately Hotel Liberty is centrally located, with rooms tailored more to affluent business travellers than to tourists looking for signs of Bohemia. Care has gone into the dignified decor and service is superb. Three suites have balconies – suite 33 has a sensational view of Prague Castle. Some rooms have whirlpool baths.
Hotel services *Air-conditioning. Beauty salon. Gym. No-smoking rooms. Sauna.* **Room services** *Bathrobe. Dataport. Minibar. Safe. TV: pay movies/satellite.*

Hotel Mejstřík Praha

Jakubská 5, Prague 1 (224 800 055/fax 224 800 056/www.hotelmejstrik.cz). Metro Náměstí Republiky/ tram 5, 14, 26. **Rates** 4,100-5,500 Kč single; 4,900-6,200 Kč double; 7,300-8,300 Kč suite. **Credit** AmEx, DC, MC, V. **Map** p309 K3.
This hotel, in the heart of Staré Město, is now back in the hands of the family that founded it in 1924. Individually decorated rooms are a hybrid of modern hotel decor and 1920s style. Art-deco elements and wood trim are a nice touch, while corner rooms offer great vantages for spying on streetlife.
Hotel services *Bar. Conference room. Disabled: adapted rooms. Limousine service. No-smoking rooms. Parking. Restaurant.* **Room services** *Dataport. Minibar. TV: satellite.*

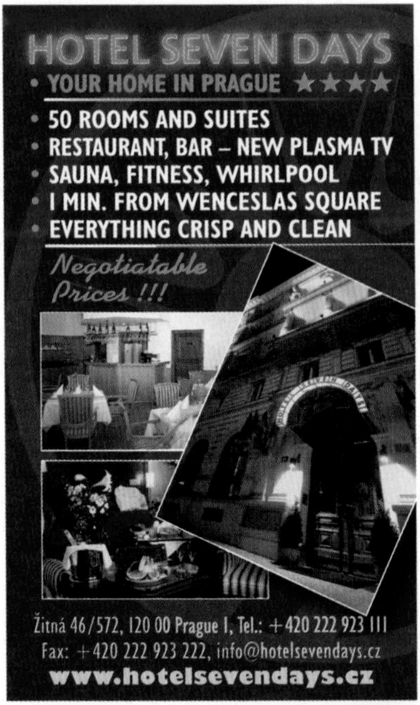

HOTEL SEVEN DAYS
• YOUR HOME IN PRAGUE ★★★★
• 50 ROOMS AND SUITES
• RESTAURANT, BAR – NEW PLASMA TV
• SAUNA, FITNESS, WHIRLPOOL
• 1 MIN. FROM WENCESLAS SQUARE
• EVERYTHING CRISP AND CLEAN
Negotiatable Prices !!!
Žitná 46/572, 120 00 Prague 1, Tel.: +420 222 923 111
Fax: +420 222 923 222, info@hotelsevendays.cz
www.hotelsevendays.cz

Hotel ****
Liberty
BOUTIQUE HOTEL
where the rooms have not only a number ... but also a soul
• Central location: at the bottom of the Wenceslas Square.
• Charming and elegant rooms: air conditioning, smoke detectors, internet access, safe, minibar, TV and SAT programs, telephone, balcony, parking available.
• Relax Club: sauna, whirlpool, excercise machines Technogym.
... A Good Choise
ul. 28. října 11 - 110 00 Praha 1
Tel.: 00420 224 239 598 • Fax: 00420 224 237 694
E-mail: info@hotelliberty.cz • www.hotelliberty.cz

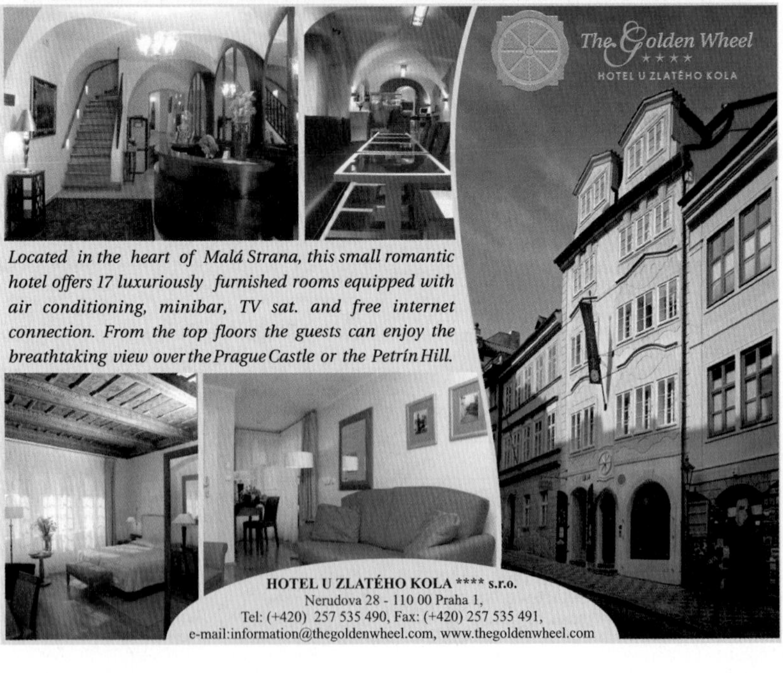

The Golden Wheel
★★★★
HOTEL U ZLATÉHO KOLA
Located in the heart of Malá Strana, this small romantic hotel offers 17 luxuriously furnished rooms equipped with air conditioning, minibar, TV sat. and free internet connection. From the top floors the guests can enjoy the breathtaking view over the Prague Castle or the Petrín Hill.
HOTEL U ZLATÉHO KOLA **** s.r.o.
Nerudova 28 - 110 00 Praha 1,
Tel: (+420) 257 535 490, Fax: (+420) 257 535 491,
e-mail:information@thegoldenwheel.com, www.thegoldenwheel.com

Hotel Metamorphis

Malá Štupartská 5 (Ungelt Square), Prague 1 (221 771 011/fax 221 771 099/www.metamorphis.cz). Metro Náměstí Republiky/tram 5, 14, 26. **Rates** 3,850-5,450 Kč single; 4,530-6,520 Kč double; 5,080-7,300 Kč suite. **Credit** AmEx, DC, MC, V. **Map** p308 J3.

The former Pension Metamorphosis has metamorphosised into the now more grown-up Hotel Metamorphis. Each room is different, but all are tastefully done, featuring wood floors and an array of comforts – some ceilings have original beams from the late 15th century. The once-empty square on which the Metamorphis stands has become a tourist mecca, jammed with craft shops, a respectable bookshop and cafés – and one of the best is on the ground floor of the Metamorphis itself. Ask for a room with view of the Týn Church. Check the hotel website for special deals.

Hotel services *Bar. Internet. Parking. Restaurants (2).* **Room services** *Air-conditioning. Dataport. Minibar. Tea/coffee-maker. TV: pay movies/satellite.*

Residence Řetězová

Řetězová 9, Prague 1 (tel/fax 222 221 800/ www.residenceretezova.com). Metro Staroměstská/ tram 17, 18. **Rates** 3,413-13,017 Kč single/double; 260-325 Kč maid service. **Credit** AmEx, MC, V. **Map** p308 H4.

A labyrinth of restored Renaissance rooms, some with timbered ceilings and lofts, makes up this easy-to-miss Staré Město gem. Genial service, a fantastic location and a homely feel make it easy to imagine retiring to this abode to live a quiet life. The spread in rates reflects, aside from deep seasonal discounts, a variety of rooms from little more than a loft to a regal apartment – all tastefully appointed, though.

Hotel services *Internet point. No-smoking rooms. Parking (off-site).* **Room services** *Hairdryer. Iron. Kitchenette. Minibar. TV: cable.*

U Zlaté studny

Karlova 3, Prague 1 (222 220 262/fax 222 221 112/www.uzlatestudny.cz). Metro Staroměstská/ tram 17. **Rates** 3,750-4,500 Kč double; 4,500-5,100 Kč suite. **Credit** AmEx, MC, V. **Map** p308 H4.

Fans of the arcane will delight in this 16th-century building and the legendary well in its cellar that gives the hotel its name. Exquisitely furnished with Louis XIV antiques and replicas, the four suites and two doubles are cavernous by Staré Město standards. Sightseers will appreciate its location halfway between Charles Bridge and Old Town Square.

Hotel services *Fax. Internet point. Laundry. Restaurant.* **Room services** *Minibar. Safe.*

Budget

Botel Albatross

Nábřeží Ludvíka Svobody (adjacent to Štefáník bridge), Prague 1 (224 810 541/fax 224 811 214). Metro Náměstí Republiky/tram 5, 8, 14, 26. **Rates** 1,260-2,520 Kč single; 1,620-3,240 Kč double. **Credit** AmEx, MC, V. **Map** p309 K1.

Essentially a floating *panelak*, the Albatross has seen better days (*see p55* ***Ahoj*, matey**). Still, it's hard to beat the price for a quiet room in Staré Město, especially if you're going to spend most your time ashore anyway. The rooms are humble, the facilities modest, and the staff somewhat salty.

Hotel services *Bar. Parking. Restaurant.*
Room services *TV.*

U krále Jiřího

Liliová 10, Prague 1 (222 220 925/224 248 797/fax 222 221 707/www.kinggeorge.cz). Metro Staroměstská or Národní třída/tram 6, 9, 17, 18, 21, 22, 23, 26. **Rates** 1,500-2,200 Kč single; 2,700-3,500 Kč double; 3,900-4,700 Kč apartment. **Credit** AmEx, MC, V. **Map** p308 H4.

This simple pension is named for King George of Poděbrady, who kept a house nearby. An easy walk from Old Town Square and the Charles Bridge, it's a fair choice for tourists who want to get the most out of their time. Basic, but great location.

Hotel services *Bar. Fax. Garden. Safe.*
Room services *Minibar. TV: satellite.*

U Medvídků

Na Perštýně 7, Prague 1 (224 211 916/fax 224 220 930/www.umedvidku.cz). Metro Národní třída/tram 6, 9, 18, 21, 22, 23, 26. **Rates** 1,500-2,300 Kč single; 2,300-3,500 Kč double. **Credit** AmEx, MC, V. **Map** p308 H5.

The Little Bears hearkens back to a number of Dark Ages. The iron doors on some rooms may remind visitors of Gothic dungeons, while the rudimentary bathrooms evoke the benighted years of communism. The traditional inn's pub keeps a constant stream of tourists and locals fed on roasted pig, even if the prices of food and drink could be lower.

Hotel services *Bar. Restaurant.* **Room services** *Minibar. Room service (24hrs). TV.*

Hostels

Travellers' Hostel

Dlouhá 33, Prague 1 (224 826 662/224 826 663/ fax 224 826 665/www.travellers.cz). Metro Náměstí Republiky/tram 5, 14, 26. **Rates** (per person) 270-370 Kč dorm; 520-620 Kč double; 380-480 Kč triple; 350-450 Kč 4-6-bed rooms; 1,500-3,000 Kč apartment. **Credit** MC, V. **Map** p309 K2.

This remarkably successful hostel organisation offers consistent value and a steady stream of young Westerners, especially at the Dlouhá street location. With internet access, drinks and sandwiches for sale in the lobby, it's got what you need, which also describes the dorm beds. Fortunately, there are also five apartments and a surprisingly romantic double suite with beamed ceilings at this branch. Both the apartments and the suite feature kitchens to save you some coppers, but be sure to book ahead. The hostel is also a booking office, connecting travellers to a network of hostels (www.czechhostels.com).

Hostel services *Bar. Fax. Internet. Laundry. No-smoking hostel. TV room.*
Other locations: throughout town.

Residence Řetězová – it's a Renaissance affair. *See p49.*

Nové Město

Prague's New Town, Nové Město (*see p94*), might lack the medieval charm of the Old Town, Staré Město, but it easily makes up for it with lower hotel rates with more rooms and better dining. And there's no need to feel like you away from the hub of the action. In minutes, the public transport system can carry you to the city centre or out to the lively districts of **Vinohrady** and **Žižkov** (for both, *see p106*).

Deluxe

Hotel Palace Praha

Panská 12, Prague 1 (224 093 111/fax 224 221 240/www.palacehotel.cz). Metro Můstek/tram 3, 9, 14, 24, 26. **Rates** 7,600-9,400 Kč single; 8,200-10,000 Kč double; 11,100-20,800 Kč suite; 25,600-32,000 Kč apartment. **Credit** AmEx, MC, V. **Map** p309 K5.

The Hotel Palace Praha is an excellent alternative to the more expensive and haughty hotels that you'll find on Wenceslas Square. The Palace offers guests a peaceful respite near the city's chicer shops on Na příkopě. The rooms are nothing to write home about, though, but you certainly won't want for comfort.

Hotel services *Disabled: adapted rooms. Interpreting services. No-smoking floors. Sauna.* **Room services** *Dataport. Minibar.*

Expensive

Radisson SAS Alcron

Štěpánská 40, Prague 1 (222 820 000/fax 222 820 100/www.radisson.com). Metro Muzeum/3, 9, 14, 24, 26 tram. **Rates** 6,270-8,850 Kč single/double; 10,050 Kč suite. **Credit** AmEx, DC, MC, V. **Map** p311 K6.

When the Alcron was built in 1930, it was the city's first luxury hotel. Restored to its original art-deco grandeur the Alcron has all the extras of a five-star hotel, plus liberal doses of history and personality. Eighth-floor rooms have views of Prague Castle – those on the sixth and seventh floors have balconies.

Hotel services *Airport transfers. Bar. Concierge. Disabled: adapted rooms. Dry-cleaning. Gym. Limousine service. No-smoking floors. Parking. Restaurant.* **Room services** *Bathrobe. Dataport. Fax. Hairdryer. Internet. Minibar. Room service (24hrs). Safe. Trouser press. Turndown. TV: cable/pay movies/satellite.*

Moderate

Andante

Ve Smečkách 4, Prague 1 (222 210 021/fax 222 210 591/www.andante.cz). Metro Muzeum or IP Pavlova/tram 4, 6, 10, 11, 16, 22, 23. **Rates** 2,500-3,300 Kč single; 3,000-4,000 Kč double; 4,000-5,200 Kč suite. **Credit** AmEx, MC, V. **Map** p311 K7.

This no-frills hotel is located near enough Wenceslas Square for most travellers to feel that they're getting a real bargain. The rooms are cheerful if spartan, and the staff is very accommodating and eager to please. Guest will feel welcome.
Hotel services *Airport transfers. Concierge. Limousine service. No-smoking rooms. Restaurant.* **Room services** *Minibar. TV: satellite.*

Carlo IV

Senovážné náměstí 13, Prague 1 (224 593 111/ fax 224 593 000/www.boscolohotels.com). Metro Náměstí republiky or Hlavní nádraží/tram 5, 9, 26. **Rates** 3,800-10,500 Kč single; 3,800-14,400 Kč double; 12,200-80,000 Kč suite. **Credit** AmEx, DC, MC, V. **Map** p309 M4.
Boscolo Hotels overcame many daunting challenges to create this masterpiece. Carlo IV's building, which was originally a bank and later a communist-era post office, has been completely re-imagined, from the preserved mouldings in the lobby to the cigar bar in the former vault to the Roman-style baths. The hotel's inward opulence and Italian accent compensates for the fact that there's not much to see on the outside.
Hotel services *Air-conditioning. Bar. Beauty salon. Concierge. Gym. Indoor pool. Internet point. Limousine service. No-smoking rooms. Parking (350 Kč per night). Restaurant.* **Room services** *Bathrobe. Hairdryer. Minibar. TV: cable/pay movies/satellite.*

Grand Hotel Evropa

Václavské náměstí 25, Prague 1 (224 228 117/ fax 224 224 544). Metro Můstek/tram 3, 9, 14, 24, 26. **Rates** 2,990 Kč single; 3,990 Kč double; 5,000 Kč apartment. **Credit** AmEx, MC, V. **Map** p309 K5.
Guests here will need a sense of humour and an appreciation of history to enjoy their stay. Behind the drop-dead gorgeous art nouveau-façade lie rooms that time forgot – or at least hasn't exchanged a civil word with since some time in the late 1970s. Unless you're accustomed to curtainless showers, battered furniture and orange rotary phones, you'll definitely know you're not in Kansas anymore. Rooms ending in Nos.01 to 05 on each floor face the square.
Hotel services *Airport transfers. Café. Concierge. Parking. Restaurant.* **Room services** *Ceiling. Four walls.*

Hotel Elite

Ostrovní 32, Prague 1 (224 932 250/www. hotelelite.cz). Metro Národní třída/tram 6, 9, 18, 21, 22, 23, 26. **Rates** 3,400-5,200 Kč single; 3,800-5,950 Kč double; 4,300-6,500 Kč suite. **Credit** AmEx, MC, V. **Map** p310 H6.
Now we're talking. The Hotel Elite stands out with a delicate balance of location, progressive attitude and old-world style. The hotel's modern amenities flesh out its 14th-century bones pleasantly, and it occupies a hip corner of Nové Město renowned for its bars and restaurants.
Hotel services *Bar. Concierge. Hairdresser. Parking. Restaurant.* **Room Services** *Dataport. Minibar. Safe. TV: satellite.*

Hotel Opera

Těšnov 13, Prague 1 (222 315 609/fax 222 311 477/www.hotel-opera.cz). Metro Florenc/ tram 8, 24. **Rates** 2,600-3,500 Kč single; 3,200-4,200 Kč double; 5,000-6,600 Kč suite. **Credit** AmEx, DC, MC, V. **Map** p309 M2.
This low-lying hotel took a soaking in the 2002 floods, but its back on it's feet and once again providing the solid, simple service it's known for. The small rooms are plain but comfortable, and the hot-pink hotel is a short walk from Staré Město.
Hotel services *Bar. Internet. Limousine service. Restaurant.* **Room services** *TV: satellite.*

Marriott

V Celnici 8, Prague 1 (222 888 888/fax 222 888 889/www.marriotthotels.com). Metro Náměstí Republiky/tram 5, 8, 9, 14. **Rates** 5,700-7,300 Kč single/double; 9,600-41,600 Kč suite. **Credit** AmEx, DC, MC, V. **Map** p309 L3.
Marriott prides itself on providing its guests with the same world-class service, regardless of the city. Brimming with conveniences (including a first-class gym, complete with swimming pool) the Prague location is no exception. If its local flavour you're after – or if you find helpful, smiling staff and good service too ordinary – keep looking.
Hotel services *Airport transfers. Babysitting. Bar. Beauty salon. Business services. Concierge. Disabled: adapted rooms. Gym. Internet point. Limousine service. No-smoking floors. Parking. Restaurant. Solarium. Swimming pool.* **Room services** *Air-conditioning. Dataport. Hairdryer. Iron. Minibar. Room service (24hrs). Safe. TV: pay movies/satellite.*

Budget

Hotel 16 U sv. Kateřiny

Kateřinská 16, Prague 2 (224 920 636/224 919 676/fax 224 920 626/www.hotel16.cz). Metro IP Pavlova/tram 4, 6, 10, 11, 16, 22, 23. **Rates** 2,300-2,500 Kč single; 3,100-3,400 Kč double; 3,200-4,600 Kč apartment. **Credit** MC, V. **Map** p311 K8.
This 14-room family-run inn is a little away from the centre, but only minutes from Staré Město via tram. Yet it's as quiet as a small Bohemian town and within easy walking distance of the Botanical Gardens.
Hotel services *Bar.* **Room services** *Air-conditioning. Minibar. Safe. TV: satellite.*

Jerome House

V Jirchářích 13, Prague 1 (224 933 207/fax 224 933 212/www.jerome.cz/jerome-house.html). Metro Národní třída/tram 6, 9, 18, 21, 22, 23, 26. **Rates** 2,000-2,300 Kč single; 2,300-2,900 Kč double. **Credit** MC, V. **Map** p310 H6.
Although technically a hotel, this budget accommodation option, with its dorm-style rooms, bears more than a passing resemblance to a hostel. The location

is convenient for sightseeing and the surrounding streets are full of nightlife. The firm also arranges tours around town and daytrips to outlying towns.
Hotel services *Safe. Terrace.*
Room services *TV: satellite.*

U Šuterů

Palackého 4, Prague 1 (224 948 235/http://usuteru.jsc.cz). Metro Můstek/tram 3, 9, 14, 24, 26. **Rates** 1,790-2,490 Kč single; 2,390-3,990 Kč double; 2,790-3,990 Kč apartment. **Credit** MC, V. **Map** p310 J6.
Traditional inns like this one are common in Malá Strana but almost unheard of so close to Wenceslas Square. The building dates back to 1383, the rooms are cosy and outfitted in comfortable, rustic charm. The pub downstairs is the neighbourhood's best.
Hotel services *Bar. Restaurant.*
Room services *Minibar. TV: satellite.*

Hostels

Charles University Dorms

Voršilská 1, Prague 1 (224 933 825/fax 224 930 361). Metro Národní třída/tram 6, 9, 18, 21, 22, 23, 26. **Rates** 200-500 Kč per person, double. **No credit cards**. **Map** p310 H6.
The central office arranges accommodation in hundreds of dorm rooms scattered throughout the city. An obvious choice for budget-minded travellers who want to meet other young people – but be prepared for some locations that involve true roughing it.
Hostel services *Bedding. Kitchen access.*

Hotel Imperial

Na Poříčí 15, Prague 1 (223 316 012/www.hotelimperial.cz). Metro Náměstí Republiky/tram 5, 8, 9, 14. **Rates** 750-1,500 Kč single; 1,180-2,360 Kč double. **No credit cards**. **Map** p309 L2.
When it was named the Imperial, it nearly deserved it. However, accommodation standards have left this once grand hotel behind, and nowadays it gets by as an ordinary hostel with a strangely ornate stairway, lobby and restaurant (*see p143*).
Hostel services *Bedding. Kitchen access. Lockers. Restaurant.*

Klub Habitat

Na Zderaze 10, Prague 2 (224 921 706/fax 224 918 252). Metro Karlovo náměstí/tram 4, 10, 16, 22, 23. **Rates** 390-500 Kč per person. **No credit cards**. **Map** 310 G7/H7.
It's spic-and-span, all proceeds go to charity and they give you free lemonade. Suspicious? Don't be. It's simply outstanding value, great service, good location – with overwhelming demand. Book ahead.
Hostel services *Bar. Kitchen.*

Further afield

Stay off-centre to mix with the locals and soak up the character of Prague (*see p103*). None of the places listed below are more than a ten- to 15-minute metro or tram ride into the city centre.

Deluxe

Andel's Hotel Prague

Stroupežnického 21, Smíchov, Prague 5 (296 889 688/fax 296 889 999/www.andelshotel.com). Metro Anděl/tram 4, 6, 7, 9, 10, 12, 14. **Rates** 7,260 Kč single; 8,250 Kč double; 10,230-11,880 Kč suite. **Credit** AmEx, MC, V.
A new beacon in Smíchov, a neighbourhood that's one of Prague's redevelopment success stories, this distinctive hotel opened its doors in June 2002. Design work throughout the hotel was done by hot-shot British architects D3A and designers Jestico+Whiles. The theme throughout (especially evident in the lobby) is ultra-modern.The rooms are unquestionably comfy, loaded with choice amenities, including DVD players and a floor-warmer under the bathroom tiles. Business services abound and most public areas are internet hot spots. Fitness facilities are outstanding. You can upgrade any room to 'Andel's Club Room Service' and enjoy extra-special touches, including room-service breakfast.
Hotel services *Air-conditioning. Beauty salon. Business centre. Concierge. Disabled: adapted rooms (2). Dry-cleaning. DVD rentals. Gym. Massage. Meeting facilities. No-smoking floors. Parking (covered). Pet-friendly. Restaurants (2). Sauna. Solarium. Steam bath.* **Room services** *Dataport. DVD player. Minibar. Safe. Trouser press. TV: satellite.*

Le Palais

U Zvonařky 1, Vinohrady, Prague 2 (234 634 111/fax 222 563 350/www.palaishotel.cz). Metro IP Pavlova or Namĕstí míru/tram 4, 10, 16, 22, 23. **Rates** 7,200-9,400 Kč single; 8,000-11,000 Kč double; 38,400-160,000 Kč suite. **Credit** AmEx, DC, MC, V.
Looking at this belle-époque palace in a garden-like corner of Vinohrady today, you'd never guess it was originally a meat-processing plant. Later, renowned Czech artist Luděk Marold moved in and is largely responsible for the pastoral touches like the ceiling frescoes. A member of the Leading Small Hotels of the World, the Palais goes all the way, with marble baths, heated floors and DVD players standard in all rooms. The gym is larger than you would expect for a hotel of this size, and features a Roman-style whirlpool, hydro-jet massage table and six varieties of aroma showers.
Hotel services *Air-conditioning. Airport transfers. Bar. Beauty salon. Concierge. Disabled: adapted rooms (1). Garden. Gym. Internet point. Limousine service. No-smoking rooms. Parking (660 Kč per day). Restaurant.* **Room services** *Bathrobe. Dataport. DVD player. Hairdryer. Minibar. Room service (24 hrs). Sauna. Trouser press. Turndown. TV: satellite.*

Prague Hilton

Pobřežní 1, Karlín, Prague 8 (224 841 111/fax 224 842 378/www.hilton.com). Metro Florenc/tram 8, 24. **Rates** 7,710-9,600 Kč single; 8,040-9,930 Kč double; 11,190-12,450 Kč suite; 23,790 Kč family apartment. **Credit** AmEx, MC, V.

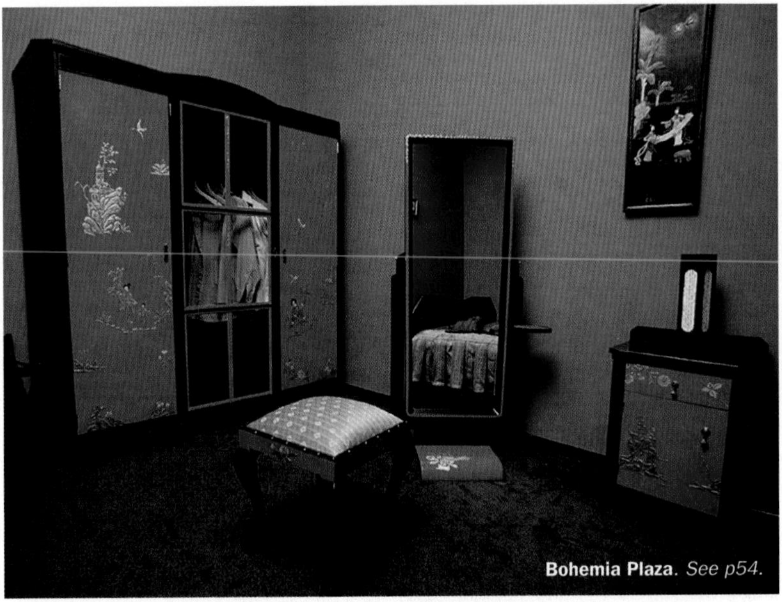
Bohemia Plaza. *See p54.*

Like a boxy spacecraft, the Hilton looms large just east of the centre. The hotel's vast central atrium is home to life-sustaining greenery and restaurants. Visiting Earthlings will appreciate such human touches as the leather armchairs and comprehensive fitness and relaxation centre. Leaders of distant civilisations like the United States like to stay here, and the expansive congress facilities can host teeming multitudes of humanity. Now, if only there were a shuttle to take guests to Planet Prague.
Hotel services *Beauty salon. Disabled: adapted rooms. Gym. Interpreting services. Massage. No-smoking floors. Putting green. Sauna. Swimming pool. Whirlpool.* **Room services** *Dataport (business-class rooms only). Minibar. Safe (business-class rooms only). TV: satellite.*

Expensive

Arcotel Hotel Teatrino

Bořvojova 53, Žižkov, Prague 3 (221 422 211/ fax 221 422 222/www.arcotel.at). Metro Jiřího z Poděbrad/tram 5, 9, 11, 26. **Rates** 4,600 Kč single; 6,300 Kč double. **Credit** AmEx, MC, V.
Only a few years ago, this former communist cultural centre was a tattered hulk destined for the dustbin of history. Now the forces of the free market, sensing the demand for an upscale hotel in Žižkov, have turned this 19th-century building into a strange amalgam of architectural styles and questionable design decisions. But, then, if it weren't quirky, it wouldn't be Žižkov.
Hotel services *Parking. Restaurant. Safe. Sauna.* **Room services** *Dataport. Laundry/ dry-cleaning. Minibar. Room service. Safe. TV: pay movies/satellite.*

Diplomat Hotel Praha

Evropská 15, Dejvice, Prague 6 (296 559 111/ fax 296 559 215/www.diplomatpraha.cz). Metro Dejvická/tram 2, 20, 26. **Rates** 6,270-7,260 Kč single; 7,260-8,250 Kč double; 11,220-14,850 Kč suite. **Credit** AmEx, MC, V.
A good antidote to historical overload, the Diplomat is a spacious oasis of modern comforts. Though it's located on the outer, unremarkable edge of the otherwise pretty Hradčany district, a quick metro or tram ride takes you back into the heart of historic Prague. Situated 20 minutes by car from the airport, the Diplomat is popular with business travellers. Children 12 and under stay free with parents – and they seem to love the basement mini-car drag strip.
Hotel services *Air-conditioning. Bar. Beauty salon. Business services. Disabled: adapted rooms. Gift shops. Gym. Interpreting services. Laundry. Limousine service. No-smoking floors. Parking. Restaurants (2). Safe.* **Room services** *Dataport. Minibar. Radio. Room service (6am-midnight). Safe. TV: pay movies/satellite.*

Mövenpick Hotel

Mozartova 1, Smíchov, Prague 5 (257 151 111/ fax 257 153 131/www.movenpick-prague.com). Metro Anděl/tram 4, 7, 9. **Rates** 5,820 Kč single; 6,420 Kč double. **Credit** AmEx, MC, V.

Yes, it may be a generic big-chain hotel and it's also far from the centre of town, but the Mövenpick offers both holiday-makers and business travellers a wide range of top-shelf amenities. The executive wing is accessible only by cable car and its breathtaking views and fine dining attract many a Czech celebrity. The peaceful park that lies below the hotel is a relaxing place for a stroll. Rooms are modern and very comfy. Ask for one overlooking the courtyard or nearby Villa Bertramka, the Mozart museum (*see p105*). It's just 15 minutes by car to the airport too.
Hotel services *ATM machine. Concierge. Conference rooms. Disabled: adapted rooms (4). Garden. Gift shop. Gym. Massage. No-smoking floors. Parking (covered). Pet-friendly. Restaurants (2). Safe. Sauna.* **Room services** *Dataport. Laundry/dry-cleaning. Minibar. Room service (24hrs). Safe. TV: pay movies/satellite.*

Moderate

Bohemia Plaza

Žitná 50, Prague 2 (224 941 000/fax 224 943 000/www.bohemiaplaza.com). Metro IP Pavlova or Muzeum/tram 4, 6, 10, 11, 16, 22, 23. **Rates** 4,500 Kč single/double; 4,800-6,400 Kč suite. **Credit** MC, V. **Map** p311 K7.

The suites at this family-owned and operated hotel are each decorated with a different theme – such as the sumptuous 'Florence' (suite five) with its rich, dark colours and tapestries. The owners here have combed Europe to find and restore the antique furniture featured throughout. Under communism, the building housed an illicit Catholic chapel on the second floor, which the family still uses for Mass. Monthly rates available.
Hotel services *Bar. Concierge. Meeting room. No-smoking rooms. Parking. Restaurant.* **Room services** *Bathrobe. Iron. Kitchenette. Minibar. Room service (24 hrs). Safe. TV: cable/satellite.*

Dorint Don Giovanni

Vinohradská 157A, Žižkov, Prague 3 (267 031 111/fax 267 036 704/www.dorint.de). Metro Želivského/tram 10, 11, 16, 19, 26, 35. **Rates** 4,400-7,600 Kč single/double; 5,600-8,400 Kč suite. **Credit** AmEx, MC, V.

Relatively isolated from the historical sights (unless you count Kafka's grave next door), the Don Giovanni can seem a little sterile. Service, however, is top-notch and the rooms, fitted with Biedermeier reproductions, are nearly as good as it gets. Potential guests will want to reserve west-facing rooms, as the view to the semi-industrial east is not entirely soothing. 'Expect More' packages include access to the hotel's library, fitness centre and rooftop garden.
Hotel services *Air-conditioning. Airport transfers. Bar. Business services. Concierge. Disabled: adapted rooms. Gym. Limousine service. No-smoking floors. Parking. Restaurant.* **Room services** *Dataport. Hairdryer. Minibar. Room service (24hrs). Safe. TV:cable/satellite/pay movies.*

Budget

Admiral Botel

Hořejší nábřeží, Smíchov, Prague 5 (257 321 302/fax 257 319 516/www.admiral-botel.cz). Metro Anděl/tram 4, 6, 7, 9, 10, 12, 14, 20, 26. **Rates** 1,880-2,980 Kč single; 2,000-3,130 Kč double. **Credit** AmEx, MC, V.

The Admiral is the swishest of Prague's floating hotels (*see p55* ***Ahoj*, matey**). Cabins are still tiny, but the fixtures are modern and the public spaces evoke an old-fashioned ocean liner. Riverside cabins afford views of Vyšehrad and Emmaus monastery.
Hotel services *Bar. No-smoking rooms. Parking. Restaurant.* **Room services** *Hairdryer. Iron. Room service. TV: satellite.*

Ametyst

Jana Masaryka 11, Vinohrady, Prague 2 (222 921 947/fax 222 921 999/www.hotelametyst.cz). Metro Naměstí míru/tram 4, 10, 16, 22, 23. **Rates** 2,500-4,600 Kč single; 2,900-6,200 Kč double. **Credit** AmEx, MC, V.

This quiet hotel is popular with German and Austrian business travellers. The rooms are comfortable if plain, but the Austro-Hungarian wine bar and restaurant, and art collection add character.
Hotel services *Airport transfers. Bar. Concierge. Disabled: adapted room (1). Limousine service. Meeting rooms. No-smoking floors. Restaurant. Sauna. Solarium.* **Room services** *Hairdryer. Minibar. Safe. TV: satellite, pay movies.*

Hotel Abri

Jana Masaryka 36, Vinohrady, Prague 2 (222 515 124/fax 224 254 240/www.abri.cz). Metro Náměstí Míru/4, 10, 16, 22, 23 tram. **Rates** 2,300-3,100 Kč single; 2,800-3,600 Kč double. **Credit** AmEx, MC, V.

An understated little hotel with no pretensions. The Abri's large rooms are modest but tasteful, decorated in soft colours – though they could do with a lick of paint. The staff is eager to please. In warm weather, you can enjoy morning coffee or a twilight beer on the terrace overlooking the leafy courtyard.
Hotel services *Disabled: adapted rooms (1). Parking (220 Kč per night). Restaurant.* **Room services** *Hairdryer. TV: satellite.*

Hotel Anna

Budečská 17, Vinohrady, Prague 2 (222 513 111/fax 222 515 158/www.hotelanna.cz). Metro Náměstí Míru/tram 4, 10, 16, 22, 23. **Rates** 1,900-2,300 Kč single; 2,500-3,100 Kč double; 3,500-4,200 Kč suite. **Credit** AmEx, MC, V.

With its classy wrought-iron railings, brass door-handles and gas fire in the lobby, the Anna retains the stateliness of an earlier era. This old-fashioned walk-up is showing its age, and is unlikely to see more modern improvements, such as its impossibly tiny lift. The top-floor suite seems an afterthought; better to go with one of the doubles below. The summer terrace is delightful.
Hotel services *Air-conditioning. Fax. Laundry. Parking.* **Room services** *Hairdryer. TV.*

Ahoj, matey

If you thought sleeping cheap in Prague meant a dim, characterless box halfway to Poland, think again. A stay in one of the city's **botels**, or floating hotels, offers convenience and character at prices that won't plunder your purse. But get aboard soon before these unique sleeps pull up their gangplanks for good.

Prague's fleet of four botels was launched in the 1960s and 1970s, when the city needed more hotel rooms. Rather than renovate older buildings – a dauntingly expensive project, even with today's foreign investment – communist city fathers took their troubles to the river and, in typical utilitarian fashion, refitted four barges with sleeping berths for the masses.

Without keels or engines, the botels' seaworthiness is limited merely to staying afloat and their hulls are coated with zinc, as they can't be towed to dry dock for repairs. The botels' upper decks were added after the barges were moored to the quays, so the they can't fit under Prague's bridges. Dire and vivid predictions of runaway barges smashing into bridges in the event of a devastating flood proved unjustified in 2002, when the highest water in centuries passed harmlessly under the floating hotels. Low-lying hotels ashore were not so lucky.

Botel cabins are tiny, much like those on more conventional craft, with little space left over for washing facilities. But have no fear of seasickness: the massive hulls are virtually insensitive to the motion of the river.

Sitting on the deck of a botel changes the Prague paradigm. Prague Castle and the city's famed spires fade away as the Vltava takes centre stage. The river is the main draw, faced on both sides by thousands of windows, laced with bridges and teeming with crafts of all sizes.

Quality varies from botel to botel. The oldest of the fleet, the **Albatross** (*see p49*), was launched in 1969 with a 30-year life expectancy, the same as its two descendants, launched not long after. This may account for the ship's general appearance of fatigue. Still, the rates are low given the central location, and the deck affords a wonderful view of riparian comings and goings. Some distance upriver, and up the spectrum, is the **Admiral** (pictured; *see p54*). Here the brass fixtures gleam, cabins sparkle and uniformed staff takes nautical pride in keeping the botel in tip-top condition. The top deck features a restaurant, dance hall and sun deck for 100 people.

No one's spotted any leaks, but there are no plans afloat to replace the fleet. Stow your gear now: this may be your last call to board.

Hotel Arbes-Mepro

Viktora Huga 3, Smíchov, Prague 5 (251 116 555/fax 257 312 380/www.arbes-mepro.cz). Metro Anděl/6, 9, 12 tram. **Rates** 1,700-3,500 Kč single; 2,200-4,000 Kč double. **Credit** AmEx, MC, V.

This hotel is located just four quick tram stops from the Charles Bridge and offers great value. It's also close to the resurgent Smíchov district. Rooms have an attention to detail not often found in this category.

Hotel services *Air-conditioning. Bar. Garden. Parking. TV room.* **Room services** *Minibar. Safe. TV: satellite.*

Hotel Tosca

Blanická 10, Vinohrady, Prague 2 (221 506 111/ fax 221 506 199/www.hotel-tosca.cz). Metro Náměstí Míru/tram 4, 10, 16, 22, 23. **Rates** 2,380-3,650 Kč single; 2,660-4,600 Kč double; 3,480-4,920 Kč apartment. **Credit** AmEx, MC, V. **Map** p313 A3.

The family-friendly Tosca is modestly furnished, but the enthusiastic staff at the hotel is very house-proud. All rooms here are no-smoking. For a true Vinohrady experience, take a room facing the tree-filled courtyard.

Hotel services *Airport transfers. Bar. Concierge. Internet point. Limousine service. Parking (320 Kč per day).* **Room services** *Hairdryer. Minibar. TV: cable/satellite.*

Ibis Praha City

Kateřinská 36, Prague 2 (222 865 777/fax 222 865 666/www.accorhotels.com). Metro IP Pavlova/tram 4, 6, 10, 11, 16, 22, 23. **Rates** 1,870-3,350 Kč single; 2,470-3,950 Kč double. **Credit** AmEx, MC, V. **Map** p311 K8.

Ibis is the Accor group's budget hotel. No surprises, no adventure, just efficient and reliable accommodation. Travellers looking for a little more may want to check out the adjoining Arcotel, with its larger rooms and enhanced services. None of the group's efficient local hotels are more than a few years old.

Hotel services *Air-conditioning. Bar. Disabled: access. Gym. Meeting rooms. Parking. Restaurant (open 24hrs). Swimming pool.* **Room services** *Hairdryer. Minibar. Room service. Safe. TV: cable/pay movies/satellite.*

Other locations: Ibis Praha Karlín, Šaldova 54, Karlín, Prague 8 (222 332 800/fax 224 812 681).

Julian

Elišky Peškové 11, Smíchov, Prague 5 (257 311 150/fax 257 311 149/www.julian.cz). Tram 6, 9, 12, 20. **Rates** 2,400-3,900 Kč single; 2,700-4,200 Kč double. **Credit** AmEx, MC, V.

A favourite of regular travellers to Prague, the Julian offers perfectly adequate, good-value comfort. On the edge of Smíchov, the Julian is slightly off the beaten track, but is just a ten-minute walk or a quick tram ride from Malá Strana. The fourth floor is air-conditioned and apartments have kitchenettes. The fireside reading room and reception area is the Julian's jewel.

Hotel services *Airport/railway station transfers (for fee). Bar. Conference room. Fax. Gym. Internet. Laundry. Massage. No-smoking rooms. Parking. Pet-friendly. Sauna. Solarium. Whirlpool.* **Room services** *Dataport. Safe. TV: pay movies/satellite.*

Pension Vyšehrad

Krokova 6, Vyšehrad, Prague 2 (241 408 455/ www.pension-vysehrad.cz). Metro Vyšehrad. **Rates** 1,000 Kč single; 1,600 Kč double. **No credit cards**.

This family-run pension offers home-style hospitality in a peaceful residential setting. Close to the tranquil green spaces of Vyšehrad, it's a good choice for travellers who like to take it slow. Pets stay free.

Hotel services *Garden. Parking.*

Hostels

A&O Hostel Prague

U Výstaviště 1, Holešovice, Prague 7 (220 870 252). Metro Holešovice/tram 5. **Rates** 330-450 Kč dorm; 900-990 Kč single; 570-660 Kč double. **No credit cards**. **Map** p312 D1.

The A&O offers reasonable bare-bones accommodation with friendly, 24-hour service. It's the best dirt-cheap option in this district, which features the National Gallery's Veletržní palác and Stromovka park. Some rooms have showers. Following a reconstruction, the breakfast cellar will double as a nightclub with live bands. Breakfast is 90 Kč.

Hostel services *Bar. Internet. Lockers. No-smoking hostel. Parking.*

Clown & Bard

Bořivojova 102, Žižkov, Prague 3 (222 716 453/ www.clownandbard.com). Metro Jiřího z Poděbrad/ tram 5, 9, 11, 26. **Rates** 250-400 Kč dorm; 400 Kč per person, 4-6-person apartment (kitchen and private bath). **No credit cards**. **Map** p313 B2.

Prague's premier party hostel attracts a hearty crowd of young backpackers. The house café is the scene of many a late-night debauch for those who can't get enough in the scores of nearby pubs.

Hostel services *Bar. Fax. Laundry.*

Hostel Boathouse

Lodnická 1, Modřany, Prague 4 (tel/fax 241 770 051/www.aa.cz/boathouse). Tram 3, 17, 21. **Rates** 330-360 Kč per person. **No credit cards**.

Despite its location (20 minutes south of the centre by tram) the Boathouse is a favourite with the backpacker set. Sitting on a pastoral Vltava riverbank, the hostel also offers rental bikes for those who really want to stretch their legs, a driving range and tennis courts. Breakfast included.

Hostel services *Internet. Laundry. Parking. Payphone.*

Sir Toby's Hostel

Dělnická 24, Holešovice, Prague 7 (283 870 635/fax 283 870 636/www.sirtobys.com). Metro Vltavská or Nádraží Holešovice/tram 1, 3, 9, 12, 15, 25. **Rates** 250-360 Kč per person, dorm; 650-750 Kč single; 450-525 Kč double. **Credit** AmEx, MC, V. **Map** p312 E2.

The former warehouse district of Holešovice holds a number of gems for the bargain hunter – this hostel one of them. The renovated art-nouveau building is cosier than some of the city's pensions, and the staff is among the friendliest anywhere.

Hostel services *Café. Garden. Internet. Kitchen access. Lockers. Parking. Payphone.*

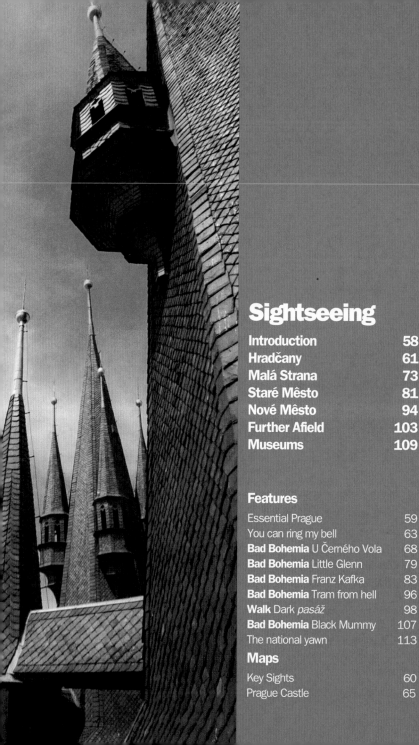

Sightseeing

Features

Maps

Introduction

Compact, ancient and mysterious, the capital of Bohemia is a living cabinet of curiosities. Stray from the path and be rewarded.

Prague's compact old centre will take you on a visual trip through every period of the last millennium. Within blocks of each other you'll encounter palaces, galleries, cellar pubs and mysterious passageways, only to emerge into the formal gardens of some count or other, in a scene straight out of *Amadeus*.

A bend of the Vltava river arcs through the heart of the city, gracing it with nine dramatic bridges, all scaled perfectly for a stroll from one side of Prague to the other. The river eventually runs north to the Baltic after curling around Letná, the high country on the left bank that first provided a strategic vantage to Stone Age peoples. The neighbouring hill of **Hradčany** (*see p61*) gave the first Czech princes, the Přemyslids, their castle foundations, which still exist today under **Prague Castle** (*see p61*). Head here for a heart-stopping overview of the town below.

Between Hradčany and the Vltava, the **Malá Strana** district (*see p73*) is a tapestry of its former histories: a craftsmen's quarter during the medieval period, prize real estate granted to nobles for supporting the crown during the late Renaissance, and a hotbed of poets bristling against foreign domination in coffeehouse cabals during the 19th century. Cottages, fabulous palaces and smoky cafés from each era stand side by side today on its narrow streets.

On the right bank, the river is also responsible for the unique underworld of flat **Staré Město** (*see p81*), the Old Town, with its subterranean drinking holes, cinemas, music halls and galleries. These countless vaulted, stone-walled spaces were once at street level, but constant flooding of the Vltava during the 13th century prompted city fathers to raise the streets one storey to the level at which they lie today. This means that ordinary-looking doorways to pubs and clubs often lead to underground labyrinths.

Prague's layers are such that no matter how deep you dig, you're constantly making new discoveries. People who have lived here for years still stop in amazement when an old passage between favourite streets is reopened (*see p98* **Dark *pasáž***). Many of these walkways through building courtyards haven't seen the light of day for over 50 years but now host designer shops and smart bars. Prague is rediscovering itself, as it digs out from its grey pre-Velvet Revolution days.

Bordering Staré Město to the south and east is **Nové Město** (*see p94*), the New Town, the first area of the city to be laid out with broad streets, planned by Charles IV in 1348. This is where the city's commerce gets done and is also where the uniquely Czech form of political dissent known as defenestration was perfected. All of Europe was plunged into chaos after the tossing out the window of city mugwumps from the New Town Hall. Nové Město's Wenceslas Square is very much the heart of modern Prague and the adjoining Na příkopě street is the place to shop for lifestyle essentials. South of the National Theatre, the area sometimes known as SONA is still blooming as a fashionable, hedonistic quarter.

To the east of the city centre lies the tumble-down district of **Žižkov** (*see p106*), boasting the highest number of pubs per capita in the world. It's also the place to see phenomenal regional music acts and indie artists trying to create conceptual cuts, and meet up with irascible Prague characters. The hippest clubs outside Staré Město are also here.

The good-value **Prague Card** (690 Kč adults, 560 Kč concessions), available at American Express (Václavské náměstí 56, Nové Město, Prague 1, 224 219 992), is valid for three days of public transit and entry to museums (*see p109*), including Prague Castle.

The whole city is, of course, one great outdoor museum, with stunning, free sights aplenty in the centre. For in-depth guided tours, try **City Walks** (608 200 912), which departs from the St Wenceslas equestrian statue, Wenceslas Square, at 9.45am daily (450 Kč, 300 Kč concessions).

Essential Prague

...in one day

The key sights

- Breakfast at the **Globe Bookstore & Coffeehouse**, or a mimosa at **Café Slavia** (for both, *see p144*) in Nové Město.
- Stroll toward the Vltava river past the **National Theatre** (*see p99*), an icon of Czech national identity.
- Cross the **Most Legií** (Legionnaire's Bridge; *see p60*), taking in the city's best view of the Charles Bridge and Prague Castle.
- Walk through **Kampa Park** in Malá Strana and catch the cosmic works by František Kupka at **Kampa Museum** (*see p76*).
- Make your way up the Castle Steps, skipping touristy Nerudova street, to **Prague Castle** (*see p61*).
- Catch the **changing of the Prague Castle guard** at the Hradčanské náměstí gate (best show at noon; *see p64*).
- Reward yourself with a perfectly tapped Kozel beer at **U Černého vola** (*see p71*).
- Catch the **No.22 tram** (*see p273*) down the hill from Hradčany, the best scenic tour of the city around for 12 Kč.
- In **Staré Město**, exit at the Novotného lavka stop and walk across the **Charles Bridge** (*see p88*); make a wish at the **Lorraine cross**.
- Continue across to Malá Strana for lunch with stunning views at **Kampa Park** (*see p125*) or **Hergetova Cihelna** (*see p118*).
- Cross back into **Staré Město** to visit the **Jewish Museum** (*see p92*).
- Stroll on to Dušní and Vězeňská streets to take in the newest monument to literary Prague, the surreal **Franz Kafka statue** (*see p92*).
- Take Pařížská down to **Old Town Square** (*see p82*), checking out the state of early 21st-century capitalism in Bohemia.
- Catch the dancing figures of the Apocalypse on the **Old Town Hall Astronomical Clock** (on the hour 8am-8pm daily; *see p85*).
- Nearby are some of Prague's most unusual permanent and temporary exhibition spaces, including the **Museum of Communism** (*see p115*), **Municipal House** (*see p97*), the **House of the Black Madonna** (*see p81*), **House at the Stone Bell** (*see p199*) and the **Galerie Rudolfinum** (*see p198*).
- Consider more beer and an improbably filling dinner at a classic like **U Medvídků** (*see p151*) or **U Pinkasu** (*see p137*).

...in two days

Style it up with art and live jazz

- Wander the **baroque gardens** of Malá Strana (*see p73*).
- Soak up live jazz at **U Malého Glena** (*see p221*), Czech rock at **Malostranská beseda** (*see p215*) or classical at the **State Opera** (*see p214*), **National Theatre** or **Rudolfinum** (for both, *see p209*).
- Take your kid, or inner kid, to the **Aquarium**, **Prague Zoo** or the **National Technical Museum** (for all, *see p187*).
- Get a taste of Bohemian style at the **Museum of Decorative Arts** (*see p93*) or the **Mucha Museum** (*see p114*).

...in three days

Art, architecture – and more beer

- Get the ghostly perspective or Kafka's angle on Staré Město with a guided **City Walk** (*see p58*).
- Take a crash course in 20th-century architecture with a stroll down **Wenceslas Square** (*see p94*) and lunch at **Jáma** (*see p134*).
- Catch Prague's own brand of mannerist/erotic Renaissance/Old Masters art at the castle: **St George's Convent** (*see p67*), the **Prague Castle Picture Gallery** (*see p64*) and **Sternberg Palace** (*see p70*).
- Wander through **Nové Město**'s attractions: the grand **New Town Hall**; the chilling **Police Museum**; and the sobering **Church of Sts Cyril & Methodius** (for all, *see p102*).
- Survive the **Ultimate Pub Crawl** (*see p149* **Bad Bohemia: Glug like Glen**) or create your own in Žižkov at the **Akropolis** (*see p155*), **Hapu** (*see p156*), **U Houdků** (*see p143*) and **U Sadu** (*see p156*).

...in four days

Go for detail

- The best of outlying **Holešovice**: peruse cosmic modern art at **Veletržní palác** (*see p103*), refresh at **Výletná** beer garden, **Fraktal** or **La Bodega Flamenca** (for all, *see p154*), then explore the extraordinary **Bílek Villa** (*see p111*).
- Seek out the **cubist architecture** of Staré Město and Nové Město (*see p23*).
- Investigate the amazing obscurantism of **Strahov Library** (*see p72*).
- Vow to stay longer and start planning a trip to the beautiful **Šumava** region (*see p264*).

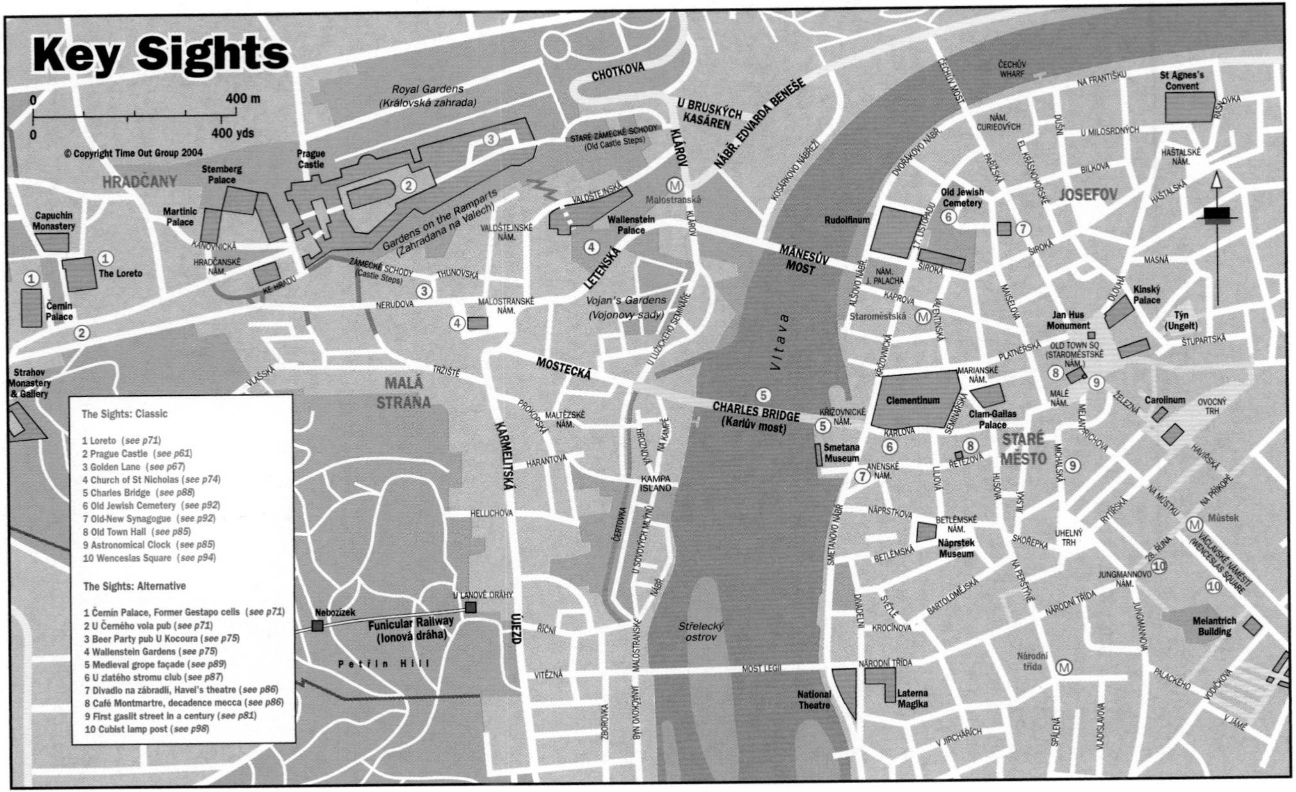
Key Sights
0 400 m
0 400 yds
© Copyright Time Out Group 2004
The Sights: Classic
1 Loreto (see p71)
2 Prague Castle (see p61)
3 Golden Lane (see p67)
4 Church of St Nicholas (see p74)
5 Charles Bridge (see p88)
6 Old Jewish Cemetery (see p92)
7 Old-New Synagogue (see p92)
8 Old Town Hall (see p85)
9 Astronomical Clock (see p85)
10 Wenceslas Square (see p94)
The Sights: Alternative
1 Černín Palace, Former Gestapo cells (see p71)
2 U Černého vola pub (see p71)
3 Beer Party pub U Kocoura (see p75)
4 Wallenstein Gardens (see p75)
5 Medieval grope façade (see p89)
6 U zlatého stromu club (see p87)
7 Divadlo na zábradlí, Havel's theatre (see p86)
8 Café Montmartre, decadence mecca (see p86)
9 First gaslit street in a century (see p81)
10 Cubist lamp post (see p98)
HRADČANY
MALÁ STRANA
STARÉ MĚSTO
JOSEFOV
Royal Gardens (Královská zahrada)
Gardens on the Ramparts (Zahradana na Valech)
Vojan's Gardens (Vojanovy sady)
Vltava
Střelecký ostrov
KAMPA ISLAND
Petřín Hill
Prague Castle
Sternberg Palace
Martinic Palace
Capuchin Monastery
The Loreto
Černín Palace
Strahov Monastery & Gallery
Wallenstein Palace
Funicular Railway (lanová dráha)
Nebozízek
CHARLES BRIDGE (Karlův most)
MÁNESŮV MOST
Rudolfinum
Old Jewish Cemetery
Clementinum
Clam-Gallas Palace
Smetana Museum
Náprstek Museum
Jan Hus Monument
Kinský Palace
Týn (Ungelt)
Carolinum
St Agnes's Convent
National Theatre
Laterna Magika
Melantrich Building
OLD TOWN SQ (STAROMĚSTSKÉ NÁM.)
Malostranská
Staroměstská
Můstek
Národní třída
CHOTKOVA
U BRUSKÝCH KASÁREN
NÁBŘ. EDVARDA BENEŠE
KLÁROV
LETENSKÁ
MOSTECKÁ
KARMELITSKÁ
ÚJEZD
NERUDOVA
ZÁMECKÉ SCHODY (Castle Steps)
STARÉ ZÁMECKÉ SCHODY (Old Castle Steps)
MOST LEGIÍ
VÁCLAVSKÉ NÁMĚSTÍ (WENCESLAS SQUARE)

Hradčany

Topped by the iconic millennium-old Prague Castle, Hradčany hill exudes both mystery and stateliness, with back corridors and lanes made for exploring.

Maps p306 & p307

The roots of the Czech nation have a tangible manifestation in **Prague Castle**, at the centre of the Hradčany district. You can't help but be affected by the dizzying heights of its Gothic spires and the flying buttresses of St Vitus's Cathedral, no matter how often you've seen them before. The coronation of Charles IV and the Nazis' march through the gates are just two moments in Hradčany's 1,000-year history that are likely to give you goose bumps. Nowhere else in Prague resonates with as much national identity and symbolism, increased by the pride Czechs take in having the castle finally returned to them in 1989. Locals and foreigners alike, wanting to escape the hordes that come here by day, will be seen rambling through late at night or on drizzly days when the ghosts of Hradčany are apparently most strongly felt.

The rest of Hradčany comprises the surrounding streets, which stretch north and west from the castle across the hilltop. It's quiet, enchanting and less touristy than the castle itself, and the Nový Svět, or New World, pocket of streets is particularly enchanting. The castle grounds themselves demand lengthy strolling, but you'll find a fair number of options for refuelling in the near vicinity and a handful of terrace restaurants visible below. Otherwise, there are richer pickings down the hill in Malá Strana (*see p73, p121 and p144*).

Prague Castle

Founded some time around AD 870 by Přemysl princes, the impressive if somewhat sombre collection of buildings that make up the castle – including a grand palace, three churches and a monastery – has been variously extended, torn down and rebuilt over the centuries. The final touches, including the present shape of **St Vitus's Cathedral** (*see p65*), were not added until the early 1900s, thus the castle can feel like an enormous festival of architectural styles, stretching all the way back to the Romanesque.

The grandiose façade enclosing the complex is the result of the Empress Maria Theresa's desire to bring some coherence to the jumble of mismatched parts that the castle had become by the mid 18th century. But the outcome of Nicolo Pacassi's monotonous design concept is uninspiring – 'an imposing mass of building in the factory style of architecture', as one 19th-century commentator put it. After Maria Theresa's son, Joseph II, attempted to turn the castle into a barracks, it was largely deserted by the Habsburgs. Václav Havel chose not to live here, although his presidential office was installed in the castle. He did his best to enliven the palace, opening it to the public and hiring the costume designer from the film *Amadeus* to remodel the guards' uniforms.

You really can't get away without spending at least half a day up at the castle. And, unfortunately, every visitor to Prague knows this. The result is a notable lack of

Grand horizons: **Prague Castle**.

You can ring my bell

Church bells in the Czech lands have always been considered guardians of the parishes in which they pealed. If a bell's ring was ever silenced, that could only be bad news – and a fearsome portent.

When one as grand as Sigismund, the greatest of St Vitus's Cathedral bells (*see p65*), forged in 1549, begins to crack up, it's surely time to bolt the door and crawl under the bed. No wonder that Czechs held their breath in terror on 15 June 2002 when Sigismund's 400-or-so-kilogram (882-pound) clapper, known in Czech as the *srdce*, or heart, broke after the fifth chime announcing St Vitus's Day. Historians, politicians, astrologers and the generally pessimistic Czech public immediately began debating what calamity must be just around the corner. Students, workers and other regulars at Prague's *pajzls* (the oldest guard of cheap Czech pubs, little changed since communism) sat up late over their beer rounds speculating about increasingly dismal scenarios.

Thus it was almost a relief to many when the first alarming development turned up: in the parliamentary elections that officially closed on the day of the accident, the communists emerged as the third most powerful party in the country. For the first time since the Velvet Revolution the repudiated party had a solid chance to be in the governing coalition with the victorious Social Democrats.

This, however, was just a taste of the biblical pox to come. A month later – tradition dictates that the parish remains in danger as long as the bell is out of action – a happening worse than anyone had foreseen struck Prague on a fine, warm summer afternoon.

The most devastating floods in the modern history of the country washed down the Vltava river from the Šumava mountains, knocking out the Metro, backing up the sewers of prime riverside real estate, washing toxic waste from a large chemical plant into the city and causing damage totalling billions of crowns. In Prague and the whole of southern and western Bohemia, tens of thousands of people were evacuated, several died, and national archives and cultural treasures were destroyed. Even a favourite baby elephant at the Prague Zoo was drowned as crowds watched helplessly – zookeepers were unable to get the terrified creature to come out of his enclosure to safety.

Despite a budget crisis, Prague Castle officials decided to dally no longer in getting Sigismund back in place, securely swinging and ringing again. 'God knows what else would befall the country in the meantime,' recalls Viktor Procházka of the department of art collections at the castle.

Though sceptics had predicted repairs to the massive bell would take up to a year and bellmaker Petr Matuš's workshop was among the destroyed riverside properties, the master craftsman, whose family has been casting bells since the Middle Ages, nevertheless came to the rescue. Salvaging the essential equipment from his base in Zbraslav, he relocated to the workshop of a fellow bell caster in east Bohemia and set to work there. Sigismund was back in action in time for the next major Czech church holiday, St Wenceslas's Day (28 September). On hearing the mother of all bells peal again, the nation heaved a collective sigh of relief. Notably silent were all the skeptics who usually scoff at old Czech superstitions.

any real city life and an awful lot of chattering tour groups and whirring video cameras. To avoid the worst of the crush, come as early or as late in the day as you can. Another frustration is the almost complete lack of labelling in English and lacklustre exhibits on the castle tour – the St Vitus crypt looks more like a concrete bunker, despite being the final resting place for the nation's most hallowed forefathers. Major renovations are planned, however, and most of the docent ladies installed around the castle and its palaces are friendly, English-speaking and forthcoming.

The first & second courtyards

The grandest entrance to the Prague Castle complex, through the **Hradčanské náměstí gates**, is overseen from a discreet distance by an approving Tomáš Garrigue Masaryk, the first president of free Czechoslovakia, whose bronze likeness was added during the cultural festival Praha 2000. The gateway has been dominated since 1768 by Ignatz Platzer's monumental sculptures of battling Titans. They create an impressive, if not exactly welcoming, entrance. The changing of the guard takes place in this courtyard, a Havel-

The high and mighty **St Vitus's Cathedral**. *See p65.*

inspired attempt to add some ceremonial pzazz to the castle. The change is carried out on the hour every day from 5am to 10pm, but the big crowd-pulling ceremony, complete with band, takes place at noon. The two tapering flagpoles are the work of Slovene architect Josip Plečnik, who was hired by President Masaryk in the 1920s to create a more uniform look for the seat of the First Republic.

To reach the second courtyard go through the Matthias Gate (Matyášova brána), a baroque portal dating from 1614, topped by a double-headed German Imperial Eagle that pleased Hitler when he came to stay in 1939. A monumental stairway is visible from inside the passage (on the lefthand side), which leads up to the magnificent gold-and-white **Spanish Hall** (Španělský sál). It's open to the public only during occasional concerts, but they are worth watching. Built in the 17th century for court ceremonies, the decor was redone in the 19th century, when the trompe l'œil murals were covered with white stucco, and huge mirrors and gilded chandeliers were brought in to transform the space into a glitzy venue for the coronation of Emperor Franz Josef I.

Franz Joseph, however, failed to show up and it was not until the 1950s that the hall was given a new use – it was here the Politburo came to discuss the success of their latest five-year plan, protected from assassins by a reinforced steel door. Behind the austere grey walls of the second courtyard lies a warren of opulent state rooms whose heyday dates from the time of Rudolf II. The state rooms of the airy second courtyard, which are rarely open to the public, housed Rudolf's magnificent art collection and such curiosities as a unicorn's horn and three nails that are supposedly from Noah's ark. The bulk of the collection was carried off in 1648 by Swedish soldiers, although some remnants are housed in the **Prague Castle Picture Gallery** (*see p111*) on the north side of the courtyard near the **Powder Bridge** (U Prašného mostu) entrance. A 17th-century baroque fountain and the **Chapel of the Holy Rood** dominate the yard. The chapel now houses a box office for castle tours and concert tickets and also rents out audio guides.

Prague Castle

Hradčanské náměstí, Prague 1 (224 373 368/ 224 372 434/old.hrad.cz). Metro Malostranská/tram 12, 22, 23. **Open** *Jan-April, Nov-Dec* 9am-4pm daily. *May-Oct* 9am-5pm daily. **Admission** 220 Kč; 120 Kč concessions. *Guided tours in a foreign language* 400 Kč for up to 5 people; 80 Kč per additional person. **Credit** AmEx, MC, V. **Map** p306 C2/D2.

There's no charge to enter the grounds of the castle, but you will need a ticket to see the main attractions. An audio guide (available in English) costs extra; pick one up from the information centre in the second courtyard. One ticket covers entrance to the Old Royal Palace, the Basilica of St George, the Golden Lane, the Powder Tower and the choir, crypt and tower of St Vitus's Cathedral (except Jan-Apr & Oct-Dec, when the tower is closed and the Golden Lane is free). Entrance to the art collection of St George's Convent (*see p110*) and the Toy Museum (*see p116*) is extra.

It's a stiff walk up to the castle from Malá Strana's Malostranská metro station. The least strenuous approach is to take the No.22 tram up the hill and get off at the Pražský hrad stop. There are a handful of adequate cafés within the castle complex, if you don't mind paying double the usual prices.

St Vitus's Cathedral

The third courtyard – the oldest and most important site in the castle – is entirely dominated by the looming towers, pinnacles and buttresses of St Vitus's Cathedral (Katedrála sv. Víta). Entry is free to the nave and chapels, but at the time of writing a ticket was required for the rest. That may change in the near future, thanks to public outcry, so check the castle website for developments.

Although the cathedral was only completed in 1929, exactly 1,000 years after the murdered St Wenceslas was laid to rest on the site, there's no doubt the magnificent building is the spiritual centre of Bohemia. This has always been a sacred place: in pagan times Svatovít, the Slavic god of fertility, was worshipped on this site, a clue as to why the cathedral was dedicated to his near namesake St Vitus (*svatý Vít* in Czech) – a Sicilian peasant who became a Roman legionnaire before he was thrown to the lions. Right up until the 18th century young women and anxious farmers would bring offerings of wine, cakes and cocks. The cathedral's Gothic structure owes its creation to Charles IV's lifelong love affair with Prague. In 1344 he managed to secure an archbishopric for the city, and work began on the construction of a cathedral under the direction of French architect Matthew of Arras. Inconveniently, Matthew died eight years into the project, so the Swabian Peter Parler was called in to take up the challenge. He was responsible for the *Sondergotik* or German late Gothic design. It remained unfinished until late 19th-century nationalists completed the work according to Parler's original plans. The skill with which the later work was carried out makes it difficult to tell where the Gothic ends and the neo-Gothic begins, but a close look at the nave, the twin towers and the rose window of the west end will reveal the telltale lighter-coloured newer stone.

From outside, as from anywhere you look at it in the town below, the **Great Tower** is easily the most dominant feature. The Gothic and Renaissance structure is topped with a baroque dome. This houses Sigismund (*see p63* **You can ring my bell**), unquestionably the largest bell in Bohemia, made in the middle of the 16th century, weighing in at a hefty 15,120 kilograms (33,333 pounds). The clapper weighs slightly over 400 kilograms (882 pounds). Getting Sigismund into the tower was no mean feat: according to legend it took a rope woven from the hair of the city's noblest virgins to haul it into position. Below the tower is the **Gothic Golden Portal** (Zlatá brána), visible

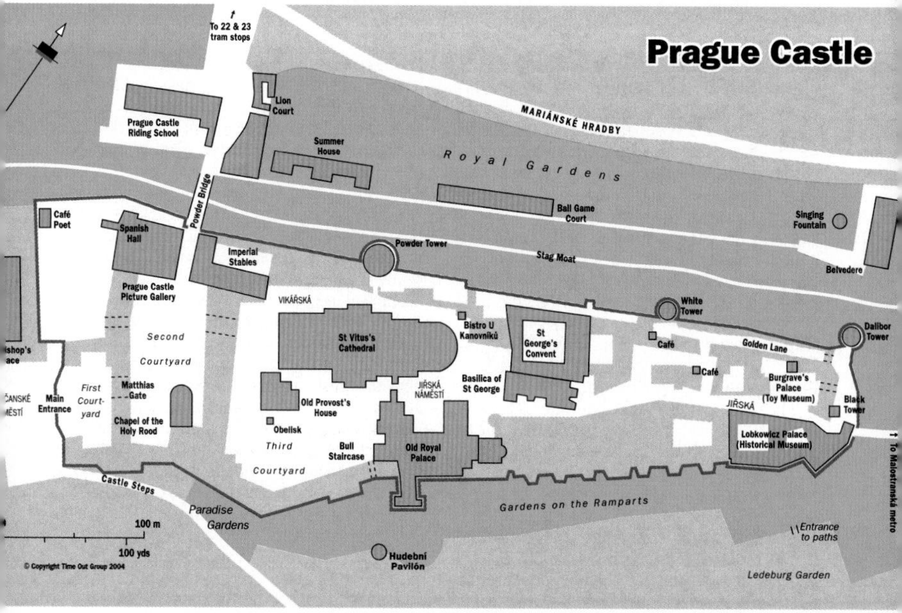

from the courtyard south of the cathedral. It's decorated with a mosaic of multicoloured Venetian glass depicting the Last Judgement. A Getty-funded project has restored its original lustre after years of refurbishment. On either side of the centre arch are sculptures of Charles IV and his wife, Elizabeth of Pomerania, whose talents allegedly included being able to bend a sword with her bare hands.

Inside, the enormous nave is flooded with multicoloured light from the gallery of stained-glass windows created at the beginning of this century. All 21 of them were sponsored during a period of nationalist fervour by finance institutions including, (third on the right) an insurance company whose motto – 'those who sow in sorrow shall reap in joy' – is subtly incorporated into the biblical allegory. The most famous is the third window on the left, in the **Archbishop's Chapel**, created by Alfons Mucha. It depicts the struggle of Christian Slavonic tribes; appropriately enough, the artwork was paid for by Banka Slavia.

On the right is the **Chapel of St Wenceslas** (Svatováclavská kaple), on the site of the original tenth-century rotunda where 'Good King' Wenceslas was buried. Built in 1345, the chapel has 1,345 polished amethysts, agates and jaspers incorporated into its design and contains some of the saint's personal paraphernalia, including armour, chain shirt and helmet. Alas, it's closed to the public – too many sweaty bodies were causing the gilded plaster to disintegrate – but you can catch a glint of its treasure trove over the railings.

Occasionally, on state anniversaries, the skull of the saint is put on display, covered with a cobweb-fine veil. A door in the corner leads to the chamber that contains the crown jewels. A papal bull of 1346 officially protects the jewels, while legend has it that fate prescribes an early death for anyone who uses them improperly. At any rate, the curse seemed to work on the Nazis' man in Prague, Reichsprotektor Reinhard Heydrich tried on the crown and was assassinated shortly afterward by the resistance. The door to the chamber is locked with seven keys, after the seven seals of Revelations, each looked after by a different Prague state or church official.

The most extraordinary baroque addition to the cathedral was the silver **tombstone of St John of Nepomuk**, the priest who was flung from Charles Bridge in 1393 as a result of King Wenceslas IV's anti-clerical wrath. The tomb, designed by Fischer von Erlach the Younger in 1733-36, is a flamboyant affair (the entry ticket is now required to get a proper look at it; *see p64*). An astonishing 2,032 kilograms (two tons) of silver was used for the pedestal, statue of the saint and fluttering cherubs holding up a red velvet canopy. The phrase 'baroque excess' scarcely does it justice. Close by is the entrance to the crypt. Below lie the remains of various Czech monarchs, including Rudolf II. Easily the most eye-catching tomb is Charles IV's modern, streamlined metal affair, designed by Kamil Roškot in the mid 1930s. However, the vault itself, hastily excavated between world wars, has a distinctly cramped, temporary look to it.

The third courtyard

After the cathedral, the second most noticeable monument in the third courtyard is the fairly incongruous 17-metre-high (50-foot) granite obelisk, a memorial to the dead of World War I, erected by Plečnik in 1928.

Close to the Golden Portal is the entrance to the **Old Royal Palace** (Starý královský palác; ticket required, *see p64*), which contains three areas of royal chambers. Six centuries of kings called the palace home and systematically built on new parts over the old. The basement, which contains the 12th-century Romanesque remains of Prince Soběslav's residence, was undergoing renovations at press time, but was due to open by summer 2004. A worthwhile highlight that is open, if worn, is the **Vladislav Hall**, designed by Benedict Ried at the turn of the 16th century. The hall boasts an exquisitely vaulted ceiling, representing the last flowering of Gothic in Bohemia, while the large, square windows were among the first expressions of the Renaissance. It is here that the National Assembly elects its new president. The specially designed **Rider's Steps**, at the east end, allowed knights to enter the hall without dismounting. On the floor above is the **Bohemian Chancellery** and the window through which the victims of the defenestration of 1618 were ejected. This room was also undergoing renovation at press time, but the chamber above, in which the Habsburgs inflicted their payback – 27 Czech nobles were sentenced to death after the Battle of White Mountain in 1621 – is now open.

The **Diet chamber** ('diet' essentially means 'parliament'), above the Rider's Steps, is the third attraction to the palace, featuring heraldic crests from all the best families of Bohemia and a few editions from the court library, catalogued before numerical systems were invented, using an imaginative system of plant and animal images on the spines.

Just east of the cathedral is Jiřské náměstí, named after **St George's Basilica** (Bazilika sv. Jiří). If you stand far enough back from the basilica's crumbling red-and-cream baroque façade, you'll notice the two distinctive Romanesque towers jutting out behind. The

Toilets turned tourist attraction – **Golden Lane** cleans up its act.

Italian craftsmen who constructed them in 1142 built a fatter male tower (Adam, on the right) standing guard over a more slender female one (Eve, on the left). The basilica, founded by Prince Vratislav in AD 921, has burned down and been rebuilt over the centuries. Its first major remodelling took place 50 years after it was originally erected, when a Benedictine convent was founded next door. A major renovation in the early 20th century swept out most of the baroque elements and led to the uncovering of the original arcades, remnants of 13th-century frescoes and the bodies of a saint (Ludmila, who was strangled by assassins hired by Prince Wenceslas's mother Drahomíra) and a saint-maker (the notorious Boleslav the Cruel, who martyred his brother Wenceslas by having him stabbed to death). The basilica's rediscovered simplicity and clean lines seem far closer to godliness than the mammon-fuelled baroque pomposity of most Prague churches.

On the left of the main entrance is an opening built to give access for the Benedictine nuns from **St George's Convent** next door (now housing part of the National Gallery's vast collections; *see p110*) and to keep to a minimum their contact with the outside world.

Vikářská lane, on the north side of the cathedral, is where Picasso and Eluard came to drink in the Vikářská tavern, now closed. It gives access to the 15th-century Mihulka or **Powder Tower** (Prašná věž). Here Rudolf II employed his many alchemists, who were engaged in attempts to distil the Elixir of Life and transmute base metals into gold. Today the tower hosts exhibits (in Czech only) about alchemy and Renaissance life in the castle.

Elsewhere on the castle grounds

Going down the hill from St George's, signposts direct you to the most visited street in Prague, **Golden Lane** (Zlatá ulička; ticket required Mar-Sept, *see p64*). The tiny multicoloured cottages that cling to Prague Castle's northern walls were thrown up by the poor in the 16th century out of whatever waste materials they could find. Some allege that the name is a reference to the alchemists of King Rudolf's days, who supposedly were quartered here. Others contend that it alludes to a time when soldiers billeted in a nearby tower used the lane as a public urinal. In fact, the name probably dates from the 17th century, when the city's goldsmiths worked here. Houses used to line both sides of the street, with barely enough space to pass between them, until a hygiene-conscious Joseph II had some of them demolished in the 18th century. Although the houses look separate, a corridor runs the length of their attics and used to be occupied by the sharpshooters of the Castle Guard. The house

Bad Bohemia U Černého vola

One of the last great holdouts against the banal forces of the free market is an unprepossessing pub – or should we say shrine – known as **U Černého vola** (pictured: *see p143*). This smoky beerhall, furnished with blocky wooden benches and tables in two rooms of yellow-stained plaster, bedecked with heraldic crests, doesn't exactly look like the leader of a non-commercial resistance movement. Yet any drinker here will immediately notice a certain spirit of defiance. Not to mention a remarkably authentic crowd, whatever that means, for a pub that sits just a few hundred strides away from Prague Castle (*see p61*).

So how has the most intransigent pub in the heart of the city's most touristy district hung on to life, still serving pub grub for 60 Kč and Primo Kozel and Pilsner Urquell beer for less than 25 Kč after 14 years? The appropriately named 'At the Black Ox' saw the writing on the wall after 1989 but stubbornly refused to change an iota of the way it had done business for 24 years.

With just one exception: owners and patrons are no longer state-run. But neither are they strictly commercial. At a time when the concept of a non-commercial, non-state organisation was utterly foreign, U Černého vola founded the civic organisation Association of the Pub at the Black Ox. It was premised on the principle that, if city hall would agree not to privatise the pub, the owners would agree to donate all profits to a neighbouring music academy for the blind.

Aside from preserving the operational status quo, the association is charged with keeping the original, local clientele coming in. 'We don't want the pub to get into the hands of some money-greedy businessmen who will turn it into one of those globalised-looking pubs that are all over Prague now, and destroy its spirit,' says Zdeněk Taichman, head of the association. He argues that the association is doing as much for the city of Prague as it is for the patrons by protecting what amounts to a national treasure of social and cultural heritage.

Founded in 1992, the nine-member association has included literati like Karel Pecka, a celebrated Czech writer whose prose and poetry was drawn from his experience as a political prisoner in the 1950s. It's an exclusive club, needless to say, and not accepting any new membership applications. It is effective, though. In 1993 the association drafted a new contract with the city to run the pub for another ten years.

The Association of the Black Ox shouldn't, however, be confused with the Society of the Friends of Beer, whose sign hangs above their official table in the back room of the pub. Although it's nearly as old as the former association, the latter appears to be still formulating just what its manifesto should be.

'I don't know what they do at their meetings,' says harried publican Bohumil Landergot, distracted for a rare moment from pulling taps. 'They meet up every Thursday at six, drink beer and just chat,

at No.22 was owned by Kafka's sister Ottla, and he stayed here for a while in 1917, reputedly drawing the inspiration from the streets for his novel *The Castle*. If he rewrote it today, he'd call it *The Souvenir Shop*. Atmospheric at night, by day the lane is logged with shuffling tourists.

At the eastern end some steps take you under the last house and out to the **Dalibor Tower** (Daliborka), named after its most famous inmate, who amused himself by playing the violin while awaiting execution. According to legend (and Smetana's opera *Dalibor*), he attracted crowds of onlookers who turned up at his execution to weep en masse. Continuing down the hill takes you past a **Lobkowicz Palace** (Lobkovický palác), one of several in the town. This one, finished in 1658, houses the Historical Museum (Jiřská 3, no phone, old.hrad.cz, closed Mon). Opposite is Burgrave House, home of the **Toy Museum** (*see p116*), adjacent to the generally more interesting **Leica Gallery** (Supreme Burgrave's House, Jiřská ulice, 233 355 757, www.leicagallery.cz, closed Mon) of photography. The statue of a naked boy in the courtyard fell victim to Marxist-Leninist ideology when President Novotný decided that his genitals were not an edifying sight for the populace and ordered them to be removed. Happily the boy and his equipment have since been reunited.

The lane passes underneath the **Black Tower** (Černá věž) and ends at the **Old Castle Steps** (Staré zámecké schody), which lead to Malá Strana, as do the **Castle Steps** (Zámecké schody) on Thunovská (accessed from the other end of the castle). Before

I think.' The Friends of Beer has one advantage over its more ambitious rival, though. Membership is highly democratic. They just 'come and go,' he says.

Fortunately, at least one person permanently on the premises remains alert and vigilant against possible threats. 'As long as I am alive this place will remain the same,' Landergot says. 'We won't let it go.' Just a bit of an ox himself, he doesn't even take kindly to questions about ongoings at the pub. 'Come and have a look,' he will tell any caller. 'I won't tell you anything.'

What he *will* tell you is what happens to unwary would-be developers who regularly wander in with ideas for a buyout: 'One of threatened me, saying "In a year and a day you no longer will be here".' Landergot simply tossed out the would-be arbitrageur. He recalls the encounter with disgust. 'This guy wanted to turn the pub into a Smirnoff bar.'

descending, pause at the top for a view over the red tiled roofs, spires and domes of the Lesser Quarter (*see p73*). An even better view can be had from the **Paradise Gardens** (Rajská zahrada; *see also p75*) on the ramparts below the castle walls (enter from the Bull Staircase or from outside the castle, to the right of the first courtyard). This is where the victims of the second and most famous defenestration fell to earth. They were fortunate that it was a favoured spot for emptying chamber pots, as the dung heap surely saved the lives of the defenestrated Catholic counsellors. The site is now marked by an obelisk, signifying ground consecrated by the victorious Habsburgs after putting down the upstart Czech Protestants.

The gardens, which were initially laid out in 1562, were redesigned in the 1920s by Josip Plečnik. The spiralling **Bull Staircase** leading up to the castle's third courtyard and the huge granite bowl are his work. Their restoration is complete after many years, and you can now make the descent to Malá Strana via the terraced slopes of five beautiful Renaissance gardens, open, like most gardens in Prague, from April to October only. The pride of the restoration is the lovely **Ledebour Gardens** (Ledeburska zahrada), featuring fountains, ornate stone stair switchbacks and palace yards, and emptying you out on to the middle of **Valdštejnská**. Fit hikers might consider ascending to the castle this way as well, though there's an entrance fee of 60 Kč whichever way you go.

The Royal Garden & the Belvedere

Cross over the **Powder Bridge** (U Prašného mostu) from the castle's second courtyard and you will reach the **Royal Garden** (Královská zahrada), on the outer side of the **Stag Moat** (Jelení příkop). Laid out for Emperor Ferdinand I in the 1530s, it once included a maze and a menagerie, but was devastated by Swedish soldiers in the 17th century.

At the eastern end of the gardens is the **Belvedere**, saved from French fire in the 18th century by a canny head gardener's payment of 30 pineapples. The stunning Renaissance structure was built by Paola della Stella between 1538 and 1564 (though work was interrupted by a fire at the castle in 1541). The strangely shaped green copper roof is supported by delicate arcades and columns. The Belvedere was the first royal structure in Prague to be dedicated to pleasure-seeking rather than power-mongering – it was commissioned by Ferdinand I as a gift for his wife, Anne – a loveshack one remove away from the skulduggery of life in Prague Castle. But the long-suffering Anne never got to see 'the most beautiful piece of Renaissance architecture north of the Alps' – as the city's gushing tourist brochures invariably call it. She drew her last breath after producing the 15th heir to the throne. The royal couple are immortalised in the reliefs adorning the façade. The Belvedere went on to become the site of all sorts of goings-on: mad King Rudolf installed his astronomers here and the communists later bricked up the windows of the upper level to prevent assassins from getting too close to the president. People come here today to see occasional art shows. In front of the palace is the so-called **Singing Fountain** (Zpívající fontána), created in bronze by Bohemian craftsmen in the 1560s. It used to hum as water splashed into its basin but sings no longer, thanks to overzealous reconstruction.

On the southern side of the garden, overlooking the Stag Moat, is another lovely Renaissance structure, completed by Bonifác Wohlmut in 1563 to house the king's **Ball Game Court** (Míčovna). The elaborate black-and-white sgraffito has to be renewed every 20 years. The last time this was done some decidedly anachronistic elements were added to the allegorical frieze depicting Science, the Virtues and the Elements: look carefully at the lovely ladies on the top of the building and you'll see that the woman seated next to Justice (tenth from the right) is holding a hammer and sickle. On the same side of the garden, by the entrance, is the quaint, mustard-coloured **Dientzenhofer Summer House**, the presidential residence from 1948 to 1989. During this period, large sections of the castle were closed to the public and huge underground shelters were excavated to connect the exalted president's residence with the remainder of the complex. No sooner were the shelters completed than it was seen that the subterranean passages might help to conceal counter-revolutionary saboteurs, and so the exit shafts were blocked off with enormous concrete slabs.

Hradčany

Hradčany owes its grand scale and pristine condition to a devastating fire in 1541, which destroyed the medieval district, and the frenzied period of Counter-Reformation building that followed the Protestant defeat at the Battle of White Mountain in 1620. Little has changed here in the last two centuries.

The area's focal point is **Hradčanské náměstí**, one of the grandest squares in the city, lined with imposing palaces built by the Catholic aristocracy, anxious to be close to the Habsburg court. It was nonetheless cut off from the castle and its temperamental inhabitants by a complicated system of fortifications and moats, which remained until Empress Maria Theresa had a grand spring clean in the mid 18th century. Along with the moat went the tiny Church of the Virgin Mary of Einsedel, which used to stand next to the castle ramp. Lovely as this was said to have been, it's hard to believe that it was lovelier than the superb panorama of Malá Strana, the **Strahov Gardens** (*see p72*) and **Petřín hill** (*see p78*) that the demolition opened up.

Over on the north side of the square, next to the castle, is the domineering 16th-century **Archbishop's Palace** (Arcibiskupský palác), which was tarted up with a frothy rococo façade in 1763-64. Next door, slotted between the palace and a lane of former canons' houses, stands the **Sternberg Palace** (Šternberský palác; *see p109*), which houses part of the National Gallery's collection of European art. Opposite stands the heavily restored **Schwarzenberg Palace** (Schwarzenberský palác), one of the most imposing Renaissance buildings in Prague. It was built between 1545 and 1563, the outside exquisitely decorated with 'envelope' sgraffito. Alas, thanks to the return of nationalised property, it no

Welcome to the New World order, in **Nový Svět.**

longer contains the Military Museum, which long had a comprehensive collection of killing instruments.

Further up Loretánská is the respected pub **U Černého vola** (*see p68* **Bad Bohemia: U Černého vola**), a Renaissance building with a crumbling mural on the façade. As a result of some direct action in 1991, it's one of the few places left in Hradčany where the locals can afford to drink. Its well-worn environs make for a just reward after a day of castle-trekking and you don't have to feel guilty about the amount you drink here – all profits from the sale of beer go to a nearby school for the blind.

The pub overlooks **Loretánské náměstí**, a split-level square on the site of a pagan cemetery. Half of it is taken up by a car park for the Ministry of Foreign Affairs in the monolithic **Černín Palace** (Černínský palác) – an enormous and unprepossessing structure; its long and imposing grey façade, articulated by an unbroken line of 30 pillars, is telling. Commissioned in 1669 by Humprecht Johann Černín, the Imperial ambassador to Venice, the construction of the palace financially ruined his family. As a result, the first people to move in were hundreds of 17th-century squatters. Gestapo interrogations were later conducted here during the Nazi occupation. Its curse surfaced again in 1948, when Foreign Minister Jan Masaryk, the last major political obstacle to Klement Gottwald's communist coup, fell from an upstairs window a few days after the takeover and was found dead on the pavement below. No one really believed the official verdict of suicide, but no evidence of who was responsible has ever come to light.

Somewhat dwarfed by the Černín Palace is the **Loreto** (*see p72*), a baroque testimony to the Catholic miracle culture that swept the Czech lands after the Thirty Years War. The façade (1721) is a swirling mass of stuccoed cherubs, topped with a bell tower. Every hour the 27 bells ring out the cacophonous melody 'We Greet You a Thousand Times'.

The streets behind the Loreto are some of the prettiest and quietest in Hradčany, and are known as **Nový Svět** (New World). The quarter was built in the 16th century for Prague Castle staff; its tiny cottages are now the most prized real estate in the city. Going down Kapucínská, you pass the **Domeček**, or Little House, at No.10, once home to the notorious Fifth Department – the counterintelligence unit of the Defence Ministry. At No.5 on the nearby Černínská is **Gambra** (Černínská 5, 220 514 527, closed Mon, Tue and Apr-Sept), a funky gallery specialising in surrealist art. Its owner, the world-renowned animator Jan Švankmajer, lives in the attached house. At the foot of the hill is Nový Svět street itself, full of brightly coloured cottages restored in the 18th and 19th centuries – all that remains of Hradčany's medieval slums. The rest were destroyed in the great fire of 1541. Tycho Brahe, the Danish alchemist known for his missing nose and breakthroughs in accurate observations of orbits, lived at No.1, the Golden Griffin.

Back up from Loretánské náměstí is Hradčany's last major square, **Pohořelec**. The passage at No.8 leads to the peaceful surroundings of the **Strahov Monastery** (Strahovský klášter; *see p72*), which contains some magnificent libraries and religious art.

Going for gold at the baroque **Loreto**.

The Loreto

Loretánské náměstí 7, Prague 1 (220 516 740). Tram 22. **Open** 9am-12.15pm, 1-4.30pm Tue-Sun. **Admission** 90 Kč; 60 Kč concessions. **No credit cards. Map** p306 B2/3.

The Loreto is probably the most outlandish piece of baroque fantasy you'll see in Prague. Its attractions include a sculpture of the bearded St Wilgefortis, the skeletons of another two female saints and the highest concentration of cherubs found anywhere in the city. It was built as part of a calculated plan to reconvert the masses to Catholicism after the Thirty Years' War.

At the Loreto's heart is a small chapel, the Santa Casa, whose history is so improbable that it quickly gained cult status. The story goes that the original Santa Casa was the home of Mary in Nazareth until it was miraculously flown over to Loreto in Italy by angels, spawning a copycat cult all over Europe. This one, dating from 1626-31, boasts two beams and a brick from the 'original', as well as a crevice left on the wall by a divine thunderbolt that struck an unfortunate blasphemer. The red colour scheme makes it look less like a virgin's boudoir and more like a place in which to hold a black mass.

The shrine was a particular hit with wealthy ladies, who donated the money for baroque maestri Christoph and Kilian Ignaz Dientzenhofer to construct the outer courtyards and the Church of the Nativity (1716-23) at the back. They also sponsored the carving of St Wilgefortis (in the corner chapel to the right of the main entrance), the patron saint of unhappily married women, who grew a beard as a radical tactic to get out of marrying a heathen, and that of St Agatha the Unfortunate, who can be seen carrying her severed breasts on a meat platter (in the Church of the Nativity). The famous diamond monstrance, designed in 1699 by Fischer von Erlach and sporting 6,222 stones, is in the treasury.

Strahov Monastery

Strahovský klášter

Strahovské nádvoří 1, Prague 1 (220 517 451/www.strahovskyklaster.cz). Tram 8, 22/bus 143, 149, 217. **Open** 9am-noon, 1-5pm daily. **Admission** 60 Kč. **No credit cards. Map** p306 A4.

The Premonstratensian monks set up house here in 1140 and soon after embarked upon their austere programme of celibacy and silent contemplation. The complex still has an air of seclusion and fragrant orchard gardens stretching down the hill to Malá Strana. Since 1990 several cowled monks have returned to reclaim the buildings nationalised by the communists in 1948. They can sometimes be seen from Úvoz street walking laps around green fields and meditating, and services are once again being held in the Church of Our Lady, which retained its 12th-century basilica ground plan after remodelling in the early 17th century.

The highlights of the complex are surely the superb libraries, which appear on posters in universities all over the world. Within the frescoed Theological and Philosophical Halls alone are 130,000 volumes. There are a further 700,000 volumes in storage and together they form the most important collection in Bohemia. Visitors cannot, unfortunately, stroll around the libraries. They are, however, generously allowed to gawp through the doors. The comprehensive acquisition of books didn't begin until the late 16th century. When Joseph II effected a clampdown on religious institutions in 1782, the Premonstratensians managed to outwit him by masquerading as an educational foundation, and their collection was swelled by the libraries of less shrewd monasteries. Indeed, the monks' taste ranged far beyond the standard ecclesiastical tracts and included such wonderful highlights as the oldest extant copy of *The Calendar of Minutiae* or *Selected Times for Bloodletting*.

The monks didn't merely confine themselves to books either: the 200-year-old curiosity cabinets house a collection of deep-sea monsters that any landlocked country would be proud to possess. In another part of the monastery complex, the Strahov Gallery exhibits a small part of the monks' considerable collection of religious art. Unlike the library, both are open to visitors.

Malá Strana

At the foot of Prague Castle, the Lesser Quarter belies its humble name with grand palaces and gardens, picturesque streets and an enchanting riverside.

Map p306 & p307

Prague's Malá Strana district is a maze of quiet lanes that lie between the Vltava river and Prague Castle, skirting the hill that makes up Hradčany (*see p61*). Historically the home of nobles in favour with the king, it's full of palaces, embassies and fantastically ornate churches; best of all, the once-private formal gardens are now open to strollers. This little left-bank area has always been home to Prague's boho poets, artists and musicians, as well, something you'll pick up on as you hear string serenades emanating from conservatories on your way to a coffee joint or a tiny jazz cellar.

Malá Strana was founded by the Přemyslid Otakar II in 1287, when he invited merchants from Germany to set up shop on the land beneath the castle walls. Very little remains of this Gothic town today – the present-day appearance of the quarter dates to the 17th century. The area was transformed into a sparkling baroque district by the wealthy Catholic aristocracy, who won huge parcels of land in the property redistribution that followed the Thirty Years' War. When the fashionable followed the court to Vienna in the 17th century, the poor took back the area. It has been the home of poets, drunks and mystics ever since, living cheek by jowl with the ambassadors and diplomats, who also inhabit what is one of Prague's two diplomatic quarters – the British, American, German, Irish, Italian and French embassies, among many others, are situated in Malá Strana.

Today, the character of the area is changing rapidly, as accountancy firms, bankers and wine bars set up shop. It's still remarkable, though, just how few businesses there are in what is one of the most central Prague districts. The first Subway sandwich shop opened here in November 2003. **Malostranské náměstí** (*see p74*) now throbs with life deep into the night, but this is mostly down to overt tourism marketing, and its many bars, restaurants and music venues (*see p144, p121, p209 and p215*). Apart from stores selling souvenirs and cut glass, there is very little shopping in the area.

The formal beauty of Prague Castle's **Paradise Gardens**. *See p75*.

Thus, the district has been lucky enough to preserve its ancient look and the back streets of Malá Strana are a favourite locale for an endless stream of film crews shooting period pieces in the city. Local residents are unfazed by the attention, however, and carry on as ever.

Malostranské náměstí & around

The short main drag between **Charles Bridge** (*see p88*) and Malostranské náměstí is **Mostecká**. It's a continuation of the Royal Route – the path taken by the Bohemian kings to their coronation – and is lined with elegant baroque dwellings. One at No.15 is the **Kaunitz Palace** (Kaunicův palác), built in 1773 for Jan Adam Kaunitz, an advisor to Empress Maria Theresa, who sycophantically had the exterior painted her favourite colours – yellow and white. It's now the embassy of the former Yugoslavia. Just off Mostecká are the **Blue Light** jazz pub (*see p144*) and the **U Patrona** restaurant (Dražického náměstí 4, *257 530 725*), both oases of quality in a stretch that is over-dominated by naff souvenir shops. At the heart of the quarter is wide, open Malostranské náměstí, a lively square edged by large baroque palaces and Renaissance, gabled townhouses perched on top of Gothic arcades. A decidedly modern touch has been added with **Square** (*see p125*), a sleek and excellent restaurant with modern minimalist design and Mediterranean cuisine. This space was known as Malostranská Kavárna for a century and inspired the tales of one of the city's most beloved Bohemian writers, Jan Neruda, author of *Prague Tales*. Nils Jebens (*see p127* **Bad Bohemia: Nils Jebens**), an iconic Prague restaurateur, is behind the transformation. Bang in the middle of the square, dividing it in two, is the girth of **Church of St Nicholas** (Chrám sv. Mikuláš; *see p75*), a monumental late-baroque affair, whose dome and adjoining bell tower dominate the skyline of Prague's left bank. Built between 1703 and 1755, it's the largest and most ornate of the city's many Jesuit-founded churches. During its construction, the Society of Jesus waged a pitched battle against local residents loath to let go of the two streets, two churches and various other structures that had to be demolished to make room for the church.

The grim block next door at No.25 is yet another Jesuit construction, built as a college for its priests and now housing harassed-looking maths students. More appealing is the **Lichtenstein Palace** (Lichtenštejnský palác; *see p210*) opposite, finished in 1791. The Lichtensteins used to be major landowners in Bohemia and the Alpine principality has been battling to regain the palace, which was confiscated in 1918. The palace is currently used as a venue for classical concerts. Also in the square, located in the former town hall at No.21, is the club **Malostranská beseda** (*see p215*), home to music of a more raucous bent. Opposite the south side of St Nicholas is a parade of pubs and restaurants. The original American backpacker hangout **Jo's Bar** (*see p145*) is on this stretch as well, but, alas, under new ownership.

Nerudova heads up from the north-west corner of the square towards Prague Castle, and is a fine place to begin deciphering the ornate signs that decorate many of the city's houses: the Three Fiddles at No.12, for example, or the Devil at No.4. This practice of distinguishing houses continued up until 1770, when that relentless modernist Joseph II spoiled all the fun by introducing numbered addresses. The street, which is crowded with restaurants, cafés, and shops aimed at the ceaseless flow of tourists to and from the castle, is, as you might expect, named after the poet and novelist Jan Neruda. He lived at No.47, the Two Suns (U dvou slunců). The house was turned into a pub and during the communist period was a favourite hangout of the Plastic People of the Universe, the underground rock band that was later instrumental in the founding of Charter77, the petition carried out in December 1976 against restrictions of the regime. The place is now a joyless tourist trap. Also to be ignored is the turquoise drinking

Church of St Nicholas.

Sightseeing

establishment at No.13 where Václav Havel, in an uncharacteristic lapse of taste, took Yeltsin for a mug of beer. A better bet is **U Kocoura** (257 530 107) at No.2. It was briefly owned by the Friends of Beer (formerly a political party, now a civic association). Although its manifesto is a bit vague, the staff's ability to pull a good, cheap pint is beyond question. The more recent **Bazaar Mediterranée** restaurant (*see p125*) at No.40 offers enviable terrace views for lunch and ridiculous striptease and drag-show entertainments with dinner.

The alley next door leads up to the British Embassy at Thunovská 14, which a diplomatic wag christened 'Czechers'. Leading up from here are the **New Castle Steps** (Nové zámecké schody), one of the most peaceful (and least strenuous) routes up to the castle and a star location in the film *Amadeus*.

There are still more embassies back on Nerudova, the Italians occupying the **Thun-Hohenstein Palace** (Thun-Hohenštejnský palác) at No.20, built by Giovanni Santini-Aichel in 1726 and distinguished by the contorted eagles holding up the portal, the heraldic emblem of the Kolowrats for whom the palace was built. The Italians were trumped for a while by the Romanians, however, who used to inhabit the even more glorious **Morzin Palace** (Morzinský palác) at No.5. Also the work of Santini-Aichel, the façade, dating from 1714, sports two hefty Moors – a pun on the family's name – who hold up the window ledge. Their toes have been rubbed shiny by passers-by who believe that touching them will bring good luck.

Nerudova also leads up to Prague Castle, with the added incentive of a fine respite from the crowds and a good midway break provided by **U zavěšenýho kafe** (*see p145*), a mellow pub farther up, where Nerudova turns into in Úvoz. Walking back down Nerudova, if you continue straight down the tram tracks instead of veering off on to Malostranské náměstí, you'll see on your left the **Church of St Thomas** (Kostel sv. Tomáše; *see p76*). Its rich baroque façade is easy to miss, tucked into the narrow side street of Tomášská. Based on a Gothic ground plan, the church was rebuilt in the baroque style by Kilián Ignaz Dientzenhofer for the Augustinian monks. The symbol of the Order, a flaming heart, can be seen all over the church and adjoining cloisters (now an old people's home) and makes a distinct impression, held tightly in the hand of St Boniface, a fully dressed skeleton who occupies a glass case in the nave.

On the corner of Josefská and Letenská is the **Church of St Joseph** (Kostel sv. Josef), a tiny baroque gem set back from the road and designed by Jean-Baptiste Mathey. Since 1989 it has been returned to the much-diminished Order of English Virgins, who were also one-time owners of the nearby **Vojan's Gardens** (Vojanovy sady), one of the most tranquil spots in the city.

Running parallel to U lužického semináře is **Cihelna**, a street named after the former brick factory now being renovated into studios. The street provides an opening on to the river and an almost perfect view of the Vltava and Charles Bridge beyond. Back on Letenská, towards Malostranská metro station, is a door in a wall leading into the best-kept formal gardens in the city. The early 17th-century **Wallenstein Gardens** belonged, along with the adjoining **Wallenstein Palace** (Valdštejn palác), to General Albrecht von Wallenstein, commander of the Catholic armies in the Thirty Years' War and a formidable property speculator. The palace (which now contains the Czech Parliament) is simply enormous. Designed by the Milanese architect Andrea Spezza in 1624-30, it once had a permanent staff of 700 servants and 1,000 horses. A little-noticed entrance to the palace gardens, just to the right of the Malostranská metro station exit, provides a wonderful way of cutting through the district and leaving tourists behind. You come out on Valdstejnšké námestî, just west of an even more impressive collection of greenery, terraces and baroque arches, the **Paradise Gardens** (Rajská zahrada; *see also p69*).

Much of the area of Malá Strana between Malostranská metro station and the square is these days sprouting cosy little bars and cafés, one of the best being **Palffy Palác** (*see p123*). Another, just uphill from Parliament, and a new favourite of its members, is restaurant **U zlaté studně** (*see p123*), up the tiny street of the same name.

Church of St Nicholas

Kostel sv. Mikuláš
Malostranské náměstí, Prague 1 (224 190 991). Metro Malostranská/tram 12, 22. **Open** 10am-4pm daily. **Admission** free. **Map** p307 D3.
The immense dome and bell tower of St Nicholas, which dominate Malá Strana, are monuments to the money and effort that the Catholic Church sank into the Counter-Reformation. The rich façade by Christoph Dientzenhofer, completed around 1710, conceals an interior and dome by his son Kilián Ignaz, dedicated to high baroque at its most flamboyantly camp – bathroom-suite pinks and greens, swooping golden cherubs, swirling gowns and dramatic gestures; there's even a figure coyly proffering a pair of handcuffs.

Commissioned by the Jesuits, it took three generations of architects, several financial crises and the demolition of much of the neighbourhood between presentation of the first plans in 1653 to

Snow-blanketed **Kampa Island** and the impressive **Kampa Museum**.

final completion in 1755. Inside, a trompe l'œil extravaganza, created by the Austrian Johann Lukas Kracker, covers the ceiling, seamlessly blending with the actual structure of the church below. Frescoes portray the life and times of St Nicholas, best known as the Bishop of Myra and the bearer of gifts to small children, but also the patron saint of municipal administration. Maybe this is why St Nicholas's was restored by the communists in the 1950s when the rest of Prague's baroque churches were left to crumble. The church tower also happened to make a favourite spy roost for teams of secret police.

Church of St Thomas

Kostel sv. Tomáše
Josefská 8, Prague 1 (257 530 556). Metro Malostranská/tram 12, 22. **Open** 11am-1pm Mon-Sat; 9am-noon, 4.30-5.30pm Sun. **Admission** free. **Map** p307 E3.

It's worth craning your neck to get a good look at the curvy pink façade of St Thomas's. The lopsided structure is the legacy of an earlier Gothic church built for the Order of Augustinian hermits. After the structure was damaged by fire in 1723, Kilián Ignaz Dientzenhofer was employed to give it the baroque touch. The newly rich burghers of Malá Strana provided enough cash for the frescoes to be completed at breakneck speed (they took just two years) and for Rubens to paint the altarpiece *The Martyrdom of St Thomas*. They even bought the bodies of two saints. The original altarpiece is now part of the National Gallery's collection on show in the Šternberg Palace (*see p109*) and has been replaced by a copy, but the skeletons of the saints dressed in period costume are still on display. Next door are 17th-century cloisters, where the monks dabbled in alchemy before realising that transforming hops into beer was easier and more lucrative than trying to make gold out of lead. A door on Letenská leads to their former brewery, now a tourist-filled restaurant.

Kampa Island

The approach to Malá Strana from Staré Město via Charles Bridge affords one of the best photo opportunities in the city: the twin towers of the bridge framing an almost perfect view of the Church of St Nicholas and the castle behind. Before continuing, however, take the flight of steps on the left leading down to **Na Kampě**, the principal square of Kampa Island. Until 1770, it was known simply as Ostrov or 'island', which understandably led to confusion with the other islands of the Vltava – especially since Kampa's southern end looks as if it's attached to land. A little fork of the Vltava, the burbling Čertovka, translated as Little Devil, runs briefly underground at the south end but resurfaces to slice Kampa from the mainland. It went by the altogether unromantic name of the Ditch until it was cleaned up and rechristened in the 19th century. The communists proposed filling the Čertovka to create a major road but were thwarted by a sudden outbreak of good sense, and this singular place, with its medieval water wheels, has survived.

Kampa is an oasis of calm on even the most crowded August day. Its verdant setting is home to the revamped **Kampa Museum** (*see p109*) and at the south end of the island is one of the loveliest parks in the city. This was created in the 19th century, when an egalitarian decision was made to join the gardens of three private palaces and throw them open to the public. Washerwomen once rinsed shirts on the banks – note the **Chapel to St John of the Laundry** (Kaple sv. Jan Na Přádle) near the southern end. Today it's taken up by snoozing office workers and bongo-beating hippies. The river and bridge views are as romantic as they

Peace 'n' love endure at the **John Lennon Wall**.

come, while the chestnut trees make shady spots for reading and recharging. In spring the park is filled with pink blossom. **Kampa Park** the restaurant (*see p125*), one of Prague's classier and pricier places to eat, is at the north end of the island, where the Čertovka runs back into the river by Charles Bridge, and offers the finest waterfront view of any dining establishment in town.

Between Kampa & Petřín hill

Across the tiny bridge on Hroznová that leads to tranquil **Velkopřevorské náměstí** is the elegant **Buquoy Palace** (Buquoyský palác), a pink stucco creation dating from 1719, which now houses the French Embassy. Opposite is the **John Lennon Wall**. During the 1980s this became a place of pilgrimage for the city's hippies, who dedicated it to their idol and scrawled messages of love, peace and rock 'n' roll across it. The secret police, spotting a dangerous subversive plot to undermine the state, lost no time in painting over the graffiti, only to have John's smiling face reappear a few days later. This continued until 1989 when the wall was returned to the Knights of Malta as part of a huge restitution package. The Knights proved even more uptight than the secret police and were ready to whitewash the graffiti when an unlikely Beatles fan, in the form of the French Ambassador, came to the rescue. Claiming to enjoy the strains of 'Give Peace a Chance' wafting through his office window, he sparked a diplomatic incident but saved the wall. In the summer of 1998 the Knights had a change of heart, the graffiti and crumbling remains of Lennon's face were removed, the wall was replastered and the Beatle's portrait repainted by artist František Flasar. The John Lennon Peace Club is encouraging modest graffiti – preferably in the form of little flowers.

Just around the corner is the quiet and lovely **Maltézské náměstí**. The Knights of Malta lived here for centuries until the communists dissolved the order. The Knights regained great swathes of property under the restitution laws. Opposite the church, is the excellent little café-restaurant **Cukrkávalimonáda** (*see p121*) and round the corner on Saska ulička are the prettiest flower shops and boutiques for club clothes in town. Prokopská street is home to the **U Maltézských rytířů** restaurant (*see p123*), which occupies a Gothic cellar that was once a hospice operated by the Knights. The baroque building on the corner of the square was once known as the Museum of Musical Instruments. It has suffered more than its fair share of misfortune: its priceless Flemish tapestries were given to Von Ribbentrop, Hitler's foreign affairs advisor, and its Stradivarius violins were stolen in 1990; now the museum is closed for good.

Although the museum is gone, the sound of students practising at the nearby conservatory provides a soundtrack for wandering around the area. The highlight of the square is the strange **Church of Our Lady Beneath the Chain** (Kostel Panny Marie pod řetězem), the oldest Gothic parts of which were built by a military-religious order to guard the Judith Bridge, which spanned the Vltava close to where Charles Bridge sits today – bits of the original bridge are visible in the lobby of the **Rezidence Lundborg** (*see p42*). Two heavy towers still stand at the entrance, but they now contain some of the most prized apartments in Prague. The Hussite wars barred the construction of the church and it was never finished. In place of a nave is an ivy-covered courtyard that leads to a baroque addition (dating from 1640-50), built in the apse of the original structure.

At the foot of Petřín Hill runs Újezd, which becomes Karmelitská as it runs north before leading into **Malostranské náměstí** (*see p74*). There are peculiar diversions along the way. The first is at the intersection of Újezd and Vítězná (the border between Malá Strana and Smíchov), where you'll find the popular **Bohemia Bagel** (*see p119*) spilling rock music and American college kids on to the street. There they mix with Death Metal fans from **Újezd** next door (*see p228*). Just to the north is the **Michna Palace** (Michnův palác), a fine baroque mansion also built in 1640-50. It was intended to rival the Wallenstein Palace (*see p75*), which was itself built to compete with Prague Castle. With these gargantuan ambitions, Francesco Caratti took Versailles as his model in designing the garden wing of Michna. Today the gardens contain little but tennis courts.

Just north up Karmelitská, at No.9, is the **Church of Our Lady Victorious** (Kostel Panny Marie Vítězné; *see below*), the first baroque church in Prague (built from 1611 to 1613). It belongs to the Barefooted Carmelites, an Order that returned to the city in 1993 and has taken charge of the church's most celebrated exhibit: the doll-like, miracle-working Bambino di Praga. Porcelain likenesses of the wonder baby fill shop windows for blocks around, and pilgrims from across the globe file into the church.

Heading left up the hill from Karmelitská is **Tržiště**, on the corner of which stands **U Malého Glena** (*see p221*), a convivial jazz pub owned by expat American Glenn Spicker (*see p79* **Bad Bohemia: Little Glenn**). A little further up is the hip **St Nicholas Café** cellar bar (*see p145*) and opposite it is the cosy little **Gitanes** (*see p121*), which is ideal for a traditional romantic dinner. The 17th-century **Schönborn Palace** (Schönbornský palác), now the American Embassy, sits at Tržiště No.15. It was built by Giovanni Santini-Aichel, who, despite his Mediterranean-sounding name, was in fact a third-generation Praguer and one of the descendants of Italian craftsmen who formed an expat community on **Vlašská** just up the hill.

From here, Tržiště becomes a tiny little lane that winds its way up the hill, giving access to some of the loveliest hidden alleys you'll find in Malá Strana. Developers have been busy converting most of the flats here into investment property, but No.22 is a great survivor, **Baráčnická rychta** (*see p144*). This is one of the most traditional – and certainly the most insalubrious – drinking establishments of the Lesser Quarter.

Vlašská runs on up the hill from Tržiště and contains the **Lobkowicz Palace** (Lobkovický palác) at No.19. One of four Lobkowicz Palaces in Prague, its design (1703-69) is based on Bernini's unrealised plans for the Louvre. In 1989 the gardens sheltered thousands of East Germans, who ignored the *verboten* signs and scaled the high walls, setting up camp in here until they were granted permission to leave for the West. Until the nationalisation of property in 1948, the Lobkowicz family was another of Bohemia's major landowners.

Vlašská ambles on upwards, fading out as it passes a hospital and chapel founded in the 17th century by the area's Italian community, and eventually leading back on to Petřín Hill.

Church of Our Lady Victorious

Kostel Panny Marie Vítězné
Karmelitská 9, Prague 1 (257 533 646). Tram 12, 22. **Open** 8.30am-6pm Mon-Sat; 9am-7pm Sun. **Admission** free. **Map** p307 D4.

The early baroque church is entirely eclipsed by its diminutive but revered occupant: Il Bambino di Praga (Pražské Jezulátko). This 400-year-old wax effigy of the baby Jesus draws pilgrims, letters and lots of cash from grateful and/or desperate believers the world over. The list of miracles that the Infant of Prague is supposed to have performed is long and impressive, and over 100 stone plaques expressing gratitude attest to the efficacy of his powers. The effigy, brought from Spain to Prague in the 17th century, was placed under the care of the Carmelite nuns, just in time to protect them from the plague. It was later granted official miracle status by the Catholic Church.

A wardrobe of over 60 outfits befits this dazzling reputation: the baby Jesus is always magnificently turned out, and his clothes have been changed by the Order of English Virgins at sunrise on selected days for around 200 years. While he's said to be anatomically correct, the nuns' blushes are spared by a specially designed wax undershirt. At the back of the church is a shamelessly commercial gift shop, jostling with miraculous souvenirs.

Petřín hill

Rising up in the west of Malá Strana is Petřín hill (Petřínské sady), the highest, greenest and most peaceful of Prague's seven hills. This area is the largest expanse of greenery in central Prague – a favourite spot for tobogganing children in winter and canoodling couples in summertime. Petřín comes from the Latin word for rock, a reference to the hill's past role as the source for much of the city's Gothic and

Bad Bohemia Little Glenn

It's difficult to quaff a *pivo*, tap your foot to music or contemplate the old regime in Prague without feeling the influence of one of Malá Strana's definitive bohemians, a New Englander known to many Praguers simply as Little Glenn.

Obviously comfortable with his diminutive stature, Glenn Spicker (pictured) opted for the name **U Malého Glena** when he and two friends launched the city's most happening jazz club in 1995. The name, which translates as At Little Glenn's, is a play on the centuries-old Czech tradition of naming houses with symbols such as U Dvou kocoura (At the Two Cats) or U Velký boty (At the Big Boot), usually represented by a relief somewhere in the house's façade or an outsize hanging boot.

The tradition predates modern address systems, but Czechs have never really given up the old habit – which in Spicker's case is a good thing. No one's really sure what the address of the club is (though we have cleverly ferreted it out for you, *see p221*), but everyone knows where Little Glen's is.

And, of course, his bagel shop down the street, **Bohemia Bagel** (*see p119*), the first to serve the Yiddish wonder bread in Prague since before World War II... and its branch in Staré Město... and the **Museum of Communism** (*see p115*)... and wasn't there a baroque palace beneath Wenceslas Square for a while that did great Thai food and hosted salsa classes led by a hot Cuban couple?

In short, if there's an untried idea for a Prague venture, Spicker is in there as often as not. Launching a bar or a music club is a thoroughly risky venture in the most developed market in the West, dependent on remaining at the top of the hip heap. How then to properly identify a vacant niche in the Wild East? Is there a method to this entrepreneurial empire-building?

'I did it for the passion and the love,' Spicker says, from his favourite corner table at U Malého Glena. Admittedly, not always the best business strategy: 'I've got a jazz club that seats 25 people. How do you pay the band from that?' But the crowds that cram into the cellar club, hidden under the floorboards of the street-level bar, seem just as happy to stand, attracted by the best players in town.

Spicker's passionate about his club – 'I put my heart and soul into this place because I love music. I just said "I'm gonna do it".' And this is perhaps what attracts them. Bass legend Robert Balzar, sax master Franta Kop, the smoking blues act Rene Trossman Band and a half-dozen others at the city's musical forefront play at the club. Which takes care of the 'hip'.

But the Museum of Communism? 'I was tired of restaurants, losing money, and people stealing,' Spicker says. 'And it was such a great idea. It was a simple idea and from a business model it made sense.'

Thus, in 2000, the former political science student set up the country's first open confrontation with its communist past. The Czech press was not a little sceptical; what could a Westerner possibly tell Czechs about communism? But Spicker brought in native scholars, invested in a stockpile of MiG fighter regalia, spy gear, Lenin and Gottwald likenesses, archival photographs and films. Then he priced tickets so that pensioners get in free and politicians are surcharged 50 per cent.

Lest anyone assume Little Glenn was only an expert on bohemian living, the popular, respected museum has now set them straight. Decadence and social consciousness do indeed make good bed partners. 'Besides,' he says with a grin, 'I couldn't believe it hadn't been done – so I went for it.'

The dazzling **Strahov Monastery** library.

Romanesque building material. The southern edge of the hill is traversed by the so-called **Hunger Wall** (Hladová zeď), an eight-metre-high (23-foot) stone fortification that was commissioned by Charles IV in 1362 in order to provide some work for the poor of the city.

The lazy (and most fun) way up to the top of the hill is to catch the funicular from Újezd, which runs roughly every ten minutes from 9.15am until 8.45pm, stopping halfway up by the touristy **Nebozízek** restaurant (Petřínské sady 411, 257 315 329). At the top is a fine collection of architectural absurdities. Ascend the 299 steps of **Petřín Tower** (Rozhledna; *see below*), a fifth-scale copy of the Eiffel Tower, for spectacular views over the city. The tower was erected in 1891 for the Jubilee Exhibition, as was the neighbouring mock-Gothic castle that houses **Zrcadlové bludiště** (Mirror Maze; *see below*), a fairground-style hall of wacky reflectors. There's a café at the base of the tower and a basic refreshment hut nearby. The third and least-frequented of the Petřín attractions is **Štefánik Observatory** (Hvězdárna; *see below*), which is at the top of the funicular.

While kids get the most out of the hilltop attractions, Petřín's meandering paths are the attraction for grown-ups. You wind through the trees for hours, seeking the statue of Karel Hynek Mácha, unofficial patron saint of lovers. The shadowy bowers are a favourite of his disciples. **Strahov Monastery** (*see p71*) and the No.22 tram stop are just a gentle stroll downhill from here.

Petřín Tower

Rozhledna

Petřín hill, Prague 1 (257 320 112). Tram 12, 22, then funicular railway. **Open** *Jan-Mar, Nov-Dec* 10am-4.30pm Sat, Sun. *Apr-Oct* 10am-7pm daily. Closed in poor weather. **Admission** 25 Kč; 5 Kč children. **No credit cards**. **Map** p306 B5.

While Parisians were still hotly debating the aesthetic value of their newly erected Eiffel Tower, the Czechs decided they liked it so much that they constructed their own version out of recycled railway tracks in a lightning 31 days for the 1891 Jubilee Exhibition. Its fiercest opponent was Adolf Hitler, who looked out of his room in the castle and immediately ordered 'that metal contraption' to be removed. Somehow it survived. It is fairly tatty these days, but the stiff climb to the top is made worthwhile by phenomenal views of the city. The view of St Vitus's Cathedral includes the complete building, not just the usual vista of a set of spires poking over the top of the rest of the castle. Just try not to think about the way the tower sways in the wind.

Štefánik Observatory

Hvězdárna

Petřín hill, Prague 1 (257 320 540). Tram 12, 22, then funicular railway. **Open** *Jan, Feb, Nov-Dec* 6-8pm Tue-Fri; 10am-noon, 2-8pm Sat, Sun. *Mar* 7-9pm Tue-Fri; 10am-noon, 2-6pm, 7-9pm Sat, Sun. *Apr-Aug* 2-7pm, 9-11pm Tue-Fri; 10am-noon, 2-7pm, 9-11pm Sat, Sun. *Sept* 11am-6pm, 8-10pm Tue-Fri; 10am-noon, 2-6pm, 8-10pm Sat, Sun. *Oct* 7-9pm Tue-Fri; 10am-noon, 2-6pm, 7-9pm Sat, Sun. **Admission** 30 Kč; free under-6s. **No credit cards**. **Map** p306 C5.

With classic old-regime inconvenient hours, Prague's observatory is nevertheless part of a proud tradition of historical astronomical connections. Both the haughty Dane Tycho Brahe and his protégé Johannes Kepler resided in the city. The duo features in the observatory's stellar displays (which contain some English). Telescopes offer glimpses of sunspots and planets during the day and panoramas of the stars and the moon on clear nights.

Zrcadlové bludiště

Mirror Maze

Petřín hill, Prague 1 (257 315 212). Tram 12, 22, then funicular railway. **Open** *Jan-Mar, Nov-Dec* 10am-4.30pm daily. *Apr-Oct* 10am-6.30pm daily. **Admission** 30 Kč; 20 Kč children. **No credit cards**. **Map** p306 C5.

Housed in a cast-iron mock-Gothic castle, complete with drawbridge and crenellations, is a hall of distorting mirrors that still causes remarkable hilarity among kids and their parents. Alongside is a wax diorama of one of the proudest historical moments for the citizens of Prague: the defence of Charles Bridge during the Swedish attack of 1648.

Staré Město

Shadowy streets, new boutiques, Old Town Square, weathered pubs, the royal coronation route and the Old Jewish Cemetery. The storybook opens here.

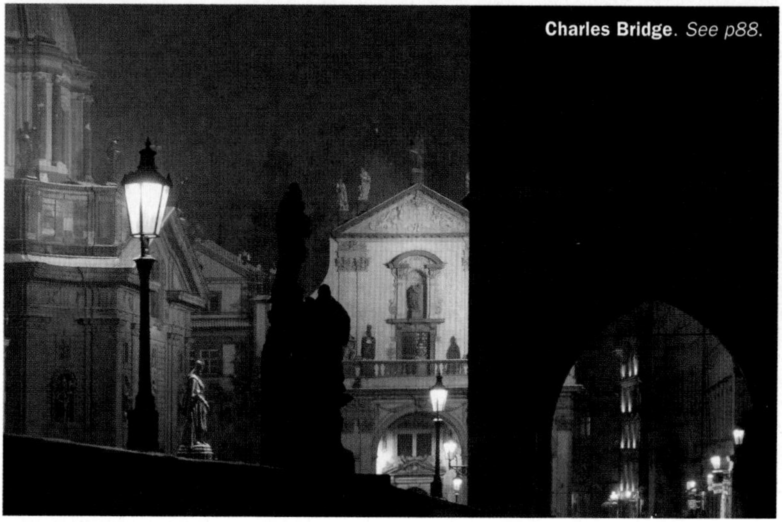

Charles Bridge. *See p88.*

Maps p308 & 309

Once a walled city and still very much a portal to the past, the old centre of Prague is a labyrinth of narrow Gothic lanes – soon to be lit up by old-fashioned gas streetlamps, such as those flickering enchantingly on Michalská . But nowadays, traditional ironmongers and shoe repair shops also stand side by side with trendy brewery-owned restaurants and modern art galleries. Staré Město's grim, blackened stone façades and arches have lined the district since the tenth century. A fair barometer for the state of the republic, this district is a microcosm; what was once the scene of bloody martyrdoms, a Jewish ghetto and official neglect is now more and more like a hip Western European capital. Yet, like a Kafka tale, the twists and turns will confound you.

The Powder Gate to Old Town Square

The **Powder Gate** (Prašná brána; *see p82*), a Gothic gateway dating from 1475 at the eastern end of Celetná, marks the boundary between the Old and New Towns. It's also the start of the so-called Královská Cesta, or Royal Route – the traditional coronation path taken by the Bohemian kings and now a popular tourist track. The first stretch runs west down Celetná, a promenade lined with freshly restored baroque and Renaissance buildings. A more recent makeover is the **House of the Black Madonna** (*see p109*) at No.34, the first cubist building in the city (built in 1913) and now housing the city's first museum of Czech cubism. **Kubista** (*see p162*), on the ground floor of this former lunch counter, is a stylish shop selling original cubist pieces and copies made according to the original technique.

On the opposite side of Celetná, an alley leads into Templová, where you'll be immersed in a part of town where ancient façades are jumbled with fresh new pastel-paint jobs, and restoration has revitalised long-dormant lanes. This hub of nightlife is where backpackers, tourists and foreign residents disappear into a warren of bars, clubs and restaurants, most of which, for some reason, have French names: **La Provence** (*see p131*), **Chateau/L'enfer Rouge** (*see p143*) and the **Marquis de Sade**

The twin towers of **Týn Church** loom over **Old Town Square**.

(*see p150*) are all within a block of each other, while the **Radegast Pub** (*see p143*), gloriously unchanged in decades, holds its ground.

Opposite is the **Basilica of St James** (Bazilika sv. Jakuba; *see below*), on Malá Štupartská – a typical baroque reworking of an older Gothic church. The city's best English-language bookshop, **Big Ben Bookshop** (*see p163*), is just across the street. From this lane you can find a sharp contrast to the sleaze of the popular bars in this neighbourhood and stroll through the crisply restored, café- and restaurant-lined square of Týn, better known by its German name of Ungelt. This square now houses upscale businesses such as **Botanicus** (*see p164*) and the **Ebel Coffee House** (*see p144*). Continuing west takes you past the ominous **Church of Our Lady before Týn** (Kostel Matky boží pod Týnem; *see p85*), Staré Město's parish church since the 1100s, and on to Old Town Square.

Church of St James

Kostel sv. Jakuba
Malá Štupartská, Prague 1 (224 828 816). Metro Náměstí Republiky/tram 5, 14, 26. **Open** 9.30am-12.30pm, 2.30-4pm Mon-Sat; 2-3.45pm Sun. **Admission** free. **Map** p308 J3.

St James's boasts a grand total of 21 altars, some fine frescoes and a desiccated human forearm hanging next to the door. The latter belonged to a jewel thief who broke into the church in the 15th century and tried to make off with gems from the statue of the Virgin. The Madonna grabbed him by the arm and kept him captive until the limb had to be cut off.

Powder Gate

Prašná brána
U prašné brány, Prague 1 (no phone). Metro Náměstí Republiky/tram 5, 14, 26. **Open** *Apr-Oct* 10am-6pm daily. **Admission** 20 Kč; 10 Kč under-6s. **No credit cards. Map** p309 K3.

The Powder Gate, or Tower, is a piece of late 15th-century flotsam, a lonely relic of the fortifications that used to ring the whole town. The bridge that incongruously connects it to the art nouveau masterpiece of the Municipal House (*p97*) used to give access to the royal palace that stood on the same site during the 10th century. By the mid 14th century Charles IV had founded the New Town, Nové Město and the city's boundaries had changed. The Powder Gate mouldered until it finally gained a purpose, and a name, when it became a store for gunpowder in 1575. This, unfortunately, made it a target for invading Prussian troops and it was severely damaged during the siege of 1757. It was once again left to crumble until the neo-Gothic master Josef Mocker provided it with a new roof and redecorated the sides in the 1870s.

Old Town Square

For centuries the beautiful Old Town Square (Staroměstské náměstí), edged by an astonishing jumble of baroque and medieval structures, has been the natural place for people visiting Prague to gravitate to. This was the medieval town's main marketplace and has always been at the centre of the action: criminals were executed here; martyrs

Bad Bohemia Franz Kafka

If Franz Kafka was a little ambivalent about his feelings for *Matka Praha*, or Mother Prague – not many sons describe their maternal figure as having claws – she clearly reciprocated.

Outside Czech lands, it's impossible to pick up a literary work on Prague that doesn't refer to Kafka. *The Trial*, *The Castle*, and maybe *Metamorphosis* are required reading for any literary student. It's a bit different in Prague itself, though. Ask a Czech to name the country's greatest writers and names such as Bohumil Hrabal, Karel Čapek and Jaroslav Seifert come up.

And Kafka? A troubled look comes with that question, then a polite suggestion something like: 'Well, he's not really Czech and, besides, I can't make head nor tale of his stories.'

Literature students may secretly be inclined to agree with the latter assessment. Kafka himself was painfully aware that the radical forms of writing he was venturing into were considered, at best, curious. Swept along by the spirit of the new 20th century, it's hard to imagine that Kafka wasn't inspired by other revolutionaries in the arts: Picasso and Scriabin abroad; the cubist architecture of Gočár; and the tone poems of Janáček at home. But his passions were traditional and it's doubtful he set out to redefine literature.

Kafka often read and wrote all night, turning up exhausted to his day job as attorney for the Workers Accident Insurance Company. He consumed Czech, German and Jewish literature and always had works by Shakespeare, Dostoevsky and Tolstoy close at hand.

Still, Kafka didn't need to be a revolutionary wordsmith to be an outsider in Prague at the turn of the 19th century. His difficulty with assimilation was part of a long history of Bohemia's troubled relationships with Judaism, the German language and even Czech identity.

The writer who did much to mythologise Prague and put the city on the world's literary map, who spent most of his life perambulating a few blocks of Staré Město and whose work was inspired by Prague, has only recently been honoured with a statue in the city. Kafka's image is plastered everywhere these days, but, until January of 2004, it was all essentially for foreign tourist consumption.

An odd, hulking bronze statue (*see p92*) now stands at Dušní and Vězeňská streets, a surrealist creation by Jaroslav Rona, depicting a golemlike headless and handless figure carrying a smaller, dapper man on his shoulders. At its base, 'Franz Kafka' is all that's inscribed.

In his own day, Kafka could hardly have ever been well-loved. He was born on the wrong side of every major national, cultural and linguistic divide of the age. Kafka arrived in the world on 3 July 1883 in the final days of Prague's Jewish ghetto. This sensitive child of an ambitious social climber, who started out as a butcher in South Bohemia, felt mainly terror at the thought of the teeming Josefov district. As a German speaker in a time of feverish Czech nation-building, his mother tongue symbolised 500 years of foreign oppression to the new powers of Prague – his lover Milena Jesenská chided him in the Czech tongue he never mastered.

And, of course, his apathy toward Judaism did nothing to keep him from being an undesirable to the anti-Semitic German bourgeoisie of Prague. Indeed, had he not died of tuberculosis in 1924, Kafka would almost certainly have ended up in the concentration camps that claimed his sister Ottla.

The sense of alienation that runs through his work is hardly surprising. Yet Kafka captured the spirit of Prague, and arguably of 20th-century alienation in general, better than any other author. Perhaps that's the real reason his name is still bound to chill conversation even among Prague's 21st-century consumer-mad, EU-citizenry. His tales hit just a bit too close to the bone.

But one comfort Kafka would surely take is the very discomfiture his work still causes at home. 'Altogether,' he wrote in 1904 to his friend Oskar Pollak, 'I think we ought to read only books that bite and sting us. If the book we are reading doesn't shake us awake like a blow on the skull, why bother reading it in the first place? So that it can make us happy, as you put it? A book must be the axe for the frozen sea within us. That is what I believe.'

Is Kafka's unforgivable sin, then, that his writing is a kind of well that reflects the soul (and the demons) of whoever gazes in? If so, it would take a society of rare courage to be able to embrace such a writer.

MUCHA
museum
ADDRESS
Panská 7,
110 00 Prague 1
OPENING
HOURS
daily 10.00 – 18.00
© MUCHA TRUST 2004
TICKETPRO
www.ticketpro.cz
COPA
The Mucha Museum invites you to discover the works of the great Czech artist, Alphonse Mucha (1860 – 1939), the Master of Art Nouveau. A comprehensive cross section of works loaned by the Mucha Foundation provides you with a unique view into the universe of the artist.

prague jewellery collection
UNIQUE JEWELLERY FROM
THE 17th CENTURY TO THE PRESENT.
HERGETOVA CIHELNA
CIHELNA 2 / PRAGUE 1 / OPEN DAILY 10.00–18.00
COPA
u(p)m
TICKETPRO

MUSEUM OF
COMMUNISM
OPEN
9.00 - 21.00
DAILY
www.museumofcommunism.com
NA PŘÍKOPĚ 10, PRAGUE
... above Mc Donald's, next to Casino
tel.: +420 224 212 966

were burnt at the stake; and, in February 1948, huge crowds greeted the announcement of the communist takeover. Most of the houses are much older than they look, with Romanesque cellars and Gothic chambers hiding behind the toy-town, pastel-coloured baroque and Renaissance façades – the communists spent an unprecedented $10 million smartening up the formerly grimy square for the 40th anniversary of the Czechoslovak Socialist Republic.

The west side is lined with stalls selling kitschy souvenirs. The grassy area behind them was provided by the Nazis, who destroyed much of the Old Town Hall on 8 May 1945, when the rest of Europe was celebrating the end of World War II. The town lost most of its archives, though gained a fine vista of the **Church of St Nicholas** (Kostel sv. Mikuláše; *see p213*).

The **Old Town Hall** (Staroměstská radnice; *see below*) was begun in 1338, after the councillors had spent fruitless decades trying to persuade the king to allow them to construct a chamber for their affairs. John of Luxembourg finally relented, but with the bizarre proviso that all work was to be financed from the duty on wine. He obviously underestimated the high-living inhabitants of Staré Město – within the year they had enough money to purchase the house adjoining the present tower.

You can still see what remains of the Old Town Hall from the Nazis' handiwork, although trying to decipher the extraordinary components of the **Astronomical Clock** (Orloj; *see below*) is more rewarding. It was constructed in the 15th century, sometime before the new-fangled notion that Prague revolves around the sun and not vice versa. Undismayed, the citizens kept their clock with its gold sunburst swinging happily around the globe.

Perhaps the finest of the houses that make up what is left of the Old Town Hall is the **Minute House** (U minuty), the beautiful black-and-white sgraffitoed structure on the south-west corner, which dates from 1611. Franz Kafka (*see p83* **Bad Bohemia: Franz Kafka**) lived here as a boy; opposite the Astronomical Clock you'll find **Café Milena** (Staroměstské náměstí 22, 221 632 602), named after Milena Jesenská, the radical journalist who was Kafka's girlfriend. The area teems with other Kafka sites. The writer was born at U Radnice 5, lived for a while at Oppelt's House on the corner of Pařížská and the square (where *Metamorphosis* takes place), went to primary school on nearby Masná and later attended the strict German Gymnasium on the third floor of the Golz-Kinský Palace. This frothy stuccoed affair in the north-east corner of Staroměstské náměstí once contained Kafka's father's fancy goods shop; it now houses the **Franz Kafka Bookshop** (No.12, 222 321 454) which carries numerous translations of his works. Adjoining the palace is the **House at the Stone Bell** (*see p199*), the baroque cladding of which was removed in the 1980s to reveal a 14th-century Gothic façade.

The focal point of the square is the powerful Jan Hus Monument dedicated to the reformist cleric, designed by Ladislav Šaloun and unveiled in 1915 (and received as a passé artistic flop). On the orders of the Pope, Hus was burnt at the stake in 1415 for his revolutionary thinking, although the Catholic Church, some 500 years after the fact, has finally formally apologised. Hus's fans may at last feel vindicated as they point to the quote on the side of his monument that reads 'Pravda vítězí' ('Truth will prevail'). Those words were also used by first working class president Gottwald in the Glorious February of 1948 accurately, as it finally turned out, in 1989.

Church of Our Lady before Týn

Kostel Matky boží pod Týnem
Staroměstské náměstí 14, Prague 1 (222 322 801). Metro Náměstí Republiky or Staroměstská/tram 17, 18. **Open** *Services* (doors open 30mins before) 5.30pm Mon-Fri; 1pm Sat; 11.30am, 9pm Sun. **Admission** free. **Map** p308 J3.

The twin towers of Týn are one of the landmarks of Staré Město. The church nave is much lighter and more inviting than its foreboding exterior would lead you to believe. The church dates from the same period as much of St Vitus's Cathedral (late 14th century; *see p61*), but whereas St Vitus's was constructed to show the power of King Charles IV, Týn was a church for the people. As such it became a centre of the reforming Hussites' movement in the 15th century before being commandeered by the Jesuits in the 17th. They commissioned the baroque interior, which blends uncomfortably with the original Gothic structure, and melted down the golden chalice in the church façade, a symbol of the Hussites, recasting it as the Virgin. At the end of the southern aisle is the tombstone of Tycho Brahe, Rudolf II's personal astronomer, famous for his false nose-piece and gnomic utterances. Look closely at the red marble slab and you'll see the former, while the lines above provide evidence of the latter, translating as 'Better to be than to seem to be'.

Old Town Hall & Astronomical Clock

Staroměstská radnice/Orloj
Staroměstské náměstí, Prague 1 (224 482 909). Metro Staroměstská/tram 17, 18. **Open** 11am-4.30pm Mon; 9am-4.30pm Tue-Sun. **Admission** *Hall* 50 Kč. *Tower* 30 Kč. **No credit cards**. **Map** p308 H3/J3.

The Old Town Hall, established in 1338, was cobbled together over the centuries out of several adjoining houses, but only around half of the original remains standing today. The present Gothic and Renaissance portions have been carefully restored since the Nazis

Crowd-pleaser? The **Astronomical Clock**.

blew up a large chunk at the end of World War II. The Old Town coat of arms, adopted by the whole city after 1784, adorns the front of the Old Council Hall, and the clock tower, built in 1364, has a viewing platform that is definitely worth the climb. The 12th-century dungeon in the basement became the headquarters of the Resistance during the Prague Uprising in 1944, when reinforcements and supplies were spirited away from the Nazis all over Staré Město via the connecting underground passages. Four scorched beams in the basement remain as a testament to the resistance fighters who fell there. On the side of the clock tower is a plaque, marked by crossed machine guns, giving thanks to the Soviet soldiers who liberated the city in 1945. There's also a plaque commemorating Dukla, a pass in Slovakia where the worst battle of the Czechoslovak liberation took place, resulting in the death of 84,000 Red Army soldiers.

The Astronomical Clock has been tick-tocking and pulling in the crowds since 1490 – even if its party trick is laughably unspectacular, prompting 'is that it?' looks from bemused spectators. Every hour on the hour, from 8am to 8pm, wooden statuettes of saints emerge from trap doors while, below them, a lesson in medieval morality is enacted by Greed, Vanity, Death and the Turk. The clock shows the movement of the sun and moon through the zodiac, as well as giving the time in three different formats: Central European Time, Old Czech Time (in which the 24-hour day is reckoned around the setting of the sun) and, for some reason, Babylonian Time. A particularly resilient Prague legend concerns the fate of the clockmaker, Master Hanuš, who was blinded by the vainglorious burghers of the town to prevent him from repeating his horological triumph elsewhere. In retaliation Hanuš thrust his hands inside the clock and simultaneously ended both his life and (for a short time at least) that of his masterpiece. Below the clock face is a calendar painted by Josef Mánes in 1865, depicting saints' days, the astrological signs and the labours of the months.

Old Town Square to Charles Bridge

The simplest and most direct route from the Old Town Square to Charles Bridge is along Karlova – the continuation from Celetná of the Royal Route. Twisting and curling as it does, the lane would not be particularly obvious were it not for the crowds proceeding along it.

Before heading down Karlova, fuel up at **U Radnice** (*see p129*), a traditional cellar restaurant on the west side of Old Town Hall. To reach Karlova, walk past the Old Town Hall into **Little Square** (Malé náměstí). In the centre is a plague column enclosed by an ornate Renaissance grille and overlooked by the neo-Renaissance Rott House, built in 1890 and entirely decorated with murals of flowers and peasants by Mikoláš Aleš.

Karlova winds past a procession of souvenir Bohemian glass shops, the third turn arriving at the massive, groaning giants that struggle to hold up the portal of the **Clam-Gallas Palace** (Clam-Gallasův palác) on Husova. Designed by Fischer von Erlach and completed in 1719, the palace now houses the city's archives; those that weren't destroyed by backing up sewers in the flood of 2002, that is.

An alternative route to Charles Bridge is Řetězová, a block south of Karlova. This walk, down a narrow lane full of funky smells, takes you past No.7, **Café Montmartre** (*see p144*), a historic scene of hedonism that's now been revived as a mellow sipping space with embroidered parlour sofas. It was here during the glory days of the inter-war First Republic that opium, absinth and jazz mixed into a potent cocktail that at one point led to black masses and orgies – or so the owners say, at any rate. A block further west on Anenské náměstí you'll find the little **Divadlo Na zábradlí** (Theatre on the Balustrade; *see p233*), the theatre where a set-builder named Václav Havel first tried his hand at absurdist play-writing and soon landed himself in jail.

Back on Karlova, the vast bulk of the **Clementinum** (Klementinum; *see p87*) makes up the right-hand side of Karlova's last stretch. After

Prague Castle, it's the largest complex of buildings in Prague. The Jesuits, storm troopers of the Counter-Reformation, set up home here and enthusiastically went about the tradition of book-burning and browbeating. Like much of Staré Město, Karlova is best viewed at night, when tour groups are safely back at their hotels. If you get peckish along the way (and aren't picky) there are two all-night eateries: **U zlatého stromu** (222 220 441, www.zlatystrom.cz) at Karlova 6, where there's a non-stop restaurant in a complex that also includes a hotel, disco and strip show, and **Pizzeria Roma Due** (*see p133*) at Liliová 18.

At the foot of Karlova, tourists have trouble crossing the road past the continuous stream of trams and cars that race through **Knights of the Cross Square** (Křižovnické náměstí). The eponymous Knights, a bunch of elderly neo-medieval crusaders, have come out of retirement and reclaimed the **Church of St Francis** (Kostel sv. František). Designed by Jean-Baptiste Mathey in the late 17th century, the church, which has a massive red dome, is unusual for Prague, not least because its altar is facing the wrong way. The gallery next door houses religious bric-a-brac that the Knights extricated from various museums, and a subterranean chapel decorated with stalactites made out of dust and eggshells, an 18th-century fad that enjoyed unwarranted popularity in Prague. On the eastern side of the square is the **Church of St Saviour** (Kostel sv. Salvátor; *see below*), marking the border of the Clementinum.

Clementinum

Klementinum

Mariánské náměstí 4, Prague 1 (221 663 111). Metro Staroměstská/tram 17, 18. **Open** *Library* 9am-7pm Mon-Fri; 8am-7pm Sat. *Chapel of Mirrors* for concerts only. **Admission** *Library* free. **Map** p308 G3/4/H3/4.

In the 12th and 13th centuries this enormous complex of buildings was the Prague headquarters of the Inquisition, and when the Jesuits moved in during the 16th century, kicking out the Dominicans who had set up home there in the meantime, they carried on the tradition of intimidation and forcible baptising of the city's Jews. They replaced the medieval Church of St Clement with a much grander design of their own (rebuilt in 1711-15 and now used by the Greek Catholic Church) and gradually constructed the building of today. It is arranged around five courtyards, and several streets and 30 houses were demolished during its construction.

The Jesuits' grandest work was the Church of St Saviour (Kostel sv. Salvátor), whose opulent but grimy façade was designed to reawaken the joys of Catholicism in the Protestant populace. Built in 1578-1653, it was the most important Jesuit church in Bohemia. The Jesuits' main tool was education and their library is a masterpiece. It was finished in 1727 and has a magnificent trompe l'œil ceiling showing the three levels of knowledge, with the Dome of Wisdom occupying the central space. However, the ceiling started crumbling and, to prevent the whole structure from collapsing, the Chapel of Mirrors was built next door in 1725 to bolster the walls. The chapel interior, decorated with fake pink marble and the original mirrors, is lovely. Mozart used to play

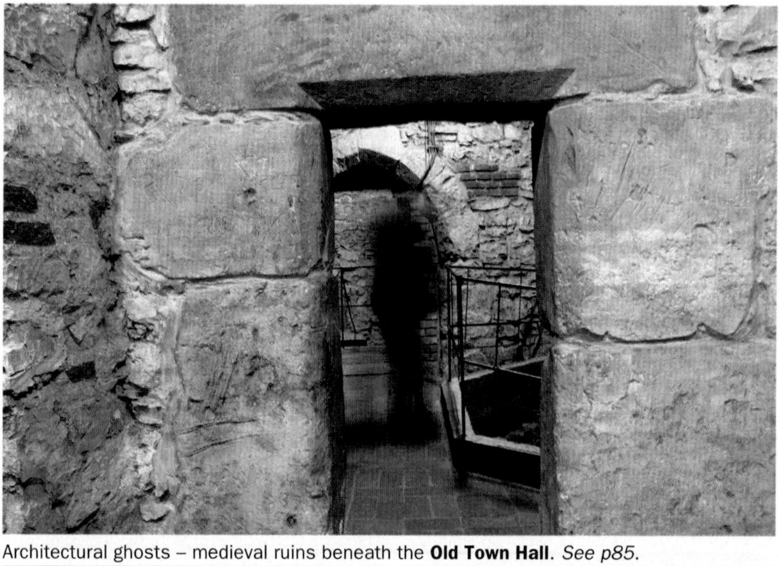

Architectural ghosts – medieval ruins beneath the **Old Town Hall**. *See p85.*

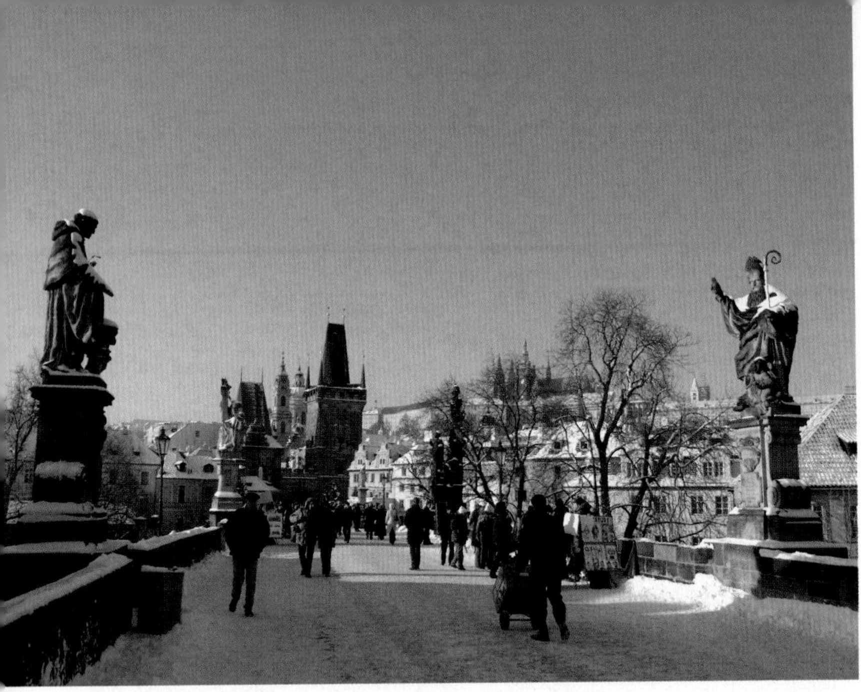

here and it is still used for chamber concerts today – the only way you can get in to see it. At the centre of the complex is the Astronomical Tower, where Kepler came to stargaze. It was used until the 1920s for calculating high noon: when the sun crossed a line on the wall behind a small aperture at the top, the castle was signalled and a cannon fired.

Charles Bridge

Charles Bridge (Karlův most) is the most popular place in the city to come and get your portrait painted, take photos of the castle, have your pocket picked or pick up a backpacker. The range of entertainment is always dodgy and diverse, from blind folk-singers to the man who plays Beethoven concertos on finger bowls.

The stone bridge was built in 1357 (replacing the earlier Judith Bridge that collapsed in a flood in 1342) and has survived over 600 years of turbulent city life. Guarding the entrance to Charles Bridge is the early 14th-century **Old Town Bridge Tower** (Staroměstská mostecká věž; *see p89*), a Gothic gate topped with a pointed, tiled hat. Climb the tower for a bird's-eye view of Prague's domes and spires, the wayward line of Charles Bridge, the naff **Klub Lávka** (*see p222*) and the most massive addition to Prague clubbing, **Karlovy Lázně** (*see p223*), all below on the river and beyond.

The statues lining Charles Bridge didn't arrive until the 17th century, when Bohemia's leading sculptors, including Josef Brokof and Matthias Braun, were commissioned to create figures to inspire the masses as they went about their daily business. The strategy proved more effective than an earlier Catholic decoration – the severed heads of Protestant nobles. More mundane statues were added in the 1800s.

The third statue on the right from the Staré Město end is a crucifixion bearing a mysterious Hebrew inscription in gold. This was put here in 1696 by a Jew found guilty of blaspheming in front of the statue, according to local lore; his punishment was to pay for the inscription 'Holy, Holy, Holy, Lord God Almighty'.

St John of Nepomuk – the most famous figure – is eighth on the right as you walk towards Malá Strana, recognisable by his doleful expression and the gold stars fluttering around his head. Legend has it that John was flung off the bridge after refusing to reveal the secrets of the queen's confession. Actually, he was just in the wrong place at the wrong time during one of Wenceslas IV's anti-clerical rages. A bronze bas-relief below the statue depicts the scene, and people stop and rub it for luck. The statue, placed here in 1683, is the bridge's earliest. Cast in bronze, it has weathered better than the sandstone statues, most of which have been replaced by copies.

Further towards Malá Strana, fourth from the end on the left, is the Cistercian nun St Luitgard, sculpted by Matthias Braun in 1710 and depicted in the middle of her vision of Christ. The statue is considered by many,

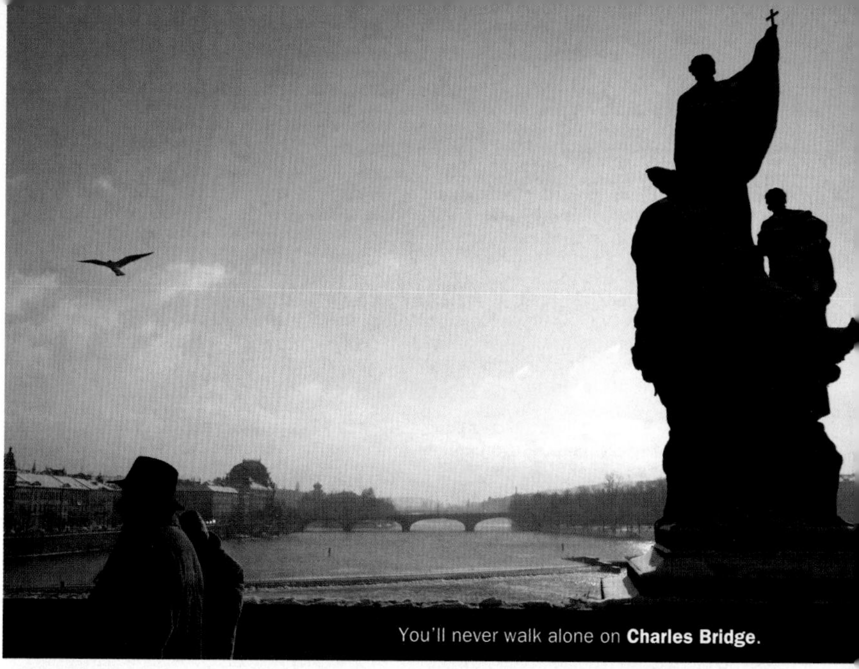
You'll never walk alone on **Charles Bridge**.

including Prince Charles, to be the finest work on the bridge; he pledged the money to save her from the elements, which threatened to wipe the look of wonder off her face. On the same side, second from the Malá Strana end, is the largest grouping on the bridge. It commemorates the founders of the Trinitarian Order, which built its reputation by ransoming Christian hostages: Saints John of Matha and Felix of Valois (accompanied by his pet stag) share space with a rogue St Ivan, included for no obvious reason. Below them is a lethargic Turk and his snarling dog framing three imprisoned true believers.

If you've fallen for the city, seek out the bronze **Lorraine cross** located on the wall halfway across the bridge on the downstream side, touch it, make a wish – and presto, it's guaranteed that you'll return to Prague.

Old Town Bridge Tower

Staroměstská mostecká věž
Křižovnické náměsti, Staré Město, Prague 1 (224 220 569). Metro Staroměstká/tram 17, 18.
Open *Jan-Mar, Nov-Dec* 10am-5pm daily. *Apr, May, Oct* 10am-7pm daily. *Jun-Sept* 10am-10pm daily.
Admission 40 Kč; 30 Kč concessions. **No credit cards**. **Map** p308 G4.

Built in 1373, along the shadow line of St Vitus's Cathedral (*see p61*), the Old Town Bridge Tower was badly damaged in 1648 by marauding Swedes, but Peter Parler's sculptural decoration on the eastern side survives. There's a dull exhibit on the tower's history, but the real reason for visiting is to take in the splendid view from the top. Don't miss the medieval groping figures on the tower's outer corners, just visible before you go under the tower coming from Staré Město, each depicts a buxom lass being felt up by a gentleman friend.

Southern Staré Město

Canny German merchants were the first to develop the area south of the Old Town Square. They built a church dedicated to St Havel (more commonly known as St Gall) when Charles IV generously donated some spare parts of the saint from his burgeoning relic collection. The onion domes of the existing **Church of St Havel** (Kostel sv. Havel), on Havelská, were added in 1722 by the Shod Carmelites – the Barefooted Carmelites settled on the other side of the river. The opposite end of Havelská is lined with bowed baroque houses precariously balanced on Gothic arcades. Prague's best open market (*see p161*) also stands in this lane.

Between here and Celetná, on Ovocný trh, is one of Prague's finest neo-classical buildings: the **Estates Theatre** (*see p213 and p232*), dubbed the 'Mozart Theatre'. Unlike Vienna, Prague loved Mozart – and Mozart loved Prague. During the composer's lifetime, the theatre staged a succession of his greatest operas, including the première of *Don Giovanni*, conducted by Wolfgang Amadeus himself. The building was paid for by Count Nostitz, after whom it was named when it opened in 1783 – aimed at promoting productions of works in German. But, by the late 19th century, most productions were being performed in Czech, and the name was changed to the Tyl Theatre, after the dramatist JK Tyl. His song 'Where Is My Home?' was played here for the first time and later adopted as the Czech national anthem.

The massive oriel window overlooking the theatre belongs to the Carolinum, the university founded by Charles IV (*see p288*). Charles never made a move without consulting the stars and ascertained that Aries was an auspicious sign for the first university in Central Europe, established on 7 April 1348.

Opposite the Estates Theatre is the former Soviet House of Science and Culture. Boutiques, a Ticketpro (*see p210*) and a dubious black light theatre occupy the complex these days.

Around Betlémské náměstí

Once the poorest quarter of Staré Město and a notorious area of cut-throats and prostitutes – whose present-day descendants can be seen lining Perlova and Na Perštýně a few blocks away – this was the natural breeding ground for the radical politics of the late 14th century. On the north side of **Bethlehem Square** (Betlémské náměstí) are the swooping twin gables of the plain **Bethlehem Chapel** (Betlémská kaple; *see p91*), a reconstructed version of the 1391 building where Jan Hus (*see p7*) and other independent Czech preachers passed on their vision of the true church to the Prague citizenry.

Across the courtyard is the **Galerie Jaroslava Fragnera** (Betlémské náměstí, 222 222 157) – offering the best collection of Czech and English-language design books and magazines in town – while **Klub Architektů** (*see p126*) serves cheap eats in the vaulted basement and, in summer, at tables outside.

On the other side of the square is the **Náprstek Museum** (*see p116*). After making his fortune by inebriating the masses, Vojta Náprstek installed a collection of ethnological knick-knacks in the family brewery. A 19th-century do-gooder, he didn't just spend his time hunting down shrunken heads, but also founded the first women's club in the country. The room, untouched for 100 years, can still be seen, although the peephole he drilled through from his office perhaps draws into question the purity of his motives.

One of the three Romanesque rotundas in the city, the **Rotunda of the Holy Cross** (Rotunda sv. Kříže), is on nearby Konviktská. The tiny 12th-century building was built entirely in the round so that the devil had no corner to hide in. If you don't manage to get a look inside, try the **Hostinec U rotundy** (Karoliny Svetle 17, 224 227 227). Covered with lovely sgraffito, it's as authentic a pub as you'll find in Staré Město.

On Husova, to the north-east, is the **Church of St Giles** (Kostel sv. Jiljí), a massive Gothic structure that looks like a fortress from the outside. It was built by the Dominicans in 1340-70, an Order that has now returned to reclaim its heritage and inhabit the monastery next door. Nearby is **U Zlatého tygra** (*see p151*), favourite watering hole of Bohumil Hrabal, the author and Nobel Prize nominee who spent half his life inside a pub and the other half writing about what goes on inside them. The pub makes a good refuelling stop before a visit to the Romanesque **House of the Lords of Kunštát and Poděbrady on Řetězová** (Dům pánu z Kunštátu a Poděbra; *see p92*).

Parallel to Konviktská is the unnaturally quiet **Bartolomějská**. Czechs still avoid its environs – a legacy of the role it played in communist times. Police departments line the street and most dissidents of note did time in the StB (Secret Police) cells in the former convent. The building, now containing the **Pension Unitas** (Bartolomějská 9, 224 385 802, www.unitas.cz), has been restored to the Sisters of Mercy and you can stay the night in the cell where President Havel was once locked up to ponder the error of his ways. The river is only a few dozen yards away, and from the west end of this street you have a perfect view across it to Kampa, with the Castle high on the hill beyond. Turning right will take you past Novotného lávka, a group of buildings jutting into the river centred around a 19th-century water tower and a small assortment of bars, and back to Charles Bridge. Turn left at the end of Konviktská to reach the National Theatre and the start of the Nové Město.

Bethlehem Chapel

Betlémská kaple

Betlémské náměstí, Staré Město, Prague 1 (224 248 595). Metro Národní třída/tram 6, 9, 18, 22. **Open** *Jan-Mar, Nov-Dec* 10am-4.30pm daily. *Apr-Oct* 10am-6.30pm daily. **Admission** 30 Kč; 20 Kč concessions. **Map** p308 H4.

The Bethlehem Chapel, a huge barn-like structure dating from 1391, was where the proto-Protestant Jan Hus delivered sermons in the Czech language, accusing the papacy of being, among other things, an institution of Satan. It's perhaps not surprising that he was burnt at the stake in 1415. His last request before being thrown to the flames was for 'history to be kind to the Bethlehem Chapel'. In response, the fanatical Jesuits bought up the site and promptly turned it into a woodshed. In the 18th century, German merchants moved in and built two houses within the walls. Hus's wish was finally fulfilled under the communists. They chose to look on him as a working-class revolutionary thwarted by the forces of imperialism and spared no expense in the extensive restoration of the chapel. Three of the original walls remain and still show the remnants of the scriptures that were painted on them to enable people to follow the service. Following the fall of communism, religious services have resumed at the chapel. Secular visits are also welcome.

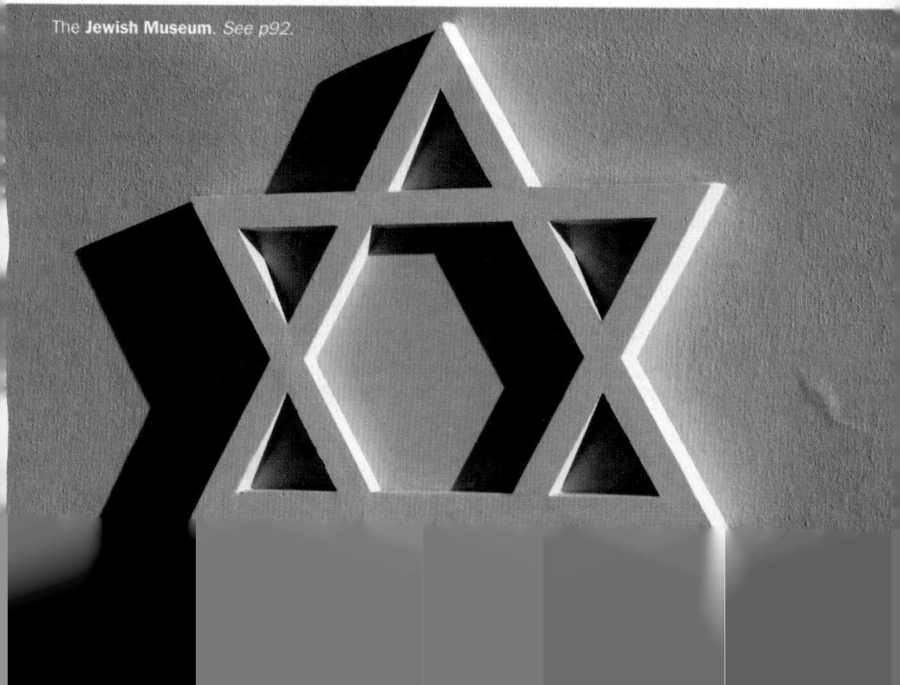

The **Jewish Museum**. *See p92.*

House of the Lords of Kunštát & Poděbrady

Dům pánu z Kunštátu a Poděbrad
Řetězová 3, Prague 1 (224 212 299 ext 22). Metro Staroměstská/tram 17, 18. **Open** *May-Sept* 10am-6pm Tue-Sun. **Admission** 20 Kč. **No credit cards. Map** p308 H4.
This house is one of the few accessible examples of Romanesque architecture in Prague. It was begun in 1250, originally built as a walled-in farmstead, but like its neighbours in Staré Město, was partially buried in the flood-protection scheme of the late 13th century, which reduced the vaulted ground floor to a cellar. By the mid 15th century it was quite palatial, a suitably grand dwelling for George of Poděbrady, who set out from here for his election as king. The upper storeys were later greatly altered. Now it houses a modern art display and an exhibition in honour of Poděbrady, whose scheme for international co-operation is hailed as a forerunner of the League of Nations.

Josefov

The main street of Josefov is **Pařížská**, an elegant avenue of designer shops, flash restaurants, expensive cocktail bars and airline offices, which leads from the Old Town Square down to the river. Here you'll find swish places like **Barock** (*see p131*) and **Bugsy's** (*see p147*). This is all, however, in sharp contrast to the rest of what was once Prague's Jewish quarter.

The spiritual heart of Josefov, the **Old-New Synagogue** (Staronová synagoga; *see p93*) stands on a wedge of land between Maiselova and Paížská. Built around 1270, it's the oldest synagogue in Europe. Legend has it that the foundation stones were flown over by angels from the Holy Temple in Jerusalem on the condition (*al tnay* in Hebrew) that they should be returned on Judgement Day, hence the name Alt-Neu in German or Old-New in English.

Next door is the former **Jewish Town Hall** (Maiselova 18), dating from the 1560s, with a rococo façade in delicate pinks and a Hebraic clock whose hands turn anti-clockwise. The money to build the Town Hall and the neighbouring **High Synagogue** was provided by Mordecai Maisel, a contemporary of Rabbi Löw's and a man of inordinate wealth and discriminating taste. The Town Hall has been the centre of the Jewish community ever since. The High Synagogue, built at the same time as the Town Hall and attached to it, was returned to the community early in 1994 and is now, once again, a working synagogue serving the Jewish community (not open to sightseers).

Further down Maiselova is the Maisel Synagogue. This, with the Pinkas, Klausen and Spanish synagogues, and the Old Jewish Cemetery and Ceremonial Hall, comprise the extraordinary **Jewish Museum** (*see p109*), also funded by the wealthy 16th-century money-lending mayor. Sadly, the current building is a reconstruction of the original (apparently the most splendid synagogue of them all), which burnt down in the great fire of 1689, when all 316 houses of the ghetto and 11 synagogues were destroyed. The present structure dates from 1892 to 1905, and houses a permanent exhibition of Jewish history.

On U starého hřbitova is the **Old Jewish Cemetery** (*see p113*), a small, unruly patch of ground that contains the remains of thousands upon thousands of bodies. Forbidden to enlarge their burial ground, the Jews buried their dead on top of each other in an estimated 12 layers, so that today crazy mounds of earth are jammed with lopsided stone tablets.

To the left of the entrance is the **Klausen Synagogue** (*see p112*), built in 1694 by the same craftsmen responsible for many of Prague's baroque churches. Inside, the pink marble Holy Ark could almost pass for a Catholic altar were it not for the gold inscriptions in Hebrew. Here you'll find displayed various religious artefacts and prints, as well as explanations of Jewish customs and traditions. Facing the synagogue is the **Former Ceremonial Hall** (*see p112*), designed in the style of a Romanesque castle at the beginning of this century, which hosts an exhibition of funeral ceremony and ornament.

On the other side of the cemetery is the **Pinkas Synagogue** (*see p114*), built as the private house of the powerful Horowitz family in 1607-25. The building is now primarily given over to a memorial to the more than 80,000 Jewish men, women and children of Prague who died in Nazi concentration camps according to German transport lists. A communist-era 'refurbishment' once obscured the names recorded on the Pinkas walls, but every one was painstakingly repainted in a two-year project started in April 1997. Josefov's final synagogue, the **Spanish Synagogue** (*see p114*), was built just outside the boundaries of the ghetto in 1868, on Dušní. It was constructed for the growing number of Reform Jews, and its façade is of a rich Moorish design. Since its return to the community it has been meticulously restored and is now a working synagogue again, with a permanent exhibition on Jewish history in the Czech lands up to the beginning of World War II.

Standing just before it is a surreal bronze statue of Franz Kafka, depicted as a dwarf figure riding on the shoulders of a headless, handless, footless giant with a striking resemblance to the Golem of Prague (*see p83* **Bad Bohemia: Franz Kafka**).

Old-New Synagogue

Staronová synagoga
Červená 2, Prague 1 (no phone). Metro Staroměstská/tram 17, 18. **Open** *Jan-Mar, Nov-Dec* 9.30am-5pm Mon-Thur, Sun; 9am-2pm Fri. *Apr-Jun* 9.30am-6pm Mon-Thur, Sun; 9.30am-5pm Fri. **Admission** 200 Kč; 140 Kč concessions; free under-6s. **No credit cards**. **Map** p308 H2.

The Old-New Synagogue is a rather forlorn piece of medievalism. The oldest survivor of the ghetto and the spiritual centre of the Jewish community for 600-plus years, it has now been returned to the community and is still used for services. The austere exterior walls give no clues to its peculiar Gothic interior. An extra rib was added to the usual vaulting pattern to avoid the symbolism of the cross. Instead the decor and structure are based on the number 12, after the 12 tribes of Israel: there are 12 windows, 12 bunches of grapes, and clusters of 12 vine leaves decorate the pillar bases. Sadly, there's not much to see once you're inside the synagogue.

The interior was left untouched for 500 years as a reminder of the blood spilled here during the pogrom of 1389, when the men, women and children who sought sanctuary in the synagogue were slaughtered by Christians. The 19th-century neo-Gothic crusaders, however, couldn't resist the temptation to 'restore' the original look and slapped a fresh coat of paint over the top. Oak seats line the walls facing the *bema*, or platform, protected by a Gothic grille, from which the Torah has been read aloud every day for more than six centuries, with the exception of the Nazi occupation. The tall seat marked by a gold star belonged to Rabbi Löw, the most famous inhabitant of the ghetto. The rabbi lived to the age of 97, and a sculpture by Ladislav Šaloun to the right of the New Town Hall (*see p102*) in Mariánské náměstí depicts the manner of his death. Unable to approach the scholar, who was always absorbed in study of the scriptures, Death hid in a rose that was offered to Löw by his innocent granddaughter. The rabbi's grave can be found in the Old Jewish Cemetery (*see p113*), recognisable by the pebbles and wishes on scraps of paper placed upon the tomb.

Precious Legacy Tours

Maiselova 16, Staré Město, Prague 1 (222 321 954). Metro Staroměstská/tram 17, 18. **Open** 9.30am-6pm Mon-Fri, Sun. **Fees** *Entrance fee* 300 Kč. *Tour with a guide* 620 Kč. **No credit cards**. **Map** p308 H3.

This Jewish travel agency purveys tickets for the various Jewish Museum sights, the Old-New Synagogue, tours of Prague and trips to Terezín (*see p256*), a small town that was used in 1941 as a camp for Jews destined for concentration camps further east. The English-speaking staff can also book meals in kosher restaurants and accommodation.

Northern Staré Město

The area along the banks of the Vltava wasn't incorporated into the new design of Josefov, and the grandiose buildings there have their backs turned upon the old ghetto. Going down Kaprova towards the river will bring you to **Jan Palach Square** (Náměstí Jana Palacha), named in memory of Jan Palach, the first of the students who set themselves on fire in 1969 to protest the Soviet-bloc invasion . Dominating the square is the breathtakingly beautiful **Rudolfinum** (*see p209*), or House of Arts, which houses the Dvořák and Suk concert halls. It was built from 1876 to 1884 (and named after Rudolf II) in neo-classical style and entirely funded by the Czech Savings Bank to display its 'patriotic, provincial feelings'. You can see the bank's corporate logo, the bee of thrift, in the paws of the two sphinxes who guard the riverfront entrance. In 1918 the concert hall became home to the parliament of the new Republic.

When Chamberlain returned to England from meeting Hitler in 1938 disclaiming responsibility for the 'quarrel in a faraway country between people of whom we know nothing', it was here that 250,000 of these people came to pledge themselves to the defence of the Republic. The Nazis turned it back into a concert hall and called it the German House of Arts. Legend has it that a statue of the Jewish composer Mendelssohn was ordered to be removed for obvious reasons, but the workmen, not knowing what Mendelssohn looked like, took their lessons in racial science to heart and removed the figure with the biggest nose – which turned out to be Richard Wagner. Opposite, with its back to the Old Jewish Cemetery, is the magnificent **Museum of Decorative Arts** (*see p114*).

Few visitors make it over to the streets of art nouveau tenement houses in northern Staré Město – most semi-derelict, but many undergoing rapid restoration these days – but they are well worth inspection, even without the attraction of **St Agnes's Convent** (*see p110*), the oldest example of Gothic architecture in the city, which now hosts the National Gallery's medieval collection. The convent's founder, St Agnes, died a full 700 years before the Pope deigned to make her a saint. Popular opinion held that miracles would accompany her canonisation, and, sure enough, within five days of the Vatican's announcement the Velvet Revolution had begun.

Nearby is **Dlouhá**, or Long Street, which contained no fewer than 13 breweries in the 14th century, when beer champion Charles IV forbade the export of hops. These days its main attraction is the atmospheric **Roxy** club (*see p222*) and the serene **Dahab** tea house (*see p144*), replete with belly dancers and Middle Eastern cheap eats; above it sits **Gallery NoD** (*see p202*), a hive of new media artists and one of the city's grooviest internet bars.

Nové Město

The place where Prague gets its business done, Nové Město is a gritty, glitzy mix that's a far cry from the horse market Wenceslas Square once was.

Maps p309, p310 & p311

The thing about Prague's New Town, Nové Město, is that it's neither. Created in the 14th century, it's hardly new, nor does it bear any resemblance to an independent town. But you would be hard-pressed to find a section of the city more emblematic of its emerging identity, encompassing the sweep of history and the ongoing transition from communism to capitalism. With its mix of grand architecture, low streetlife, glitzy stores and crumbling remnants, and reminders of life under foreign oppressors, Nové Město embodies the zeitgeist of an entire nation seeking to establish its place in 21st-century Europe.

The area is bounded roughly to the north and east by Národní, Na příkopě and Revoluční, which form the border with Staré Město, the Old Town (*see p81*). The heavy traffic arterial Wilsonova forms a natural barrier on the south, turning into Mezibranska. Heading west from there along Žitná or Ječná takes you through the back streets and past some of the more historic buildings in Nové Město to the Vltava river.

Wenceslas Square

The hub of Nové Město (and for that matter, the entire city) is Wenceslas Square, a broad, sloping boulevard nearly one kilometre (0.63 miles) long. Almost every major historical event of Prague's past century has unfolded here, or at least passed through. Masses assembled in Wenceslas Square for the founding of the Czechoslovak Republic in 1918, and again in 1939, when Nazi troops marched in to establish the Protectorate of Bohemia and Moravia. In 1968 the brief hope of Prague Spring was born and died here. And, when the communist regime was finally toppled with the Velvet Revolution in 1989, the world watched throngs celebrating in Wenceslas Square.

Only faint echoes of those events are discernible now, mostly in the form of monuments and plaques that are easy to miss. The tone is commercial, with a busy mix of hotels, shops, restaurants, clubs and tourist services. Cabs buzz up and down the boulevard, which is often cluttered with construction work, parked cars and police pulling over traffic violators. The pedestrian mix is lively and varied. By day, office workers, shoppers and vendors mingle with the tourist crowds. After dark, the night people emerge – hustlers trying to draw people into clubs, hookers openly soliciting startled passers-by, and boisterous groups of drunken tourists careening from pub to pub.

Indeed, night is when Wencelsas Square is most alive. The glow of neon signs high atop the buildings; the smell of sausages frying in the food stands; the mix of languages, laughter and come-ons as you stroll the broad pavements – it's like a carnival, with crystal shops and brightly lit souvenir shops glittering along both sides of the central promenade.

A tour of the square

At the top of Wenceslas Square, sits the **National Museum** (*see p116*), overlooking the boulevard. Built from 1885 to 1890, this neo-Renaissance palace is covered in decades of grime and the street graffiti that has become common in Prague since the Velvet Revolution. Nevertheless, the building merits a visit, as every niche, corner and column top boasts elaborate nationalist stonework. The soaring lobby and grand staircase inside are also worth a look, far more so than the actual contents of the museum (*see p113* **The national yawn**).

In front of the museum, twin mounds in the cobbled street mark the site of two self-immolations. In January 1969 the Czech student named Jan Palach set himself on fire to protest Soviet oppression. The following month, Jan Zajic did the same. Usually covered with flowers and candles, the mounds also mark a more recent tragedy. In March 2003 a disturbed teenager named Zdeněk Adamec set himself ablaze on the same spot, kicking off a wave of copycat acts throughout the country. Even Czechs were at a loss to explain the phenomenon, which lacked a political subtext.

One of the most popular meeting spots in Prague is across Wilsonova in the gigantic form of the Czech patron saint: the statue of Wenceslas astride a horse, surrounded by Saints Agnes, Adelbert, Procopius and Ludmila, Wenceslas's grandmother. (The good king takes a satirical ribbing nearby, inside the Lucerna complex at the corner of Štěpánská, where he hangs from the ceiling in an inverted version, the work of art prankster David Černý.) A few steps below 'the horse', as the stately monument is known, a headstone with the images of Palach and Zajic stands as a **memorial to the victims of communism**.

The modern glass-and-stone structure just east of the National Museum is the new **Parliament building**, where the Federal Assembly met until the split of the Czech and Slovak republics in 1993. Now the home of **Radio Free Europe**, it's better known to the station employees as 'the fortress', owing to the concrete barriers and tight security that surround it. Continuing post-9/11 security concerns – the station's prime focus is broadcasting to Muslim fundamentalist audiences – make a move for RFE likely in the near future. These days, the current Czech Parliament is ensconced in the more fashionable **Wallenstein Palace** (*see p75*).

The next building along is the **State Opera** (*see p214*), which opened in 1888 as the New German Theatre. Stepchild of the city's performing arts establishment, the theatre is perennially underfunded and perpetually trying to compensate with creativity and enthusiasm. It's worth the price of a ticket just to see the sumptuous neo-rococo performance hall.

Just past the State Opera beauty is the beast, **Hlavní nádraží** (*see p270*), the city's main train station – also known as Wilsonovo nádraží, or Wilson Station. Overdue for renovation, the station no longer retains even faded glamour. Dirty inside and out, it's a haven for the homeless, junkies and cruising rent boys. The upstairs rotunda, which houses a rough café, offers glimpses of bygone glory: dull brass rails, dusty statues and peeling murals that disappear into the dark curve of the dome. The lower level, where escalators connect with the Metro, is a prime example of late communist design.

Heading down Wenceslas Square, historical monuments quickly give way to capitalist totems like McDonald's and KFC. At No.56 you'll find **Jégr's Sports Bar** (224 032 481, www.jagrsportbar.cz), a Western-style drinking emporium with prices to match, owned by Czech hockey hero Jaromir Jagr. (If you need a sports fix though, you're better off going around the corner to **Hvězda Sport Bar**, which shows more than just hockey and football; *see p152*).

Along with the upside-down horse, the **Lucerna** shopping passage offers one of the last survivors of pre-war Czech grandeur (*see p98* **Dark *pasáž***). This tattered art-nouveau gem is a labyrinth of shops ranging from high-fashion boutiques to a Ticketpro (*see p210*), where you can buy tickets to most entertainment events. Walk through the passage for a flavour of everyday Prague, the small-scale cafés, second-hand camera shops and wedding dress rentals characterising the lifeblood of the city. Take the big staircase from the main lobby up to the **Lucerna** cinema bar (*see p193*), a classy, rundown art-nouveau relic.

Continuing along Wenceslas Square, the building fronts become more ornate. Sit on any bench, look up, and you'll discover stone angels, griffins, muscular atlantes and all manner of ornamental filigree. There's a particularly impressive set of murals on the **Wiehl**

'The horse' in **Wenceslas Square**. *See p94.*

Bad Bohemia Tram from hell

Perhaps 'dreaded' is too harsh a word for the experience, but it's certainly with ambivalent disdain that anyone caught out after 12.10am when the Metro shuts down (whose coffers won't stretch to a taxi), considers their only remaining option: the night tram. Though not entirely recommended, night trams are an option for those with a sense of adventure.

Waiting at Lazarská and Spálená streets in Nové Město, squinting through the rain or graffiti at a schedule for a 50s-numbered tram, you may begin to feel like a lost soldier separated from his regiment behind enemy lines. If you have less than half an hour to wait, and the tram stops anywhere near your bed, you're in, well... one could call it luck.

Relief and revulsion vie for supremacy as the warm glow of an approaching car is spotted. The door opens, revealing a solid wall of humanity and a wave of smell. Stale alcohol, wet dogs, falafel aroma and body odour blast out like the bad breath of a jungle animal. Inebriated? Congratulations. Not being in full possession of your faculties is a distinct advantage.

All rules of personal space and politeness (not Prague's strong point at the best of times) are suspended. Force your way in, grab on to a pole and hold tight, as the driver takes the corner like he's at Le Mans. Don't even hope to get a seat. They're always full, occupied by scraggly, besotted street people. For some, the night tram is their only alternative to sleeping outside.

Younger, stronger riders somehow sleep while standing, hand gripping the pole above, head tucked into the crook of the elbow, and no way to fall – the press of bodies prevents that.

For the party crowd, it's just a cheap club on wheels. You'll hear them before you see them, the sounds of drunken outpourings mixing with the clink of beer bottles. Still, this lot only serves to enhance the generally loose and convivial atmosphere. Since it's the only way home, everyone is on the night tram – locals, tourists, expats – talking in a riotous polyglot babel.

The late hour and the alcohol intake fuel drama. Fist fights are rare – fortunately, there just isn't the space. The night tram does, however, provide stage space for heated arguments, intimate encounters and other happenings. Indeed, these steamy cars are rich laboratories of social science, revealing what makes Prague's citizens laugh or cry: warring couples produce sighs of relief as they disembark; drunken missteps or bad singing are seen as free entertainment; overheated heavy-petting sessions result in studied indifference; smiles and coos erupt when a dog of any kind is brought on board – the latter an instant feel-good for Czechs.

Perplexing by day (when did this route change?) a tram ride can be truly baffling at night, with pit stops between stops, nobody getting on or off, a warning buzzer (wake up!), then the car lurching on again. What's more, disembarking requires strategic planning, starting several stops ahead. Each time someone exits the show, edge closer to the door. When the big moment arrives, plunge ahead in a stream of 'pardons' and 'sorrys', nudge aside skate punks and a drunk or two, dive down the steps and leap out the door, praying it doesn't close on you. The night air never felt so good. Now, which way is home?

House (1896) at No.34, while Blecha's **Supich Building** (1913-16) at Nos.38-40 has likeably bizarre Assyrian-style masks adorning its façade. The second-floor balcony of the **Melantrich Building** (No.30) became the unlikely venue for one of the most astounding events of the Velvet Revolution: on 24 November 1989, in front of over 300,000 people, Václav Havel and Alexander Dubček stepped forward here and embraced, signifying the end of 21 years of 'normalisation'. Within weeks the entire cabinet had resigned.

For an interior version of gorgeous art-nouveau mural and stained-glass work, stop in at the **Grand Hotel Evropa** (*see p51*) at No.25, the hotel time forgot. From here, the growing number of familiar Levi's and Nike logos means you're approaching the cobbled walkway at the bottom of Wenceslas Square.

Northern Nové Město

From the end of Wenceslas Square, **Na příkopě** runs north-east along what was once a moat surrounding Staré Město, though there's no hint of that now. Instead, the street has some of the city's poshest shops and most impressive examples of 'adaptive reuse' – in this case, turning stately baroque buildings into shopping meccas. **Palác Koruna**, at the junction of Wenceslas Square and Na příkopě, is a prime example.

Across the way, the **Star Café** (224 232 173) at No.3 is noteworthy not for its coffee, but for the blithe manner in which former socialist countries expropriate capitalist symbols. This is no Starbucks, though everything from the green-and-white logo out front to the 'Starpuccino' on the menu inside does its best to blur the distinction. You'll see other examples of this throughout the city, such as the all-Czech **Hard Rock Café** (220 108 148) a few doors west.

The **Prague Information Service** (*see p291*) at Na příkopě 20 is a good place to pick up leaflets, schedules and maps. Just beyond, the swanky and successful **Slovanký dům** shopping mall seems an improbable renovation of the former offices of the Gestapo and the Communist Party. Somewhere, totalitarians are spinning in their graves over the sushi bar, multiplex cinema and U2-owned **Joshua Tree** club (220 108 148).

Opposite is one of Prague's cultural treasures, the resplendent **Municipal House** (Obecní dům; *p209*). The city's finest art-nouveau orgy, built from 1905 to 1911, it serves as a multipurpose facility housing the 1,500-seat performance hall of the Prague Symphony Orchestra (*see p209*), galleries, offices, meeting rooms and restaurants. The entranceway is crowned with a dome and arched gable framing a monumental tile mosaic, *Homage to Prague* by Karel Špillar. The walls and floors inside are also covered with fabulous tile work and murals, some of the latter by Alfons Mucha.

The forbidding Gothic structure attached to the Municipal House is the **Powder Tower** (*see p67*), built in 1475 and renovated many times since. Originally called New Tower, its current name derives from the storage of gunpowder there beginning in the early 1800s. Centuries earlier, the tower marked the beginning of the 'Royal Route', which coronation parades took through Staré Město, across Charles Bridge (*see p88*) and up to Prague Castle (*see p61*).

A brief loop around two streets running east from the Municipal House offers a capsule view of a city in transition. **V celnici** could be almost anywhere in Western Europe, with the modern **Marriott** (*see p51*) and **Renaissance** (V Celnici 7, 218 211 111) hotels facing each other across the street and two upscale shopping malls: **Millennium Plaza** and **Stará Celnice**, the latter with a Christian Dior shop.

The street ends at **Masarykovo nádraží** (*see p271*), the Masaryk train station, a smaller and cleaner version of Hlavní nádraží. A left turn up Havlíčkova brings you to the **Café Imperial** (*see p143*), a high-ceilinged and high-spirited remnant of First Republic decadence with eye-popping, floor-to-ceiling ornamental porcelain tile work. (Check your bill here carefully – the waiters like to mark it up imaginatively.)

A left on Na Poříčí takes you back toward the Municipal House, past a dreary row of hole-in-the-wall shops and second-hand clothing stores. The dreary pall of socialist economics still hangs heavy here, even with the occasional internet café sign. If the YMCA building at No.12 is open, stop in for a look at a working paternoster, a cross between a dumbwaiter and a lift that's a thrilling fright to ride.

Southern Nové Město

Back at Wenceslas Square, **Října** stretches from the north end of the square south-west to Jungmannovo náměstí. The **Adria Palace** at No.28, built from 1923 to 1925, is perhaps the city's finest example of Rondocubist architecture. You can skip the tacky wax museum inside, but don't miss the **Church of Our Lady of the Snows** (Kostel Panny Marie Sněžné) – its towering black-and-gold baroque altarpiece is awe-inspiring. Also worth seeking out here, is the church's side chapel (accessible

Dark *pasáž*

One of the most bandied-about words in the Czech capital, since asset stripping became a popular sport post-1989 is *tuneling*. Adapted from 'tunnelling', the term implies taking all the worth of a big firm and secretly siphoning it off, leaving the workers and shareholders screwed, with only a shell, just as if a tunnel had been dug into the centre of a bank and all the gold removed during the night. Perhaps it's only appropriate, then, that meandering through the city centre can be done with equal stealth and cunning, making use of Prague's many *pasažes* or a *myší díra* (mouse hole) or two – some of which are so clandestine, they don't even have names to call their own.

These secret shortcuts, most of which were built in the 1920s as the forerunners to modern department stores, take you into a private world rarely glimpsed by non-natives – and there's a great series of them running from **Wenceslas Square** to **Opatovická**.

From the top of Wenceslas Square walk down and make a left on **Krakovská**. On your right is the **Blaník pasáž**, a shopping arcade of tarnished brass and a cinema mosaic depicting muses. Continue to **Ve Smečkách**, go left, run the gauntlet between sex-biz rivals **Darling Club Cabaret** (*see p231*), **Cabaret Atlas** (*see p231*) and the **Buggy Buggy Bar** (608 029 913) and duck into the next passage on the right. This marbled collection of anaemic businesses is the place to pick up, should you so desire, bargain stretchy underwear from China and permanently marked-down polyester suits from EGOist.

At the west end, cross **Štepánská**, go right and enter the **Lucerna** *pasáž* on your left, easily Prague's best assortment of second-hand camera shops, bridal dress shops and **Lucerna** cinema bar (*see p97 and p193*), the most atmospheric art-nouveau movie-house lobby bar in town. This *pasáž*, built from 1912 to 1916 by a consortium, which included Václav Havel's grandfather, is a ground-breaking piece of early modern architecture for its reinforced concrete structure with suspended ceiling. Despite an unfortunate 1960s redecoration, it still impresses with an air of faded grandeur.

Exit the west side of Lucerna on to **Vodičkova**, cross and enter the **Světozor** *pasáž* by the tram stop. Grab a fruit ice at **Ovocný Světozor** (Vodicková 41, no phone), an ancient sweet shop, and note also the extraordinary stained glass advertisement for the old Czech electronics company Tesla.

Making a left into the **Franciscan Gardens** (*see below*), idle, ogle or make out with someone as you please, then stroll out at the north-west end, cutting through another shopping *pasáž* to **Jungmannova** and past the **Teta Tramtárie** children's arcade (*see p166 and p187*). Now head south on Jungmannova, turning left into the *pasáž* one street along. Pay your respects to the statue of Josef Hlávka, a leading light of Czech scholarship during the tumultuous 19th century.

Turn right on **Vodičkova**, make another right at the end of the street and head into the *pasáž* of **Divadlo Komedie** (224 222 734), a frenetic Czech theatre company well supplied with bran from **Country Life** (*see p119 and*

via a door on the right in the rear), where you can gawp at the trio of gruesome crucifixes.

Outside the church stands the world's only **cubist lamp post**. Everywhere else, cubism was confined to painting; in the Czech Republic it shaped everything from furniture to this bizarre, solitary creation. Leading off in the other direction, a path takes you to the **Franciscan Gardens** (Františkánská zahrada), an oasis of green and calm.

Heading west from Jungmannovo náměstí along Národni brings you to **Tesco** (*see p158*), five floors of bustling department-store capitalism. In the basement supermarket expats forage for non-Czech grocery items. Gather here after clubbing to catch a night tram (*see p96* **Bad Bohemia: Tram from hell**). Across **Spálená**, you'll find the first of two great cafés. **Café Louvre** (*see p152*), accessible via a lobby and staircase entrance from the street, was once a hangout for Prague's literary and intellectual crowd. Cleaned up and modernised, it's now the ideal place to people-watch and mix with locals.

Further down the street, **Slavia** (*see p144*) was a famous dissident meeting place during the 1970s and 1980s, and a storied haven for literati like Tolstoy and Kafka for a century before. There's no plotting now and precious little inspiration, just a pricey menu and one of the best riverside views in town. Grab a window seat for a glamour shot of Prague Castle after dark.

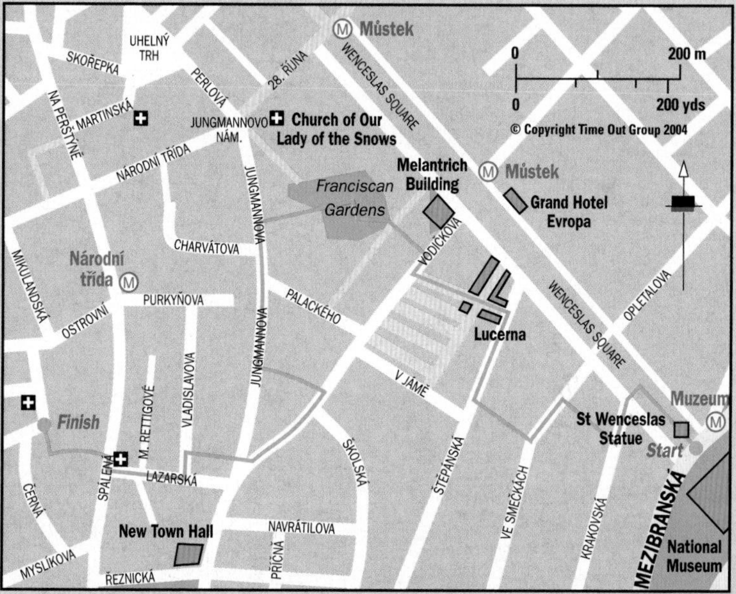

p171). Browse the latest pirate Czech videos at the low-budget stall here, then continue on out the other side, and right (west) on **Lazarská**.

Pass the impressive **Diamant** house, a cubist showroom that was standing empty at press time, and cross **Spalená** to the last and most easily overlooked mouse hole on your route at No.15. Open most weekdays, this dark, narrow shortcut takes you into what you would swear is a dead end outside the classrooms of the **Vyšší odborná škola publicistiky**, where all of tomorrow's Czech marketing geniuses are put through their paces. Exit onto cobbled little Opatovická and you've three great choices for celebrating your personal dark passage: the hip **Velryba** tearooms (*see p153*), boho **Jazz Cafe č.14** (*see p152*) and cool **Tulip Café** (*see p119*).

Next to the entrance for Louvre, you'll notice photos of Bill Clinton playing the saxophone in the basement jazz club, **Reduta** (*see p221*) at No.20. Little of that vibe has been left behind, though – the club feels like it's still run by the old regime. For a funkier hangout try the adjoining **Rock Café** (*see p215*) or the basement club **Vagon** (*see p220*) across the street at No.25.

Národni ends at the Vltava river, where the breathtaking **National Theatre** (Národní divadlo; *see p232*) anchors the nation's culture. Topped by a crown of gold and with statues of bucking stallions lining the balustrade, the building is a product and symbol of the fervour of 19th-century Czech nationalism. It took 20 years to raise the money to begin construction, and from 1868 to1881 to build it. Then, just days before the curtain was to be raised for the first performance, it was gutted by fire. Construction started all over again, and, in 1883, the building finally opened with *Libuše*, an opera written for the occasion by Smetana. The theatre's hall is only open for performances, but it's a stunning place, perfect for a swish night on the town.

Just before you reach the National Theatre, you'll see its bastard offspring, **Laterna Magika**, or Magic Lantern (*see p237*). A frosted-glass monstrosity, it was built from 1977 to 1981 as a communist showpiece. The interior is all made from expensive imported marble – the floors, walls, even the banisters

Czech and proud:
the **National Theatre**. *See p99.*

– and every seat is upholstered in leather, now well-worn and patched. The black light shows and other multimedia fare that play here are not worth the admission, which is perhaps in keeping with an unintentionally ironic socialist relic.

Directly across the street, however, is a high Renaissance delight: the Czech **Academy of Sciences** (Akademie Věd), built from 1858 to 1862 as a Czech savings bank. The façade, fashioned after St Mark's Library in Venice, is crowned with an allegorical figure receiving the savings of the people. Inside, stone lions guard the entrance hall, and, in the spacious library beyond, ornate female figures of Economy and Thrift watch over the stacks.

Following the river south takes you past **Slovanský Island**. In the days before slacking became an art form, Berlioz came here and was appalled at the 'idlers, wasters and ne'er-do-wells' who congregated on the island. With a recommendation like that it's hard to resist the outdoor café here or spending a few lazy hours in one of the rowing boats for hire. There's also a fine statue of Božena Němcová, as seen on the front of the 500 Kč note. She was the Czech version of George Sand, a celebrated novelist whose private life scandalised polite society.

The island is home to the newly restored cultural centre **Žofín** (224 934 880, www.zofin.cz) – a large yellow building dating from the 1880s that hosted tea dances and concerts until just before World War II. Today you're more likely to find lectures and concerts here, along with one of the sweetest riverside beer gardens in Prague. At the southern tip is **Galerie Mánes** (*see p202*), a 1930s functionalist building oddly attached to a medieval water tower. Named for Josef Mánes, the 19th-century artist and nationalist, the building also houses a restaurant and dance club. The intelligentsia used to gather here between the wars, while in 1989 this was where the Civic Forum churned out posters and leaflets. Some of that spirit lives on in the gallery's shows, which feature mostly contemporary Czech artists.

Back on the riverside, continuing south along Masarykovo nábřež brings you to the corner of Resslova and the **Dancing Building** (Tančící dům), a collaboration between Czech architect Vlado Milunic and American architect Frank Gehry, completed in 1996. Also known as 'Fred and Ginger' – he's the rigid vertical half, she's the swaying glass partner – the project presaged Gehry's later, more prominent work, such as the Guggenheim Museum in Bilbao, Spain. According to Gehry, the original inspiration for the pinch in the middle of the glass tower came from wanting to protect a neighbour's view of Prague Castle.

Two blocks further south, **Palackého náměstí** is dominated by a huge Stanislav Sucharda sculpture of 19th-century historian František Palacký, who took 46 years to write a history of the Czech people. The solemn Palacký sits on a giant pedestal, oblivious to the beauties and demons flying around him. Behind him rise the two modern spires of the altogether more ancient **Emmaus Monastery** (Klášter Na Slovanech), which was founded by Charles IV. The spires were added after the baroque versions were destroyed by a stray bomb during World War II.

Around Karlovo náměstí

The streets that lie between the National Theatre and the Dancing Building, moving east back toward **Splálená**, comprise one of the lesser-known yet more entertaining nightlife areas of the city. The name SONA (south of Národni) was floated for a while but never really stuck, which is probably just as well. Part of this area's charm is its amorphous character; there are interesting pubs and restaurants on almost every street, although they never quite coalesce into a scene. Given that, and the tendency of these places to appear and disappear with alarming regularity, you always feel like you're exploring.

For years the **Globe Bookstore & Coffeehouse** (*see p144 and p163*) was the centre of expat life in Prague, but now that's not so true. A quick glance at the menus posted outside the entrances of neighbouring restaurants shows one reason why: most are in both Czech and English, an indication of how English-friendly the central city has become. There are also other English-language bookshops in Prague now (*see p163*) and plenty of places to get online (*see p282*).

U Fleků (*see p153*), at Křemencova 11, remains a tourist mainstay, mostly for the busloads of Germans who disembark ready to quaff 13-degree dark beer and sing along with the accordion players. Its entrance is marked by a picturesque old clock hung like a tavern sign. But there are plenty of hip, relaxed and far better-value pubs nearby. Walk north to the corner of **Opatovická** and you'll see a host of places accommodating a variety of budgets and tastes – the hip **Tulip Café** (*see p119*) at No.3, **H2O** (No.5, no phone) and **Cheers** (Křemencova 17, no phone) all feature cocktail menus reflecting how worldly (or globally uniform) Prague has become, at least in its boozing. Cuba Libre, Long Island Iced Tea and, of course, the obligatory Sex on the Beach are served at the lot. The more you walk, the more places you'll discover – including, by day, some entertaining antique shops, such as **Hamparadi Antik Bazar** (*see p162*).

The south-east corner of the area drops you into **Karlovo náměstí**, a sprawling square that used to be a cattle market and the site of Charles IV's relic fair. Once a year he would wheel out his collection of sacred saints' skulls, toenails and underwear, causing cripples to throw down their crutches and the blind to miraculously regain their sight.

On the north end of the park that forms the area's spine, the handsome **New Town Hall** (Novoměstská radnice) dates back to the 14th century, though the current version was built during the 19th and early 20th centuries. This was the notorious site of Prague's first defenestration. Across the square is the splendidly restored Jesuit **Church of St Ignatius** (Kostel sv. Ignác), a typically lush early-baroque affair, with gold-trimmed cream, pink and orange stucco. Built from 1665 to 1670, it features a wonderful collection of angels in its arches and nave. At the south-west corner of the park sits the **Faust House** (Faustův dům), an ornate 17th-century building that has more than a few legends attached to it. Edward Kelly, the earless English alchemist once lived here, as did a poor student who was lured into making a Faustian pact with the Prince of Darkness: the impoverished kid was offered riches in exchange for his soul, which Satan then snatched through a hole in the roof.

Walking east on Ječná will bring you to No.14, where Dvořák died. But rather than staring at the plaque on the wall, go to the **Dvořák Museum** nearby (*see p115*), where you can catch a chamber recital. It's quartered in a lovely summerhouse designed by Kilian Ignaz Dientzenhofer – the Villa Amerika, though, these days, it's surrounded by incongruous modern bits of concrete.

At the far end of the street is a museum of a very different sort – the **Police Museum** (*see p116*). Brek, the stuffed wonder dog responsible for thwarting the defection of several hundred dissidents, has been given a decent burial, but there are still plenty of gruesome exhibits here to delight the morbid.

If it all gets to be too much, seek sanctuary in the unusual church next door, dedicated to Charlemagne, Charles IV's hero and role model. The octagonal nave of **Na Karlově** was only completed in the 16th century, and for years the superstitious locals refused to enter it for fear that it would collapse. The gilt-frescoed walls inside were restored after the building was partially destroyed in the Prussian siege of 1757, but bullets can still be seen embedded in them. From the garden there are extensive views across the Nusle Valley to Vyšehrad on the other side.

A few blocks to the west on Vyšehradská is the **Church of St John on the Rock** (Kostel sv. Jan Na skalce), a fine Dientzenhofer structure built in the 1730s, perched at the top of an impressive double stairway. And a little further to the south from that are the delightful, though little-visited, **Botanical Gardens** (Botanická zahrada), with tranquil terraces.

Walking the other way on Ječná (west, toward the river), the street turns into Resslova and quickly brings you to the baroque **Cathedral of Sts Cyril and Methodius** (Kostel sv. Cyrila a Metoděje; *see below*).

Orthodox Cathedral of Sts Cyril & Methodius

Kostel sv. Cyrila a Metoděje
Resslova 9, Prague 2 (224 920 686). Metro Karlovo náměstí/tram 4, 7, 9, 12, 14, 16, 18, 22, 24. **Open** *Jan-Apr, Oct-Dec* 10am-4pm Tue-Sun. *May-Sept* 10am-5pm Tue-Sun. At other times, ring the administrator's bell to be admitted. **Admission** 50 Kč adults; 20 Kč concessions. **No credit cards. Map** p310 H8.

This baroque church, built in the 1730s, was taken over and restored by the Czech Orthodox Church in the 1930s. A plaque and memorial outside, together with numerous bullet holes, still attract tributes and flowers today, and are a clue to what happened inside during World War II. On 29 December 1941 two Czech paratroopers trained in England were flown into Bohemia, together with five colleagues, to carry out, among other resistance acts, the assassination of Reinhard Heydrich, Reichsprotektor of Bohemia and Moravia, and the man who chaired the infamous 1942 Wannsee Conference on the Final Solution. Josef Gabčík, Jan Kubiš and their co-conspirators were given sanctuary in the crypt here after the event, until they were betrayed to the Germans. In the early hours of 18 June, 350 members of the SS and Gestapo surrounded the church and spent the night bombarding it with bullets and grenades. The men, who managed to survive until dawn, used their final bullets to shoot themselves.

The incident did not end there. Recriminations were swift, brutal and arbitrary. Hundreds of people, many of them Jews, were rounded up in Prague and shot immediately, while five entire villages and most of their inhabitants were liquidated, the most famous being Lidice. The events brought about a turning point in the war. Britain repudiated the Munich Agreement and Anthony Eden declared that Lidice had 'stirred the conscience of the civilised world'. The story of the assassination and its aftermath is movingly told in the crypt of the church (entrance on Na Zderaze), where the Czech paratroopers made their last stand.

An excellent collection of photos is on display, along with the tunnel through which the assassins tried to dig their way out, in a failed effort to reach the city sewer. They came within centimetres of reaching their goal.

Further Afield

Stretch your legs and try daily life as Czechs live it: modern art, communist tombs, green space, a surreal radio tower and the best of the local locals.

Holešovice, Letná & Troja

Maps p312 & 313

The somewhat blighted look of **Holešovice** is your first clue that you've found out-of-centre neighbourhood life – although, Prague is so small that Staré Město, the Old Town (*see p81*), to the south over the Vltava river, is still in view from some parts of the district. The ostensibly unremarkable 19th-century suburb has a lot more going for it than grimy tenement blocks – alongside increasingly spruced-up ones – factories and one of Prague's two international train stations, **Nádraží Holešovice** (*see p270*). Indeed, this district is also home to two of Prague's finest green spaces, Stromovka (*see below*) and Letná park (*see p104*), and has become one of Prague's hippest areas.

Down towards the river on Kostelní is the **National Technical Museum** (*see p116*), a constructivist building dating from 1938-41, whose dull name belies a fascinating collection of Czechnology that instantly wows kids. Five minutes' walk east is Holešovice's main drag, **Dukelských hrdinů**. Here stands a sleeker constructivist building, the modern-looking **Veletržní palác**. Built in the mid 1920s to house the trade fairs that had long outgrown Výstaviště, it was gutted by fire in 1974 but has been splendidly restored. The stunning white-painted atrium rises up seven storeys and is lined with sweeping guard rails, giving it the feel of ża massive ocean liner. Pop in to peak at the atrium, even if you don't have time to take in the **National Gallery** collection of 19th-, 20th- and 21st-century art (*see p109*) within.

A couple of minutes' walk to the north is **Výstaviště** (*see p104*), a fairground fronted by an unusual wrought-iron pavilion erected for the Jubilee Exhibition of 1891 and considered the first expression of art nouveau in the city. Here, in the **Lapidárium** (*see p104*), you'll find an intriguing collection of reject monuments that once stood around the city. But don't go expecting much laughable communist-era public art: the collection here is mainly historic baroque and Gothic statuary, including most of the original statues from the Charles Bridge (those there now are almost all copies; *see p88*), moved here years ago to protect them from the elements. Beyond the pavilion is **Lunapark** (*see p104*), featuring a roller-coaster and Ferris wheel – always a fave with local teens and lovers – from which there are fine views over the woody environs of **Stromovka**, a park to the west, laid out by Rudolf II in the 16th century as a place for him to commune with nature. His favoured companion here was English alchemist John Dee, who got the job when he claimed to understand both the language of the birds and the one Adam and Eve spoke in Eden. Today the leafy park makes a wonderful spot for a stroll or picnic – though you may have to dodge the hordes of in-line skaters. Just south of Stromovka lie two of the city's hotbeds of late-night lifestyling: **Fraktal**, the semi-trashed bar where you'll find performance artists and affable international drunks sitting around tattered, hand-carved furnishings, and **La Bodega Flamenca** (for both, *see p154*), the Czech-owned cellar-haven of sangria sipping, one

The space-age **Žižkov Tower**. *See p108*.

Church of Sts Peter and Paul. *See p106.*

of the area's best after-hours refuelling options. For some of the city's hottest clubbing, with proper elbow room and a stylish long bar, try the Holešovice dance haven known as **Mecca** (*see p221*), on the eastern side of the district.

For a breath of fresh air, take the half-hour walk back to Staré Město via the sedate embassy-land of **Bubeneč**, just to the west of these bars and clubs, and ramble on past the **AC Sparta** stadium (*see p239*) and through **Letná** park (Letenské sady). This was where the biggest demonstration of 1989 took place, attended by nearly a million people. On the edge of the park sits the plinth, which now houses a giant metronome, in the place where the massive statue of Stalin once stood. Letná features its own hot new dance space, **Výletná** (*see p154*), which masquerades as a great garden barbecue pub.

Alternatively, a 20-minute walk north of Stromovka (or bus No.112 from Metro Nádraží Holešovice) brings you to the elaborate **Troja Chateau** (Trojský zámek; *see below*), recently restored after suffering massive damage from the flood of 2002. The inmates of the less salubrious **Prague Zoo** (*see p187*) across the road (still being rebuilt from flood damage at press time) can only curse their historical mistiming – at Troja, the count's horses were provided with a vast, sumptuous stable block, with marble floors and decorated with frescoes of their noble forebears.

Troja Chateau

Trojský zámek
U trojského zámku 1, Holešovice, Prague 7 (283 851 625/283 851 625). Metro Nádraží Holešovice/bus 112. **Open** *Jan-Apr, Oct-Dec* 10am-6pm Tue-Sun. *Mar-Nov* 10am-5pm Sat, Sun. **Admission** 120 Kč. **No credit cards**.

After winning huge tracts of land in the property lottery that followed the Thirty Years War, Count Šternberg embarked upon creating a house worthy of his ego. An 18th-century Czech nobleman, he was anxious to prove his loyalty to the Habsburg emperor and literally moved mountains to do so. The hillside had to be dug out to align the villa with the royal hunting park of Stromovka (*see p103*), still accessible via footbridge from the embankment, and the distant spires of St Vitus's Cathedral (*see p61*). The result, built by a French architect and Italian craftsmen, is a paean to the Habsburgs, modelled on a classical Italian villa and surrounded by formal gardens in the French style. The chateau's interior is replete with stunning trompe l'œil murals and on the massive external staircase gods hurl the rebellious giants into a dank grotto. In the Grand Hall the virtuous Habsburgs enjoy a well-earned victory over the infidel Turks. This, a fascinating though slightly ludicrous example of illusory painting, is Troja's main attraction. To see it you have to don huge red slippers to protect the marble floors. An insensitive pre-flood restoration programme essentially destroyed the villa's atmosphere, and the installation of a small collection of 19th-century Czech painting has done little to redeem it.

Výstaviště

Prague 7 (220 103 111/220 103 484/ www.incheba.cz). Metro Nádraží Holešovice/tram 5, 12, 17. **Open** 2-9pm Tue-Fri; 10am-9pm Sat, Sun. **Admission** free Tue-Fri; 20 Kč Sat, Sun; free under-6s. **No credit cards**. **Map** p312 D1/C1.

Built out of curvaceous expanses of wrought iron to house the Jubilee Exhibition of 1891, Výstaviště signalled the birth of the new architectural form in Prague. During the 1940s it became the site of various communist congresses, but today it is mainly used to house trade shows for every industry from information technology to porn. It's worth dodging past the salesmen to see the interior.

The industrial feeling of the wrought-iron structure is offset by vivid stained glass and exquisite floral decorations. The best view of the exterior is gained from the back, where a monumental modern fountain gushes kitschily at night, in time to popular classics and also accompanied by a light show. The grounds are filled with architectural oddities such as the Lapidárium, a working model of Shakespeare's Globe theatre and the delightfully dilapidated funfair Lunapark, which pulls in the weekend crowds of Czech families.

Dejvice & further west

Some of the most exclusive residences in the city are located in **Prague 6**, the suburbs that lie beyond Prague Castle (*see p61*). This neighbourhood is filled with embassies and the former residences of court and republic retainers of all stripes. You'd never guess this, though, from the rather desolate hub of the area, **Vítězné náměstí**, where another statue of Lenin used to stand.

Leading north from the square is the wide **Jugoslávských partyzánů** (Avenue of Yugoslav Partisans), at the end of which you'll find the **Crowne Plaza Hotel** (Kuolova 15, 296 537 111), formerly known as Hotel International. This monumental piece of 1950s socialist realism is one of the last remaining bastions of Marxist-Leninist decor in the city. The façade over the main entrance features Russian war heroes being greeted by grateful Czech peasants – they feel a bit out of place now, juxtaposed as they are with the bars inside the lobby, which are frequented by yuppies and foreign business folk who look like they use the hotel's new fitness centre. Very much a sign of the times.

On the hill above the hotel are the **Baba Villas** (Přírodni památka Babě), a colony of constructivist houses built after, and inspired by the huge success of, the 1927 Exhibition of Modern Living in Stuttgart. Under the guidance of Pavel Janák, all 33 of the houses were individually commissioned to provide simple but radically designed living spaces for ordinary families. However, they were quickly snapped up by leading figures of the Czech avant-garde and many of them are still decorated with original fixtures and fittings. None, alas, open to the public, but they are still a must-see for any fan of modern architecture. Take bus No.131 to U Matěje and walk up Matějská to reach the estate.

On the western fringe of the city, just off Patočkova, is the **Břevnov Monastery** (Benediktinské opatství Břevnov), inhabited by Benedictine monks since AD 993 and modelled on 'God's perfect workshop'. Since the Velvet Revolution the monks have purged all traces of the Ministry of the Interior, which for the last 40 years had used the **Basilica of St Margaret** (Bazilika sv. Markéta) as a warehouse for its files on suspicious foreigners. This Romanesque church was remodelled by the Dientzenhofer father-and-son act in the early 18th century and is one of their most triumphant commissions, with a single high nave and unfussy interior.

Close by, near the terminus of tram No.22, a small stone pyramid marks the site of **Bílá Hora**, or White Mountain, the decisive first battle of the Thirty Years' War, fought in 1620. In the park is the **Hvězda Hunting Lodge** (Letohrádek Hvězda), an extraordinary product of the Renaissance, its angular walls and roof arranged in the pattern of a six-pointed star (*hvězda* in Czech). It was built in the 1550s for Archduke Ferdinand of Tyrol, who was obsessed with numerology, and is conceived as an intellectual conundrum.

North of here, off Evropská, is the extensive and wonderfully wild **Divoká Šárka** (*see p243*), a fine place to stroll, swim or cycle away from the city crowds and fumes. There's a nude sunbathing area in summer by the murky lake.

Smíchov & Barrandov

Smíchov has undergone some changes since Mozart stayed here in 1787. Rapid industrialisation rather spoilt the ambience of the aristocracy's summer houses and the area was until recently dominated by factories (including the Staropramen Brewery) and factory workers. Now it has exploded with sleek new malls, multiplexes and office complexes. However, a few remnants of proletarian glories are commemorated in a couple of surviving socialist realist murals in Anděl metro station. To get an idea of what Smíchov was once like visit **Bertramka**, the house with lilac gardens that belonged to František and Josefina Dušek, now a museum to their most famous house guest, Wolfgang Amadeus Mozart (*see p115*).

South of Smíchov is **Barrandov**, the Czech version of Hollywood. On the cliffs below there are even white Hollywood-style letters that spell out 'Barrande' – though this is actually in homage to the 19th-century geologist after whom the quarter takes its name. Vast studios were built here in the 1930s, which have been the centre of the Czech film industry ever since.

Vyšehrad

Vyšehrad, the rocky outcrop south of Nové Město, the New Town (*see p94*), is where all the best Prague myths were born. Here Libuše, the mythic mother of Prague, fell into a trance and sent her horse out into the countryside to find her a suitable spouse, the ploughman called Přemysl, after whom the early Bohemian kings take their name. The true story is that a castle was founded here in the first half of the tenth century, enjoying a period of importance when King Vratislav II (1061-92) built a royal palace on the rock. Within 50 years, though, the Přemyslid rulers had moved back to Prague Castle and Vyšehrad's short-lived period of political pre-eminence was over.

Sightseeing

The easiest way to reach Vyšehrad is to take the metro to the Vyšehrad stop, under the enormous road bridge spanning the **Nusle Valley**. Built in the 1970s, the bridge was hailed as a monument to socialism, a description that was hastily dropped when chunks of concrete began falling on passing pedestrians and it became the most popular spot for suicides in the city. Walk away from the towering **Corinthia** (Kongresová 1, Prague 4, 261 191 111) and past the unappealing, monolithic **Congress Centre** (*see p217*), completed in 1980 as the supreme architectural expression of the Soviet-imposed 'normalisation' years, then through the baroque gateway into the park. The information centre (V pevnosti, no phone) to the right can provide maps of the area.

One of the first sights you will pass is the over-restored **Rotunda of St Martin** (Rotunda sv. Martina). Dating from the second half of the 11th century, it's the oldest complete Romanesque building in Prague and now hosts evening mass. There's been a church on the same site at Vyšehrad since the 14th century, but it was apparently irrevocably damaged when Lucifer, angered by an insubordinate cleric, threw three large rocks through the roof. The granite slabs (known as the **Devil Pillars**) can be found close to the **Old Deanery**, but the holes are gone. Joseph Mocker's neo-Gothic **Church of Sts Peter and Paul** (Kostel sv. Petr a Pavel) dates from the beginning of the 20th century. Restoration has brought out the best of the splendid polychrome interior, decked out with art nouveau-style saints and decorative motifs.

Next door is **Slavín**, Vyšehrad's cemetery, conceived by the 19th-century National Revival movement and last resting place of the cream of the country's arts worthies, including the composers Dvořák and Smetana, writers Karel Čapek and Jan Neruda, and painter Mikoláš Aleš. The Slavín (meaning 'pantheon') was designed by Antonín Wiehl and jointly commemorates further artistic big cheeses such as painter Alfons Mucha and sculptor Josef Václav Myslbek. Surrounded by Italianate arcades, the cemetery contains an abundance of fine memorials, many of them displaying art nouveau influences. The cemetery is very much a sacred intellectual ground in Czech history.

On the south side of the church are four monumental sculptural groups by Myslbek depicting mythological heroes from Czech history; the couple nearest to the church are Přemysl and Libuše. The park extends to the cliff edge overlooking the Vltava, from where there are lovely views across to Prague Castle.

If you continue down the hill from Vyšehrad along Přemyslova, you'll find one of the city's most outstanding pieces of cubist architecture, a corner apartment block designed by Josef Chochol at Neklanova 30 (1911-13). Some way south is a railway bridge popularly known as the **Bridge of Intelligence** because it was built by members of the intellectual elite who ended up working as labourers after losing their jobs during the purges of the 1950s.

Vinohrady & Žižkov

Map p313

Vinohrady came into existence in what the communist guidebooks called the period of Bourgeois Capitalism, and it's an area of magnificent, if crumbling, fin-de-siècle tenements. The heart of the neighbourhood is **Náměstí Míru**, a round 'square' spiked by the twin spires of the neo-Gothic **Church of St Ludmila** (Kostel sv. Ludmila) and faced by the opulent **Vinohrady Theatre** (Divadlo na Vinohradech; Náměstí Míru 7, 224 254 813). The **Radost FX** café, gallery and nightclub complex (*see p119 and p222*), still one of Prague's premier clubs, is nearby on Bělehradská. The **Medúza** café (*see p155*) on quiet Belgická is one of the city's cosiest, if threadbare, winter hideout spots, and, just over on the border of **Prague 10**, the **Café Atelier** (*see p141*) on Na Kovárně is one of the most accomplished local eateries. The area south of Náměstí Míru has become a centre of Prague's gay scene, with bars, clubs and pensions (*see p205*).

The main artery of Vinohrady, however, is **Vinohradská**, a little further north. Formerly called Stalinova třída, it saw some of 1968's fiercest street battles against Warsaw Pact troops. Art-nouveau apartment blocks line Vinohradská, looking out on to the **Church of the Sacred Heart** (Nejsvětější Srdce Páně), one of the most inspiring pieces of modern architecture in the city, dominated by its huge glass clock. It was built in 1928-32 by Josip Plečnik, the pioneering Slovenian architect who also redid Prague Castle.

Fans of ecclesiastical modernism might also enjoy Pavel Janák's 1930s **Hussite Church** (Husův sbor) on the corner of U vodárny and Dykova, as well as Josef Gočár's functionalist **Church of St Wenceslas** (Kostel sv. Václav) on Náměstí Svatopluka Čecha.

Near Plečnik's church is the scary **Žižkov Tower** (*see p108*), which was completed in 1989. A couple of nearby venues worthy of note are **Hapu**, a contender for top living-room cocktail bar, and **U Sadu** (for both, *see p156*), cheap and Czech, with well-located outside seating in the summer.

Down the hill to the north and east is **Žižkov**. This district, notorious for its iniquitous pubs, and for its large Romany population, is loved for its quirky outlandishness. Žižkov, always a working class district, not surprisingly became a popular interment place for post-war presidents. The massive **National Memorial** (Národní památník; *see p108*) on top of **Vítkov hill** is a mausoleum with the largest equestrian statue in the world, a 16.5-ton (16,764-kg) effigy of Hussite hero Jan Žižka. The corpses were ejected from the mausoleum in 1990; now it's an eerie place that occasionally hosts raves (if you fancy your chances of attending one, check out www.techno.cz/party).

Further east on Vinohradská are two fine cemeteries. The first, **Olšany Cemetery** (Olšanské hřbitovy; *see p108*), is the largest in Prague. Since 1989 the cemetery has begun to suffer from graffiti and grave-robbing. The cemetery extends from the Flora metro station to Jana Želivského, and includes a Garden of Rest, where the Red Army soldiers who died liberating Prague are buried.

Next door is the **Jewish Cemetery** (Židovské hřbitovy), not to be confused with the Old Jewish Cemetery (*see p92 and p113*) in Staré Město. Here fans of Franz Kafka come to pay respects at his simple grave (follow the sign at the entrance by Zelivského metro station; it's

Bad Bohemia Black Mummy

A district long famous for grotty worker pubs and even more grotty venues – and apartments and studios – **Žižkov** (*see p106*) is both bizarre and beloved. Wander into Žižkov's favourite drinking hole/performance space, **Akropolis** (*see p215*), for example, and you'll find an interior by surrealist Czech sculptor František Skala, while one of the most popular new dance clubs, **Matrix** (*see p224*) is a former frozen meat warehouse.

The area is also known for producing the odd good rock band or two. Few artists personify the spirit of Žižkov better than a band known as **Black Mummy** (sometimes Blaq Mummy; pictured), who are raising the standard of the district's bars with their brand of psychobilly surf rock. Not entirely unlike The Cramps meets the Butthole Surfers and fed back through a badly dinged amp with a few loose tubes, Black Mummy's loud, fast and furious sound has been known to get them booted offstage – as happened early in their career when an irritable hostel owner cancelled a performance after one song.

Their credentials as Žižkov icons thus unquestionably established, Black Mummy's concerts are invariably preceded by much rumour and speculation. That may be because they are rarely announced more than a few days ahead of time and are usually promoted via word of mouth.

Or, it may just be that Black Mummy tends to thrive in an aura of mystery. Even their origins are a bit hazy, though most often traced to a Halloween party in 1997, from whence time the band has been inextricably associated with unearthly occurrences. Naturally, there's a curse and a statistically improbable number of strange, usually minor, catastrophes that coincide with their concerts.

During one recent show, local poet and rocker Phil Shöenfelt encountered an alarming sensation of heat in his loins, which was traced to a pepper pot, somehow mistakenly put down his pants. The story makes marginally more sense as told on the band's website **blackmummy.tripod.com**.

The appealingly lurid, low-budget site explains that the band's image and name were inspired by a cheesy Mexican horror film, which haunted founder Reverend Vincent Feedback, aka Farnsworth. A band, the vision told him, 'could combine Egyptology, human transcendence and strains of [Farnsworth's] own possible Gypsy ancestry, all while playing cheap covers of three-chord rock 'n' roll.'

He reflects upon the moment, and the band's chequered history, with reverence to this day: 'I think it's basic stuff,' says Farnsworth, 'but everyone says it's weird.

approximately 200 metres/660 foot down the row by the southern cemetery wall). Though founded in 1890, only a fraction has been used since World War II – the neglect is obvious.

National Memorial

Národní památník

U památníku, Prague 3 (222 781 676). Metro Florenc/bus 133, 168, 207. **Open** times vary. **Map** p313 C1.

One of the city's best-known and least liked landmarks is this hulking mass of concrete. The immense constructivist block and enormous equestrian statue high up on Vítkov hill can be seen from around the city. It was built in 1925 by Jan Zázvorka as a dignified setting for the remains of the legionnaires who fought against the Austro-Hungarian Empire in World War I. In 1953 the communist regime turned it into a mausoleum for Heroes of the Working Class. The mummified remains of Klement Gottwald, first communist president, were kept here, tended by scientists who unsuccessfully tried to preserve his body for display, Lenin-style, before the project was abandoned and the decaying body fobbed off on Gottwald's family in 1990.

Opening times are unpredictable, but it doesn't really matter as most of what you might want to see can be seen from the outside. In front stands the massive equestrian statue of one-eyed General Žižka, scourge of 14th-century Catholics and the darling of the communists, who subsequently adopted him in an effort to establish genuine Bohemian credentials.

Olšany Cemetery

Olšanské hřbitovy

Vinohradská/Jana Želivského, Prague 3 (272 739 364). Metro Flora or Želivského. **Open** dawn-dusk daily. **Map** p313 D2/E2.

The overgrown yet beautiful Olšany Cemetery contains impressive memorials to two unlikely bed fellows: the first communist president, Klement Gottwald, who died after catching a cold at Stalin's funeral, and the most famous anti-communist martyr, Jan Palach, the student who set fire to himself in Wenceslas Square in 1969. In death their fates have been strangely linked, as neither's mortal remains have been allowed to rest in peace. Palach was originally buried here in 1969, but his grave became such a focus of dissent that the authorities disinterred his body and reburied it deep in the Bohemian countryside. In 1990 he was dug up and brought back to Olšany. His grave is to the right of the main entrance. Gottwald is harder to locate, hidden away in section five and sharing a mass grave with various other discredited party members. In 1990 his mummified remains were ejected from the National Memorial (*see above*) and returned to the family.

Žižkov Tower

Mahlerovy sady, Prague 3 (267 005 778). Metro Jiřího z Poděbrad/5, 9, 26 tram. **Open** 11am-11pm daily. **Admission** 60 Kč; free under-10s. **No credit cards. Map** p313 C2.

The huge, thrusting, three-pillared television tower in Žižkov has long been dubbed the Pražský pták, or Prague Prick, by local fans. Seemingly modelled on a Soyuz rocket ready for blast-off, or maybe something out of Thunderbirds, it has been more of a hit with space-crazy visitors than with the locals. The tower also has a made guest appearance in the film *Blade II*. It was planned under the communists (who tore up part of the adjacent Jewish Cemetery to make room for it), completed early in 1989, and no sooner started operating in 1990 than it came under attack from nearby residents who claimed it was guilty of, among other things, jamming foreign radio waves and giving their children cancer. You can take a lift up to the eighth-floor viewing platform or have a drink in the fifth-floor café, but in many ways standing at the base and looking up the 216m (709ft) of grey polished steel is even more scary. More than 20 TV channels broadcast from behind the white plastic shielding that defends against the elements. Transmitters lower down deal with radio stations and emergency services. The tower is now the subject of public art, with several large black babies crawling on its exterior. The intriguing, rather disturbing *Miminka* are the work of Czech bad-boy artist and satirist David Černý.

Jižní Město & Háje

To the south and east of the city centre lies the wilderness of **Prague 4**. Though parts are very old and beautiful, the postcode has come to mean only one thing for Praguers: *paneláky*.

Panelák is the Czech word for a tower block made from prefabricated concrete panels. These blocks sprouted throughout the 1960s and 1970s as a cheap solution to the post-war housing crisis. **Jižní Město**, or Southern Town, has the greatest concentration, housing 100,000 people, and now inspires Czech rap music polemics by its more youthful residents. There have been intermittent efforts to individualise the buildings with pastel exteriors, but this has only made the district look like a nightmarish toy town.

Háje, the last metro stop on the red Line C, is another good place to see the best of the worst. Before 1989, **Háje** used to be known as Kosmonautů, a nod in the direction of the USSR, and a rather humorous sculpture of two cosmonauts is outside the metro station. **Galaxie** (Arkalycká 877, Háje, Prague 4 (bookings 267 900 567, programme information 296 141 414, www.cinemacity.cz). Central Europe's first multiplex cinema and perhaps the only place in the world that sells pork-flavoured popcorn, is nearby, as is the popular swimming spot of **Hostivař Reservoir** (Prague 15; take tram No.s 22 or 26 to the end of the line), usually thronged by semi-clad sun-seekers all summer.

Museums

Whether it's art, history, technology or inscriptions on a hair, Prague has an incredible collection of collections. Just dive in.

For a city of its size Prague has an absurd number of exhibitions from design to Rudolfine arcanery. The city's museums also reflect Bohemia's location on the crossroads of Europe, where successive waves of cultures have left behind a toothsome variety of artefacts. Many reveal the tantalising tastes of eras and fashions long since abandoned, or particular Czech genius in the decorative arts. Revolution and restitution have taken their toll, of course, but the city's best offerings finally seem to be settled for the most part in good, permanent homes.

Recent times have brought some welcome news. **Kampa Museum** (Muzeum Kampa; *see p111*), located on the banks of the Vltava river, was particularly hard hit by the 2002 flood. But in September 2003 it was finally able to unveil its permanent display of works from the storied collection of museum founder Meda Mládkova and her late husband, Jan Mládek. And, while the flood didn't touch it, the **House of the Black Madonna** (Dům u Černé Matky Boží; *see p111*) also made a remarkable comeback in 2003. Once again, cubist works are on display at this impressive cubist building near Old Town Square. A collection of cubist art, under the control of the Czech Museum of Fine Arts, had been displayed here, but closed three years ago. Now operating under the auspices of the **National Gallery** (Národní Galerie; *see p110*), the museum features paintings, sculptures and furniture. The building itself is an incredible feat of cubism by Josef Gočar. **Sternberg Palace** (Šternberský palác; *see p110*), just outside the gates of Prague Castle, was recently renovated and now houses the National Gallery's European Old Masters collection. The brand-new **Prague Jewellery Collection** (Pražský kabinet šperku; *see p114*), located on the river near the Charles Bridge, brings together an impressive assortment of jewellery, including Fabergé eggs.

The sites that make up the **Jewish Museum** (Židovské Muzeum; *see p111*) still never fail to impress. On the other end of the spectrum, the Museum of Torture Instruments and the Sex Machine Museum in Prague's Old Town, Staré Město, are unabashed tourist traps posing as museums – you have been warned.

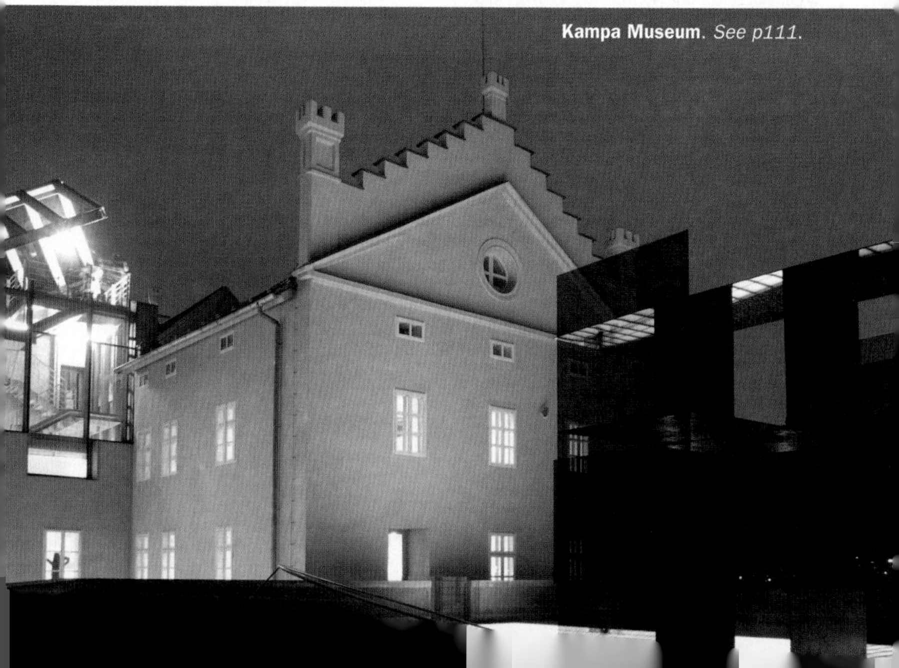

Kampa Museum. *See p111.*

National Gallery

National Gallery Collection of 19th-, 20th- & 21st-Century Art

Sbírka moderního a současného umění
Veletržní palác, Dukelských hrdinů 47, Holešovice, Prague 7 (224 301 122/www.ngprague.cz). Metro Vltavská/tram 5, 12, 17. **Open** 10am-6pm Tue-Sun. **Admission** 100 Kč 1 floor; 150 Kč 2 floors; 200 Kč 3 floors; 250 Kč all floors . *Temporary exhibitions* 50 Kč; free under-10s. **No credit cards. Map** p312 D2.

This functionalist building, designed by Oldřich Tyl and Josef Fuchs and opened in 1929, hosted trade fairs until 1951; later it served as headquarters for foreign trade companies. It has housed the National Gallery's collections of modern and contemporary art since its reconstruction in 1995. The 19th-century collection, here since 2000, is on the fourth floor. Highlights include paintings by Karel Purkyně, informed by a thorough knowledge of Old Master techniques, and the mystical strain of 19th-century Czech art represented by symbolists Max Švabinský and František Bílek. On the third floor is Czech art from 1900 to 1930, plus the gallery's impressive holdings of French art. The groundbreaking abstract artist František Kupka is the major figure here, where you'll also find the Czech cubists, surrealists and 1920s social art. The second floor covers art from 1930 to the present, including surrealist works by Toyen and Jindřich Štýrský, Stalin-era socialist realism and existentialist Art Informel from the same period. Also part of the international contemporary collection is Siah Armajani's installation *Glass Porch* for Walter Benjamin in the entrance hall.

Convent of St Agnes of Bohemia

Klášter sv. Anežky České
U milosrdných 17, Staré Město, Prague 1 (224 810 628/www.ngprague.cz). Metro Náměstí Republiky/tram 5, 8, 14. **Open** 10am-6pm Tue-Sun. **Admission** 100 Kč; 150 Kč family; free under-10s. **No credit cards. Map** p308 J1.

St Agnes's convent, Prague's first Gothic building, now houses a collection highlighting Bohemian and Central European medieval art from 1200 to 1550. Prague, after all, was at the forefront of European artistic development during the reign of Charles IV and one of the greats of the end of the 14th century was the Master of Třeboň. Here you can see his altarpiece featuring the *Resurrection of Christ* and his *Madonna of Roudnice*, an example of the Beautiful Style that prevailed until the Hussite wars. Gothic remained popular in Bohemia up to the 16th century, as seen in the extraordinary wood carving by monogrammist IP, depicting the half-decomposed figure of Death brushed aside by the risen Christ. The convent is fully wheelchair-accessible.

St George's Convent

Klášter sv. Jiří
Jiřské náměstí 33, Hradčany, Prague 1 (257 535 829/www.ngprague.cz). Metro Malostranská, then up the Old Castle Steps/tram 18, 22, 23. **Open** 10am-6pm Tue-Sun. **Admission** 100 Kč; 150 Kč family; free under-10s. **No credit cards. Map** p307 D2.

The newly restored **Sternberg Place**.

St George's Convent features mannerist and baroque art, including paintings from the collections of whimsically whacked-out Rudolf II (1576-1611). A highlight is the stylised work of Bartholomaeus Spranger, the Antwerp innovator whose sophisticated colours, elegant eroticism and obscure themes typify mannerism at its best. The baroque selection begins with Karel Škréta, whose down-to-earth canvases contrast with the religious work of Michael Leopold Willmann and Jan Krystof Liška. The tendency in baroque painting and sculpture to borrow from each other is seen in the paintings of Petr Brandl, the most acclaimed Czech artist of the early 18th century. His work is displayed near that of the two great sculptors of the time, Mathias Bernard Braun and Ferdinand Maxmilián Brokof. A workshop was recently opened, offering glimpses of the tools and methods of the masters.

Sternberg Palace

Šternberský palác
Hradčanské náměstí 15, Hradčany, Prague 1 (233 090 570/www.ngprague.cz). Metro Malostranská/tram 22, 23. **Open** 10am-6pm Tue-Sun. **Admission** 150 Kč; free under-10s. **No credit cards. Map** p306 C2.

Enlightened aristocrats trying to rouse Prague from provincial stupor founded the Sternberg Gallery here in the 1790s. The palace, just outside the gates of Prague Castle, now houses the National Gallery's European Old Masters. Not a large or well-balanced collection, especially since some of its most famous works were returned to their pre-war owners, but some outstanding paintings remain, including a brilliant Frans Hals portrait and Albrecht Dürer's *Feast of the Rosary*. The gallery finished renovations in spring 2003, making space for more paintings from the repositories and restoring ceiling frescoes and mouldings that had long been covered up.

Zbraslav Chateau

Zámek Zbraslav
Bartoňova 2, Zbraslav, Prague 5 (257 921 638/ www.ngprague.cz). Metro Smíchovské nádraží, then 129, 241 or 243 bus to Zbraslavské náměstí. **Open** 10am-6pm Tue-Sun. **Admission** 100 Kč; 150 Kč family. **No credit cards.**

This baroque chateau at the southern tip of Prague houses the National Gallery's surprisingly good collection of Asian art. The Chinese and Japanese holdings are particularly fine. There's also a smattering of Indian, South-east Asian and Islamic pieces, plus a handful of Tibetan scrolls crawling with fire demons and battling monks. A 30-minute bus ride from the metro. The ground floor is wheelchair accessible.

Other collections

Bílek Villa

Bílkova vila
Mickiewiczowa 1, Hradčany, Prague 1 (224 322 021). Metro Hradčanská/tram 18, 22. **Open** *Jan-mid May, mid Oct-Dec* 10am-6pm Sat, Sun. *Mid May-mid Oct* 10am-6pm Tue-Sun. **Admission** 100 Kč. **No credit cards. Map** p312 A3.

This must be the only building in the world designed to look like a wheatfield. Built in 1911-12 by mystic sculptor František Bílek as his studio and home, it still contains much of his work. Bílek went to Paris to study as a painter but discovered that he was partially colour-blind. He then turned to sculpture and illustration. The wheatfield, representing spiritual fertility and the harvest of creative work, was one of his many motifs. The results range from the sublime to the repellent. If the Hobbitlike wooden figures out front takes your fancy, you should have a look inside.

House at the Golden Ring

Dům U Zlatého prstenu
Týnská 6, Staré Město, Prague 1 (224 827 022). Metro Náměstí Republiky/tram 5, 8, 14, 26. **Open** 10am-6pm Tue-Sun. **Admission** 60 Kč; 120 Kč family; free under-6s. **No credit cards. Map** p308 J3.

The collection comprises a broad spectrum of 20th-century Czech works, organised intriguingly by theme rather than by artist or period. There's a fine basement exhibition space for temporary installations, often well-curated, fresh and international, though the gallery itself has limited space.

House of the Black Madonna

Dům u Černé Matky Boží
Celetná 34, Staré Město, Prague 1 (224 211 732). Metro Náměstí Republiky/tram 5, 8, 14. **Open** 10am-6pm Tue-Sun. **Admission** 100 Kč; 150 Kč family. **No credit cards. Map** p309 K3.

Renovated and reopened in November 2003, this fantastic cubist building and collection of paintings and sculptures strive to present a totally plane-defying environment. Worth a visit for the Josef Gočár-designed building alone, this is perhaps the finest example of cubist architecture in Prague. Considering its new lease of life under the umbrella of the National Gallery, English-language information on displays remains frustratingly scarce – and an hour with an English-speaking guide is a costly 1,200 Kč. These days, the Madonna, a treasured artefact that once adorned the outside corner in a gilded cage, is kept indoors for safekeeping and a copy has replaced it.

Kampa Museum

Muzeum Kampa
U Sovových mlýnů 2, Kampa, Prague 1 (257 286 147/www.museumkampa.cz). Tram 6, 9, 22. **Open** 10am-6pm daily. **Admission** 120 Kč. **No credit cards. Map** p307 F4.

This new museum in a completely overhauled mill, one of the city's oldest, makes a suitably stunning home for the first-rate collection of modern Czech and Central European art amassed by Czech émigré Jan Mládek and his widow, Meda. The permanent collection contains works by the abstract artist Frantisek Kupka, cubist sculptor Otto Gutfreund, and contemporary works by artists from the Czech Republic, Slovakia, Poland, Hungary and the former Yugoslavia. The 2002 flood hit the riverside building hard, but the newly renovated Museum Kampa opened in September 2003. By December of that year it had made headlines by premiering a temporary exhibition by Yoko Ono.

Prague Castle Picture Gallery

Obrazárna Pražského hradu
Prague Castle (2nd courtyard), Hradčany, Prague 1 (224 373 368/old.hrad.cz). Metro Malostranská/ tram 18, 22, 23. **Open** 10am-6pm daily. *Tours* Tue-Sun. **Admission** 100 Kč; 50 Kč concessions; 150 Kč family; free under-6s. **No credit cards. Map** p306 C2.

This collection of Renaissance and baroque works is home to Giuseppe Archimboldo's infamous mannerist work *Vertumnus*, which cast Rudolf II as a Roman harvest god. The gallery also includes works by Rubens, Tintoretto, Titian, Veronese and lesser-known masters. Though there's no hope of ever piecing together the emperor's original collection, the Castle has recently bought back on the open market a handful of works from the scattered cache.

Jewish Museum

The Jewish Museum, founded in 1906, strives to preserve the historical monuments of the former Jewish ghetto. By a gruesome irony, Hitler was responsible for today's comprehensive collections, though the story that he wanted a 'museum of an extinct race' is debated. Another suggestion is that Prague's German overlords allowed museum workers to catalogue and store the property of the 153 Czech Jewish communities, the better to eventually plunder them. The loot remained here after World War II since there was nobody to whom it could be returned. The museum, comprising five buildings and the **Old Jewish Cemetery** (Starý židovský hřbitov; *see p113*), is one of Prague's busiest – and most costly – tourist draws. You have to buy a ticket for all six parts of the museum. Tickets are sold at the **Klausen** (Klausová synagoga; *see below*), **Maisel** (Maiselova synagoga; *see p113*), **Pinkas** (Pinkasova synagoga; *see p114*) and **Spanish** Synagogues (Španělská synagoga; *see p114*). English-language tours run Sunday through Friday from the Maisel Synagogue (call the Jewish Museum beforehand for details and reservations; *see below*). The **Old-New Synagogue** (Staronová synagoga), though not officially part of the Jewish Museum, can be found nearby in Josefov (*see p92*).

Jewish Museum

Židovské Muzeum

Josefov, Prague 1 (222 317 191/www.jewish museum.cz). Metro Staroměstská/tram 17, 18. **Open** *Jan-Mar, Nov-Dec* 9am-4.30pm Mon-Fri. *Apr-Oct* 9am-6pm Mon-Fri. Closed Jewish holidays. **Admission** 300 Kč; 200 Kč concessions; under-6s free. *Old-New Synagogue* 200 Kč. **No credit cards**. **Map** p308 H2/3.

These directions, hours and rates apply to the six museum sites listed below; buy tickets at any one for the entire complex.

Former Ceremonial Hall

Obřadní sín

U starého hřbitova 3A, Josefov, Prague 1 (222 317 191/www.jewishmuseum.cz). **Map** p308 H2.

The Romanesque turrets and arches of this building at the exit of the cemetery make it appear as old as the gravestones. In fact, it was built in 1906 for the Prague Burial Society, which used the building for only 20 years. It hosts fascinating temporary exhibitions on such topics as Jewish customs and traditions, focusing on illness and death.

Klausen Synagogue

Klausová synagoga

U starého hřbitova 3A, Josefov, Prague 1 (222 310 302/www.jewishmuseum.cz). **Map** p308 H2.

The great ghetto fire of 1689 destroyed the original Klausen Synagogue along with 318 houses and ten other synagogues. The existing synagogue, constructed on the same site in 1694, has much in common with Prague's baroque churches, as it was built by the same craftsmen. Its permanent exhibition explores religion in the lives of the ghetto's former inhabitants. The best view of the synagogue is from the Old Jewish Cemetery (*see p113*), where the simple façade rises behind ancient gravestones, topped by two tablets of the Decalogue.

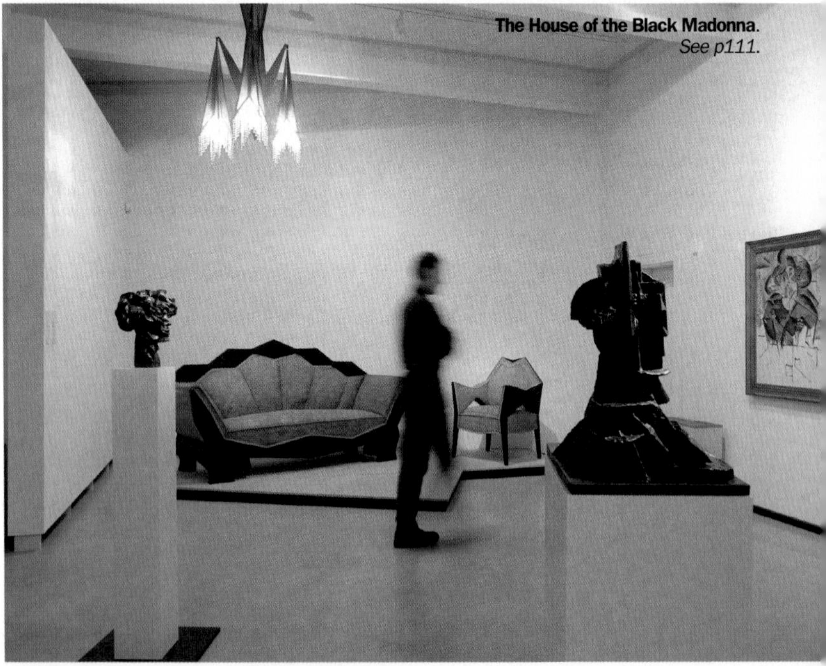

The House of the Black Madonna. *See p111.*

The national yawn

Like the Warsaw Pact invaders of 1968, tourists flooding into Prague following the Velvet Revolution got the wrong idea about the **National Museum** (*see p116*). Russian tank drivers back in the day mistakenly thought the striking building at the top of Wenceslas Square was Parliament and opened fire. The post-Revolution tourists on the other hand, a bit less sinister, and generally better-dressed, mistakenly thought the museum might be interesting. One can only guess what the tank drivers said upon learning of their mistake, but the refrain of the early 1990s tourists is well-documented: 'Gorgeous building! But there *must* be a better use of this space.'

More than a decade later not a lot has changed. Occasionally, rumours float that the museum is going to upgrade its collections of dusty mineral samples, stuffed mastodons, rusty spearheads, broken pottery and busts. Then, the story goes, captivating temporary exhibits will pull in those crowds.

Thus far, in a grudging nod to foreigners, English-language labelling now abounds, but the museum's meat and potatoes remain bland. And captivating temporary exhibits? Visitors in early 2004 were fascinated to learn the ins and outs of water. Yes, water. Veteran barmen will tell you that water holds great appeal when mixed in small quantities with a fine whisky. As a museum topic, though? Take it from the canny Prague museum intelligentsia: the previous show on wood was way better.

Still, the fact remains that the National Museum is among the most impressive buildings in the city, both inside and out, and it certainly merits an 80 Kč ticket and an hour or two of your time, if only for architectural reasons (though one of the chamber concerts periodically held on the Museum steps, with red pillows thoughtfully provided for sensitive backsides, might be a slightly less painful way to experience that). Marble floors and columns, wide staircases, and striking bronze busts of all the great Czech thinkers are everywhere. Think outtakes from *Titanic* meet Disneyland's Haunted Mansion.

The setting was impressive enough for the crew of *From Hell*, certainly, who cast the building as a piece of Jack the Ripper's London. Perhaps it's best, then, to ignore the exhibits entirely and just stroll through at your leisure, soaking up the atmosphere – you can even try the aforementioned water theory at the well-stocked snack bar.

If you do insist on taking in an exhibit, neophyte anthropologists will dig the collection on the prehistoric settlers of Bohemia, Moravia and Slovakia. And, admittedly, kids do enjoy the zoology floor, which features hundreds of stuffed, furry friends, along with the skeleton of a whale. Unfortunately, this is one area of the museum that remains light on translations – but 'big fishy!' is the same in any language, right?

Some hope remains that the museum will one day house a collection that's as remarkable as its setting. For now, though, don't be surprised if you walk away more impressed by the package than the contents.

Maisel Synagogue

Maiselova synagoga

Maiselova 10, Josefov, Prague 1 (222 325 172/ www.jewishmuseum.cz). **Map** p308 H3.

Mordecai Maisel (1528-1601), mayor of the Jewish ghetto during the reign of Rudolf II, was one of the richest men in 16th-century Europe. Legend traces Maisel's wealth to a lucky intervention by goblins, but more realistic historians suggest that Rudolf II granted Maisel a lucrative trading monopoly. The original building on this site, funded by Maisel, was apparently the most splendid of all the quarter's synagogues until it burned down along with most of the others in 1689. The present structure, sandwiched between apartment blocks, has a core dating to the 1690s; the rest was redone between 1892 and 1905. The synagogue houses exhibitions on the Jewish history of Bohemia and Moravia.

Old Jewish Cemetery

Starý židovský hřbitov

Široká 3, Josefov, Prague 1 (no phone/www.jewishmuseum.cz). **Map** p308 H2.

The Old Jewish Cemetery, where all of Prague's Jews were buried until the late 1600s, is one of the eeriest remnants of the city's once-thriving Jewish community. The 12,000 tombstones crammed into this tiny, tree-shaded patch of ground are a forceful reminder of the lack of space accorded to the ghetto, which remained walled until the late 1700s. Forbidden to enlarge the burial ground, the Jews were forced to bury the dead on top of one another. An estimated 100,000 bodies were piled up to 12 layers deep. Above them, lopsided stone tablets were then crammed on to mounds of earth. Burials began here in the early 15th century, although earlier gravestones were brought in from a cemetery nearby. Decorative reliefs on the headstones indicate the name of the deceased or their occupation: a pair of scissors, for example, indicates a tailor. The black headstones are the oldest, carved from 15th-century sandstone; the white ones, of marble, date from the 16th and 17th centuries.

Pinkas Synagogue

Pinkasova synagoga
Široká 3, Josefov, Prague 1 (222 326 660/ www.jewishmuseum.cz). **Map** p308 H2/3.
The story goes that a Rabbi Pinkas founded this synagogue in 1479 after falling out with the elders at the Old-New Synagogue. The building was enlarged in 1535, and a Renaissance façade added in 1625. In the 1950s the names of more than 80,000 men, women and children of Bohemia and Moravia who died in the Holocaust were inscribed on the synagogue's walls as a memorial. In 1967, after the Six-Day War, the Czechoslovak government expelled the Israeli ambassador and closed the synagogue for 'restoration'. In the ensuing 22 years, the writing became indecipherable. Not until after 1989 could the museum begin restoring the names, a job completed in 1994. The Pinkas also houses a powerful exhibition of drawings by children interned in Terezín (*see p256*), the last stop en route to the death camps in the east.

Spanish Synagogue

Španělská synagoga
Vězeňská 1, Josefov, Prague 1 (224 819 464/ www.jewishmuseum.cz). **Map** p308 J2.
The Old Synagogue, or Altschul, older still than the Old-New Synagogue, stood on this site as an island amid Christian territory, to which Jews could cross from the main ghetto only at certain times. It became a Reform synagogue in 1837, then the prospering congregation rebuilt it in 1868 in the then-fashionable Moorish style. After painstaking reconstruction, the long-decrepit building reopened in 1998. Its lovely domed interior glows with hypnotic floral designs traced in green, red and faux gold leaf, lit by stained-glass windows. It houses varied and inspired exhibitions on Jewish history and, in its upper-floor prayer hall, an exhibition of synagogue silver. It occasionally hosts concerts; tickets are available in the lobby.

Decorative arts

Mucha Museum

Muchovo muzeum
Kaunický palác, Panská 7, Nové Město, Prague 1 (221 451 333/www.mucha.cz). Metro Můstek/tram 3, 9, 14, 24. **Open** 10am-5pm daily. **Admission** 120 Kč. **No credit cards. Map** p309 K4.
Opened in 1998, this museum is dedicated to perhaps the most famous of all Czech visual artists, Alfons Mucha (1860-1939). Known for commercial work such as mass-produced decorative panels and posters for Sarah Bernhardt's theatre performances, Mucha exercised his greatest influence through his *Encyclopaedia for Craftsmen* (1902), a catalogue of art nouveau decorative elements, forms and designs. Mucha created a stained-glass window for St Vitus's Cathedral (*see p61*) and the *Slavonic Epic*, a series of gigantic narrative oil paintings now in Moravsky Krumlov castle, south-west of Brno. Also displayed in the musem are drawings, sketches, notebooks and a video on his life.

Museum of Decorative Arts

Uměleckoprůmyslové muzeum
Ulice 17. listopadu 2, Staré Město, Prague 1 (251 093 111). Metro Staroměstská/tram 17, 18. **Open** 10am-6pm Tue-Sun. **Admission** 120 Kč; free under-10s. **No credit cards. Map** p308 G2.
This neo-Renaissance museum, built from 1897 to 1900, is a work of art in itself, boasting richly decorated halls, stained- and etched-glass windows, and intricately painted plaster mouldings. Exhibits group objects according to material. In addition to the stellar 20th century collection, the permanent, pre-20th-century collections comprise lavishly crafted pieces, including exquisite furniture, tapestries, pottery, clocks, books, a beautifully preserved collection of clothing, and fine displays of ceramics and glass.

The Prague Jewellery Collection

Pražský kabinet šperku
Hergetova Cihelna, Cihelna 28, Malá Strana, Prague 1 (257 535 738). Metro Malostranská/tram 6, 9, 22. **Open** 10am-6pm daily. **Admission** 60 Kč; 50 Kč concessions. **No credit cards. Map** p307 F3.
Housed in a magnificently reconstructed brickyard on the river and just a stone's throw from the Charles Bridge, this new museum is a collaboration between the Museum of Decorative Arts and the private COPA company. The collection brings together an impressive assortment of jewellery and goldsmithing, documenting the evolution of the art from the 17th century to the present. Included are Tiffany artworks and Fabergé eggs, along with some Czech pieces once exhibited at the Expo '58 world's fair in Brussels.

History

Museum of the City of Prague

Muzeum hlavního města Prahy
Na Poříčí 52, Nové Město, Prague 1 (224 816 772/ www.muzeumprahy.cz). Metro Florenc/tram 3, 8, 24. **Open** 9am-6pm Tue-Sun. **Admission** 60 Kč; 120 Kč family; free under-6s; 1 Kč 1st Thur of mth. **No credit cards. Map** p309 M2.
Antonín Langweil spent 11 years of the early 1800s building an incredibly precise room-sized paper model of Prague. Now this museum's prize exhibit, it is the only complete depiction of what the city looked like before the Jewish ghetto was torn down. Other displays follow the city's development from pre-history through to the 17th century, with some English labels provided in the rooms devoted to medieval and later events. The upstairs galleries host temporary exhibitions and the original of the Josef Mánes painting reproduced inside the Old Town Hall's astronomical clock tower.

Planes, trains and automobiles at the **National Technical Museum**. *See p116.*

Museum of Communism

Muzeum komunismu

Na příkopě 10, Nové Město, Prague 1 (224 212 966/www.museumofcommunism.com). Metro Můstek/tram 3, 9, 14, 24. **Open** 9am-9pm daily. **Admission** 180 Kč. **Credit** AmEx, MC, V. **Map** p308 J4.

Opened in 2001 as the first of its kind in the country, the museum puts the communist era in historical perspective through its ample archive photographs with explanatory texts, as well as hundreds of relics. Co-founded by American restaurateur Glenn Spicker (*see p79* **Bad Bohemia: Little Glenn**), the museum has mock-ups of a school room from the period, with Czechoslovak and Soviet flags hanging side by side and a Russian lesson on the blackboard. More eerie is the interrogation room like those used by the Czechoslovak secret police. And just to keep Lenin spinning, the museum is directly above a McDonald's and shares a floor in the building with a casino.

Music & musicians

Dvořák Museum

Muzeum Antonína Dvořáka

Villa Amerika, Ke Karlovu 20, Nové Město, Prague 2 (224 918 013). Metro IP Pavlova/tram 4, 6, 11, 16, 22, 23, 34. **Open** 10am-5pm Tue-Sun. **Admission** 40 Kč. **No credit cards. Map** p311 K8.

Hidden away behind wrought-iron gates, the Dvořák Museum is housed in an elegant, early 18th-century baroque summer palace. This small red-and-ochre villa was built by Kilian Ignaz Dientzenhofer in 1720 for Count Jan Václav Michna, then became a cattle market in the 19th century. It now houses the Dvořák Society's well-organised tribute to the most famous Czech composer. Memorabilia and photographs make up the ground-floor display. Upstairs are further exhibits and a recital hall, decorated with frescoes by Jan Ferdinand Schor. Concerts held here are the best way to appreciate the building's past as a retreat for the composer. Outdoor recitals in warm weather are particularly evocative.

Mozart Museum

Bertramka

Mozartova 169, Smíchov, Prague 5 (257 318 461/www.bertramka.cz). Metro Anděl/tram 4, 7, 9, 10. **Open** *Jan-Mar, Nov-Dec* 9.30am-4pm daily. *Apr-Oct* 9.30am-6pm daily. **Admission** 90 Kč; free under-6s. *Concerts* 230-450 Kč. **No credit cards.**

Villa Bertramka – a former vineyard manor house that has been restored to its 18th-century glory – is a welcome refuge in its walled park next to the Mövenpick hotel (*see p53*). Mozart stayed here several times as a guest of the villa's owners, composer František Dušek and his wife, Josefína. And it was here, in 1787, that he composed the overture to *Don Giovanni*, the night before its première in the Nostitz Theatre, now called the Estates Theatre (*see p210 and p232*). Bertramka showcases memorabilia of Mozart and the Dušeks, including personal keepsakes, musical instruments, manuscripts and letters. Tranquillity, however, is the villa's greatest asset – mid-morning or late afternoon, it is possible to linger over cappuccino in the courtyard café and remain relatively undisturbed by tour groups. There are also occasional evening recitals on the terrace.

Natural history & ethnography

Náprstek Museum

Náprstkovo muzeum

Betlémské náměstí 1, Staré Město, Prague 1 (224 221 426/www.aconet.cz/npm). Metro Můstek or Národní třída/tram 6, 9, 17, 18, 22, 23. **Open** 9am-5.30pm Tue-Sun. **Admission** 60 Kč; free under-6s; free 1st Fri of mth. **No credit cards. Map** p308 G4/5.

The 19th-century nationalist Vojta Náprstek had two passions: modern technology and primitive cultures. While the gadgets he collected are now in the National Technical Museum (*see below*), the ethnographic oddities that he acquired from Czech travellers are here in an extension to his house. The displays concentrating on native peoples of the Americas, Australasia and the Pacific Islands are interesting and exemplarily arranged. Temporary exhibitions favour travelogues of exotic cultures by Czech photographers.

National Museum

Národní muzeum

Václavské náměstí 68, Nové Město, Prague 1 (224 497 111/www.nm.cz). Metro Muzeum/tram 11. **Open** *Jan-Apr, Oct-Dec* 9am-5pm daily. *May-Sept* 10am-6pm daily. Closed 1st Tue of mth. **Admission** 100 Kč; 120 Kč family; free under-6s; free 1st Mon of mth. **No credit cards. Map** p311 L6/7.

The vast edifice dominates the top of Wenceslas Square, its neo-Renaissance flamboyance promising an intriguing interior. Instead, it is filled with rooms of dusty fossils, rocks and stuffed animals. The museum is arguably worth a visit, if only to take in the grand environs. The architecture and interior decorations are the most appealing features, designed as they were by Josef Schulz and finished in 1890 as a proud symbol of the Czech National Revival. The exterior still has scars from shelling, when Warsaw Pact tanks invaded Prague in 1968. As at Prague Castle, here's an almost complete lack of labels in English, but an audio guide in English is available for an extra 200 Kč. (*See also p113* **The national yawn**.)

Miscellaneous

Miniatures Museum

Muzeum miniatur

Strahovské nádvoří 11 (grounds of Strahov Monastery), Hradčany, Prague 1 (233 352 371/ www.muzeumminatur.cz). Metro Malostranská/ tram 22, 23. **Open** 9am-5pm daily. **Admission** 50 Kč; 20 Kč children. **Credit** AmEx, DC, MC, V. **Map** p306 A4.

With the aid of magnifying glasses and microscopes, you'll be able to see truly tiny works of art – portraiture on a poppy seed, a caravan of camels painted on a grain of millet, a prayer written out on a human hair, and minuscule copies of masterpieces by the likes of Rembrandt and Botticelli. Absorbing, but perhaps not fascinating enough to merit the schlep up to the Strahov Monastery (*see p71*), where the museum is located.

National Technical Museum

Národní technické muzeum

Kostelní 42, Holešovice, Prague 7 (220 399 111/ www.ntm.cz). Metro Hradčanská or Vltavská/tram 8, 25, 26. **Open** 9am-5pm Tue-Fri; 10am-6pm Sat, Sun. **Admission** 70 Kč; 150 Kč family. **No credit cards. Map** p312 C3.

Don't let the mundane name put you off: the National Technical Museum is a fascinating collection, enjoyable for both kids and adults. The museum traces the development of technology and science in Czechoslovakia, which, until the communist era, was among Europe's most innovative and industrially advanced nations. The Transport Hall contains steam trains, vintage motorcycles, racing cars and biplanes, while the claustrophobic 'mine' in the basement has sinister coal-cutting implements in place in mock tunnels. Guided tours of the mine are available in English. There's also an extensive photography and cinematography section, and a collection of rare astronomical instruments.

Police Museum

Muzeum policie CR

Ke Karlovu 1, Nové Město, Prague 2 (224 923 619/ www.mvcr.cz/policie/muzeum.htm). Metro IP Pavlova/ tram 6, 11. **Open** 10am-5pm Tue-Sun. **Admission** 30 Kč; 50 Kč family. **No credit cards. Map** p311 K10.

Prague's surprisingly interesting Police Museum resides in a former convent attached to the Karlov Church. In the section on crime detection techniques you can take your own fingerprints or try to reconstruct events at a creepy scene-of-the-crime mock-up. Kids love it, though parents are warned that some of the photographs are quite graphic. The final room contains an arsenal of home-made weaponry that would please James Bond: sword sticks, makeshift pistols, pen guns, even a lethal lighter. The texts, though, are almost entirely in Czech.

Toy Museum

Muzeum hraček

Jiřská 6, Hradčany, Prague 1 (224 372 294/ www.muzeumhracek.cz). Metro Malostranská/ tram 12, 18, 22, 23. **Open** 9.30am-5pm daily. **Admission** 50 Kč; 80 Kč family; free under-5s. **No credit cards. Map** p307 E1/2.

Part of Czech émigré Ivan Steiger's large collection is displayed on the two floors of this museum in the Castle grounds. Brief texts accompany cases of toys, from teddy bears to an elaborate tin train set. Kitsch fans will love the robots and the enormous collection of Barbie dolls clad in vintage costumes throughout the decades. Good for a rainy day, but probably better for the young at heart rather than the actual young, most of whom greatly prefer playing with toys than looking at them from a historical perspective.

Eat, Drink, Shop

Features

Restaurants

The scene is set for fresh taste, less pretence, solid values and – dare we say it? – good service.

Any country where all the restaurants were once an arm of state central planning and waiters were trained as secret agents will probably have a bit of evolving to do, if they hope to win over fussy free-market diners. But Prague chefs and restaurateurs, inspired by a handful of foreigners who have drawn crowds like a house fire, have gone back to the planning table, consequently leaping forward aeons in style and service.

If you drop in on places at random, you're still likely to encounter at least one pizza served with ketchup – and a server who's hoping that you'll go away if he ignores you for long enough. But, with a bit of counter intelligence, you'll be rewarded with wood-fired Neapolitan pies at **Hergetova Cihelna** (*see p123*), fiery Thai at **Lemon Leaf** (*see p134*) or authentic Czech pork and dumplings at **Celnice** (*see p136 and p222*) or **Kolkovna** (*see p128*).

All these recently opened establishments set the standard for affordable, elegant but unpretentious dining, and the latter two represent the most popular new wave in Prague dining: the brewery-owned pub. **Potrefená husa** (*see p156*), another in this mould, is a phenomenally successful Czech chain owned by Staropramen, offering traditional potato soup, chicken Caesar salads and pastas – they take no culinary risks but provide consistent service with a smile, and that seems enough to have them packed with diners seven days a week. A few of these cleaned-up classic pubs for a new generation feature an added twist, such as Celnice's sushi menu. Still, that's about as bold as innovation gets in Prague's mainstream restaurants for the time being.

Nevertheless, it all adds up to a palpable move in a positive direction, perfectly timed for the new competition involved in being an EU-member country – even if that's also accompanied by a rise in the five per cent restaurant value-added tax, to 19 per cent. Boldness doesn't always win points anyway, at least when it turns into overstyling and snobbery. The absurdly haughty designer showcases of recent years (the ones specialising in Plexiglas furnishings, swarms of smarmy waiters and tiny dinners presented à la Jackson Pollock) have steadily fallen by the wayside in favour of real food for real people.

A few genuine gems at the high end have proven their staying power with elegant gusto, such as **Opera Garden** (*see p138*), the Four Seasons' **Allegro** (*see p126*), and the beloved French **Le Bistrot de Marlène** (*see p137*).

Prague's expat community can always be counted on to open restaurants when they can't find satisfying brunches, bagel shops and Sonoran Mexican food. The latest crop includes **Tulip Café** (*see p134*) and **Picante** (*see p134*), a cheap, all-night fast-food joint that still serves the best Mexican in town. And then there's the ever-popular **Bohemia Bagel** (*see p121*).

The Michelin stars in Prague may lag far behind Paris's, London's or even Berlin's, but Prague still beats them all hands-down for price. Besides, dining here, like most things, is still an adventure. Where's the fun in knowing you'll always be well catered to? So brace yourself for the occasional waiter with suspect maths, annoyingly short opening hours and the ever-arduous hunt for vegetarian food.

This meat-loving culture does offer **Radost FX Café** (*see p140*) for non-carnivores, as well as the buffet-style **Country Life** (*see p133*). Otherwise, it may come down to *smažený sýr*, the fried cheese served at most pubs – just mind they don't slip in ham (*šunka*).

Menus are available in both English and Czech. Otherwise, should you have trouble deciphering the dishes at the Czech restaurant that doesn't, *see p134* **What's on the menu?**

TIPPING AND ETIQUETTE

Tables are often shared with other patrons who, like you, should ask *'Je tu volno?'* (Is it free?) and may also wish each other *'Dobrou chut'* before tucking in. Prague dines with a relaxed dress code and reservations are necessary at only the fanciest spots in town – you should have little trouble making a phone booking in English at swankier establishments, but everywhere else it might be easier to book in person.

Waiters record your tab on a slip of paper, which translates at leaving time into a bill. Pay the staff member with the folding wallet in their waistband, not your waiter (*'Zaplatím, prosím'* means 'May I pay, please?'). A cover charge and extra charges for milk, bread and the ubiquitous accordion music are standard, as is tipping by rounding the bill up to the nearest 10 Kč.

Hradčany

Asian

Malý Buddha

Úvoz 46, Prague 1 (220 513 894). Tram 8, 22. **Open** 1-10.30pm Tue-Sun. **Main courses** 100-250 Kč. **No credit cards. Map** p306 A3.

An incongruously serene space for light noodles and spring rolls, mainly vegetarian, which nicely complement the dozens of teas. The Little Buddha also features a handy shrine at the back in case an offering is in order. The laid-back owner, who's always on hand, supervises with fluid motions. Mellow doesn't half describe it. No smoking.

Czech

U Ševce Matouše

Loretánské náměstí 4, Prague 1 (220 514 536). Tram 22. **Open** 11am-4pm, 6-11pm daily. **Main courses** 180-280 Kč. **Credit** AmEx, MC, V. **Map** p306 A3.

The house special, green-pepper steak, or your choice of a dozen other varieties, is served without fuss on to the old wooden bench tables with the requisite pint of Czech pilsner (bottled, alas, not on tap). Generous servings are the rule, and fish and chips provide the variety in this former shoemaker's workshop – where it was once possible to get your boots repaired while lunching. Reasonable prices given the prime location.

The best Restaurants

For Bohemian meat and dumplings
U Radnice (*see p129*) – classic, over-lit, hearty grub on Old Town Square.

For dining in a palace
Palffy Palác (*see p123*) has culinary prowess to match its palatial setting.

For dining with the city spread at your feet
Enjoy fettuccine among the roof gables at **Bazaar Mediterranée** (*see p125*).

For intimate space and dreamy cuisine
Le Bistrot de Marlène (*see p137*) serves it up in streamlined splendour.

For late eats/vegetarian/good old-fashioned brunch
Radost FX Café (*see p140*) still does it all, and not so badly.

For local celeb-spotting
Make the scene at **Tulip Café** (*see p134*).

For prime riverside romancing
Impress your date with an affordable splurge at **Hergetova Cihelna** (*see p123*).

For the state of Czech nouvelle
Celnice (*see p136*): playful, never intimidating.

Palatial kitsch at **Palffy Palác**. *See p123.*

Malá Strana

Americas

Bohemia Bagel

Újezd 16, Prague 1 (257 310 694/www.bohemiabagel.cz). Tram 6, 9, 12, 22. **Open** 7am-midnight Mon-Fri; 8am-midnight Sat, Sun. **Main courses** 100-250 Kč. **No credit cards.** **Map** p307 E5.

A breakfast diner in Prague serving chocolate chip muffins, bottomless cups of filtered coffee, and, yes, fresh bagels. Top them with scrambled eggs and ham, grab a booth and browse your issue of the *Prague Post*. No one will ever guess you're not local! Glenn Spicker of U Malého Glena fame (*see p79* **Bad Bohemia: Little Glenn**) created this place after he finally had enough of pining for comfort food from home. There's also usually something of interest – courses, places to rent, exhibitions – on the bulletin board.

Other locations: Masná 2, Staré Město, Prague 1 (224 812 560).

Continental

C'est la Vie

Říční 1, Prague 1 (257 321 511). Tram 12, 22. **Open** 11.30am-midnight daily. **Main courses** 1,000-1,600 Kč. **Credit** AmEx, MC, V.

The great riverside location in Malá Strana doesn't translate into embankment tables, but the progressive menu and fleet-footed service have attracted the attention of the expense-account crowd looking for casual elegance to go with the truffles and tuna tartare, and grilled chicken in tamarind sauce.

Cukrkávalimonáda

Lázeňská 7, Prague 1 (257 530 628). Metro Malostranská/tram 12, 22. **Open** 8.30am-8pm daily. **Main courses** 100-300 Kč. **No credit cards.** **Map** p307 E4.

This simple eaterie is a breath of fresh air. Both hip and homely, it's just a block off the main tourist drag leading from the Charles Bridge but seems miles away with a short, well-chosen wine list and daily specials of chicken roulades with heaps of mashed potatoes. Expect tall lattes, a casually alert service, designer benches and slick magazines for leafing through.

David

Tržiště 21, Prague 1 (257 533 109/www.restaurant-david.cz). Metro Malostranská/tram 12, 22. **Open** 11.30am-11pm daily. **Main courses** 360-700 Kč. **Credit** AmEx, MC, V. **Map** p307 D3.

Conservative in menu, but few places do the classics better. A quaint house of old is now a respected restaurant that wins over A-list celebrities with its discreet location, seen-it-all waiters and pampering, old-club style. Roast duck with red-and-white sauerkraut, or rabbit fillet with spinach leaves and herb sauce is rarely brought off better. Booking essential.

Gitanes

Tržiště 7, Prague 1 (257 530 163/www.gitanes.cz). Metro Malostranská. **Open** noon-midnight daily. **Main courses** 150-290 Kč. **Credit** MC, V. **Map** p307 D3.

Up the style ante at **Hergetova Cihelna**. *See p123.*

A bracing taste of spice in traditional, safe central Europe, this two-room place just off the district's main square serves Yugoslavian favourites like sheep's cheese, stuffed peppers, home-made bread with paprika milk-fat spread, and hearty red wine. Warm service, gingham and doilies give you the feeling you're visiting your Balkan granny's house, only with much cooler music – emanating from speakers hidden in the birdcages. Don't miss the private table available for curtained-off dalliances.

Hergetova Cihelna

Cihelna 2b, Prague 1 (257 535 534/www.cihelna.com). Metro Malostranská/tram 12, 18, 22. **Open** noon-2am daily. **Main courses** 300-500 Kč. **Credit** AmEx, MC, V. **Map** p307 F4.

The latest star of restaurateur Nils Jebens (*see p127* **Bad Bohemia: Nils Jebens**), this former brick factory combines inspired cuisine (the pizza chef is a native of Naples and sticks religiously to his home recipes) with a swanky upstairs lounge bar. All at remarkably affordable prices and with knock-out riverside tables, complete with blankets for when it's chilly. Nice Belgian ales too.

Palffy Palác

Valdštejnská 14, Prague 1 (257 530 522/www.palffy.cz). Metro Malostranská/tram 12, 18, 22. **Open** 11am-11pm daily. **Main courses** 130-270 Kč. **Credit** AmEx, MC, V. **Map** p307 E2.

The kind of place only possible in Prague – a baroque palace room, complete with crystal chandeliers, once used as the lunchroom for the music conservatory that still owns the building. Meet here or on the small terrace outside for a dream date of a classy brunch. The saltimbocca of veal sirloin is impressive, as is the fillet of roebuck marinated in honey and juniper, but the quail *confit* is gone after a few bites . The crêpes and salads are generous and delicate affairs. All in all, excellent value for money.

Czech

U Karlova mostu

Na Kampě 15, Prague 1 (257 531 430/www.nakampe15.cz). Metro Malostranská/tram 12, 22. **Open** 11am-11pm daily. **Main courses** 90-200 Kč. **Credit** AmEx, DC, MC, V. **Map** p307 F4.

An unpretentious pub-restaurant serving potato thyme soup and *topinka*, or Czech fried toast with raw garlic, this close to the Charles Bridge? Just don't tell the package tourists – and mind that you don't accidentally wind up in the pricey restaurant at this same address. Swing around the corner to the pub with the mustard walls for the real thing. The scattering of outdoor tables on the edge of Kampa Park is among the perks.

U Maltézských rytířů

Prokopská 10, Prague 1 (257 533 666/www.umaltezskychrytiru.cz). Tram 12, 22. **Open** 11am-11pm daily. **Main courses** 260-540 Kč. **Credit** AmEx, MC, V. **Map** p307 E4.

A candlelit, Gothic cellar, once an inn for the eponymous Knights of Malta, this place is justly proud of its venison chateaubriand. Mrs Černíková, whose family runs the place, does a nightly narration on the history of the house, then harasses you to eat the incredible strudel. Booking essential.

U Sedmi Švábů

Jánský vršek 14, Prague 1 (257 531 455/www.viacarolina.cz). Metro Malostranská/tram 12, 22, 23. **Open** 11am-11pm daily; kitchen closes at 10pm. **Main courses** 150-350 Kč. **Credit** AmEx, MC, V. **Map** p306 C3.

A *krčma*, or Czech medieval tavern, the Seven Swabians is a trippy, if borderline tacky experience, with occasional live troubadour music, traditional sweet honey liqueur and salty platters of pork knuckle. Only in Prague.

U Zlaté studně

U Zlaté studně 166, Prague 1 (257 533 322/www.zlatastudna.cz). Metro Malostranská/tram 12, 22, 23. **Open** 11am-midnight daily. **Main courses** 400-600 Kč. **Credit** AmEx, MC, V. **Map** p307 E2.

Dine like a prince in this hillside space at the foot of Prague Castle, perfectly situated to reward a day's tramping about the grounds – you can walk right in from the castle gardens. Owned by the management of Palffý Palác (*see above*), At the Golden Well offers spectacular views, sharp service and a menu that starts off with decadent choices like duck livers marinated in armagnac. Czech classics of game, beef, pork and dumplings follow. It's not to be mistaken for the Staré Město hotel of the same name, though.

French

Bar Bar

Všehrdova 17, Prague 1 (257 312 246). Tram 12, 22. **Open** noon-2am daily. **Main courses** 80-140 Kč. **Credit** MC, V. **Map** p307 E5.

A decadent, lively, red basement room for light dinners of salads and savoury crêpes served amid junk-shop decor. Locals crowd in early for this alternative to heavy pub food, and alternative to the usual gruff service of Prague. If you can find the entrance, your reward awaits: dinner pancakes of fresh cream and mushrooms, English-style dessert pancakes with lemon and sugar.

U malířů

Maltézské náměstí 11, Prague 1 (257 530 000/www.umaliru.cz). Tram 12, 22. **Open** 11.30am-midnight daily. **Main courses** 500-1,000 Kč. **Credit** AmEx, MC, V. **Map** p307 E4.

Not one for the faint of heart, Prague's most pricey restaurant lurks within a quaint 16th-century house with original painted ceilings. Authentic, quality French cuisine – game sautéd Burgundy-style – plus local treasures like trout in beer sauce. Well-arranged *prix fixe* menus, and seasonal menu, which

range from snails or paté served with Sauternes to sea bass, lobster, lamb and squab. An excellent cheeseboard and wine list – although the price of a bottle will double the cost of a meal already qualified mainly for expense accounts. Stiff service.

Italian

Bazaar Mediterranée

Nerudova 40, Prague 1 (257 535 050/ www.restaurantbazaar.cz). Tram 12, 22. **Open** noon-midnight daily. **Main courses** 250-500 Kč. **Credit** AmEx, MC, V. **Map** p307 D3.

A hit mainly for its knockout terrace views of Malá Strana from the garden, this surreal labyrinth of cellars and stairs presents, simply, pasta – as if it were the pride of the kitchen. Unfortunately, it is. Not that this matters much to anyone sipping a Chardonnay in mild weather on the terrace – lap blankets roll out if it's cool. Hint: the terrace is up the winding stairs at the back. For some reason, the cellar bar trots out nightly oddball entertainment ranging from drag shows to striptease acts, as does its kitschy sister establishment, Banana Bar & Café (*see p147*).

Mediterranean

Square

Malostranské Náměstí 5, Prague 1 (257 532 109/www.squarerestaurant.cz). Metro Malostranská/tram 12, 22, 23. **Open** 8am-midnight daily; kitchen closes at 11pm. **Main courses** 650-1,200 Kč. **Credit** AmEx, MC, V.

The house specialities – high-concept Spanish tapas, and *nouvelle* seafood delights like tiger prawns and squid fritters – go along with the other Mediterranean treats at Square, such as pumpkin risotto with Italian sausage and pecorino – all in a celebration of cool, modern design that features running waterfalls and padded, creamy walls. Several fine wines by the glass, killer lunch specials and a reasonable breakfast menu, with tables on the Malá Strana's main square.

Seafood

Kampa Park

Na Kampě 8B, Prague 1 (257 532 685/ www.kampapark.com). Metro Malostranská/ tram 12, 22. **Open** 11.30am-1am daily; kitchen closes at 11pm. **Main courses** 300-650 Kč. **Credit** AmEx, MC, V. **Map** p307 F4.

One of the city's first foodie meccas, with stunning riverside views on to the Charles Bridge, Kampa Park is probably due for some kind of medal after ten years. Alfresco dining on oysters or Thai tuna steak in summer complements a slick bar-room scene inside, favoured by the business crowd. Tasteful wood and glass accents, punchy Scandinavian sauces and notably sharp service.

Staré Město & Josefov

Americas

Brasiliero

U Radnice 8, Staré Město, Prague 1 (224 234 474/www.ambi.cz). Metro Staroměstská/tram 17, 18. **Open** 11am-midnight daily. **Main courses** 650-800 Kč. **Credit** AmEx, MC, V. **Map** 308 H3/4.

Part of a local runaway hit, the Ambiente group, this restaurant specialises in hearty Brazilian butchery, complete with a well-armed staff of knife-wielding servers laden with enough sausage, chops and fillets to stop any normal healthy heart in short order.

Red Hot & Blues

Jakubská 12, Staré Město, Prague 1 (222 314 639). Metro Náměstí Republiky/tram 5, 14, 26. **Open** 9am-11pm daily. **Main courses** 120-230 Kč. **Credit** AmEx, MC, V. **Map** p309 K3.

Perhaps best on Sunday mornings for brunch on the patio (assuming you're not trumped by a stag party), Red Hot & Blues, a requisite expat institution, brought Cajun and heaping Mexican platters to Bohemia. With the requisite blues player on a stool by night, and the patio now conveniently heated and enclosed for winter, the restaurant is reliable and relaxed. You're best off avoiding the overpriced drink specials.

Asian

Ariana

Rámová 6, Staré Město, Prague 1 (222 323 438/ ariana.dreamworx.cz). Metro Náměstí Republiky/ tram 5, 8, 14. **Open** 11am-11pm daily. **Main courses** 280-360 Kč. **Credit** AmEx, MC, V. **Map** p308 J2.

A postage-stamp Afghan restaurant on a short back street that's well worth tracking down for *Qabuli uzbeki* (minced mutton in split pea sauce) and great lunch specials starting at 89 Kč. Sumptuous vegetarian *chalou* of spinach leaves, aubergine and basmati rice is a winner as well, all served under a fringed, arched ceiling with familial service that makes you consider a life in Kabul.

Arsenal

Valentinská 11, Staré Město, Prague 1 (224 814 099). Metro Staroměstská/tram 17, 18. **Open** 10am-midnight daily. **Main courses** 300-600 Kč. **Credit** AmEx, DC, MC, V. **Map** p308 H3.

Newly renovated, but still featuring pricey designer Thai and Japanese *teppan* fare, Arsenal is a showplace for glass artist Bořek Šípek, which admittedly does its cuisine with no spice spared. While Arsenal is no longer the fashionable favourite and the abstract furnishings and cruet sets now seem a tad lonely, it still makes for a memorable night.

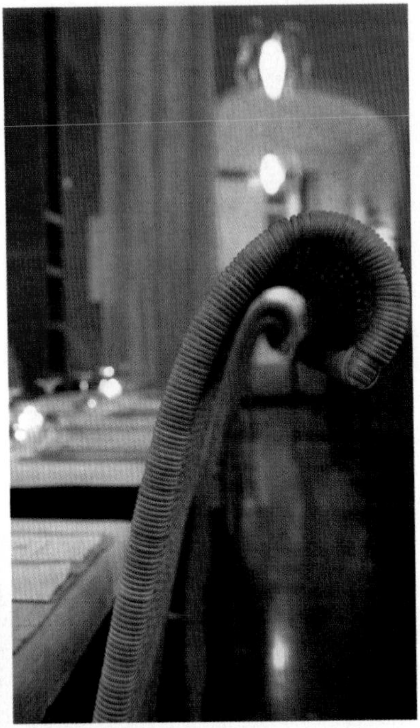

Red Fish gets the green light for sushi.

Orange Moon

Rámová 5, Staré Město, Prague 1 (222 325 119/www.orangemoon.cz). Metro Náměstí Republiky/tram 5, 8, 14. **Open** 11.30am-11.30pm daily. **Main courses** 180-350 Kč. **Credit** AmEx, DC, MC, V. **Map** p308 J2.

A bright, warm cellar space for Thai, Burmese and Indian – *kaeng phed kai*, or basil chicken curry with bamboo shoots, Orange Moon is a treat. Unpretentious, eager servers bringing on the platters and Czech beer. The restaurant entrance is easy to miss, but the voices of customers celebrating will lead you down the right stairs. The bar section's also a popular hangout.

Red Fish

Betlémská 9, Staré Město, Prague 1 (222 220 716/www.redfish.cz). Metro Staroměstská/ tram 17, 18. **Open** 11.30am-midnight daily. **Main courses** 250-500 Kč. **Credit** AmEx, MC, V.

Red Fish serves some of the best-priced sushi in a town where it's still thought of as something exotic. The *nagiri* and noodles are a light delight, served up in a setting of comfy wicker chairs, picture windows and pink walls. On a street that's hidden off Betlémské náměstí, it's hard to fault – just mind the tempura Czech veggies (mostly fat carrots and yellow onions).

Restaurance po Sečuánsku

Národní třída 25, Staré Město, Prague 1 (221 085 331). **Open** 10am-11pm daily. **Main courses** 59-220 Kč. **No credit cards**. **Map** p308 G5.

Tucked away in the Palác Metro shopping passage, this is a handy, clean, bright option for Chinese food, with a vast list of *rychlé*, or quick, items for 59 Kč. *Kung pao*, sweet-and-sour chicken and fried rice all come in these light sizes.

Sushi Sandwich

Divadelní 24, Staré Město, Prague 1 (222 221 117/ www.sushisandwich.cz). Metro Národní třída or Staroměstská. **Open** 11am-4pm Mon-Fri. **Main courses** 80-200 Kč. **No credit cards**. **Map** p308 G5.

Just off the river embankment, but hidden away behind a small park, stands this peaceful Zen temple of a sushi place. Lunch specials are the thing, with big *maki* shaped into rice sandwiches, miso soup, green tea and fresh-baked sweet beancakes. Take away or eat in among the blonde-and-black wood – you'll get a gracious smile either way.

Continental

Allegro

Veleslavínova 2A, Staré Město, Prague 1 (221 426 880/www.fourseasons.com). Metro Staroměstská/ tram 17, 18. **Open** *Restaurant* 6.30am-11.30pm daily. *Bar* until 12.30am. *Terrace* until 9pm. **Main courses** 500-1,200 Kč. **Credit** AmEx, MC, V. **Map** p308 G3.

Continental, Mediterranean and Bohemian cuisine are given an inspired touch by Chef Vito Mollica, Prague's star of kitchen feats since the Four Seasons (*see p46*) opened at this prime location across the Vltava from Prague Castle. From handmade gnocchi with fricassee of rabbit to tranche of swordfish with fennel seeds, it's a splurge to savour. Don't miss the exquisite Italian cheeses drizzled in 13-year-old *balsamico*. The terrace is sublime in warm weather, though the interior is traditional hotel all the way.

Bellevue

Smetanovo nábřeží 18, Staré Město, Prague 1 (222 221 438/www.pfd.cz). Metro Národní třída/tram 17, 18. **Open** noon-3pm, 5.30-11pm Mon-Sat; 11am-3.30pm (jazz brunch), 7-11pm Sun. **Main courses** 490-790 Kč. **Credit** AmEx, MC, V. **Map** p308 G5.

From the pumpkin ravioli with *girolle* mushrooms and truffles to the New Zealand lamb with lemon thyme and aubergine, the menu's always been hard to better, and the service is generally head and shoulders above the competition. Formal and traditional, but with stunning views of Prague Castle and a ritzy Sunday jazz brunch. Booking is essential.

Klub Architektů

Betlémské náměstí 5A, Staré Město, Prague 1 (224 401 214/www.klubarchitektu.com). Metro Národní třída/tram 6, 9, 18, 22, 23. **Open** 11.30am-midnight daily. **Main courses** 70-140 Kč. **Credit** AmEx, DC, MC, V. **Map** p308 H5.

Bad Bohemia Nils Jebens

Sexy dining seems to be an issue for Prague. Though increasingly sophisticated in most other areas of style, Czechs are perhaps a bit too fond of cheap goulash, pork and sauerkraut to have achieved much of lasting value in the areas of low-light restaurants, aphrodisiac cocktails, groovy table settings, sultry servers, views and Marvin Gaye on the soundtrack.

All hail Nils Jebens, then, a force majeur in the field of sensual wining and dining. Jebens, along with partner Tommy Sjöö, has been behind the city's hottest restaurants for over ten years: places like **Barock** (*see p131*), **Pravda** (*see p131*) – both now owned by Sjöö – and Jebens' own **Square** (*see p125*), **Kampa Park** (*see p125*), **Hergetova Cihelna** (*see p123*) and the lobby café at one of the most stylish hotels in town, the **Aria** (*see p38*).

Each of these spaces has that indefinable something that attracts both foodies and lounge lizards. Each is a place where the casual visitor feels welcome but local media types and international celebs also have favourite tables. And they attract bold young chefs from all over, dreaming of the chance to live in Prague.

What's the formula? 'You can't be only trendy,' Jebens says. 'You have to have substance. If you're not already Alain Ducasse, you shouldn't try to make a Michelin three-star. If I don't know how to make a hamburger well, I take it off the menu.'

Never mind that Jebens, a Norwegian and former naval commando officer had no restaurant experience when he and Sjöö opened Kampa Park in 1994 on a lot next to the Charles Bridge, where an old house stood surrounded by willows and weeds. The glowing reviews it quickly earned in *The New York Times* would suggest Jebens is either a quick student or knows how to find and keep pros.

Second: 'It has to fit into the area.' In this case, that means a lot more than neighbourhood harmony – Jebens and Sjöö minted the practice of sending their Czech chefs abroad to soak up wisdom and inspiration, then gave them a free hand to develop what would work in Prague.

The result has been consistent raves for the finest rack of New Zealand lamb, beef carpaccio and Scandinavian seafood in hearty sauces, among many other delights.

Jebens's reputation around town as a bit of a party animal raises a vexing question, though. How ecactly does he manage to balance the demands of full-on Bohemian living with running such a tight culinary ship?

'When I take it out, I take it out all the way,' he says. 'It's normally once a week. It's a very Scandinavian thing.'

Then he's all business again Monday... OK, maybe Tuesday morning.

'I got these places because I have a good balance sheet,' he says. 'Developers want to see that.' Indeed, his business model has to be spot-on to offer some of the lowest-priced fine cuisine in town, as he does at his latest venture, Hergetova Cihelna. 'To have it this, cheap you have to have it full.'

That's what it's been since day one, with a creative restaurant below, a cool-cat lounge bar up top, riverside terrace seating, and a decadent, modern atmosphere throughout. The formula (or perhaps Jebens's naval training?) has proven formidable. While '*styl*' restaurants all over town have gone under in recent years, Jebens's establishments bounced back from the worst flood in recent history. The rising Vltava turned Kampa Park and Hergetova into swamps in 2002, but business was going so well that both were reconstructed in months, despite a still unresolved dispute with the insurance company – don't miss the high-water mark, displayed with pride at the entrance to Hergetova.

Jebens declares his manifesto in *Park Life*, a lush new book on Kampa Park, its adventures, chefs and recipes: 'I knew I would never get rich doing restaurants. But I did think it would be a lot of fun along the way.'

Does it get any more bohemian than that?

In a stony Gothic cellar lit with cool, modern fixtures, this student haven, attached to an architecture and design gallery, is a bit better at style than fine cuisine. But the summer patio offers quiet respite, rare in Staré Město, with low prices and decent vegetarian dishes. Cheapish Pilsner Urquell on tap.

Metamorphis

Malá Štupartská 5, Staré Město, Prague 1 (224 827 058/www.metamorphis.cz). Metro Náměstí Republiky/ tram 5, 14, 26. **Open** 9am-midnight daily. **Main courses** 280-420 Kč. **Credit** AmEx, MC, V. **Map** p308 J3.

With a handy location just streets from Old Town Square, this sedate and capable family-run place has gone modern of late. It does both venison on stewed apples and crab claws with hot sauce. Metamorphis is also a hotel (*see p49*) with a separate pizzeria.

N11

Národní 11, Staré Město, Prague 1 (222 075 705). Metro Národní třída/tram 6, 9, 17, 18, 22, 23. **Open** 4pm-4am daily. **Main courses** 300-600 Kč **Credit** AmEx, MC, V.

Considering the crazy late hours this underground restaurant and dance club is open, you could do far worse. With 40 international wines available by the glass and decent marinated aubergine and flank steaks, it's a damn good find at 3am. *See also p215.*

Století

Karolíny Světlé 21, Staré Město, Prague 1 (222 220 008/www.stoleti.cz). Metro Národní třída. **Open** noon-11pm daily. **Main courses** 300-450 Kč. **Credit** AmEx, MC, V. **Map** p308 G5.

A roast chicken and kiwi salad named after Jerry Lee Lewis is a typical starting point at this refreshingly imaginative Staré Město eaterie. Not everything succeeds, surely, but it's a classy room in a baroque building where a decent veggie polenta, spinach soufflé and tender steaks go along with the old-world decor and swift service.

V Zátiší

Liliová 1, Betlémské náměstí, Staré Město, Prague 1 (222 221 155/www.pfd.cz). Metro Národní třída/tram 6, 9, 18, 22, 23. **Open** noon-3pm, 5.30-11pm daily. **Main courses** 400-600 Kč. **Credit** AmEx, MC, V. **Map** p308 G4.

Celebs and foodies are often spied slipping into this old townhouse on a narrow lane, apparently seduced by the call of delicate gourmet risottos, sashimi, monkfish and saffron sauce, venison with rosehip sauce or a maple and herb-crusted rack of New Zealand lamb. Owned by the management of Bellevue (*see p126*), this is one of the city's most elegant dining rooms with consistently bold culinary inspirations and some fine French vintages. Stops short of heaven, however, with unreliable service, always an issue in Prague (sigh), and enthusiastic wine inflation – stick to the imports: at least these are arguably worth the price.

Czech

Kolkovna

V kolkovně 8, Staré Město, Prague 1 (224 819 701/www.kolkovna.cz). Metro Staroměstská/tram 17, 18. **Open** 11am-midnight daily. **Credit** AmEx, MC, V. **Map** p308 J2.

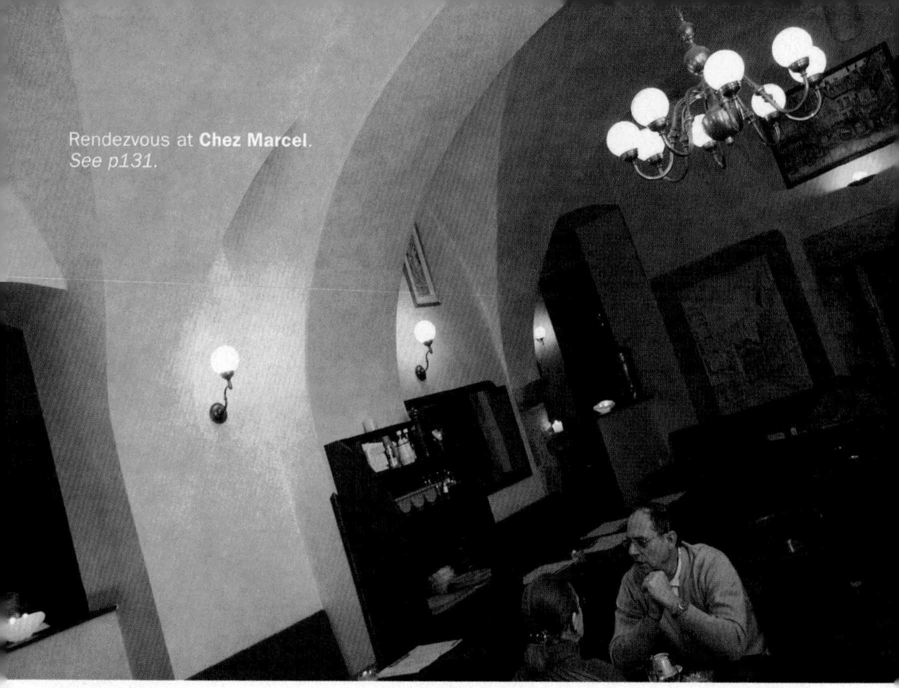

Rendezvous at **Chez Marcel**. *See p131.*

Crowds of post-1989-generation locals pack this pretty re-creation of the kind of place Prague was famous for before World War II. Owned by the brewery Pilsner Urquell, Kolkovna offers an art-nouveau interior, excellent beer on tap and a menu of traditonal pub food like dumplings stuffed with *uzeniny*, or smoked meat.
Other locations: V celnice 4, Prague 1 (224 212 240); Vítězná 7, Prague 5 (251 511 080).

Pivnice u Pivrnce

Maiselova 3, Josefov, Prague 1 (222 329 404). Metro Náměstí Republiky/tram 5, 8, 14. **Open** 11am-midnight daily; kitchen closes at 11.30pm. **Main courses** 120-230 Kč. **Credit** MC, V. **Map** p308 H3.
Rough and ready and looking set to stare down the next century unchanged, this pub prides itself on traditional Czech pork and dumplings with above-average presentation. *Svíčková* (beef in lemon cream sauce), duck with sauerkraut and walls covered with crude cartoons guaranteed to offend. Radegast here is well tapped and nicely priced.

U Bakaláře

Celetná 13, Staré Město, Prague 1 (224 817 369/ www.ubakalare.euweb.cz). Metro Náměstí Republiky/ tram 5, 8, 14. **Open** 9am-7pm Mon-Fri; 11am-7pm Sat, Sun. **Main courses** 40-70 Kč. **No credit cards**. **Map** p308 J3.
A life-saver for nearby Charles University students, this Staré Město lunch buffet is a stalwart example of that pre-revolutionary classic, the workers' cafeteria. Situated across the street from one of the university colleges, U Bakaláře is still an excellent standby for a quick, cheap toasted sandwich, savoury pancake or soup when you need to refuel for sightseeing. You'll find communal seating, friendly-ish service and far too much salt in everything.

U modré kachničky

Michalská 16, Staré Město, Prague 1 (224 213 418/www.umodrekachnicky.cz). Metro Staroměstská/tram 17, 18. **Open** 11.30am-11.30pm daily. **Main courses** 500-800 Kč. **Credit** AmEx, DC, MC, V. **Map** p308 H4.
A branch of the famous original in Malá Strana, there may be fewer film stars here but the atmosphere is this location is just as sedate, old-fashioned and classy. Seek out this obscure side street of Staré Město for fine interpretations of classics like duck roasted with pears and boar steak with mushrooms. The restaurant also offers an array of excellent Moravian wines.
Other locations: Nebovidská 6, Malá Strana, Prague 1 (257 320 308).

U Radnice

U radnice 2, Staré Město, Prague 1 (224 228 136). Metro Staroměstská/tram 17, 18. **Open** 11am-midnight daily. **Main courses** 50-100 Kč. **Credit** AmEx, DC, MC, V. **Map** p308 H3.
U Radnice is one of the last places around Old Town Square with traditional food served at prices that are meant for the locals. The tasty Czech specialities such as goulash or beef in cream sauce go for a pittance. Alas, a recent restoration cleaned it up a bit too much, but the communal tables still create a comfortable pub atmosphere.

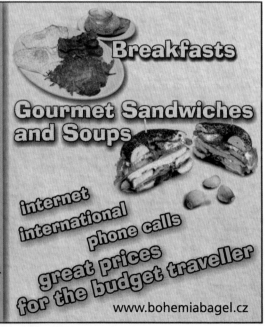

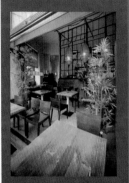

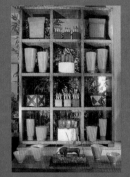

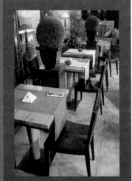

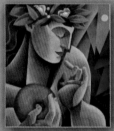

U Sádlů

Klimentská 2, Staré Město, Prague 1 (224 813 874/www.usadlu.cz). Metro Náměstí Republiky/ tram 5, 14, 26. **Open** 11am-1am Mon-Sat; noon-midnight Sun. **Main courses** 120-230 Kč. **Credit** MC, V. **Map** p309 K2.

OK, it's medieval kitsch – but efficient, tasty and affordable medieval kitsch. The Armour Hall is the place to score a table if you can, then hoist a mead and lay on the pepper steak or boar – if you can work out the illuminated menu. Nice helmets in the bar. **Other locations**: Balbínova 22, Vinohrady, Prague 2 (222 252 411).

French

Le Café Colonial

Široká 6, Josefov, Prague 1 (224 818 322). Metro Staroměstská/tram 17, 18. **Open** 10am-midnight daily. **Main courses** 300-550 Kč. **Credit** AmEx, DC, MC, V. **Map** p308 H3.

The restaurant side, where local chefs go to dine, is austere, dark and decadent, serving delightful rabbit and perch in delicate sauces with heavenly salads. The café section has teak accents, wicker sofas and a menu of miniature quiches, roasted duck and more delightful salads. Resolutely French.

Chez Marcel

Haštalská 12, Staré Město, Prague 1 (222 315 676). Metro Náměstí Republiky/tram 5, 8, 14. **Open** 8am-1am Mon-Sat; 9am-1am Sun. **Main courses** 200-350 Kč. **No credit cards**. **Map** p308 J2.

As thoroughly French as it gets, this brasserie invariably attracts a local crowd with its appealing brass accents, copies of *Le Monde* and views on to a lovely Old Town Square. It also makes the deepest quiche in town, which goes well with the big baskets of crispy fries, dappled with Dijon mustard. By night this is a favourite rendezvous for clubbers and by day it offers highchairs (rare in Prague restaurants) and a non-smoking section. **Other locations**: Brasserie le Molière, Americká 20, Vinohrady, Prague 2 (222 513 340)

Francouzská restaurace

Municipal House, Náměstí Republiky 5, Staré Město, Prague 1 (222 002 770/ www.obecnidum.cz). Metro Náměstí Republiky/ tram 5, 8, 14. **Open** noon-3pm, 6-11pm Mon-Sat; 11.30am-3pm, 6pm-midnight Sun. **Main courses** 250-500 Kč. **Credit** AmEx, DC, MC, V. **Map** p309 K3.

Though the service is heavy-handed and the cuisine passable, the aesthetics rarely get any better. The city's pre-eminent shrine to art nouveau (and one of its top concert halls) was painstakingly renovated, including this space, which acts as its dining room. Service is laid on thick rather than well, as in many an upmarket Prague restaurant, but the rabbit in mustard sauce and the French cheese plate are both treats, and you could spend several times more for the same fare in Staré Město.

La Provence

Štupartská 9, Staré Město, Prague 1 (222 324 801/ reservations 257 535 050/www.laprovence.cz). Metro Náměstí Republiky/tram 5, 8, 14. **Open** *Restaurant* noon-midnight daily. *Bar* 8pm-2am daily. *Café* 11am-2am daily. **Main courses** 130-270 Kč. **Credit** AmEx, MC, V. **Map** p308 J3.

Veal with morrel sauce and mascarpone polenta looks to signify an improvement in the conservative cuisine of recent years, but the wine list is still over-hyped and understocked. Billed as a 'restaurant, bistro and tapas bar' and sharing its premises with the cheesy Banana Bar& Café (*see p147*), this place still suffers from an identity crisis but has improved its service to meet the standards you'd expect for these prices. Just be prepared to elbow through a beefcake and hair-product mob at the café to access the cellar restaurant.

Global

Barock

Pařížská 24, Josefov, Prague 1 (222 329 221). Metro Staroměstská/tram 17, 18. **Open** 8.30am-1am Mon-Fri; 10am-2am Sat; 10am-1am Sun; kitchen closes at 10.45pm. **Main courses** 250-500 Kč. **Credit** AmEx, DC, MC, V. **Map** p308 H2.

Glitz and glam all the way, this is where models gather and their boyfriends pick up the tab. Gleaming zinc bar, floor-to-ceiling windows, and a credible sushi platter with suitably aesthetic *nigiri*. A reasonably priced breakfast menu of croissants, sandwiches and powerhouse lattes attracts a contemplative morning crowd to the street tables.

DaMúza

Řetězová 10, Staré Město, Prague 1 (222 221 749/www.damuza.cz). Metro Staroměstská/ tram 17, 18. **Open** 11am-12.30am daily. **Main courses** 150-300 Kč. **Credit** AmEx, MC, V. **Map** p308 H4.

No major awards due for the predictable fare, but the garlic soups and schnitzels are fine examples of the form. Just across from the Café Montmartre (*see p147*), this is the official café of the Academy of Dramatic Arts, whose Czech acronym is contained in the restaurant's name. Six kinds of beer are on tap, as are fairly substantial steaks – an unusual option for a Prague café. Schedules on the tables list the irregular theatre pieces and concerts performed in the cellar. Nice glass-roofed garden.

Pravda

Pařížská 17, Josefov, Prague 1 (222 326 203). Metro Staroměstská/tram 17, 18. **Open** noon-11pm Mon-Thur; noon-midnight Fri-Sun; kitchen shuts 1hr before closing times. **Main courses** 330-670 Kč. **Credit** AmEx, DC, MC, V. **Map** p308 H2.

World cuisine presented with style by waiters well-versed in the Asian, African and Czech specialities. Pravda's owner Tommy Sjöö, who was instrumental in bringing fine dining to post-1989 Prague (*see p127*

Bloomin' marvellous **Tulip Café**. *See p134.*

Bad Bohemia: Nils Jebens), presides over a multi-level establishment on fashionable Pařížská, where chicken in peanut sauce vies against Vietnamese *nem* spring rolls and borscht, all credibly done.

La Veranda

Elišky Krásnohorské 2, Josefov, Prague 1 (224 814 733/www.laveranda.cz). Metro Staroměstská/tram 17, 18. **Open** 11am-11pm daily. **Main courses** 700-1,200 Kč. **Credit** AmEx, MC, V. **Map** p308 H2.

Another full-on style-and-fashion food assault, this 'concept' restaurant has the usual complement of crews of waiters bringing on platter after platter of precious, exotic little creations. Admittedly, you'll probably enjoy the baked arctic char with white tomato sauce or guinea hen with cardamom sauce and mushroom barley, and prices are fair for such fare – but you may feel lonely unless business picks up soon.

Indian

Rasoi Restaurant/Bombay Café

Dlouhá 13, Staré Město, Prague 1 (222 324 040/www.rasoi.cz). Metro Náměstí Republiky or Staroměstská/tram 5, 8, 14. **Open** *Restaurant* noon-11pm daily. *Bar* 5pm-4am Mon-Thur, Sun; 5pm-5am Fri, Sat. **Main courses** 280-480 Kč. **Credit** AmEx, MC, V. **Map** p308 J2.

Head to the cellar for *tawa* lamb tikka or a fiery vindaloo in this tandoori haven. With pan-cooked regional specialities from the subcontinent, and an appealingly twee dining room, it's also a bar at street level that packs in the Czuppies – but mixes a killer Bombay Gin Martini.

Italian

Amici Miei

Vězeňská 5, Staré Město, Prague 1(224 816 688/www.amicimiei.cz). Metro Můstek. **Open** noon-4pm, 6.30-11pm daily. **Main courses** 350-550 Kč. **Credit** AmEx, DC, MC, V. **Map** p308 J2.

Hidden behind wispy white fabric covering the street windows is this outstanding panelled hall. Amici's Miei's expertly done scampi in garlic and tender *scaloppini al limone* go with warm service and an exceptional wine list.

Don Giovanni

Karolíny Světlé 34, Staré Město, Prague 1 (222 222 060/dongiovanni.cz). Metro Staroměstská/tram 17, 18. **Open** 11am-midnight daily. **Main courses** 200-500 Kč. **Credit** AmEx, DC, MC, V. **Map** p308 G5.

An institution among Italian expats in Prague, this formal but understated eaterie hosts some of the finest Italian dining in town. Owner Avelino Sorgato oversees the home-made fettuccine, and pappardelle with boar and porcini mushrooms, and the Parma ham is the real stuff. Sample from one of over 30 grappas or stick to the noteworthy, if expensive, Italian wine list.

Kogo Pizzeria & Caffeteria

Havelská 27, Staré Město, Prague 1 (224 214 543/www.kogo.cz). Metro Můstek/tram 6, 9, 18, 22. **Open** *Restaurant* 11am-11pm daily. *Café* 8am-11pm daily. **Main courses** 150-300 Kč. **Credit** AmEx, DC, MC, V. **Map** p308 J4.

The flagship of a growing empire of restaurants, this Staré Město venue is still the most popular. One side serves quick pizza, pasta and tiramisu, while the other offers more extensive menus and relaxed but capable white-linen service. An espresso or mushroom pizza is served faster than any place around, and the other location, in the Slovanský dům mall, is perfect for pre-cinema dining and courtyard views. It stocks a good selection of Chiantis too.
Other locations: Na Příkopě 22, Nové Město, Prague 1 (221 451 259).

Maestro

Křížovnická 10, Staré Město, Prague 1 (222 320 498). Metro Staroměstská/tram 17, 18. **Open** 11am-11pm daily. **Main courses** 130-270 Kč. **Credit** AmEx, DC, MC, V. **Map** p308 G3.
A short walk from the Rudolfinum (*see p93*), this corner pizza place is really much more. Wicker chairs, baroque trompe-l'œil on the walls and, yes, wood-fired pizzas. The sauce is one of the best in town, service is generally on target and it's still a fair bargain. The chicken cacciatore is inspiring too.

Modrá Zahrada

Národní třída 37, Staré Město, Prague 1 (224 239 055). Metro Národní třída/tram 6, 9, 17, 18, 22, 23. **Open** 11am-11.30pm daily. **Main courses** 120-280 Kč. **Credit** AmEx, MC, V. **Map** p308 H5.
Popular and utilitarian pizza joint with a moody blue decor and art-deco theme. At street level you'll find the futuristic bar, with vanity tables in the window for exhibitionists. One level up (stairs hidden at the back) the regulars gather from all around for cheap, pleasant pies – a safer bet than the fairly dodgy salads, nearly all of which contain some kind of meat. It's a relaxing place and a bargain given the location. Service can be somewhat dizzy, though.
Other locations: Široká 114, Josefov, Prague 1 (222 327 171); Vinohradská 29, Vinohrady, Prague 2 (222 253 829).

Pizzeria Roma Due

Liliová 18, Staré Město, Prague 1 (222 222 515). Metro Staroměstská/tram 17, 18. **Open** 24hrs daily. **Main courses** 70-150 Kč. **No credit cards**. **Map** p308 G4.
A last-ditch chance for 3am food, the pizza merits mention only because it's cheap, warm and available right around the clock. It's also usefully within stumbling distance of many trendy nightspots, including the Roxy (*see p222*) and Chateau (*see p143*).
Other locations: Jagellonská 16, Žižkov, Prague 3 (222 714 154).

Kosher

King Solomon

Široká 8, Josefov, Prague 1 (224 818 752/www.kosher.cz). Metro Staroměstská/tram 17, 18. **Open** noon-11pm Mon-Thur, Sun (kitchen closes at 10.30pm); 11am-90mins before sundown Fri; open by request with reservation Sat. **Main courses** 200-500 Kč. **Credit** AmEx, MC, V. **Map** p308 H3.
Just a block from the Jewish Museum, this is an incongruous but solid addition. An upscale kosher restaurant with Sabbath menu, Hebrew-speaking staff and certified cuisine still unavailable in any Czech eaterie. With the atrium in the back, the long and authoritative Israeli wine list and austere sandstone- and-iron decor, it may be an odd setting for the traditonal comfort food like *gefilte* fish, chicken soup and carp with prunes, but Solomon's a hit with visiting groups. And the portions, darling!

Middle Eastern

Dunia

U Milosrdných 4, Staré Město, Prague 1 (224 813 706). Metro Staroměstská/tram 17, 18. **Open** noon-11pm Tue-Sun. **Main courses** 350-550 Kč. **Credit** AmEx, MC, V.
Entering the latest Staré Město craze in Middle Eastern food is like coming upon an old street market in Marrakech, with credibly done Lebanese meze and North African tagines. Great value for money and an utter escape from Bohemia.

Seafood

Reykjavík

Karlova 20, Staré Město, Prague 1 (222 221 218/www.reykjavik.cz). Metro Staroměstská/tram 17, 18. **Open** 11am-midnight daily. **Main courses** 250-500 Kč. **Credit** AmEx, MC, V. **Map** p308 G4.
Blanched cod and perch are done to perfection with classic and Scandinavian sauces at this surprisingly high-quality restaurant for its location. Smack-bang on the main tourist route to Charles Bridge, the comfortably elegant restaurant still offers reasonable prices. The Icelandic owner has fish and lobster flown in and the local crowds lap it up. There's a street terrace in summer, but the upstairs loft offers the quietest seating.

Vegetarian

Country Life

Melantrichova 15, Staré Město, Prague 1 (224 213 366). Metro Národní třída/tram 6, 9, 18, 22, 23. **Open** 9am-8.30pm Mon-Thur; 9am-3pm Fri; 11am-8.30pm Sun. **Main courses** 50-100 Kč. **No credit cards**. **Map** p308 H4.
Not inspired, to be sure, but the soups, a Czech passion, are hearty, cheap and part of an all-vegetarian menu – rare in meat-loving Prague. Though this place has expanded from a shop with salad bar (*see p171*) into a full cafeteria with seating and beautiful Staré Město views, Country Life has managed to remain a low-key source of organically grown fare. DIY salads, fresh carrot juice, and crunchy wholegrain breads go along with slightly disquieting mashed-potato casseroles. By all means avoid the lunchtime crush.
Other locations: Jungmannova 1, Nové Město, Prague 1 (257 044 419).

Nové Město

Americas

Jáma

V jámě 7, Prague 1 (224 222 383/www.jamapub.cz). Metro Můstek/3, 9, 14, 24 tram. **Open** 11am-midnight Mon, Sun; 11am-1am Tue-Sat; kitchen closes at 11.40pm. **Main courses** 100-260 Kč. **Credit** AmEx, MC, V. **Map** p311 K6.

Still a lunch and brunch fave after all these years, American-owned and outfitted Jáma has a prime patio space (and kids' playground) out back and a bank of internet terminals by the door to boot. It's kept the loud college vibe that made its name. Czech scenesters are here by day and young business types by night. Lunch specials and happy-hour deals are a big draw, as is the Czech-Mex menu and well-poured Gambrinus. The video-rental counter also does brisk business.

Picante

Revoluční 4, Prague 1 (222 322 022/www.picante.cz). Metro Náměstí Republiky/tram 5, 8, 14. **Open** 24hrs daily. **Main courses** 100-200 Kč. **No credit cards.**

Oddly enough, this over-lit, all-night, fast-food counter does the finest home-made salsas, steamed pork *carnitas* and soft maize tacos in town. The mission from God of two once-frustrated Californians is a godsend for hungry revellers from the Roxy club (*see p222*).

Tulip Café

Opatovická 3, Prague 1 (224 930 019/www.tulipcafe.cz). Metro Národní třída/tram 6, 9, 17, 18, 22, 23. **Open** 11am-midnight Mon-Thur; 11am-2am Fri, Sat; 11am-11pm Sun. **Main courses** 300-500 Kč. **Credit** MC, V. **Map** p310 H6.

Amazingly popular across the Czech and expat scenes, this groovy café, complete with newly outfitted basement music lounge, offers up imaginative variations on American diner food, plus lentil soup and home-baked treats at consistently affordable prices. The back deck is a heavenly summer oasis.

Asian

Lemon Leaf

Na Zderaze 14, Prague 2 (224 919 056/www.lemon.cz). Metro Karlovo náměstí/tram 3, 4, 16, 17, 18, 22, 24. **Open** 11am-11pm Mon-Thur; 11am-12.30am Fri; 12.30pm-12.30am Sat; 12.30-11pm Sun. **Main courses** 250-400 Kč. **Credit** AmEx, MC, V.

What's on the menu?

You'll find that Czech menus generally list two categories of main dishes: *minutky*, cooked to order (which may take ages), and *hotová jídla*, ready-to-serve fare. The usual accompaniments to these dishes are rice, potatoes or the fried béchamel dough known as *krokety*, all of which should be ordered separately. When dining in pubs, the closest thing served to fresh vegetables is often *obloha*, which is a garnish of pickles, or a tomato on a single leaf of cabbage. Tasty appetisers to try are Prague ham with horseradish or rich soups (*polévka*), while a dessert staple is *palačinky*, filled pancakes.

Meals (*jídla*)

snídaně breakfast; **oběd** lunch; **večeře** dinner.

Preparation (*příprava*)

bez masa/bezmasá jídla without meat; **čerstvé** fresh; **domácí** home-made; **dušené** steamed; **grilované** grilled; **míchaný** mixed; **na roštu** roasted; **pečené** baked; **plněné** stuffed; **smažené** fried; **špíz** grilled on a skewer; **uzené** smoked; **vařené** boiled.

Well-done, unabashed Thai and Burmese in a warm, yellow and dark wood setting with bargain lunch specials have kept Lemon Leaf close to capacity since its opening in 2002. No compromises for spice-phobic Czechs have been made with the *tom ka kai*, or prawn curries.

Millhouse Sushi

Slovanský dům, Na Příkopě 22, Nové Město, Prague 1 (221 451 771). Metro Náměstí Republiky/tram 5, 8, 14. **Open** 11am-11pm daily. **Main courses** 400-800 Kč. **Credit** AmEx, DC, MC, V. **Map** p309 K4.

Handy if you're in the shopping mall catching a film but not the place to save your travel funds. The trendiest sushi bar in town does do *maki* and *nagiri* in lovely, quick fashion, it must be said.

Other locations: Sokolovská 84-6, Karlín, Prague 8 (222 832 583).

Thanh Long

Ostrovní 23, Staré Město, Prague 1 (224 933 537). Metro Národní třída/tram 6, 9, 18, 22, 23. **Open** 11.30am-11pm daily. **Main courses** 100-200 Kč. **Credit** AmEx, DC, MC, V. **Map** p310 H6.

One of the old standby Chinese places in Nové Město, it's really still distinguished mainly by its central location and blissfully over-the-top trappings, such as the revolving 'Lazy Susan' tables, pagoda lanterns and the moving-light painting in the back. Cuisine blanded down to suit Czech tastes.

Continental

Červená Tabulka

Lodecká 4, Prague 1 (224 810 401/www.cervenatabulka.cz). Metro Náměstí Republiky. **Open** 11.30am-11pm daily. **Main courses** 400-700 Kč. **Credit** AmEx, DC, MC, V. **Map** p309 L2.

Here you'll find whimsical playschool decor and lava-grilled lamb plus a variety of poultry comfort foods – which all make the Red Tablet a Nové Město star. The baked duck leg with bacon dumplings, apple and sauerkraut is cheerily served up alongside rabbit skewer with a cream and lime sauce. The decadent desserts and a rare kids' menu here make this restaurant a definite weekend family favourite.

Chaoz

Masarykovo nábřeží 26, Prague 1 (224 933 657). Metro Národní třída/tram 6, 9, 17, 18, 22, 23. **Open** noon-midnight daily. **Main courses** 130-270 Kč. **Credit** AmEx, DC, MC, V. **Map** p310 G6.

Basics (*základní*)

chléb bread; **cukr** sugar; **drůbež** poultry; **karbanátek** patty of unspecified content; **máslo** butter; **maso** meat; **ocet** vinegar; **olej** oil; **omáčka** sauce; **ovoce** fruit; **pepř** pepper; **rohlík** roll; **ryby** fish; **smetana** cream; **sůl** salt; **sýr** cheese; **vejce** eggs; **zelenina** vegetables.

Drinks (*nápoje*)

čaj tea; **káva** coffee; **mléko** milk; **pivo** beer; **pomerančový džus** orange juice; **sodovka** soda; **víno** wine; **voda** water.

Appetisers (*předkrmy*)

boršč Russian beetroot soup (borscht); **chlebíček** meat open-sandwich; **hovězí vývar** beef broth; **kaviár** caviar; **paštika** pâté; **polévka** soup; **uzený losos** smoked salmon.

Meat (*maso*)

biftek beefsteak; **hovězí** beef; **játra** liver; **jehně** lamb; **jelení** venison; **kančí** boar; **klobása, párek, salám, vuřt** sausage; **králík** rabbit; **ledvinky** kidneys; **slanina** bacon; **srnčí** roebuck; **šunka** ham; **telecí** veal; **tlačenka** brawn; **vepřové** pork; **zvěřina** game.

Cuisine actually lives up to the lush art-nouveau entrance on the Nové Město embankment. Risottos, roast duck and the Waldorf salad are standouts, while the salmon in pastry with wild rice does very well solo.

Dynamo

Pštrossova 220-29, Prague 1 (224 932 020/ www.mraveniste.cz). Metro Národní třída/tram 6, 9, 18, 22, 23. **Open** 11.30am-midnight daily. **Main courses** 170-330 Kč. **Credit** AmEx, DC, MC, V. **Map** p310 G6.

Though you may feel like you're posing for a designer photo-shoot, eating here is nonetheless a treat for other senses. This sleek diner typifies the food and drink renaissance sweeping through the area south of the National Theatre (an area sometimes called SONA). The steaks-and-pasta cuisine doesn't quite keep up with the streamlined decor, but the collection of single-malt Scotches makes Dynamo's bar a connoisseur's favourite.

Czech

Celnice

V celnice 4, Prague 1 (224 212 240/www. celnice.com). Metro Náměstí Republiky/tram 5, 8, 14. **Open** 11am-2pm Mon-Thur, Sun; 11am-4am Fri, Sat; light menu only after 11.30pm. **Main courses** 250-400 Kč. **Credit** AmEx, MC, V. **Map** p309 K3.

By far the hippest of the new wave of Pilsner-owned restaurants, Celnice is a mix of a classic brick-and-brass restaurant with updated Bohemian classics like *kyselo*, or sauerkraut soup, pickled Prague ham and pastas, and a sleek, modern sushi bar with DJ dance fare on weekends that packs in the bright young things (*see p222*).

Other locations: Vítězná 7, Prague 5 (251 511 080).

Novoměstský Pivovar

Vodičkova 20, Prague 1 (222 232 448/ www.npivovar.cz). Metro Můstek/tram 3, 9, 14, 24. **Open** 10am-11.30pm Mon-Fri; 11.30am-11.30pm Sat; 10am-10pm Sun. **Main courses** 120-230 Kč. **Credit** AmEx, DC, MC, V. **Map** p310 J6.

A reliable source of artery-blocking Czech classics, Novoměstský Pivovar is one of surprisingly few brew-pubs in Prague. The vast underground warren of rooms is fascinating to explore and, perhaps unsurprisingly, a good glass of beer is served here. On the other hand, in the rush, the bills can occasionally get confused, so it's worth taking the time to check your total.

What's on the menu ? (continued)

Poultry & fish (*drůbež a ryby*)

bažant pheasant; **husa** goose; **kachna** duck; **kapr** carp; **křepelka** quail; **krocan** turkey; **kuře** chicken; **losos** salmon; **pstruh** trout; **úhoř** eel.

Main meals (*hlavní jídla*)

guláš goulash; **řízek** schnitzel; **sekaná** meat loaf; **smažený sýr** fried cheese; **svíčková** beef in cream sauce; **vepřová játra na cibulce** pig's liver stewed with onion; **vepřové koleno** pork knee; **vepřový řízek** fried breaded pork.

Side dishes (*přílohy*)

brambor potato; **bramborák** potato pancake; **bramborová kaše** mashed potatoes; **hranolky** chips; **kaše** mashed potatoes; **knedlíky** dumplings; **krokety** potato or béchamel dough croquettes; **obloha** small lettuce and tomato salad; **rýže** rice; **salát** salad; **šopský salát** cucumber, tomato and curd salad; **tatarská omáčka** tartar sauce; **zelí** cabbage.

Cheese (*sýr*)

balkán a saltier feta; **eidam** hard white cheese; **hermelín** soft, similar to bland brie; **Madeland** Swiss cheese; **niva** blue cheese;

ague 1 (224 219 357). Metro ky/tram 5, 8, 14. **Open** 7.30am- 8am-6pm Sat; 10am-6pm Sun. 40-75 Kč. **No credit cards**.

t of a breed, this chrome-covered, eria is a survivor of the pre-revolu- ;, the workers' canteen. The cast of m servers in worn white aprons to ing customers in white socks and emain. So do the incredibly cheap lumplings and *chlebíčky* (open-faced nd meat sandwiches).

t de Marlène

ague 2 (224 921 853/ marlene.cz). Metro Karlovo náměstí/ 17. **Open** noon-2.30pm, 7-10.30pm .30pm Sat. **Main courses** 500-1,000 mEx, MC, V. **Map** p310 G10.

market-fresh meals of fine traditional ité cuisine in a newly redone, sleek and n with red accents. Simple, expertly pre-

ananas pineapple; **banány** banana; **borůvky** blueberries; **broskev** peach; **hrozny** grapes; **hruška** pear; **jablko** apple; **jahody** strawberries; **jeřabina** rowanberries; **mandle** almonds; **meruňka** apricot; **ořechy** nuts; **pomeranč** orange; **rozinky** raisins; **švestky** plums; **třešně** cherries.

Desserts (*moučník*)

buchty traditional curd-filled cakes; **čokoláda** chocolate; **dort** layered cake; **koláč** cake with various fillings; **ovocné**

uit dumplings; **palačinka** **ár** ice-cream sundae; **šlehačka** eam; **zákusek** cake; **závin** strudel; oread pudding with apples and **zmrzlina** ice-cream.

ohrases

the menu? Mohu vidět ek? **Do you have...?** Máte...? **getarian** Jsem vegetarián/ ıka (m/f). **How is it prepared?** připravené? **Did you say 'beer** Říkal jste 'pivní sýr'? **Wow, lls!** Páni, to smrdí! **Can I have it .?** Mohu mít bez...? **No ketchup za, please** Nechci kečup na pizzu, **didn't order this** Neobjednal jsem si to. **How much longer will it be?** Jak dlouho to ještě bude? **The bill, please** Účet, prosím. **I can't eat this and I won't pay for it!** (use with extreme caution) Nedá se to jíst a nezaplatím to. **Takeaway/to go** S sebou. **A beer, please** Pivo, prosím. **Two beers, please** Dvě piva, prosím. **Same again, please** Ještě jednou, prosím. **What'll you have?** Co si dáte? **Not for me, thanks** Pro mě ne, děkuji. **No ice, thanks** Bez ledu, děkuji. **He's really smashed** Je totálně namazaný.

pared, always fresh fare of fussily chosen ingredients – the pheasant, venison and boar are the only things not imported. The sea bass and spinach, *filet mignon* and *chèvre* salads have become a cause célèbre among Prague foodies. Attentive, warm service, phenomenal value for the price and reservations a must.

La Perle de Prague

Rašínovo nábřeží & Resslova streets, Prague 2 (221 984 160/www.laperle.cz). Metro Karlovo náměstí/tram 17. **Open** 7-10.30pm Mon; noon-2pm, 7-10.30pm Tue-Sat. **Main courses** 470-730 Kč. **Credit** AmEx, DC, MC, V. **Map** p310 G8.

With prices as heavenly as the views, this eyrie atop Frank Gehry's 'Fred and Ginger' building (*see p101*) was once king of the hill. For some time after it opened, the chance to eat on top of the dancing building was enough to bring the diners in. These days it's mostly a business crowd taking in the skyline and the rack of lamb in thyme and rosemary sauce. No great adventure and, in truth, the views are a bit disappointing.

Universal

V Jirchářích, Prague 1 (224 934 416). Metro Národní třída/tram 6, 9, 17, 18, 22, 23. **Open** 11.30-12.30am Mon-Sat; 11am-midnight Sun. **Main courses** 250-350 Kč. **Credit** DC, MC, V. **Map** p310 G6.

There's far more to the appeal of Universal than a cosy red-and-cream train-carriage interior and old-fashioned French tin advertisements. The servers here know their stuff and tip you to the daily specials (cod in white sauce, tender flank steak and rolled veggie lasagne are all typical), which come with delectable sides of fresh spinach or roasted gratin potatoes. The vegetarian-friendly menu is clearly created by chefs who exercise a French passion for tasty greens. The coffee is characteristically supercharged and goes down well with a massive lemon tart.

Global

Opera Garden

Legerova 75, Prague 1 (224 239 685/ www.zahradavopere.cz). Metro Muzeum/tram 11. **Open** 11.30am-1am daily; kitchen closes at midnight. **Main courses** 165-440 Kč. **Credit** AmEx, DC, MC, V. **Map** p311 L6.

Start off with smoked trout and almond salad, then debate mains like spinach tagliolini with roasted calamari and scampi or pheasant with shiitake mushrooms and watercress. Dessert platters are almost too beautiful to eat. It's rarely full and the menu's not as imaginative as it once was. Still, Opera Garden (or *Zahrada v opeře* in Czech) has zen style to spare, with airy, minimalist decor and gliding waiters.

Greek

Řecká Taverna

Revoluční 16, Prague 1 (222 317 762). Metro Náměstí Republiky/tram 5, 8, 14. **Open** 11am-midnight daily. **Main courses** 180-250 Kč. **Credit** AmEx, MC, V. **Map** p309 K2.

Good food, decent beer *and* a swanky setting – **Celnice** tops the popularity polls. *See p136.*

Fast food

Gyrossino

Spálená 47, Prague 1 (no phone). Metro Národní třída/tram 6, 9, 18, 22, 23. **Open** 24 hrs daily. **Main courses** 50-80 Kč. **No credit cards. Map** p310 H6.

Many a drunken party-goer has given thanks for the light of the Gyrossino sign while fending off the frostbite and waiting for a night tram. This is actually two places, side by side, separated by a building entryway. The left half is a bakery; the right serves up roast chicken, falafel, kebabs and just-edible mini-pizzas.

U Pinkasů

Jungmannovo Náměstí 16, Prague 1 (221 111 151/www.upinkasu.cz). Metro Můstek/ tram 3, 9, 14, 24. **Open** *Restaurant* 11am-10pm. *Pub* 9am-11pm. **Main courses** 300-500 Kč. **Credit** AmEx, MC, V. **Map** 308 J5.

This historic Pilsner pub (the first, in fact, circa 1843) is a smoky, packed, dependable source for gruff, utterly authentic service and classic pub grub meat platters including leg of hare or duck with red-and white-cabbage and potato dumplings.

U Rozvařilů

Na Poříčí 26, Prague 1 (224 219 357). Metro Náměstí Republiky/tram 5, 8, 14. **Open** 7.30am-8.30pm Mon-Fri; 8am-6pm Sat; 10am-6pm Sun. **Main courses** 40-75 Kč. **No credit cards. Map** p309 L2.

One of the last of a breed, this chrome-covered, mirrored cafeteria is a survivor of the pre-revolutionary classic, the workers' canteen. The cast of characters, from servers in worn white aprons to harassed-looking customers in white socks and sandals, all remain. So do the incredibly cheap soups, *guláš*, dumplings and *chlebíčky* (open-faced mayonnaise and meat sandwiches).

French

Le Bistrot de Marlène

Plavecká 4, Prague 2 (224 921 853/ www.bistrotdemarlene.cz). Metro Karlovo náměstí/ tram 3, 7, 16, 17. **Open** noon-2.30pm, 7-10.30pm Mon-Fri; 7-10.30pm Sat. **Main courses** 500-1,000 Kč. **Credit** AmEx, MC, V. **Map** p310 G10.

Enchanting, market-fresh meals of fine traditional Franche-Comté cuisine in a newly redone, sleek and modern room with red accents. Simple, expertly pre-

pivní sýr beer-flavoured semi-soft cheese; **primátor** Swiss cheese; **tavený sýr** packaged cheese spread; **tvaroh** soft curd cheese.

Vegetables (*zelenina*)

česnek garlic; **chřest** asparagus; **cibule** onion(s); **čočka** lentils; **fazole** beans; **feferonky** chilli peppers; **hrášek** peas; **kukuřice** corn; **květák** cauliflower; **mrkev** carrot; **okurka** cucumber; **petržel** parsley; **rajčata** tomatoes; **salát** lettuce; **špenát** spinach; **žampiony** mushrooms; **zelí** cabbage.

Fruit (*ovoce*)

ananas pineapple; **banány** banana; **borůvky** blueberries; **broskev** peach; **hrozny** grapes; **hruška** pear; **jablko** apple; **jahody** strawberries; **jeřabina** rowanberries; **mandle** almonds; **meruňka** apricot; **ořechy** nuts; **pomeranč** orange; **rozinky** raisins; **švestky** plums; **třešně** cherries.

Desserts (*moučník*)

buchty traditional curd-filled cakes; **čokoláda** chocolate; **dort** layered cake; **koláč** cake with various fillings; **ovocné knedlíky** fruit dumplings; **palačinka** crêpe; **pohár** ice-cream sundae; **šlehačka** whipped cream; **zákusek** cake; **závin** strudel; **žemlovka** bread pudding with apples and cinnamon; **zmrzlina** ice-cream.

Useful phrases

May I see the menu? Mohu vidět jídelní lístek? **Do you have...?** Máte...? **I am a vegetarian** Jsem vegetarián/ vegetariánka (m/f). **How is it prepared?** Jak je to připravené? **Did you say 'beer cheese'?** Říkal jste 'pivní sýr'? **Wow, that smells!** Páni, to smrdí! **Can I have it without...?** Mohu mít bez...? **No ketchup on my pizza, please** Nechci kečup na pizzu, prosím. **I didn't order this** Neobjednal jsem si to. **How much longer will it be?** Jak dlouho to ještě bude? **The bill, please** Účet, prosím. **I can't eat this and I won't pay for it!** (use with extreme caution) Nedá se to jíst a nezaplatím to. **Takeaway/to go** S sebou. **A beer, please** Pivo, prosím. **Two beers, please** Dvě piva, prosím. **Same again, please** Ještě jednou, prosím. **What'll you have?** Co si dáte? **Not for me, thanks** Pro mě ne, děkuji. **No ice, thanks** Bez ledu, děkuji. **He's really smashed** Je totálně namazaný.

pared, always fresh fare of fussily chosen ingredients – the pheasant, venison and boar are the only things not imported. The sea bass and spinach, *filet mignon* and *chèvre* salads have become a cause célèbre among Prague foodies. Attentive, warm service, phenomenal value for the price and reservations a must.

La Perle de Prague

Rašínovo nábřeží & Resslova streets, Prague 2 (221 984 160/www.laperle.cz). Metro Karlovo náměstí/tram 17. **Open** 7-10.30pm Mon; noon-2pm, 7-10.30pm Tue-Sat. **Main courses** 470-730 Kč. **Credit** AmEx, DC, MC, V. **Map** p310 G8.

With prices as heavenly as the views, this eyrie atop Frank Gehry's 'Fred and Ginger' building (*see p101*) was once king of the hill. For some time after it opened, the chance to eat on top of the dancing building was enough to bring the diners in. These days it's mostly a business crowd taking in the skyline and the rack of lamb in thyme and rosemary sauce. No great adventure and, in truth, the views are a bit disappointing.

Universal

V Jirchářích, Prague 1 (224 934 416). Metro Národní třída/tram 6, 9, 17, 18, 22, 23. **Open** 11.30-12.30am Mon-Sat; 11am-midnight Sun. **Main courses** 250-350 Kč. **Credit** DC, MC, V. **Map** p310 G6.

There's far more to the appeal of Universal than a cosy red-and-cream train-carriage interior and old-fashioned French tin advertisements. The servers here know their stuff and tip you to the daily specials (cod in white sauce, tender flank steak and rolled veggie lasagne are all typical), which come with delectable sides of fresh spinach or roasted gratin potatoes. The vegetarian-friendly menu is clearly created by chefs who exercise a French passion for tasty greens. The coffee is characteristically supercharged and goes down well with a massive lemon tart.

Global

Opera Garden

Legerova 75, Prague 1 (224 239 685/ www.zahradavopere.cz). Metro Muzeum/tram 11. **Open** 11.30am-1am daily; kitchen closes at midnight. **Main courses** 165-440 Kč. **Credit** AmEx, DC, MC, V. **Map** p311 L6.

Start off with smoked trout and almond salad, then debate mains like spinach tagliolini with roasted calamari and scampi or pheasant with shiitake mushrooms and watercress. Dessert platters are almost too beautiful to eat. It's rarely full and the menu's not as imaginative as it once was. Still, Opera Garden (or *Zahrada v opeře* in Czech) has zen style to spare, with airy, minimalist decor and gliding waiters.

Greek

Řecká Taverna

Revoluční 16, Prague 1 (222 317 762). Metro Náměstí Republiky/tram 5, 8, 14. **Open** 11am-midnight daily. **Main courses** 180-250 Kč. **Credit** AmEx, MC, V. **Map** p309 K2.

Good food, decent beer *and* a swanky setting – **Celnice** tops the popularity polls. *See p136.*

U Pinkasů. See p137.

With all the kitsch seascape you'd find on Rhodes painted on the walls, this still-affordable, authentic Greek place offers a breath of fresh air in meat-loving Prague. Just across the street from Staré Město and a block from the hip Roxy club (*see p222*) this array of mezes – stuffed vine leaves in tsatsiki, spinach pie and *saganaki* cheese – stands alongside savoury souvlakia and kebabs. Ouzo, retsina and cold frappé coffee are on hand, of course.

Indian

Himalaya

Mikovčova 7, Prague 2 (224 231 581). Metro IP Pavlova/tram 4, 6, 10, 16, 22. **Open** 11am-11pm Mon-Fri; noon-11pm Sat, Sun. **Main courses** 150-200 Kč. **No credit cards.**

Cheap Indian street eats finally arrive in Prague – though they're probably not on a par with the best of London ethnic offerings, Himalaya's arrival has nevetheless been met with tears of joy. Indeed, the lunch special Madras curries, biryanis and samosas eaten at the counter or takeaway have perhaps started a craze. Let's hope so.

Italian

Cicala

Žitná 43, Prague 1 (222 210 375). Metro IP Pavlova/tram 4, 6, 16, 22, 23. **Open** 11.30am-10.30pm daily. **Main courses** 200-400 Kč. **No credit cards. Map** 311 K7.

Almost worth hunting down for the familial atmosphere alone, Cicala has an Italian owner known for driving in fresh *sardelle* and calamares weekly. It's all presented like a work of art – and for a prodigal sum. This easily missed subterranean two-room eaterie on an otherwise unappealing street is well worth seeking out as a bastion of home cooking and a mainstay of Prague's Italian community.

Pizza Coloseum

Vodičkova 32, Prague 1 (224 214 914/www.pizzacoloseum.cz). Metro Můstek/tram 3, 9, 14, 24. **Open** 10am-11.30pm Mon-Sat; noon-11.30pm Sun. **Main courses** 100-200 Kč. **Credit** AmEx, DC, MC, V. **Map** p310 J6.

Here you'll find some of the most respected pies in town, topped with a fair selection of Italian cheeses, peppers, sausage and, if you like, aubergine. An easy-to-miss entrance just off Wenceslas Square leads into this mellow cellar. Excellent bruschetta, flame-baked pizza and big, saucy pastas complement well-stocked wine racks, an oil-heavy antipasto bar and a familiar range of decent steak and fish dishes.

Other locations: Ovocný trh 8, Staré Město, Prague 1 (224 238 355); Nádražní 25, Smíchov, Prague 5 (257 322 622).

Il Ritrovo

Lublaňská 11, Prague 2 (224 261 475/www.ilritrovo.cz). Metro IP Pavlova/tram 4, 6, 11, 22, 23. **Open** noon-3pm, 6-11pm daily. **Main courses** 130-270 Kč. **Credit** MC, V. **Map** p311 L8.

Just a short walk from Wenceslas Square, this restaurant features 30 varieties of pasta, several home-made, with zingy twists on traditional sauces. Try the antipasto bar, *panzerotti* with mushrooms, ravioli in cream and sage, and, if you fancy it, a stately brandy.

Seafood

Alcron

Štěpánská 40, Prague 1 (222 820 038). Metro Můstek/tram 3, 9, 14, 24. **Open** 5.30-10.30pm Mon-Sat. **Main courses** 600-1,200 Kč. **Credit** AmEx, DC, MC, V. **Map** p311 K6.

It's all too easy not to notice the seafood wonders being laid out at the seven tables off the lobby of the SAS Radisson Hotel, but that is a pity as it features some of the best scallops, tenderest crab and lightly poached pike-perch in the republic. Chef Jiří Štift is a master of the savoury sauce, while the decor outshines even that of the swanky surroundings. The hotel was known as the Alcron between the wars, but the name now applies only to the tiny dining room, not to be mistaken for the larger restaurant here, La Rotonde.

Vegetarian

Radost FX Café

Bělehradská 120, Prague 2 (224 254 776/ www.radostfx.cz). Metro IP Pavlova/tram 4, 6, 11, 16, 22, 34. **Open** *Restaurant* 8.30am-4am Mon-Fri; 11am-6am Sat, Sun. *Club* 10pm-4am Thur-Sat. **Main courses** 150-300 Kč. **No credit cards. Map** p311 L8.

An all-night vegetarian eaterie with house music might be old news in a lot of European cities, but in Prague Radost continues to rule the roost with precisely that. A constant turnover in the tiny kitchen unfortunately means inconsistent quality, but the trippy atmosphere and good-looking servers more than compensate. Comforting pesto fettuccine , meatless meatballs and Mexican food are perhaps better options than the frozen spinach pizza. After partying hard at the club downstairs (*see p222*), it's unlikely anyone will complain – especially if Johnny Depp drops in, as visiting celebs tend to do.

U Govindy Vegetarian Club

Soukenická 27, Prague 1 (224 816 631). Metro Náměstí Republiky/tram 5, 8, 14, 26. **Open** 11am-5pm Mon-Fri. **Main courses** 75 Kč set meal. **No credit cards. Map** p309 L2.

Clean, efficient and very mild in taste – it's run by Krisnas, who consider bulb spices like onion and garlic unclean – U Govindy is a friendly, cheap and healthy student hangout. A basic self-service vegetarian Indian meal costs a mere 75 Kč and can be embellished with an extra pakora for another 30 Kč or so. Share a table while seated on floor cushions or opt for a real table and chairs. Virtually all of the ingredients served here are grown on the U Govindy organic farm outside Prague.

Other locations: Na Hrází 5, Palmovka, Prague 8 (284 823 805).

Himalaya. *See p139.*

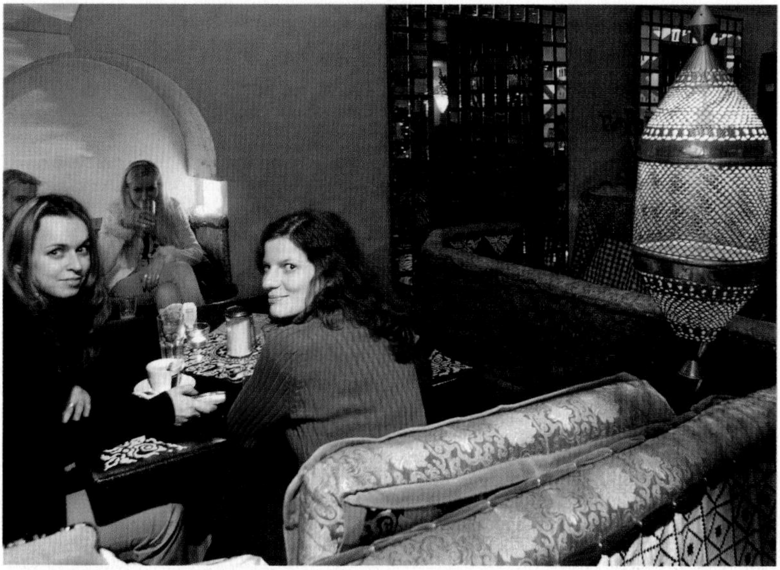

Radost FX Café's A-list credentials entice hungry clubbers around the clock.

Further afield

Americas

Barracuda

Krymská 2, Vinohrady, Prague 2 (271 740 599/ www.barracuda-cafe.cz). Metro Náměstí Míru/tram 4, 22. **Open** *Upstairs* 11.30am-midnight Mon-Fri; 5pm-midnight Sat, Sun. *Downstairs* 5-11.30pm Mon-Fri. **Main courses** 130-270 Kč. **Credit** AmEx, MC, V.

Once a top draw for Mexican in Prague, Barracuda is worth a visit if you're in the neighbourhood. The fajitas aren't exactly hot news any more, but the tacos are a hit.

Asian

The Sushi Bar

Zborovská 49, Smíchov, Prague 5 (mobile 603 244 882/www.sushi.cz). Tram 6, 9, 12, 22. **Open** noon-10pm daily. **Main courses** 300-600 Kč. **Credit** DC, MC, V.

Small and welcoming with clean lines and an excellent *maki* bar, the fish is as fresh as it comes in Prague. The *nigiri* is served on small, beautiful enamel plates.

Balkan

Modrá řeka

Mánesova 13, Vinohrady, Prague 2 (222 251 601). Metro Muzeum/tram 11. **Open** 11am-11pm Mon-Fri; 5-11pm Sat, Sun. **Main courses** 130-270 Kč. **No credit cards. Map** p313 A2.

Out of the way, to be sure, but think of it as a visit to the Yugoslavian home you never knew you had. Muhamed Londrc and his wife run this simple eaterie, which might be mistaken for a pub were it not for the folk art hanging from the walls. Customers are very nearly adopted as children, then stuffed senseless with home-made *somun* bread and *Šarena dolma* (lamb-stuffed vine leaves with peppers and onions).

Czech

Včelín

Kodaňská 5, Vršovice, Prague 10 (271 742 541). Tram 4, 22, 23. **Open** 11am-midnight Mon-Fri; 11.30am-1am Sat; 11.30am-11pm Sun. **Main courses** 250-400Kč. **Credit** V.

The Beehive is a well-named gathering spot for up- and-coming Prague creative types, but without the attitude that ruins most such places. The quick, amiable servers hustle from table to table bearing any of three great Czech beers on tap – Kozel, Radegast and Pilsner Urquell. The house special, gnocchi in spinach sauce, is the hit of this little room, which is done up with graphic-design magazine covers.

French

Café Atelier

Na Kovárně 8, Vršovice, Prague 10 (271 721 866/ www.restaurantatelier.cz). Tram 4, 22, 23. **Open** noon-11pm Mon-Sat. **Main courses** 350-550 Kč. **No credit cards**.

This incredible-value French cuisine restaurant is well worth riding out of the centre for. The rabbit in *basquaise* sauce and veal *osso-bucco* in orange sauce is served up in an intimate, modern space that's often booked solid. Fortunately Café Atelier has opened a new terrace for warm-weather dining or sipping from one of the city's best wine collections, which are priced a good deal better than a lot of plonk. For dessert, the indulgent chocolate mousse is pure sin.

La Crêperie

Janovského 4, Holešovice, Prague 7 (220 878 040/www.lacreperie.cz). Metro Vltavská/tram 1, 8, 14, 25. **Open** 9am-11pm Mon-Sat; 9am-10pm Sun. **Main courses** 150-300 Kč. **No credit cards. Map** p312 D2.

The decadent little cellar setting looks like a scene straight out of a vintage Truffaut film, from where the French-owned niche restaurant serves generous-sized crêpes, both sweet and savoury – all for a pittance. Seating here is in a comfortable but closet-sized basement, so it's probably not ideal for big parties. There's also an above average wine list, and fresh croissants.

Global

Akropolis

Kubelíkova 27, Vršovice, Prague 3 (296 330 913/ www.palacakropolis.cz). Metro Jiřího z Poděbrad/ tram 11. **Open** 10am-midnight Mon-Fri; 4pm-midnight Sat, Sun. **Main courses** 80-170 Kč. **No credit cards. Map** p313 B2.

As an eating destination, the Akropolis is no Michelin-star contender, but if you're clubbing here or rocking out in the attached concert space (*see p215*), a Czech chicken curry may indeed just do the job. Maybe a fried, battered mushroom as a vegetarian option? Whatever you go for, just drown them with beer and focus on the surrounding environment, which is a dining room designed by surrealist artists. The service is laid-back to say the least, but the crowd is ever-lively.

Indian/Pakistani

Mailsi

Lipanská 1, Žižkov, Prague 3 (222 717 783). Tram 5, 9, 26. **Open** noon-3pm, 6-11.30pm daily. **Main courses** 250-350 Kč. **Credit** AmEx, MC, V. **Map** p313 C1.

Mailsi is simply a comfortable, friendly neighbourhood Pakistani restaurant – but it's the district's only one. Even though there's not much atmosphere here, there is plenty of good, solid Pakistani food to be had, which goes down well in Žižkov, one of Prague's few truly ethnically mixed districts. The kebabs, dahl and other traditional dishes are all expertly prepared and spiced and served up with fast and friendly gusto by competent waiting staff.

Italian

Grosseto Pizzeria

Francouzská 2, Vinohrady, Prague 2 (224 252 778/ www.grosseto.cz). Metro Náměstí Míru/tram 4, 16, 22, 23. **Open** 11.30am-11pm daily. **Main courses** 100-200 Kč. **No credit cards. Map** p313 A3.

A zingy, four-cheese pie is made here by chefs working next to the entrance, who slide their creations from the wood-fired traditional oven on to your plate. With two booming locations, Grosseto does the most popular pizzas in town, if not necessarily the very finest. The minestrone is hearty too, and the carpaccio in tomato sauce is perfect for sopping up with the complimentary fresh hot peasant bread.
Other locations: Jugoslávských partyzánů 8, Dejvice, Prague 6 (233 342 694).

Puccelini

Tusarova 52, Holešovice, Prague 7 (283 871 134). Metro Vltavská/tram 1, 3, 14, 25. **Open** 11am-11pm Mon-Fri; noon-11pm Sat, Sun. **Main courses** 450-550 Kč. **Credit** AmEx, MC, V. **Map** p312 E2.

This fine Italian joint is housed in a red-brick dining room decorated with old musical instruments. Perfect if you're dancing at Mecca (*see p222*), Puccelini is the other redeeming venue in the bleak semi-industrial district of Holešovice. Adorned throughout with music scores and lamps hidden inside trumpets, it serves up wood-fired pizzas dappled with excellent, punchy sauce. But starters like baked stuffed aubergine and mozzarella, and potato-and-thyme soup are just as impressive. There's a fairly good wine list here and the house tiramisu is a wonder.

Ristorante da Emanuel

Charles de Gaulla 4, Dejvice, Prague 6 (224 312 934). Metro Dejvice/tram 25. **Open** noon-11pm daily. **Main courses** 250-450 Kč. **Credit** AmEx, MC, V.

Impossible to get a table without a reservation and this far from the centre? *Mama mia*, it's got to be good. With new menu additions like swordfish carpaccio and *pappardelle al cinghiale* (mildly spiced ground boar), this neighbourhood pasta joint always requires a booking these days. Expat Italians commute across Prague to eat at the tiny tables in an atmosphere of doting servers and terrible seaport decor.

Seafood

Café Savoy

Zborovská 68, Smíchov, Prague 5 (251 511 690/ www.cafesavoy.cz). Tram 6, 9, 12, 22. **Open** 11am-10pm Mon-Sat. **Main courses** 300-600 Kč. **Credit** AmEx, MC, V.

Just out of the way enough to merit a walk across the Most Legií from Staré Město this bright, high-ceilinged 19th-century café is now streamlined, elegant and stocked with an excellent menu of fresh mussels, courtesy of its new owner, the seafood importer across the street. Classy service and a fashionable crowd.

Cafés, Pubs & Bars

Drinking is a national pastime in Bohemia, of course. But added to the classic pub is the newest wave of coffeehouses and late, late cocktail bars.

Though beer remains king of the heap in Prague, and is likely to remain so, the younger generation is turning to more adventurous imbibing and bars, cafés and modern, cleaned-up beerhalls have answered the demand.

Aside from the runaway-success brewery-owned pubs like **Kolkovna** (*see p118*) and **Celnice** (*see p118 and p222*), there's been a rise in atmospheric emporiums, with chiselled bar staff mixing Mojitos as fast as patrons can throw them down: glitzy places like **Ocean Drive** (*see p150*), or the über-cool **M1 Secret Lounge** (*see p150*) and rambunctious **Dusk till Dawn** (*see p148*).

All this goes hand in hand with shaking it – another thing you can't do in the pubs of the older gen – and the DJ action is fast and furious at places like **Železné dveře** (*see p154*), **Chateau/L'enfer Rouge** (*see p147*) and **Solidní nejistota** (*see p152*).

This, then, leaves the classic pubs to the classic pub lovers. Though, increasingly, a café by day may serve beer and become a bar by night, a hardcore Bohemian pub is hard to kill off – and plenty are still left for purists.

With their 500-year history as a nation of brewmasters, the Czechs pour, raise and down beer like they perform Dvořák – with a gusto nothing shy of religious. The shrines to *pivo* drinking, too numerous to count, are here to stay and a representative night out can be found at **U Černého vola** (*see p144*) or **Radegast Pub** (*see p150*). Or just use the magic words '*pivo, prosím*' ('beer, please') at any of the traditional working-class pubs of źthe Žižkov district (famed for having more per capita than any other place on earth). There's still no place better for pub-crawling in terms of both affordability and quality than Prague (*see p149* **Bad Bohemia: Glug like Glen**). And alongside the workhorses of Pilsner Urquell, Radegast, Staropramen and Gambrinus, many of the classic pubs now serve new, zestier beers as well, like the ruby red Staropramen Granát.

By summer, it's best quaffed under the trees, of course, at places like **Letenský zámeček** (*see p154*), **Výletná** (*see p154*) or **U Houdků** (*see p156*). Suitably rough and ready food is usually on hand for the brave – smoked meat platters and/or magnificently smelly *pivní sýr* (beer cheese). Other than that, you may find surprisingly little to eat out after 10pm (for restaurants that serve food until later *see p118*).

Café culture in Prague, the traditional passion of dangerous intellectuals ever since the Industrial Age, offers everything from imperial elegance to American experiments these days. With secret police now gone, the *kavárna* has rebounded. Jam doughnuts fly at the legendary **Café Imperial** (*see p152*),

The best Pubs & Bars

For an inspiring visit from Kafka's ghost
Franz Kafka Café (*see p148*); dark, gloomy and unchanged by time.

For an intimate Gin and Tonic for two
St Nicholas Café (*see p145*) – always dim and moody.

For a killer mocha and brownies between sights
Bakeshop Praha (*see p147*) puts love in the oven.

For a late mulled wine in winter
Cosy **Blatouch** (*see p147*), a haven for the sleepless.

For a perfect Sex on the Beach
Ocean Drive (*see p150*) mixes it up in top form.

For experiencing the rush-hour crush, only hotter
Chateau/L'enfer Rouge (*see p147*), where drinking's a contact sport.

For forgetting you're in Prague
Dahab (*see p148*) for mint tea and belly dancers.

For running into a local accordion band
U zavěšenýho kafe (*see p145*), Malá Strana's watering hole.

while the cosy **Café Montmartre** (*see p147*) has bounced back from the *bon vivant* days when it hosted black masses during the 1930s. The **Slavia** (*see p151*), where dissidents like Václav Havel and Jiří Kolář once planned, penned and plotted, has been slightly too cleaned up, alas. Meanwhile, expat caffeine addicts get their fix at **Ebel Coffee House** (*see p148*), **Café Break** (*see p151*) and **The Globe Bookstore & Coffeehouse** (*see p152*).

A newer Prague tradition, dating back only to the Velvet Revolution of 1989, has brought to the city a host of haremlike demi-mondes such as **Dahab** (*see p148*). This is the highest form of the *čajovna* or tearoom. These dim, terminally mellow places come fully equipped with Persian seating, belly-dancing shows and mint tea.

All smashed up

Czechs have a vast vocabulary for conditions related to drinking. When you've really had enough, '*mam vopici*', or 'I have a monkey', best sums it up. If someone's already nabbed that line, there's always '*zpitý pod čáru*', 'to be drunk under the line'; '*zlitej jak dán*', 'to be drunk as a Dane'; '*být pod vobraz*', 'to be under the picture'; '*být na kaši*', or 'to have turned to mush' (a favourite of teens). This often happens after 'drinking like a mushroom' or '*nasávat jak houba*'. Do so quickly enough and you'll find yourself throwing a sabre or '*hodit šavli*' – or, if you prefer, a scythe or '*hodit kosu*'. That's vomiting, to the less imaginative.

Hopefully, before that stage one can at least enjoy 'having a head like a searching balloon' or '*mít hlavu jako pátrací balón*'. Do try to maintain some composure, however, lest you 'swear like a cobblestone layer' or '*nadávat jako dlaždič*'. This is perhaps more forgivable when on a boys' night out, or '*pánská jízda*', or at a hen party, '*dámská jízda*', both of which, curiously, translate literally as a 'ride'.

You should be careful not to 'stick the axe in' or '*zaseknout sekeru hluboko*' lest you run up a big tab. Better to call it quits while you can still 'slither like a snail' or '*plazit se jako šnek*'. Just don't be surprised the following morning when your mind is found to be 'outside' or '*být mimo*' – that is, useless.

Worse still, you could find you have your 'brain swept up like leaves' or '*nametený*', or, if you've really overdone it, have a 'head like a piece of broken glass' or '*mít hlavu jako střep*'.

Hradčany

U Černého vola

Loretánské náměstí 1, Prague 1 (220 513 481). Tram 22. **Open** 10am-10pm daily. **No credit cards. Map** p306 B3.

The definitive classic Czech pub, At the Black Ox looks like it's been here forever, but in fact the pub is a newcomer for Prague, built only after World War II and put under the current management in the '60s. Its superb location, right above Prague Castle, made it a prime target for redevelopment in the post-1989 building frenzy, but the rugged regulars took to civic action to ensure that local bearded artisans would have at least one place where they could afford to drink. The Kozel beer is perfection and the basic snacks line the stomach for long sessions. (*See also p69* **Bad Bohemia: U Černého vola.**)

Malá Strana

Baráčnická rychta

Tržiště 23, Prague 1 (257 532 461). Metro Malostranská/tram 12, 22, 23. **Open** noon-1am daily. **No credit cards. Map** p307 D3.

A survivor from the days of old, this former hall of barons and landlords has made only grudging nods to the present, with designer lamps now illuminating its heavy, communal tables. Czechs cling passionately to this oasis of indigenous pub culture – immortalised in Jan Neruda's *Prague Tales* – that thrived in Malá Strana from the 19th century onwards. Behind a series of archways, the pub is split into two: a small beerhall frequented by hardcore *pivo* drinkers and a downstairs music hall.

Blue Light

Josefská 1, Prague 1 (257 533 126). Metro Malostranská/tram 12, 22, 23. **Open** 6pm-3am daily. **No credit cards. Map** p307 E3.

Dim and crumbling, the Blue Light is a thoroughly insider hangout, with funk sounds on the stereo, spontaneous dancing around the bar in the wee hours and jazz posters all over the dilapidated walls. By day it's a convivial spot to sit with a friend. At night it gets more rowdy, with an infectious vibe.

Café El Centro

Maltézské náměstí 9, Prague 1 (257 533 343/ www.elcentro.czrb.cz). Metro Malostranská/tram 12, 18, 22, 23. **Open** noon-midnight daily. **Credit** AmEx, MC, V. **Map** p305 E4.

With decent portos, rums and Sangria by the jug, this sunny Malá Strana bar jives with mambo soundtracks and tropical cocktails. Efforts to expand into a full restaurant specialising in paella aren't winning over the Daiquiri lovers, but the patio at the rear is a boon.

Laid-back lounging at **Tato Kojkej**.

Jo's Bar

Malostranské náměstí 7, Prague 1 (257 531 422). Metro Malostranská/tram 12, 22, 23. **Open** 11-2am daily. **Credit** AmEx, DC, MC, V. **Map** p307 E3.

No longer the drinking haven that it once was, the legendary Jo's Bar was bought out a few years back and has been endlessly copied since its opening in 1992, when it was a shining beacon of friendly drunkenness and junky furnishings. The street-level bar is an adjunct to the downstairs Jo's Bar & Garáž (*see p223*), which fills with backpackers come summer. It's still a good place to meet fellow travellers, but it lacks soul these days.

Petřínské Terasy

Seminářská zahrada 13, Prague 1 (257 320 688/ www.petrinsketerasy.cz). Metro Malostranská/tram 12, 18, 22, 23. **Open** noon-11pm Mon-Fri; 11am-11pm Sat, Sun. **Credit** AmEx, DC, MC, V. **Map** p306 C4.

One of two tourist traps on Petřín hill, the Petřín Terraces offer exquisite views of Prague Castle and the city; unfortunately alongside expensive Krušovice and indifferent service.

St Nicholas Café

Tržiště 10, Prague 1 (257 530 204). Metro Malostranská/tram 12, 22, 23. **Open** noon-3am daily. **Credit** AmEx, DC, MC, V. **Map** p307 D3.

Now with a passable pizza oven, this is also an atmospheric vaulted cellar decked out with steamer trunk tables, painted arches and Pilsner Urquell on tap. A mellow but lively crowd gathers in the nooks for late-evening conversation.

Tato Kojkej

Kampa Park (no phone). Metro Malostranská/ tram 22, 23. **Open** 10am-midnight daily. **No credit cards. Map** p306 E5.

A wonderfully run-down gallery café hidden on the shore side of Kampa Park, this former millhouse still features a wooden water wheel. Inside is a long list of cocktails – though the staff is no expert at making them – and a short one of cheap red wine. Sofas, second-hand chairs, abstract sculpture and a terrace are the trump cards. Sunday-night movie screenings are a laugh.

U zavěšenýho kafe

Úvoz 6, Prague 1 (257 532 868/www. uzavesenyhokafe.com). Metro Malostranská/ tram 12, 22, 23. **Open** 11am-midnight daily. **No credit cards. Map** p306 C3.

As good for Czech duck as for a quick beer, the pub known as At the Hanging Coffee Cup is a mellow, thoroughly Czech spot with plank flooring, traditional grub and a long association with local artists and intellectuals. The name comes from an old tradition of paying for a cup of coffee for someone who may arrive later without funds – in which case the coffee, or *kafe*, is considered to be 'hanging' for them.

Staré Město & Josefov

Au Gourmand

Dlouhá 10, Staré Město, Prague 1 (222 329 060). Metro Staroměstská/tram 17, 18. **Open** 8.45am-7pm Mon-Fri; 9am-7pm Sat, Sun. **No credit cards. Map** p308 J3.

Pretty as an art-nouveau postcard, it's also the richest little French bakery in town, with savoury baguette sandwiches and quiches on one side, luscious pear tarts and Black Forest cakes on the other. Sit down at a wrought-iron table in the middle, surrounded by unique, fin-de-siècle tile interiors, and watch half of Prague slip in for a bite of sin.

Bakeshop Praha

Kozí 1, Josefov, Prague 1 (222 316 823). Metro Staroměstská/tram 17, 18. **Open** 7am-7pm daily. **Credit** MC, V. **Map** p308 J2.

Authentic American muffins, cookies and brownies draw Czechs and homesick Westerners in, but the savoury nut breads and zesty quiches are just as popular, as are sandwiches to go (*see p171*). Great coffee, and counterspace for eating here too.

Banana Bar & Café

Štupartská 9, Staré Město, Prague 1 (222 324 801/ www.laprovence.cz). Metro Náměstí Republiky/tram 5, 8, 14. **Open** 11-3am daily. **Credit** AmEx, DC, MC, V. **Map** p308 J3.

A magnet for beefy Czuppies, this pretentious bar above the La Provence restaurant (*see p131*) is usually as packed with suits as a Samsonite. The attached café features overpriced standard grub, while the downstairs restaurant goes for a mass-produced French country inn ethos. Good for a laugh.

Blatouch

Vězeňská 4, Staré Město, Prague 1 (222 328 643). Metro Staroměstská/tram 17, 18. **Open** noon-1am Mon-Thur; noon-3am Fri; 2pm-3am Sat; 2pm-midnight Sun. **No credit cards**. **Map** p308 J2.

Ever packed with students, artists and scribblers drinking cheap red wine, this gentle café is run by two sisters. A long-time favourite among new bohemians, the Mudflower plays jazz and soul through the narrow, high-ceilinged space and up the metal stairwell to a cosy loft. The food offerings aren't recommended, though.

Bugsy's

Pařížská 10 (entrance on Kostečná), Josefov, Prague 1 (224 810 943/www.bugsysbar.cz). Metro Staroměstská/tram 17, 18. **Open** 7pm-2am daily. **Credit** AmEx, MC, V. **Map** p308 H3.

Once the only source for proper cocktails in town, these days Bugsy's attracts an older crowd, many suits and not a few hustlers, all soaking up its swish Pařížská location. Its claim to fame is the drinks list, including 200 cocktails, and a bar staff good enough to mix them properly. Prices prohibit all but flush tycoons, but it's still packed most evenings.

Café Indigo

Platnéřská 11, Staré Město, Prague 1 (no phone). Metro Staroměstská/tram 17, 18. **Open** 9am-midnight Mon-Fri; 11-midnight Sat, Sun. **No credit cards**. **Map** p308 G3.

The place to meet a nicotine-fiend philosophy student, Indigo is a post-industrial, yet comfortable, art café with huge streetside windows and a limited menu of toast, soups and dubious omelettes. It's a favourite with students from Charles University, which means a lot of smoke, cheap wine and a consistently upbeat vibe. Children's corner in the back.

Café Konvikt

Bartolomějská 11, Staré Město, Prague 1 (224 232 427). Metro Národní třída/tram 6, 9, 18, 22, 23. **Open** 9-1am Mon-Fri; noon-1am Sat, Sun. **No credit cards**. **Map** p308 G5/H5.

This popular, well-lit Staré Město spot attracts Prague's new generation of penniless creatives – who appear to have a taste for poor wine. Small, edible sweets are served, but it's really just about drink, talk and smoke here.

Café Montmartre

Řetězová 7, Staré Město, Prague 1 (222 221 244). Metro Staroměstská/tram 17, 18. **Open** 9am-11pm Mon-Fri; noon-11pm Sat, Sun. **No credit cards**. **Map** p308 H4.

Today's successors of Czech literati like Gustav Meyrink, Jaroslav Hašek and Franz Werfel – who all tippled here before it became a Jazz Age hotspot – hang out here these days. Pilsner Urquell and Velvet are on tap, but wine is better suited to the crowd of creative miscreants that gather around the battered tables for late-night talks.

La Casa Blů

Kozí 15, Josefov, Prague 1 (224 818 270/ www.lacasablu.8k.com). Metro Staroměstská/ tram 17, 18. **Open** 11-2am daily. **No credit cards**. **Map** p308 J2.

Tequila shots, cheap red wine and above-average Mexican food are on offer, served among decorative rugs draped over hard-back chairs and Mexican street signs. It's a pleasant break from beerhall rowdiness, with a new Mexican menu, and is generally packed. Try the buzzer even if the door is locked – people routinely wheedle their way in past closing.

Chateau/L'enfer Rouge

Jakubská 2, Staré Město, Prague 1 (222 316 328/www.chateau-bar.cz). Metro Náměstí Republiky/tram 5, 14, 26. **Open** noon-3am Mon-Thur; noon-4am Fri; 4pm-4am Sat; 4pm-2am Sun. **No credit cards**. **Map** p308 J3.

One of Prague's most attitude-heavy bars is nevertheless packed nightly with young things on the make. It has much in common with hell, being unbearably hot, loud and red. But it also has great DJs, such as Liquid A, who spins Latin and reggae on Thursday, and blowout parties at all other times.

Cream & Dream

Husova 12, Staré Město, Prague 1 (224 211 035). Metro Staroměstská. **Open** 11am-10pm daily. **No credit cards**. **Map** p308 H4.

Not another of Prague's many sex clubs, just a nice, clean ice-cream shop. But admittedly one with sinful waffle cones stuffed with *frutti di bosco* or caramel. If you can make it past the gleaming freezer, however, a micro-bar awaits in the back.

Dahab

Dlouhá 33, Staré Město, Prague 1 (224 827 375/www.dahab.cz). Metro Náměstí Republiky/tram 5, 8, 14. **Open** noon-1am Mon-Sat; noon-midnight Sun. **Credit** AmEx, DC, MC, V. **Map** p309 K2.

By far the most elaborate of Prague's tearooms, Dahab is nothing less than a harem tent strewn with pillows and teak, providing a perfect candlelit counterpoint to the crazed antics at the Roxy (*see p222*) next door, complete with pistachio sweets, Turkish coffees and occasional belly-dancing. Otherwise, thoroughly calming. Dahab's other location is called Boršov, where you have to pull the bell to enter this hideaway oasis.

Other locations: Boršov 2, Staré Město, Prague 1 (222 221 430).

Duende

Karoliny Světlé 30, Staré Město, Prague 1 (604 269 731/www.duende.cz). Metro Národní třída/tram 6, 9, 17, 18, 22, 23. **Open** 11-1am daily. **No credit cards**. **Map** p308 G5.

A second home to many, this Latin-flavoured café-bar, is a good deal more than the sum of its parts: Russian mandolin-playing on Friday nights, bizarre movies screened on Sundays, tattered sofas and fringed lampshades, which splash diffused light in the backroom. The walnut liqueur (*Ořechovka*) is a rare treat.

Dusk till Dawn

Týnská 19, Staré Město, Prague 1 (224 808 250). Metro Staroměstská/tram 17, 18. **Open** 5pm-4am daily. **No credit cards**. **Map** p308 J3.

Nice 'n' sleazy dim bar that's forever packed with the friends of the friends who recently launched it. Appealing specials and naughty cocktails named for unmentionable activities go nicely with the lounge seating, bar perches and party atmosphere that is characteristic of this popular meeting place.

Ebel Coffee House

Týn 2, Staré Město, Prague 1 (224 895 788/ www.ebelcoffee.cz). Metro Náměstí Republiky/tram 5, 8, 14. **Open** 9am-10pm daily. **Credit** AmEx, DC, MC, V. **Map** p308 J3.

A caffeine-junkie heaven, this wood-trimmed room is where Malgorzata Ebel brews more than 30 prime arabica coffees stocked in her neighbouring shop, Vzpomínky na Afriku (*see p173*). Ebel serves fine blends any way you like them, plus passable quiches, bagels and brownies are offered on tables in Prague's most fashionable Staré Město courtyard.

Érra Café

Konviktská 11, Staré Město, Prague 1 (222 220 568). Metro Národní třída/tram 6, 9, 18, 22, 23. **Open** 10am-midnight daily. **No credit cards**. **Map** p308 G5.

With glamour to spare, it's as if a copy of Czech *Elle* exploded in a Staré Město cellar – even the menu poses: salads of apple and walnut are artfully arranged for lunch, as are the garlic-sesame chicken baguettes and rich banana milkshakes. The service is great by Prague standards, but the chairs are slightly less comfortable. Gay-friendly scene by night, when the permanent house-music soundtrack seems more appropriate.

Franz Kafka Café

Široká 12, Josefov, Prague 1 (222 318 945). Metro Staroměstská/tram 17, 18. **Open** 10am-9pm daily. **No credit cards**. **Map** p308 H2/3.

Café Montmartre – the place to sip wine and let the words flow. *See p147.*

Bad Bohemia Glug like Glen

Take it from the man who launched three of Prague's hippest bars – Jo's Bar and the former Repre and Iron Door pubs. **Jo's Bar** (*see p145*) has since been sold off, but Canadian engineer Glen Emery (*pictured*) still keeps tabs on the best taps in town. Here's his hit list, which exposes you to three of the five classic 12-degree brews expertly tapped: Kozel, Pilsner Urquell and Budvar. The other two, Radegast and Krušovice, are common at pubs all over town.

Start near Prague Castle at the most legendary classic pub in town (and very nearly its own political party), **U Černého vola** (*see p144*), for a half-litre of Kozel and a strictly local crowd. At the Black Bull is one of the few pubs that pumps ambient air, not just gas into the beer, in keeping with what brewers intended.

From there, make your way down the hill to **U Kocoura**, or At the Cat (Nerudova 2, 257 530 107), for a Budvar. 'The beer isn't that good, but it's a famous pub' says Emery. Fair enough.

'The best Pilsner in Malá Strana' can be found just around the corner at **U Hrocha**, or At the Hippo (Thunovská 10, 257 316 890).

Retrace your steps now, past the Church of St Nicholas, to **Divadlo Rubin** (Malostranské náměstí 8, no phone), a grotty, but highly credentialled hangout for local thesps. The easy-to-miss entrance is down some stairs at the back of a hallway. Expect smoke, late-night gabbing and no one taking any notice if you wear your pants on your head.

From here, it's a short walk across the square towards the Charles Bridge, but don't cross or you'll miss the equally grotty, favourite hangout of visiting actors and directors, **Blue Light** (*see p144*). Behind a smoke-tinted glass door, this cave of a bar is far from a classic Czech pub but has a thoroughly decadent vibe, with names carved in every available surface – and it only really gets going about 1am. 'You can walk into there and run into Charlie Sheen or Jerry Bruckheimer,' imparts Emery.

Now cross the Charles Bridge and find your way to **U Zlatého tygra** (*see p151*), former haunt of the Czech writer Bohumil Hrabal. Another fine Pilsner awaits if you get there before 11pm. Otherwise, expect a cold shoulder – or maybe expect one anyway: 'They're surly and burly,' Emery says of Hrabal's surviving friends.

If you've left it too late, no worries: **U Medvídků** (*see p151*) stays open until 3am and is one of the few places left to serve the hoppy Budvar, or Budweiser in German, not to be confused with the watery American beer of the same name. It's 'the best pint of Bud in the old centre.'

Had enough? If not, there's always **Marquis** (*see p150*), **Chateau** (*see p147*), **Tretter's**, (*see p151*), **M1** (*see p150*)...

Dim, old-world and almost austere, this little coffeehouse is a trip back in time: there's frosted glass, dark, deep wooden booths, old engravings of the Jewish Quarter (it's just around the corner from the Jewish Cemetery) and, naturally, lots of Kafka portraits. The decent coffee here and convivial tables on the street make it a convenient stop when touring Josefov.

Kavárna Obecní dům

Náměstí Republiky 5, Staré Město, Prague 1 (222 002 763/www.vysehrad2000.cz). Metro Náměstí Republiky/tram 5, 14, 26. **Open** 7.30am-11pm daily. **Credit** AmEx, MC, V. **Map** p309 K3.

Easily the most epic café space in town, this balconied, art-nouveau sipping space with grand piano is situated at street level in the magnificently restored Municipal House. Replete with elaborate secessionist brass chandeliers, odd characters and always a few grand dames, there's no more memorable venue for an espresso in Prague.This place should be a must on your 'to do' list.

Kozička

Kozí 1, Josefov, Prague 1 (224 818 308/ www.kozicka.cz). Metro Náměstí Republiky/tram 5, 8, 14. **Open** noon-4am Mon-Fri; 6pm-4am Sat, Sun. **Credit** MC, V. **Map** p308 J2.

It's hip, it's blue, it's **Ocean Drive**.

Wall-to-wall people on any weekend night, this cellar grill bar is a late-night refuge for the party hearty set. It's hard to beat, with intimate nooks throughout, mighty steaks served until 11pm and Krušovice on tap.

M1 Secret Lounge

Masná 1, Staré Město, Prague 1 (221 874 256). Metro Staroměstská/tram 17, 18. **Open** 6pm-4am daily. **No credit cards. Map** p308 J2.

A bit heavy on attitude but a late option with an appealingly lurid style. This is just a bar with red velour and wavy iron décor, but the crowd that assembles here can be counted on to get up to some manner of mischief. Stick to the beer and the shots here.

Marquis de Sade

Templová 8, Staré Město, Prague 1 (no phone). Metro Náměstí Republiky/tram 5, 14, 26. **Open** 2pm-2am daily. **No credit cards. Map** p309 K3.

Dark, decadent and known for sofas with the stuffing knocked out, the Marquis is an institution. Peeling red vinyl seating runs around the perimeter of the bar, which manages to be dim even in broad daylight. Prime seating is on the balcony, the perfect place to spot a drunken patron doing something indiscreet. The bar's nothing to write home about and the service gets pretty slack, but occasional live blues or jazz compensates somewhat.

Molly Malone's

U Obecního dvora 4, Staré Město, Prague 1 (224 818 851/www.mollymalones.cz). Metro Náměstí Republiky/tram 5, 14, 26. **Open** 11-1am Mon-Thur, Sun; 11-2am Fri, Sat. **Credit** AmEx, MC, V. **Map** p308 J2.

Prague's first Irish bar started an invasion that's never slowed down. Complete with roaring log fire, mismatched chairs and tables constructed out of old beds and sewing machines, incessant Pogues in the background and 'traditional Irish food', it attracts backpackers and rowdy English businessmen. The bar is great for propping up, the Guinness is excellent, the food is decent, and in winter there's a warm and welcoming atmosphere.

Ocean Drive

V kolkovně 7, Josefov, Prague 1 (224 819 089/ www.tretters.cz). Metro Staroměstská/tram 17, 18. **Open** 4pm-2am daily. **Credit** AmEx, MC, V.

The latest hotspot for well-mixed cocktails and well-rehearsed chat-up lines is this classy, West Coast-style cousin to the well-established hit next door, Tretter's (*see p151*). Count on Ocean's Drive's gorgeous clientele, tempting cocktails, which set the scene for getting into trouble.

Radegast Pub

Templová 2, Staré Město, Prague 1 (222 328 069). Metro Náměstí Republiky/tram 5, 14, 26. **Open** 11-12.30am daily. **Credit** AmEx, DC, MC, V. **Map** p309 K3.

This defiantly unchanged place is one of the last typical Czech pubs in this central drinking hub. Apart from the absence of foreigners, its main attractions are the excellent beer and pub food – you could easily pay an extra 400 Kč in a swanky restaurant and not find a better goulash. Semi-enclosed tables give an air of privacy, but the service can be iffy – orders have been known to get lost in the smoke or added up imaginatively.

Scandals

Dlouhá 7, Josefov, Prague 1 (224 817 703/www.czrb.cz/scandals). Metro Staroměstská/tram 17, 18. **Open** 11-2am daily. **No credit cards. Map** p308 J2.

A foxy, decadent, red-walled cocktail bar that manages English breakfasts and bacon sandwiches to boot. This new Staré Město bar is a winner. Alas, it does attract annoying Brit stag parties, but, these days, they're at every bar this large.

Slavia

Smetanovo nábřeží 2, Staré Město, Prague 1 (224 218 493/www.cafeslavia.cz). Metro Národní třída/tram 6, 9, 17, 18, 22. **Open** 9am-11pm daily. **Credit** AmEx, DC, MC, V. **Map** p308 G5.

Its literary credentials unquestionable, the Slavia remains the mother of all Prague cafés, where Karel Tiege, Jiří Kolář and a struggling Václav Havel once tippled, penned and plotted the overthrow of communism. Unfortunately, the café would hardly be recognised by its former customers today. The art-deco fixtures and crisp service were overdue but are not the stuff of Jaroslav Seifert's classic poem *Café Slavia*. Still, it does offer stunning castle views, a decent salmon toast and a fine Staré Město respite.

Tretter's

V kolkovně 3, Josefov, Prague 1 (224 811 165/www.tretters.cz). Metro Staroměstská/tram 17, 18. **Open** 7pm-3am Mon-Sat; 7pm-2am Sun. **Credit** AmEx, MC, V. **Map** p308 J2.

With red walls, a blues singer on Mondays and over 50 special cocktails created by owner Mike Tretter, this is a delightfully cosmopolitan scene, with beautiful, competent bar staff. Try the newest sensation, the Caipikahlua, at the grand old 1930s-style tile bar, watching for film and music types in the crowd. The staff has garnered several bartending and mixing awards at international competitions.

Týnská literární kavárna

Týnská 6, Staré Město, Prague 1 (224 826 023/www.knihytynska.cz). Metro Staroměstská/tram 17, 18. **Open** 9am-11pm Mon-Fri; 10am-11pm Sat, Sun. **No credit cards. Map** p308 J3.

Classic, vinegary wine, watery coffee, stale pastries and students who couldn't love it more. They file in to smoke, cavort, sit outside on the patio in summer and get steadily wasted. An arty location with a spacey staff.

U Medvídků

Na Perštýně 7, Staré Město, Prague 1 (224 211 916/www.umedvidku.cz). Metro Národní třída/tram 6, 9, 18, 22, 23. **Open** 11.30am-11pm Mon-Sat; 11.30am-10pm Sun. **Credit** AmEx, MC, V. **Map** p308 H5.

Noisy, over-lit and friendly as they come, At the Little Bears has five centuries as a beerhall behind it. Having brushed off communism as a passing fad, the bar keeps the fine, cheap Budvar coming until you tell the waiter to stop. Don't be sidetracked by the modern bar to the left of the entrance (unless it's 2.30am and the main one's closed); the real thing is on the right. The menu is a step up from pub grub.

U Vejvodů

Jilská 4, Staré Město, Prague 1 (224 219 999/ww.restauraceuvejvodu.cz). Metro Můstek/tram 3, 9, 14, 24. **Open** 10am-2am daily. **No credit cards. Map** p308 H4/5.

Another brewery-owned mega-beerhall, in this case one of Pilsner Urquell's, this vast pub caters to big tour groups – stick to the smaller front room to avoid them. But it does offer quick service and old-style wood interiors, accented by the obligatory huge copper beer vat lids. For a ye olde pub feel, fine brews and traditional pub fare, this one's hard to beat.

U Zlatého tygra

Husova 17, Staré Město, Prague 1 (222 221 111). Metro Staroměstská/tram 17, 18. **Open** 3-11pm daily. **No credit cards. Map** p308 H4.

Small, full of cranky old locals and an equally testy staff, At the Golden Tiger was once the second home of Prague's favourite writer, the famously crotchety Bohumil Hrabal. This bar has lost virtually all its appeal since its famous patron fell to his death from a hospital window in 1997. Tourists still besiege the place, which may explain why the Pilsner Urquell is no bargain.

Žíznivý pes

Elišky Krásnohorské 5, Josefov, Prague 1 (222 310 039/www.thirstydog.cz). Metro Staroměstská/tram 17, 18. **Open** 11-2am Mon-Fri; noon-2am Sat, Sun. **No credit cards. Map** p308 H2.

Once a shrine to the golden days of expat slacking, when its original location was still open and Nick Cave sat and wrote a song about the place. Nowadays it's about burgers, Murphy's Stout and Staropramen with cavorting Yanks, Brit stag parties and a handful of Czechs. Summer breezes waft through the *psí bouda* (dog kennel) patio out back.

Nové Město

Café Archa

Na Poříčí 26, Prague 1 (221 716 117). Metro Náměstí Republiky or Florenc/tram 3, 24. **Open** 9am-10.30pm Mon-Fri; 10am-10pm Sat; 1-10pm Sun. **No credit cards. Map** p309 M2.

Theatre cafés are some of the coolest spots in Prague to catch a culture wave, owing to the city's long-held passion for the stage. This glass fish tank, with dangling lamps as bait, has hooked a young, laid-back clientele with cheap drinks, pristine surfaces and posters and photos from the theatre and rock worlds.

Café Break

Štěpánská 32, Prague 1 (222 231 065). Metro Můstek/tram 3, 9, 14, 24. **Open** 8am-10pm Mon-Fri; 10am-7pm Sat, Sun. **No credit cards. Map** p311 K6.

A remarkable find just off Wenceslas Square, this café is bright and lively. Window seats offer a prime spot for people-ogling, while your formally polite waiter brings on Irish breakfast platters, fresh muffins and sandwiches. Nearly as popular for white wine- or beer-drinking, in low light, by evening.

Café Imperial

Na Poříčí 15, Prague 1 (222 316 012/ www.hotelimperial.cz). Metro Náměstí Republiky/ tram 5, 8, 14, 26. **Open** 9am-midnight daily. **Credit** AmEx, MC, V. **Map** p309 L2.

A bit like a ghost ship from another age, this *Marie Celeste* is at least full of patrons. Once the very picture of decadence during Czechoslovakia's First Republic, the Café Imperial has yet to really finish being renovated. Nevertheless, it's an only-in Prague experience, with incredible floor-to-ceiling, art-nouveau, sculpted porcelain tiles. Order the Saturnin's Bowl of *koblihy* (jam doughnuts) if you'd like to spend 1,943 Kč for the privilege of throwing them at anyone you like. It's good to know that the attached hostel (*see p52*) is also a major bargain.

Café Lamborghini

Vodičkova 8, Nové Město, Prague 1 (222 231 869). Metro Můstek/tram 3, 9, 14, 24. **Open** 8am-10pm Mon-Sat; 10am-10pm Sun. **Credit** MC, V. **Map** p310 J6.

Burning rubber in the race to be Prague's hottest café, this clean, streamlined space with slate grey accents serves killer Italian coffee, imaginative salads with tropical fruit and gorgonzola, and the best *pappardelle carbonara* in town. Grind your own fresh parmasan and take in the colourful cast of casual-cool patrons.

Café Louvre

Národní třída 20, Prague 1 (224 930 949/ www.kavarny.cz/louvre). Metro Národní třída/ tram 6, 9, 18, 22. **Open** 8am-11.30pm Mon-Fri; 9am-11.30pm Sat, Sun. **Credit** AmEx, DC, MC, V. **Map** p308 H5.

Popular since the 19th century, this lofty café somehow manages to get away with a garish cream-and-turquoise colour combination, perhaps because it leads to a fine backroom with pool tables. Solid weekend breakfasts and vested waiters.

French Institute Café

Štěpánská 35, Prague 1 (222 231 782). Metro Můstek/tram 3, 9, 14, 24. **Open** 8.30am-7.30pm Mon-Fri. **No credit cards**. **Map** p311 K6.

An island of Left Bank-espirit, this convivial, smoky café is a crucial source of croissants, philosophy and strong espresso. The French Institute is a Gallic nerve centre, with an unapologetically Francophile art gallery downstairs and cinema adjoining. An elegant, prime posing space, with an open courtyard and a fair chance of starting an intellectual romance.

The Globe Bookstore & Coffeehouse

Pštrossova 6, Prague 1 (224 934 203/ www.globebookstore.cz). Metro Národní třída/ tram 6, 9, 18, 22, 23. **Open** 10am-midnight daily. **Credit** AmEx, DC, MC, V. **Map** p310 G7.

Far more than a bookshop with coffee, the Globe was something of an icon from day one (*see also p101 and p163*). The city's original expat bookshop-café has been pegged as the literary heart of post-revolutionary Prague – and blamed for encouraging all the wannabe Hemingways. The Globe still carries the burden graciously, offering a cosy reading room and comfortable café surroundings to scribblers of both novellas and postcards. Passable pasta salads and such do for food, easily surpassed by the tall lattes and enormous brownies. There's strong support for local writers, who do regular readings. The internet terminals and bulletin board are lifelines for expat life.

Hvězda Sport Bar

Ve Smečkách 12, Praha 1 (296 222 292/sportbar.cz). Metro Muzeum/tram 11. **Open** 11am-11pm Mon; 11-2am Tue-Thur; 11-4.30am Fri; noon-4.30am Sat; noon-midnight Sun. **Credit** AmEx, MC, V. **Map** 310 K7.

The district's cosiest sports bar has all the big matches, conveniently marked well ahead on a calendar near the entrance and shown on several screens, and a spacious, low-lit interior of wooden tables and old tin advertisements. There's reasonable service too.

Jáma

V jámě 7, Prague 1 (224 222 383/www.jamapub.cz). Metro Můstek/tram 3, 9, 14, 24. **Open** 11am-midnight Mon, Sun; 11am-1am Tue-Sat. **Credit** AmEx, MC, V. **Map** p311 K6.

A lively, sometimes rowdy, joint for a beer or six with your pals, this long bar serving Mexican food is the choice of the post-1989 generation, local and foreign. The Americans who run it also sponsor the literary quarterly *Prague Revue*, but you'd never guess it from the noisy, beery atmosphere, the extensive menu of cocktails (often on special), faux cacti, video counter or bank of internet terminals. A beer garden in the back offers a break from the noise within.

Jazz Café č.14

Opatovická 14, Prague 1 (no phone). Metro Národní třída/tram 6, 9, 18, 22, 23. **Open** 10am-11pm Mon-Fri; noon-11pm Sat, Sun. **No credit cards**. **Map** p310 H6.

Always smoky and filled with second-hand knick-knacks and struggling students, the Jazz Café makes for a cosy winter hideaway. Service is patchy and jazz is only on CDs, while very basic snacks do for victuals – *medovník*, or honey cake, is about it. But the *svařák*, or mulled wine, is warming indeed.

Le Patio

Národní třída 22, Nové Město, Prague 1 (224 934 402). Metro Národní třída/tram 6, 9, 18, 22, 23. **Open** 8am-11pm Mon-Fri; 10am-11pm Sat, Sun. **Credit** AmEx, MC, V. **Map** p308 H5.

Opulent and well-stocked, with decadent sweets and serious coffee, this French-owned emporium of imported and locally made decorative art doubles as an atmospheric café.

Solidní nejistota

Pštrossova 21, Prague 1 (224 933 086/ www.solidninejistota.cz). Metro Národní třída/ tram 6, 9, 17, 18, 22, 23. **Open** 6pm-6am daily. **No credit cards**. **Map** p310 G7.

Go-faster coffee at Café Lamborghini.

A shrine to posing and pick-ups, Solid Uncertainty comes equipped with the now standard blood-red interior and grill bar. Occasional live rock shows draw in the crowds.

U Fleků

Křemencova 11, Prague 1 (224 934 019/ www.ufleku.cz). Metro Národní třída/tram 3, 6, 14, 18, 24. **Open** 9am-11pm daily. **Credit** AmEx, DC, MC, V. **Map** p310 H7.

Unfortunately, this pub has made it on to 90% of the web pages about Prague and, though it's always been a tourist trap, it continues to rake them in. The city's most famous pub has indeed been brewing fine 13-degree dark beer on the premises for centuries so, if you must try it, just be prepared. Basic Bohemian meat and two veg is also available, but it's automatically assumed you're here for the beer. Never accept the over-priced Becherovka when it's suggested by your smiling waiter. The picturesque courtyard is shaded by cherry trees, enclosed by a graffitied wall and leaded windows. Inside and out, the long tables are invariably filled with Germans swinging glasses to oompah music.

Ultramarin

Ultramarin, Ostrovní 32, Prague 2 (224 932 249/www.ultramarin.cz). Metro Národní třída. **Open** 10.30-4am daily. **Credit** AmEx, DC, MC, V. **Map** p310 H6.

A cool combination of ancient townhouse and modern art bar, Ultramarin is one of the city's most stylish bars, if still alcoholically challenged. The atmospheric retro jazz on the sound system, Santa Fe chicken salad on the menu, and blond wood and mottled wall paint throughout would be better complemented by real cocktails and decent wines. Still, it's about the best option going for late-night refuelling and chilling. Downstairs, the Ultramarin dance club attracts hip Czechs (*see p222*).

U Sudu

Vodičkova 10, Prague 1 (222 232 207). Metro Karlovo náměstí/tram 3, 9, 14, 24. **Open** 1pm-2am Mon-Fri; 2pm-3am Sat; 3pm-1am Sun. **No credit cards. Map** p310 J6.

Very local, very trashed and very worthwhile, U Sudu was originally a small, dark wine bar on the ground floor only. Over the years it's expanded into three Gothic cellars. The cellars have been claimed by students, while upstairs sees everyone from artists to business types to little old ladies. The wine is nothing to write home about, except when the *Burčák* (a half-fermented, traditional Czech wine punch; *see also p182*) arrives in September.

Velryba

Opatovická 24, Prague 1 (224 912 391). Metro Národní třída/tram 6, 9, 18, 22, 23. **Open** 11am-midnight daily. **No credit cards. Map** p310 H6.

Starving-student heaven, with perpetual blasting rock on the sound system, a fog of cigarette smoke, greasy, cheap grub and barely drinkable wine. The Whale combines clamorous front-room dining on pastas and chicken steaks with back-room chess and a cellar gallery specialising in fringe art and photography. The bar only serves bottled Gambrinus.

Vesmirna

Ve Smečkách 5, Prague 1 (222 212 363). Metro Muzeum/tram 11. **Open** 8.30am-10pm Mon-Fri; 2-10pm Sat. **No credit cards. Map** 310 K7.

Železné Dveře, fired up for fun.

This is an earthy, warm coffeehouse serving fresh-squeezed juices and satisfying light meals, many of which are made from organic produce. Excellent service, fluent in many languages. The grapefruit juice with echinacea, the organic couscous with cheese and vegetables, and the hot apple pie are all highly recommended.

Železné dveře

Křemencova 10, Prague 1 (224 932 052). Metro Národní třída/tram 6, 9, 17, 18, 22, 23. **Open** 7pm-5am daily. **No credit cards. Map** p310 H7.

This maze of underground rooms in Prague's ghetto of cool, the area south of the National Theatre, is a favourite with party animals and attracts an undiscriminating mob of students looking to get blitzed fast. Joining the pack can be a laugh.

Further afield

Dejvice

Café Orange

Puškinovo náměstí 13, Dejvice, Prague 6 (mobile 603 894 499). Metro Hradčanská. **Open** 10am-11pm Mon-Sat; 11am-3pm Sun. **No credit cards.**

Certainly out of the way, but a is discreet, warm space ideal for a secret rendezvous. The first day-time venue in Prague 6 with fresh orange juice, lattes, mozzarella ciabattas and street tables, it's on a quiet square that's hard to find.

Holešovice

La Bodega Flamenca

Šmeralova 5, Prague 7 (233 374 075). Metro Vltavská/tram 1, 8, 25, 26. **Open** 4pm-1am Mon-Thur, Sun; 4pm-3am Fri, Sat. **No credit cards. Map** p312 C2.

A refreshing taste of salsa and Sangria, this easily missed Spanish tapas bar resides two doors north of Fraktal (*see below*). Owner Ilona oversees the bar, serving up tapas such as marinated olives, *patatas fritas*, garlic mushrooms and fresh bread in little ceramic plates. Bench-style seats line the walls and fill up fast and, in true Spanish style, things only really start hotting up after 1am.

Fraktal

Šmeralova 1, Prague 7 (no phone). Metro Vltavská/tram 1, 8, 25, 26. **Open** 11am-midnight daily. **No credit cards. Map** p312 C2.

Very nearly a Berlin-style squatter pub, this mecca for neighbourhood expats and locals is out-of-centre, but no less popular. It's a scruffy yet cosy little drinking hole, with occasional live music and/or book launches. Like most Czech bars, it still serves mostly beer, but a few cocktails are worth noting: Mojitos and Tequila Gold with orange and cinnamon are a treat.

Letenský zámeček

Letenské sady 341 (in Letná Park), Prague 7 (233 375 604/www.letenskyzamecek.cz). Metro Hradčanská/tram 1, 8, 25, 26. **Open** *Beer garden* 11am-11pm daily. *Restaurant* 11.30am-3pm, 6-midnight daily. **Credit** AmEx, MC, V. **Map** p312 C3.

Though the Little Palace has gone upmarket of late, with designer seating and haughty waiters, the trashy beer garden opposite remains rough and loud. This leafy enclave on the hill above the Vltava is arguably the city's finest summer beer garden. A local crowd gathers under the chestnut trees for beer in plastic cups late into the evening, every evening.

Výletná

Letenské sady 32, Prague 7 (no phone). Metro Hradčanská/tram 1, 15, 25, 26. **Open** 11-1am daily. **No credit cards. Map** p312 C3.

Situated just off the tennis courts in Letná park, this rustic little pub serves bargain barbecue fare on its terrace by summer and often gets taken over for parties and, at press time, literary slams were a happening Monday night ritual (*see p29*).

Smíchov

Kavárna v sedmém nebi

Zborovská 68, Prague 5 (257 318 110). Tram 6, 9, 12, 22. **Open** 10-1am Mon-Fri; 2pm-1am Sat, Sun. **No credit cards.**

A peaceful, arty café-bar, with a whimsical loft from which to spy on those in the comfy junk-shop chairs below. This meeting place for the local film community is half work of sculpture, half living room. The menu is limited to coffee and tea, along with *bábovka*, a Czech cake, *bundt*, toasted sandwiches and crisps.

U Buldoka

Preslova 1, Prague 5 (257 329 154). Metro Anděl/tram 6, 9. **Open** 11am-midnight Mon-Thur; 11-1am Fri; noon-midnight Sat; noon-11pm Sun. **No credit cards.**

At once old-world and modern, At the Bulldog is one of the last classic pubs in this district. Well-tapped Staropramen beer and excellent traditional grub go with an international sensibility, quick service and a cool dance club below deck (*see p228*). All-day specials of *halušky* (Slovak gnocchi with bacon) and *guláš* soup go with the light and dark beer, plus a nice collection of Czech herbal liqueurs at the bar.

Vinohrady

James Bond Café

Polská 7, Prague 2 (222 733 871/www.jamesbondcafe.cz). Metro Jiřího z Poděbrad/tram 11. **Open** 6pm-2am daily. **No credit cards.**

A license to kill seems to be sufficient for the flow of young style-conscious Czechs who gather about the retro-cool furnishings, monster fish tanks, cocktail bar and terrace. The soundtrack doesn't always match, but overall it delivers the bullet as promised.

Kaaba

Mánesova 20, Prague 2 (222 254 021). Tram 11. **Open** 8am-10pm Mon-Sat; 11am-10pm Sun. **No credit cards.**

Wacky furnishings from '60s and '70s communist kitsch, all done over in pastel colours, make for a groovy environment with great street windows. Coffees and cocktails don't quite live up to the look, but an easygoing art crowd doesn't seem to mind.

Medúza

Belgická 17, Prague 2 (222 515 107/www.volny.cz/cafe_meduza). Metro Náměstí Míru/tram 4, 22, 34. **Open** 11am-1am Mon-Fri; noon-1am Sat, Sun. **No credit cards. Map** p311 M9.

This beloved women-run café is a peaceful, classy, threadbare kind of place. Good coffee, Czech liqueurs and a limited menu of snacks go with the odd furniture, antique mirrors and faded photos on the walls, complemented by classical music or old Czech chansons playing in the background. A great place to chill.

První Prag Country Saloon Amerika

Korunní 101, Prague 2 (224 256 131). Metro Náměstí Míru/tram 16. **Open** 11am-11pm Mon; 11am-midnight Tue-Fri; 5pm-midnight Sat; 6-11pm Sun. **No credit cards. Map** p313 B3.

Head 'em up, move 'em out! Live Czech country-and-western bands – must be seen to be believed – fiddle nightly. Would-be cowboys and their gals crowd into the hardwood seating, tuck into steaks and admire the animal skins on the walls. The hardcore but incredibly friendly crowd here risked jail under the old regime for collecting Americana. *See also p221.*

Žižkov

Akropolis

Kubelíkova 27, Prague 3 (296 330 911). Metro Jiřího z Poděbrad/tram 11. **Open** 11.30-1am daily. **No credit cards. Map** p313 B2.

Still the most popular bar in the district for the post-1989 generation, the Akropolis is a longtime Žižkov institution of drinking, indie music concerts and networking for arty types. It has four separate pubs on site, each with its own crowd and vibe. The street-level Akropolis restaurant serves cheap and decent food with the passable beer (*see p142*); the Kaaba Café is a small, well-lit place to meet up and get a

Shooters

The *panák* – or 'little clown', as shots are known – is a serious business in the Czech drinking world. If you'll take a shot with someone and match them one for one all night, you're to be trusted and will have a lifelong friend. That is, if they remember who you are the next day.

Becherovka, a ubiquitous, sweetish, yellow herbal liqueur from Karlovy Vary, is drunk straight or cut with tonic, in which case it's known as *beton* – 'concrete'. Fernet, a bitter local liqueur inspired by Fernet-Branca, goes better with beer. This too can be lightened with tonic water to create a *Bavorské pivo*, or 'Bavarian beer' – which, of course, has no beer in it and is unknown in Bavaria. The cheapest ticket to oblivion, and thus favoured by local drunks, is *Tuzemský* rum, made from beets. With sugar, hot water and a slice of lemon it actually makes a good warming grog in winter. *Borovička* is a juniper brandy, more Slovak than Czech and not unlike Dutch Jenever, while *Slivovice* (plum brandy), if not home-made, is smooth and goes down a treat.

Absinth, at a staggering 70 proof, has long been banned in most countries. It's a wormwood distillate but contains a slightly smaller (and allegedly less brain-damaging) percentage of wood alcohol than the version that once pickled the best minds of Paris. It's a translucent green liquid that tastes much like alcoholic shampoo.

The proper ritual is to soak a spoonful of sugar with absinth then set the sugar alight in the spoon to caramelise it. When the fire goes out, dump the spoonful back into the glass and stir. Then hang on to your socks.

caffeine fix; the Divadelní Bar is a hot, intense vortex of DJ action and surreal woodcarvings; the Malá Scena, on the other hand, is a red-washed chill-out space with a post-industrial look and battered tables.

Blind Eye

Vlkova 26, Prague 3 (no phone). Metro Jiřího z Poděbrad/tram 11. **Open** 10-5am daily. **No credit cards. Map** p309 2B.

A late-night hideout for the district's sleep-starved bohemians of all nationalities, the open but unfinished Blind Eye, offers rambling conversations at the wavy iron-top bar, beer at a booth table or a cult movie of your choice from its built-in video rental.

Le Clan

Balbínova 23, Prague 3 (736 673 894). Metro Muzeum/tram 11. **Open** 8pm-3am Mon-Fri, Sun; 8pm-4am Sat. **No credit cards. Map** p313 2A.

Impossible to spot if you don't know it's here, this dim hideaway offers plush sofas, cocktails, house music and the occasional go-go dancer. Le Clan has become a mecca for local Francophile clubbers.

Clown & Bard

Bořivojova 102, Prague 3 (222 716 453/ www.clownandbard.com). Metro Jiřího z Poděbrad/ tram 5, 9, 26. **Open** 5pm-midnight daily. **No credit cards. Map** p313 B2.

A lively spot for a bottled Budvar, cheap shots or a chess game, the Clown & Bard is about as entertaining as hostel bars get (for information on the hostel, *see p56*). And, actually, that can be quite entertaining if you come on a night when one of the undiscovered bands that regularly plays here is any good.

Hapu

Orlická 8, Prague 3 (no phone). Metro Flora/tram 11, 16, 26, 51, 58. **Open** 6pm-2am Mon-Sat. **No credit cards. Map** p313 C2/3.

Essentially a living room with great cocktails, this tattered Žižkov drinking hole was opened by a couple who imagined their ideal bar, then created it for their friends. Fresh mint leaves adorn the tasty rum Mojito; rum, cream, chocolate and yet more mint goes into the house special, *horká novinka*, or 'hot news'. Shooters range from 40-70 Kč.

Park Café

Riegrovy sady, Prague 3 (222 717 247). Metro Muzeum/tram 11. **Open** 11am-midnight daily. **No credit cards. Map** p313 B2.

Kids, dogs, beer and sunshine. Park Café is the biggest outdoor venue in the east end of central Prague, attracting people from three adjoining neighbourhoods, who are drawn by battered benches, the pleasant shade of chestnut trees and cheap Krušovice by the half-litre. Dogs run yapping between the tables, bands take to the stage on weekends and there are grassy knolls all around for more private moments.

Potrefená husa

Vinohradská 104, Prague 3 (267 310 360). Metro Jiřího z Poděbrad/tram 11. **Open** 11.30-1am daily. **Credit** AmEx, MC, V. **Map** p313 E2.

The kind of place that you'd find in every suburb of a Western city, The Wounded Goose is a runaway success in Prague. It offers a better menu and service than a lot of Prague restaurants – but that's not terribly difficult. Seems enough, though, for it to be the new-generation, stylish, almost-too-clean pub of the 21st century. Part of a national chain, it's nearly always packed with young professionals sipping Velvet beer and noshing on chicken wings and ribs while taking in cable TV sports.

Other locations: Kolínská 9, Prague 3 (267 310 360); Bílkova 5, Prague 1 (222 326 626).

Shakespeare & Sons

Krymská 12, Prague 10 (271 740 839/ www.shakes.cz). Metro Náměstí Míru/tram 4, 22. **Open** noon-midnight daily. **Credit** MC, V.

Aside from the best selection of second-hand English-language books in town, this cosy café-bar is a gathering point for readings, jazz and a colourful cast of literati. Out of the way, but worth the trip, with delectable Bernard beer and proper coffee.

U Houdků

Bořivojova 110, Prague 3 (222 711 239). Metro Jiřího z Poděbrad/tram 11. **Open** 11am-11pm daily. **No credit cards. Map** p313 B2/C2.

Just a cheap, neighbourhood pub untouched by time, where you can sit out in the garden behind and sip away in the sunshine. It's also a blast of South Bohemia: Eggenberg and Budvar, hearty brews from the Český Krumlov area, are served both light and dark, alongside mounds of typical Czech pub grub for pocket change. Every student and worker in the district seems hooked.

U Sadu

Škroupovo náměstí 5, Prague 3 (222 727 072). Metro Jiřího z Poděbrad/11 tram. **Open** 10-2am daily. **No credit cards. Map** p313 B2.

This classic Czech pub-restaurant in the heart of old-style Žižkov is popular with students and holds its own against the hundreds of earthy pubs around. The chilli goulash, schnitzels and fried cheese are a marvellously unhealthy treat, the Pilsner and Gambrinus are well-tapped and service is thoroughly gruff. It doesn't get any more authentic than this. The kitchen is open late too, for Prague.

U vystřelenýho oka

U božích bojovníků 3, Prague 3 (222 540 465). Metro Florenc, then bus 135 or 207. **Open** 4.30pm-1am Mon-Sat. **No credit cards. Map** p313 C1.

Thoroughly surreal. The Shot-Out Eye sits beneath the ominous giant statue of General Jan Žižka, the renowned warrior whose battle injury inspired the gory name. Žižkov has more pubs than any other area of Prague, but this is one of the best, at least for fans of garage rock and weird art. A three-level outdoor beer garden serves bargain-basement Měšťan, while the taps indoors flow non-stop to a soundtrack of local anarcho-rockers Psí Vojáci and a backdrop of grotesque paintings by the artist Martin Velíšek.

Shops & Services

Once a shopper's nightmare, Prague has cottoned on to supply and demand.

In 1998 a Malá Strana shop assistant was heard discouraging a customer from buying an item. 'It's the last one,' she told the shopper. 'If you buy it, we'll have to order more.'

While such communism-inspired reluctance is still not unheard of in Prague's shops, smiles now greet shoppers as often as frowns. Increasingly, convenience is the order of the day. Credit and debit cards are more commonly accepted and consumers no longer need to leave work early to get their shopping done before the stores close.

The new wave of commercialism is led by the capital's fleet of shopping malls (*see p158*). The vanguard of Western-style consumption, these juggernauts stay open well into the evening Monday through Sunday and pause only briefly to observe major holidays. They have parking for everyone's new cars and, worryingly, some of the coolest bars in town.

The challenge for the Czech retail sector during the first ten years after the collapse of communism was finding a way to supply the much-desired Western goods to locals at a price they could afford. The average Czech salary still hovers around 15,000 Kč (about 457) a month. Clothing merchants like C&A, Kenvelo and Mango have found success marketing stylish, inexpensive clothing of reasonable quality. All the major grocery stores are multinationals now, with volume giving them leverage over prices, sounding a death knell for the *potraviny*, the family-run cornershop, but generally delighting consumers. Bargain shops abound, offering factory seconds and overruns. Even such luxury retailers as Louis Vuitton, Hugo Boss and Versace are increasing their presence on the market but are generally so devoid of shoppers that one wonders how they stay in business.

Happily, while the practical side of shopping has improved greatly, hunting for treasure is still an arcane business, accomplished by trawling the markets, diving down narrow alleys or drifting far from the centre to uncover First Republic loot or communist-era booty. The city centre is thick with high-quality Czech crystal, glass and porcelain, and jewellery of local amber and garnet. Browsing street-market stalls can reward you with unique grandmother-made lace or bizarre imported kitsch, but shoppers should be aware that street markets are plagued with disreputable sellers of bootleg CDs, liquor and sport clothes knock-offs.

Designer clothes shops are less common but worth seeking out for truly original fashions and high-quality garments (*see p167* **Bad Bohemia: Faux Pas**).

Shop clerks will ask '*Máte přání*' ('Do you have a wish?') when you walk into a shop and may ask '*Ještě něco?*' ('Anything else?) or '*Všechno?*' ('Is that all?') when they ring up your purchase. Ask '*Kolik to stojí?*' to find out what something costs.

SHOPPING AREAS

Unless you get caught without film or overpriced bottled water, there's really no reason to shop in Hradčany. The prices of touristy goods are almost always in inverse relation to their distance from Prague Castle. Malá Strana is a good for marionettes, a porcelain holy infant and a few boutiques, but for the most part shopping is done on the Staré Město–Nové Město (Old Town–New Town) line. **Na příkopě** has the fashion shops, as does Pařížská, with its leafy pavement cafés. If it's a souvenir you seek, prowl **Michalská**,

The best Shops

For cheap 19th-century tomes
Antikvariát Galerie Můstek, **Antikvariát Kant** and **Antikvariát Pařížská** are worth the dust (for all, *see p164*).

For a cubist ashtray
Kubista (*see p162*) is a gallery worth visiting in its own right.

For fresh halibut
La Bretagne (*see p171*) trucks it in.

For a guilt offering
Charita Florentinum (*see p174*) does it with spirit.

For raiding communist kitsch
Papírnictví Týnská Ulička (*see p180*), the paper shop time forgot.

For wild Czech togs
Devátá vlna (*see p166*) and **Mýrnyx Týrnyx** (*see p165*) go their own way.

Železná and other streets radiating from Old Town Square. **Pařížská** has posh luxury goods and not-always-pricey jewellery. Antique hounds will do well to explore **Karlín** and **Holešovice**, but out-of-print books (and some surprisingly affordable new ones) are still to be found from **Celetná** to **Malá Štupartská** and in **Týn**, known as Ungelt Square.

Most neighbourhoods hold some sort of rarity, like **Shalamar** (*see p173*) in Žižkov for those curry cravings or **Shakespeare & Sons** (*see p156*) in Vršovice for a great selection of second-hand English-language books. Vinohrady has the mega-shopping and entertainment centre **Palác Flóra** (*see below*), Smíchov has its counterpart, **Nový Smíchov Centrum** (*see below*), and far-flung satellites like Letňany and Zličín have mega-malls nearly as large as historic Prague itself. These, for better or worse, are where you'll find most under-40 Praguers.

One-stop shopping

Department stores

Kotva

Náměstí Republiky 8, Staré Město, Prague 1 (224 801 111). Metro Náměstí Republiky/tram 5, 8, 14. **Open** *Department store* 9am-8pm Mon-Fri; 10am-7pm Sat; 10am-6pm Sun. *Supermarket* 7am-8pm Mon-Fri; 9am-6pm Sat; 10am-7pm Sun. **Credit** AmEx, MC, V. **Map** p309 K3.

Generally quite ugly but also well-stocked. Work your way up past the glossy cosmetics stalls; a pharmacy; a bakery; the bed linen, fashion, sports gear and car accessories departments; and end up at the fairly naff furniture and lighting section.

Tesco

Národní třída 26, Nové Město, Prague 1 (222 003 111). Metro Můstek or Národní třída/tram 6, 9, 18, 21, 22, 23. **Open** *Department store* 8am-9pm Mon-Fri; 9am-8pm Sat; 10am-8pm Sun. *Supermarket* 7am-10pm Mon-Fri; 8am-8pm Sat; 9am-8pm Sun. **Credit** AmEx, MC, V. **Map** p308 H5.

This is what became of Máj, the pride of communist Czechoslovakia's retail industry. Soon after the revolution it was sold to American chain K-mart, which revamped the shop and sold it to Tesco in 1996. It now has a nice mix of Czech and Western products, and a popular supermarket with a good bakery. The street-level off-licence is well-stocked.

Malls

Prague's first malls were forced to employ marketing teams to explain the concept to Czechs. They also sold cheap potatoes in the basement to bring in the crowds. Czech teens have since worked out that they should spend Saturdays here, and Czechs of all ages are firmly on board with the idea of one-stop shopping as the malls get more and more modern. The city's latest ventures are the **Nový Smíchov Centrum** and **Palác Flora** (for both, *see below*).

Černá růže

Na příkopě 12, Nové Město, Prague 1 (221 014 111). Metro Můstek/tram 3, 9, 14, 24. **Open** 10am-8pm Mon-Fri; 10am-7pm Sat; 11am-7pm Sun. **Credit** AmEx, MC, V. **Map** p309 K4.

An easily overlooked entrance next to McDonald's leads from a main pedestrian drag into this rather sterile three-level complex full of fashion boutiques, an Adidas store, other shoe shops, a few designer furniture outlets and some wine shops.

Dětský dům

Na Příkopě 15, Staré Město, Prague 1 (272 142 401). Metro Můstek/tram 3, 9, 14, 24. **Open** 9am-8pm Mon-Sat; 10am-8pm Sun. **Credit** AmEx, MC, V. **Map** p309 K4.

Once a communist centre for kids' clothing, the Children's House has reopened with a thoroughly capitalist 21st-century attitude. Instead of the aisles of matching grey jumpers of the past, it's now packed with shops such as Bim Bam Bum, stocking Ralph Lauren for tykes. The mall also features occasional puppet shows and the odd fashion shop for Mum. At press time, the whole place was under reconstruction.

Myslbek Centre

Na Příkopě 19-21, Staré Město, Prague 1 (224 239 550). Metro Můstek/tram 3, 9, 14, 24. **Open** 8.30am-8.30pm Mon-Sat; 9.30am-8.30pm Sun. **Credit** AmEx, MC, V. **Map** p309 K4.

Familiar shops like Calvin Klein Jeans, Marks & Spencer, Next, Tie Rack, Mothercare, Kookai and Vision Express fill this busy central mall. There's a café upstairs, where you can refuel on cappuccino, fresh juices and desserts. For a lesson in insensitive modern architecture, see how the back of the mall utterly fails to relate to the surrounding Ovocný Square. Most shops follow the above hours.

Nový Smíchov Centrum

Plzeňská 8, Smíchov, Prague 5 (257 284 111). Metro Anděl/tram 4, 6, 7, 9, 10, 14. **Open** 7am-midnight daily. **Credit** AmEx, MC, V.

This busy, spacious mall in the rapidly redeveloping Anděl area features loads of retail shops, including H&M, Clinique and Sephora. You can also spend your time and money at a huge game arcade, a Carrefour supermarket (*see p173*) and a food court. Live entertainment is often part of the experience.

Palác Flóra

Vinohradská 149, Vinohrady, Prague 3 (255 741 700/www.palacflora.cz). Metro Flóra/tram 5, 10, 11, 16. **Open** 10am-midnight daily. **Credit** AmEx, MC, V. **Map** p313 D2.

The shiny and new **Palác Flóra** mall.

A·R·Z·E·N·A·L
Cross Culture Junction Asian Gourmet Cuisine
conceived and designed by the renowned architect and artist Bořek Šípek, combines a top class design, fashion and styles meet. ARZENAL allows every quest to appreciate a full scope of Bořek Šípek´s genius - architecture, glass and furniture design - while putting it´s functionality to test sampling Thai gourmet food.
ARZENAL, a.s.
Valentinská 11/56
Praha 1
open daily 10 - 24
Tel.: 224 814 099, Fax: 224 810 722, galerie@arzenal.cz, www.arzenal.cz

BIG BEN BOOKSHOP
The Biggest selection of english books in town
▪ fiction ▪ travel guides ▪ poetry
▪ drama ▪ children's books ▪ non fiction
... and more
BIG BEN BOOKSHOP
Malá Štupartská 5 • 110 00 Prague 1
tel.: 224 826 565 • fax: 224 826 559
e-mail: books@bigbenbookshop.com
OPENING HOURS
Mon – Fri 9 – 18:30
Sat – Sun 10 – 17

Located outside the city centre, but only a short metro ride away, Prague's newest mall is so ultra-modern and upscale that it's hard to remember you're still in Prague. Something for everyone here, with trendy shops for teens; big-name label stores like Guess Jeans and Puma; a chemist; supermarket; dry-cleaners; and gift-wrapping service, to mention but a few. Edible offerings range from fast-food chains to surprisingly appealing outside-facing cafés and full-service restaurants. The mall is also the home of Prague's IMAX theatre (*see p193*).

Slovanský Dům

Na Příkopě 22, Nové Město, Prague 1 (221 451 400/information 2421 1295/www.slovanskydum.cz). Metro Můstek/tram 3, 9, 14, 24. **Open** 10am-8pm daily. **Map** p309 K4.

The newest addition to this central strip of shopping centres, housing fashion shops like Mexx and Escada Sport. Decent Italian and sushi restaurants can be found, but the major draw is the multiplex cinema.

Markets

In general Prague's outdoor markets are mostly fruit and veg affairs, although Christmas and Easter markets spring up seasonally along the main tourist routes. If you catch one of the **Christmas markets** in Old Town Square, Václavské náměstí or Náměstí Republiky, warm yourself with a nice glass of steaming mulled wine – *svařené víno* or *svařák*.

Havelský Market

Havelská, Nové Město, Prague 1 (no phone). Metro Můstek or Národní třída/tram 6, 9, 18, 22. **Open** 7.30am-6pm Mon-Fri; 8.30am-6pm Sat, Sun. **No credit cards**. **Map** p308 J4.

Officially known as Staré Město Market but universally referred to by its location, this is Prague's best market for greens and a taste of daily Bohemian life. Fresh fruit and vegetables are crammed alongside wooden toys, puppets, tourist trinkets and bad art. Good for gifts, and flowers are a tremendous bargain. Visit in the morning before the trinket hawkers take over three-quarters of the stalls. Caution: Havelská is a prime pickpocket hunting-ground.

Market at the Fountain

Spálená 30, Nové Město, Prague 1 (no phone). Metro Národní třída/tram 6, 9, 18, 22. **Open** 7.30am-7pm daily. **No credit cards**. **Map** p308 H5.

Excellent fruit and vegetable market just outside Tesco (*see p158*), with some of the nicest-looking produce in the city – usually cheap too. There is a wide variety of roasted nuts for sale here – the perfect snack to take with you on a trek around the city.

Antiques

There are dozens of antiques shops in Prague, but there are also numerous junk shops, selling everything from old irons and typewriters to

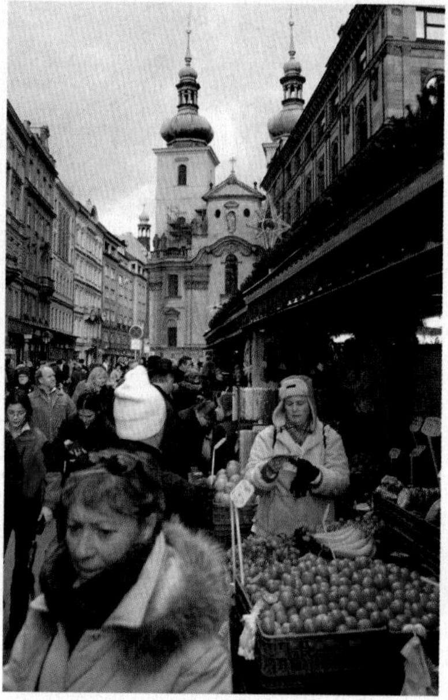

Get your five a day at **Havelský Market**.

prints by Alfons Mucha. If an antiques shop is on a main tourist route, you can be fairly sure that the prices are aimed at foreigners. For cheaper and more unusual items, seek out a bazaar. Some are listed here, but more can be found in the *Zlâté stránky* (Yellow Pages) – look for the index in English at the back.

Antique

Kaprova 12, Staré Město, Prague 1 (222 329 003). Metro Staroměstská/tram 17, 18. **Open** 10am-7pm Mon-Sat; 10am-6pm Sun. **Credit** AmEx, MC, V. **Map** p308 G3.

Expensive but rewarding, specialising in glass, jewellery, paintings and religious icons. Check out the antique art-deco watches – stylish and affordable.

Antique Ahasver

Prokopská 3, Malá Strana, Prague 1 (257 531 404). Metro Malostranská/tram 12, 18, 22, 23. **Open** 11am-6pm Tue-Sun. **Credit** MC, V. **Map** p307 E4.

Antique formal gowns, traditional folk clothing, linens, mother-of-pearl hairpins, beaded purses, brooches and trays of charming oddments. The English-speaking sales assistants are always ready to supply a story and help you decide.

Art Deco

Michalská 21, Staré Město, Prague 1 (224 223 076). Metro Staroměstská or Národní třída/ tram 6, 9, 17, 18, 22, 23. **Open** 2-7pm Mon-Fri. **Credit** AmEx, MC, V. **Map** p308 H4.

Hamparadi Antik Bazar – eclectic, to say the least.

The remains of a golden era, when Prague was the fashion centre of Eastern Europe. Vintage 1920s-50s clothes and costume jewellery at fair prices.

Bric a Brac

Týnská 7, Staré Město, Prague 1 (224 813 240). Metro Staroměstská or Náměstí Republiky/tram 5, 8, 14, 17, 18. **Open** 10am-6pm daily. **Credit** AmEx, MC, V. **Map** p308 J3.

A comprehensive collection of antiques that could keep you browsing for hours through everything from old movie cameras to leather coats and exquisite jewelled purses. Bric a Brac also owns a tiny shop around the corner, stocked with every kind of timepiece imaginable.

Hamparadi Antik Bazar

Pštrossova 22, Nové Město, Prague 2 (224 931 162). Metro Národní třída/tram 6, 9, 18, 21, 22, 23. **Open** 10.30am-6pm daily. **No credit cards. Map** p310 G7.

The toys, comic figurines and old advertisements scattered throughout this antique bazaar give it a mood of fond nostalgia. Plenty of the usual porcelain and glass, along with quirky treasures such as a stage make-up chest straight from *Vaudeville*.

Jan Huněk Starožitnosti

Pařížská 1, Staré Město, Prague 1 (222 325 122). Metro Staroměstská/tram 17, 18. **Open** 10am-6pm daily. **Credit** AmEx, MC, V. **Map** p308 H3.

Specialising in exquisite and expensive Czech porcelain and glass from the 18th century to the 1930s. Be sure to check out their selection of gorgeous red-coloured crystal pieces.

Kubista

Dům u Černý Matky Boží, Celetná 34, Staré Město, Prague 1 (224 236 378/www.kubista.cz). Metro Námestí Republiky/tram 5, 8, 14. **Open** 10am-6pm daily. **Credit** MC, V. **Map** p309 K3.

Original cubist porcelain and furniture, lovingly wrought re-creations and art books from the museum shop of the National Gallery's excellent museum of cubism at the House of the Black Madonna (*see p109*). Pricey, but very Prague and utterly unique.

Military Antique Army Shop

Křemencova 7, Nové Město, Prague 1 (224 930 952/mobile 603 210381). Metro Národní třída/tram 6, 9, 18, 21, 22, 23. **Open** 11am-5pm Mon-Fri. **Credit** AmEx, MC, V. **Map** p310 H6/7.

The Military Antique Army Shop stocks just about everything you'd need to re-enact the Normandy landings. World War II flyers' headgear, goggles, bayonets, swords, badges and lots of those ever-so-handy ammo boxes. The owner tends to close up at random hours, so it's advisable to call in advance and negotiate the time of your visit.

Modernista

Konviktská 5, Staré Město, Prague 1 (222 220 113/www.modernista.cz). Metro Můstek or Národní třída/tram 6, 9, 18, 21, 22, 23. **Open** 2-6pm Mon-Fri; 11am-4pm Sat. **Credit** AmEx, MC, V. **Map** p308 G5.

Specialist collectors of Czech cubist, art-deco, functionalist and other exquisite modernist pieces, this engaging shop features restored desk chairs and armoires from the early to mid-20th century. It also sells reproductions of works by leading Czech architects and designers. More (or less) portable acquisitions run from gleaming chrome lamps to huge prints of communist propaganda.

Bookshops & newsagents

English-language books in Prague are often reasonably priced by Western standards, if outrageously priced by local standards. Most bookshops listed here can order in new books, but there's often a wait of three to five weeks.

Anagram Bookshop

Týn 4, Staré Město, Prague 1 (224 895 737/ www.anagram.cz). Metro Náměstí Republiky/ tram 5, 8, 14. **Open** 10am-8pm Mon-Sat; 10am-7pm Sun. **Credit** DC, MC, V. **Map** p308 J3.

This outlet has, in addition to a wide selection of topical books on Prague and Central Europe, a great second-hand English-language rack, with an emphasis on philosophy, self-help and alternative medicine – everything that's generally hard to find in Prague.

Big Ben Bookshop

Malá Štupartská 5, Staré Město, Prague 1 (224 826 565/www.bigbenbookshop.com). Metro Náměstí Republiky/tram 5, 8, 14. **Open** 9am-6.30pm Mon-Fri; 10am-5pm Sat; noon-5pm Sun. **Credit** AmEx, MC, V. **Map** p308 J3.

If you've used up all your reading material, this welcoming establishment has the standard books on Prague, several shelves of bestsellers, lots of English-language newspapers and magazines, plus the best children's books in English around. The staff knows its stock and writers better than most.

The Globe Bookstore & Coffeehouse

Pštrossova 6, Nové Město, Prague 2 (224 916 264). Metro Národní třída/tram 6, 9, 18, 21, 22, 23. **Open** 10am-midnight daily. **Credit** AmEx, MC, V. **Map** p310 G7.

One of the most famous bookstores in the world, this expat literary heart is in a multi-level, hardwired space in Nové Město. Fine second-hand paperbacks still line the walls, and it now has internet terminals and a sleek balcony. The list of international authors doing readings is star-studded, and there are regular live music performances. Basic salads, soups and snacks are also served (*see p144*).

Knihkupectví U Černé Matky Boží

Celetná 34, Nové Město, Prague 1 (224 222 349). Metro Náměstí Republiky/tram 5, 8, 14. **Open** *Jan-Easter, Oct-Dec* 9.30am-7pm Mon-Fri; 10am-6pm Sat. *Easter-Sept* 9.30am-7pm Mon-Fri; 10am-6pm Sat; 10am-6pm Sun. **Credit** AmEx, MC, V. **Map** p309 K3.

It's worth tracking down this arty bookshop just to gaze at the building's wonderful cubist exterior. The bookshop itself is good for gift-hunting, with hundreds of maps, art prints, T-shirts, translated Czech novels, coffee-table books and calendars.

Trafika Můstek

Václavské náměstí, Nové Město, Prague 1 (no phone). Metro Můstek/tram 3, 9, 14, 24. **Open** 8am-10pm daily. **No credit cards. Map** p308 J5.

The two green magazine stands at the bottom of Wenceslas Square stock everything from *Forbes* to *Film Threat*. If you can't find a Western periodical here, you won't find it in Prague.

Buy into the Prague literary tradition at **Big Ben Bookshop**.

Old books & prints

Prague's second-hand bookshops are known as *antikvariáty*. These are the places for one-of-a-kind Prague souvenirs, like an old communist coffee-table book or a dirt-cheap print by an unknown Czech artist. *Antikvariáty* are also good for second-hand novels in English.

Antikvariát Galerie Můstek

Národní 40, Nové Město, Prague 1 (224 949 587). Metro Národní třída/tram 6, 9, 18, 21, 22, 23. **Open** 10am-7pm Mon-Fri; noon-4pm Sat; 2-6pm Sun. **Credit** AmEx, MC, V. **Map** p308 H5/J5.

A discriminating *antikvariát* with fine antiquarian books (19th-century natural history especially) and a reliable stock of major works on Czech art.

Antikvariát Kant

Opatovická 26, Nové Město, Prague 1 (224 934 219/www.antik-kant.cz). Metro Národní třída/ tram 6, 9, 18, 21, 22, 23. **Open** 10am-6pm Mon-Fri; 10am-3pm Sat. **Credit** AmEx, MC, V. **Map** p310 G6/H6.

An eclectic mix of prints and dust-encrusted tomes. There's an impressive selection of second-hand titles in English, from *Jaws* to Germaine Greer. You may bump into one of the last Czech aristocrats here, Sir Schwarzenberg; he likes to hang out and chat with other customers.

Antikvariát Pařížská

Pařížská 8, Staré Město, Prague 1 (222 321 442). Metro Staroměstská/tram 17, 18. **Open** 10am-7pm Mon-Fri; 10am-6pm Sat, Sun. **Credit** AmEx, MC, V. **Map** p308 H3.

This welcoming shop is filled from floor to ceiling with gorgeous prints and maps dating from the 16th to 19th centuries, giving it the feel of a venerable library. You can also find an array of antique stamps, postcards and books, plus a staff that's ready to help.

Computers

HSH Computer

Nádražní 42, Smíchov, Prague 5 (257 310 910/ fax 257 310 911/www.hsh.cz). Metro Muzeum/ tram 11. **Open** 9am-6pm Mon-Fri. **Credit** MC, V.

In addition to the sales and service of Compaq, HP, IBM and Toshiba computers, this shop rents notebooks, printers and video cameras.

Service centre: Gorazdova 5, Nové Město, Prague 2 (224 912 163).

Other locations: Kotva, Náměstí Republiky 8, Staré Město, Prague 1 (224 801 337); Bílá labuň, Na poříčí 23, Prague 1 (222 320 581).

MacSource

Bělehradská 2, Vinohrady, Prague 2 (222 515 455/fax 222 515 456/www.macsource.cz). Metro IP Pavlova/tram 6, 11. **Open** 9am-6pm Mon-Fri. **Credit** AmEx, MC, V. **Map** p311 M9.

The local leader in Mac sales and repairs, MacSource services both Mac and PC systems for such institutions as Radio Free Europe. It also carries a range of hardware, software and other electronics.

Cosmetics & perfumes

In addition to the places listed below, most of the department stores above have big-name cosmetic booths on their ground floors.

Body Basics

Myslbek Centre, Na Příkopě 19-21, Staré Město, Prague 1 (224 236 800). Metro Můstek/tram 3, 9, 14, 24. **Open** 9am-8pm Mon-Sat; 10am-19pm Sun. **Credit** AmEx, MC, V. **Map** p309 K4.

This Body Shop lookalike has affordable, pleasant-smelling cosmetics that are guaranteed not to have been tested on animals.

Other Locations: Marriott, V Celnici 10, Nové Město, Prague 1 (228 818 55); Pavilon, Vinohradská 50, Vinohrady, Prague 2 (222 097 105). Ruzyně Airport, Ruzyně, Prague 6 (220 113 595); Nový Smíchov Centrum, Plzeňská 8, Smíchov, Prague 5 (257 322 947).

Dr Stuart's Botanicus

Týskný Dvůr 3, Staré Město, Prague 1 (224 895 446/www.botanicus.cz). Metro Náměstí Republiky/tram 5, 8,14, 26. **Open** 10am-8pm daily. **Credit** AmEx, MC, V. **Map** p308 J3.

Botanicus is all-Czech, earthy cosmetics shop. You'll find stacks of soaps, shampoos, body lotions and creams infused with herbs and other natural ingredients, which all come lovingly wrapped in brown paper once you've made your purchase.

Other locations: Lucerna, Štěpánská 61, Nové Město, Prague 1 (224 221 927); Michalská 2, Staré Město, Prague 1 (224 212 977); Veselská 663, Letňany, Prague 9 (284 014 369); Centrum Černý Most, Chlumecká, Prague 9 (281 917 726).

Lush

Kaprova 13, Staré Město, Prague 1 (603 164 362). Metro Staroměstská/tram 17, 18. **Open** 10am-7pm Mon-Sat; 2-6pm Sun. **Credit** AmEx, MC, V. **Map** p308 G3.

It seems nowhere can escape the overwhelming aromas that waft from the doors of this British chain. Prague's outlet of Lush is no different, boasting the usual counter of 'fresh, handmade cosmetics', from luxurious soaps and hair care to bath products, each made of natural ingredients.

Dry-cleaners & laundrettes

All the laundrettes in the city charge roughly the same for washing and drying, so your choice chiefly depends on location.

CleanTouch

Dlouhá 20, Staré Město, Prague 1 (224 819 257). Metro Náměstí Republiky/tram 5, 8, 14, 26. **Open** 8am-7pm Mon-Sat. **No credit cards. Map** p311 K7.

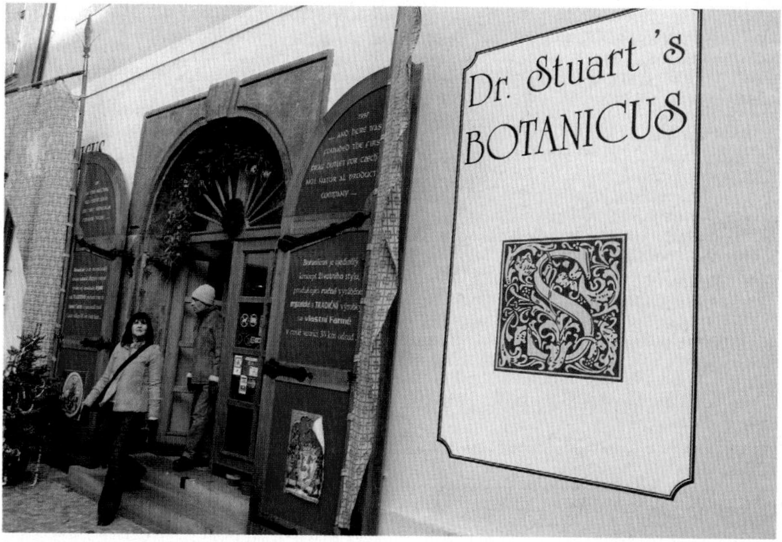

Scrub up with natural cosmetics from sweet-smelling **Botanicus**. *See p164.*

CleanTouch offers dry-cleaning at reasonable prices with a quick turnaround in modern surroundings. **Other locations**: Na Rybníčku 1329, Vinohrady, Prague 2 (296 368 500); Supermarket Delvita, Jeremiášova 7A, Stodůlky, Prague 5 (5162 6371).

Prague Laundromat

Korunní 14, Vinohrady, Prague 2 (222 510 180/www.volny.cz/laundromat). Metro Náměstí Míru/tram 4, 10, 16, 22, 23. **Open** 8am-8pm daily. **No credit cards. Map** p313 A3.

The self-proclaimed 'first internet-laundromat in Europe' will do everything your laundry needs. The English-speaking staff provides service washes andcan help you with self-service washes. There's also dry-cleaning, plus internet access, beer and coffee in spotless surroundings.

Electronics

Tesco (*see p158*) stocks most of the basic electronic equipment that you might want. But, if you need something special, you may have to trek out to **Electro World**, all the way out in Zličín.

Datart

Národní 60, Prague 1 (221 105 311/fax 221 105 312/www.datart.cz). Metro Národní třída/tram 6, 18, 19, 22, 23. **Open** 9am-8pm daily. **Credit** AmEx, MC, V. **Map** p308 H5/J5.

This electronics retailer advertises 'lowest prices' and offers extended warranties on the washing machines, kitchen appliances, home entertainment systems, computers and everything else it sells.

Electro World

Řevnická 1, Zličín, Prague 5 (235 002 800). Metro Zličín. **Open** 9am-9pm daily. **Credit** MC, V.

Bright, modern supermarket owned by the UK's Dixons and stocking everything from computers to sleek household appliances, with something appealing usually on sale. Digital cameras at fair prices too. **Other locations**: Česlice, Obchodní 117, Prague Česlice (267 227 700); Černý Most, Chlumecká 1531, Prague 9 (281 028 555).

Fashion

Budget

Mýrnyx Týrnyx

Saská ulička, Malá Strana, Prague 1 (257 321 111/www.myrnyxtyrnyx.com). Metro Malostranská/tram 12, 18, 22, 23. **Open** 11am-7pm Mon-Sat. **No credit cards. Map** p307 E3.

Prague's hippest second-hand fashion shop doesn't waste any of its closet-sized space on boring run-of-the-mill togs. You'll find Day-Glo 1960s vinyl hangs alongside feather boas and homburg hats. Owner Mia Květná also buys pieces from indie Czech designers and runs an 'alternative models agency' out of the shop, which does casting for commercials shooting in Prague.

Šatna

Konviktská 13, Staré Město, Prague 1 (no phone). Metro Národní třída/tram 6, 9, 18, 21, 22, 23. **Open** 11am-7pm Mon-Fri; 11am-6pm Sat. **No credit cards. Map** p308 G5/H5.

A friendly second-hand shop run by a North American proprietor with taste – this shop actually wouldn't feel out of place in Chicago or Berkeley. Piles of jeans abound, and be sure to check out the leather jackets and coats.

Senior Bazar

Senovážné náměstí 18, Nové Město, Prague 1 (224 235 068). Metro Náměstí Republiky/tram 3, 5, 9, 14, 24, 26. **Open** 9am-5pm Mon-Thur. **No credit cards. Map** p309 L4.

A Prague institution and one of the best second-hand clothes shops in the city, Senior Bazar gets its stock straight from Prague's most stylish citizens – that's the octogenarians. Pick up a handmade 1950s summer dress or leather coat for peanuts. But get there early, as the *Elle* and *Cosmo* magazine girls who work nearby do a clean sweep during their lunch breaks.

Other locations: Karolíny Světlé 18, Staré Město, Prague 1 (222 333 555).

Children

Lapin House

Pařížská 3, Staré Město, Prague 1 (224 236 525). Metro Staroměstská/tram 17, 18. **Open** 10am-8pm Mon-Sat; 10am-6pm Sun. **Credit** AmEx, MC, V. **Map** p308 H3.

This French, luxury children's clothing chain offers high quality you will pay for dearly. The tiny gowns, rich with satin and lace, are heirloom-quality. More casual shoes and clothes for tots, from the basic (T-shirts) to the ridiculous (tiny, fringed suede skirts) are also on offer.

Teta Tramtárie

Jungmanova 28, Nové Město, Prague 1 (no phone/ www.tetatramtarie.cz). Metro Mustek or Narodni trida/tram 6, 9, 18, 21, 22, 23. **Open** 7.30am-8pm daily. **Credit** MC, V. **Map** p308 J5.

Teta Tramtárie is kid heaven in a city still learning to cater to them as valuable customers. This two-storey building comprises a toy shop, a children's bookshop, a miniature movie theatre continuously showing children's films and cartoons (some in English), a puppet theatre, two pizza restaurants and an ice-cream parlour with a large indoor jungle gym. *See also p187.*

Costume & formal dress hire

Every school and major workplace holds its own *ples*, or ball, sometime between November and April – there are annual balls for hunters, miners and Moravians alike. Attending one is an excellent inroad to old Prague tradition. If you're invited to a ball and have apparently forgotton your dressing up box, try the following for suitably fantastical attire. Be sure to reserve several days in advance and take your passport as proof of identity.

Barrandov Studio, Fundus

Kříženeckého náměstí 322, Barrandov, Prague 5 (267 072 210/www.barrandov.cz). Metro Smíchovské nádraží, then bus 246, 247, 248. **Open** 7am-3pm Mon-Fri. **No credit cards.**

Prague's main film studio rents everything you can imagine – from bear costumes to Prussian military uniforms – from its extensive wardrobe of over 240,000 costumes and accessories, including 9,000 wigs. None of this comes cheap. There's a fee of 600-1,000 Kč for a one- to seven-day hire, plus you'll need another 3,000-9,000 Kč for a deposit.

Designer

Prague was the fashion capital of Eastern Europe in the brief, shining period between the two world wars. In many ways Prague is still recovering from the communist regime's death knell to style, but the small and scattered local fashion scene is steadily expanding as more designers set up shop and residents earn more disposable income.

Devátá vlna

Národní 25, Nové Město, Prague 1 (221 085 207/ www.devatavlna.cz). Metro Můstek or Národní třída/tram 6, 9, 18, 21, 22, 23. **Open** 11am-7pm Mon-Fri, Sun; 10am-7pm Sat. **Credit** AmEx, MC, V. **Map** p308 H5.

Devátá vlna, or Ninth Wave, was founded in 1994 by three Czech twentysomething women and focuses on street- and clubwear for the young and hip. Amid the moderately priced jeans and over-sized trousers, T-shirts and breezy little sundresses are fun surprises, such as cartoon-covered bags and disco-queen gold lamé dresses. Devátá vlna's workshop also does custom orders.

Fashion Galerie No.14

Opatovická 14, Nové Město, Prague 1 (no phone). Metro Národní třída/tram 6, 9, 18, 22. **Open** noon-7pm Mon-Sat. **Credit** AmEx, MC, V. **Map** p310 H6.

Irena Jarošová's Nikkita line features feminine, delicate designs in touchable fabrics: chiffon, cut velvet and silk. The focus is on beautiful dresses, but there's also casual- and clubwear. Each piece is a complete original, and the prices reflect it. Handmade beaded jewellery by Inkognito and cute kids' clothes by Bim Bam Bum add variety.

Faux Pas

Újezd 26, Malá Strana, Prague 1 (603 783 684/ 257 315 261). Metro Malostranská/tram 12, 22, 23. **Open** 11am-7pm Mon-Fri; 11am-4pm Sun. **No credit cards. Map** p307 E4/5.

This showcase for designer Jolana Izbická (*see p167* **Bad Bohemia: Faux Pas**) is a bright little spot on the Prague fashion map. Izbická's imaginative designs for the fashion-forward individual feature bright colours, eye-catching details and a sly sense of humour. Unique originals from other Czech and German designers are also represented.

Klára Nademlýnská

Dlouhá 3, Staré Město, Prague 1 (224 813 723/ www.klaranademlynska.cz). Metro Staroměstská/ tram 17, 18. **Open** 10am-7pm Mon-Fri; 11am-6pm Sat. **Credit** AmEx, MC, V. **Map** p308 J2/3.

Fine tailoring is the hallmark of this Czech designer, the kind of workmanship that makes her suits, separates and eveningwear a treasured find. Original pieces from the designer's shows are also available, along with spangly jewellery, perfect for dressing up basics.

Krab

Husova 8, Staré Město, Prague 1 (224 229 808). Metro Národní třída/tram 6, 9, 18, 21, 22, 23. **Open** 11am-7pm Mon-Fri. **Credit** MC, V. **Map** p308 H4.

This 'textile gallery' features tactile clothes and accessories, both with a New-Age bent. The wide-ranging accessories you'll find at Krab are made by different designers but tend to feature silver wire, coloured glass and geometrical style. The shop also offers a selection of well-crafted handmade bags, which are decorated with unique and imaginative details.

Other locations: Janovského 9, Prague 7 (266 711 508); Jana Masaryka 58, Prague 2 (222 510 031).

Life Style

Štěpánská 51, Nové Město, Prague 1 (224 214 106). Metro Můstek/tram 3, 9, 14, 24. **Open** 10am-7.30pm Mon-Fri; 10am-5pm Sat. **Credit** AmEx, MC, V. **Map** p311 K6.

Bad Bohemia Faux Pas

'I love people when they wear what makes them individual,' says Czech fashion designer Jolana Izbická. Her designs under the **Faux Pas** label, sold from her shop of the same name in Malá Strana since 1995 (*see above*), surely qualify as individual. They have the stamp of the unique and the expressive, from knitted women's underwear complete with pompom balls at each hip to Day-Glo yellow outfits inspired by construction workers' uniforms.

Izbická, 35, strayed from the conventional path very young. She started sewing for herself when she was ten, influenced by her father, who made marionettes. Her first self-designed dress was made out of one of the Russian flags that were waved every 1 May in the old days to celebrate International Workers' Day.

After the Velvet Revolution, Izbická revelled in her new freedom and travelled to many parts of the globe with her English husband, working odd jobs and soaking it all in. 'My father said, "Who knows, the border could close again, you should go while you can."' Fashion-wise, Izbická was especially enthralled with London and its tradition of street style.

Street fashion is still a big player in Izbická's designs, which often set out to push boundaries. Her collection of vinyl pieces, she says, is partly a confrontation of a society that still has a lot of taboos about sexuality. Not that sex isn't a part of Czech society, she adds, but she does find it restrictive, like the buckled and binding vinyl and latex clothes she designs. Sexuality in the Czech Republic, she says, is presented as 'Boys sucking from blonde girls' bellies. It's not shown with a nice feeling. It's ugly.'

She admits that many of her vinyl pieces are meant to shock, but also to make way for acceptance – to convey that outrageous clothes don't make someone a 'pervert'. Expressing your sexuality – and fashion – is different altogether.

Izbická ultimately takes inspiration from the people she makes clothes for: 'I like to help finish people's dreams. I'm not a dictator. I can learn from other people and still build myself.

Eat, Drink, Shop

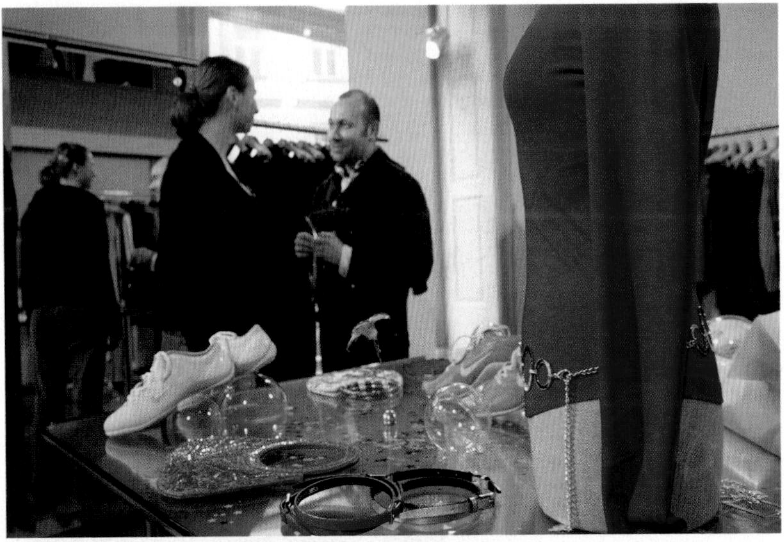

Ditch the Eurotrash, **Klára Nademlýnská** is simply chic. *See p167.*

Like a little piece of Asia, this shop is a welcome respite when its grey in Prague. Along with ceramics and teas, it offers unique fashions based on traditional Asian clothes, designed under the La Femme Mimi label and manufactured in Prague and Vietnam. The jewel-coloured brocades and silks are a delight.

Tatiana

Dušní 1, Staré Město, Prague 1 (224 813 723/ www.tatiana.cz). Metro Staroměstská/tram 17, 18. **Open** 10am-7pm Mon-Fri; 11am-4pm Sat. **Credit** AmEx, DC, MC, V. **Map** p308 J3.

Elegant clothes in rich fabrics for the fashionable career woman who wants to stay away from staid work-wear. The suits and separates feature unique details: leather trim or subtle but stylishly patterned fabrics. Gorgeous, classic coats. Prices are steep, but sales offer relief.

Fur & leather

Kreibich Kožešiny & Rukavice

Michalská 14, Staré Město, Prague 1 (224 222 522/ www.kreibich.cz). Metro Staroměstská or Národní třída/tram 6, 9, 17, 18, 22, 23. **Open** 9.30am-6pm Mon-Fri. **Credit** AmEx, MC, V. **Map** p308 H4.

When the cold hits Prague, the furs and skins hanging outside this little shop on charming Michalská street draw in locals and tourists alike looking for stylish insulation. Inside, the place is packed with quality fur and leather in all colours and styles, most of it handmade. The shop specialises in gloves and also does custom orders and repairs.

Other locations: Hybernská 30, Staré Město, Prague 1 (224 222 924).

Jewellery & accessories

Prague is well known for its jewellery, especially garnets and amber. There are a multitude of shops where you can buy either, especially in the more tourist-orientated areas. Prices tend to be pretty similar, but it usually pays to look around a bit before you buy.

Belda Jewelry Design

Mikulandská 10, Nové Město, Prague 1 (224 933 052). Metro Národní třída/tram 6, 9, 18, 22. **Open** 10am-12.30pm, 1.30-6pm Mon-Thur; 10am-12.30pm, 1.30-5pm Fri. **Credit** AmEx, MC, V. **Map** p308 H5/p310 H6.

Breaking away from traditional garnet-and-gold jewellery, Belda offers a forward-thinking alternative modern, unique and very expensive. The small collection of earrings, bracelets, rings, cuff links and pendants here, some made of unusual materials like titanium, tends toward simple geometric shapes.

Galerie Vlasta

Staroměstské náměstí 5, Staré Město, Prague 1 (222 318 119). Metro Staroměstská/tram 17, 18. **Open** 10am-6pm Mon-Fri; 10am-1pm Sat. **Credit** MC, V. **Map** p308 J3/H3.

The pieces of jewellery designed by Valerie Wasserbauerová are more works of art than mere adornment. The shop feels like a gallery, with pieces displayed on walls, stands and gleaming shelves. Gold and silver woven wire pieces range from dangling, geometric earrings to Egyptianesque collars.

Lingerie

Chez Parisienne

Pařížská 8, Staré Město, Prague 1 (224 817 786). Metro Staroměstská/tram 17, 18. **Open** 10am-7pm Mon-Fri; 10am-6pm Sat. **Credit** AmEx, DC, MC, V. **Map** p308 H3.

High-quality boxers, lingerie and pyjamas at sky-high prices. Also a small selection of dressy, tailored blouses to go over the pretty underthings.

Dessous-Dessus

Králodvorská 7, Staré Město, Prague 1 (224 811 779). Metro Náměstí Republiky/tram 5, 8, 14. **Open** 10am-7pm Mon-Fri; 10am-6pm Sat. **Credit** AmEx, MC, V. **Map** p309 K3.

It would be incredibly easy to spend a fortune here on the vast selection of super-sexy lingerie or even on a pair of designer tights. Great range of colourful bras and knickers, from boy-cut lacy ones to G-strings, as well as pyjamas and chemises.

Other locations: Železná 547/3 Staré Město, Prague 1 (224 217 854).

Skiny

V Jámě 2, Nové Město, Prague 1 (224 212 535). Metro Můstek/tram 3, 9, 14, 24. **Open** 10am-7pm Mon-Fri; 10am-4pm Sat. **Credit** AmEx, DC, MC, V. **Map** p311 K6.

Especially good for sporty cotton lingerie and other bodywear for both women and men. Along with well-stocked shelves, Skiny also offers impressive quality and a wide range of colours.

Mid-range

Madeo Boutique

Vodičkova 28, Nové Město, Prague 1 (no phone). Metro Můstek/tram 3, 9, 14, 24. **Open** 10am-7pm Mon-Fri; 10am-3pm Sat. **Credit** AmEx, MC, V. **Map** p310 J6/307 K5.

Madeo features primarily stylish casualwear with boutique service and a constantly updated collection. While prices vary depending on what you're buying, bargains are to be found in the sales.

Modes Robes

Benediktská 5, Staré Město, Prague 1 (224 826 016/www.cabbage.cz/modes-robes). Metro Náměstí Republiky/tram 5, 8, 14. **Open** 10am-6pm Mon-Fri; 10am-4pm Sat. **Credit** MC, V. **Map** p309 K2.

Run by a collective of seven local designers, with natural, not-too-outrageous-to-wear skirts, shirts and suits, mostly for women. This is everything a fringe fashion shop should be, with industrial cable twisted into postmodern clothes racks and walls used as canvases for artwork.

Vivienne Butique

Vodičkova 20, Nové Město, Prague 1 (222 232 444). Metro Můstek/tram 3, 9, 14, 24. **Open** 10am-5.30pm Mon-Fri; 10.30am-3pm Sat. **Credit** AmEx, MC, V. **Map** p310 J6.

Vivienne, with three locations, offers unique, eye-catching fashions that run the gamut from tailored suits to transparent shirts that shouldn't go anywhere near the office unless you work in a disco.

Other locations: Královodvorská 5, Staré Město, Prague 1 (222 323 837); Rytířská 22, Staré Město, Prague 1 (221 094 314).

Shoes

While clothes-shopping in Prague can be a frustrating experience, finding a pair of shoes is another matter. The streets are lined with shoe shops and the selection is good. Italian imports are very popular, but there are also plenty of Czech and other European chains that offer more reasonable prices.

The ART

Štěpánská 33, Nové Město, Prague 1 (222 230 598). Metro Můstek/tram 3, 9, 14, 24. **Open** 9.30am-7pm Mon-Fri; 9.30am-5pm Sat. **Credit** AmEx, MC, V. **Map** p311 K6.

Rows and rows of Doc Martens and other substantial but stylish shoes, along with platform boots and mile-high heels.

Other locations: Národní 36, Nové Město, Prague 1 (224 948 828).

Baťa

Václavské náměstí 6, Nové Město, Prague 1 (224 218 133). Metro Můstek/tram 3, 9, 14, 24. **Open** 9am-9pm Mon-Fri; 8am-8pm Sat; 9am-8pm Sun. **Credit** AmEx, MC, V. **Map** p308 J5.

The Baťa family, whose shoe-making operation was one of the world's first multinational companies, saw trouble coming in 1938, so the owners fled the country and re-established their headquarters in Canada. Whatever was left of the parent company after the war was nationalised ten years later. Now back in the driving seat, the Baťa family has refurbished its original 1928 modernist shop in Wenceslas Square, with plenty of other locations throughout the city.

Other locations: Bubenský náb. 306, Prague 7 (220 804 329); Dejvická 30, Dejvická, Prague 6 (224 314 185); Fr. Křížka 11, Prague 7 (233 378 333); Jindřišská 20, Nové Město, Prague 1 (222 247 349); Moskevská 27, Vršovice, Prague 10 (271 721 860); Plzeňská 8, Smíchov, Prague 5 (251 512 847); Vinohradská 149, Prague 3 (255 740 028).

Francesca Lecca

Pařížská 14, Staré Město, Prague 1 (222 311 030). Metro Staroměstská/tram 17, 18. **Open** 10am-7pm daily. **Credit** AmEx, MC, V. **Map** p308 H3.

Quality Italian shoes, fashionable but not too trendy. This may be one of the few places in Prague where you can still find sandals on sale in November.

Humanic

Národní třída 34, Nové Město, Prague 1 (224 920 295). Metro Můstek or Národní třída/tram 3, 6, 9, 14, 18, 22, 23, 24. **Open** 9am-8pm Mon-Fri; 9am-7pm Sat; 10am-6pm Sun. **Credit** MC, V. **Map** p308 H5.

This busy shop specialises in cheap and cheerful fashion shoes. It's especially popular among trendy teenagers on tight budgets.

Vicini

Pařížská 24, Staré Město, Prague 1 (224 815 976). Metro Staroměstská/tram 17, 18. **Open** 10.30am-12.30pm, 1.30-7.30pm Mon-Fri; 11am-12.30pm, 1.30-7.30pm Sat; noon-7pm Sun. **Credit** AmEx, MC, V. **Map** p308 H2.

The shoes in this modern and elegant shop are more works of art than footwear. The unique creations define high style, with exquisite craftsmanship and details; rhinestones and fur create a sense of fun without veering into the outrageous.

Shoe repairs

There are shoe repair shops in **Baťa** (*see p169*) as well as **Tesco** and **Kotva** supermarkets (for both, *see p158*). Failing that, check the *Zlaté stránky* (Yellow Pages) under '*obuv-opravy*'.

Jan Ondráček

Navrátilova 12, Nové Město, Prague 1 (222 231 960). Metro Národní třída/tram 3, 9, 14, 24. **Open** 8am-6pm Mon-Thur; 8am-5pm Fri. **No credit cards. Map** p310 J7.

This central shoe repair shop offers all the services you need to make your favourite pair last more than a little bit longer.

Florists

Giving flowers is a big Czech tradition, so there's no shortage of florists in Prague. Your local corner *květinařství* is likely to be as good as the centrally located places listed below.

Bohemia Flowers

Opletalova 22, Nové Město, Prague 1 (224 213 033/www.flowers.cz). Metro Muzeum/tram 3, 9, 14, 24. **Open** 8am-8pm Mon-Fri; 10am-2pm Sat. **Credit** MC, V. **Map** p309 L5.

An expat-run venture that delivers tasteful, speedy, custom arrangements across town or anywhere else via Interflora. Choose from simple sprigs to wedding bouquets, viewing your selection online through the helpful website. The real-life shop is handily located just north of Wenceslas Square.

Květinařství U Červeného Lva

Saská ulička, Malá Strana, Prague 1 (mobile 604 855 286). Metro Malostranská/tram 12, 22, 23. **Open** 9am-7pm Mon-Sat; 11am-7pm Sun. **Credit** MC, V. **Map** p307 E3.

The tiny Red Lion is situated in a picturesque little spot on a back street around the corner from the Charles Bridge. Its high-quality, fresh-cut flowers, charming ceramic pots and tasteful arrangements are prepared with care.

Food & drink

Looking for something a little more exotic than standard Czech groceries? Fret not, foodies, the following shops have got it covered.

Specialist

Angel Food & Wine

Dřevná 4, Prague 2 (224 921 325). Metro Karlovo náměstí/tram 3, 4, 6, 10, 14, 16, 18, 22, 23, 24. **Open** 10am-7pm Tue-Sat; 11am-4pm Sun. **No credit cards. Map** p310 G9.

Here's your source for delicious chutneys, fresh bread and herbs, fish paste, organic pasta and other rare delectables. The delicatessen also offers a small menu of imaginative pastries, pies and soups.

Bakeshop Praha

Kozí 1, Staré Město, Prague 1 (222 316 823/ www.bakeshop.cz). Metro Staroměstská/tram 17, 18. **Open** 7am-7pm daily. **Credit** AmEx, MC, V. **Map** p308 J2.

A godsend for those who have had their fill of sour, brown Czech bread and woody pastries, the Bakeshop offers such tempting loaves as potato dill and walnut, as well as tasty croissants and quiches, sandwiches and spreads. The Staré Město location has a small counter where you can enjoy your *rugalah* with a cup of tea. The Malá Strana shop offers full-service dining (*see p147*).

Other locations: Lázeňská 19, Malá Strana, Prague 1 (257 534 244).

La Bretagne

Široká 22, Staré Město, Prague 1 (224 819 672). Metro Staroměstská/tram 17, 18. **Open** 9.30am-7.30pm daily. **No credit cards. Map** p308 H2.

Anyone who tells you there's no fresh fish outside the Vltava hasn't been to this cheerful fishmonger's. Take home your ice-packed, imported catch – or a portion of the house paella – and a bottle of imported wine, and enjoy the best seafood bargain in town.

Country Life

Melantrichova 15, Staré Město, Prague 1 (224 213 366/www.countrylife.cz). Metro Můstek/tram 3, 9, 14, 24. **Open** 9.30am-6.30pm Mon-Thur; 10am-3pm Fri; 11am-6pm Sun. **No credit cards. Map** p308 H4.

Health nuts flock to the shop for grains, meal, tofu and other good-for-you goodies. The adjoining buffet restaurant (*see p119*) draws a steady stream of diners seeking reliable vegetarian eats.

Other locations: Jungmannova 1, Nové Město, Prague 1 (257 044 419).

Cream & Dream

Husova 12, Staré Město, Prague 1 (224 211 035/ www.cream-dream.com). Metro Národní třída/tram 6, 9, 18, 21, 22, 23. **Open** 11am-10pm daily. **No credit cards. Map** p308 H4.

Imagine you've died, gone to heaven, and they serve ice-cream. Choose – if you can – from roughly two dozen flavours of fine Italian-style *gelato* made fresh on the premises from real, rich cream and fresh fruit. Enjoy it here with a cup of coffee or take it with you, in a waffle cone or by the litre. They deliver too.

Fruits de France

Jindřišská 9, Nové Město, Prague 1 (222 511 261/ www.fdf.cz). Metro Můstek/tram 3, 9, 14, 24. **Open** 9.30am-6.30pm Mon-Fri; 9.30am-1pm Sat. **Credit** MC, V. **Map** p309 K5.

In a city where the phrase 'forbidden fruit' takes on new, disturbingly broad meaning, this oasis of imported produce, cheeses and wines is a positive debauch. Grab a light gourmet lunch at the Jindřišská location, which specialises in wine, fruit and vegetables; the Bělehradská shop focuses on fish, pâtés and armagnac. Not for the faint of wallet.

Other locations: Bělehradská 94, Vinohrady, Prague 2 (222 511 261).

Interlov Praha

Jungmannova 25, Staré Město, Prague 1 (224 949 516/www.interlov.cz). Metro Národní třída/tram 6, 9, 18, 21, 22, 23. **Open** 9am-5.30pm Mon-Fri. **No credit cards**. **Map** p308 J5.

You needn't carry a gun or a hunting license to bring home fresh boar, pheasant, rabbit and venison. This game butcher also sells sausages, spices, recipe books and wine especially suited to wild meat. Of course, if you really want to dress up like Elmer Fudd, there's a hunting-clothes shop just next door.

Jarmark lahůdky

Vodičkova 30, Nové Město, Prague 1 (224 162 619). Metro Můstek/tram 3, 9, 14, 24. **Open** 8am-8pm Mon-Fri; 9am-midnight Sat. **No credit cards**. **Map** p310 J6.

Meat market

Health consciousness may be on the rise among young Czechs, but in a country where a meatless meal still raises eyebrows, the butcher's shop isn't going anywhere for a while. And while supermarkets' gleaming cases and refrigerated stacks of meat in sealed plastic are gaining popularity, an *uzeniny* like **Maso Tomáš Turek** (*see p173*) near Wenceslas Square looks as busy today as at any time before 1989: filled with workers from offices all around hungrily eyeing old-fashioned glass cases and slicers full of the more gristly varieties of fresh and smoked pork and beef.

Not exactly a bucolic country butcher's, Turek's shop is a utilitarian affair where a slow, muttering queue of shoppers circumambulates the room, while assistants in stained white smocks and hairnets pluck, weigh and bag orders without ceremony.

The Czech meat-packing industry traces its roots back to the Middle Ages, when butchers' guilds were some of the most prosperous and influential in town. With the exception of royal tables, culinary culture revolved around stewed meat dishes like the ubiquitous *guláš* (actually an import from Hungary), which can turn the most recalcitrant hunk of leather into a delight.

Prime steak remains a stranger to most Czech tables today, and a fittingly unromantic approach to butchery prevails at Turek's; most of the beef sold here is in the form of brisket, flank and shoulder roasts for stewing.

Meat consumption in the Czech Republic has been declining steadily since the collapse of communism. And, free of state control, the price of meat has soared. The combined effect of those factors is that in 1990 the average Czech ate 97 kgs (214 lbs) of meat; five years later, that figure was down to 82 kg (181 lbs) a year.

All of which is gravy for the local *uzeniny*. Higher prices give Czechs even more excuse, if any were needed, to buy the cheaper cuts Turek stocks for stew. No tenderloin around here, thank you very much. Sausages and salami are good enough for these red-blooded *Mareks* and *Matějs*. Bone-in cuts like pork knuckle are also big sellers, along with liver, hearts and kidneys.

Czech beef consumption hardly dipped even after BSE was recently discovered at an isolated beef-processing plant. Czech authorities continually test the country's meat supply now, and turn up a new case once or twice a year but conventional wisdom has it that the Czech beef supply is safe, and less than ten per cent of the meat Czechs eat comes from abroad.

With chronically low profit margins, meat-processing plants operating below capacity, companies forced to streamline and the increased demands of EU standards, could it finally be that red meat production and consumption may begin to drop to levels similar to those in the West?

Naah. One look at the queue of salivating, florid customers at Turek's and it's clear there's only one thing that could clear out this *uzeniny*: blood clots.

The restaurant moguls behind the Jarmark eatery just across the way and the Coloseum pizzerias around town have got the deli market covered as well. In addition to the sliced meats and cheeses, sandwiches and mayonnaise salads, they also stock an abundance of Italian biscotti, coffees, wines and pastas.

Koruna Pralines Chocolaterie

V Jamě 5, Nové Město, Prague 1 (606 222 651). Metro Můstek/tram 3, 9, 14, 24. **Open** 9am-8pm Mon-Fri; 9am-6pm Sun, Sat. **Credit** MC, V. **Map** p310 J6/p311 K6.

Chocoholics, rejoice. This little shop has more truffles, pralines, chocolate sculptures and other sinful sweets per square metre than any other corner of the city. There's gift baskets make for great last-minute saves and also a decent wine selection.

Lesa

Haštalská 10, Prague 1 (224 812 832). Metro Náměstí Republiky/tram 5, 14, 26. **Open** 10am-7pm Mon-Fri; 10am-2pm Sat. **Credit** MC, V. **Map** p308 J2.

A well-kept secret among Prague gourmets, this hidden nook offers wholesale and retail sales of Italian wine, prosciutto, cheeses, grappa and countless other Italian culinary marvels.

Maso Tomáš Turek

Jindřišská 23, Prague 1 (224 230 968). Metro Můstek/ tram 3, 9, 14, 24. **Open** 8am-6pm Mon; 7am-6pm Tue, Wed, Fri; 7am-6.30pm Thur; 8am-12.30pm Sat. **No credit cards. Map** p309 K5.

All the cheap meat you shouldn't eat. If you really must try a *klobása* and don't want it hot off a street vendor, this is the place (*see p172* **Meat market**).

Potraviny U Cedru

Československé armády 18, Dejvice, Prague 6 (233 342 119). Metro Dejvická/tram 20, 25. **Open** 7am-11pm daily. **No credit cards.**

Hungry for houmous? Pining for vine leaves? Take the A train (erm, metro) to Dejvice and shop to your heart's content at this little Lebanese grocery.

Shalamar

Lipánská 3, Žižkov, Prague 3 (603 495 260). Metro Jiřího z Poděbrad/tram 5, 9, 26. **Open** 10am-7pm Mon-Fri; noon-7pm Sat, Sun. **No credit cards. Map** p313 C1.

Whether you're looking for a bulk bag of basmati rice, a little lime pickle or the best of Bollywood, you're bound to find it here at Prague's premier shop for treats from the Subcontinent. You can pick up inspiration at the Pakistani restaurant Mailsi next door (*see p142*).

Teuscher

Malá Štupartská 5, Staré Město, Prague 1 (224 828 050). Metro Náměstí Republiky/tram 5, 8, 14. **Open** 10.30am-7.30pm daily. **No credit cards. Map** p308 J3.

Champagne- and Becherovka-filled truffles number among the fine Swiss chocolates on hand here. Don't miss the twee marzipan goodies.

La Vecchia Bottega

Na Perštýně 10, Staré Město, Prague 1 (224 234 629). Metro Národní třída/tram 6, 9, 18, 21, 22, 23. **Open** 9am-6pm Mon-Fri; 10am-4pm Sat, Sun. **Credit** AmEx, MC, V. **Map** p308 H5.

This shop stocks an amazing variety of Italian wines, plus countless pestos, pastas, vinegars and sweets. Duly inspired by the ingredients, you can hit the annexe next door and pick up the utensils to do the job properly.

Vzpomínky na Afriku

Rybná & Jakubská, Staré Město, Prague 1 (603 544 492/www.ebelcoffee.cz). Metro Náměstí Republiky/tram 5, 14, 26. **Open** 10am-7pm daily. **Credit** AmEx, MC, V. **Map** p309 K2/3.

You know you're getting close when you catch the irresistible scent of fresh-roasted coffee. More varieties of beans than you can shake a biscotti at. Have a cup here or take it home, whole-bean or freshly ground. Note: credit cards accepted only on purchases over 500 Kč.

Supermarkets

In addition to the places listed below, there are centrally located supermarkets in the **Kotva** and **Tesco** department stores (for both, *see p158*).

Carrefour

Radlická 1, Smíchov, Prague 5 (257 284 111/ www.carrefour.cz). Metro Anděl/tram 4, 6, 7, 9, 10, 14. **Open** 7am-midnight daily. **Credit** AmEx, DC, MC, V.

The supermarket that ate the world: in addition to the lorry-loads of day-to-day fare, this enormous food shop stocks a staggering selection of imported specialities, spices, produce and fresh fish.

Other locations: Stodůlky, Prague 13 (251 173 111).

Delvita

Bělehradská 50, Nové Město, Prague 2 (222 562 292). Metro IP Pavlova/tram 4, 6, 11, 16, 22, 23. **Open** 9am-9pm daily. **Credit** MC, V.

This local favourite has polished its image and is increasingly offering a wider variety of baked goods, fresher vegetables and better cuts of meat. There are over two dozen branches across town.

Other locations: throughout town.

Food delivery

Délicatesse

Kostelní 6, Holešovice, Prague 7 (tel/fax 220 571 775/www.delicatesse.cz). Metro Vltavská/tram 1, 3, 14, 25. **Open** 9am-9pm Mon-Fri. **No credit cards. Map** p312 C3/D3.

This French bakery delivers a bevy of freshly made sandwiches and panini, quiches, salads and sweets. You can order from anywhere in Prague. Minimum order 200 Kč, plus delivery of 60-80 Kč per order.

Food Taxi

(777 171 394/603 171 394/www.foodtaxi.cz). **Open** 10am-3.30pm, 5.30-10pm Mon-Fri; 11am-10pm Sat. **No credit cards**.
Brilliant! This delivery service has no kitchen of its own, just a fleet of cars which Food Taxi uses to deliver food from an array of restaurants, including Chinese, Mexican and Thai. Oh, yeah, and pizza. Order by phone or online.

Pizza Go Home

Sokolská 31, Nové Město, Prague 2 (283 870 000/www.pizzagohome.cz). Metro IP Pavlova/tram 4, 6, 11, 16, 22, 23, 34. **Open** 24 hrs daily. **No credit cards**. **Map** p311 K7/8.
It's 3am and you're craving pizza. Only one pizzeria is generous enough to bake you a cheap pie and deliver it, and you're going to complain about the meagreness of toppings? Ingrate. Pizza Go Home's delivery fees are 20-170 Kč.
Other locations: Argentinská 1, Prague 7 (283 870 000); Odborů 3, Prague 2 (283 870 000).

Wine & beer

Blatnička

Michalská 6, Staré Město, Prague 1 (224 233 612). Metro Národní třída/tram 6, 9, 18, 22, 23. **Open** 10am-6pm Mon-Fri. **No credit cards**. **Map** p308 H4.
A favourite among the locals, this little wine bar also keeps *sudová vina*, or jug wine, on hand and sells cheap litres of local plonk – bring a bottle.

Cellarius

Lucerna Passage, Štěpánská 61, Nové Město, Prague 1 (224 210 979/www.cellarius.cz). Metro Můstek/tram 3, 9, 14, 24. **Open** 9.30am-9pm Mon-Sat; 3-8pm Sun. **Credit** AmEx, MC, V. **Map** p311 K6.
This friendly little shop has an excellent selection of Moravian wines and vintages from Bulgaria, Hungary, Slovakia and elsewhere. Guests at the Vinohrady location can enjoy the wares in the cellar or the garden, weather permitting.
Other locations: Budečská 29, Vinohrady, Prague 2 (222 515 243).

Dionýsos

Vinařického 6, Vinohrady, Prague 2 (224 922 237). Metro Karlovo náměstí/tram 7, 18, 24. **Open** 10am-6pm Mon-Fri. **Credit** AmEx, MC, V. **Map** p310 H10.
If you're looking for a local grape, the knowledgeable staff here will be proud to show off the wares and help you find one to your liking. Foreign wines are available too.

Monarch

Na Perštýně 15, Staré Město, Prague 1 (224 239 602/www.monarchvinnysklep.cz). Metro Národní třída/tram 6, 9, 18, 21, 22, 23. **Open** 11am-7pm Mon-Sat. **Credit** AmEx, MC, V. **Map** p308 H5.
This wine seller has excellent stock from the southern hemisphere as well as from California and southern Europe. Not many French wines, but there are also some lovely numbers from Moravia. Take a seat in the adjoining wine bar and explore the possibilities over a plate of cheese.

Pivni galerie

U Průhonu 9, Holešovice (220 870 613/ pivnigalerie@post.cz). Metro Nádraží Holešovice/ tram 12, 25. **Open** 10am-8pm Mon-Fri; 10am-3pm Sat. **No credit cards**. **Map** p312 E1.
Connoisseurs can sample from the hundreds of small and rare brews from all over Bohemia and Moravia. The rest of us can take home a couple cold ones. A must for the bottle collector.

Vinotéka u Svatého Štěpána

Štěpánská 7, Nové Město, Prague 2 (221 901 160). Metro Muzeum/tram 3, 9, 14, 24. **Open** 10am-7pm Mon-Fri. **Credit** AmEx, MC, V. **Map** p311 K6.
This small shop stocks wines from all corners of the map, including some real gems from Moravia, plus champagnes, liqueurs and whiskies.

Gifts

While there's no shortage of chum about, Prague rewards the determined seeker of the unusual. The city's antique shops (*see p161*) are treasure troves of the rare and just plain strange. Merchants have sussed the demand for folksy handicrafts, some of which are actually charming, and there's always the celebrated Czech beer and Becherovka. Shopping for the collector or art junkie? Prague's many museums (*see p109*) often have an exciting selection of coffee-table books and calendars.

Candles Gallery

Karlova 23, Staré Město, Prague 1 (224 219 990/www.candle-gallery.com). Metro Staroměstská/ tram 12, 18, 22, 23. **Open** 10am-8pm daily. **Credit** MC, V. **Map** p307 E5.
It's almost a shame to set a match to the wax masterpieces that are on sale here. Choose, for instance, from modern numbers, the Mexican-inspired cubes, or the art-nouveau capital letters.

Charita Florentinum

Ječná 4, Nové Město, Prague 2 (224 921 501). Metro Karlovo náměstí/tram 4, 6, 16, 22, 34. **Open** 8am-6pm Mon-Fri; 9am-1pm Sat. **No credit cards**. **Map** p310 J8.
Robes, votive candles and other clerical gear. Sorry, no holy water.

Manufaktura

Karlova 26, Staré Město, Prague 1 (221 632 480). Metro Staroměstská/tram 17, 18. **Open** 10am-8pm Mon-Thur, Sun; 10am-9pm Fri, Sat. **Credit** AmEx, DC, MC, V. **Map** p308 H4.
The name of the shop is intended to evoke 'handmade', not factories; hence the oh-so-cute folk accents of straw, wood and textiles. Finds include rustic jumpers or throws, and natural cosmetics.

Charita Florentinum offers up gifts from the crypt. *See p174.*

Slovenská Izba

Jilská 1, Staré Město, Prague 1 (224 947 130). Metro Staroměstská/tram 17, 18. **Open** 10am-12.30pm, 1.30-6pm Mon-Fri. **No credit cards. Map** p308 H4.

You can't get much more obscure than this specialist in all things Slovak. You might be surprised to know how many CDs the Czechs' cousins to the east have produced, not to mention books, ceramics and embroidery. If your curiosity is piqued, the Slovak Cultural Centre is just down the street.

Včelařské potřeby

Křemencova 8, Nové Město, Prague 2 (224 934 344/ www.beekeeping.cz). Metro Karlovo náměstí/tram 4, 6, 16, 22, 34. **Open** 9am-5pm Mon, Wed; 9am-6pm Tue, Thur; 9am-2pm Fri. **No credit cards. Map** p310 H6/7.

Comb the city and you won't find a more unusual gift. For the busy beekeeper, gloves and headgear. For the enthusiast, everything imaginable from the hive, including honeys, cosmetics and mead.

Hair & beauty

Those after the simplest of cuts should be able to get a decent trim in any *kadeřnictví* (hairdresser's) or *holičství* (barber's). But just because you're in the former East bloc doesn't mean you have to go without the kind of cut you'd expect from a top Western salon. The rates of chic stylists are pricey for locals, but anyone thinking in terms of Western currency can find a decent bargain.

Andrew Jose

Michalská 17, Staré Město, Prague 1 (224 232 029/www.andrewjose.com). Metro Staroměstská or Národní třída/tram 6, 9, 17, 18, 22, 23. **Open** 9am-6pm Mon, Tue, Sat; 9am-8pm Wed-Fri. **Credit** MC, V. **Map** p308 H4.

An offshoot of the salon of the same name in London, Andrew Jose has a devoted following among the better-heeled Prague citizens. The mixed Czech and foreign staff is on top of the latest trends. Cuts for women are usually 700-1,500 Kč; for men, 550-990 Kč.

James Hair

Malá Štupartská 9, Staré Město, Prague 1 (224 827 373/www.jameshair.cz). Metro Náměstí Republiky/tram 5, 8, 14. **Open** 8am-8pm Tue-Fri; 9am-5pm Sat. **No credit cards. Map** p308 J3.

This international stylist and his crew have star status on the Prague fashion scene. Dream cuts and makeovers are all in a day's work, and the customer raves have spread throughout town. A cut runs from 650 Kč to 1,150 Kč. Most of the staff speak English.

The Salon

Dušní 6, Staré Město, Prague 1 (224 817 575). Metro Staroměstská/tram 17, 18. **Open** 9am-9pm Mon-Fri; 11am-6pm Sat. **No credit cards. Map** p308 J3.

The devotees of Libor Šula's salon agree that the Italian-born Czech delivers on his promise of 'an international salon without any Czech attitude'. He's personally booked months in advance, but you can usually get an appointment to see one of his well-trained English-speaking staff within a week or two. Cuts for women start at 490 Kč and can go up to 1,500 Kč if you want highlights or colour. Cuts for men are usually under 300 Kč.

Salon Joshua

Slovenská 2, Vršovice, Prague 10 (222 520 126/ www.joshua.cz). Metro Náměstí Míru/tram 22, 23. **Open** 9am-11pm Mon-Fri. **Credit** AmEx, MC, V.

Way off the beaten track in Prague 10, über-hip Salon Joshua offers a lot more than just a haircut (*see p177* **Bad Bohemia: Salon Joshua**). While stylists can do any style, the salon specialises in cutting-edge and street looks, with tattoos and even 'intimate design' for those who want their more private areas to be just as stylish as the hair on their heads. Not much English spoken, but the friendly receptionist does and is ready to help. Tanning and massage. Cuts for women are usually 700-800 Kč; for men, 350-400 Kč.

Thai World

Týnská 9, Staré Město, Prague 1 (224 817 247/ 606 116 272/www.thaiworld.cz). Metro Staroměstská/ tram 17, 18. **Open** 11am-9pm daily. **Massage** 495 Kč/hr; 295 Kč/30mins. **No credit cards.** **Map** p308 J3.

This relaxation haven in Staré Město has a staff that are certified from the Wat Po medical school in Bangkok and offers traditional Thai massage (which focuses on pressure points in the body), reflexology, Swedish oil massage or combinations.

Household

Bauhaus

Budějovická 1A, Pankrác, Prague 4 (241 732 014/www.bauhaus.cz). Metro Pankrác. **Open** 8am-8pm Mon-Sat; 8am-7pm Sun. **Credit** AmEx, MC, V.

Think timber, not Gothic art rock. When the landlord doesn't come through, Bauhaus does, with anything you could possibly need in the way of DIY.

Other locations: Ústecká 822, Chabry, Prague 8 (255 715 211).

Ikea

Skandinávská 1, Zličín, Prague 5 (251 610 110). Metro Zličín. **Open** 10am-8pm daily. **Credit** MC, V.

The Swedish furniture giant IKEA really hit the proverbial nail on the head when it came to the Czech Republic and its huddled masses cramped in their tiny *panelák*, or prefab, apartments. Locals consider Ikea near the height of interior design, one stop short of designer furniture, often surpassing that.

Le Patio

Národní 22, Nové Město, Prague 1 (224 934 853). Metro Národní třída/tram 6, 9, 17, 18, 22, 23. **Open** 10am-7pm Mon-Sat; 11am-7pm Sun. **Credit** AmEx, MC, V. **Map** p308 H5.

Le Patio's collection of inspired furniture and accents have a warm, romantic touch that says 'home' in a Bohemian sort of way. It also has a great online catalogue.

Other locations: Pažížská 20, Staré Město, Prague 1 (222 320 260); Týn 640, Staré Město, Prague 1 (224 895 773).

Potten & Pannen

Václavské náměstí 57, Nové Město, Prague 1 (224 214 936/www.pottenpannen.cz). Metro Muzeum/tram 3, 9, 14, 24. **Open** 10am-7pm Mon-Sat. **Credit** AmEx, MC, V. **Map** p309 K6.

If it cuts, squeezes, scalds or pours, it's in stock. Have a cappuccino in the shop's café and try not to drool on the fabulous gadgetry and gourmet kit.

Key-cutting & locksmiths

Add 'lost keys' to 'death and taxes'. You can cut an extra set at a *zamečnictví* such as those at **Tesco** or at the bottom of the escalators at the entrance to the **Kotva** supermarket (for both, *see p158*). When you're locked out at 3am, try the following.

KEY Non-Stop

Dukelských hrdinů 7, Holešovice, Prague 7 (220 878 016). Metro Vltavská/tram 1, 5, 25, 26. **Open** 24hrs daily. **No credit cards.** **Map** p312 D2.

Lock-picking, cheap cutting and copying – there's no need to go to them; Key Non-Stop comes to you.

Music

Records, tapes & CDs

Bontonland Megastore

Palác Koruna, Václavské náměstí 1, Nové Město, Prague 1 (224 235 356/www.bontonland.cz). Metro Můstek/tram 3, 9, 14, 24. **Open** 9am-8pm daily. **Credit** AmEx, MC, V. **Map** p310 J6.

With stacks of rock and pop, a couple truck-loads of jazz, and a smattering of classical and country, the stock at Bontonland Megastore largely reflects the musical tastes of the nation. In addition to CDs and cassettes, you'll find videos, fan gear and listening posts.

Disko Duck

Karlova 12, Staré Město, Prague 1 (221 213 696/www.diskoduck.cz). Metro Staroměstská/ tram 17, 18. **Open** noon-7pm daily. **Credit** MC, V. **Map** p308 G4.

Hip hop is the rule at this Staré Město vinyl shop, but you'll also find nearly every kind of 12-inch, from Goa to drum 'n' bass. DJs can pick up all sorts of gear and mix it up with the locals on Disko Duck's turntables.

Maximum Underground

Jilská 22, Staré Město, Prague 1 (222 541 333). Metro Můstek, Národní třída or Staroměstská/ tram 3, 9, 18, 22, 23. **Open** 11am-7.30pm Mon-Sat; 1-7pm Sun. **No credit cards.** **Map** p308 H4.

Within a sort of alternative shopping mall that includes clothing stores, tattoo and piercing parlours, this friendly shop stocks mainly CDs, with some cassettes and vinyl. If you're into acid jazz, break beats or psychobilly, this is your place.

Music shop-antikvariát

Národní třída 25, Nové Město, Prague 1 (221 085 268). Metro Národní třída/tram 6, 9, 18, 22. **Open** 10.30am-7pm Mon-Sat. **Credit** AmEx, MC, V. **Map** p308 H5.

A collector's paradise, with hundreds of used CDs and LPs from the 1920s onwards. The selection includes jazz, blues, country, folk, Czech pop/rock, classical and a pricey stack of rarities and bootlegs.

Music World

Benediktská 2, Staré Město, Prague 1 (224 827 830). Metro Náměstí republiky/tram 5, 14, 26. **Open** 7.30am-7.30pm Mon-Fri; 8am-6pm Sat. **Credit** AmEx, MC, V. **Map** p309 K2.

For a small fee, you can join this recording 'owner's club' and rent CDs and DVDs by the night. As an owner, you are naturally entitled to make a personal copy. Everyone, including the police across the street, assumes there's something illegal about that, but no one seems able to pin down just what it is. Music World also sells mobile phones and photo and video gear.

Pohodlí

Benediktská 7, Staré Město, Prague 1 (224 827 026/www.etno.cz). Metro Náměstí Republiky/tram 5, 14, 26. **Open** 11am-7pm Mon-Fri; 10am-4pm Sat. **No credit cards. Map** p309 K2.

Looking for new tunes for your belly-dancing music? Indian classical? Fanfare Ciocarlia? This tiny, family-run ethnic music store carries everything from Zimbabwean marimba music to Nusrat Fateh Ali Khan, plus a fair selection of Moravian folk and Czech alternative.

Bad Bohemia Salon Joshua

Lukáš Černý, a handsome 29-year-old Czech with tousled bleach-blond hair, a ready smile and halting English, spent a month living in a Berlin squat when he was 17. At the time, not long after the fall of the Wall, Berlin presented a new world to Černý and he soaked up the youth culture fast – wild, wonderful fashion, crazy hair and a whole in-your-face lifestyle.

Two years later, back in Prague, Černý started a hair salon in the back of the Mystic Skate shop on Štepánská, calling it **Salon Joshua** (*see p176*), in tribute to a drummer friend from his Berlin days. At first Černý, who had no real training in hairstyling, would just do wild punk and skate styles for his friends, basically for beer money. But his venture kept growing, evolving into its current incarnation, a full-service salon off the beaten path in Prague 10 which also includes massage services and tattooing. Černý and his staff also work on films and fashion shows.

Salon Joshua is situated in an old sports hall, and the entrance is a bare-bones Czech-style pub full of guys named Honza huddled over their beers under the fluorescent lights – men not often seen with blue hair and dreadlocks. But walk up the stairs and it's a different world. A huge spider-web-shaped window dominates the salon – in fact, it was this feature that inspired Černý to build here. The salon is modern but warm, with lots of glass and metal, hardwood floors, hip lifestyle magazines in the racks and a techno soundtrack.

Černý aims to create a different world for both his staff and clients. To him, Salon Joshua has never been simply about hair. The venture is equally about image, lifestyle, 'how you see the world' and how you express that vision. It's a place where the young and avant-garde – and even thirtysomethings, who are perhaps a bit less radical – can feel welcome and celebrate their own personal sense of style.

U zlatého kohouta.

Supraphone

Jungmannova 20, Nové Město, Prague 1 (224 948 718). Metro Národní třída or Můstek/tram 3, 9, 14, 24. **Open** 9am-7pm Mon-Fri; 9am-1pm Sat. **Credit** AmEx, MC, V. **Map** p308 J5.

The former state recording company has its own shop, where selections run the gamut from classical to jazz to pop to country. To see what's in stock, flick through the files that are on the counter. Knowledgeable staff and an excellent selection of cheap Czech classical recordings.

Musical instruments

Hudební nástroje – Radek Bubrle

Náprstkova 10, Staré Město, Prague 1 (222 221 110/www.nastroje-hudebni.cz). Metro Můstek or Staroměstská/tram 17, 18. **Open** 10am-6pm Mon-Fri; 10am-4pm Sat. **Credit** DC, MC, V. **Map** p308 G4.

This small, cheery shop specialises in acoustic guitars of Czech manufacture, including Furch, Procházka and Rieger-Kloss. The staff is happy to help professionals and beginners alike with sales, repairs and accessories. CDs and ticket sales too.

Pianosalon Petrof

Jungmannovo náměstí 17, Prague 1 (224 222 501/ www.petrof.com) Metro Můstek/tram 3, 9, 14, 24. **Open** 10am-7pm Mon-Fri; 10am-3pm Sat. **Credit** AmEx, MC, V. **Map** p308 J5.

The Petrof family began making fine pianos in 1864. After the collapse of Czech communism, they regained control of their factories and have been busy restoring the company's reputation. The piano salon shares the same address with a number of other instrument shops.

Praha Music Centre

Soukenická 20, Nové Město, Prague 1 (226 011 111/www.pmc.cz). Metro Náměstí Republiky/tram 5, 14, 26. **Open** 9am-6pm Mon-Fri. **Credit** MC, V. **Map** p309 L2.

Praha Music caters to plugged-in musicians in need of a new axe. Pick up a second-hand amp and choose a new drummer from the bulletin board.

Other locations: Revoluční 14, Staré Město, Prague 1 (222 311 693).

U zlatého kohouta

Michalská 3, Staré Město, Prague 1 (224 212 874). Metro Můstek or Národní třída/tram 3, 9, 14, 24. **Open** 10am-noon, 1.30-6pm Mon-Fri. **Credit** AmEx, MC, V. **Map** p308 H4.

The craftsmen here will restore not only your violin, viola, cello or double bass, but also your faith in quality workmanship. The shop also supplies new string instruments, accessories and rare CDs.

Opticians

Eiffel Optic

Na příkopě 25, Nové Město, Prague 1 (224 234 966/ www.eiffeloptic.cz). Metro Můstek/tram 3, 9, 14, 24. **Open** 8am-8pm Mon-Fri; 9am-8pm Sat; 9.30am-7pm Sun. **Credit** AmEx, MC, V. **Map** p309 K4.

This shop stocks thousands of frames, ranging from modest to haute couture, and offers express service that will fill your prescription in an hour.

The on-site optician also offers free eye tests and can fit you for glasses, contact lenses or coloured contacts should you have any problems with those you brought along with you.
Other locations: Ječná 6, Nové Město, Prague 2 (224 913 173); Jungmannovo náměstí 1, Prague 1 (224 232 744); Celetná 38, Staré Město, Prague 1 (225 113 302); Bělehradská 102, Nové Město, Prague 2 (222 512 431); Centrum Černý Most, Prague 9 (281 917 258); Palác Flóra, Prague 3 (255 742 006); Europark Štěrboholy, Prague 10 (272 701 775).

GrandOptical

Myslbek Centre, Na příkopě 19-21, Staré Město, Prague 1 (224 238 371/www.grandoptical.cz). Metro Můstek/tram 3, 9, 14, 24. **Open** 9.30am-8pm Mon-Fri; 10am-7pm Sat; 10am-6pm Sun. **Credit** AmEx, MC, V. **Map** p309 K4.
Owned and run by Vision Express, GrandOptical is well known for its fast, precision lens-crafting. and helpful (English-speaking staff) – all of which comes at a premium.
Other locations: Shopping Park Praha-Zličín, Prague 5 (251 613 375); Metropole Zličín, Prague 5 (257 952 696); Nový Smíchov Centrum, Prague 5 (257 321 620); Nakupní centrum Letňany, Prague 9 (284 014 360).

Photocopying

Copy General

Senovážné náměstí 26, Nové Město, Prague 1 (224 230 020/www.copygeneral.cz). Metro Náměstí Republiky/tram 3, 5, 9, 14, 24, 26. **Open** 24hrs daily. **Credit** MC, V. **Map** p309 L4.
It happens: sometimes you need glossy, colour A3s at 4am. Thankfully, Copy General understands. Other services available include binding and digital printing, plus pick-up and delivery.
Other locations: Národní 11, Prague 1 (222 075 650); Jugoslavská 11, Prague 2 (221 181 181); Milady Horákové 4, Holešovice, Prague 7 (233 370 013); Na Bělidle 40, Smíchov, Prague 5 (257 316 653).

Photography

Camera shops & repairs

AZ Foto

Vodičkova 39, Nové Město, Prague 1 (224 947 561/224 948 003/www.azfoto.cz). Metro Náměstí Republiky/tram 3, 5, 9, 14, 24, 26. **Open** 8.30am-6pm Mon-Fri; 9am-noon Sat. **Credit** MC, V. **Map** p309 K4.
This helpful shop offers a variety of both new and second-hand cameras and various accessories. AZ Foto has other convenient locations around town for general photography needs.
Other locations: Celetná 8, Staré Město, Prague 1 (224 239 170); Václavské náměstí 23, Prague 1 (222 245 901); Senovážná 8, Nové Město, Prague 1 (224 226 020); Revoluční 6, Prague 1 (224 814 769); Lidická 26, Prague 5 (257 329 162).

Foto Škoda

Palác Langhans, Vodičkova 37, Nové Město, Prague 1 (222 929 029/fax 222 926 016/www.fotoskoda.cz). Metro Můstek/tram 3, 9, 14, 24. **Open** 8.30am-8pm Mon-Fri; 9am-6pm Sat. **Credit** AmEx, DC, MC, V. **Map** p308 J6.
One-stop shopping for the professional photographer. You'll find a wider range of film here than anywhere in Prague, plus tripods, lights, enlargers, and both second-hand and new cameras. Prices tend to be a little higher than at smaller shops. Upstairs the Langhans Gallery displays historic portraiture.

Jan Pazdera obchod a opravna

Lucerna, Vodičkova 30, Nové Město, Prague 1 (224 216 197). Metro Můstek/tram 3, 9, 14, 24. **Open** 10am-6pm Mon-Fri. **No credit cards**. **Map** p309 K5.
This shop features used cameras, video cameras, enlargers, filters, microscopes, telescopes, tripods and just about every other photographic accessory you can imagine. It also stocks plenty of affordable second-hand cameras from the former East bloc – pieces currently quite fashionable among photographers in the West. Simple camera repairs too.

Photo developing

Photo shops are rife all over the tourist areas, so finding a place to get your prints is never a problem. The shops below are noted for providing quality work – sloppy developing is otherwise all too common.

Česká tisková kancelář (ČTK)

Opletalova 5-7, Nové Město, Prague 1 (222 098 353). Metro Muzeum/tram 3, 9, 14, 24. **Open** 8am-7pm Mon-Fri; 9am-1pm Sat. **Credit** MC, V. **Map** p311 K6.
This professional developing shop also serves the country's leading news agency. As such, it's one of the only places to get black-and-white photos printed 'quickly' – meaning a week, or three days if you fork out a 50% 'rush' fee. You'll probably want to take your holiday snaps elsewhere for printing.

Fotoplus

Na příkopě 17, Nové Město, Prague 1 (224 213 121). Metro Náměstí Republiky/tram 5, 14, 26. **Open** 7.30am-9pm; Mon-Fri; 9am-7pm Sat; 10am-7pm Sun. **Credit** AmEx, MC, V. **Map** p309 K4.
Fotoplus offers quality, one-hour developing and able to handle black and white printing up to A3 size, but not developing. This place also has a quite nice selection of photo albums. A little English spoken.

Stationery & art materials

If it's made of paper, chances are it's available at your local *papírnictví*, where they sell everything from envelopes to loo roll. If you can't find what you want there, try **Kotva**, **Tesco** (for both, *see p158*) or one of the shops listed below.

AKM Papírnictví

Vinohradská 151, Palác Flóra, Žižkov, Prague 3 (255 742 134). Metro Flora/tram 5, 10, 11, 16. **Open** 9am-9pm daily. **Credit** MC, V. **Map** p313 D2.
All sorts of office and school supplies, from fine writing instruments to notepads. Get organised.

Altamira

Jilská 2, Staré Město, Prague 1 (224 219 950/ http://vytvarnepotreby.cz). Metro Národní třída/tram 6, 9, 18, 21, 22, 23. **Open** 9am-7pm Mon-Fri; 10am-5pm Sat. **No credit cards. Map** p308 H4.
Crammed with stretchers, easels, canvases, paints, chalks and brushes, this specialist art shop has everything you need to release the Picasso within. If you find him, the friendly staff can help you with matting and framing.
Other locations: Skořepka 2, Nové Město, Prague 1 (224 220 923).

Loco Plus

Palackého 10, Prague 1 (224 947 732). Metro Můstek/tram 3, 9, 14, 25. **Open** 8.30am-6.30pm Mon-Thur; 8.30am-6pm Fri; 9am-noon Sat. **No credit cards. Map** p310 J6.
An old-school *papírnictví*, where they fairly shriek at you if you don't pick up a shopping basket on your way in. You'll need assistance to examine the pens, but you can peruse the wrapping paper, notepads and a mystifying selection of receipts more or less unmolested. Basic photocopy service.

Papírnictví Týnská Ulička

Týnská ulička 10, Staré Město, Prague 1 (222 314 869/www.papirnictvi-tynska.cz). Metro Staroměstská/tram 17, 18. **Open** 8am-6pm Mon-Fri. **No credit cards. Map** p308 J3.
This curious Staré Město shop offers paper for printing, scribbling, sketching and wrapping. It also does a delightful trade in obscure flags, calendars and other strange things.

Toys

Although you'd like to think that Czech children still ride broomstick horses and play with marionettes when they're not practising the dulcimer, the truth is you can hardly get them away from the PlayStation long enough to pick up their Pucca gear. This leaves more hand-made wooden toys, puppets and dolls for youngsters abroad. The shops listed below are some of the better spots to find toys for culturally enlightened kids.

Ivre

Veleslavinova 3, Staré Město, Prague 1 (222 313 523). Metro Náměstí Republiky/tram 5, 14, 26. **Open** 11am-5pm daily. **Credit** AmEx, MC, V. **Map** p309 K3.
Small children who haven't yet begun to demand toys with Intel chips will be delighted with the soft playthings and handmade puppets on offer here.

Modely, Stavebnice, Hračky

Benediktská 9, Staré Město, Prague 1 (224 827 818/mac.distribution.cz). Metro Náměstí Republiky/ tram 5, 14, 26. **Open** 10am-6pm Mon-Fri. **Credit** MC, V. **Map** p309 K2.
The name of this shop means 'models, construction kits, toys', to wit: replicas of classic and rare automobiles like the Trabant 601, models of Soviet military hardware and a staggering array of durable toys for small and big kids alike.

Sparky's Dům hraček

Havířská 2, Staré Město, Prague 1 (224 239 309/ www.sparkys.cz). Metro Můstek/tram 3, 9, 14, 24. **Open** 10am-7pm Mon-Sat; 10am-6pm Sun. **Credit** AmEx, MC, V. **Map** p308 J4.
Four floors of toys guaranteed to send the spawn into a veritable frenzy. Sparky's House of Toys stocks quality stuff for boys and girls of all ages and interests, including a menagerie of plush animals, action figures and dolls, games, and children's party costumes and favours.

Video rental

The following video rental shops stock DVDs and videos in both PAL and NTSC format. If you don't find what you're looking for at those listed below, you could also try **Music World** (*see p177*).

Video Gourmet

Jakubská 12, Staré Město, Prague 1 (222 323 364). Metro Náměstí Republiky/tram 5, 8, 14. **Open** 11am-11pm daily. **Credit** AmEx, MC, V. **Map** p309 K3.
Attached to Red Hot & Blues (*see p125*), this video-rental shop offers microwave-ready take-out portions of the restaurant's more popular dishes, plus other imported foods like English bacon and Californian wines. Great for homebodies.

Video to Go

Čelakovského sady 12, Prague 1 (224 235 098). Metro Muzeum/tram 11. **Open** 10am-10pm daily. **Credit** MC, V. **Map** p311 L7.
Video to go has reliable supply of hits on video and DVD, as well as a goodly number of children's movies, but at slightly higher prices than you'll find elsewhere. Look for discount offers. Leave your DVD player in your other suitcase? Video to Go will lend you one.
Other locations: Vítězné náměstí 10, Dejvice, Prague 6 (224 318 981).

Virus Video

Templova 8, Staré Město, Prague 1 (728 820 133). Metro Náměstí Republiky/tram 5, 8, 14. **Open** 2-11pm daily. **No credit cards. Map** p309 K2.
If it's fringe cinema you're after, look no further – or not: this peripatetic rental shop tends to move house every couple of years and often ignores its own posted hours. It promises to stay at its present location, in an alcove of the Marquis de Sade bar (*see p150*) until at least 2006.

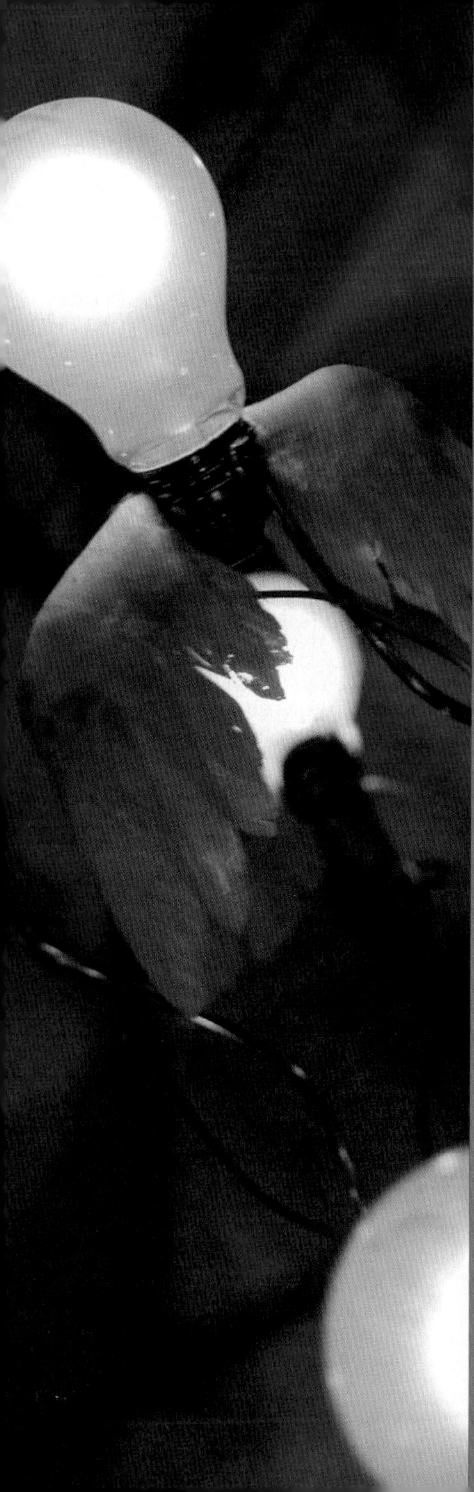

Arts & Entertainment

Features

Festivals & Events

Prague's changing colours mean angels and devils at Christmas, witches in spring and fireworks all year round.

St Nicholas's Eve. *See p186.*

The life cycles of Prague are dramatic and full of ancient rites. Czechs know the approximate day and certainly the order of every blossom arriving in spring, have their favourite summer weekend coordinated with 12 sets of friends months in advance, hunt down the mushrooms of autumn with alacrity (*see p184* ***Houby*** **to you**) and never miss a **St Nicholas's Eve** (*see p186*) street party in winter. It's a completely different city each season.

In April and May people seem to blossom along with the lilacs and chestnut trees, and emerge like moles into the sunlight. Beer gardens fill up even when the crowd is shivering at dusk. Off come the layers, as **Stromovka** park (*see p103*) fills with runners training for the **Prague International Marathon** (*see p183*). Soon after, the **Prague Spring Festival** (*see p184*) heralds the warm weather, as it has for half a century.

With the hot days of June and July, locals (including the staff of most cultural institutions, which go dark until September) tend to clear out to avoid the flood of tourists and head for the country. If you can get an invitation, you may get to experience the joy of the *chata* (cottage) and blueberry-picking. The city bears its own sweet fruit during the summer months, though, with music festivals and the **Tanec Praha** (*see p185*) modern dance performances.

In autumn symphonies, operas and balls return to town, and with them **Prague Autumn** (*see p185*) – and not a little of the sneak-attack libation known as ***Burčák*** (*see p185*). And, of course, with the tourists finally gone, Prague citizens get their beautiful city back to themselves – just as it begins to fill with ice and smog.

Miserable though winter can be, it has its rewards: the glorious spires that tower above Staré Město, the Old Town, are an incomparable sight in the snow. The city may be a sleepy, grog-guzzling, grey and melancholy place, but its **Christmas markets** (*see p186*) are enchanting. And, once the carp has been bashed into submission at the fishmongers' stands for the traditional festive supper, fireworks have people diving for cover in the same square on **New Year's Eve** (Silvestr; *see p186*).

TICKETS & INFORMATION

You can book for most ticketed events through **Ticketpro** (*see p210*), which accepts payments by credit card. Tickets are sometimes also available on the door, but it's advisable to phone ahead and note that credit cards are unlikely to be accepted at venues.

Be sure to check out *The Prague Post* (www.praguepost.cz) before and during your stay or check organisers' website for current listings and further information on events.

Spring

Matejská pouť

Výstaviště, Holešovice, Prague 7 (220 103 204). Metro Vltavská/tram 5, 14, 25. **Admission** 30-50 Kč. **Date** Feb-Mar.

The St Matthew's Fair marks the arrival of warm weather with cheesy rides for the kids at a run-down funfair at Prague's exhibition grounds, Výstaviště (*see p103*). Dodgem cars at 10 Kč a pop and the Ferris wheel bring out the juvenile in all.

Prague Jazz Festival

Various venues (222 211 275/www.agharta.cz). **Admission** varies according to venue. **Date** Mar-Oct. **Map** p309 K7.

One of the hottest jazz fests in Central Europe, the Prague Jazz Festival features world-class players like John Scofield and Richard Bona. Sponsored by the AghaRTA club (*see p221*), the festival is small and sporadic, carrying on intermittently throughout the spring, summer and autumn and offers intimate performances, mainly at the Lucerna Music Bar (*see p215*).

Easter

Date Mar/Apr.

Men rush around the country beating women on the backside with willow sticks. Women respond by dousing the men with cold water but also by giving them painted eggs. Then everyone does a lot of shots of alcohol. This ancient fertility rite is rarely seen in Prague these days, but painted eggs and willow sticks (*pomlaska*) are on sale all over the city.

Witches' Night

Date 30 Apr.

A tradition that rolls the best of Halloween and Bonfire Night into one: *Pálení čarodějnic*, or Witches' Night, marks the death of winter and the birth of spring. Bonfires are lit to purge the winter spirits, an effigy of a hag is burnt – a relic of historical witch hunts – and the more daring observers of the custom leap over the flames. Most fires are in the countryside, but occasionally there's a pyre in the capital, sometimes on Petřín hill in Malá Strana (*see p78*).

Labour Day

Date 1 May.

There's little danger of being run over by a tank in Wenceslas Square these days, but May Day is still a good excuse for a demonstration. The communists, in an attempt to keep the faith alive, usually have a small rally in Letná park (*see p103*) and encourage pensioners to moan about the rigours of the free market. Prague's anarchists sometimes hold an uncharacteristically orderly parade.

May Day

Petřín hill, Malá Strana, Prague 1. Metro Malostranská/tram 6, 9, 12, 22, 23. **Date** 1 May. **Map** p306 C5.

Czech lovers of all ages, their sap rising, make a pilgrimage to the statue of Karel Hynek Mácha on Petřín hill (*see p78*) to place flowers and engage in snogging. Mácha, who was a 19th-century Romantic poet, gave rise to many myths, several bastards and the epic poem *Máj* ('May'). It's actually a melancholy tale of unrequited love, but nobody lets that spoil their fun.

VE Day

Date 8 May.

The Day of Liberation from Fascism is actually 9 May, the date on which the Red Army reached Prague in 1945. In its eagerness to be a good Euro-citizen, however, the Czech government moved the celebration to 8 May, in line with the rest of the continent. Flowers and wreaths are laid on Soviet monuments such as Náměstí Kinských in Smíchov, where a Soviet tank used to stand.

Prague International Marathon

Throughout the city, route varies (224 919 209/ www.pim.cz). **Registration fee** 300-600 Kč. **Credit** (online registration only) MC, V. **Date** May.

Runners from around the world now fly in for the biggest race of the year and have a city-wide street party afterwards, where more than just water is gulped by runners and a few thousand less healthy types. Those not up to the full 28km (18-mile) race still have a shot at the 10km (6-mile) race.

Prague Writers' Festival

Various venues (information 224 931 053/ www.pwf.pragonet.cz). **Admission** varies. **Date** May.

Czech and international literati gather in Prague to read extracts, hobnob and compare their royalty contracts. This is your chance to observe Ivan Klíma's improbable hairdo and the quirks of other local literary lions.

Mezi ploty

Ústavní 91, near Bohnice Psychiatric Hospital, Prague 8 (272 730 623/www.meziploty.cz). Metro Nádraží Holešovice, then bus 200. **Admission** 200 Kč/day; 370 Kč/weekend. **Date** last weekend in May.

This unique festival brings together professional, amateur, and mentally or physically disadvantaged artists, dancers and musicians for two days of events on the grounds of the city's main psychiatric hospital. *See also p238.*

Prague Spring

Hellichova 18, Malá Strana, Prague 1 (257 311 921/257 310 414/www.festival.cz). Metro Malostranská/tram 12, 22, 23. **Admission** varies according to venue. **Date** mid May-early June. **Map** p307 D4.

The biggest and best of Prague's music festivals begins on the anniversary of Smetana's death with a performance of his tone poem *Má Vlast* ('My Country'). The festival is hugely popular, drawing symphony orchestras and virtuosi from around the world, who perform at the city's finest venues, so book in advance if possible. *See also p209.*

Summer

Khamoro

Various venues (222 518 554/www.khamoro.cz). **Admission** free-200 Kč. **Date** May.

This festival features concerts, seminars and workshops on Roma culture, focusing on traditional Gypsy music, customs and art. Concerts run the gamut from swing guitar jams to a Hungarian all-violin Roma orchestra

Respect

Various venues (222 710 050/603 461 592/ respect.inway.cz). **Admission** from 120 Kč. **Date** June.

Houby to you

On autumn days, especially following a rainy spell, Czechs drop everything and head for the forest. They're prowling the woods, as Slavic people have for ages, seeking *houby*, the Czech word for mushrooms (and also, curiously, the expression for 'bollocks!').

The most prized catches are Boletes, often called by their Italian name, Porcini, but known to every Czech as *hřiby*. The best varieties look like an oven-baked bun on top with the undersides of their caps covered in tiny tubes rather than gills. These are eaten with abandon during mushrooming season – and find their way into everything from soups to egg dishes to goulash. What can't be consumed while fresh will quickly be sliced up and left to sun dry for the off-season. Top priority: having enough dried *hřiby* on hand for the traditional Christmas dish *Černý Kuba*, a mix of pearl barley and *Boletes*.

Since mushrooms do the majority of their growing overnight, Czechs hit the forest early, when the light makes the hunt easier on the eyes and before woodland creatures can get to them. Maggots are especially fond of mushrooms – gather later in the day and you risk uncovering an invasion. They start munching from the ground up, though, so there may still be a chance to save for hunters who've slept in.

Mushroom-hunting etiquette is serious business and woe to those who trample through the woods without proper respect for forest inhabitants or fellow mushroomers. Careful harvesting – cutting a mushroom with a knife slightly above its base – will protect the mycelium fungus, of which the mushroom is the fruiting body, so that the bounty will grow back one day. Rip out mushrooms by their roots, or – God forbid – kick a mushroom, and you'll rue the day you did. Trim and clean the mushroom as much as possible on the spot before adding it to your basket.

And what of all those stories about, um, poisonous mushrooms and felled gourmets?

The deadly *Amanita phalloides* can look to a beginner rather like an innocent *champignon*, and lots of non-fatal mushrooms can cause plenty of pain. Don't even think of touching that bright-red beauty with the white dots, the ubiquitous Fly Agaric, known to all from fairytale illustrations. Even the delicious Honey Mushroom, known locally as the *Václavka* because it always grows around the name day of St Wenceslas or Václav on 28 September, wreaks digestive havoc if not thoroughly boiled or deep-fried. So save the aggro and bring a Czech. Most, having picked since childhood, are seasoned pros.

But, if the lure of the hunt proves too great, and no expert is at hand, the **Czech Mycological Society** (Ceská mykologická společnost, Karmelitská 14, Malá Strana, Prague 1, closed Thur-Sun), will identify a questionable mushroom for you. If nothing else, remember this: there are old mushroom hunters and bold mushroom hunters, but no old, bold mushroom hunters. If in doubt, throw it out.

Light entertainment: **Wenceslas Square Christmas market**. *See p186.*

The world and ethnic music high point of the year features Balkan folk and Gypsy music, with performers such as Taraf de Haidouks, and its Prague counterparts. The organiser is Prague's main underground and ethnic music label, Rachot. Concerts are usually at the Akropolis (*see p215*).

Tanec Praha

Various venues (224 817 886/www.tanecpha.cz). **Admission** from 200 Kč. **Date** June.

Eagerly anticipated by audiences all year, Tanec Praha, or Dance Prague, is an international gala of modern dance which has become one of the more successful performance festivals in Prague. International participants perform in major theatres and venues across the city and sometimes conduct workshops and symposiums. *See also p232.*

Summer Old Music Festival

Collegium Marianum, Melantrichova 19, Staré Město, Prague 1 (224 229 462/www.tynska.cuni.cz). Metro Staroměstská/tram 17, 18. **Admission** from 120 Kč. **Date** July.

Growing in popularity, this gala of Renaissance and baroque music, performed on period instruments and in historic settings, is one of the few native musical offerings during the summer holidays. It also attracts some of the highest-quality performers around.

Autumn

Prague Autumn

Various venues (222 540 484/www.prazskypodzim.cz). **Date** mid Sept-early Oct. **Admission** varies according to venue.

Garnering more respect every year, the next best thing to Prague Spring is this festival of world-renowned classical talents. Performances are held in the city's finest concert venues, including the splendid Rudolfinum (*see p209*).

Burčák arrives

Date late Sept-early Oct.

Burčák – a cloudy, half-fermented, early-season wine – arrives in Prague sometime in the autumn months. It's a speciality of Moravia, where it would appear that the locals haven't got the patience to wait for their alcohol to finish aging. Served straight from the barrel into special jugs, *Burčák* looks like murky wheat beer, tastes like cherryade and – beware – will sneak up on you if you don't treat it with respect.

Festival of Best Amateur & Professional Puppet Theatre Plays

Various venues (241 409 293). **Admission** varies according to venue. **Date** Oct.

This is an unusual festival that celebrates Bohemia's long tradition of puppet-making. Puppets are a big thing in the Czech Republic – some of the country's most innovative artists continue to use them, and a faculty at the university is devoted to the craft.

Anniversary of the birth of Czechoslovakia

Date 28 Oct.

The country no longer exists, but that's no reason to cancel a public holiday – so the people still get a day off. Lots of fireworks – as on every other possible occasion – and it takes forever to get a tram.

All Souls' Day

Date 2 Nov.

Surely the best time of year to visit any one of the city's cemeteries. Whole families turn out to light candles, lay wreaths and say prayers for the dead. The best place to go is the enormous Olšany Cemetery (*see p107*).

Anniversary of the Velvet Revolution

Národní třída & Václavské náměstí, Nové Město, Prague 1. Metro Národní třída or Můstek/tram 3, 6, 9, 14, 18, 22, 23, 24. **Date** 17 Nov. **Map** p308 H5.

Surprisingly understated observances to commemorate the demonstration that began the Velvet Revolution. Flowers are laid and candles lit in Wenceslas Square near the equine statue and on the memorial on Národní třída near No.20.

Winter

St Nicholas's Eve

Around Charles Bridge & Staroměstské náměstí. Staré Město, Prague 1. Metro Staroměstská/tram 17, 18. **Date** 5 Dec. **Map** p306 H3.

Grown men spend the evening wearing frocks, drinking large amounts of beer and terrorising small children. They wander the streets in threesomes, dressed as St Nicholas, an angel and a devil, symbolising confession, reward and punishment. Rather than a red cloak, St Nicholas usually sports a long white vestment, with a white mitre and staff. The angel hands out sweets to children who have been good, while the devil is on hand to dispense rough justice to those who haven't.

Christmas

In the week leading up to the Vánoce (Christmas) holiday, the streets sport huge tubs of water filled with carp, the traditional Czech Christmas dish and there are Christmas markets in Old Town Square and Wenceslas Square. The feasting and exchange of gifts happen on the evening of 24 December, when – apart from midnight masses, the finest of which is at St Vitus's Cathedral (*see p61*) – pretty much everything closes down. Things don't start opening up again until the 27th.

New Year's Eve

Václavské náměstí & Staroměstské náměstí, Prague 1. Metro Můstek or Staroměstská/tram 3, 9, 14, 24 or 17, 18. **Date** 31 Dec. **Map** p309 K5.

Bring your helmet? On New Year's Eve, Silvestr, the streets are packed with a ragtag crowd of Euro-revellers, with much of the fun centred on Wenceslas Square and Old Town Square. Fireworks are let off everywhere and flung around with frankly dangerous abandon, then champagne bottles are smashed.

Anniversary of Jan Palach's death

Václavské náměstí, Nové Město, Prague 1. Metro Muzeum/tram 11. **Date** 16 Jan. **Map** p311 L6.

Jan Palach set himself ablaze on 16 January 1969 in Wenceslas Square to protest the Soviet occupation that killed off the promise of cultural freedoms allowed the previous year. His grave at Olšany Cemetery (*see p107*) is adorned with candles and flowers all year round. Many people visit Olšany or the memorial to the victims of communism (*see p95*) near the St Wenceslas statue to lay a few more.

Masopust

Akropolis, Kubelíkova 27, Žižkov, Prague 3 (www.palacakropolis.cz). Metro Jiřího zPoděbrad/tram 11. **Date** mid Feb (7th Sun before Easter). **Map** p313 B2.

Traditionally, groups of 12 carolers accompanied by people in masks parade about in this whimsical celebration of what the rest of the world knows as Shrove Tuesday, the eve of Ash Wednesday (the original tradition seen in the Czech lands has the holiday on Sunday). According to custom, everyone who meets this procession should be invited to the evening feast, a great opportunity to stuff yourself with a freshly slaughtered pig and wash it down with rivers of beer. More manageable might be the version of the Masopust street party centred around Prague's Žižkov district, where a slate of activities revolve around the Akropolis club (*see p215*).

Out of town

Karlovy Vary International Film Festival

Hotel Thermal, IP Pavlova 11, Karlovy Vary (221 411 011/www.kviff.cz). **Admission** varies. **Date** July.

This genteel spa town hosts the Czech version of Cannes. While hardly in the same league, the festival shows an interesting mix of foreign and home-grown features. *See also p196.*

Barum Rally

Start/finish line: Interhotel Moskva, Práce náměstí 2512, Zlín (www.rallysport.cz/barum). **Admission** free. **Date** Sept.

A classic road race dating back decades, this still attracts drivers from across Europe and has recently been ranked one of the best. Moravian roads roar to life as amateur and pro drivers compete for the big *pohár*, the winner's cup. Autoklub Barum Zlín sponsors the event and an entry form in English can be downloaded from its website listed above.

Velká Pardubice Steeplechase

Pražská 607, Pardubice (www.pardubice-racecourse.cz). **Admission** 200-2,000 Kč. **No credit cards. Date** 2nd weekend in Oct.

The star steeplechase event in the annual calendar is also a controversial one: horses and riders are often injured on the difficult course. Celebrity horse people pour in from all over Europe, putting box seats at a premium. A full price list can be found on the above website along with instructions for ordering an advance ticket.

Children

Fairytale Prague has always enchanted children of all ages. Now more grown up, with a new aquarium, it's family-friendly too.

The storybook splendour of Prague won't be lost on your little princes and princesses. From the dramatic gates of Prague Castle to the winding medieval streets of Staré Město and Josefov, it's a city that fires the imagination. Thankfully, it's also becoming a city that's more and more geared to the special needs of kids. There are all sorts of diversions, some quaint and low-tech like the **Zrcadlové Bludiště**, or Mirror Maze (*see p188*), on picturesque Petřín hill, a favourite for generations, while more high-tech developments include the cybercombat **Laser Game** (*see p189*). **Puppet theatre** (*see p190*) is another evergreen option and other favourites include indoor jungle gyms at kids' mini-mall **Teta Tramtárie** (*see p190*) and **Jungleland** (*see p189*), **outdoor playgrounds** (*see p190*), a trip to **Prague Zoo** (*see p188*) and a visit to the new **Sea World** aquarium (*see p188*).

When it's time to feed hungry little ogres, the good news is an increasing number of restaurants can satisfy the whole family. One popular pizzeria, **Rugantino** (*see p190*) even lets kids make their own pizza. More shops also cater to the needs of children, and it's now possible to rent prams and car seats (*see p190*). Parents gagging for a night out will appreciate the host of babysitting agencies providing English-speaking care-givers too (*see p191*).

Finding a suitable area for baby-changing isn't always easy. **Mothercare** (*see p191*) has one on the first floor, with two changing tables, a sink and a bottle warmer. **Nový Smíchov** shopping centre (*see p158*) has one on the first floor near lifts and adult toilets, including toilets for toddlers – but be prepared to wait, as the mall is popular with mums. **Tesco** (*see p158*) has a changing table on the first floor. Request a key from any cashier there. Teta Tramtárie also has facilities.

Sightseeing

Some attractions, such as the **Astronomical Clock** (*see p85*) and climbable towers like the **Petřín Tower** (*see p80*), **Old Town Bridge Tower** (*see p88*) and the **Powder Gate** (*see p81*), are as suited to children as to adults. Note that most towers are closed during winter.

Museums

National Museum

Národní muzeum
Václavské náměstí 68, Holešovice, Prague 7 (224 497 111/www.nm.cz). Metro Muzeum.
Open *Jan-Apr, Oct-Dec* 9am-5pm daily. *May-Sept* 10am-6pm daily. Closed 1st Tue of mth.
Admission 80 Kč; 40 Kč children, students; free under-6s; 90 Kč family; free to all 1st Mon of mth.
No credit cards. Map p311 L6.

Many of the displays in this natural history museum are a little dull, but children still seem to be fascinated by the stuffed animal exhibits on the top floor (*see also p116*).

National Technical Museum

Národní technické muzeum
Kostelní 42, Holešovice, Prague 7 (220 399 111/www.ntm.cz). Metro Hradčanská or Vltavská/tram 1, 8, 25, 26. **Open** 9am-5pm Tue-Fri; 10am-6pm Sat-Sun. **Admission** 70 Kč; 30 Kč children, students; 150 Kč family. **No credit cards.**
Map p312 C3.

This museum is a sure hit with kids interested in planes, trains and automobiles. It's full of original vehicles, some of which can be climbed on to afford

The best Kids' stuff

For coal mining in the city (and cool planes)
The **National Technical Museum** (*see above*) has all the best conveyances.

For light-pulsing evil enemies
Laser Game (*see p189*) zaps 'em good.

For monkeying around
The **Prague Zoo** (*see p188*) is a fave of boys and gorillas.

For old-fashioned laughs – and a good hike
Zrcadlové Bludiště (*see p188*) is a bendy mirror-ful of fun.

For riding to the zoo in style
Pražská paroplavební společnost (*see p189*) steams almost to the gate.

Animal-action at **Prague Zoo**.

a good look at the interiors, and the temporary exhibitions are quite interesting. A popular coal mine replica tunnels through the basement, and English-speaking tours can be arranged in advance. The museum is located next to the lovely Letná Park.

Sights

Prague Zoo

Zoologická zahrada v Praze

U Trojského zámku 3, Trója, Prague 7 (296 112 230/www.zoopraha.cz). Metro Nádraží Holešovice, then bus 112. **Open** *Jan, Feb, Nov, Dec* 9am-4pm daily. *Mar* 9am-5pm daily. *Apr-May* 9am-6pm daily. *June-Aug* 9am-7pm daily. *Sept-Oct* 9am-6pm daily. **Admission** 80 Kč; 50 Kč children, students; 230 Kč family; free under-3s. **No credit cards.**

The flood of 2002 hit the Prague Zoo hard. There was, however, a silver lining to the storm clouds. Numerous improvement projects that had been on the shelf were put into play not long after the waters receded. The temporary downside is that visitors can expect to encounter construction work at various places. Stromovka Park is nearby.

Sea World

Mořský svět

Výstaviště, Holešovice, Prague 7 (220 103 275/ www.morsky-svet.cz) Metro Nádraží Holešovice/tram 5,12,17. **Open** 10am-7pm daily. **Admission** 120 Kč; 70 Kč children; 100 Kč concessions; 330-350 Kč family. **No credit cards. Map** p312 C1.

A trip underwater to see some sharks makes for a great break from musty castle tours. A soundtrack of waves crashing and seagulls crying gives the impression you've left this landlocked country. The aquarium has a collection of over 300 species.

Zrcadlové Bludiště

Mirror Maze

Petřín Hill, Malá Strana, Prague 1 (257 315 212). Tram 12, 22, 23, then funicular to Petřín hill. **Open** *Jan-Mar, Nov, Dec* 10am-4.30pm daily. *Apr-Oct* 10am-6.30pm daily. **Admission** 30 Kč; 20 Kč children. **No credit cards. Map** p306 C5 .

This mirror maze has been a staple with Czech children for decades, where kids are guaranteed to belly-laugh at their distorted images. There's also a wax diorama of the Swedes' unsuccessful 1648 attack on the Charles Bridge. While you're on the hill, check out the Stefanik Observatory (*see p80*).

Activities & events

Boating

Slovanský Island & Charles Bridge, Staré Město, Prague 1. Metro Staroměstská/tram 17, 18. **Open** *Mar-Oct* 10am-6pm. **Rates** 80-120 Kč per hour. **No credit cards. Map** p310 M6/p308 G4.

Rowing- or paddleboats can be rented at Novotného lávka, south of the Staré Město end of Charles Bridge or at Slovanský Island, near the National Theatre.

Historic tram 91

296 124 901. **Open** *Apr-Nov* hourly, noon-6pm Sat, Sun & national holidays. **Fare** 25 Kč; 10 Kč children. **No credit cards.**

This quaint, wood-framed tram travels a loop from Výstaviště, trundling along the banks of Malá Strana, across the Legionnaires' Bridge to the National Theatre, up through Wenceslas Square and then back to Výstaviště via Náměstí Republiky. Hop on the antique at any stop along the route.

Horse-drawn carriages

Staroměstské náměstí, Staré Město, Prague 1 (no phone). Metro Staroměstská/tram 17, 18. **Rides** 10am-6pm daily. **No credit cards. Map** p308 J3.
Hitch a ride on an old-time, horse-drawn carriage. Rides begin near the clock tower on Old Town Square and are offered during peak tourist months.

Matějská pouť

Výstaviště, Holešovice, Prague 7 (220 103 204) Metro Vltavská/tram 5, 14, 25. **Date** Feb-Mar. **Admission** 30-50 Kč. **No credit cards. Map** p312 C1.
This popular springtime carnival is a hit with kids. For a month, the grounds of Výstaviště fairground (*see p103*) are jam-packed with rides, bumper cars and shooting galleries, and the air is filled with the pungent smells of doughnuts and candyfloss.

Pražská paroplavební společnost

Docked on the embankment below Palackého náměstí, Nové Město, Prague 1 (224 931 013/224 930 017/ www.paroplavba.cz). Metro Karlovo náměstí/tram 3, 4, 10, 16, 17, 21. **Open** Various times daily (call or check website for details). **Tickets** 80 Kč; 40 Kč children; free under-6s. **Credit** MC, V. **Map** p310 G9.
Great in combination with a trip to the Prague Zoo (*see p188*), which this steamship serves via the Vltava river, the PPS is a leisurely 75-minute ride, operated late March to November. This company also offers 55- and 90-minute sightseeing rides year-round. There are several cruises each day.

Entertainment & sport

Jungleland

Výmolova 298/2A, Radlice, Prague 5 (251 091 437). Metro Radlická. **Open** 9am-7pm daily. **Admission** 50 Kč children for 90mins (accompanying adults free); 25 Kč disabled children. **No credit cards.**
Children aged one to 13 can burn off energy at this huge padded jungle gym, which features much more than your standard slide and box of plastic balls. Kids will have a blast climbing, balancing on a rope bridge, crawling under obstacles and navigating their way through the labyrinthine playground. Parents can relax at an elevated café, while babies and toddlers can enjoy a separate soft-play area.

Laser Game

Národní 25, Staré Město, Prague 1 (224 221 188). Metro Národní třída/tram 6, 9, 18, 21, 22, 23. **Open** 10am-midnight daily. **Admission** 149 Kč per 15 mins. **No credit cards. Map** p308 G5.
If family tensions are running high, work them out with cyberblast pulse guns. Children transform into Terminators in this dark basement labyrinth, shooting laser guns at light sensors on their adversaries' belts to score a kill, while trying to dodge shots at their own belts. Adults should be mindful of low-clearance ceilings in the dark.

Teta Tramtárie

Jungmanova 28, Nové Město, Prague 1 (www.tetatramtarie.cz). Metro Mustek or Narodni trida/tram 6, 9, 18, 21, 22, 23. **Open** 7.30am-8pm daily. **Credit** V, MC. **Map** p308 J5.

Teta Tramtárie is a ball for kids: an entire mini-mall of toy shop, children's bookshop, kid-sized cinema, with endless children's films and cartoons (some in English), puppet theatre, two pizza restaurants and an ice-cream parlour (*see p166*). By far the favourite is the large indoor jungle gym. Centrally located, pushchair-friendly, and with a baby-changing station and toilets adapted for small people.

Outdoor playgrounds

Happily, Prague finally has a good number of playgrounds newly outfitted with the latest swings, slides, merry-go-rounds and more – most generally have equipment suitable for toddlers too. Below are some central ones, all open from 8am until sunset daily.

Kampa

Malostranské nábřeží 1, Malá Strana, Prague 1. Metro Malostranská/tram 6, 9, 12, 20, 22, 23. **Map** p307 F4.

The walled playground on the side of Kampa Park closest to the river (not to be confused with the nearby restaurant of the same name) is a consistent hit with local kids.

Kinského zahrada

Újezd 1, Smíchov, Prague 5. Metro Anděl/ tram 6, 9,12, 20.

Located just off naměsti Kinský. To reach the playground, enter the park via the arched iron gate, then follow the pavement to the right.

Petřín hill

Újezd & Vítězná streets, Malá Strana, Prague 1. Metro Malostranská/tram 6, 9, 12, 20, 22, 23. **Map** p307 D5.

Walk up Petřín hill past the funicular stop (lanová dráha), then take the pedestrian bridge to the right. That path leads directly to the playground.

Puppet theatre

Puppet theatre has a rich history in Bohemia. The **National Marionette Theatre** (*see p237*) stages regular kid-pleasing shows for foreigners, while a handful of theatres across the city host puppet performances (*see p233*). Another option is a non-verbal multimedia performances at the **Magic Lantern** theatre (*see p237*). Current listings appear in *The Prague Post*. If your little darling wants a marionette of their own, a number of quality puppet shops are along Jilská and Karlova streets in Staré Město. **Krásná Dišperanda** (Jilska 7, 224 235 579) is recommended.

Eating out

More restaurants in Prague are providing highchairs upon request, though finding a suitable baby-changing area remains a challenge. Also, restaurant owners often side with the cigarette puffers, neglecting to provide non-smoking sections for families. Still, **Pizzeria Rugantino** (Dušní 4, Staré Město, Prague 1, 222 318 172), minutes from Old Town Square, has a friendly staff, provides crayons and paper, offers kid-sized portions and has a non-smoking section. From 4-6pm kids can even make their own pizzas – booking is essential.

The Staré Město branch of **Bohemia Bagel** (*see p119*), with its token play corner and quick, child-friendly food, remains a favourite of English-speaking parents. For dessert, treat your kids to a pilgrimage to fruit-ice heaven – also known as **Ovocný Světozor** (Vodičkova 39, Nové Město, Prague 1, 224 946 826), located in the Světozor passage, just off Wenceslas Square. Don't be put off by the crowds – service is quick. Good sundaes and milkshakes too.

Practicalities

Baby requirements

As in any European capital, disposable nappies and baby food are widely available. Any larger, full-service supermarket will stock all your basic baby supplies. For the basics, plus additional items like bottles, nipples, nursing supplies, formula, lotions and so on, head to a hypermarket such as **Carrefour** (*see p173*) or **Tesco** (*see p158*), or to a pharmacy (*lékárna*). For late-night emergencies, each district in Prague has a 24-hour pharmacy. The Prague 1 *lékárna* is at Palackého 5 (224 946 982). It accepts credit cards on purchases over 300 Kč. Note there's a small surcharge on purchases after 7pm on weekdays, after noon on Saturday and all day Sunday.

If you're in need of clothes and other supplies for your sprog, try the following.

Baby Shop Sparky's

Slovanský dům, Senovážné náměstí 28A, Nové Město, Prague 1 (221 451 790). Metro Můstek/ tram 3, 9, 14, 24. **Open** 10am-7pm daily. **Credit** AmEx, MC, V. **Map** p309 K4.

The upscale Sparky's stocks a wide variety of all things baby-related, including clothes, pushchairs, cots and toys. It specialises in the needs of babies up to 12 months old. Just outside the shop, you'll find Sparky's small, fenced-in play area.

The **National Museum**. *See p187.*

Mothercare

Myslbek Pasáž, Na Příkopě 19-21, Staré Město, Prague 1 (222 240 008). Metro Můstek/tram 3, 9, 14, 24. **Open** 9.30am-7pm Mon-Fri; 9am-6pm Sat; 11am-6pm Sun. **Credit** MC, V. **Map** p309 K4.
Everything for little ones, from pushchairs to clothes. There's also a spacious baby-changing area.

Baby gear rentals

Ajuty

Plzeňská 20, Smíchov, Prague 5 (257 320 032, www.ajuty.cz). Metro Anděl/tram 4, 6, 7, 9, 10, 12, 14, 20. **Open** 9.30am-6pm Mon-Fri; 9am-noon Sat. **Credit** MC, V.
Pushchairs rent for 300-600 Kč per week. Car seats go for 385-420 Kč per week. A deposit is required.

Childminding

Large hotels usually offer a babysitting service. Otherwise, try the following, whose rates tend to be cheaper than hotel rates. These agencies all provide sitters who speak English. Be prepared to pay transport costs for sitters who stay after midnight.

Agentura Admina

Americká 10, Prague 2 (608 281 280/603 421 542). **Rates** 140-200 Kč per hr. **No credit cards.** **Map** p309 A3.
This agency also has an indoor play area for short-term childminding.

Agentura Aja

603 886 736. **Rates** 100-150 Kč per hr. **No credit cards.**
This agency will book a sitter for any schedule and send them to you at rates of 100-150 Kč, depending on the time of day and the number of children.

Agentura Pohoda

274 772 201/602 252 873/www.agpohoda.cz. **Rates** 130-150 Kč per hr. **No credit cards.**
This agency specialises in minding foreigners' kidsand does a lot of work with local film studios, even looking after Bruce Willis's son and daughter.

Health

For sore throats, scuffed knees, or worse, call the following English-speaking care providers:

First Medical Clinic of Prague

První Pražská Zdravotní
Ladova 7, Nové Město, Prague 2 (224 919 121/ emergencies 603 555 006/www.medicover.com). Metro Karlovo Náměstí/tram 3, 16, 17, 21. **Open** 7am-7pm Mon-Fri. **Credit** AmEx, MC, V. **Map** p310 G10.
This clinic specialises in paediatrics.

Poliklinika na Národní

Národní třída 9, Nové Město, Prague 1 (222 075 120/www.poliklinika.narodni.cz). Metro Národní třída/tram 6, 9, 18, 21, 22, 23. **Open** 8.30am-5pm Mon-Fri; by appointment Sat, Sun. **Credit** AmEx, MC, V. **Map** p310 H5.
A highly professional staff, including a paediatrician, and a central Nové Město location. Handy for crises.

Transport

In Prague children up to six years old travel free on public transport, while those aged 6-15 travel for half-price. On the metro, many stations lack escalators or lifts from ground level down to the entrance vestibule. Czechs are accustomed, however, to helping mums carry their strollers up or down the stairs. They may approach you offering help but if no one volunteers, don't be shy about asking – just say '*Pomoc, prosím*' ('Help, please'). If you're at a busy tram stop, it's a good idea to wave to the approaching driver to let him know you'll be getting on with a pram. People with prams must enter and exit by the tram's rear door; on buses, look for the pram sticker indicating which door to use. As you reach your stop, push the button above the door (not the red emergency one) to signal that you'll require a little extra time getting off.

Film

'Cinematic' doesn't half capture Prague, with Hollywood crews and indie productions both shooting here, and newly plush theatres. Cue camera.

Czech film companies, which used to have a near monopoly on the city's studio space, can now seldom afford to rent the top-line facilities, which have been taken over by foreign production companies. So local films now tend to be shot on location, which, if anything, adds to their indie spirit. New Czech films like the wartime melodrama *Želary* and the black comedy *One Hand Can't Clap* (*Jedna ruka netleská*) still manage to be among the biggest domestic box-office draws, even if – or because – they lack dazzling effects and megastars. *Smart Philip* (*Mazaný Filip*), a parody of 1940s Hollywood detective films, used one of the smaller stages at Barrandov – a huge Czech facility where the Nazis once made propaganda films – to re-create the stage-bound look of Hollywood's Golden Age. *Smart Philip* also shows another new trend in savvy Czech filmmaking: conspicuous product placement is taking over as state funding dries up.

The first international splash in Czech filmmaking came with *Ecstasy* (*Extáze*) in 1932, which featured a nude bathing scene and a young Hedy Lamarr. Until the mid '60s, though, very few Czech films – with the exception of Karel Zeman's *The Fabulous World of Jules Verne* (*Vynález zkázy*, 1958) – won attention abroad.

The Czech New Wave, from 1963 to 1968, brought Miloš Forman, Jiří Menzel and Ivan Passer to prominence. Menzel' s *Closely Observed Trains* (*Ostře sledované vlaky*) won an Oscar in 1968. The Soviet-led invasion in 1968 all but killed off creativity for another 20 years. But, recently, young filmmakers referred to as the Velvet Generation have been helping to put Czech cinema back on the international map with films such as *Kolya*, *Divided We Fall* and *Loners*.

Foreign productions, meanwhile, are so eager to exploit Czech filmmaking mastery and affordability that Barrandov is no longer enough. Prague Studios, built in a converted MiG factory, is nearly always booked, just as Barrandov is, and has plans for expanding. Disused factories and warehouses are pressed into service when demand still isn't met. Recent Prague-made films include *Blade II*, *XXX*, *Shanghai Knights*, *Van Helsing*, *The League of Extraordinary Gentlemen* and *The Brothers Grimm*. Often shooting spills over into the streets of Prague, everyone's favourite backdrop, and the stars themselves are known for hitting Prague clubs like **Radost FX** and **Mecca** (for both, *see p222*).

For audiences, the stakes are also steadily climbing. A few years ago there was just one multiplex, but the cinema-building in Prague

Želary.

has just about reached capacity now, with a wave of construction producing 11 multiplexes boasting more than 100 screens.

The newest addition to cinema devlopment was the opening of an **IMAX** screen at **Cinema City Flóra** (*see below*) in late 2003. Few of the screenings are in English, however. The single-screen cinemas that were sold out for the weekend by most Fridays in the '90s are now struggling to maintain a handful of customers. Many of these gems of pre-Velvet Revolution discomfort and bad sound have at least upgraded to high-tech stereo sound systems, but the seats and concession stands lag far behind the times. Some even cling to the old five-person rule: if fewer than five customers turn up, the screening is cancelled. These theatres offer that extra frisson to your thriller.

They have other appeal, as well: while tickets for the multiplexes run around 150 Kč (and more for special seating), the smaller theatres hold the line closer to 100 Kč. Some have bars or cafés that draw a crowd, including regulars without the slightest interest in film. The programming for many single-screeners is also more imaginative: second-run films mixed with art-house fare. **Blaník** (*see below*) offers live performances on days when it doesn't show films. French- and Spanish-language films have been making headway on to schedules, but the majority of films screened in the city are mass-appeal blockbusters, with a few token indie English-language pictures thrown in.

The most ornate of the grand-dame theatres is the **Lucerna** (*see below*). The art nouveau interior is a fine change from the assembly-line sterility of the multiplexes. For a peek into cinema-going of the past, check the film archives at **Ponrepo** (*see p194*) – you need to fill out an application for membership before getting to see a film.

There's generally a sign at the box office explaining what version the film is in. *Dabing* films are dubbed into Czech but usually only children's films get this treatment. By and large, films are screened *s českými titulky*, or simply *č t* (with original soundtrack and Czech subtitles). Important Czech films are sometimes screened with English subtitles; look for *s anglickými titulky*.

Tickets have assigned seat numbers and you can usually pick your spot from a computer screen at the box office. Unless you want some latecomer to argue that you're in their place, be sure to find the row (*řada*) and seat (*sedadlo*) that are printed on the ticket.

Film times are available in *The Prague Post* (www.praguepost.cz), as well in a number of smaller but ever-changing Czech publications, usually available for free. Big posters at many tram stops and kiosks offer a fairly complete schedule. All the multiplexes and many of the smaller art-house cinemas post listings online.

In addition, some nightclubs and cafés like **NoD** in **Roxy** (*see p222*) or **Rock Café** (*see p215*) show videotapes or DVDs, but sometimes these are dubbed and it can be hard to predict.

Commercial cinemas

Blaník

Václavské náměstí 56, Nové Město, Prague 1 (224 032 172). Metro Muzeum/tram 11. **No credit cards. Map** p311 K6.

Still hanging on, thanks to its prime location, this pleasant if plain single-screen theatre has undergone an extensive renovation and alternates between recent hit films and live theatrical productions, usually in the form of musicals.

Lucerna

Vodičkova 36, Nové Město, Prague 1 (224 216 972). Metro Můstek/tram 3, 9, 14, 24. **No credit cards. Map** p311 K6.

Still holding on to quickly fading glory, this art-nouveau masterpiece is a reminder of cinema's glory days. The elevated lobby bar has large windows with views over the 1920s-era shopping arcade (*see p98* **Dark pasáž**) below, and occasionally somebody still tickles the ivories on the piano. The coat-check still functions, you can still access the balcony and there's even a real curtain in front of the screen. Recently, the Lucerna has been moving towards fewer Hollywood and more European films in its programme.

Multiplexes

Cinema City Flora

Vinohradská 149, Žižkov, Prague 3 (255 742 021/www.cinemacity.cz) Metro Flora/tram 11. **No credit cards. Map** p313 A3.

The presence of the city's only IMAX cinema, capable of 3-D screenings, distinguishes this shopping mall cinema located on the upper floors of Palác Flora from the other multiplexes.

Palace Cinemas Nový Smíchov

Plzeňská 8, Smíchov, Prague 5 (257 181 212/ www.palacecinemas.cz). Metro Anděl/tram 6, 9, 12. **No credit cards.**

With 12 screens and 2,702 seats, this holds claim to the most popular multiplex in terms of attendance, and the largest screen (excluding IMAX; *see above*). It's right across the street from Village Cinemas Anděl City (Radlická 3179, 251 115 100, www. villagecinemas.cz). If a film is sold out here, it isn't too far a walk to try again.

Palace Cinemas Slovanský dům

Na Příkopě 22, Nové Město, Prague 1 (257 181 212/ www.palacecinemas.cz). Metro Náměstí Republiky/ tram 5, 8, 14. **No credit cards. Map** p309 K4.

A touch of classic glamour at the **Lucerna** bar. *See p193.*

This is the most centrally located multiplex. It sometimes shows recent Czech films with English subtitles or original-language versions of animated films that are dubbed elsewhere. The cinema also boasts a high-tech digital projector that can simulcast live concerts or show digital films. In January the annual Febiofest (*see p196*) takes over the entire complex.

Art-house cinemas

Evald

Národní třída 28, Nové Město, Prague 1 (221 105 225/www.cinemart.cz). Metro Národní třída/tram 6, 9, 18, 22. **No credit cards. Map** p308 H5.

The best central art-house is also rather small. The owners also distribute films, so they often have exclusive bookings on some European art films, independent American films and Czech films, which are sometimes shown with English subtitles. Advance booking is recommended for new films. There's no snack bar, but the cinema does have a decent restaurant with Czech food specialities.

French Institute

Štěpánská 35, Nové Město, Prague 1 (221 401 011/www.ifp.cz). Metro Můstek/tram 3, 9, 14, 24. **No credit cards. Map** p311 K6.

New and classic French films – around half with English subtitles – are shown here in a full-scale, fairly comfortable basement cinema. Tickets are incredibly cheap at 40 Kč. But *sacre bleu!* Don't even think of bringing food or drinks into the screening room.

Kino Aero

Biskupcova 31, Žižkov, Prague 3 (271 771 349/ www.kinoaero.cz). Metro Želivského/tram 1, 9, 16. **No credit cards.**

No cinema makes more of an effort than Aero. This 70-year-old movie palace goes beyond the offerings of local distributors to get prints from all over. Luckily, the imports of foreign films often have English subtitles, with Czech translations broadcast to headsets. On occasion, filmmakers such as Terry Gilliam and Paul Morrissey come along to introduce their films. The cinema is also home to several festivals (*see below*). Tickets can be booked in advance online. *See also p195* **Aero takes off**.

MAT Studio

Karlovo náměstí 19, Nové Město, Prague 1 (224 915 765/www.mat.cz). Metro Karlovo náměstí/tram 3, 4, 6, 14, 16, 18, 22, 24. **No credit cards. Map** p310 H7.

Definitely the smallest cinema in town, this intimate screening room shows a fair mix of offbeat films, Czech classics with English subtitles and rare selections from the Czech TV vaults. The cinema's bar has movie props and old posters from Czech films.

Ponrepo

Bio Konvikt Theatre, Bartolomějská 13, Staré Město, Prague 1 (no phone). Metro Národní třída/tram 6, 9, 18, 22. **Annual membership** 150 Kč; tickets 30 Kč. **No credit cards. Map** p308 H5.

This is the screening room for the Czech Film Archive, though the managment seem to discourage patrons from coming to enjoy old films: a photo ID is required for all screenings. The schedule features Czech and Slovak films, plus world classics. Make sure the film doesn't have a live Czech translation announced directly into the hall (denoted by *s překl.*), since it will be impossible to hear the original soundtrack.

Festivals & special events

Some film festivals have become relatively well established. Others tend to float a bit in terms of time and location, so be on the

Arts & Entertainment

Aero takes off

Prague's most cherished source of vintage and world film – and, naturally a beer to go with it – is known as **Kino Aero** (*see p194*). Situated in the out-of-the-way neighbourhood of Žižkov (*see p106*), the cinema is one of those relaxed places where people go, especially in summer, to hang out as often as to see a film. The vibe is thoroughly indie, yet it's not such a far cry from what cinema-goers experienced here between the wars. Opened in 1932, much of the building and some parts of the interior are still the original pieces.

Located in the courtyard of a block of crumbling apartments, the place maintains its old-fashioned charm but now features Dolby Digital sound, seats wired with headphone jacks for simultaneous translation and a digital projector, added in 2000. Oh, and one other thing: some of the most progressive programming in Bohemia takes place here, with early Scorsese retrospectives, Italian New Realism nights and the occasional Gothic silent film with live orchestral accompaniment (*Nosferatu* packed 'em in last Halloween).

One of the most telling new additions is the three-hole drink holders that swing down from the back of each seat to accommodate a plastic beer mug, a juice cup and a large shot glass. Having a shot or two while watching a classic art film is emblematic of the Aero agenda: always informal, always provocative. Images of one of the cinema's sternest bartenders are flashed on the screen before films to remind you that plastic cups are preferred inside the cinema, while real glasses aren't supposed to leave the bar.

The bar, added in 1998, proved to be an inspired addition. It now generates one third of the cinema's income, and some people who frequent the bar have probably never seen a film there. 'The bar is an important source of revenue that can be spent on programming,' says manager Ivo Andrle (pictured). 'It gives us greater freedom.'

In the summer picnic tables are set up outside the cinema, which turns it all into a quiet beer garden with a strict 10pm curfew – typical of Prague, where cranky neighbors invariably get annoyed at any street noise after that time and start ringing the police or tossing pitchers of water on to revellers.

Aero's neighbours are beginning to get accustomed to the antics of film freaks, though. During a recent retrospective of Finnish films, the sight of nude film patrons leaving the travelling sauna that came with the festival raised a few eyebrows, but curious residents seemed satisfied when told that this is proper behaviour in Finland – and that the sauna would only be there for a few days.

Andrle's involvement with Aero was something he never really planned. Before coming on board, he worked in international trade, but had been a film addict since he saw Wim Wenders' *Wings of Desire* at age 15. 'I never stopped looking for similar experiences since then.'

The first big project that Aero screened was, fittingly enough, a Wim Wenders retrospective. 'The success of the retrospective made us believe there is an audience for these kinds of films,' says Andrle. 'Since then we organised more than 30 series of this kind.'

A surprising list of filmmakers has made it out to this unprepossessing corner of the city, thanks to Aero. Former Pythons Terry Jones and Terry Gilliam have both screened films here, as has Godfrey Reggio, who came for the third part of his *Qatsi* trilogy, and Agnieszka Holland, for a retrospective.

But you get the feeling that glitz is not exactly what Aero's about. Andrle agrees. His stars, he says, are 'the community of people that works for the cinema or helps it without getting paid at all, and who are very loyal and friendly. That's a precious thing to all of us.'

Maybe even as good as filmmakers who bring their own sauna.

Arts & Entertainment

lookout for the occasional embassy-sponsored event, such as the **Days of Swedish Film** or selections of recent British, German or Italian films. Most of these offer English-subtitled versions when possible. Many of these smaller festivals have moved around but are slowly finding a permanent home in **Kino Aero** (*see p194*). *The Prague Post* (www.praguepost.cz) carries listings for film festivals. Interest in summer outdoor cinema is waning – the one at Střelecký Island has been going it alone recently. Look out for posters around town during the summer months.

Days of European Film

224 215 538/www.eurofilmfest.cz. **Date** early Mar.
More than a decade old, this approximately ten-day festival screens films from European Union members and candidates at Lucerna (*see p193*) and Aero (*see p194*). Many offerings have English subtitles, and a number of filmmakers come to introduce their works. A few of the films have gone into local distribution, but most are just screened once or twice. There are usually a few gems hidden in the pile.

Febiofest

224 214 815/www.febiofest.cz. **Date** late Jan.
The multiplex at Slovanský dům (*see p193*) houses the largest of the local festivals. The selection of films has a wide scope, with groups of films, both old and new, from all over the globe and on select topics. One constant problem, though, is that it's hard to tell which ones have English subtitles, in spite of promises made in the catalogue. The festival also includes concerts and other events. Recent guests have included Roman Polanski.

French Film Festival

221 401 011/www.ifp.cz. **Date** late Nov.
Some French stars come to introduce their recent films and not all of them are as arty as you might expect. Some mainstream French comedies and crime films also make a rare appearance. Half the festival happens at the French Institute, while the other half has moved around several cinemas over the years. A few of the flicks have English subtitles.

Karlovy Vary International Film Festival

Info: Film Service Festival Karlovy Vary, Panská 1, Staré Město, Prague 1 (221 411 011/www.kviff.com). **Date** early July.
The main event for cinema is outside of Prague in the spa town of Karlovy Vary (*see p246*). Festival headquarters is at the Hotel Thermal, but every available screening room in the city is used. This is the only film festival in the country to be accredited by the FIAPF, the group that sanctions the Cannes, Berlin and Venice festivals. High-profile guests, including Morgan Freeman, Gus van Sant and Michael Douglas, have come in the past and the festival has worked through initial growing pains and now runs fairly smoothly. While there are many gems to be seen, the festival has recently been showcasing big Hollywood blockbusters as well. Most films sell out, but it's possible to get in to some screenings without a ticket if space allows.

One World Human Rights Film Festival

www.oneworld.cz. **Date** late Apr.
Attendance has shot up from about 3,000 viewers in 1999 to 30,000 in 2003 for this festival of documentaries and features about human rights issues. The venues are spread out and can include Aero (*see p194*), Lucerna (*see p193*) and NoD (*see p222*). Usually, one of the venues has a schedule of films in English or with English subtitles. The same films can turn up at other venues with Czech subtitles, so be careful.

Films on video & DVD

It's easier to see films in the original language now that DVDs are widely available. Several shops and two major restaurants hire out imported videos and DVDs.

Video Express

Prokopská 3, Malá Strana, Prague 1 (251 535 139/ mobile 604 302 126/www.videoexpress.cz). **Open** noon-10pm daily. **Membership** 400 Kč. **Rental** 60-100 Kč. **No credit cards. Map** p311 K7.
The large catalogue of films on tape or DVD in American and European formats can be searched online, and popcorn and soda can be added to the delivery order. Films can be dropped off at drop-boxes in either of the two Bohemia Bagel restaurants (*see p119*). Delivery is also available but fairly pricey.

Video Gourmet

Jakubská 12, Staré Město, Prague 1 (222 323 364). Metro Náměstí Republiky/tram 5, 8, 14. **Open** 11am-11pm daily. **Membership** free. **Rental** 50-75 Kč. **No credit cards. Map** p309 K3.
Videos in both PAL and NTSC formats make up the bulk of the selection, but the small number of DVDs is slowly starting to grow. Wine and takeaway meals are available for easy one-stop dinner-and-a-movie shopping. Food items include some hard to find ingredients for Asian cooking and lean bacon. If you want to eat out instead, the shop is in the same building as Red Hot & Blues (*see p125*).

Videopro

Vodičkova 17, Nové Město, Prague 1 (224 949 544/ www.videopro.cz). Metro Můstek. **Membership** 50 Kč. **Rental** 40 Kč. **No credit cards. Open** noon-10pm Mon-Sat. **Map** p310 J6.
Choose online or in person from a fairly mainstream selection that's fast approaching 2,000 DVDs. Delivery is available, and not that expensive, in a fairly wide area. Drop-boxes are scattered throughout the city to make returns easier. This is also one of the few places where you can hire out DVD players. The shopfront is hidden in a little courtyard accessible from Vodičkova or Jungmannova streets.

Galleries

Artist-run galleries and indie art spaces are breathing fresh life into a fractious and underfunded Prague art scene.

Galerie Jiří Švestka. See p202.

As if on cue, an impulse towards internationalism is rolling on to the Prague gallery scene just as the Czech Republic joins the European Union. This drive is starting to push aside the remnants of a provincialism that has perpetually dogged it and owes much to the hard work and worldly vision of the city's new independent and artist-run spaces.

But others are also giving the scene a push from the outside. The editors of the Italian *Flash Art* magazine (www.flashartonline.com) recognised the Czech capital as a place in need of a self-image boost, and, seeing the city's potential as host to a gathering of contemporary international art, they organised the first Prague Biennale in the summer of 2003 (www.praguebiennale.org). While it may not have had the clout of Venice, it was nevertheless pulled off for a tiny fraction of the budget that other biennales enjoy. Artists, curators and art lovers poured into Prague from around the globe. And the tradition looks set to continue in 2005.

Around the same time as biennale fever was raging, the art world welcomed a fantastic new arts complex to the traditional working-class district of Smíchov. **Futura** (*see p201*) established its position in record time, snagging the prestigious annual show of finalists for the Chalupecký Award for under-35s – the Czech answer to the Turner Prize – just months after its opening.

A new crop of independent galleries is also wielding the international baton. The spunky **Galerie Display** (*see p201*), a graffiti-covered space, continually puts on provocative shows by young artists from central Europe and beyond, with an emphasis on conceptual installation and video work. Elsewhere, the **Home Gallery** (*see p204*), the effort of three women artists, presents art from beyond the Czech borders, exposing Prague audiences to artists from Slovenia to Australia, in addition to staging group shows by younger Czech artists.

Other new spaces like **Gallery Art Factory** (*see p202*), housed in the industrial space where the *Rudé právo* (Red Truth) newspaper used to crank out communist propaganda, are focusing on shows that connect Czech artists with their counterparts from abroad – in this instance, mainly Slovakia. The gallery is also behind bold initiatives, including 'Sculpture Grande', for which a dozen monumental-scale sculptures by local and international artists were erected

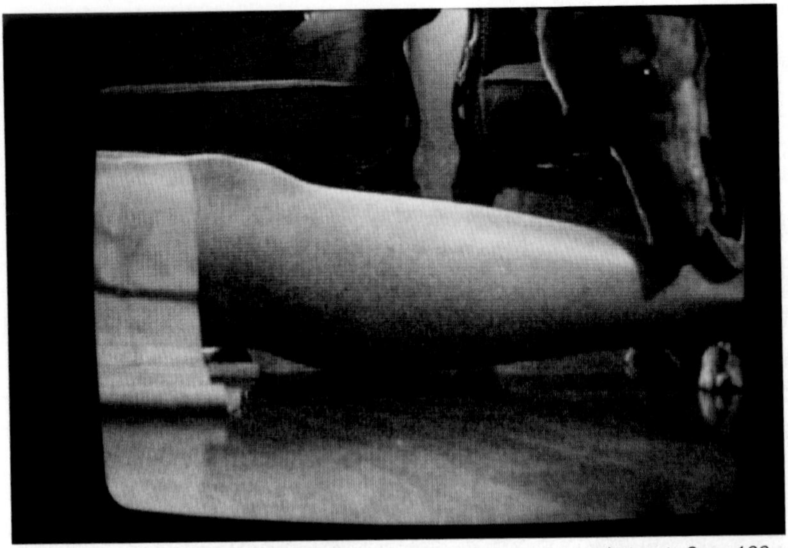

'Reality Check' at the **Galerie Rudolfinum**, Prague's contemporary art hotspot. *See p199.*

up and down Wenceslas Square. The gallery also inspired the Czech and Slovak representatives at the 2003 Venice Biennale, the art groups Kamera skura and Kunst-Fu, to collaborate on a special project for Prague.

Photography is going strong too – the country has nurtured a disproportionate number of world-class photographers for its small size. Expansive historical overviews of Czech, Slovak and German photography have all been displayed at such major spaces as the **Municipal Library** (*see p201*) and the **Rudolfinum** (*see p199*), while exquisite small shows of art photography regularly take place at venues like the **Josef Sudek Atelier** (*see p204*), Sudek's former studio.

Meanwhile, among the old standby exhibition spaces, the **National Gallery** (*see p109*) and **Prague Castle Picture Gallery** (*see p111*) have had to reckon with dwindling budgets and are consequently scaling back their programmes. A changing of the guard at Prague Castle ushered in a change of direction in what kind of 'culture' is considered to be in the 'Czech national interest' and thus worthy of a show at the castle. A new mandate for art shows to break even unfortunately leaves most shows of contemporary and experimental art in the lurch. The National Gallery has similarly been holding to a more conservative line, tending towards sure-fire shows of popular artists, including 19th-century artists Václav Brožík and the Mánes.

Happily, however, the **Prague City Gallery** (www.citygalleryprague.cz), which is one of the other major organisers of art exhibitions in the city, continues to boldly mix it up, presenting important big shows, as well as championing the youngest artists by giving them their first solo shows in its **Old Town Hall** location (*see p201*). The City Gallery is especially keen on displaying the creativity of a new breed of painters who are emerging from the nation's art academies. So far, this has culminated in the high-profile 2003/4 show titled 'Constantly Inflated Prices', which attempted to put a finger on the pulse of Czech painting and so signal a revival of this classic medium among the up-and-coming generation of artists. And the consensus? The academies are still instilling a high level of technical competence in their students – and a sense of irony remains a hallmark of Czech painting.

WHO'S WHO

The senior generation of such artists as Adriena Šimotová and Zdeněk Sýkora continues to hold its own, while gracefully making way for the middle generation of rebel artists such as Vladimír Kokolia and the Maneses, who fought their way under communism and are now mature, well-established artists. As if time has passed at double-speed, two waves of artists have subsequently emerged since 1989.

The first artists to rise to attention in the years following the revolution – Kateřina Vincourová and Veronika Bromová, for example – made their mark by criticising the new orthodoxy of consumerism and bringing feminist and identity issues into the open. A second, only slightly younger, crew is represented by Krištof Kintera. David Černý remains the bad boy of Czech art, his latest provocation being an installation in the courtyard of the new Futura gallery of two enormous bums, inside which you can spy a politically provocative video.

This chapter covers the principal public exhibition spaces for temporary shows and the more interesting private, non-profit and commercial galleries. For permanent art collections and museum exhibitions, *see p109*.

INFORMATION

For information on exhibitions, consult *The Prague Post*, *Culture in Prague* (Kultura v Praze – a listings booklet available in English from newsstands at some central locations) or *Atelier*, a Czech fortnightly broadsheet with an English summary and listings of all exhibitions in the country. *Umělec* (Artist) magazine features reviews of recent shows and articles on the contemporary Czech scene and is now available in separate English and Czech editions in some galleries and selected central newsstands.

Most galleries and museums in Prague are closed on Mondays, and some private spaces take a holiday in August, but it's always best to check before setting out that the one you want to visit hasn't closed temporarily for 'technical reasons'.

Exhibition spaces

Exhibition spaces come and go in Prague, but the main organising bodies are the **National Gallery** (*see p109*), **Prague City Gallery** (*see p198*) and **Prague Castle Picture Gallery** (*see p111*), though the castle is currently rethinking its exhibition plan and may soon forgo splashy blockbusters for less ambitious shows that won't break the bank.

Czech Museum of Fine Arts

Husova 19-21, Staré Město, Prague 1 (222 220 218/www.cmvu.cz). Metro Staroměstská/tram 17, 18. **Open** 10am-6pm Tue-Sun. **Admission** 50 Kč. **No credit cards. Map** p308 H4.

Housed in an attractive block of renovated Renaissance townhouses, this museum exhibits mainly 20th-century Czech art, with the occasional exhibition by a foreign artist. The gallery especially goes in for sweeping themes, such as people, nature or technology. Experimental art is often shown in the atmospheric Romanesque cellar, which provides a perfect setting for site-specific installations.

Galerie Rudolfinum

Alšovo nábřeží 12, Staré Město, Prague 1 (227 059 346/www.galerierudolfinum.cz). Metro Staroměstská/tram 17, 18. **Open** 10am-6pm Tue-Sun. **Admission** 100 Kč; free under-15s, concessions. **No credit cards. Map** p308 G2.

This gallery remains one of the best venues for catching Czech and international contemporary art. The only space in the city with a European Kunsthalle model, its exhibitions lean toward themes of identity and mindscapes. Contemporary Chinese art is a strong speciality. A steady stream of touring shows (Cindy Sherman, for one) bring an updated feel to the grand, naturally lit rooms of the 19th-century Rudolfinum concert building (*see p209*).

House at the Stone Bell

Dům U Kamenného zvonu

Staroměstské náměstí 13, Staré Město, Prague 1 (224 827 526/www.citygalleryprague.cz). Metro Staroměstská/tram 17, 18. **Open** 10am-6pm Tue-Sun. **Admission** 90 Kč; 50 Kč concessions. **No credit cards. Map** p308 J3.

Operated by the Prague City Gallery, this Gothic sandstone building on the east side of Old Town Square features a gorgeous baroque courtyard and three floors of exhibition rooms, some of which have their original vaulting still in place. It favours retrospectives of Czech artists such as Toyen, Emila Medková and Zdeněk Rykr and is also the traditional venue for the Zvon biennale of young Czech and central European artists.

Kinský Palace

Staroměstské náměstí 12, Staré Město, Prague 1 (224 810 758/www.ngprague.cz). Metro Staroměstská/tram 17, 18. **Open** 10am-6pm Tue-Sun. **Admission** 100 Kč; 150 Kč family; free under-10s. **No credit cards. Map** p308 J3.

The National Gallery's renovated Kinský Palace opened with a bang in 2000 with the polemical 'End of the World' show but has recently been adhering to a less provocative programme. The palace is home to the National Gallery's extensive collection of drawings and graphics though, for some reason, these works are only on view to the public during temporary exhibitions. *See also p111.*

Municipal House Exhibition Hall

Obecní dům

Náměstí Republiky 5, Staré Město, Prague 1 (222 002 101/www.obecni-dum.cz). Metro Náměstí Republiky/tram 5, 8, 14. **Open** 10am-6pm daily. **Admission** 100 Kč for exhibitions. **Credit** AmEx, MC, V. **Map** p309 K3.

A stunning exhibition space producing shows on themes, including historic art glass and architectural greats like Jan Kotěra. The best shows are those that harmonise with the stunning space itself, which is an art-nouveau masterpiece. A ticket to an art show or concert is the only way to see the gorgeous upper floors.

Municipal Library

Mariánské náměstí 1 (entrance on Valentinská), Staré Město, Prague 1 (222 310 489/www.citygalleryprague.cz). Metro Staroměstská/tram 17, 18. **Open** 9am-6pm Tue-Sun. **Admission** 100 Kč. **No credit cards. Map** p308 H3.

Newly renovated, the extensive well-lit rooms in this space located within the Municipal Library run by the Prague City Gallery (*see p198*). Important shows bolstered by imaginative installation work tend toward those with historical importance and a strong curatorial point of view, such as 1960s action art or a show spanning the history of German photography.

Old Town Hall

Staroměstské náměstí, Staré Město, Prague 1 (224 810 036/224 482 751/www.citygalleryprague.cz). Metro Staroměstská/tram 17, 18. **Open** *Jan-Mar, Nov-Dec* 9am-5pm Tue-Sun. *Apr-Oct* 10am-6pm Tue-Sun. **Admission** 40 Kč. **No credit cards. Map** p308 H3.

There are two separate spaces for exhibitions within the Old Town Hall. The one entered from the ground floor presents a mixed bag of larger shows, favouring photojournalism and portrait photography, while the more adventurous space on the second floor, operated by the Prague City Gallery (*see p198*), usually displays work by young artists like Štepánka Šimlová. Lately there's been a series of solo shows featuring the youngest Czech painters on the art scene.

Wallenstein Riding School

Valdštejnská jízdárna

Valdštejnská, Klárov, Malá Strana, Prague 1 (257 073 136/www.ngprague.cz). Metro Malostranská/tram 12, 18, 22, 23. **Open** 10am-6pm Tue-Sun. **Admission** 100 Kč; 50 Kč concessions. **No credit cards. Map** p307 D2.

Part of the Wallenstein Palace complex and operated by the National Gallery (*see p109*), this space has established itself as host to some of Prague's most popular and well-attended exhibitions. These range from explorations of social issues to overviews of Czech artists from symbolist Max Švabinský to the Tvrdohlaví (Stubborn Ones) art group. Art walks, in which an English-speaking docent guides visitors, are another new addition to the programme here.

Private & independent galleries

Prague has a still-developing commercial scene, best viewed at a smattering of galleries around town. A number of these spaces have very high standards. Among these, outstanding galleries such as **Galerie Jiří Švestka** (*see p202*) show tantalising artworks, as do contemporary breeding grounds such as **Galerie Behémót** (*see below*). Several non-profit spaces, whose funding doesn't hinge on appealing to mainstream tastes, are bringing some of the most interesting work to public attention.

Futura

Holečkova 49, Smíchov, Prague 5 (251 511 804/www.futuraprojekt.com). Metro Anděl/tram 4, 7, 9. **Open** noon-7pm Wed-Sun. **Admission** free. **No credit cards.**

This new arts complex has quickly risen to the top ranks of the Prague gallery circuit. A brilliantly renovated building houses multiple exhibition halls, ranging from white-cube to atmospheric cellar spaces, with a labyrinthine series of nooks devoted to video works. It's proving to be a great place to see an eclectic blend of established and up-and-coming Czech artists, including Jiří David and Veronika Bromová – at the same time, it's also a welcoming home for bright young stars of European art like Annika Larsson. Don't miss David Černý's provocative installation in the gallery's courtyard.

Galerie AM 180

Bělehradská 45, Vinohrady, Prague 2 (605 407 320/732 750 444/www.am180.org). Metro Náměstí Míru/tram 6, 11. **Open** 6-9pm Tue-Thur or by appointment. **Admission** free. **No credit cards.**

This new artist-run space is a collective effort of an energetic group of young people. Shows tend to be imaginatively titled and, even when the art is a tad unpolished, the young artists exhibiting here often show great promise.

Galerie Behémót

Elišky Krásnohorské 6, Staré Město, Prague 1 (606 744 120/www.behemot.cz). Metro Staroměstská/tram 17, 18. **Open** 11am-6pm Tue-Sat. **Admission** free. **Credit** AmEx, MC, V. **Map** p308 H2.

Gallery owner Karel Babíček believes that display conditions are nearly as important as the original creative act and thus favours installations, often with the artists creating their works directly on the gallery walls. More portable work in a separate showroom can be viewed upon request. The resulting exhibitions are some of the most dynamic in Prague. Behémót's stable of artists is mostly of the generation that came of age before 1989, such as Martin Mainer, Všclav Stratil, Vladimír Kokolia and Otto Placht, but younger artists like Krištof Kintera also exhibit.

Galerie Display

Bubenská 3, Holešovice, Prague 7 (mobile 604 722 562/www.galerie.display.cz). Metro Vltavská/tram 1, 3, 8, 14, 25. **Open** 3-6pm Wed-Sun. **Admission** free. **No credit cards. Map** p312 D2.

This graffiti-covered shopfront gallery is an energetic new player on the scene. In addition to a risk-taking exhibition programme, which is connecting Prague audiences with young artists from abroad, especially from other central European countries, it also holds film screenings and discussion evenings with artists.

Galerie Gambit

Mikulandská 6, Nové Město, Prague 1 (224 910 508). Metro Národní třída/tram 6, 9, 18, 21, 22, 23. **Open** noon-6pm Tue-Sat. **Admission** free. **No credit cards. Map** p308 H5.

This waistcoat-pocket gallery has recently beefed up its exhibition programme in order to concentrate on small shows of new works by well-known names on the Czech scene – Michael Rittstein, Petr Kvíčala and Karel Nepraš, for instance. The gallery also occasionally exhibits foreign artists and displays contemporary design.

Galerie Jelení

Jelení 9, Hradčany, Prague 1 (224 373 178/ www.fcca.cz). Metro Malostranská/tram 22, 23. 10am-5.30pm Mon-Fri. **Admission** free. **No credit cards. Map** p306 A1/B1.

This space, which is operated by and provides the base for the Centre for Contemporary Art, puts on some of the most progressive shows in the city, including student exhibitions. It occasionally casts its happenings on the web and additionally sponsors residencies for experimental artists. The attached café has brilliant occasional jazz nights.

Galerie Jiří Švestka

Biskupský dvůr 6, Nové Město, Prague 1 (222 311 092/www.jirisvestka.com). Metro Náměstí Republiky/tram 5, 8, 14, 24. **Open** noon-6pm Tue-Fri; 11am-6pm Sat. **Admission** free. **No credit cards. Map** p309 M2.

Returned émigré Jiří Švestka recently moved his space from the former Mozarteum to larger digs in a former photography atelier. Since 1995 he has been specialising in bold, internationally recognised Czech artists, such as Stanislav Kolíbal, Jan Kotík from the senior generation and Kateřina Vincourová among the younger artists. The gallery also exhibits international names like Donald Flavin and Dan Graham. You can view classic Czech modernist works here too.

Galerie Kritiků

Jungmannova 31, Nové Město, Prague 1 (224 494 205/www.galeriekritiku.cz). Metro Národní Třída/tram 6, 9, 18, 21, 22, 23. **Open** 10am-6pm Tue-Sun. **Admission** 40 Kč; 20 Kč concessions. **No credit cards. Map** p308 J5.

This elegant space in the Adria Palace, with its grand pyramid skylight, has quickly proved itself to be a class act, particularly in its strong shows of mainly contemporary Czech art.

Galerie Mánes

Masarykovo nábřeží 250, Nové Město, Prague 1 (224 930 754/www.galeriemanes.cz). Metro Karlovo náměstí/tram 17, 21. **Open**10am-6pm Tue-Sun. **Admission** 100 Kč; 50 Kč concessions; free children. **No credit cards. Map** p310 G7.

The largest and most prominent of the Czech Fund for Art Foundation's network of galleries, Mánes is also a beautiful, if run-down, piece of 1930s functionalist architecture by Otakar Novotný. This riverside gallery usually hosts anything from international travelling shows to exhibitions of contemporary Czech artists like Vladimír Kokolia and Lukáš Rittstein. Be sure to look up at the cubist ceiling frescoes on the lower level.

Galerie NoD

Dlouhá 33, Staré Město, Prague 1 (224 826 330/ www.roxy.cz). Metro Náměstí Republiky/tram 5, 8, 14. **Open** 1pm-1am Mon-Sat. **Admission** free. **No credit cards. Map** p309 K2.

Sharing premises with the Roxy club (*see p222*), this space shows experimental work by young and, increasingly, more established artists. A particular speciality is the eclectic, thematic group show, mixing established and up-and-coming artists. Funding from the attached dance club supports and cultivates indie artists, new media and fringe culture cells, all of whom tend to rotate around the surreal-industrial internet bar adjoining the gallery.

Galerie Tvrdohlaví

Vodičkova 36, Nové Město, Prague 1 (296 236 494/www.tvrdohlavi.cz). Metro Můstek/tram 3, 9, 14, 24. **Open** 10am-10pm daily. **Admission** free. **No credit cards. Map** p311 K6.

Through the foyer of the lovely Lucerna cinema (*see p193*), this gallery is the showcase for works by members of the still-impressive Tvrdohlaví (Stubborn Ones) art group, which was rattling the local art establishment before the revolution. Now the members rank among the country's blue-chip artists. Changing exhibitions tend to feature one or more of the group's members, which include well-known names like Petr Nikl, Jiří David and Michal Gabriel, together with a selected 'guest artist' from outside the group.

Galerie Václava Špály

Národní Třída 30, Nové Město, Prague 1 (224 946 738/www.nadacecfu.com). Metro Národní třída/ tram 6, 9, 18, 21, 22, 23. **Open** 10am-noon, 12.30-6pm Tue-Sun. **Admission** free. **No credit cards. Map** p308 H5.

Until recently, this venue run by the Czech Fund for Art Foundation, with two floors of exhibition space plus a basement, kept its programme on a consistently high level. Sadly, however, a recent shake-up in management has put this once-venerable gallery in the same boat as other foundation venues, with only those shows that can afford the high rental fees able to secure a space on the roster.

Gallery Art Factory

Václavské náměstí 15, Nové Město, Prague 1 (224 217 585/www.galleryartfactory.cz). Metro Můstek/ tram 3, 9, 14, 24. **Open** 10am-6pm Mon-Fri. **Admission** 50 Kč. **No credit cards. Map** p309 K5.

Located in the former printing house of the main communist-era newspaper, this spacious gallery keeps the factory feel of the space's former function, with grey-painted cement floors and some of the old industrial hardware as part of the interior architecture. One speciality of the gallery is two-person shows pairing important Czech and Slovak artists.

Seeking Sudek

The name Josef Sudek crops up all over Prague. From Staré Město to Malá Strana and Hradčany, you'll find art galleries that bear the name of this revered photographer.

Sudek, born in Kolín in 1896, carried out his major work from the 1920s through the 1960s. With his lyrical vision, by turns boldly modern and unabashedly romantic, he paved the way for modern Czech photography. Loved by the citizens of Prague, Sudek also served to immortalise his adopted home-town in his studies of the cycles of Prague Castle and his panoramas of the city. His hard-to-pigeonhole individualism may have sat uncomfortably in the ideological regime, but his images, which were neither 'shocking' nor 'political', nevertheless won grudging recognition from the communists.

Seeing original Sudek prints may be more challenging, but finding books with his work is no problem. Any photography gallery that stocks art books will certainly have at least one volume on Sudek. A major retrospective took place several years ago at Prague Castle. Hit the timing just right, and you may be able to catch a retrospective of his work there.

If you don't manage to catch a Sudek exhibition, however, you'll find that his spirit lives on in the many spaces around town where the photographer lived and worked. The studio from which he observed and recorded nature from 1927 to 1958 has been lovingly restored in an effort spearheaded by photo historian Anna Farová, the leading authority on Sudek's work. Situated in a cottage in the courtyard of a residential building, the picturesque bungalow is found at the end of a winding path. In addition to occasional shows of Sudek's own photography, the **Josef Sudek Atelier** (*see p204*) in Malá Strana puts on small, high-quality exhibitions of art photography.

Even when he moved his studio in the late 1950s to a house in Úvoz street near Prague Castle, he always kept his darkroom down in Malá Strana. The ghost of Sudek seems ever present in this narrow house in Hradčany, which is now the **Josef Sudek Gallery** (*see p204*). Looking out on to picturesque Petřín hill, the gallery is an outpost of the Museum of Decorative Arts (*see p114*) and puts on shows drawn from the museum's stellar collection, with an emphasis on interwar Czech photography. The third of the galleries bearing his name, the **Josef Sudek House of Photography** (*see p204*), is just off Old Town Square, where contemporary documentary photography and reportage are the specialities.

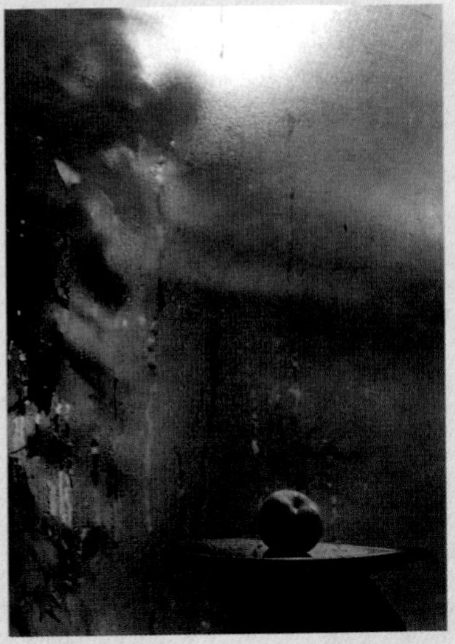

Gandy Gallery

Školská 7, Nové Město, Prague 1 (296 233 066/www.gandy-gallery.com). Metro Karlovo náměstí/tram 3, 9, 14, 24. **Open** 1.30-6.30pm Tue-Fri; 10am-noon Sat. **Admission** free. **No credit cards. Map** p310 J6.

Owned by Frenchwoman Nadine Gandy, the gallery deals in known Western artists, especially French ones, hosting minor exhibitions by not-so-minor names such as Lydia Lunch and Nan Goldin. Recently the gallery has been presenting shows of limited editions in various materials, including glass and soap.

Home Gallery

Truhlářská 8, Nové Město, Prague 1 (224 819 658/ www.homegallery.cz). Metro Náměstí Republiky/tram 5, 8, 14. **Open** 1-8pm Wed-Sun. **Admission** free. **No credit cards. Map** p309 L2.

Founded by a trio of women artists, this airy space has been putting on some of the most progressive shows in the city, splitting its programme between solo and group shows of foreign artists and thought-provoking exhibitions featuring local artists.

Photography galleries

In photography, the long and well-established Czech tradition is still carried on today by practitioners such as Jindřich Štreit, Pavel Baňka and, among the younger generation, Markéta Othová and the duo of Martin Polák and Lukáš Jasanský. For more on the late forerunner of modern Czech photography, Josef Sudek, who lends his name to three galleries around town, *see p203* **Seeking Sudek**.

Galerie Velryba

Opatovická 24, Nové Město, Prague 1 (224 233 337) Metro Národní Třída/tram 3, 6, 9, 18, 21, 22, 23. **Open** noon-9pm Mon-Fri; 11am-9pm Sat. **Admission** free. **No credit cards. Map** p310 H6.

Located in the basement of the trendy Velryba café (*see p153*), this gallery is the showcase for students in the photography department of the Czech film academy FAMU.

Josef Sudek Atelier

Újezd 30, Malá Strana, Prague 1 (251 510 760/ www.sudek-atelier.cz). Metro Malostranská/tram 9, 22, 23. **Open** noon-6pm Tue-Sun. **Admission** 10 Kč; 5 Kč students. **No credit cards. Map** p307 E5.

This little gallery, where Josef Sudek long had his photography studio, is accessible through a residential building courtyard. Select shows of quality art photography are held in the intimate exhibition room, while Sudek memorabilia is on view in a separate small room.

Josef Sudek Gallery

Úvoz 24, Hradčany, Prague 1 (257 531 489). Metro Malostranská/tram 22, 23. **Open** 11am-5pm Wed-Sun. **Admission** 10 Kč; 5 Kč students. **No credit cards. Map** p306 B3.

The father of modern Czech photography almost seems to be hanging about the corners in this house, where he lived and worked from 1959 to 1976. It once displayed a collection of Sudek's own photographs but now presents a fine programme of changing exhibitions organised by the Museum of Decorative Arts (*see p114*), including work by Sudek contemporaries such as Jindřich Štyrský.

Josef Sudek House of Photography

Maiselova 2, Josefov, Prague 1 (224 819 098). Metro Staroměstská/tram 17, 18. **Open** 11am-6pm Tue-Sun. **Admission** 20 Kč; 10 Kč concessions. **Credit** DC, MC, V. **Map** 308 H3.

One of the three photography galleries in town bearing Sudek's name, this space just off Old Town Square leans towards documentary photography and reportage, with a programme of fresh young talent.

Langhans Galerie

Vodičkova 37, Nové Město, Prague 1 (222 929 333/www.langhansgalerie.cz). Metro Můstek/tram 3, 9, 14, 24. **Open** noon-6pm Tue-Fri; 11am-4pm Sat. **Admission** 60 Kč; 30 Kč concessions. **No credit cards. Map** p311 K5.

This beautifully renovated building was once home to the Jan Langhans Atelier, where anyone who was anyone in interwar Prague had their portrait made. The rich tradition was recently reborn in this new entry among photography galleries. The emphasis is on historic shows, especially drawing on the Langhans archives, mixed in with shows of work by established photographers.

Leica Gallery Prague

Burgraves House, Prague Castle, Hradčany, Prague 1 (233 355 757/www.leicagallery.cz). Metro Malostranská/tram 22, 23. **Open** 10am-6pm daily. **Admission** 40 Kč; 30 Kč concessions. **Credit** MC, V. **Map** p307 E2.

This is the place for top-shelf documentary photography and reportage. The gallery snags high-quality travelling shows of such names as Sebastičo Salgado and Mary Ellen Marks. Shows by members of the Magnum Photo Agency also gravitate here. Work by local photographers and a good selection of photography books can be purchased in the lobby bookshop.

Prague House of Photography

Václavské náměstí 31, Nové Město, Prague 1 (222 243 229/www.php-gallery.cz). Metro Muzeum/tram 3, 9, 14, 24. **Open** 11am-6pm daily. **Admission** 30 Kč; 15 Kč concessions. **Credit** AmEx, MC, V. **Map** p308 J2.

The peripatetic PHP seemed to have finally settled down in a Staré Město courtyard until the devastating floods in the summer of 2002 drowned its showroom there. Temporarily located in Wenceslas Square, it's planning a move to a new permanent space on Revoluční street. At press time renovations were in progress, with a scheduled opening in late autumn 2004. When it reopens, it will be reborn as an institution with state funding, with the space – some 2,600 sq m (27,976 sq ft) in two separate halls – to stage major retrospectives and group shows.

Gay & Lesbian

Gay clubbing, saunas and bars are more genteel, while the lesbian scene is quietly hotting up and offering more options.

Prague's slow but steady gay revolution is being fomented in the ubiquitous underground cellar bars. Though this is a gay-friendly city, you'll find no Love Parade here and rainbows are few and far between. Yet there's no need for double lives: *Amigo*, a provocative gay guide to the city, is on sale at most newsagents – and polls show 90 per cent of Czechs are just fine with gays.

A number of gay bars increasingly feature big, but generally harmless blokes at heavy metal doors, with buzzers you ring to get in – despite the build-up though, they're usually just bars. And it's worth venturing in, as many of these bars and some of Prague's gay cafés now hold warm-up parties for the big gay nights, and straight clubs, such as **Mecca** (see *p222*) and **Radost FX** (*see p222*), also have regular gay nights. Before heading out, you'll find that there are architectural and culinary glories at gay-owned **Pálffy Palác** (*see p123*). Even gay-friendly oddities like **La Provence** (*see p131*) and the attached **Banana Bar** (*see p147*), with decent dining, strip and cabaret shows, can be a laugh.

Prague's lesbian scene has been a much slower starter in comparison with the 'European Bangkok' of gay Prague, perhaps because it lacks the economic engines of prostitution. However, the **A-Club** (*see p206*) has finally been joined by clubs like **TERmix** (*see p207*) and **MaLer Ladies' Club** (*see p206*), broadening the city's options, and lesbian nights out are now on discussion boards at **www.expats.cz**. For gays, note that Czech-language pick-up sites like **www.xko.cz** and **www.xchat.cz** do have English-speaking users. An online escort service is available for men at **www.callboys.cz**.

The Czech Republic has a relatively low AIDS and HIV infection rate, owing mainly to the country's closed borders until 1989. The Czech Ministry of Health reported a total of 650 HIV-infected people in 2003, but the actual infection rate is probably higher. Condoms are widely available in supermarkets, select clubs and in vending machines at some metro stations. For more information on health and helpful organisations, *see p279*.

The age of consent is 15 in the Czech Republic although, if money changes hands, the age rises to 18 years, and visitors have been busted that way. Most clubs with butterflies, or prostitutes, are run with discretion and supervision, as at **Drake's** and **Escape** (for both, *see p206*). Others near the main rail station have no supervision and attract a less salubrious clientele and the interest of the police. By and large, though, the city is safe, particularly the venues listed here.

Do be aware that pickpockets favour clubs and dark rooms, and always discuss financial matters and any boundaries before getting down to business. Most gay clubs are home to a varying number of prostitutes, so be prepared to accept or reject advances during your evening.

Spartacus, the international gay guide, is useful for planning, as is **www.planetout.com** or **www.gayguide.net**. Meanwhile, **Rainbow Travel** (www.rainbowtravel.cz) is a well-recommended gay-owned, gay-run and straight-friendly accommodation agent.

HELP AND INFORMATION

The website **prague.gayguide.net** has the most complete and up-to-date listings on Prague's gay scene and acts as a booking agent for many gay pensions and hotels.

Associations

Fiminismus Gender Studies

Gorazdova 20, Nové Město, Prague 1 (224 915 666/www.feminismus.cz). Metro Karlovo náměstí/ tram 3, 6, 14, 18, 22, 24. **Open** by appointment. **Map** p310 G8.

The organisation's English website is under construction and will be a useful resource for mainly lesbian activities.

Accommodation

Agencies

Prague Center Guest Residence

www.gaystay.net/PragueCenter. **Rates** 1,700-3,400 Kč. **No credit cards**.

Book via the website with Bob, the American owner, who rents some Ikea-inspired rooms and apartments, one with a fireplace. Some have shared bathrooms and living rooms, but service and locations are above average. Reservations required.

Toucan Apartments

www.gaystay.net/Toucan. **Rates** 1,800-5,800 Kč. **Credit** AmEx, MC, V.

This Dutch-owned agency has over 30 apartments available in Prague 1, 2, 3 and 10, all of which can be booked via the website. Some apartments are wood-beam attic niches, some are studios and some have a washing machine – but all are simple, clean and comfortable, and the website offers information on nearby nightlife options. All staff are gay. Book ahead.

Hotels

Arco Pension

Voroněžská 24, Vršovice, Prague 10 (271 740 734/fax 7174 0734/www.arco-guesthouse.cz). Metro Náměstí Míru/tram 4, 16, 22, 23. **Rates** (incl breakfast) 1,300 Kč double; 1,900 Kč apartment. **No credit cards.**

Occupying various addresses on the same street, Arco is a comfortable and relaxed collection of apartments, from fairly basic to quite luxurious. The main plus is the location and friendly restaurant, bar and internet cafe. Reservations are required.

Ron's Rainbow Guest House

Bulharská 4, Vršovice, Prague 10 (271 725 664/ mobile 604 876 694). Metro Flóra/tram 6, 7, 22, 24, 34. **Open** 9am-9pm daily. **Rates** 1,815-2,475 Kč per room. **Credit** MC, V.

The Rainbow comprises four comfortable apartments – one with a whirlpool – in residential Prague bordering gay-centric Žižkov. Reservations required.

Bars

Non-Czech-speaking visitors may feel a tad neglected in the more local hangouts listed here, although the younger the crowd is, the more likely you'll find English spoken. If you're given a drink card upon entering a bar, don't lose it or you'll be charged a minimum of 1,000 Kč. Listed closing times generally tend to be ignored, depending on how much fun is being had.

A-Club

Milíčova 25, Žižkov, Prague 3 (222 781 623). Metro Jiřího z Poděbrad/tram 10, 11, 16, 51. **Open** 7pm-3am Mon-Sat. **Admission** free Mon-Thur; 25-50 Kč Fri, Sat. **No credit cards. Map** p313 C1.

This lesbian bar is women-only on Fridays but otherwise is open to all persuasions. There's the usual mix of central European techno pop and some gems, plus transvestite or *travesti*, and lesbian strip shows. The space also doubles as a clubhouse for a variety of lesbian interest groups; check the notice board.

Alcatraz

Bořivojova 58, Žižkov, Prague 3, (222 711 458/ mobile 603 510 510/www.run.to/alcatraz). Metro Jiřího z Poděbrad/tram 10, 11, 16, 51. **Open** 10pm-4am daily. **Admission** 80 Kč; 100Kč party nights. **No credit cards. Map** p313 C2.

A hard-core leather and rubber venue in an appropriately dark though well-maintained cellar, with run-off troughs, slings, cages, equipment, dark rooms, cabins, videos, and glory holes. Quite possibly everything you could imagine, plus underwear and the occasional hard-core theme party.

Bar 21

Símská 21, Vinohrady, Prague 2 (724 254 048). Metro Náměstí Míru/tram 4, 10, 16, 22, 23, 51, 57. **Open** 4pm-4am daily. **Admission** free. **No credit cards. Map** p311 M7.

With a predominantly queer audience, this is a chilled out bar in a cellar, close to the clubbing options. The music is dance-inspired, as is the young crowd, and Bar 21 is a hip place to spend a Friday night if you're not up to mad dancing and prefer to sit, chat and chew a light meal.

Drake's

Zborovská 50, Smíchov, Prague 5 (no phone). Metro Anděl/tram 6, 9, 12, 22, 57, 58. **Open** 24hrs daily. **Admission** 500 Kč. **No credit cards.**

For an older and more 'beefy' crowd, pay the (high) admission price and enjoy the myriad services and entertainments for 24 hours. Drake's can be slow at times; a happening dance club bar it may not be, but a popular after hours place it is. Drake's is, after all, the Grande Dame of the Prague scene. There are video booths, daily strip shows at 9pm and 11pm, glory holes and an S&M Dungeon.

Escape to Paradise

V Jámě 8, Nové Město, Prague 1 (mobile 606 538 111/www.escapetoparadise.cz). Metro Můstek/ tram 3, 9, 14, 24, 58. **Open** *Disco* 9.30pm-3am daily. *Restaurant* 8pm-2am daily. **Admission** 50 Kč Fri, Sat. **No credit cards. Map** p310 J6.

There are mega-strip shows here with more than twenty twinks getting naked and then staying naked all night long – be prepared to talk or dance with carefree naturists. Also, body paint, oil and live sex shows make an appearance. There isn't much cruising action, but for a glimpse of the state of decadence, escape to Escape.

MaLer Ladies Club

Blanická 28, Vinohrady, Prague 2 (222 013 116). Metro Náměstí Míru/tram 4, 10, 16, 22, 23, 51, 57. **Open** 9am-11pm Mon-Thur; 9am-4am Fri, Sat; 1-10pm Sun. **Admission** free. *Party nights* 50Kč. **No credit cards. Map** p313 A3.

A nondescript door leads to a cellar bar devoted to the hedonistic delights of ladies – though no one is barred entry. Everyone seems to know each other or is getting to know each other, and fun dominates the slow grooves or the raunchy gyrations of table-top dancers – there's even a pole. A welcome addition to the lesbian scene.

Rudolf II Party Club

Slovenská 19, Vinohrady, Prague 2 (603 731 012). Metro Náměstí Míru/tram 4, 22, 23, 57. **Open** 8pm-5am daily. **Admission** free. **No credit cards.**

A new venue, sometimes known as G Club, with a small dancefloor, mirror ball, DJ and wooden tables. A passable restaurant is on the ground floor. The club is downstairs behind the locked door – ring the bell.

Tingl Tangl

Karolíny Světlé 12, Staré Město, Prague 1 (224 238 278/www.tingltangl.cz). Metro Národní třída/tram 6, 9, 18, 21, 22, 23, 51, 54, 57, 58. **Open** 8pm-5am Wed-Sat. **Admission** 120 Kč. **No credit cards. Map** p308 G5.

A new venue at an old address (U Střelce occupied these premises until the floods of 2002), Tingl Tangl serves a short menu of international cuisine upstairs and in the quiet courtyard. Downstairs are the borderline-cliché cabaret and transvestite shows, which trade off with more unusual performers until the DJ takes over. Reservations are recommended.

Clubs

All the clubs we've listed in our nightlife chapter (*see p222*) offer cool nights of tunes and moves, where gays won't feel particularly noticed. But for decidedly gay options, try the following.

Angel

Kmochová 8 (corner of Grafická), Smíchov, Prague 5 (257 316 127/www.clubangel.cz). Metro Anděl/tram 4, 7, 9, 10, 58. **Open** 7pm-3am Mon-Thur, Sun; 7pm-6am Fri-Sat. **Admission** free Sun-Thur; 35Kč Fri-Sat. **No credit cards.**

A mirror-balled, LP decorated '80s throwback of a dance club, and a very local hangout – hence the Czech and Slovak hits played on Friday nights. It's also out of the way and difficult to find, so take a taxi if Thursday's Karaoke Night appeals. Otherwise it's the admittedly popular weekend-long dance party.

Gejzeer

Vinohradská 40, Prague 2 (222 516 036/www.gejzeer.cz). Metro Náměstí Míru/tram 4, 10, 16, 22, 23, 51, 57. **Open** 6pm-5am Thur; 9pm-5am Fri, Sat. **Admission** free Thur; 100 Kč Fri; 150 Kč Sat. **No credit cards. Map** p313 A3.

Gejzeer is a hopping club dedicated to gay men but is fun for all. People chill and cruise in the corridor by the toilets, while beautiful lollipop men parade in sarongs. Strip shows, videos and a dark room are also options, while young, available men circle subtly around. Note: the dry ice can be suffocating and avoid the crap free 'cocktail'.

TERmix

Třebízského 4A, Vinohrady, Prague 2 (222 710 462/www.club-termix.cz). Metro Jiřího z Poděbrad/tram 10, 11, 16, 51. **Open** 8pm-5am daily. **Admission** free. **No credit cards. Map** p313 B3.

Dedicated to the pure ideal of gay and lesbian drinks, dancing and sex, TERmix fulfils its obligations beautifully. Ring the bell and descend into the sleek and chic club, past the long glass bar, large-screen TV, sofas and a car parked in the wall. The dancefloor is regularly packed as DJs throw on theme-night music: Latin and Czech hits are popular, while Thursday's Hot Night is a chilled get together evening of candles and easy music. A chill-out room, make-out room and two dark rooms, cabins and a shower complete the facilities.

Cruising

Prague's long, hot summers tempt all towards outdoor escapades, and the metronome atop **Letná** park (*see p104*) beckons men and women with its rhythmic movements. Petřín hill is no longer a popular cruising area, although the terrace at the hill's **Petřínské Terasy** restaurant (Seminářská zahrada 13, 290 000 457) remains a favoured spot. The nudist beach at the lake in **Šárka** park (*see p243*) has a gay section – the area nearest the dam. The **Podolí** swimming pool (*see p244*) is a hotspot for hooking up, with its nude sunbathing galore, but note that families share the grounds. Prague's main train station **Hlavní nádraží** (*see p270*) is a seedy meeting point for male prostitutes and their mostly German clients.

The **Gejzeer** club.

Everybody's welcome at **Downtown Café** – gay, lesbian, naked or otherwise.

Restaurants & cafés

As well as the two eateries listed below the **Érra Café** (*see p148*) in Staré Město is popular with the gay and lesbian crowd, as are the restaurants **Pálffy Palác** (*see p123*), **La Provence** (*see p131*) and the **Banana Bar** (*see p147*).

Café Café

Rytířská 10, Prague 1, Staré Město (224 210 597/ www.cafe-cafe.cz). Metro Můstek/tram 6, 9, 18, 22, 51, 54, 57, 58. **Open** noon-11pm Mon-Fri; 10am-11pm Sat, Sun. **Main courses** 150-350 Kč. **Credit** MC, V. **Map** p308 J4.

This jam-packed café features large, old-fashioned murals and mirrors to improve the scoping action among the absurdly beautiful people who frequent it. Café Café attracts a gay crowd, but its Staré Město location makes it equally popular with anyone looking to hobnob, and the salads aren't bad either. Large windows and pavement tables make this a handy spot for assignation, planned or impromptu.

Downtown Café

Jungmannovo náměstí 21, Nové Město, Prague 1 (724 111 276). Metro Můstek/tram 6, 9, 18, 22, 51, 54, 57, 58. **Open** 10am-11pm Mon-Fri; 10am-midnight Sat, Sun. **Main courses** 150-350 Kč. **No credit cards**.

Being deliciously central, with delicious waiters (not all of whom are gay) this a popular place for all persuasions. Booths and tables fill the space around the central bar, which serves up sandwiches, baguettes, cakes, coffees and alcohol.

Saunas

In addition to saunas, many of the following feature whirlpools, limited gym facilities, steam rooms, video rooms and massage. There's always a bar on the premises and usually some chill-out space.

Sauna Babylonia

Martinská 6, Staré Město, Prague 1 (224 232 304/ www.amigo.cz/babylonia). Metro Můstek/tram 3, 9, 14, 25. **Open** 2pm-3am daily. **Admission** 250 Kč full use; 80Kč gym only. **No credit cards**. **Map** p308 H5.

Babylonia is the most popular gay sauna in Prague, with an active crowd of regulars. Babylonia wins out with modern facilities and a central location, but some men here are clearly too young and beautiful to be just hanging out.

Sauna Marco

Lublaňská 17, Nové Město, Prague 2 (224 262 833). Metro IP Pavlova/tram 4, 6, 11, 16, 22, 23. **Open** 2pm-3am daily. **Admission** 180-200Kč. **No credit cards**.

Marco remains popular and not too crowded. A well-known meeting spot, it's also handy for the main gay clubbing options in the Vinohrady district (*see p106*).

Shops

Amigo Shop & Gay Info

Příčná 7, Nové Město, Prague 1 (222 233 250/www.amigo.cz). Metro Můstek/tram 3, 9, 14, 24, 58. **Open** 11am-7pm Tue-Sat. **Credit** MC, V. **Map** p310 J7.

You can pick up copies of *Amigo*, a general interest gay paper (you'll need a Czech friend to help you translate the Czech) and other publications here, plus all the sex aids you could care for and the latest info on the scene.

Special events

Aprilfest

Various venues (www.lesba.cz/apriles). **Date** Apr.

The premier lesbian festival, organised through the A-Club (*see p206*), is a welcoming forum for new artists, musicians and speakers. Now in its tenth year, the festival is drawing an increasingly international crowd.

Music: Classical & Opera

Concertos are in the Czech DNA and the city's dozens of halls and theatres range from epic to cloistered. Then there are the world-class festivals, of course. Bring your tux.

Prague is heir to a stellar musical heritage that resounds throughout the Bohemian city, from modest basement nooks to grand concert halls. Reaching back to adopted son Mozart and running through proud Czech masters Smetana, Dvořák and Janáček, this is one of the greatest concentrations of musical wealth in central Europe. At times it seems the very pulse of the city is classical music, wafting from open windows, drawing passers-by into cherub-filled churches and filling the numerous venues across the city every night.

Indeed, Prague boasts three opera houses, five major orchestras and countless smaller ensembles. International stars like Andrea Bocelli and Dmitri Hvorostovsky come through on a regular basis and in bunches during the **Prague Spring** (*see p214*) and **Prague Autumn** (www.prazskypodzim.cz) festivals. The former remains the premier classical music festival, attracting star performers and conductors to the city in May every year. The latter, held in September, brings in orchestras from cities like St Petersburg and Budapest, and mixes in strains of world music.

The **Czech Philharmonic** (227 059 352, www.ceskafilharmonie.cz) is top of the heap, a world-class orchestra that has flourished of late and whose tours have drawn rave reviews, while the capable **Prague Symphony Orchestra** (222 002 336, www.fok.cz) has a wider repertoire that includes a strong commitment to Russian symphonic works.

The **Radio Prague Symphony Orchestra** (221 551 400) lacks the recognition of the former two but generally produces more than creditable performances of contemporary works. Find out concert details from the Rudolfinum box office (*see p211*) or check www.heartofeurope.cz for regular postings. The **Prague Chamber Philharmonic** (224 232 488, www.pkf.cz), founded and conducted by Prague Symphony Orchestra conductor Jiří Bělohlávek, is an excellent ensemble of younger musicians. The **Czech National Symphony Orchestra** (225 273 909, www.icn-cnso.cz) has pioneered interesting new paths, playing with unorthodox guests like American jazz musician and composer Chris Brubeck.

Czech conductors such as Bělohlávek and Libor Pešek have established themselves on the international circuit, as have divas Eva Urbanová, Dagmar Pecková and Magdalena Kožená. Russian-born pianist-conductor Vladimir Ashkenazy was a key part of the country's growing profile until his stormy departure in the spring of 2003.

Outside the two major festival dates, you can still catch the above orchestras at the same stunning venues used during the festival – **Municipal House** (*see p211*), the **Rudolfinum** (*see p211*) and the **National Theatre** (*see p214*) are treats in themselves.

The **Prague Spring Festival**. *See p214.*

Baroque beauties **Collegium Marianum**.

Works by Czech musical giants Bedřich Smetana and Antonín Dvořák are regularly heard in the performance halls of Prague. The bolder, more modern Leoš Janáček and Bohuslav Martinů aren't so well represented, although Janáček's operas are given increasingly frequent airings at the National Theatre. Josef Suk, Dvořák's son-in-law, is another talented Czech composer to keep an eye out for on programmes. His heir, a violin virtuoso also named Josef, often performs in Prague. Zděnek Fibich, a contemporary of Smetana and Dvořák, who is known for his lyrical piano pieces, is another discovery, .

Contemporary composers such as Martin Smolka and Ivan Acher are also finally finding an audience, mostly through the **Agon Orchestra** (233 312 459, www.musica.cz/agon), Prague's superb modern music ensemble. The city's strong, developing avant-garde scene is showcased at festivals like the **Modern Music Marathon**, which is held in November at the **Archa Theatre** (*see p233*).

Unfortunately for summer visitors, every major symphony, orchestra and opera company shuts down at the end of June for a two-month holiday. If you're visiting then, your choices will be mostly among the small ensembles that perform clichéed renditions of *A Little Night Music* and the *Four Seasons* at every vacant church and palace in town – usually at prices higher than those charged for major concerts by any of the principal orchestras. Look instead for the few serious ensembles still working in summer, such as open-air operas at **Lichtenstein Palace** (*see p213*) and summertime baroque music concerts by the first-rate **Collegium Marianum** ensemble (224 229 462, www.tynska.cuni.cz).

Prague opera, a particularly fractious world, has had new life breathed into it by the innovative repertoire of the **State Opera** (*see p214*). The artistic risks taken don't always work, but its bold programming is admirable. And that has prodded the National Theatre into shaking off its staid traditions too, staging works by contemporary composers such as John Adams and Philip Glass. The **Estates Theatre** (*see p213*), run by the National Theatre, mounts competent operas in season and is a shrine for Mozart lovers.

TICKETS AND INFORMATION

Ticketpro (*see p211*) books for most of the big classical venues, with a small surcharge that's far less than many other agencies charge foreigners. If buying directly from the venue's box office, don't worry if a show is 'sold out'. Touts buy up all the remaining seats for popular shows, so just wait around the entrance until the last minute when the touts have to sell or lose their investment. Prices for concerts vary and some (in smaller churches) are free, but the cost is usually around 250 Kč to 600 Kč.

Information can be haphazard, but **Bohemia Ticket International** (*see p211*) has an online calendar prepared months in advance and accepts bookings and credit card payment from abroad. Also keep an eye on *The Prague Post* (www.praguepost.cz) for listings of current and forthcoming events. Prague has a tradition of subscription evenings, so you may find certain glittering occasions difficult to get into.

Bohemia Ticket International

Malé náměstí 13, Staré Město, Prague 1 (224 227 832/fax 224 237 727/www.ticketsbti.cz). Metro Můstek or Národní třída/tram 6, 9, 18, 22, 23. **Open** 9am-5pm Mon-Fri; 9am-1pm Sat. **No credit cards. Map** p309 K4.

This is the best non-travel agency for buying tickets in advance from abroad for opera and concerts at the National Theatre, Estates Theatre and State Opera, plus other orchestral and chamber events.

Other locations: Na příkopě 16, Nové Město, Prague 1 (224 215 031).

Čedok

Na příkopě 18, Nové Město, Prague 1 (224 197 242/www.cedok.cz). Metro Můstek or Náměstí Republiky/tram 5, 8, 14, 26. **Open** 9am-7pm Mon-Fri; 9.30am-1pm Sat. **Credit** AmEx, MC, V. **Map** p309 K4.

Tickets for various events, with some concerts.

Other locations: Václavské námestí 53, Nové Město, Prague 1 (221 965 243); Rytířská 16, Staré Město, Prague 1 (224 224 461).

Ticketpro

Old Town Hall, Staré Město, Prague 1 (224 223 613/www.ticketpro.cz). Metro Staroměstská/tram 17, 18. **Open** 9am-6pm Mon-Fri; 9am-5pm Sat, Sun. **Credit** AmEx, MC, V. **Map** p308 H3.

Advance booking for major concerts and various smaller events. The automated freephone number works for all branches – mostly found at Prague Information Service offices (*see p291*) and hotels.

Other locations: Štěpánská 61, Lucerna, Nové Město, Prague 1 (224 818 080); Rytířská 31, Staré Město, Prague 1 (2161 0162); Václavské náměstí 38, Rokoko, Prague 1 (224 228 455).

Principal concert halls

Municipal House

Obecní dům

Náměstí Republiky 5, Nové Město, Prague 1 (222 002 336/222 002 100/www.obecni-dum.cz). Metro Náměstí Republiky/tram 5, 14, 26. **Open** *Box office* 10am-6pm Mon-Fri. **Tickets** 150-1,100 Kč. **Credit** AmEx, MC, V. **Map** p309 K3.

A stunning example of Czech art nouveau, the Municipal House is built around the Smetana Hall, home to the Prague Symphony Orchestra. The orchestra launches the Prague Spring Festival (*see p214*) here every year, as it has done for over half a century. Listen to Smetana variations on folk tunes while gazing at the ceiling mosaics of old Czech myths for an authentic Bohemian national cultural experience. *See also p97.*

Rudolfinum

Alšovo nábřeží 12, Staré Město, Prague 1 (227 059 309/227 059 352/www.rudolfinum.cz). Metro Staroměstská/tram 17, 18. **Open** *Box office* 10am-6pm Mon-Fri. Closed mid July-mid Aug. **Tickets** 200-1,100 Kč. **Credit** AmEx, MC, V. **Map** p308 G2.

One of the most beautiful concert venues in Europe, the Rudolfinum was built in the neo-classical style at the end of the 19th century and has two halls: the Dvořák Hall for orchestral works and major recitals, and the Suk Hall for chamber, instrumental and solo vocal music. Opinion is divided about the acoustics of the Dvořák Hall, but the grandeur of the building's interior – plus the high standard of musicianship on offer – makes an evening here eminently worthwhile. *See also p93.*

Other venues

Venues for chamber music and instrumental recitals are legion. Practically every church and palace offers concerts. Programming is mainly from the baroque and classical repertoire, with the emphasis on Czech music. Performances are usually of a high standard. Tickets for performances can generally be bought from the venue one to two hours before a performance is scheduled to start, while **Bohemia Ticket International** (*see above*) also sells tickets for some events.

Basilica of St James

Bazilika sv. Jakuba

Malá Štupartská 6, Staré Město, Prague 1 (224 828 816). Metro Náměstí Republiky/tram 5, 14, 26. **Open** *Box office* 1hr before performance. **Tickets** 200-400 Kč. **No credit cards. Map** p308 J3.

St James's is a prime example of Czech baroque architecture, complete with resounding organ acoustics and an over-the-top façade above the entrance, depicting the Fall. In addition to large-scale sacred choral works, music for Sunday mass (usually 10am) is impressive. Concerts are held from Easter through September.

Bertramka

Mozartova 169, Smíchov, Prague 5 (257 317 465/ www.bertramka.cz). Metro Anděl/tram 4, 7, 9, 10, 12, 14. **Open** 9.30am-5pm daily. **Tickets** 110-450 Kč. **No credit cards**.

The house where Mozart stayed when in Prague is now a museum devoted to him (*see p115*) that puts on regular concerts. Nearly all include at least one work by the Austrian, who has been all but adopted into the Czech musical pantheon.

Chapel of Mirrors

Zrcadlová kaple

Klementinum, Mariánské náměstí, Staré Město, Prague 1 (221 663 111/221 663212). Metro Staroměstská/tram 17, 18. **Open** *Box office* 2hrs before performance. **Tickets** from 650 Kč. **No credit cards. Map** p308 G4.

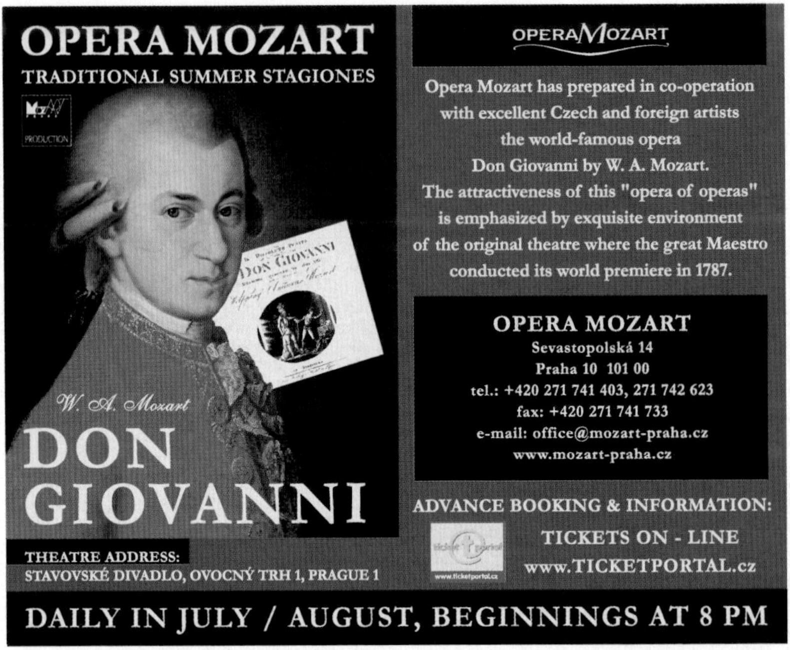
OPERA MOZART
TRADITIONAL SUMMER STAGIONES
PRODUCTION
W. A. Mozart
DON GIOVANNI
THEATRE ADDRESS:
STAVOVSKÉ DIVADLO, OVOCNÝ TRH 1, PRAGUE 1
OPERA MOZART
Opera Mozart has prepared in co-operation with excellent Czech and foreign artists the world-famous opera Don Giovanni by W. A. Mozart. The attractiveness of this "opera of operas" is emphasized by exquisite environment of the original theatre where the great Maestro conducted its world premiere in 1787.
OPERA MOZART
Sevastopolská 14
Praha 10 101 00
tel.: +420 271 741 403, 271 742 623
fax: +420 271 741 733
e-mail: office@mozart-praha.cz
www.mozart-praha.cz
ADVANCE BOOKING & INFORMATION:
TICKETS ON - LINE
www.TICKETPORTAL.cz
DAILY IN JULY / AUGUST, BEGINNINGS AT 8 PM

ZAHRADA V OPEŘE
RESTAURANT
Nejlépe střeženou zahradu světa najdete v sousedství Radia Svobodná Evropa a Státní opery.
Vyhlášená mezinárodní kuchyně a mimořádný interiér vytváří oázu klidu mezi magistrálami (nad Václavským náměstím).
Parkování možné v garážích Slovan přímo vedle Státní opery Praha.
The safest and best guarded garden in the world you can find near by Radio Free Europe and State opera.
Famous international cuisine and especial interior originate a restful oasis of coziness between motorways (above Wenceslav Square).
Parking in garage Slovan next to State opera house.
Legerova 75 / tel. 224 239 685 / e-mail restaurant@zahradavopere.cz
www.zahradavopere.cz / 11.30 – 01.00

This pink-marble chapel in the vast Clementinum complex (*see p86*), features all manner of Romantic, baroque and original chamber recitals and is seemingly an age away from the tourist hordes outside. Concerts here usually start at 5pm and 8pm.

Church of St Nicholas

Chrám sv. Mikuláše
Malostranské náměstí, Malá Strana, Prague 1 (224 190 991). Metro Malostranská/ tram 12, 22. **Open** *Box office* 2hrs before performance. **Tickets** 250-450 Kč. **No credit cards. Map** p307 D3.
This is one of Prague's most celebrated churches, with a stunning baroque interior. Irregular choral concerts and organ recitals are just as grand as the setting itself. *See also p74.*

Church of St Nicholas

Kostel sv. Mikuláše
Staroměstské náměstí, Staré Město, Prague 1 (no phone). Metro Staroměstská/tram 17, 18. **Open** noon-4pm Mon; 10am-4pm Tue-Sat. **No credit cards. Map** p308 H3.
St Nicholas's hosts regular organ, instrumental and vocal recitals in a somewhat plain setting. The emphasis is on baroque music. *See also p85.*

Church of St Simon & St Jude

Kostel sv. Šimona a Judy
Dušní & U Milosrdných, Staré Město, Prague 1 (222 321 352). Metro Staroměstská/tram 17. **Open** *Box office* 1hr before performance. **Tickets** 200-600 Kč. **No credit cards. Map** p308 H2.
Renovated with cunning trompe l'œil work, this deconsecrated church is now a full-time venue for chamber music. The Prague Symphony Orchestra, which also promotes selected ensembles, is responsible for the programming. Concerts start at around 7.30pm.

Lichtenstein Palace

Lichtenštejnský palác
Malostranské náměstí 13, Malá Strana, Prague 1 (257 534 205). Metro Malostranská/tram 12, 22. **Open** 10am-7.30pm daily. **Tickets** 30-100 Kč. **Credit** MC, V. **Map** p307 E3.
The Lichtenstein Palace is the home of the Czech Academy of Music. Regular concerts (usually starting at 7.30pm) are given in the Gallery and in the Martinů Hall, although the real star is the summer open-air series of popular operas that take place in the courtyard.

Lobkowicz Palace

Lobkovický palác
Jiřská 3, Hradčany, Prague 1 (257 535 121/ 257 534 578). Metro Malostranská/tram 22. **Open** 11am-1pm daily. **Tickets** 390 Kč. **No credit cards. Map** p307 D2.
Concerts of baroque and Romantic chamber works are held in the imposing banquet hall of the Lobkowicz Palace, which has frescoes by Fabián Harovník. Concerts usually begin at 1pm on Saturdays and Sundays.

The **Estates Theatre** – Mozart heaven.

St Agnes's Convent

Klášter sv. Anežky české
U milosrdných 17, Staré Město, Prague 1 (221 879 270). Metro Staroměstská or Náměstí Republiky/tram 5, 14, 26. **Open** 10am-6pm Tue-Sun. **Tickets** 250-550 Kč. **No credit cards. Map** p308 J1.
The acoustics here are not without their critics, but the convent has a Gothic atmosphere and high-quality chamber music, with an emphasis on Smetana, Dvořák and Janáček. *See also p93.*

Opera

Estates Theatre

Stavovské divadlo
Ovocný trh 1, Staré Město, Prague 1 (information 224 228 503/box office 224 215 001). Metro Můstek or Staroměstská/tram 3, 9, 14, 17, 18, 24. **Open** *Box office* 10am-6pm daily. **Tickets** 30-1000 Kč. **Credit** MC, V. **Map** p308 J4.
A shrine for Mozart lovers, this is where *Don Giovanni* and *La Clemenza di Tito* were first performed. The theatre was built by Count Nostitz in 1784; its beautiful dark-blue-and-gold auditorium was almost over-renovated after the Velvet Revolution. It began life as the Prague home of Italian opera but in 1807 became the German opera, with Carl Maria von Weber as its musical director (1813-17). Today much of the programming is given over to theatre, but there's still regular opera here – including, of course, *Don Giovanni. See also p89 and p232.*

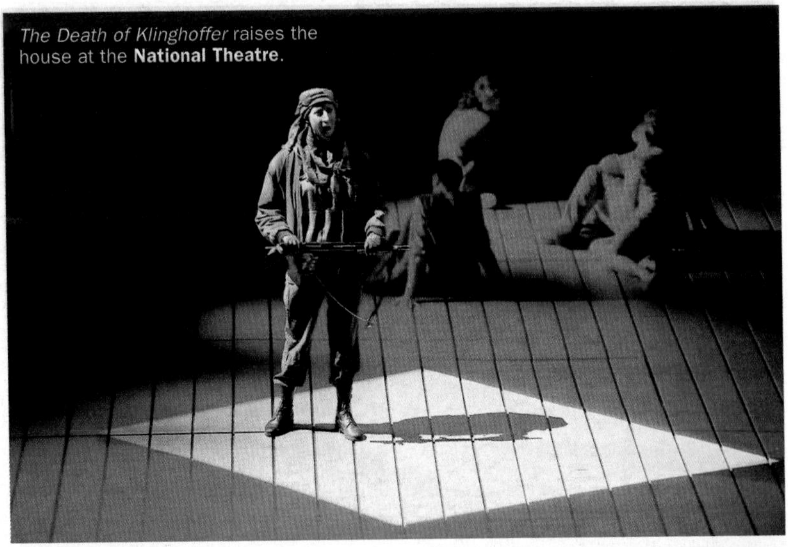

The Death of Klinghoffer raises the house at the **National Theatre**.

National Theatre

Národní divadlo

Národní 2, Nové Město, Prague 1 (224 901 448/ www.narodni-divadlo.cz). Metro Národní třída/ tram 6, 9, 17, 18, 22. **Open** *Box office* 10am-6pm daily. Closed July & Aug. **Tickets** 30-900 Kč. **Credit** AmEx, MC, V. **Map** p310 G6.

Smetana was a guiding light behind the establishment of the National Theatre, a symbol of Czech nationalism that finally opened in 1883 with a performance of his opera *Libuše*. In keeping with tradition, the theatre concentrates on Czech opera, the core of the repertoire being works by Smetana and Dvořák (including lesser-known works such as Dvořák's *The Devil and Kate* and Smetana's *The Kiss*), together with some Janáček. Operas by non-Czech composers and some impressive ballets are also performed here – there's generally three major new productions a year. *See also p99 and p232.*

State Opera

Státní Opera

Wilsonova 4, Nové Město, Prague 2 (224 227 266/www.opera.cz). Metro Muzeum/tram 11. **Open** *Box office* 10am-5.30pm Mon-Fri; 10am-noon, 1-5.30pm Sat, Sun. **Tickets** 200-900 Kč. **No credit cards. Map** p311 L6.

The State Opera (originally the German Theatre) opened in 1887 and was regarded as one of the finest German opera houses outside Germany until World War II. After the war it changed its name to the Smetana Theatre and became the second house of the National Theatre. Today it's a separate organisation and presents consistently bold contemporary opera alongside standards from the Italian, German, French and Russian repertoires.

Festivals

The major event in the Prague music calendar is the **Prague Spring Festival** (*see below*). Several summer festivals are also held out of town, for more information contact the **Prague Information Service** (*see p291*).

Opera Mozart

Žatecká 1, Staré Město, Prague 1 (224 819 324/ www.mozart.cz). Metro Staroměstská/tram 17, 18. **Open** 10am-8pm daily. **Date** July, Aug. **Tickets** 690-1,950 Kč. **Credit** AmEx, MC, V. **Map** p308 H3.

A heavily promoted production of *Don Giovanni*, performed by a travelling foreign troupe, moves into the Estates for the summer. While not a bad rendition, it's aimed squarely at tourists and priced accordingly.

Prague Spring Festival

Festival office: Hellichova 18, Malá Strana, Prague 1 (257 310 414/www.festival.cz). Metro Malostranská/ tram 12, 22. **Date** May, June. **Tickets** from 200 Kč. **Credit** AmEx, MC, V. **Map** p307 D4.

Since the Velvet Revolution the Prague Spring Festival has had a much stronger international flavour and attracts first-class international performers. The festival opens with Smetana's patriotic cycle of symphonic poems, *Má Vlast* (My Country), and concludes with Beethoven's Ninth. Many of the major events sell out quickly. It's best to obtain tickets from the festival office rather than from ticket agencies, which add a hefty mark-up. The office opens one month before the festival and there are two price ranges – one for tickets sold in Prague and one for those booked from abroad. If possible, get a Czech friend to buy them for you or wait until you get here.

Music: Rock, Roots & Jazz

In a word, Prague rocks. With funky venues, major and minor tours, world-class jazz and a growing world music scene, there's always something shakin'.

Prague's reputation as a non-stop bacchanalia, whether deserved or not, keeps it a popular destination on many a major band's European tour, but fringe bands, who know the city well, seem to gig here on permanent rotation. And the city's lack of sonically perfect major halls means you'll catch these bands up close and personal at places like the threadbare **Lucerna Music Bar** (*see p218*), the cutting-edge **Archa Theatre** (*see also p233*), with its occasionally off-the-wall live acts and avant-garde performances, or, less often, at the **Rock Café** (*see p218*). Better still, ticket prices are aimed at the Czech market, so seeing an act like the Flaming Lips won't break the bank.

On the dance scene things are less ideal for live music lovers. In the city centre, it's still a chancy business dropping into music clubs, and, with the exception of the new **N11** (*see p218*), you'll be hard-pressed to find a band playing accessible, danceable music. More than in most cities, DJs rule the scene these days, with live music left mainly to festivals, cover bands and jazz and blues clubs.

Fortunately, there are dozens of festivals each year, the best of them, like **Respect** (respect.inway.cz; *see p184*), offering up rocking Roma sounds, *klezmer* and world music. And a few fine venues, like the **Akropolis** (*see p217*) and the bunkerlike **Klub 007** (*see p218*), still frequently book musicians, focusing on regional underground acts.

Czech rock doesn't export well and many of the iconic bands, like **Už jsme doma** and **Psí vojáci**, are acquired tastes with a bristling independence born of a long history of oppression. Bands like **Plastic People of the Universe** helped spark the Velvet Revolution, after all. Their descendants today can produce introspective, moody sounds punctuated with squawks of pain that make a night out something to savour.

Not to worry, though: more recent bands (*see p216* **Bad Bohemia: Sound Czech**) are focusing on interesting alchemies, fusing Latin, African and Middle Eastern elements with Czech and traditional rock, breathing new life into the Akropolis, **Roxy** (*see p220*) and **Malostranská beseda** (*see p218*).

The use of event-only spaces such as the massive industrial space **Abaton** (*see p216*) has added a new dimension and capacity for mega-parties, and it is surely worth a trip if you happen to spy a fly poster for one (check the bulletin board at **Radost FX** (*see p119*) or **The Globe Bookstore & Coffeehouse** (*see p144 and p163*). While you're perusing the flyers, check for summer raves – there's a thriving party scene in the countryside surrounding Prague where you'll meet Glastonbury survivors by the hundreds. Details are invariably posted on **www.techno.cz/party**, usually with at least a bit of English text to help in deciphering directions and contacts.

The best Music clubs

For catching the latest wave
If they're out there, they'll be doing the **Roxy** (*see p220*).

For catching a legend up close
Lucerna Music Bar (*see p218*) gets everybody in blues and soul.

For epic parties in a weird space
Abaton (*see p216*) lets you shake it among the turbines.

For experiencing NYC jazz of the '50s
The spirit of Gil Evans has moved to **U Malého Glena** (*see p221*).

For modern-day supper clubbing
Jazz Club Železná/Mecca (*see p221*) mixes live virtuosi, top DJs and a fine French dressing.

Czech jazz has never brought in huge crowds, though it's had a stellar reputation for such a small country ever since the early days, and produced such stars as George Mraz and Jan Hammer. And the **Prague Jazz Festival** (www.agharta.cz; *see p183*) brings world-class talents such as John Scofield or Maceo Parker to the Lucerna Music Bar from spring to autumn.

Look out for the just-announced jazz and blues shows are invariable on the flyers posted at **Bohemia Bagel** (*see p119*), or listed in *The Prague Post* (www.praguepost.cz).

TICKETS AND INFORMATION

Tickets should be booked in advance for big-name concerts. For the smaller, funkier ones you'll need to buy directly from the venue.

Ticketpro

Old Town Hall, Staroměstské náměstí, Staré Město, Prague 1 (224 223 613/www.ticketpro.cz). Metro Staroměstská/tram 17, 18. **Open** 9am-6pm Mon-Fri; 9am-5pm Sat, Sun. **Credit** AmEx, MC, V. **Map** p308 H3.

Ticketpro offers easy one-stop advance ticket sales for the great majority of events and concerts in Prague these days. Book with your credit card over the internet, then pick up the tickets before the show at the branch nearest the concert venue.

Other locations: Štěpánská 61, Lucerna, Nové Město, Prague 1 (224 818 080); Rytířská 31, Staré Město, Prague 1 (221 610 162); Václavské náměstí 38, Rokoko, Nové Město, Prague 1 (224 228 455).

Venues

Enormous gigs

Prague's largest venue, the 200,000-capacity **Stadium Strahov** (*see p217*) has been graced in the past by President Havel's mates, the Rolling Stones. Shows are far more frequent at **T-Mobile Arena** (good enough for Bowie; *see p217*), though the sound quality at both is appalling.

Abaton

Na Košince 8 (off Povltavská), Libeň, Prague 8 (no phone/www.fanonline.cz/abaton). Metro Palmovka/tram 12, 14, 24.

Bad Bohemia Sound Czech

The Prague sound is a haunting and unique one, having evolved from elements of Slavic folk, Renaissance madrigals and a major infusion of early Velvet Underground, which was worshipped during the crackdowns of 1968. These days, though, a new generation has clearly taken charge, bringing in more modern inspirations from travels abroad, uncensored radio waves and rampant file-sharing over the net.

For an up-to-date sampling of what's out there, the formerly pirate **Radio 1** is a good source (listen in online at www.radio1.cz). DJ Sedloň's nightly CD Nonstop show is an insightful hour-plus that introduces an entire album of whatever local or international group has caught his fancy. But fresh local and touring talent are interviewed and have their albums played all day on Radio 1, which is the city's most respected non-commercial rock station – just be ready to turn down all the non-commercial commercials.

The live music scene tends to orbit around the mother-ship of the **Akropolis** club (*see p217*) in the wild and woolly Žižkov district, where bands are deliberately nurtured. Tuesday evening shows, with an entrance fee of a nominal 20 Kč are an invitation to new groups to perform and are always spontaneous. Free Monday nights at the **Roxy** (*see p220*) are also showcases for new talent, though generally DJs or hybrids of digital and live sound.

Surprisingly enough, the **Bontonland Megastore** (*see p176*) in Wenceslas Square is a reliable source of new musical talent – CDs are so cheap to record and publicise in the Czech Republic that even the hungriest indie band has one and they're generally stocked here.

Good local labels to watch out for are **Rachot** (www.rachot.cz) for world music, **East Authentic** for drum 'n' bass, **Beeswax** (www.beeswax.cz) for the latest dance material, and **Indies** for everything else. The love for classic, loud rock and funk is evident from the current wave of top chart Czech bands such as **MiG21** (www.mig21.cz), **Priessnitz** (www.priessnitz.com) and **Support Lesbiens** (www.supportlesbiens.cz). **Monkey Business** (www.monkeybusiness.cz) is strictly about funk, good times, bass and dancing. Hip hop is a major influence for **Tatabojs** (www.tatabojs.cz), which raps about life in the pre-fab apartment blocks, while **Čechomor** (www.cechomor.cz) gets back to Czech roots with an inspired blend of traditional folk music and modern rock.

Swingers: Havelka and His Melody Makers at the **Lucerna Music Bar**. *See p218*.

The former Interplast factory is now the site of the city's most outrageous parties and concerts, sometimes filled with sofas, bars and cigarette girls at other times just fitted out with thundering amps and world-music stars from Congo. Tickets and information are usually available at the Ticketpro website (www.ticketpro.cz). Concerts here usually start at around 8.30pm.

Congress Centre

Kongresové centrum
5 května 65, Vyšehrad, Prague 4 (261 171 111/ www.kcp.cz). Metro Vyšehrad/tram 18, 24.
Once the pride of the Party, the former Palace of Culture has been renamed as the Congress Centre in an effort to leave behind its past as a communist convention facility. It has also better sound and lights installed, but concerts here still tend to feel institutional – in the main hall, overstuffed seats allow no room for dancing.

Stadium Strahov

Diskařská 100, Břevnov, Prague 6 (233 014 111). Metro Karlovo náměstí, then bus 176 or tram 22 to Újezd, then funicular. **Map** p306 A5.
The biggest show in town is a concrete monstrosity built before World War II without much to offer besides its size to accommodate epic rock shows. It's a trek out of the centre, but a special bus service is laid on for big gigs.

T-Mobile Arena

Výstaviště, Za elektrárnou 319, Holešovice, Prague 7 (266 727 411). Metro Nádraží Holešovice/tram 5, 12, 17. **Map** p312 D1.
A skating rink when not a concert hall, this barn has all the acoustics you'd expect from such. But it's the only indoor spot in Prague that can accommodate thousands.

Small to middling gigs

Akropolis

Kubelíkova 27, Žižkov, Prague 3 (296 330 911/ www.palacakropolis.cz). Metro Jiřího z Poděbrad/tram 5, 9, 11, 26, 55, 58. **Open** *Divadelní Bar* 7pm-5am daily. *Malá Scená Bar* 7pm-3am daily. *Concerts* 7.30pm. **Admission** from 90 Kč. **No credit cards**. **Map** p313 B2.
The heart of indie rock and world music in Prague, this club hosts series such as United Colours of Akropolis and Jazz Meets World to promote a rich array of artists and avant-garde acts, from throat-singing monks to Berlin *klezmer*. The downstairs Divadelní (theatre) Bar offers nightly DJs and MCs free of charge, while the Malá Scena features live jams and red-lit sofas. The main basement stage, a former cinema hall, has lights and sound as good as any in Prague, but groups you won't find anywhere else. At street level is a pub with just-passable curries vastly surpassed by the Staropramen beer. *See also p142*.

Batalion Music Club

28 şijna 3, Staré Město, Prague 1, (220 108 147/www.batalion.cz). Metro Můstek/tram 3, 9, 14, 24. **Open** 24hrs daily. *Concerts* various start times. **Admission** free. **No credit cards**. **Map** p308 J5.

Arts & Entertainment

A club with a worn out sign (two signs, in fact, the other impersonating the Hard Rock Café, with which it has no connection) just off Wenceslas Square is not the place you'd expect to find edgy, enthralling bands. Correct! But Batalion is open all night, has fun, cheesy live rock, cheap beer and, if you don't mind the skate punks, can be a laugh.

Futurum

Zborovská 7, Smíchov, Prague 5 (257 328 571/ www.musicbar.cz). Metro Anděl/tram 6, 9, 12. **Open** 8pm-3am daily. *Concerts* 9pm. **Admission** from 100 Kč. **No credit cards.**

The former National House of the Smíchov district, a kind of local ballroom/lecture hall every major district once had, houses this club. Fully made over with powerhouse sound, video and a wavy bar, Futurum has been hosting more live music of late, usually Czech rock favourites such as Tony Ducháček and Garage.

Klub 007

Vaníčkova 5, Koleje ČVUT dorm 7, Strahov, Prague 6 (257 211 439). Metro Dejvická, then bus 143, 149, 217. **Open** 7pm-midnight Mon-Sat. *Concerts* 9.30pm. **Admission** 40-100 Kč. **No credit cards.**

Student dorm heaven – or hell, depending on how you look at it. If you can find this place (in the concrete basement of dorm, yes, 007), you'll never believe it could be a must on any international ska tour of central Europe. But that it is, as you'll soon discover when the bands start up. As authentic a youth vibe as you'll find, complete with cheap beer in plastic cups – just mind the bass player doesn't knock your beer over during riffs as you're practically in each other's lap.

Lucerna Great Hall

Vodičkova 36, Nové Město, Prague 1 (224 225 440/www.lucpra.com). Metro Můstek/tram 3, 9, 14, 24, 52, 53, 55, 56. **Open** *Concerts* start 7-8pm. **Admission** 200-900 Kč. **Credit** AmEx, MC, V. **Map** p309 K5.

Run independently from the Lucerna Music Bar (*see below*), this vast, pillared, underground performance hall hosts big-time acts from Maceo Parker to the Cardigans. Its art-nouveau ballrooms, balconies, grand marble stairs and wooden floors add a palatial feel to rock shows. Though it feels big and the sound can echo, you're always reasonably close to the band. There are no regular box office hours so book ahead through an agent like Ticketpro (*see p216*).

Lucerna Music Bar

Vodičkova 36, Nové Město, Prague 1 (2421 7108/www.musicbar.cz). Metro Můstek/tram 3, 9, 14, 24, 52, 53, 55, 56. **Open** 8pm-3am daily. *Concerts* 9pm. **Admission** 80 Kč; 80-300 Kč concerts. **No credit cards. Map** p309 K5.

An incredible list of rock, jazz and blues talents roll through this neglected old cellar concert space, from Kinsey Report to Richard Bona. But then it has always featured greats, including the likes of Satchmo and Josephine Baker. Enter from the faded 1920s Lucerna Passage off Wenceslas Square and descend into what's best described as a multi-level dive with wood-panelled balconies. Frighteningly popular '80s disco nights take over on Fridays when there isn't a touring artist passing through.

Malostranská beseda

Malostranské náměstí 21, Malá Strana, Prague 1 (257 532 092). Metro Malostranská/tram 12, 22, 57. **Open** 5pm-midnight daily. *Concerts* 8.30pm or 9.30pm. **Admission** 80 Kč. **No credit cards. Map** p307 E3.

Threadbare it may be, but this unimposing former lecture salon hosts the hottest local live acts in town. It's home to the Sto Zvířat, a popular Czech ska band, among dozens of other acts that play the back room regularly. Bottled beer is the only drawback to an otherwise welcoming bar. Weird art lines the walls, battered wood surfaces and windows overlooking Malá Strana's main square add appeal. Malostranská beseda also has a well-stocked jazz and alternative CD shop, open 11am-7pm Mon-Sat.

Meloun

Michalská 12, Staré Město, Prague 1 (224 230 126/ www.meloun.cz). Metro Můstek/tram 3, 9, 14, 24, 51, 52, 53, 54, 55, 56, 57, 58. **Open** 11am-3am daily. *Concerts* 9pm. **Admission** 80-100 Kč. **No credit cards. Map** p308 H4.

Ever packed with local pop and disco fans, the Meloun occasionally breaks the bad DJ habit with a good blues night. More often, it's album tracks better left in the pre-1989 community hall of a small Bohemian village. With occasional film screenings as well, this cellar pub covers all bases. For the summer, the attached garden pub offers traditional Czech schnitzels and the like.

N11

Národní třída 11, Nové Město, Prague 1 (222 075 705/www.n11.cz). Metro Národní třída/tram 6, 9, 18, 22, 51, 54, 57, 58. **Open** 4pm-4am daily. *Concerts* various start times. **Admission** 80-150 Kč. **No credit cards. Map** p308 H5.

One of the better sound systems and light racks makes this small club a good pick for taking in a pop-rock band. The venue is the immaculately restored headquarters of the *New Presence*, a monthly opinion journal with roots dating back to the interwar First Republic. Sunday blues acts like Stan the Man keep the crowd on its feet. The attached restaurant and bar are friendly, capable and open late (*see p128*).

Rock Café

Národní třída 20, Nové Město, Prague 1 (224 914 414/www.rockcafe.cz). Metro Národní třída/ tram 6, 9, 18, 22, 51, 54, 57, 58. **Open** 10am-3am Mon-Fri; 5pm-3am Sat; 5pm-1am Sun. *Concerts* 9pm. **Admission** 90-150 Kč. **No credit cards. Map** p308 H5.

Sometimes booking rising local stars, Rock Café is one to watch, although it more often draws the backpacker crowd. Once a post-revolution rock pioneer,

The Tiger Lilies at the **Archa**. *See p215*.

Chicago blues guitarist Rene Trossman gets lost in music at **U Malého Glena**.

these days it's only occasionally a hot ticket and features endless rockumentary screenings and Czech 'revival' bands. Not much in the way of atmosphere.

Roxy

Dlouhá 33, Staré Město, Prague 1 (224 826 296/ www.roxy.cz). Metro Náměstí Republiky/tram 5, 14, 26, 51, 53, 54. **Open** 7pm-2am Mon-Thur; 7pm-4am Fri, Sat. *DJ events* from 10pm. *Live acts* from 8pm. **Admission** *DJs events* 100-250 Kč. *Live acts* 150-450 Kč. **No credit cards. Map** p308 J3.

Although dominated by digital dance tracks, the Roxy also hosts live acts, generally to accompany the digital stuff but occasionally standing alone. When it does, the band is usually impressive, with names such as Mad Professor, or a crazed local act like Ohm Square. The space itself is a wonder of a crumbling former movie house that attracts (and sponsors) artists of all genres so long as they're weird. *See also p222.*

Vagon

Národní třída 25, Nové Město, Prague 1 (221 085 599/www.vagon.cz). Metro Národní třída/tram 6, 9, 17, 18, 22, 23. **Open** 6pm-5am Mon-Sat; 6pm-1am Sun. *Concerts* 9pm. **Admission** 60 Kč. **No credit cards. Map** p308 H5.

A smoky little cellar with bands playing, fresh, unrecorded rock, jam nights and reggae, both live and on the sound system. Vagon is just a student bar, but one with a love for chilled-out, dreadlocked hanging out. Don't miss the entrance, hidden as it is in a shopping passage.

Jazz & blues

Prague's jazz history stretches back to the 1930s, when Jaroslav Ježek led an adored big band as colleague RA Dvorský established a standard of excellence that survived Nazi and communist oppression. Karel Velebný, of the renowned Studio 5 group, continued that tradition after the war, while Czech-Canadian novelist Josef Škvorecký chronicled the eternal struggle of Czech sax men in book after book.

These days, the jazz scene occupies a lower echelon of the club world, but a corps of talented players works the city circuit – to such an extent that you'll find the same dozen top players in any venue you choose. A handful have managed to release original works on CD through the **AghaRTA** label and club (*see p221*) . 'Creative isolation' is a favoured phrase among those who perpetually jam at **U staré paní** (*see p221*), but they seem unable to get far beyond the borders.

Blues is a relative newcomer to Prague but has quickly acquired a dedicated contemporary following at U staré paní.

Concerts by the likes of BB King invariably fill the city's biggest halls. Among local 12-bar practitioners watch out for guitarman Spyder and Luboš Andršt, both of whom play frequent gigs around town.

AghaRTA

Krakovská 5, Nové Město, Prague 1 (222 211 275/ www.agharta.cz). Metro Muzeum or IP Pavlova/tram 4, 6, 10, 16, 22. **Open** *Club* 7pm-midnight daily. *Concerts* 9pm. *Jazz shop* 5pm-midnight Mon-Fri; 7pm-midnight Sat, Sun. **Admission** 100 Kč. **No credit cards. Map** p311 K6.

Named after Miles Davis's most controversial LP, this club off Wenceslas Square is one of Prague's best spots for modern jazz and blues. A fairly even mix of Czechs and foreigners mingles in the relatively small but comfortable space – which is perfect for sitting back and enjoying solo performances from artists such as guitarman Roman Pokorny. As at many Prague jazz clubs, there's a CD shop selling local recordings for 150-400 Kč. Look for releases on the club's own ARTA label.

Jazz Club Železná/Mecca

U průhonu 3, Holešovice, Prague 7 (283 870 522/www.mecca.cz). Metro Vltavská/tram 1, 3, 12, 25, 54. **Open** *Club* 8pm-2am Mon-Thur, Sun; 8pm-6am Fri-Sat. *Restaurant* 10am-11pm Mon-Thur; 10am-6am Fri; 8am-6am Sat. *Concerts* 9pm. **Admission** 100-300 Kč. **No credit cards. Map** p312 E2.

At press time, this hot, progressive little jazz club had moved to the Mecca night club (*see p222*), where it has added live jams to the heady cocktail already on offer at the comfortably cool space in the semi-industrial Holešovice district. The move also means that the cuisine has improved vastly of late, as Mecca is run by successful restaurateur Roman Řezníček. Here you can catch hot young players on the rise or a seasoned pro like František Kop, a Czech sax legend. The marriage of Mecca's long bars, subdued lighting and clean angles with jazz is one that will hopefully last – but it's best to check the club's website.

Reduta

Národní třída 20, Nové Město, Prague 1 (224 933 487/www.redutajazzclub.cz). Metro Národní třída/tram 6, 9, 18, 22, 51, 54, 57, 58. **Open** *Box office* 5-9pm daily. *Club* 9pm-12.30am daily. *Concerts* 9pm. **Admission** 200 Kč. **No credit cards. Map** p308 H5.

Virtually unchanged since the Velvet Revolution, this old chestnut of a club steadfastly hangs on to its cramped, awkward seating, overpriced beer and a coat-check guy who demands your jacket in hopes of a tip. That Bill Clinton once played sax here to entertain Václav Havel hardly makes up for the high prices – though it's still certainly affordable by Western standards. Admittedly, some of the best musicians in town often sit in with the evening's band, and the club, unusually, has a good sound system and a proper baby grand piano.

U Malého Glena

Karmelitská 23, Malá Strana, Prague 1 (257 531 717/www.malyglen.cz). Metro Malostranská/tram12, 22, 57. **Open** 8am-2am daily. *Concerts* 9pm . **Admission** 100-150 Kč. **No credit cards. Map** p307 D4.

While this is easily the most crammed club in town, patrons forget about the knee-bashing tables the minute the bands start up in the tiny cellar space. The freshest jazz players in the country have made Little Glenn's their home for nearly a decade. The sound system has been improved and there's even talk of putting some padding on the rock-hard seats. So squeeze in and order some nachos from the pub at street level before the set begins, with great Czech players like Najponk or the Wednesday night Chicago blues masters known as the Rene Trossman Band. (*See also p79* **Bad Bohemia: Little Glenn**.)

U staré paní

Michalská 9, Staré Město, Prague 1 (224 228 090/ www.ustarepani.cz). Metro Můstek/Národní třída/ tram 6, 9, 18, 22. **Open** 7pm-2am daily. *Concerts* 9pm. **Admission** 150 Kč. **Credit** AmEx, MC, V. **Map** p307 H4.

With a modern makeover and the same old cheap wine and grub, The Old Lady also features the same hot players as ever, with jams that last till dawn on a good Friday or Saturday. Conveniently, this is also a Staré Město hotel in a great location. The best players in town tend to gravitate here to do their own thing after performing for tourists at other venues.

Ungelt Jazz & Blues Club

Týn 2 (entrance on Týnská ulička), Staré Město, Prague 1 (224 895 748/www.jazzblues.cz). Metro Můstek or Náměstí republiky/tram 3, 5, 9, 14, 24, 26. **Open** 8pm-12.30am daily. **Admission** 150-300 Kč. **No credit cards. Map** p308 J3.

The highest-priced jazz club (drinks included) won't catch much of a local crowd, but it's still pretty reasonable by Western standards and does offer a serious line-up of jazz, funk and groove players in an atmospheric stone-walled space.

Folk/country & western

The folk, country and western vein runs surprisingly deep in the Czech lands. The American cowboy lifestyle has been romanticised here ever since Bohemians settled in Prague, Texas and 'trampers' – avid hikers and campers – sing old campfire tunes when they escape from their block housing and hit the countryside, often without speaking a word of English.

První Prag Country Saloon Amerika

Korunní 101, Vinohrady, Prague 2 (224 256 131). Metro Náměstí Míru/tram 4, 10, 16, 22. **Open** 11am-11pm Mon; 11am-midnight Tue-Fri; 5pm-midnight Sat; 6pm-1am Sun. **Admission** 20 Kč. **No credit cards. Map** p313 B3.

Still the place for an all-Czech cowboy fiddle jam (*see also p215*).

Nightlife

Eats to the beats, pop disco along the river, electronica in derelict buildings, plus dice and vice. It could be a long night.

Deep beats rock the **Roxy**, where all Prague's hottest parties are held. *See p225.*

Prague's been one of the key party cities in Europe ever since the days of dotty Emperor Rudolf II, so it's a good bet that wherever you land, folks will not be holding back. There are a number of venues where you'll come up against some cut-throat competition for the hippest wardrobe prize and places where no one would really notice if you arrived in your underwear. In between lies a new generation of classy little dance spaces attached to restaurants and bars that are successful in their own right. Two typical examples are **Celnice** (*see p223*) and **Mecca** (*see p224*), both usually packed.

Other places that double as eateries are **Duplex** (*see p223*), **Zvonařka** (*see p229*), **Ultramarin** (*see p228*), **Solidní nejistota** (*see p227*) and **Radost FX** (*p225*), but generally, you'll find beer is the only source of protein to be had while out late (with the exception, of course, of the late-night eats options listed in the restaurants chapter; *see p118*).

DJ culture reigns supreme in Prague, but it's dominated by techno, as seen and heard at **Roxy** (*see p225*) and Mecca, and the only alternatives are usually places that favour top-40 pop, such as **Klub Lávka** (*see p224*) or **Double Trouble** (*see p223*). Clubs for danceable funk, soul or R&B are virtually nonexistent. Good thing Radost FX comes through with at least one night a week that's not just for early-twentysomethings.

Closures and openings are constant, as in the clubbing world anywhere, only even more so in Prague since clubs tend to share buildings with residential spaces and Czechs are early risers. The other unique aspect of clubbing in Prague is a feeling of anarchy that could only be achieved in a place with virtually no safety regulations or PC culture. Bar-top stripping, crumbling walls and rampant use of stimulants can all be found within blocks of each other in Staré Město on any Friday night.

Just remember that if yo're caught with drugs, you're on your own. Czech Police arrest anyone in possession of what they deem 'more than a little' of a controlled substance and the jails are full of people still not convicted of a thing. Gambling, however, is completely legal and high rollers will find the city has no shortage of casinos, though none are as classy as the **Palais Savarin** or the **Millennium** (for both, *see p231*). Would-be beatniks and Charles Bukowskis, on the other hand, will find a plenitude of material in Prague's ubiquitous *herna* bars and many smoky dives lined with electronic one-armed bandits.

Note that any tram with a number in the 50s is a night tram. And, at the end of a long night, taking a night tram is definitely an experience in itself (*see p96* **Bad Bohemia: Tram from Hell**)

Clubs

Celnice

V celnice 4, Nové Město, Prague 1 (224 212 240/www.celnice.com). Metro Náměstí Republiky/tram 5, 8, 14. **Open** 11am-2am Mon-Thur, Sun; 11am-4am Fri, Sat. **Admission** free-200 Kč. **Credit** AmEx, MC, V. **Map** p309 K3.

With a space-age mod sushi bar and dance club in the cellar, this fairly conventional restaurant (*see p118*) has become a shining star on the Czech party scene. DJs spin happy house and the crowd dresses to kill, knows its moves and shakes it until late. Be buff or prepared to buy a lot of cocktails to get much attention.

Delta

Vlastina 887, Liboc, Prague 6 (233 312 443/www.noise.cz/delta). Tram 20, 26, 51/night bus 510. **Open** 7pm-midnight Thur, Fri. **Admission** from 80 Kč. **No credit cards**.

With solid local fringe rock credentials, but waaay out in the midst of suburban apartments on the city's north-western border, Delta is a club that attracts a local crowd that's young, bored and aching to break out. A steady supply of uncommercial DJs and once-banned live bands such as Echt! perform irregularly.

Double Trouble

Melatrichova 17, Staré Město, Prague 1 (221 632 414/www.doubletrouble.cz). Metro Můstek or Staroměstská/tram 3, 6, 9, 14, 18, 22, 24, 52, 53, 55, 56, 57, 58. **Open** 6pm-4am daily. **Admission** free-180 Kč. **No credit cards**. **Map** p308 H4.

Looks like a lively scene at first, but only after venturing in do you see it's crammed with backpackers, happily paying heavily for drinks, admission and crap pop tracks. That said, they do seem to be enjoying themselves dancing on the bar and stripping off.

Duplex

Václavské náměstí 21, Nové Město, Prague 1 (224 490 440/www.duplexduplex.cz). Metro Můstek/tram 3, 9, 14, 24, 51, 52, 53, 55, 56, 58. **Open** *Café* 10am-midnight daily. *Club* 9.30pm-2am Tue-Thur; 9.30pm-5am Fri, Sat. *Restaurant* noon-midnight daily. **Admission** 150 Kč. **Credit** AmEx, MC, V. **Map** p308 J5.

The attitude here is so thick you can cut it with your stiletto heels, but if you have to experience a Wenceslas Square disco, this one's as good a candidate as any. Friday Funk'n Motion parties and go-go dancers come with the penthouse views, overpriced drinks and hustlers. In April the Italian students who walk all over Staré Město in formation land here. Still, the programming has improved lately and the cuisine, while inconsistent, has won raves. Plus, there is a remarkable chill-out space on the terrace, where meals are also served.

La Fabrique

Uhelný trh 2, Staré Město, Prague 1 (224 233 137). Metro Můstek or Národní třída/tram 6, 9, 18, 22, 53, 57, 58. **Open** 8pm-4am daily. **Admission** free. **Credit** AmEx, MC, V. **Map** p308 H5.

Disco lovers cram into this subterranean Staré Město club to hear pop, along with nightmarish DJs who love to announce things over the songs. Done up throughout in factory decor, it's a maze of rooms with a narrow entrance just off the Havelská fruit market. Revellers pack into a sweaty throng inside.

Guru

Rokycanova 29, Žižkov, Prague 3 (777 155 103/www.guruclub.wz.cz). Metro Jiřího z Poděbrad/tram 5, 9, 26, 58. **Open** 11pm-5am daily. *Shows* 8pm or 9pm. **Admission** 30-50 Kč. **No credit cards**.

Very irregular programme and, in that sense, very Žižkov. With the right act, it can be a brilliant experience in a dive bar, but ask around before heading out unless you enjoy a gamble. A strange, worn-out, subterranean space with split-level dancefloor, balconies and dazed bar tenders. Staff ask for a deposit on glass beer mugs, which gives you an idea of how rowdy the crowds get.

Jo's Bar & Garáž

Malostranské náměstí 7, Malá Strana, Prague 1 (257 531 422). Metro Malostranská/tram 12, 20, 22, 23, 57. **Open** 8pm-4am daily. **Admission** free-100 Kč. **Credit** AmEx, MC, V. **Map** p305 E3.

Another stone cellar dance club? Say it ain't so! The handiest one in Malá Strana can be a good time for brainless bouncing to the Red Hot Chili Peppers, but just as often there's nothing on at all except desultory beer drinking. Worth checking if you're in the neighbourhood.

Karlovy Lázně

Novotného lávka 1, Staré Město, Prague 1 (no phone, www.karlovylazne.cz). Metro Staroměstská/tram 17, 18, 53. **Open** *Café* 11am-4am daily. *Club* 9pm-5am daily. **Admission** 50-100 Kč. **No credit cards**. **Map** p308 G4.

Make a pilgrimage to **Mecca**.

Prague's unabashed commercial mega-club is in a former bathhouse next door to the Charles Bridge. And it's every bit as original as you'd expect in that location. The four levels of Karlovy Lázně cover every baseline. Paradogs does techno on the fourth floor, Kaleidoskop does retro hits on the third, Discotheque does radio pop, and the MCM café, the only part of the club open by day, books occasional jazz and funk combos. Huge with teens.

Klub Lávka

Novotného lávka 1, Staré Město, Prague 1 (222 222 156/221 082 278/www.lavka.cz). Metro Staroměstská/tram 17, 18, 53. **Open** *Bar* 24hrs daily. *Disco* 10pm-4am daily. **Admission** 50 Kč. **Credit** AmEx, MC, V. **Map** p308 G4.

A lovely river terrace out back, go-go dancers, funk and disco tracks on the sound system and all within spitting distance of the Charles Bridge. There's no challenging digital music here but, in the black light, where everyone's underwear dances, no one seems to mind.

Mánes

Masarykovo nábřeží 250, Nové Město, Prague 1 (224 931 112). Metro Karlovo náměstí/tram 17, 18, 53, 57, 58. **Open** 11am-11pm daily. **Admission** 50 Kč. **Credit** AmEx, MC, V. **Map** p310 G7.

This classy 1930s functionalist gallery space is more than living art history. It's also a run-down riverside dance venue with an amazing location. For a while it specialised in Tropicana nights on Friday and Saturday, with hot mambo kings. These days, the programme is unpredictable, but a beer on the terrace (open until 11pm) is never a bad idea.

Matrix

Koněvova 13, Žižkov, Prague 3 (222 780 423/ www.matrixklub.cz). Metro Florenc, then bus 133 or 207. **Admission** free-120 Kč. **No credit cards**. **Map** p313 A1.

This former frozen meat plant is a big teen scene for techno and good, grotty partying, with Gambrinus beer on tap. Occasional local DJ stars like Babe LN play, as do international bands willing to do nearly free shows, but generally it's a fringe line-up.

Mecca

U průhonu 3, Holešovice, Prague 7 (283 870 5220/www.mecca.cz). Metro Vltavská/tram 1, 3, 12, 25, 54. **Open** *Club* 10pm-6am Fri, Sat. *Restaurant* 10am-11pm Mon-Thur; 10am-6am Fri; 8am-6am Sat. **Admission** 100-300 Kč. **No credit cards**. **Map** p312 E2.

The biggest hit on the party scene is this club for grown-ups. A disused factory made over into a stylishly modern, large-scale dance palace with respectable restaurant service, Mecca is worth a pilgrimage. Theme parties, a line-up of the city's top DJs and live jazz are the trophies. The C Lounge downstairs offers chill-out space and the most mellow of the club's three glossy bars.

Punto Azul

Kroftova 1, Smíchov, Prague 5 (no phone/www. puntoazul.cz). Tram 6, 9, 12, 20, 57. **Open** 8pm-2am daily. **Admission** 40 Kč. **No credit cards**.

This club is so underground you'll need canaries to test the air. There's nothing Spanish about this place apart from the name; it's just a student drinking dive on every wirehead's map, despite the fact that the techno dance space isn't much bigger than a circuit board. Nevertheless, a consistent groove is achieved through a line-up of the city's more avant-garde house DJs.

Radost FX

Bělehradská 120, Nové Město, Prague 2 (224 254 776/www.radostfx.cz). Metro IP Pavlova/ tram 4, 6, 10, 11, 16, 22, 51, 56, 57. **Open** 11am-4am Mon-Sat; 10.30am-4am Sun. *Club* 10pm-5am Thur-Sat. **Admission** 120-250 Kč. **No credit cards**. **Map** p311 L8.

The original house party in Prague is going strong after more than a decade in service. Radost FX still offers the best all-night mix you'll find in the city: a combination of creative veggie café, spaced-out back-room lounge, and small but slick downstairs club featuring absurdly glam theme parties, provide a first-class venure for endless fashion shows, local stars of house and techno, and one of the best Sunday brunches in town (*see p119*).

Resort

Vinohradská 40, Vinohrady, Prague 2 (222 511 997/www.resort.cz). Metro Jiřího z Poděbrad/ tram 11, 53. **Open** 9pm-4am Tue-Sat; 4pm-midnight Sun **Admission** free-100 Kč. **No credit cards**. Map p313 A3.

Newly kitted out, Resort is the latest venture to occupy this space, where 350 beautiful people can just squeeze in. The club's consistent programme (SuenoLatino on Wednesdays, Soul Jam on Saturdays) goes along with the hypermodern décor and, less fortunately, non-expert cocktail mixing.

Roxy

Dlouhá 33, Staré Město, Prague 1 (224 826 296/ www.roxy.cz). Metro Náměstí Republiky/5, 8, 14, 26, 53 tram. **Open** 7pm-2am Mon-Thur; 7pm-4am Fri, Sat. *Party nights* 10pm-5am. **Admission** *DJ nights* 100-250 Kč. *Live events* 150-450 Kč. **No credit cards**. **Map** p306 J3.

The crumbling Roxy is Prague's top destination for house, R&B and jungle, thanks in large part to one of Central Europe's best party organisers, David Urban. Star acts no other club could afford, from Arrested Development to Transglobal Underground, get talked into doing Roxy shows, in addition to local kings of the decks . Meanwhile the Galerie NoD (*see p202*) fills out the venue with multiple floors of edgy, non-commercial culture and fringe art. Free Mondays pack the place with kids. *See also p215.*

Sedm vlků

Vlkova 7, Žižkov, Prague 3 (222 711 725/www.sedmvlku.cz). Metro Jiřího z Poděbrad/tram 5, 9, 26, 55, 58. **Open** 6pm-3am Mon-Sat. **Admission** free. **No credit cards. Map** p313 B2.

Newly redone with surrealist art, low light and bendy ironwork, The Seven Wolves remains one of the hippest bar-cum-club spaces in the party mecca that is the Žižkov district. With hot-and-cold running jungle on the decks, there's basically just beer for quality libation, but that's fairly standard in Prague clubs. The crisp sound system is another reason this club has stolen the thunder of the more established clubs around, such as the neighbouring Akropolis (*see p215*) and the respected bar Hapu (*see p156*).

Solidní nejistota

Pštrossova 21, Nové Město, Prague 1 (224 933 086/www.solidninejistota.cz). Metro Národní třída/tram 6, 9, 17, 18, 22, 23, 51, 52, 53, 54, 55, 56, 57, 58. **Open** 6pm-6am daily. **Admission** free. **No credit cards. Map** p308 G7.

Ever dependable, Solid Uncertainty is the most shameless meat market in Prague, with the world-weary bar staff manning the taps at the centre of the

Bad Bohemia DJ Tim Otis

A survivor of the Los Angeles and San Francisco club scenes of the '80s, DJ Tim Otis (pictured) is on a mission where Prague is concerned. From his pulpit at Radio 1 (www.radio1.cz), where he hosts the only English-language show, on Fridays at 8pm, he informs and provokes. Invariably plugged into the most significant parties, clubbing developments and art events in Bohemia, his broadcasts are generally streets ahead of any listings in the free party 'zines that come and go in Prague on an almost monthly basis.

And, unlike the glossies, he delivers the goods without any of the attitude. Which is not to say he can't be prickly. About the better part of the dance scene in Prague he says: 'They're just robots. And the funny thing is, they're all being sold individuality by MTV and Nike.'

But, if there's something of a herd mentality to clubbing in Prague, which may well be related to the number of cover bands and knock-off bars in the city, Otis feels compelled to do more to challenge it. His live DJ gigs at **Radost FX** (*see p225*) – and, lately, at some of the hipper weddings held at castles organised by the Lobkowicz family – have attracted a cult following. Revellers tired of endless variations of house and hip hop, seek out Otis's nights for exposure to indie tracks, rare groove and even spoken-word sounds.

A former student of design, Otis tries to lay out soundscapes that contrast elements and may also encourage – gasp – discussion. 'It's not about popping e and getting stupid,' he says, summing up the positive direction of clubbing circa 2004.

Doesn't sound like a dance club? It may well not be. More and more lounge spaces like **Celnice** (*see p225*) the newly redone **Radost FX** back lounge and **Jet Set** (Radlická 1C-1D, Smíchov, Prague 5, 257 327 251) are stealing clubs' thunder these days. Other alternatives like the hulking **Abaton** (*see p216*) are making waves with events and parties that share little with the predictable parties of most Prague clubs.

None of which means things will be any less wild, of course. He sums up the Prague after-hours scene aptly: 'It's the ultimate target market for tobacco and booze.'

room, around which every creature looking to hook up rotates, scanning the possibilities. If the new Prague aquarium (*see p187*) is closed, this is just as good a spot to watch the sharks. The grill, at least, is open late into the night, but it looks like the beefy doormen are the only ones who use it.

U Bukanyra

Na Františku emankement (near Čechuv bridge), Staré Město, Prague 1 (777 891 348/www.bukanyr.cz). Metro Staroměstská/tram 17, 18. **Admission** free-100 Kč. **No credit cards**.

This floating barge party is a curative smoky disco on summer nights, but programming can be iffy. House-music DJs maintain sway when At the Buccaneer is operating, but it's not unheard of for it to be dark for weeks. Worth checking on, since it's right in the centre and good fun if you're in luck.

U Buldoka

Preslova 1, Smíchov, Prague 5 (257 329 154/www.ubuldoka.cz). Metro Anděl/tram 4, 6, 7, 9, 10, 12, 14, 20, 52, 58. **Open** 11am-midnight Mon-Fri; noon-midnight Sat, Sun. **Admission** 30-50 Kč. **No credit cards**.

With well-tapped Staropramen beer and excellent traditonal grub, the Bulldog is a classic cheap Czech pub that cleverly conceals a groovin' music club downstairs. The space is done up in the prevailing retro style, with the usual crew of Czech DJs: Loutka, Tráva and Liquid A.

Újezd

Újezd 18, Malá Strana, Prague 1 (no phone). Metro Malostranská/tram 6, 9, 12, 20, 22, 23, 57, 58. **Open** *Bar* 11am-4am daily. *Café* 3pm-4am daily. *Pub* 8pm-4am daily. **Admission** free. **No credit cards**. **Map** p307 E5.

In its earlier days as Borát, this three-storey madhouse was an important alternative music club. Today, with its surrealist ironwork decor, a young Czech crowd in dreads and thick, smokey atmosphere, Ujezd is home to some loud, badly amplified Czech rock tracks, battered wooden chairs in the café upstairs and shouted conversation in the bar below. And the venue is not an iota less popular for it.

Ultramarin

Ostrovní 32, Nové Město, Prague 2 (224 932 249/www.ultramarin.cz). Metro Národní třída/tram 6, 9, 17, 18, 22, 23, 51, 52, 53, 54, 55, 56, 57, 58. **Open** 10.30am-4am daily. **Admission** free. **Credit** AmEx, MC, V. **Map** p308 H6.

Lesser-known DJs rock the small stone cellar space and critical mass seems to be easily achieved making Ultramarin an engaging place to stay up late and get sweaty. At street level its an art bar with a small menu of salads and Czech-Mex and seating made from designer materials like layered cardboard. You'll find a grown-up crowd here and it's in a handy location, just streets from Staré Město.

U zlatého stromu

Karlova 6, Staré Město, Prague 1 (222 220 441/ www.zlatystrom.cz). Metro Staroměstská/tram 17, 18, 53. **Open** *Club* 8pm-6am daily. *Restaurant* 24hrs daily. **Admission** 80 Kč. **Credit** AmEx, MC, V. **Map** p308 G4.

Here's one of the strangest combinations in the Staré Město area: a non-stop disco, striptease, bar, restaurant and hotel. Descend into the cellar labyrinth of bad pop and strippers, and you could end up in a peaceful outdoor garden or a nook for conversing. The upstairs café has a full menu plus coffee and drinks.

Wakata

Malířská 14, Holešovice, Prague 7 (233 370 518/ www.wakata.cz). Metro Vltavská/tram 1, 8, 25, 26, 51, 56. **Open** 5pm-3am Mon-Thur; 5pm-5am Fri, Sat; 6pm-3am Sun. **Admission** free. **No credit cards**. **Map** p311 L8.

A down-and-dirty teenage wasteland, this bar can deliver great jungle mixing, but more often it feels like you've stepped into a cheap horror film. At least it stays open way past official hours, has motorcycle seats for bar stools and is, errm, away from it all.

XT3

Pod plynojemem 5, Libeň, Prague 8 (284 825 826/ www.xt3.cz). Metro Palmovka/tram 1, 3, 8, 10, 12, 19, 24, 52, 54, 55. **Open** 4pm-2am Mon-Thur, Sun; 4pm-5am Fri, Sat. **Admission** from 30 Kč. **No credit cards**.

XT3 features breakbeat, lots of smoke and cheap beer – all packed into a venue foreigners won't stumble upon. Don't forget your skateboard, and bring Czech teen friends if you want to blend in with the serious crowd of vinyl fanatics.

Zvonařka

Šafaříkova 1, Vinohrady, Prague 2 (224 251 990). Metro Náměstí Míru/tram 6, 11, 56. **Open** 11.30am-midnight Mon-Fri; noon-midnight Sat, Sun. **Admission** free-200 Kč. **Credit** MC, V.

A bit like a cruise ship inside, this happening disco was transformed by yet another hyper-modernist design from a popular Czech pub, with a terrace that overlooks Prague's southern suburbs. The circular bar and blue and silver motifs set the stage for high-energy parties when the place is busy. And, when the DJs aren't up to much, at least the food's reliable.

Gambling

Gambling is big business in Prague – and seems to get bigger every year. First came the *hernas* ('gambling halls', which are essentially bars full of one-armed bandits). Then came the bigger casinos that now line Wenceslas Square. Regulation is questionable, so, if you want to roll the dice, stick with the respectable international chains, which are geared towards tourists, encourage small-time

Sin City

It's not that Prague has lost any of the decadent behaviour that made the word 'bohemian' synonymous with a dissipated life in the 19th century. It's just that sin and the newly restored free-market economy have combined in a way that can be, well, a bit baffling.

There are more than 40 *noční kluby*, or nightclubs, in Prague offering services extending well beyond the usual definition of a few drinks. The Finance Ministry has estimated that the potential revenues from a tax on prostitution would be in the billions of crowns. And you only have to walk around Wenceslas Square after dark to see that it has become a gauntlet of hawkers from brothels, all thinly disguised as bars or 'cabarets', competing for customers.

Construction crews can constantly be seen renovating the clubs near Wenceslas Square, knocking down walls, taking over neighbouring businesses and painting enormous street windows with slogans such as 'room and pleasure from 1,200 Kc'. As older clubs keep expanding and new ones sprout up, it's apparent that the city's sex entrepreneurs are going full steam to keep up with insatiable demand.

Venturing into one of these halls is a memorable experience – like something out of a David Lynch film. At the high end there's the **Darling Club Cabaret** (*see p231*), which, inside, looks like a dim, baroque bus stop, with lithe women in lingerie standing in every aisle and lined up at the bar. Should you take a table and a drink you'll shortly be joined by one or two of them, who will politely ask where you're from – and little else – and lean in close to point out the rates for 'private shows' – an international business clientele seems happy to pay (or expense?) 2,800 Kč for a 30-minute show here. A waitress will then stop by almost immediately and try to get you to buy your new dates drinks priced at four or five times the usual rate. If, however, the ladies at your table don't appear to strike your fancy, another pair will take their place. Somewhere in the background a striptease will be happening, but it goes unnoticed with all the other eyeing-up going on in the room.

The popular **K5** (Korunní 5, Vinohrady, Prague 2, 224 250 505, www.k5relax.cz) provides another variation on the theme, with a smaller lounge bar area on the top floor. Like Darling, K5 owns an entire apartment building. Some of the women working in clubs like this live on site and generally have rental agreements that make them legally responsible for their own activities, though the house always gets a cut, which is considered rent. A similar system works for women to work out of the clubs part-time – although the rooms they rent aren't residential apartments, they're the Jungle Room, the Moon Room or the Harem Room.

At the other end of the spectrum the new **Red Light Bar** (Pražská tržnice, Bubenské nábřeží, Holešovice, Prague 7, www.redlight.cz) features a fairly standard bar – except that waitresses have added firting, dancing and stripping to their duties. The club packs in Marines, truckers and stag parties with its Saturday night parties. *Nadržené Školačky*, or 'horny schoolgirls', was a recent theme, and all parties feature the bar's signature 'body shots' – cheap whisky drunk from the cleavage or navel of your server. Of course the real action is next door at the carnival-like 'Sex Park', where secretaries, receptionists and even policewomen offer their own private shows for closer to 1,000 Kč per half hour.

In light of prostitution being illegal, a scandal in 2003 over the extent of child prostitution along the German border, and the Czech Republic's entry in 2004 into the European Union, one might just wonder what the state has to say about all this.

Well, to borrow from Bob Marley, 'Legalise it.' So proposes Jitka Gjuricová, director of the Interior Ministry's crime-prevention department, who has drafted a resolution for parliament that would do just that. In her view, 'legalisation is a way of having women be their own bosses.'

Aid organisations like Pleasure Without Risk, agree, adding that keeping prostitution illegal is likely to lead to a gradual increase in sexually transmitted diseases.

As far as Lenka, a worker at another popular club, is concerned, it all comes down to doing simple maths: 'I could work for a month in Prague in an office and make 10,000 Kč. Here I can make that in one night.'

If Adam Smith ever could have imagined!

betting and have fairly relaxed atmospheres. The *hernas* cater mostly to locals, pay a maximum of 300 Kč for a 2 Kč wager and operate on a legally fixed ratio of 60 to 80 odds.

Casinos

Millennium

V celnici 10, Nové Město, Prague 1 (221 033 401). Metro Náměstí Republiky/tram 5, 8, 14, 24, 26, 52, 53. **Open** 3pm-4am daily. **Credit** AmEx, MC, V. **Map** p309 L3.

Plush, classy and palatial, this James Bond-esque casino is part of a spick-and-span hotel and retail complex just east of Staré Město. Free drinks for players add to the fun if you can keep your head.

Palais Savarin

Na příkopě 10, Nové Město, Prague 1 (224 221 636/www.czechcasinos.cz). Metro Můstek/ tram 3, 5, 8, 9, 14, 26, 51, 52, 53, 55, 56, 58. **Open** 1pm-4am daily. **Credit** DC, MC, V. **Map** p309 K4.

One of the most established operations in town, with candelabras and baroque frescoes, it's a world apart from most of the betting rooms on Wenceslas Square. Just about worth a look even if you don't gamble – but if you do, drinks are on the house. American roulette and stud poker are offered along with all the traditional games of chance. Bets from 20 Kč to 5,000 Kč.

Herna bars

Herna Můstek

Inside Můstek metro station, Nové Město, Prague 1 (no phone). Metro Můstek/tram 3, 9, 14, 24, 52, 53, 55, 56, 58. **Open** 24hrs daily. **No credit cards. Map** p309 K5.

Most *herna* bars are pretty seedy, but this one, inside Prague's main metro station, is not too threatening.

Reno

Vodičkova 39, Nové Město, Prague 1 (224 949 133). Metro Můstek/tram 3, 9, 14, 24, 52, 53, 55, 56, 58. **Open** 11am-6am daily. **No credit cards. Map** p310 J6.

Patronised by nervous-looking types. Light food is served, but is not recommended.

Adult clubs

Prostitution, though technically illegal in the Czech Republic, is practiced openly at many clubs. Stag party favourites are **Darling Club Cabaret** (*see below*), **Red Light** (*see p230* **Sin City**) and **Cabaret Atlas** (*see below*). Bordellos usually operate officially as strip clubs and don't pressurise visitors to go any further than the bar. Sufficient funds are usually squeezed out of customers by then already, with ruinous drink prices and strippers encouraged to drink with the gullible customers.

Cabaret Atlas

Ve Smečkách 31, Nové Město, Prague 1 (296 326 042). Metro Muzeum/tram 4, 6, 10, 16, 22, 51, 53, 55, 56, 57, 58. **Open** 7pm-7am daily. **Admission** 200 Kč. **Credit** MC, V. **Map** p311 K6.

Striptease, a crowd of businessmen who can expense the drinks and whirlpools at a mere 3,500 Kč an hour – and that's just for starters.

Captain Nemo

Ovocný trh 13, Staré Město, Prague 1 (224 210 356). Metro Náměstí Republiky/tram 5, 8, 14, 53. **Open** 8pm-5am daily. **Admission** 300 Kč. **Credit** MC, V. **Map** p309 L3.

This is a handy Staré Město club that employs mainly local talent and goes for a nautical theme, though it's not clear that anyone's noticed yet.

Caroica

Václavské náměstí 4, Nové Město, Prague 1 (296 325 314). Metro Můstek/tram 3, 9, 14, 24, 51, 53, 55, 56, 57, 58. **Open** 9pm-2am daily. **Admission** 200 Kč. **No credit cards. Map** p308 J5.

Deep under Wenceslas Square in what looks like an imperial bedroom, Caroica was formerly one of the city's best jazz holes. The baroque red-and-gold setting has remained, but new management has launched a cabaret: dancers with top hats and canes alternate with strippers in what could almost be called entertainment appropriate for a date – though with the usual quadrupled drink rates.

Darling Club Cabaret

Ve Smečkách 32, Nové Město, Prague 1 (no phone, www.kabaret.cz). Metro Můstek/tram 3, 9, 14, 24, 51, 53, 55, 56, 57, 58. **Open** 8pm-8am daily. **Admission** 200 Kč. **Credit** AmEx, MC, V. **Map** p311 K6.

The biggest bacchanalia in town and a stopover for travelling 'entertainers' from around the world, Darling wins a flood of patrons with two plush bars, dizzying drink prices and loads of improbably beautiful women.

Goldfingers

Václavské náměstí 5, Nové Město, Prague 1 (224 193 571). Metro Můstek/tram 3, 9, 14, 24, 51, 53, 55, 56, 57, 58. **Open** 9pm-4am daily. **Admission** 450 Kč. **Credit** AmEx, MC, V. **Map** p308 J5.

Viva Prague's Vegas, with drinks named for James Bond foils, a theatrical setting and dizzy dancers. And it's strictly dancing they do, so all's fairly innocent in the end, perhaps to the disappointment of all the stag parties.

Satanela

Vilová 9, Strašnice, Prague 10 (274 816 618). Metro Strašnická/tram 7, 19, 26, 51, 55. **Open** 10am-2am daily. **Admission** varies. **No credit cards.**

Whips and chains, lab coats and fetish.

Theatre & Dance

The curtain rises on avant-garde performances, Czech interpretations of the classics and an edgy dance scene. Encore.

The **Archa Theatre**.

The central European passion for tragi-comedy in life, often of a romantic or Gothic stripe, combined with a history of world-class visual arts has created fertile soil for contemporary performance art in the Czech Republic. The thriving theatre and dance scenes in Prague are diverse and vibrant.

Dance, with its universal language and a range of styles, from classical hits to cool contemporary, dance theatre to truly alternative, is a good choice for English speakers. Contemporary dance has particularly flourished in the city since the Velvet Revolution – under the former regime only classical ballet and folk dance were supported – and several annual festivals of the latter survive to this day. The famous non-verbal theatre and dance courses at the **Prague Academy** (Malostranské náměstí 13, Malá Strana, Prague 1, 257 534 205) or the **Duncan Centre Conservatory for Modern Dance** (Branická 41, Braník, Prague 4, 244 461 342) have spawned an offbeat generation of young contemporary artists of international recognition. Halka Třešňáková and Petra Hauerová are names to watch out for, as is the cutting-edge theatre-dance company **Déja Donné** (*see p235* **Déja Donné**). Festivals such as the mainstream **Tanec Praha** (Dance Prague), experimental **Konfrontace** (Confrontations) and the truly alternative **Čtyři dny v pohybu** (Four Days in Motion; for all, *see p238*) feature these and international contemporary dance artists.

The larger stages such as the **National Theatre** (*see p235*), **Estates Theatre** (*see p233*) and **State Opera** (*see p235*) present a full programme of classical ballets, as well as an increasingly courageous and exciting collection of new works set or created for local dancers by visiting choreographers.

Theatre presented in English is on the increase. For several years an excellent and far-reaching **Prague German-Language Theatre Festival** (222 232 303, www.theater.cz) has taken place in the city every November, but English-language productions have been limited to self-produced ex-pat shows (of varying quality) and simplistic

black light theatre (*see p237*). This is changing fast and the choice available to visitors is now vastly improved. The **Prague Fringe Festival** (*see p238*) is a notable addition to the theatre calendar, presenting a host of varied performances from around the world, the vast majority in English.

The newest venue on the scene is **Švanda Theatre** (Švandovo Divaldo; *see p237*) in the up-and-coming district of Prague 5. Smartly reconstructed and reopened (after a turn-of-the century heyday and dark days under communism) it shows high-quality and avant-garde theatre by local artists. Those committed theatre buffs who are determined to see a Czech performance should take heart as many Prague productions are colourful adaptations of familiar works by the likes of Dostoevsky, Samuel Beckett or Shakespeare. Czech actors and directors tend to be increasingly warm and expressive, with recent productions combining striking symbolic, minimalist design with a vivid, physical acting style.

For family or for more light-hearted entertainment, there are always the traditional Czech staples of **puppetry** (*see p237*) and black light theatre.

TICKETS AND INFORMATION

Many box office clerks have at least a rudimentary command of English, but you're better off buying tickets through one of the central agencies. These accept credit cards (unlike many venues), you can book via their websites or by telephone in English, and there are numerous outlets throughout the city. **Bohemia Ticket International** (*see p210*) is the best agency for making advance bookings from abroad for the National Theatre, Estates Theatre and State Opera. **Ticketpro** (*see p210*) also sells tickets for some events.

Ticket touts cluster at the National Theatre, Estates Theatre and State Opera. You can often get into sold-out (*vyprodáno*) performances, at a price. Wait until the last bell for the best deal.

For the latest theatre and dance listings, pick up a copy of *The Prague Post* or drop into your nearest branch of the **Prague Information Service** (*see p291*) or check out its website www.pis.cz.

Czech Theatres

Alfred ve Dvoře Theatre

Divadlo Alfred ve Dvoře
Františka Křížka 36, Holešovice, Prague 7 (233 376 985/www.alfredvedvore.cz). Metro Vltavská/ tram 1, 5, 8, 12, 17, 25, 26. **Open** *Box office* 1hr before performance. **Tickets** 130 Kč; 80 Kč students. **No credit cards**. **Map** p312 D3.
A curious and appealing modern building constructed inside a residential courtyard. Physical, visual, non-verbal and experimental theatre plays here, as well as some dance and mime artists. Some performances and programme notes in English.

Archa Theatre

Divadlo Archa
Na Poříčí 26, Nové Město, Prague 1 (221 716 333/www.archatheatre.cz). Metro Náměstí Republiky or Florenc/tram 3, 8, 24, 26. **Open** *Box office* 10am-6pm Mon-Fri and 2hrs before performance. **Tickets** 100-300 Kč. **Credit** AmEx, MC, V. **Map** p309 M2.
The superb Archa Theatre brings international avant-garde luminaries of contemporary dance, theatre and music (*see p215)* to its versatile, well-equipped space. It also features the cream of the Czech avant-garde crop – such as Filip Topol, Petr Nikl and Agon orchestr. Archa's unique 'English Friendly' programme provides subtitles, translation or original English material for many quality productions, discussions and lectures.

Divadlo Na zábradli

Theatre on the Balustrade
Anenské náměstí 5, Staré Město, Prague 1 (222 868 868/www.nazabradli.cz). Metro Staroměstská/tram 17, 18. **Open** *Box office* 2-4pm, 4.30-8pm Mon-Fri; 2hrs before performance Sat, Sun. **Tickets** 100-290 Kč. **No credit cards**. **Map** p308 G4.
Founded in 1958, this theatre lay the groundwork for Czech Theatre of the Absurd. It was the focus of much secret police attention prior to 1989, when it harboured such dissidents as Václav Havel and New Wave filmmaker Jiří Menzel. Havel's celebrated play *The Garden Party* premièred here, and his works are still part of the repertoire.

Estates Theatre

Stavovské divadlo
Ovocný trh 1, Staré Město, Prague 1 (224 215 001). Metro Můstek/tram 3, 9, 14, 24. **Open** *Box office* 10am-6pm daily. **Tickets** 30-1,000 Kč. **Credit** MC, V (for advance sales only). **Map** p308 J4.
Opened in 1783, this baroque wedding-cake of a building is a venue of the National Theatre company – along with the National Theatre. The theatre, which hosted the world première of Mozart's *Don Giovanni* (conducted by the composer himself), also produces ballet, modern dance and opera. Caution: there is pre-recorded orchestration at times. Extensive English and German programmes.

Galerie NoD

1st Floor, Dlouhá 33, Prague 1 (224 826 330/ www.roxy.cz). Metro Staroměstská or Náměstí Republiky/tram 5, 8, 14. **Open** 1pm-1am Mon-Sat. **Tickets** 60-80 Kč. **No credit cards**. **Map** p308 K2.
Best described as 'very Prague', this artists' hang-out, decked out in surrealist decor, stages off-centre theatre events, political discussions and comedy nights. It also houses an art gallery and hip internet café-bar. Supported by the Linhart Foundation, a major funder of Czech alternative culture, it offers radical, though sometimes hit-and-miss, work.

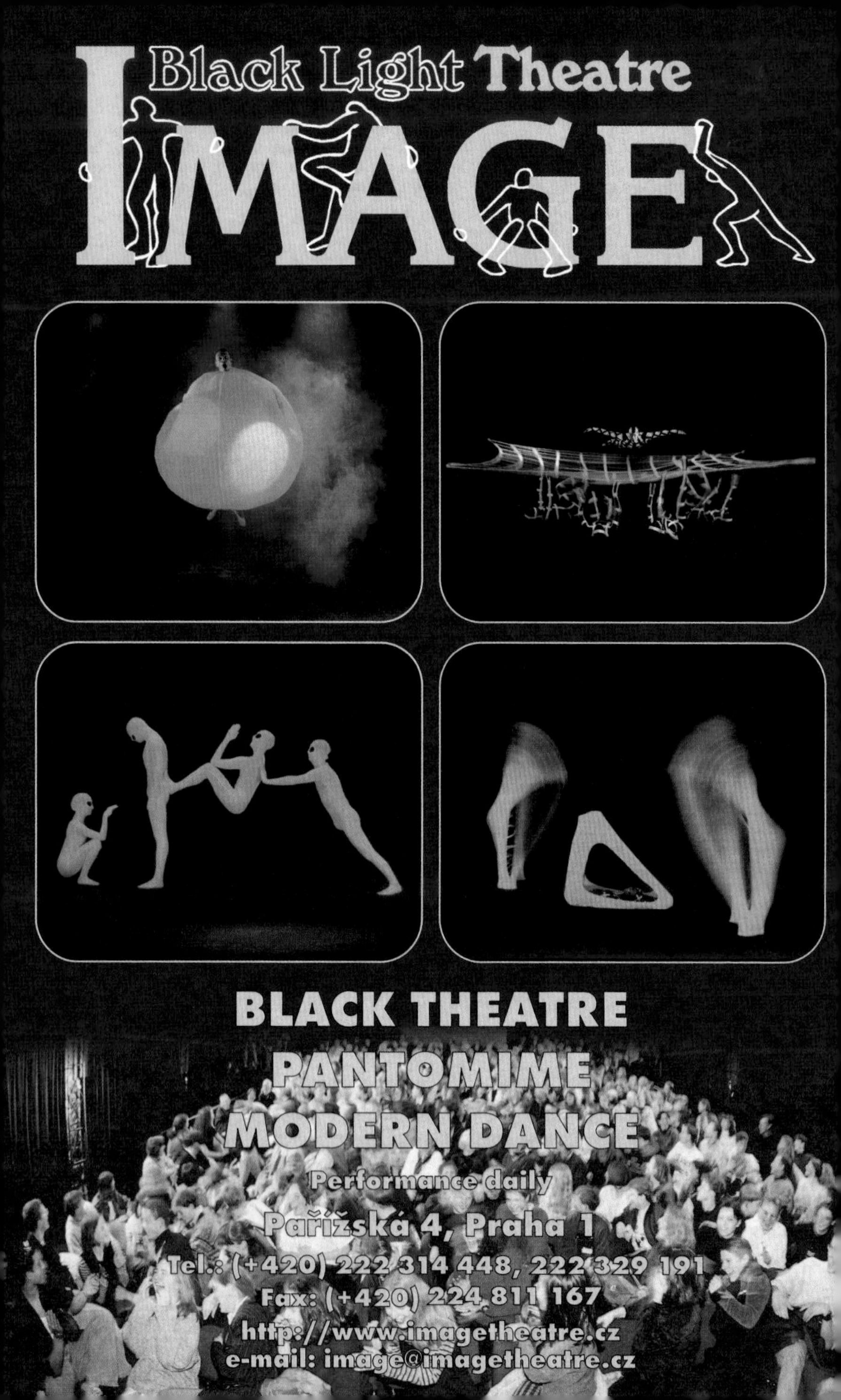
Black Light Theatre
IMAGE
BLACK THEATRE
PANTOMIME
MODERN DANCE
Performance daily
Pařížská 4, Praha 1
Tel.: (+420) 222 314 448, 222 329 191
Fax: (+420) 224 811 167
http://www.imagetheatre.cz
e-mail: image@imagetheatre.cz

National Theatre

Národní divadlo

Národní 2, Nové Město, Prague 1 (224 901 448/ www.narodni-divadlo.cz). Metro Národní třída/tram 6, 9, 17, 18, 22. **Open** *Box office* 10am-6pm daily. **Tickets** 30-900 Kč. **Credit** AmEx, MC, V. **Map** p310 G6.

This architectural ode to Slavic myth, first completed in 1881, reopened following a fire in 1883 to the strains of Smetana's opera *Libuše*, commissioned for the occasion and based on the tale of the prophet who envisaged Prague. Productions include drama, ballet and operas in their original language, with a Czech and sometimes English translation projected above the stage. You can reserve tickets through the theatre website up to three months in advance but, they must still be bought at the box office – with a 20% surcharge for reserving on the internet if you book more than 30 days before curtain. Many visitors are drawn to see the playhouse itself. Tours are available daily.

Ponec

Husitská 24A, Žižkov, Prague 3 (224 817 886). Metro Florenc, then bus 133 or 207. **Open** *Box office* 6-8pm performance days. **Tickets** 140-250 Kč. **No credit cards**. **Map** p313 1B.

This converted cinema is the home of the Tanec Praha (Dance Prague) association, which is dedicated to producing new contemporary dance work in the theatre, as well as the annual festival of the same name (*see p238*). Both local and international dance work can be seen here. Book a week ahead and the Ponec can provide babysitting services for theatre-goers for a fee.

State Opera

Státní Opera

Wilsonova 4, Nové Město, Prague 2 (224 227 266/www.opera.cz). Metro Muzeum/tram 11. **Open** *Box office* 10am-5.30pm Mon-Fri; 10am-noon, 1-5.30pm Sat, Sun. **Tickets** 200-900 Kč. **No credit cards**. **Map** p311 L6.

As elegant and sumptuous a building as the other large venues, the State Opera nevertheless offers a more parochial and inferior programme than those at the recently revitalised **National** (*see above*) or **Estates** (*see p233*) theatres. Children's ballets are excellent, however, and well worth a visit for central European charm and humour, although the modern classical dance and opera productions often lack innovation and style. Programmes in English and German.

Déja Donné

It's been called the epitome of Czech absurdist comedy and credited with a love of dark human truth. It could only be the **Déja Donné** dance company, based at the **Divadlo Komedie**, or Komedie Theatre, (Jungmannova 1, Nové Město, Prague 1, 224 222 734).

Created in 1996 by Czech dancer-turned-choreographer Lenka Flory and her partner Italian dancer-choreographer Simone Sandroni, Déja Donné has attracted audiences and acclaim for its forceful, funny and gloriously shambolic dance theatre pieces. The hit *Aria Spinta* (Over-the-top Aria) portrays a desperate group of inept performers who blunder on as their show literally collapses around them. *Bella Copia*, meanwhile, is a merciless look at human pride and aspirations. Each piece has had over 100 performances in 18 countries. Déja Donné has also collaborated with avant-garde Czech folk-music diva Iva Bittová. The company's newest piece, *There Where We Were*, won the Total Theatre award at the Edinburgh Festival in 2003 and takes a more serious turn, engaging in vicious, flashy and explosive dance.

Déja Donné prises open that mysterious chasm between idealised, imaginary lives and the actual people whom we find we are. How do we reconcile our fantasy selves and our unfulfilled dreams with reality? Through tenderness, laughter and tears, says Déja Donné – by living the imperfect present in brilliant technicolour, and by realising and accepting the essential absurdity and frailty of life.

Flory began her life and career in Prague, returning after stints dancing abroad to teach and to set up the annual cutting-edge dance festival **Konfrontace** (*see p238*). She then met Sandroni in the early 1990s, when they both danced in Belgium for Wim Vandekeybus' Ultima Vez Company. They became known for a powerful, physical style to which they have added humour, humility and gentle irony.

Performers for Déja Donné have been recruited from all over the world to co-create, and accompany Sandroni on stage. They work directly from the performers' personal desires and responses, which results in original and idiosyncratic pieces. Sandroni explains: 'At an artistic level, we were clear that we wanted to create shows that moved people and that were artistically independent of fashionable forms or themes. Our major commitment is to social and political content, which penetrates reality and flips it over to show the reverse.

Švanda Theatre

Švandovo Divadlo
Štefánikova 57, Smíchov, Prague 5 (234 651 111/ www.svandovodivadlo.cz). Metro Anděl/tram 6, 9. **Open** *Box office* 2-7pm daily; 2-9pm performance days. **Tickets** 100-240 Kč. **No credit cards.**
A brand-new addition to the scene, this venue is slick and modern after thorough refurbishment and stages experimental and alternative modern Czech productions, including Czech adaptations of English-language classics. The theatre is also a lively venue for music and lectures. A tiny studio in the theatre's stone vaulted basement is still more offbeat.

Black light theatre

The luminous 'black light' tradition has been all the rage here since Czech performers blew the audience away at the World Expo '58 in Brussels. Modern practitioners use fluorescent paint, black lights, dance, pantomime and a large dose of kitsch to aim at tourists, generally without text, or, if there is text, it tends to be offered in several languages. 'Black light' is sometimes referred to as 'Magic Lantern' after the venue that helped popularise it (*see below*).

Black Light Theatre of Jiří Srnec

Černé divadlo Jiřího Srnce
Reduta, Národní 20, Prague 1 (257 923 397/ box office 224 933 487). Metro Národní třída/ tram 6, 9, 18, 22, 23. **Open** *Box office* 9am-7.30pm daily. **Tickets** 490 Kč. **No credit cards. Map** p308 H5.
Founding father of Czech black light theatre and co-author of productions at Laterna Magika (*see below*), Jiří Srnec has been putting on work for 40 years. His shows, staged here and then moving from theatre to theatre, are the true item in a genre that's normally all kitsch grotesque and sentimentality.

Image Theatre

Divadlo Image
Pařížská 4, Prague 1 (222 314 448/222 329 191/ www.imagetheatre.cz). Metro Staroměstská/tram 17, 18. **Open** *Box office* 9am-8pm daily. **Tickets** 400 Kč. **No credit cards. Map** p308 H3.
With more dancing, modern jazz and pantomime than some black light theatres, this epitomises the modern style. There are three to four productions per month here, and clips from all shows are medleyed in a monthly 'Best of Image' production.

Magic Lantern

Laterna Magika
Nová Scéna, Národní třída 4, Nové Město, Prague 1 (224 931 482/www.laterna.cz). Metro Národní třída/tram 6, 9, 17, 18, 22, 23. **Open** *Box office* 10am-8pm Mon-Sat. **Tickets** 300-600 Kč. **No credit cards. Map** p310 G6.
Famous for pioneering the Magic Lantern style, this company's glossy, high-tech multimedia productions are professional, though no longer at the cutting edge; more slick modern dance than traditional black light theatre, but still with emphasis on visual tricks. The company's home is the Nová Scéna, the impressive glass addition to the National Theatre (*see p235*) designed by Karel Prager in 1983.

Suzanne Vega sings out at the **Švanda**.

Puppet theatre

Puppetry is not just for children in Bohemia – it formed an intrinsic part of the Czech National Revival in the 1800s. Though much puppet theatre is aimed at tourists, high-quality Czech puppeteers and productions appear frequently and continue to develop the medium. The **Dragon Theatre** (Divadlo Drak) and **Buns & Puppets** (Buchty a Loutky) troupes put on inspired and entertaining shows that should not be missed.

National Marionette Theatre

Národní divadlo marionet
Žatecká 1, Staré Město, Prague 1 (224 819 324/ www.mozart.cz). Metro Staroměstská/tram 17, 18. **Open** *Box office* 10am-8pm daily. **Tickets** 490 Kč. **Credit** AmEx, MC, V. **Map** p308 H3.
This touristy company presents unchallenging, if popular, productions of *Don Giovanni* set to recorded music. Admittedly, the puppetry is skillful and the set designs add interest.

Home-grown theatre company Krepsko lights up **Prague Fringe Festival**.

Theatre Minor

Divadlo Minor

Vodičkova 6, Prague 1 (222 231 351/www.minor.cz). Karlovo náměstí/tram 3, 9, 14, 24. **Open** *Box office* 9am-1.30pm, 2.30-8pm Mon-Fri; 11am-8pm Sat, Sun. **Tickets** 80-120 Kč. **No credit cards**. **Map** p310 J6.

A lively and progressive Czech puppet theatre for both children and young adults. All directors and designers are contemporary guest artists invited from the worlds of opera and film as well as puppet theatre. Clown performances and productions are without words and therefore good for foreigners.

Festivals

Tickets for festivals can be purchased in advance from **Ticketpro** (*see p211*).

Four Days in Motion

Čtyři dny v pohybu

Various venues (www.ctyridny.cz). **Date** Oct. **Tickets** 100-200 Kč. **No credit cards**.

Annual festival of dance and visual theatre that brings practitioners of experimental international movement theatre and multimedia performance to an assortment of makeshift theatres inside industrial spaces around Prague. Recent festivals have been located creatively in spaces such as a former sewerage plant and an ancient sports complex. An English programme is available and there are some English-language productions.

Konfrontace

Confrontations

Various venues (www.dejadonne.com/confrontations). **Date** Oct. **Tickets** 100-250 Kč. **No credit cards**.

For lovers of top-notch avant-garde dance, this festival is a treat. Focusing on the recent work of respected and idiosyncratic individuals from Europe and the USA it brings the best of the new to Prague.

Prague Fringe Festival

Various venues (www.praguefringe.com). **Date** June. **Tickets** 100-200 Kč. **No credit cards**.

The city's newest theatre festival combines the best of Czech and international companies in a host of unusual venues, such as the catacombs of Vyšehrad (*see p105*). As with the other 36 fringe festivals worldwide, any company is welcome to join in so the result is an unpredictable cocktail – anything from cabaret to multimedia. Several English-language productions and full English programme.

Mezi ploty Festival

Areál PL Bohnice, Ústavní 91, Bohnice, Prague 8 (272 773 727/www.meziploty.cz). Metro Nádraží Holešovice, then bus 152 or 200. **Date** late May, Oct. **Tickets** 100-200 Kč. **No credit cards**.

The Mezi ploty biannual two-day theatre, music and art festival is staged on the grounds of the Bohnice mental hospital on the outskirts of Prague. It features performances by top Czech theatre companies.

Tanec Praha

Dance Prague

Various venues (www.tanecpha.cz). **Date** June. **Tickets** 150-250 Kč. **No credit cards**.

This annual festival is the biggest and longest running dance event in Prague, featuring world renowned companies as well as lesser known Czech and international dance and dance-theatre troupes.

Sport & Fitness

Fighting fit, the Czechs have learned that competition is as crucial on the field as it is in the free market.

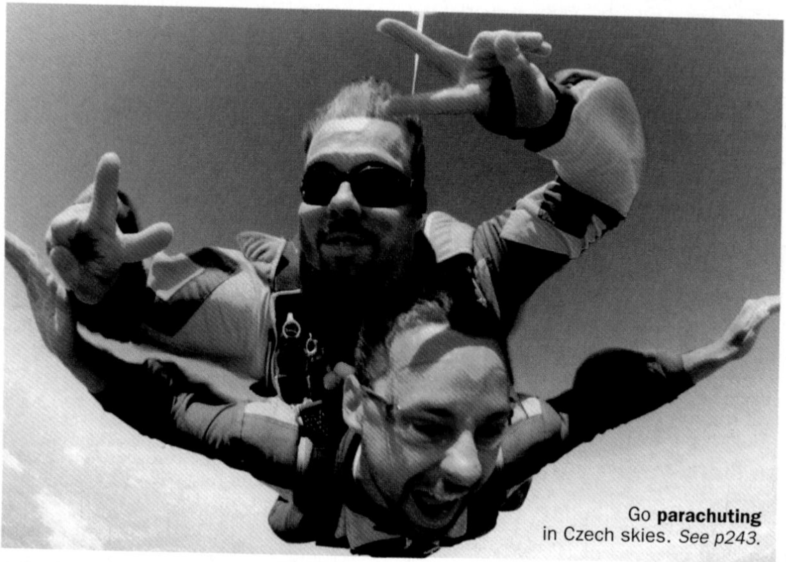

Go **parachuting** in Czech skies. *See p243.*

A decade and a half since the end of communism, Czech sport is still punching above its weight. For a nation of 10.5 million people, the profile of the country's sportsmen and sportswomen remains remarkably high. Captained by 2003 European Footballer of the Year Pavel Nedvěd, the national football team roared unbeaten through qualification for the 2004 European Championship. Alongside Nedvěd, a younger generation of star players has proven that Czech talent can succeed without hefty state support.

Similarly, young Czech players continue to flood into North America's top ice hockey league, the NHL, and the national team remains a force to be reckoned with, even if it hasn't been able to repeat its success in the 1996 Winter Olympics. Prague's hosting of the World Ice Hockey Championships in 2004 should also be a big step forward for the city's sport. The tournament will be the biggest international sports event the country has hosted since the Velvet Revolution, while the multi-purpose Sazka Arena should eventually provide a worthy addition to Prague's sporting infrastructure. There's even talk of a bid for the Summer Olympics in 2020.

But it's not all been good news. The harsh realities of being a small market in a post-communist world have hit some sports hard. The country no longer boasts tennis superstars to rival Ivan Lendl, Martina Navrátilová or Jana Novotná, and Prague has been stripped of its ATP tournament. Similarly, the country that gave the world running legend Emil Zátopek is going through a lean spell in athletics, picking up just one medal (a silver) at the 2003 World Championships in Paris. Quite how the sporting landscape will be changed by the ongoing shift from state-sanctioned, club-based sporting activities to more diverse, individualistic pursuits (anything from bungee jumping to golf) remains to be seen. In the meantime, the obscure Czech passion for cycle ball, *kolová*, is still going strong (*see p242* **Wheel of fortune... NOT**) – that's football on bicycles for anyone not in the know.

From a visitor's point of view, however, the change is definitely good news. Whereas Prague's sporting facilities were once a closed shop, catering mainly to clubs of serious athletes, there's now a wide range of facilities across the city that are open to everyone.

Spectator sports

Football

AC Sparta Praha

Toyota Arena, Milady Horákové 98, Holešovice, Prague 7 (220 570 323/www.sparta.cz). Metro Hradčanská/tram 1, 8, 15, 25, 26. **Admission** *European games* 400-900 Kč. *League games* 60-160 Kč. **No credit cards. Map** p312 2B.

Though its dominance of the domestic league has been challenged of late by provincial upstarts such as Slovan Liberec and Baník Ostrava, Sparta remains the team to beat in Czech football. Economically, Sparta is a poor relation in European competition, but this hasn't stopped the team from pulling off some mighty upsets against wealthier opponents. Their 18,500-capacity stadium, known as Letná, is the country's best and hosts big international matches.

FK Viktoria Žižkov

Stadion FK Viktoria Žižkov, Seifertova 130, Žižkov, Prague 3 (222 722 045/www.fkviktoriazizkov.cz). Tram 5, 9, 26. **Admission** 60-80 Kč. **No credit cards. Map** p313 B1.

Despite dismal support, 'Viktorka' has enjoyed several impressive seasons in the past, along with significant redevelopment of its compact stadium. At time of writing, however, the team was back in the relegation zone and showing few signs of health.

SK Slavia Praha

Stadion Evžena Rošického, Strahov, Prague 6 (233 081 751/www.slavia.cz). Bus 143, 149, 176, 217. **Admission** 30-120 Kč. **No credit cards.**

For all its history, abundant talent and romantic ideals, Slavia struggles to maintain a distant second place behind rival Sparta, and is forced to play at Strahov's soulless Evžen Rošický stadium while their 'Eden' home in Vršovice undergoes reconstruction.

Horse racing

The **Chuchle** racecourse (*see below*) on the outskirts of Prague offer a regular chance to spend a day at the races. A highlight of the Czech sporting calendar is the **Velká Pardubice steeplechase**, the world's longest race, held at **Dostihový spolek** (*see below*).

Chuchle

Radotínská 69, Radotín, Prague 5 (257 941 431/www.velka-chuchle.cz). Metro Smíchovské nádraží, then bus 129, 172, 241, 243, 244, 255. **Tickets** 100-350 Kč. **No credit cards.**

Flat racing. Races start at 2pm Sundays. The season runs from April to October.

Dostihový spolek

Pražská 607, Pardubice, 110km (68 miles) east of Prague (466 797 111/www.pardubice-racecourse.cz). Metro Florenc, then ČSAD bus to Pardubice. **Tickets** 110-4,400 Kč. **No credit cards.**

The Velká Pardubická Steeplechase is held here on the second Sunday in October. The facilities are basic, with outdoor seating and indoor monitors for watching the action, plus a handy selection of dilapidated bars and restaurants. Betting works in a similar way to the British system, with two agents accepting minimum bets, of 20 Kč and 50 Kč, respectively. You can bet to win (*vítěz*) or place (*místo*), or you can bet on the order (*pořadí*). Regular race meetings are also held every Saturday from May to October.

Ice hockey

HC Slavia Praha

Stadion SK Slavia Praha, Vršovice, Prague 10 (267 311 417/www.hc-slavia.cz). Tram 6, 7, 19, 22, 23, 24. **Open** *Box office* 90mins before games. **Admission** 50-100 Kč. **No credit cards.**

Slavistas rejoiced in 2003 when their team won the championship for the first time in its history. Visitors to the tiny arena, known as 'Eden' to locals, would be hard-pressed to identify it as the home of national champions but, for sound and fury, it's hard to beat. Don't expect comfort, however: the arena is unheated and it's usually standing room only, but downing a few beers may help to ease the pain.

HC Sparta Praha

T-Mobile Arena, Za elektárnou 419, Holešovice, Prague 7 (266 727 443/www.hcsparta.cz). Tram 5, 12, 14, 15, 17. **Open** *Box office* 7.30am-11am, noon-4pm Mon-Thur; 7.30am-noon Fri. **Admission** 50-100 Kč. **No credit cards. Map** p312 D1.

Sparta's home ice rink, like Wembley Arena, was state-of-the-art when it was built, but today it's showing signs of wear and tear. The team itself, though, is well-financed and always competitive. The large arena doesn't really come alive until the play-offs; regular season games are often poorly attended. Tickets can be bought in advance from the box office at entrance 30 or online through the Ticketpro agency (www.ticketpro.cz; *see p210*).

Active sports

Bungee Jumping

K Bungee Jump

Nechánice 263, Eastern Bohemia, 75km (47 miles) south of Prague (602 250 125/www.bungee.cz). **Rates** 700 Kč/jump. **No credit cards.**

During the summer months, this company based outside Prague organises regular jumps from Zvíkovské podhradí, a bridge high over the Vltava. Call ahead.

Climbing

Boulder Bar

V jámě 6, Nové Město, Prague 1 (222 231 244/www.boulder.cz). Metro Můstek/tram 3, 9, 14, 24. **Open** 8am-10pm Mon-Fri; noon-10pm Sat; 10am-10pm Sun. **Rates** 70 Kč/2hrs. **No credit cards. Map** p310 J6.

Tackle the climbing wall, then sink a few beers (rather than the other way round) at this curiously Czech combination of sports facility and hip bar.

Sport Centrum Evropská

José Mártiho 31, Vokovice, Prague 6 (220 172 309/ www.sportcentrumevropska.cz). Metro Dejvická then tram 20, 26. **Open** 7am-11pm Mon-Sun. **Rates** 60 Kč/hr. **No credit cards**.

A popular and impressive indoor wall within the Charles University's sports faculty. Booking essential.

Cycling

City Bike

Královdvorská 5, Staré Město, Prague 1 (776 180 274). Metro Náměstí Repupliky/tram 5, 8, 14. **Open** *Apr-Oct* 9am-7pm daily. **Rates** *Rental* 100 Kč/hr. *Tours* 250-600 Kč. **No credit cards. Map** p309 K3.

Cycle tours of the city, three times a day: 10am, 2pm and sunset. Reasonable rental fees too.

Fitness

In addition to the following, the central **Marriott** hotel also has a good gym (*see p51*).

Cybex

Hilton Prague, Karlin, Prague 8 (224 842 375/www.cybexprg.cz). Metro Florenc/tram 8, 24. **Open** 6am-10pm Mon-Fri; 7am-10pm Sat, Sun. **Admission** 600-900 Kč/day. *Squash* 500 Kč/hr. **Membership** 3,960 Kč monthly; 33,000 Kč annual. **Credit** AmEx, MC, V.

This swanky new fitness centre based in the Hilton hotel also offers spa and beauty treatments.

Delroy's Gym

Zborovská 4, Smíchov, Prague 5 (257 327 042/ www.delroys-gym.cz). Metro Anděl/tram 4, 7, 10, 14. **Open** 7am-10pm Mon-Fri; 9am-10pm Sat, Sun. **Admission** *Gym* 100 Kč/90mins; 1,400 Kč/20 visits. *Taebo* 100 Kč/class. *Thai/kick boxing* 100 Kč/class. *Karate* 150 Kč/class. **No credit cards**.

Delroy's specialises in martial arts and boxing but offers courses ranging from aerobics to self-defence.

Fitness Club Inter-Continental

Náměstí Curieových 43, Staré Město, Prague 1 (296 631 525/www.prague.intercontinental.com). Metro Staroměstská/tram 17. **Open** 6am-11pm daily. **Admission** *Gym* 250 Kč/90mins. *Pool, sauna & hot tub* 350 Kč/2hrs. *Turbo solarium* 20 Kč/min. **Credit** AmEx, MC, V. **Map** p308 H1.

Popular among the rich and moderately famous, this posh workout palace in a posh hotel features good cardio machines and an eager staff of trainers.

HIT Fitness Flora

Chrudimská 2, Žižkov, Prague 3 (267 311 447/ www.hitfitness.net). Metro Flora/tram 5, 10, 11, 16. **Open** 7am-11pm Mon-Fri; 8am-11pm Sat, Sun. **Admission** *Gym* 80 Kč. *Solarium* 7 Kč/min. *Squash* 200-380 Kč. **No credit cards. Map** p313 A3.

The HIT Fitness Flora is a well-equipped, modern and reasonably priced gym, located not too far from the centre of town.

Go-karting

Kart Centrum

Výpadová 1335, Radotín, Prague 5 (602 757 475/www.kart-centrum.cz). Bus 172 or 244 from Smíchovské nádraží to Přeštínská. **Open** 3pm-midnight Mon-Fri; 11am-midnight Sat, Sun. **Rates** 200 Kč/hr. **No credit cards**.

This loud, colourful and cheerfully tacky indoor go-karting centre in far-flung Radotín claims to be Europe's largest. There's even a water feature.

Golf

Once shunned by the communists, golf continues to gain popularity among the country's business classes, but Prague itself is relatively poorly served. The city has only one course, the **Golf Club Praha** (*see below*). Outside the city, in Central Bohemia, there are 18-hole courses in **Poděbrady** (Golf Club Poděbrady, 325 610 982, www.golfpodebrady.cz), **Karlštejn** (Golf Resort Karlštejn, 311 684 716, www.karlstejn-golf.cz) and **Konopiště** (Golf Resort Konopiště, 317 784 044, www.gcko.cz).

Erpet Golf Centrum

Strakonická 4, Smíchov, Prague 5 (257 321 177/www.erpet.cz). Metro Anděl then tram 12, 14, 20. **Open** *Jan-Mar, Nov, Dec* 8am-11pm daily. *Apr-Oct* 7am-midnight daily. **Rates** *Golf simulators* 300-400 Kč/hr. *Squash* 120-300 Kč/hr. *Tennis* 250-600 Kč/hr. *Membership* 18,000 Kč annual. **Credit** AmEx, MC, V.

An indoor golf centre catering to the new-money set. Golf simulators offer the only 18-hole course in Prague's city limits (virtual, of course). There are also squash courts and tennis in the summer.

Golf Club Praha

Plzeňská 215, Smíchov, Prague 5 (257 216 584/ www.gcp.cz). Metro Anděl, then tram 7, 9, 10. **Open** 8am-dusk daily. **Rates** 450-500 Kč/9 holes; 900-1,000 Kč 18 holes. **No credit cards**.

A nine-hole course and driving range on a hilltop. The course can get very dry in the summer.

Horse riding

Velkostatek Tetín Equestrian Centre

Tetín, Central Bohemia (602 633 775). **Rates** *Group lessons* 600 Kč/50mins. *Private lessons* 800 Kč/50 mins. *Trail riding* 600 Kč/hr. **No credit cards**.

This Canadian-Austrian centre, 30 minutes outside Prague, offers English-language lessons, plus trail riding. Phone ahead.

Ice skating

USK Praha Hotel Hasa Zimní stadion

Sámova 1, Vršovice, Prague 10 (271 747 128). Tram 6, 7, 24. **Open** 9-11am Mon, Tue, Thur, Fri; 9-11am, 4-5.30pm Wed; 10am-noon Sat, Sun. **Admission** 30 Kč. **No credit cards.**

This big hall attracts figure skating and ice hockey teams when it's not given over for public skating.

Zimní stadion Štvanice

Ostrov Štvanice 1125, Holešovice, Prague 7 (602 623 449/www.stvanice.cz). Metro Florenc or Vltavská/tram 5, 8, 12, 14, 17. **Open** 10.30am-noon Mon; 10.30am-noon, 4.30-6pm Tue, Thur; 10.30am-noon, 8-9.30pm Wed, Fri; 9-10.30am, 4-5.30pm, 8-9.30pm Sat; 9-10.30am, 2.30-4pm, 8-9.30pm Sun. **Admission** 60 Kč; 80 Kč skate rental. **No credit cards. Map** p312 E3.

This rickety-looking structure houses two rinks, with generous opening hours, on an island in the Vltava.

Wheel of fortune... NOT

Despite the high-profile achievements of the Czech Republic's football and ice hockey teams, Bohemian sport clearly isn't all about fortune and glory. Witness, for instance, what near-legend status has done for the country's cycle ball, or *kolová*, players.

Days after taking the gold medal at cycle ball's 2003 World Championships in France, triumphant Czech duo Miroslav Berger and Jiří Hrdlička were back at work, Berger selling ball bearings and Hrdlička waxing cars.

Cycle ball isn't a purely Czech phenomenon, but few countries have adopted the game with such passion. The inspiration for this bizarre sport came from Swiss-American trick cyclist Nicholas Edward Kaufmann. As part of his act, Kaufmann used the front wheel of his bike to gently knock his dog Mops around the stage. This somewhat questionable display of dexterity was converted into the sport of cycle ball in 1893. Cycle ball has since gained a small but loyal following across Europe and in Japan. The first world championships were held in 1929 and the sport now has the backing of the UCI, cycling's international governing body.

Played by teams of two on specially modified bicycles, the game is effectively a mounted version of indoor football. The catch, however, is that players aren't allowed to touch the ball with their feet or hands (unless goalkeeping). Instead, players use their front wheels to direct a 650-gram (23-ounce) ball stuffed with horsehair towards the opposition's goal.

This might all sound rather clumsy, but the sport's best players are able, with apparent ease and a deft twist of their handlebars, to ping the ball high into the corner of their opposition's two-metre-by-two-metre goal.

While Germany and Switzerland have semi-professional teams, Berger has resisted the lure of foreign currency and stayed faithful to his local team, Favorit Brno, in the Czech Republic's second city.

But, if the Czech sport offers its star players few commercial benefits, it has brought Czech teams more international success than any other sport.

At the grand old age of 42, with two world championships to his name, Berger says that he has no plans to retire, although he does have some way to go before he matches the success of cycle ball legends Jan and Jindřich Pospíšil. The Czech brothers won the last of their 20 world championship titles in 1988, when Jan was 43 and Jindřich was 46.

Like Berger and Hrdlička, the Pospíšil brothers are from Moravia, the eastern half of the Czech Republic and, because of their fame, the region is something of a *kolová* hotbed. In Prague cycle ball devotees must look to the city's sole club, **TJ Pankrác sports club** (Lomnického 1, Prague 4, 222 243 851). The team celebrated its centenary here in 1999.

Jogging

Prague's infamous pollution makes jogging, even in the parks of the central part of the city, a relatively serious health hazard. But if you must run, try one of the following areas, which are far enough from the worst of the pollution to make the endeavour somewhat less risky.

Divoká Šárka

Nebušice, Prague 6. Metro Dejvická, then tram 20, 26 or bus 119, 218.

Challenging, hilly trails for joggers, with bulbous rock formations and thick forests. The reservoir at the west end of the park attracts hordes of people in summer. Šárka is most easily accessible from Evropská, towards the airport.

Stromovka

Holešovice, Prague 7. Metro Nádraží Holešovice, then tram 5, 12, 14, 15, 17. **Map** p312 A/B/C1.

The most central of Prague's large parks. After the initial sprint to avoid the Výstaviště crowds, you can have the meadows to yourself.

Parachuting

Paraškola Impact

Dolní 12, Nusle, Prague 4 (261 225 431/www. paraskolaimpact.cz). Metro Muzeum, then tram 11. **Rates** *Tandem jumps* 3,200 Kč for 3,000m; 3,500 Kč for 4,000m. *Basic course* 1,900 Kč. *Advanced course* 800 Kč. **No credit cards**.

This unfortunately named but well-established parachuting school offers basic and advanced courses along with tandem jumps.

Skyservice

Kunětická 2, Nové Město, Prague 2 (222 253 399/ www.skyservice.cz). Metro Muzeum then tram 11. **Rates** *Tandem jumps* 3,100 Kč Mon-Fri; 3,500 Kč Sat, Sun. **No credit cards**. **Map** p313 A2.

This Prague office organises jumps from airfields in Příbram or Mladá Boleslav.

Pool

Billard Centrum

V cípu 1, Prague 1 (224 009 235/www.billard centrum.cz). Metro Můstek. **Open** 11am-2am daily. **Rates** *Pool* 69-99 Kč/hr. *Snooker* 89-120 Kč/hr. *Ten-pin bowling* 150-250 Kč/hr. **No credit cards**. **Map** p309 K5.

This endearingly seamy pleasure palace on a back street not far from Wenceslas Square offers an impressive range of bar-room pursuits.

Harlequin

Vinohradská 25, Vinohrady, Prague 2 (224 217 240). Metro Muzeum, then tram 11. **Open** 2pm-4am daily. **Rates** 80 Kč/hr. **No credit cards**. **Map** p311 M6.

Play serious pool late into the night or unwind with one of Prague's best selection of arcades games.

Shooting

AVIM Praha

Sokolovská 23, Karlín, Prague 8 (222 329 328). Metro Florenc/tram 8, 24. **Open** 10am-10pm daily. **No credit cards**.

A shooting range close to the centre. Phone ahead and ask for George to ensure English-language assistance.

Skateboarding

Aside from the **Mystic Skate Park** (*see below*), skaters head to the pavilion next to the National Theatre ticket office (*see p235*) and the area around the metronome in Letná park (*see p104*).

Mystic Skate Park

Ostrov Štvanice 38, Holešovice, Prague 7 (222 232 027/www.mysticskates.cz). Metro Florenc or Vltavská/tram 5, 8, 12, 14, 17. **Open** *Jan-Apr, Oct-Dec* noon-9pm daily. *May-Sept* 9am-10pm daily. **Rates** *BMX, in-line skates* 80-120 Kč. *Skateboard* 50-80 Kč. **No credit cards**. **Map** p312 E3.

Popular skate park on Štvanice Island in the Vltava, which also hosts the high-profile Mystic Skate Cup.

Skiing & snowboarding

Although most of the Czech Republic's winter resorts offer equipment rental, it's also possible to secure skis and boards in advance in the capital. Both of these shops also offer repairs.

Happy Sport

Národní obrany 16, Dejvice, Prague 6 (224 325 560/www.happysport.cz). Metro Dejvická/tram 2, 8, 20, 26. **Open** 9am-6pm Mon-Fri; 10am-1pm Sat. **No credit cards**.

Happy Sport's snowboard rentals start at 220 Kč per day, with ski rentals at 70 Kč per day, though you'll also have to pay insurance of 20-40 Kč and leave a deposit of 1,500-3,500 Kč, depending on the package. **Other locations**: Beranových 127, Letňany, Prague 9 (286 920 112); Na Pankráci 1598, Pankrác, Prague 4 (241 401 465).

Sport Slivka

Újezd 40, Malá Strana, Prague 1 (257 007 231). Metro Malostranská, then tram 12, 20, 22, 23. **Open** 10am-6pm Mon-Fri. **Credit** MC, V. **Map** p307 E5.

Good, reasonable rentals for skiers – a complete package costs 160 Kč per day.

Squash

See also p241 **Erpet Golf Centrum**.

Squash & Fitness Centrum Arbes

Arbesovo náměstí 15, Smíchov, Prague 5 (257 326 041). Metro Anděl, then tram 6, 9, 12, 20. **Open** 7am-11pm daily. **Rates** 150-340 Kč/hr. **No credit cards**.

Smart fitness centre with courts and a reasonably central location.

Squashové centrum Václavské náměstí
Václavské náměstí 13-15, Nové Město, Prague 1 (224 232 752/www.asbsquash.cz). Metro Můstek/tram 3, 9, 14, 24. **Open** 7am-11pm Mon-Fri; 8am-11pm Sat, Sun. **Rates** 140-420 Kč/hr. **No credit cards. Map** p308 J5.
Three courts and a central location draw Prague's business community to this underground facility.

Swimming

Pool facilities have markedly improved since 1989, when hygiene was a genuine concern. These days, a more significant problem is selecting a pool that isn't block-booked by swimming clubs or jam-packed with hysterical children and amorous teenagers. If you prefer open-air swimming, dam reservoirs are usually murky as soup but wildly popular among the locals, especially the one at **Šárka park** (*see below*). Other options are area hotels that have fitness centres with pools (*see p38*).

Divoká Šárka
Nebušice, Prague 6 (no phone). Metro Dejvická, then tram 20, 26 or bus 218, then 5mins walk. **Open** *May-mid Sept* 9am-7pm daily. **Admission** 20 Kč; 10 Kč children. **No credit cards.**
An outdoor pool in an idyllic setting with a sweet lawn area on which to lounge.

Hotel Axa
Na Poříčí 40, Nové Město, Prague 1 (222 323 967). Metro Florenc or Náměsti Republiky/tram 3, 8, 24, 26. **Open** 6-9am, noon-1pm, 5-10pm Mon-Fri; 9am-9pm Sat, Sun. **Admission** 1 Kč/min (100 Kč deposit). **No credit cards. Map** p309 M2.
The pool in this hotel is a good length and is free of shrieking children in the morning. Decent sauna facilities too (100 Kč per hour; 200 Kč deposit).

Plavecký Stadion Podolí
Podolská 74, Podoli, Prague 4 (241 433 952/ www.pspodoli.cz). Metro Palackého náměstí, then tram 17, 21. **Open** 6am-9.45pm (last entry 9pm) Mon-Fri; 8am-7.45pm (last entry 7pm) Sat, Sun. **Admission** *Indoor* 60 Kč/90mins. *Outdoor* 120 Kč/day. **No credit cards.**
Prague's biggest (and perpetually packed) swimming centre lies in the south of the city, along the river. A survivor from the old regime, it features outdoor lap swimming open year-round plus a 50m indoor pool that attracts serious swimmers.

Ten-pin bowling

Billard Centrum (*see p243*) also has an alley.

Bowling Bar Kingpin
Milady Horákové, Dejvice, Prague 6 (224 396 264). Metro Hradčanská/tram 1, 15, 18, 20, 25, 26. **Open** noon-2am daily. **Rates** 200 Kč/hr before 6pm; 280 Kč/hr after 6pm. **No credit cards.**
Ignore the intimidating graffiti-covered exterior and check out the smart interior: three Brunswick lanes at reasonable prices, complete with ultra-violet lighting and glow-in-the-dark bowling balls.

Bowling centrum RAN
V Celnici 10, Nové Město, Prague 1 (221 033 020). Metro Náměstí Republiky/tram 3, 5, 14, 24, 26. **Open** noon-2am daily. **Rates** 270-390 Kč/hr. **No credit cards. Map** p309 L3.
Eight professional AMF lanes underneath the Marriott hotel (*see p51*).

Tennis

The Czech Republic has long been renowned for its tennis stars – notably Ivan Lendl and Martina Navrátilová. Although both defected to the West, they're still national heroes here. The sport has struggled to come to terms with post-communist economics, but while participation no longer reaches communist-era levels of fanaticism, there's still plenty of interest.

1. ČLTK
Ostrov Štvanice 38, Holešovice, Prague 7 (222 316 317/www.cltk.cz). Metro Florenc or Vltavská/tram 5, 8, 12, 14, 17. **Open** 7am-midnight daily. **Rates** 300-600 Kč/hr. **No credit cards. Map** p312 E3.
Ten outdoor clay courts, three of which are floodlit, plus sparkling indoor facilities (four hard courts, two clay courts), newly reconstructed since 2002's floods. Booking essential.

Tenisový klub Slavia Praha
Letenské sady 32, Holešovice, Prague 7 (233 374 033). Metro Hradčanská, then tram 1, 8, 15, 25, 26. **Open** *Jan-Mar, Nov, Dec* (indoor only) 7am-10pm daily. *Apr-Oct* 7am-9pm daily. **Rates** *Indoor* 600 Kč/hr. *Outdoor* 200-250 Kč/hr. **No credit cards. Map** p312 B3.
Eight floodlit outdoor clay courts, plus a tennis bubble for the winter months on Letná plain.

Yoga

Aruna Singhvi
Fitcentrum Týn, Týnská 19, Staré Město, Prague 1 (220 930 073). Metro Náměstí Republiky/tram 5, 8, 14. **Rates** 400 Kč/2hr session. **No credit cards. Map** p308 J3.
Dr Singhvi offers classical and Ashtanga hatha yoga tuition for all levels in English, Czech and German, and organises weekend retreats.

Jógacentrum Blanická
Blanická 17, Vinohrady, Prague 2 (224 253 702/www.joga.cz/praha). Metro Náměstí Míru/ tram 11. **Rates** 145-160 Kč/session. **No credit cards. Map** p313 A3.
The Blanická centre offers a huge range of yoga classes, mainly in Czech, plus information on other yoga centres across Prague.

Trips Out of Town

Features

Getting Started

Stretch those legs beyond the city streets – Bohemia and Moravia offer plenty of reason to get out of Prague and get a taste of the simpler life.

While the Czech capital never comes up short on attractions, it's certainly a world apart from the countryside that surrounds it. Central Europe is the setting for countless fairytales for a reason. It's an easily accessible land of rolling hills, ruins and impossibly picturesque towns that specialise in time travel. So leave behind the noise, exhaust fumes and stresses of Prague city life – if only for a short break – and hit the highways of greater Bohemia and Moravia.

The trains of the former Eastern bloc are an excellent resource: a survivor of communist times, they may be somewhat shabby and overheated, but they're also cheap, efficient and scenic, and they go just about everywhere. Alternatively, cars can be rented for around 600 Kč a day if you shop around (*see p275*) and buses, which are also very cheap, go everywhere that the trains don't – though their drivers may cost you in other ways if you're prone to nerves. But any of these modes of transport will take you happily in to the heartland of central Europe and expose you to people and places and a laid-back lifestyle totally apart from that of the capital. You're likely to learn far more about modern Czech life by joining the locals, hiking through the countryside or pottering around a small town for an afternoon than you ever could from Old Town tours, relentless Mozart concerts and kitschy beerhalls.

Our suggested excursions are divided into the following categories: **Day trips** are places that are feasible to get to even if you had one too many beers the night before and don't make it out of bed until mid morning (*see p248*). As well as some stunning towns, we've also included a selection of the classic Central Bohemian **castles** (*see p248*). The overnighters are places worth spending a bit more time on – bearing in mind both the journey time and how much there is to see and do when you get there. We've subdivided these longer trips into **Overnighters: Town & Village** (*see p257*) and **Overnighters: Country** (*see p264*). Most destinations that are listed have been included with ease of access by public transport in mind. We've also included highlights of the Czech Republic's wine country, which lies in the eastern province of Moravia and is well suited to a driving tour (*see p266* **Ready for Moravíno, Jacques?**).

If you want a city break with minimal effort, try one of the trips to **Terezín** (*see p256*), **Karlštejn** (*see p248*), or **Karlovy Vary** (*see p252*) available through the travel agents **Čedok** (*see p252*). Rafting and cycling trips are also a breeze when the logistics are left to the likes of **Central European Adventures** (Jáchymova 4, Staré Město, Prague 1, 222 328 879, members.tripod.com/cea51).

If you're thinking of staying overnight at any of these destinations, the tourist offices listed in the following chapters should be able to help you book accommodation. Private houses all over the country also offer rooms, and this can be a chance to savour something of small-town real life.

A TOUR OF THE COUNTRY

Divided into the provinces of **Bohemia** in the north-west and **Moravia** in the south-east, the terrain of the Czech Republic offers surprisingly diverse countryside. Graced with wooded hills and little valleys, Moravia is prettiest in autumn, when a leisurely week could be spent vineyard-hopping, combing through the region's caves, and getting your music and culture fix in **Brno**, the Czech Republic's second city (*see p257*).

North Bohemia, despite inheriting a sad legacy of pollution from heavy industry, also offers the beautiful **Český ráj** (Czech Paradise; *see p264*), which is a playground for hikers and clean-air addicts. Here striking sandstone cliffs line the banks of the **Labe** (Elbe) river.

Green, mountainous southern Bohemia, with its carp ponds and dense woods, attracts pilgrims from spring to autumn, and quaint, ancient towns like **Kašperské Hory** (*see p267*) and **Český Krumlov** (*see p259*) make great jumping-off points for hikes, road trips and also mushrooming expeditions (*see p184* ***Houby* to you**).

In western Bohemia, the stars still shine as they touch the earth during the **Karlovy Vary International Film Festival** (*see p252*), but the hilly landscape around the famed spa towns is enchanting at any time of year, with spruce forests and hot springs.

Getting around

By bus

Many inter-city bus services depart from **Florenc** coach station (*see p271*). Bus services are more frequent in the morning. It's worth checking the return times before you leave, as the last bus back may depart disappointingly early (often before 6pm). A few buses also leave from **Nádraží Holešovice** station (*see p270*). The state bus company **ČSAD** (Ke Štvanici 6, Nové Město, Prague 8, 900 149 044, timetable. svt.cz/iBus) covers most destinations. It's best to pick up tickets a day beforehand for popular weekend trips, and note that you'll need a local friend to get any use out of the Czech-only information line, which operates 24 hours, but costs 14 Kč per minute. A number of private services now offer competitive prices and times and arguably better service and coaches. One of the largest of these, **Čebus** (Ke Štvanici 6, Nové Město, Prague 8, 224 811 936, www.cebus.cz, ticket office closed weekends), operates out of the Florenc metro station.

By car

There are just a few motorways in the Czech Republic, although more are planned, so drivers are often confined to local roads. Petrol stations (some marked by a big *benzína* sign) are ubiquitous these days and now come fully stocked with microwaveable junk food and coffee machines. Petrol comes in two grades, super and special; the latter is recommended for most West European cars. Unleaded is called *natural* and diesel is *nafta*. The speed limit is 50kph (31mph) in built-up areas, 110kph (68mph) on motorways, and 80kph (56mph) everywhere else. If you have an accident, call the **Emergency Road Service** on 1240. Prices for car hire vary widely depending on whether you're renting from an international or local company (*see p275*).

By train

Trains often follow more scenic routes than buses but cover less ground and usually take longer. There are four main railway stations in Prague, but no real fixed pattern as to which destinations, or even part of the country, they serve. **Hlavní nádraží** (*see p270*) is the most central station and one of two principal departure points for international services, as well as some domestic services. Timetables can be obtained at the information windows (don't queue for at *mezinárodní* info window unless you want an international train).

Brno. *See p257.*

Nádraží Holešovice (*see p270*) is also principally used for international services. **Masarykovo nádraží** (*see p271*) serves most destinations in northern and eastern Bohemia. Domestic routes to the south and west leave from **Smíchovské nádraží** (*see p271*). Train travel is priced by the kilometre and, despite recent price hikes, is still a resounding bargain by Western European or American standards.

Hitchhiking

The usual rules of courtesy and common sense, especially for women, apply to hitchhiking within the Czech Republic. It's a time-honoured method of transport, particularly among students. As with hitching a ride in any country, travel with a friend and position yourself just outside the city limits with a sign bearing your destination of choice. You should offer to help with petrol money, though your money will most likely be waved away.

Day Trips

Shake off your hangover – there are spa towns to heal and castle keeps, a medieval silver mine and a former Nazi concentration camp to explore.

Castles

Around an hour's train journey or drive from Prague will land you at the foot of the palatial **Karlštejn** (*see below*), the architecturally impressive **Konopiště** (*see below*) or the Gothic **Křivoklát** (*see p251*) castle.

Karlštejn

Jutting up like the royal crown it is, Karlštejn was once Charles IV's summer palace, perched over a lush bend of the Berounka river some 30 kilometres (19 miles) to the south-west of Prague. But it's said by castle aficionados that Karlštejn looks better from without than from within. Indeed, it was largely rebuilt in neo-Gothic style in the 19th century, but its interiors are sadly neglected.

It's also the Czech Republic's most visited castle, so it inevitably comes with some jostling. The approach is an obstacle course of overpriced snack bars and hawkers of postcards, crystal and lace. At least this 14th-century stronghold, former home to the royal jewels, offers spectacular views to reward visitors for the short but strenuous hike up to the castle entrance from the train station. And one rewarding feature inside is the **Holy Rood Chapel**. Its walls are adorned with semi-precious stones and painted wooden panels by Master Theodoric, Charles IV's court portrait artist, plus an altar with a diptych by Tomaso da Modena. The remaining rooms can't match this splendour. Karlštejn is also an easy and convenient trip but best done early or late in the season.

Karlštejn Castle

Karlštejn (311 681 617/274 008 154/www.hradkarlstejn.cz). **Open** *Mar* 9am-noon, 1-3pm daily. *Apr, Oct* 9am-noon, 1-4pm daily. *May, June, Sept* 9am-noon, 1-5pm daily. *July, Aug* 9am-noon, 1-6pm Tue-Sun. *Last tour* 1hr before closing. **Admission** *Castle tour* 200 Kč; 100 Kč children, students. *Castle tour (incl Chapel)* 300 Kč; 150 Kč children, students. **No credit cards**.

There are two tours of the castle in English, but they are thoroughly tedious in any language. The second tour includes the Holy Rood Chapel but must be booked ahead and only runs July to mid November.

Where to eat

U Janů

Karlštejn 90 (311 681 210). **Open** *Jan, Mar-Dec* 11am-10pm Tue-Sun. *Feb* 11am-10pm Sat, Sun. **Main courses** 160-180 Kč. **No credit cards**.

A cosy, old-fashioned place with antlers hanging from the ceiling, a pleasant terrace garden and assorted schnitzels and goulash.

Koruna

Karlštejn 13 (311 681 465). **Open** *Jan, Mar-Dec* 10am-10pm daily. **Main courses** 190 Kč. **Credit** AmEx, MC, V.

The Koruna pub is a local favourite frequented by village beer drinkers.

Getting there

By car

Karlštejn is 30km (19 miles) south-west of Prague. Take the E50-D5 or Route 5 towards Plzeň, then leave the motorway at exit 10 and follow the signs for Karlštejn.

By train

Trains leave Prague's Smíchovské nádraží or Hlavní nádraží stations for Karlštejn about every hour. The trip takes about 40mins. It's a 10min walk from the station up to the village, and a further 15mins from there up to the castle.

Konopiště

With more architectural appeal than Karlštejn and of equal historical significance, Konopiště is an exceptional castle in a land of hundreds. Built with seven French-style tower fortifications defending a rectangular bailey, Konopiště's contents are more stirring than most, as well, particularly the fantastic collection of weapons – and gruesomely extensive display of hunting trophies.

This castle, which dates back to the 14th century, was refurbished by the Habsburgs as a hunting lodge to satisfy the passions of its most famous occupant, Archduke Francis Ferdinand. He resided here with his Czech wife, Sophie, who was shot along with him at Sarajevo in 1914. The assassination, aside from triggering World War I, spoiled Ferdinand's accession to the throne to which

Konopištê. *See p248.*

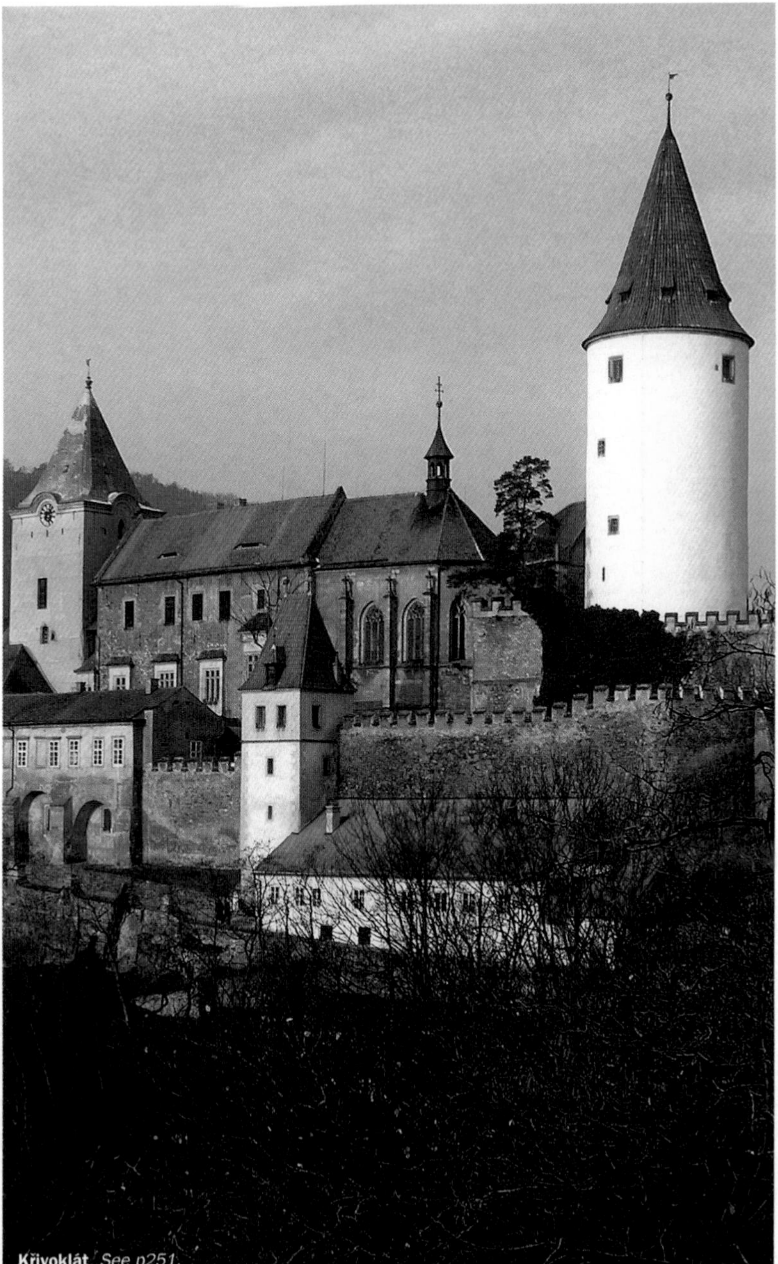
Křivoklát. See p251.

he was heir. As you meander through his decadent digs it will become apparent that he, nevertheless, managed to do enough damage. Ferdinand slaughtered nearly every kind of fauna imaginable from the surrounding Sázava river woods and the countless trophies here represent only one per cent of the total collection. He supposedly felled an average of 20 animals a day, every day for 40 years.

The tour takes in sedate rooms featuring collections of wooden Italian cabinets and Meissen porcelain. A second tour of the castle, requiring a separate ticket, takes you through the Archduke's private chambers, the chapel and a Habsburg version of a gentlemen's club.

The castle has large grounds in which the peacocks and pheasants aren't affixed to a wall. Bears pace incessantly in the dry moat, oblivious to their unluckier brethren within.

Konopiště's popularity is second only to that of Karlštejn, so expect lots of coach parties.

Konopiště Castle

Konopiště (317 721 366/602 349 068/www.zamek-konopiste.cz). **Open** *Apr, Oct* 9am-noon, 1-3pm Tue-Fri; 9am-noon, 1-4pm Sat, Sun. *May-Aug* 9am-noon, 1-5pm daily. *Sept* 9am-noon, 1-4pm daily. *Nov* 9am-noon, 1-3pm Sat, Sun. **Admission** 140 Kč; 250 Kč English-speaking guide. **Credit** MC, V.

Getting there

By bus

Buses leave from Florenc station nearly every 45mins; the trip lasts a little over an hour.

By car

Konopiště is 35km (22 miles) from Prague. Go south on the D1 and exit near Benešov, following the signs for Konopiště.

By train

Hourly trains to Benešov from Hlavní nádraží take about an hour. The castle is a 2km (1.25-mile) walk from the station, or you can catch one of the infrequent buses.

Křivoklát

Not just a Gothic fortress, founded in 1109, Křivoklát is also a kind of living museum to medieval life with resident artists and craftspeople operating a smithy and offering wares wrought by ancient carpentry, ceramics and weaving techniques. It's also the perfect counterpoint to overtrafficked Karlštejn. Just inconvenient enough to remain peaceful, Křivoklát boasts one of the finest interiors in the country, featuring a magnificent knights' hall and royal hall plastered in late Gothic paintings and sculptures.

The drive there is lovely too, following the course of the Berounka river past fields, meadows and a forested hill before the castle dramatically appears before you, standing atop a lofty promontory.

Křivoklát was originally a Přemyslid hunting lodge, which was then later converted into a defensible castle at the beginning of the 12th century by King Vladislav I. Fires followed, along with a spate of rebuilding by the Polish King Vladislav II Jagellon, whose trademark 'W' can be seen throughout the castle. A fine altarpiece in the chapel portrays Christ surrounded by sweet-looking angels holding medieval instruments of torture. A more varied selection awaits in the dungeon, where you'll find a fully operational rack, a thumbscrew and the Rosary of Shame (a necklace made of lead weights), along with the Iron Maiden. The castle's enormous Round Tower dates from 1280. English alchemist Edward Kelley was confined here after Rudolf II tired of waiting for him to succeed at turning base metals into gold.

Křivoklát Castle

Křivoklát (313 558 120/www.krivoklat.cz). **Open** *June-Aug* 9am-noon, 1-5pm daily. *May, Sept* 9am-noon, 1-4pm daily. *Mar, Apr, Oct* 9am-noon, 1-3pm Tue-Sun. **Admission** *Long tour* 160 Kč; 80 Kč concessions. *Short tour* (tower only) 80 Kč; 40 Kč concessions. **No credit cards.**

Two English-language castle tours set off every half-hour up to one hour before closing time. However, for the tours to run, there has to be a minimum of five English speakers willing to take part – or a smaller number willing to pay for the cost of five tickets.

Where to eat

Hotel u Dvořáků

Roztoky 225, Křivoklát (313 558 355). **Open** *Jan-May, Oct-Dec* 10am-11pm. *June-Sept* 5-11pm. **Main courses** 150 Kč. **No credit cards.**

This is the only real place to eat near the castle and serves a decent menu of the usual Czech fare.

Getting there

By car

Křivoklát is 45km (28 miles) from Prague. Take the E50-D5 in the direction of Beroun. Turn off at junction 14 and follow the Berounka valley west, as if going to Rakovník.

By train

Direct trains to Křivoklát are infrequent, so take one to Beroun, which leaves from Smíchovské nádraží or Hlavní nádraží about every half-hour (journey time around 45mins), and change at Beroun for Křivoklát (a further 40mins).

Towns

With the spa town of **Karlovy Vary** (*see below*), the fascinating silver mines of **Kutná Hora** (*see p253*), postcard-perfect **Mělník** (*see p254*) or dark wartime history of **Terezín** (*see p256*) to pick from, Bohemia's and Moravia's towns make for ideal trips out of Prague – the only problem is having to choose which one to fit in to your day.

Karlovy Vary

The promenades and colonnades of this West Bohemian town evoke the feeling of its past as a celebrated spa destination. Aristocrats and artists from Russia to the capitals of Western Europe once trekked to Karlsbad, as it was known until this century, for luxurious cures and to hobnob. Though the streets are quiet these days, and it's almost too pretty, Karlovy Vary is surely the grandest and most venerated of the nation's collection of natural hot springs. The Russian influx has jumped hugely of late, outnumbering the usual crowd of Germans. Things hot up considerably during the midsummer **Karlovy Vary International Film Festival** (*see p186 and p196*). It's then that this assortment of boulevards and thermal fountains becomes the Hollywood Boulevard of Central Europe, with endless screenings and celebrity-spotting.

Local lore has it that Karlovy Vary began its ascent to steamy fame and fortune in 1358 when one of Charles IV's hunting hounds leapt off a steep crag in hot pursuit of a more nimble stag. The unfortunate dog fell to the ground and injured its paw, then made a miraculous recovery as it limped through a pool of hot, bubbling water. (Everyone say 'ahhh'.) Experts were summoned to test the restorative waters and declared them beneficial for all kinds of ills. From that moment, Karlovy Vary's future was ensured.

The Ohře river runs through the centre of town and disappears beneath the hulking **Hotel Thermal** (IP Pavlova 11, 359 001 111, www.hotel.cz/thermal, 1,750-1,820 kč single, 2,700-3,100 kč double) – which stands as a fascinating symbol of the communist notion of luxury, especially when contrasted with the gracious elegance of the **Grand Hotel Pupp** (*see below*). As for the town itself, the garish boutiques and inescapable wafer shops may not be your idea of relaxation – but you can always retreat to the parks, which are adorned with busts of some of the spa's more famous guests, or self-medicate with a few *Becherovkas* – the famous local herbal liqueur that works magic with its base of the region's pure spring water.

Vojenský State Baths

Lázně 3, Mlýnské nábřeží 5 (353 225 641). **Open** 7am-3pm Mon-Sat. **Admission** 400 Kč. **Credit** AmEx, MC, V.
Not as plush as the Pupp baths (*see below*), naturally, but you'll get a thorough and renewing treatment here, administered by no-nonsense pros.

Where to stay & eat

Grand Hotel Pupp

Mírové náměstí 2 (353 109 111/www.pupp.cz). **Open** *Baths* 7-10am, noon-3pm, 6-10pm daily. *Restaurant* 8am-11pm daily. **Rates** 3,140-7,500 Kč single; 3,900-9,500 Kč double; 9,500-13,200 Kč suite. **Main courses** 350-600 Kč. **Credit** AmEx, MC, V.
If you splurge on this lavish hotel – said to be the finest in the country – ask for a room that has not yet been refurbished; several have been unsympathetically 'modernised'. If you're feeling flush, the elegant restaurant is worth a visit, as is the hotel spa.

Promenáda

Tržiště 31 (353 225 648). **Main courses** 150-300 Kč. **Credit** AmEx, MC, V.
This respectable restaurant, still something of a rarity in Karlovy Vary, is a cut above the usual goulash-and-dumplings places – with reasonably quick service, freshwater trout and steaks. If you can't afford the Pupp's dining room (*see above*), try dinner here.

Resources

Čedok

Dr Davida Bechera 21 (353 222 994). **Open** 9am-5pm daily. **No credit cards**.
Information and tickets for festivals and concerts other than the Karlovy Vary International Film Festival (*see above*).

Tourist information

Information Centre of town of Karlovy Vary, Lázeňská 1 (353 224 097). **Open** *Jan-Mar, Nov-Dec* 8am-5pm Mon-Fri; 10am-4pm Sat, Sun. *April-Oct* 8am-6pm Mon-Fri; 10am-6pm Sat, Sun. **No credit cards**.
The staff here is helpful, multilingual and has information and tickets for all events, except the Karlovy Vary International Film Festival (*see above*).

Getting there

By bus

Buses run at least every hour from Prague's Florenc station starting at 5.30am (journey time about 2hrs 30mins).

By car

Karlovy Vary is 130km (81 miles) west of Prague on the E48.

By train

Trains leave Prague's Hlavní nádraží three times a day (journey time about 4hrs).

The Gothic glory of **Kutná Hora**'s cathedral.

Kutná Hora

The twin peaks of Kutná Hora's cathedral are visible for miles around the town, testifying to its former role as a key source of wealth in Bohemia. An ancient gem which has served as a movie set more than once, Kutná Hora's fame and status were secured in the late 13th century with the discovery of silver. A Gothic boom town was born, and for 250 years Kutná Hora was second in importance only to Prague in this part of the nation.

Don't be put off by the blighted concrete tower blocks when you get off the train in **Sedlec**. The UNESCO-designated old centre is only a couple of kilometres (1.25 miles) to the south-west. But first you might want to stop at Sedlec's incredible bone chapel, the **Ossuary** (*see below*), where 40,000 skeletons have been used as decoration. The Cistercian abbey, founded in 1142 and now housing a tobacco factory, established the ossuary a few hundred metres north of the church on Zámecká.

It's a long walk or a short bus ride (take the bus marked 'Centrum') through Sedlec to Kutná Hora's centrepiece, the **Cathedral of St Barbara** (*see below*). Designed in Peter Parler's workshop, it's a magnificent 1388 building with an exterior outclassing Parler's St Vitus's Cathedral in Prague (*see p61*). St Barbara was the patron saint of silver miners and their guild emblems decorate the ceiling. For an idea of life in a medieval mine, head to the Hrádek or Little Castle. Here, the **Czech Silver Museum** (*see below*) kits you out in protective suits and hard hats for a trip into the tunnels.

Cathedral of St Barbara

Kostel sv. Barbory
Barborská (327 512 378). **Open** *Jan-Apr, Nov, Dec* 9am-noon, 2-4pm Tue-Sun daily. *May-Sept* 9am-6pm daily. **Admission** 30 Kč; 15 Kč children. **No credit cards**.

Czech Silver Museum & Medieval Mine

České museum stříbra
Barborská 28 (327 512 159). **Open** *Apr, Oct* 9am-5pm Tue-Sun. *May, June, Sept* 9am-6pm Tue-Sun. *July, Aug* 10am-6pm Tue-Sun. Last entry 90mins before closing time. **Admission** 400 Kč; 200 Kč children. **No credit cards**.
If you want to see the silver mine, a guided tour is compulsory. Booking is advisable.

Sedlec Ossuary

Kostnice
Zámecká (327 561 143). **Open** *Jan-Mar, Nov-Dec* 9am-noon, 1-4pm daily. *Apr-Sept* 8am-6pm daily. *Oct* 8am-noon, 1-5pm daily. **Admission** 35 Kč; 15 Kč children. **No credit cards**.
The Ossuary is a gruesome collection of human bones, arranged over the ages into fantastic shapes and chandeliers by monks.

Terezín. *See p256.*

Where to eat

Harmonia

Husova 105 (327 512 275). **Open** 11am-11pm daily. **Main courses** 170-190 Kč. **No credit cards.**
Traditional Czech food served on a beautiful terrace.

Resources

Tourist information

Tourist Information Kutná Hora, Palackého náměstí 377 (327 515 556). **Open** *Jan-Mar, Oct-Dec* 9am-5pm Mon-Fri. *Apr-Sept* 9am-6.30pm Mon-Fri; 9am-5pm Sat, Sun. **No credit cards.**
Staff can arrange accommodation in private houses.

Getting there

By bus

Buses leave 11 times a day from Florenc station (journey time about 75mins).

By car

Kutná Hora is 70km (44 miles) from Prague. Head out through Žižkov and follow signs to Kolín to Route 12; then change to road 38 to Kutná Hora. A scenic alternative is Route 333 via Říčany, further south.

By train

Trains run from Hlavní nádraží or Masarykovo nádraží daily and take 50mins. The main Kutná Hora station is actually located in Sedlec. Local trains meet express trains coming from Prague and take visitors into Kutná Hora proper.

Mělník

An important town in the transplanting of viniculture from France to the Czech lands, Mělník is a quiet little hamlet within easy reach of Prague, offering pastoral views from its impressively restored castle. Just 33 kilometres (20 miles) north of Prague, the town also features a bizarre ossuary to go with its bucolic appeal. The castle vineyards produce Ludmila wine, which is the tipple that Mozart supposedly drank while he composed *Don Giovanni*.

The main sights are concentrated near the lovely **castle**, now more chateau than stronghold. It occupies a prime position on a steep escarpment overlooking the confluence of the Vltava and Labe rivers, the inspiration for Smetana's anthem to Bohemia, *Ma Vlast* ('My Country').

Although a settlement has existed here since the tenth century, it was Charles IV who introduced vines to the region from his lands in Burgundy. He also established a palace for the Bohemian queens, who would come here to escape Prague until the end of the 15th century.

The castle was rebuilt during the 16th and 17th centuries. Recent restitution laws have returned it to the Lobkowicz family, some of the most powerful magnates in Bohemia before they were driven into exile by the communists.

You can tour the castle's interior and, even better, take a separate tour round the splendidly gloomy wine cellars, wherein viticulture is followed by tastings and a chance to walk over an arrangment of thousands of upturned bottles.

Opposite the castle is the late-Gothic **Church of Sts Peter and Paul** (Kostel sv. Petr a Pavel). The ossuary in the crypt consists of skulls and bones piled to the ceiling. Two speakers precariously balanced on top of a stack of femurs broadcast a breathless English commentary delivered in Hammer horror style, accompanied by Bach organ music. The site was established as a burial place for plague victims in the 16th century and sealed off for the next few hundred years. However, in 1914 a professor from Charles University cracked open the vault and brought in his students to arrange the 15,000 skeletons he found within. The end result includes the Latin for 'Behold death!' spelled out in skulls, and a cage displaying the remains of people with physical deformities.

The main square below the castle, **Náměstí Míru**, is lined with typically Bohemian baroque and Renaissance buildings. The fountain dates from considerably later.

Mělník Castle

Svatováclavská 19 (315 622 127/www.lobkowicz-melnik.cz). **Open** *Jan, Feb, Nov, Dec* 11am-4pm Mon-Fri. *Mar-Oct* 10am-5pm daily. **Admission** *Castle tour* 60 Kč; 40 Kč children. *Wine-tasting tour* 110 Kč. **No credit cards**.

Ossuary

Kostnice

Church of Sts Peter & Paul (315 621 2337). **Open** 10am-4pm Mon, Sat, Sun; 9.30am-12.30am, 1.15pm-4pm Tue-Fri. **Admission** 40 Kč; 20Kč children. **No credit cards**.

Where to eat

Castle vinárna

Svatováclavská 19 (315 622 121). **Open** 11am-6pm Tue-Sun. **Main courses** 250 Kč. **Credit** AmEx, MC, V.

The Castle vinárna is the swankiest dining room in town: the crockery is embossed with the Lobkowicz insignia, the vaulted walls are painted a delicate peach colour and it's one of the best places in Bohemia to splash out on an expensive meal.

Restaurace Stará škola

Na vyhlídce 159 (no phone). **Open** 11am-11pm daily. **Main courses** 190 Kč. **No credit cards**.

This basic restaurant, close to the Church of Sts Peter and Paul (*see above*), does a decent plate of steak and chips with a more than decent backdrop: the terrace has a stunning view over the surrounding countryside and the Vltava/Labe confluence.

Resources

Tourist information

Náměstí Míru 30 (315 627 503). **Open** *Jan-Apr, Oct-Dec* 9am-5pm Mon-Fri. *May-Sept* 9am-5pm daily.

Getting there

By bus

There are roughly 10 departures a day from Prague's Florenc station (journey time 50mins).

By car

Mělník is 33km (21 miles) from Prague. Head north out of Prague on Route 608; follow signs to Zdiby, then Mělník on Route 9.

Terezín

Originally known as Theresienstadt, when it was built as a fortress town in 1780 on the orders of Emperor Joseph II to protect his empire from Prussian invaders, Terezín was briefly given its old name back when the Nazis took it over in 1941. It was here that the Red Cross inspectors were duped with propaganda while the entire town was functioning as a holding camp for Jews en route to death camps further east. Of 140,000 men, women and children who passed through Terezín, 87,000 were sent east, most of them to Auschwitz. Only 3,000 were to return alive. Another 34,000 people died within the ghetto of Terezín itself.

Now little more than a Czech army barracks town, Terezín's atmosphere is still distinctly eerie, with lifeless, grid-pattern streets. The Nazis expelled the native population, few of whom chose to return after the war.

The **Ghetto Museum** (*see below*) screens documentary films of wartime life here in several languages. Possibly the most chilling contains clips from the Nazi propaganda film *The Führer Gives a Town to the Jews*, part of the sophisticated strategy to hoodwink the world. Red Cross officials visited the camp twice and saw a completely staged self-governing Jewish community with a flourishing cultural life.

The harrowing ground-floor exhibition of artwork produced by the children of Terezín has been removed to Prague's Pinkas Synagogue (*see p92*). Upstairs is a well laid-out exhibition on the Nazi occupation of Czechoslovakia. Decrees of discriminating measures against Jews are detailed – including the certificate that a customer in a pet shop intending to buy a canary was required to sign, which promised that the pet would not be exposed to any Jewish people.

A 15-minute walk back down the Prague road brings you to the **Small Fortress** (*see below*), which was built at the same time as the larger town fortress. The Gestapo established a prison here in 1940, through which 32,000 political prisoners passed. Some 2,500 died within its walls.

The approach to the Small Fortress passes through a cemetery containing 10,000 graves of Nazi victims. In the middle is a giant wooden cross – an insensitive memorial considering the tiny percentage of non-Jews buried here.

The whole fortress is now a museum, and a free map (available from the ticket office) assists exploration of the Gestapo's execution ground and of courtyards and cells, some of which held more than 250 inmates at a time. The former SS commander's house is now a museum with displays detailing the appalling physical condition of the inmates.

Ghetto Museum

Muzeum ghetta

Komenského 411, Terezín (416 782 577/www.pamatnik-terezin.cz). **Open** *Jan-Apr, Oct-Dec* 9am-5.30pm daily. *May-Sept* 9am-6pm daily. **Admission** *Museum* 160 Kč; 130 Kč children, students. *Museum & Small Fortress* 180 Kč; 140 Kč children, students. **No credit cards.**

Small Fortress

Malá pevnost

Malá pevnost, Terezín (416 782 577). **Open** *Jan-Apr, Oct-Dec* 8am-4.30pm daily. *May-Sept* 8am-6pm daily. **Admission** 160 Kč; 130 Kč children, students. *Fortress & Ghetto Museum* 160 Kč; 130 Kč children, students. **No credit cards.**

Guided tours run for groups of ten-plus. Book ahead.

Where to eat

Light meals can be had in the former guards' canteen inside the entrance to the Small Fortress.

Atypik

Máchova 91, Terezín, (416 782 780). **Open** 9.30am-10pm. **Main courses** 100Kč. **Credit** AmEx, MC, V.

The best bet for a goulash within Terezín town.

Hotel Salva Guarda

Mírové náměstí 12, Litoměřice (416 732 506). **Open** 11am-11pm daily. **Main courses** 150 Kč. **Credit** AmEx, DC, MC, V.

A traditional restaurant, serving decent Czech cuisine.

Resources

Tourist information

Náměstí ČS armády 85, Terezín (416 782 616). **Open** *Apr-Sept* 8am-5pm Mon-Thur; 8am-midnight Fri.

Getting there

By bus

Buses leave Florenc station about once every 2 hrs (journey time 60-75mins).

By car

Terezín is 50km (31 miles) from Prague. Join Route 8 or the E55 at Holešovice, via Veltrusy.

Overnighters: Town & Village

Moravia's capital Brno is a feast of spires and clubbing; the wine country entices; and ancient towns offer strongholds to bring out the inner Hussite.

Brno

Compact, party-loving and spiked by tall medieval spires the town of Brno, is a cultural and visual oasis in the middle of the otherwise placid rolling hills and plains of the region of Moravia, the Czech Republic's eastern half. Its population of 400,000, which is almost half that of Prague, makes it the Republic's second city and it has a lot more going for it than just cathedrals, crypts and cobbled streets. A thriving culture scene and nightlife nearly as varied as Prague's add up to an engaging but easygoing city without the capital's pretensions.

Having originated as a ford across the Svratka river – the city's name is derived from the old Slavonic word for mud – around 1100 Brno prospered from its location on important trade routes and swiftly became the capital of the Great Moravian Empire of old before it was annexed by the Czechs.

The transfer thoroughly Catholicised the city and Brno's greatest treasures today reflect that. Rising above the old centre of town is the vertiginous **Petrov Cathedral** (*see below*). Although the cathedral is a bit of a disappointment inside, it balances atop a suitably dramatic hill in defiance of the heretics. Its 'noon' bells sound at 11am, a tradition that originated during the Swedish siege of Brno, when the town was supposedly saved by an ingenious monk who knew that the attackers had decided to fight only until noon and then move on.

The **Capuchin Crypt** (*see below*), just below Petrov and adjoining the former coal market, **Zelný trh**, features a sobering confrontation with the hereafter. Through the action of constant draughts, several nobles and monks buried here have mummified and are now on display, many still in their original garb. If you haven't exceeded your squeamishness quota, further lugubrious sights await in the 13th-century fortress of **Špilberk** (*see below*), on a hill even higher than Petrov's, across Husova from the old centre. Here you can visit the labyrinth of dungeons, the *kasematy*, where Emperor Joseph II had prisoners suspended on the dank walls. Thankfully, they are no longer on display.

Back in the fresh air, Brno's streets revive you with engaging walking possibilities. Centuries-old pubs such as Pegas, as well as the fruit and veg market on Zelný trh and half a dozen impressively ornate baroque cathedrals are within strolling distance of the main square, **náměstí Svobody**. A sight that almost every tourist sees is the **Dragon of Brno** – actually an overstuffed crocodile – hanging outside the tourist information bureau. It is said to be the gift of a Turkish sultan who rather exaggerated its status – hence the name.

Perhaps inspired by the beast, Červený drak, or Red Dragon, is a popular Moravian beer that is becoming gradually more available in clubs throughout the republic. The club scene in Brno is hopping and the influence of local talents is typified by Iva Bittová, an avant-garde singer/violinist. You might even run into a local rocker or performance artist at **Spolek** (*see p259*), the city's newest bookshop-café, which is also a good spot to try Moravia's greatest claim to fame: the delectable white wines.

For information on trips to the **Moravský kras**, or Moravian Caves, near Brno, *see p268*.

Capuchin Crypt

Kapucínská krypta

Kapucínské náměstí (542 213 232). **Open** 9am-noon, 2-4.30pm Tue-Sun; 11-11.45am, 2-4.30pm Sun. **Admission** 40 Kč; 20 Kč concessions. **No credit cards**.

Špilberk Castle

Špilberk 1 (542 123 611). **Open** *Jan-Apr, Oct-Dec* 9am-4.15pm Tue-Sun. *May, June, Sept* 9am-5.15pm Tue-Sun. *July, Aug* 9am-5.15pm daily. **Admission** *Castle & dungeon* 60 Kč; 30 Kč concessions. *Dungeon only* 20 Kč; 10 Kč concessions. **No credit cards**.

Petrov Cathedral

Katedrála sv. Petr a Pavla

Biskupská & Petrská streets (543 235 030). **Open** 8am-6pm daily. **Admission** 30 Kč; 15 Kč concessions. **No credit cards**.

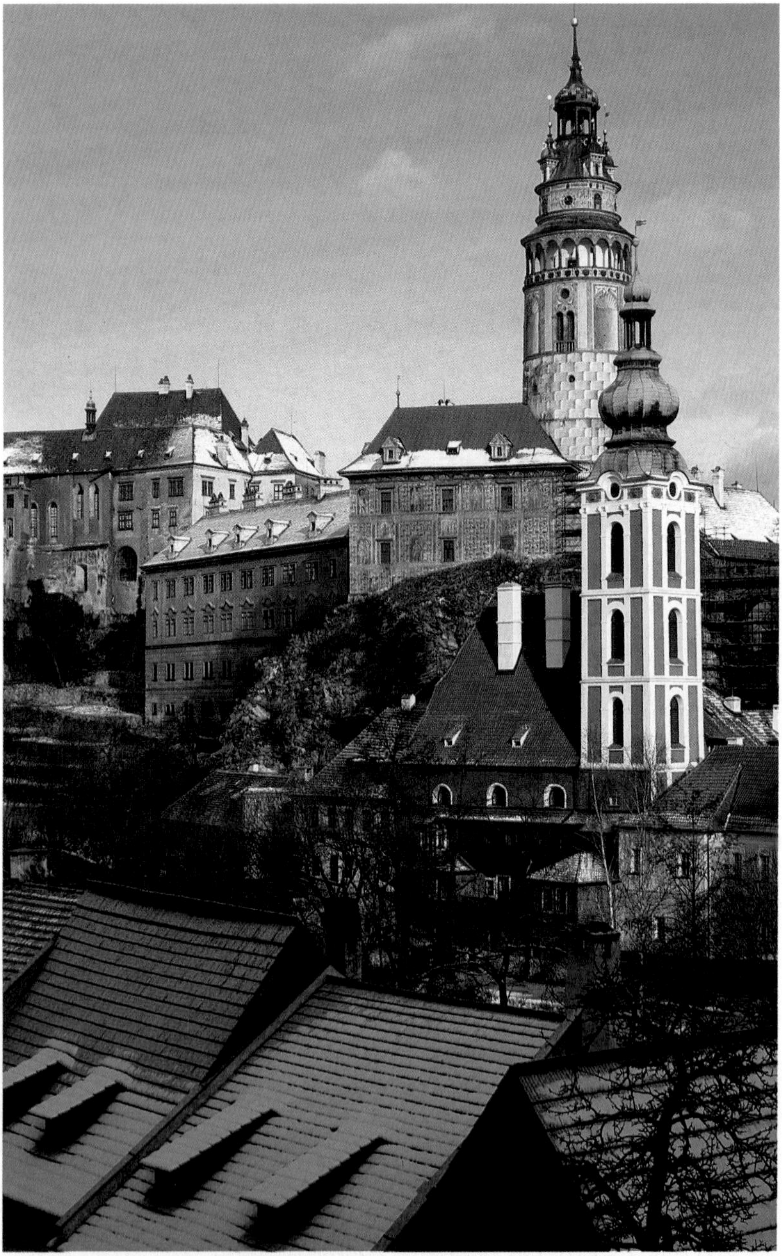

Follow the Prague crowd to **Český Krumlov**. *See p259.*

Nightlife

Charlie's Hat

Kobližná 12 (542 210 557). **Open** *Bars* 5pm-4am Mon-Thur; 5pm-5am Fri; 6pm-5am Sat; 6pm-4am Sun. *Garden* 11am-11pm Mon-Thur; 11am-midnight Fri; noon-midnight Sat; 3-11pm Sun. **No credit cards.**
Handy labyrinth of bars and a patio with DJ action and local bands.

Where to eat & drink

Restaurant Pegas

Jakubská 4 (542 210 104). **Open** 9am-midnight Mon-Sat; 10am-10pm Sun. **Main courses** 150 Kč. **Credit** AmEx, DC, MC, V.
A classic, grand-scale beerhall with its own brew, served in wheat and cinnamon varieties. Foodwise, expect schnitzel and goulash galore, credibly done.

Šermířský klub LAC

Kopečná 50 (543 237 068). **Open** 11am-midnight Mon-Fri; 5pm-midnight Sat, Sun. **Main courses** 150 Kč. **No credit cards.**
The waiters in medieval tunics at this ye olde Moravian inn serve up massive stuffed potato pancakes. This is also the headquarters of the local historic sword-fighting club.

Spolek

Orlí 22 (054 221 9002). **Open** 10am-10pm daily. **No credit cards.**
A short walk from the bus station, this bookshop-café is a hip but unpretentious hangout.

Where to stay

Hotel Amphone

Třída kapitána Jaroše 29 (545 211 783/fax 545 211 575/amphone@brn.czn.cz). **Rates** (incl breakfast) 990 Kč single; 1,390 Kč double. **Credit** AmEx, MC, V.
Although it's not situated in a particularly enchanting building, Amphone is one of the most convenient and friendly hotels in Brno.

Hotel Royal Ricc

Starobrněnská 10 (542 219 262/fax 542 219 265/ www.romantichotels.cz). **Rates** (incl breakfast) 3,200-3,500 Kč single; 3,500-4,000 Kč double; 5000 Kč suite. **Credit** AmEx, MC, V.
Royal Ricc is set in luxurious Renaissance-era quarters, with timbered ceilings, stained-glass windows and a pampering staff. Modern amenities nicely balance the historic trappings.

Resources

Tourist information

Tourist Information Brno, Radnická 8, Brno (542 211 090/www.kultura-brno.cz). **Open** 8am-6pm Mon-Fri; 9am-5pm Sat, Sun. **No credit cards.**
Staff here can book rooms at hotels and pensions.

Getting there

By bus

Buses leave Prague for Brno every 2hrs on weekdays, less frequently on weekends, from Florenc station, platform 10. The trip takes around 2hrs 30mins.

By car

Brno is 110km (77 miles) east of Prague. Take the E50/E65 motorway directly to Brno.

By train

Trains leave from Hlavní nádraží 11 times a day and take about 3hrs 30mins.

Český Krumlov

Český Krumlov is a beloved escape from Prague. Its rocky setting in the foothills of the **Šumava mountains** makes it ideal for sport activities and hiking – all of which can be coordinated through the tourist information centre (*see p260*) – while the town itself has both a fine castle to explore and a lively, lovely centre, with a delectable beer of its own. It's dominated by an enormous and well-cared-for **castle complex**, which seems to grow straight out of a rocky escarpment, overlooking lovely countryside, gabled inns and pubs overflowing with fine dark Eggenberg and Budvar, the local brews.

In 1992 the tiny town so impressed UNESCO with its beauty that it was declared second in importance only to Venice on the World Heritage list. Krumlov's fantastic pink Renaissance tower rises high above the town, idyllically positioned on a double loop of the Vltava river on the eastern edge of the forested region. The streets below are a labyrinth of cobbled alleyways filled with medieval architecture, craft shops and homely eateries.

The castle is one of the most extensive complexes in central Europe, with 40 buildings in five courtyards. Founded before 1250, the fortress was adopted by the Rožmberk clan in 1302. As the family's wealth and influence increased, it was transformed into a palace.

Cross the dry moat to enter, noting the bored bears that roam below. The tower was redone as a whimsical pink and yellow Renaissance affair in 1591, topped with marble busts and gold trimmings. The five-tiered **Plášťový Bridge** is equally spectacular, linking sections of the palace perched on two steep escarpments. For the best view descend to the **Stag Gardens** (Jelení zahrada) and look upwards. In summer, the extensive formal garden is one of the venues that hosts the **Český Krumlov International Music Festival** (*see p260*), which features everything from classical ensembles to costumed period performances to Roma music.

The highlights of the castle tour include a gilded carriage built in 1638 to convey presents to the Pope, and the Mirror and Masquerade Halls, both of which are triumphs of the arts of stucco and trompe l'œil.

On the opposite side of the Vltava from the **Castle district** (Latrán) is **Nové Město** (New Town), laid out a mere seven centuries ago. On Horní street is the impressive **Church of St Vitus** (Kostel sv. Víta), circa 1439, the long tower of which is visible from all parts of town.

It's not just a tourist town. Residents work in graphite mining, at the Eggenberg Brewery or at the nearby paper mills. Before World War II, Český Krumlov was part of the predominantly German-speaking Sudetenland and so was annexed by Hitler in 1938. The majority of the region's German-speaking inhabitants were then expelled in 1945 and the town's centuries-old bicultural life came to an end.

Český Krumlov Castle

380 704 738/380 704 712. **Open** *Apr, Oct* 9am-noon, 1-4pm Tue-Sun. *May, Sept* 9am-noon, 1-5pm Tue-Sun. June-Aug 9am-noon, 1-6pm Tue-Sun. **Admission** 150 Kč; 80 Kč children. **Credit** MC, V.
The only way to see the castle is to take an hour-long tour. Last entry is one hour before closing time.

Český Krumlov International Music Festival

Various venues (Auviex 241 445 404/www.auviex.cz). **Admission** varies according to venue. **Date** Aug.

Where to eat, drink & stay

Hospoda Na louži

Kajovská 66 (380 711 280). **Open** 10am-10pm daily. **Rates** 1100-1500 Kč all rooms. **Main courses** 200 Kč. **No credit cards**.
A good place to sample some South Bohemian cuisine, Na louži is an old-fashioned and central pub with traditional food and walls covered in tin signs. The rooms are a bit like your granny's spare room, with creaky floors but wall-to-wall charm.

Hotel Růže

Horní 154 (380 772 100/www.hotelruze.cz). **Open** *Restaurants* 7am-10pm daily. **Rates** 2,400-4,600 Kč single; 2,580-4,780 Kč double; 3,400-6,400 Kč suite. **Main courses** 350-700 Kč. **Credit** AmEx, MC, V.
A restoration of this towering Renaissance pile, a former Jesuit college, has created one of the country's most luxurious hotels. The carved wood furnishings, ceiling beams, three restaurants, cellar bar and amazing views fit the town perfectly. The modern attractions feel almost out of place: a fitness centre and pool, business amenities, top-notch service and a disco.

Hotýlek a Hospoda u Malého Vítka

Radniční 27 (380 711 925/www.krumlos.cz). **Rates** (incl breakfast) 550-700 Kč single; 1,050-1,600 Kč double; 1,800-2,500 Kč suite. **Credit** MC, V.
A restored Renaissance inn just off the main square of the city's Vnitřní město district. Kids and pets welcome. A lobby pub sells light snacks.

Pension Ve věži

Pivovarská 28 (380 711 742). **Rates** (incl breakfast) 1,200 Kč single, 1,800 Kč double. **No credit cards**.
Phone well ahead to reserve one of the four rooms inside this fortress tower with metre-thick walls.

Resources

Tourist information

Tourist Information Český Krumlov, Náměstí Svornosti 1 (380 711 183). **Open** 9am-8pm daily. **No credit cards**.
In addition to finding rooms, staff can book canoe and boat tours down the Vltava.

Vltava Travel Agency

Kájovská 62 (380 711 978/www.ckvltava.cz). **Open** *Jan-Mar* 9am-noon, 12.30-5pm Mon-Sat. *Apr-Dec* 9am-noon, 12.30-5pm daily. **Credit** MC, V.
The staff here can book rooms, horseback rides, canoe trips and other numerous activities in the area.

Getting there

By car

Český Krumlov is 136km (85 miles) from Prague. Either leave on the Brno motorway (D1-E50) and then take the E55 at Mirošovice past Tábor and České Budějovice, then the 159 road; or go via Písek leaving Prague on Route 4, towards Strakonice.

By train

The trip from Hlavní nádraží takes 5hrs and includes a change at České Budějovice.

Olomouc

Fairly remote, located some 280 kilometres (174 miles) east of Prague in the heart of Moravia, Olomouc is worth a stop if touring the region, for its picturesque town centre – a UNESCO World Heritage site – and for its willingness to stay up late, unlike other pretty old Czech hamlets, thanks to its university students. Strolling through the main squares (the town has three, cascading downhill from **Václavské náměstí** to **Horní náměstí** to **Dolní náměstí**) of an evening, you'll see parties heading to the latest happening bar or club, such as **Barumba** (*see p261*).

Otherwise, the town is a quiet, friendly escape from Prague or a good stop off on the way to Poland, the **Jeseniky mountains** or the impressive nearby **Bouzov Castle**. Dating back at least to 1017, Olomouc was a prize city in the Czech Přemyslid land grab that ended the Great Moravian Empire. During the Hussite wars, the town, like much of Moravia,

Olomouc. *See p260.*

sided with the Catholics, saw Hussite rebels executed on its squares and was rewarded with a dozen handsome churches.

The **Old Town** (Staré Město) is defined by a bend of the Morava river and is criss-crossed by tiny lanes that twist up to **St Wenceslas Cathedral** (*see below*). No doubt it was the last thing Václav III saw before he was murdered in the chapter house in 1306. It later inspired an 11-year-old Mozart to compose his *Sixth Symphony*. The neighbouring **Přemyslid Palace**, with foundations dating back to 1204, is an evocative pile with Romanesque windows but no other pulse-quickening contents.

Don't miss the socialist-realist make-over of the **Town Hall Astronomical Clock Tower** on Horní náměstí, which includes a mosaic of a scientist discovering better living for all through chemistry.

St Wenceslas Cathedral

Kostel sv. Václav
Václavské náměstí (585 224 236). **Open** 9am-6pm daily. **Admission** free.
The towering spire of this neo-Gothic wonder more than merits the hike to the city's uppermost square.

Nightlife

Barumba

Mlýnská 4 (608 081 267/www.barumba.cz). **Open** noon-midnight Mon-Thur; noon-2am Fri, Sat. **Admission** free-120 Kč. **No credit cards.**
Barumba is a combination internet café, split-level student bar and dance club, which often has DJs and live acts from Prague on its programme. It's a major scene at weekends.

Where to eat, drink & stay

Arigone

Universitní 20 (585 232 351/www.arigone.web.worldonline.cz). **Rates** (incl breakfast) 1,690 Kč single; 1,990 Kč double; 2,990 Kč suite. **Open** *Restaurant* 6am-midnight daily. **Main courses** 60-300 Kč. **No credit cards.**
This restored townhouse hotel, with raftered ceilings and warm service, also boasts a popular restaurant and bar.

Restaurace U Kapucínů

Dolní náměstí 23 (585 222 700). **Open** 10am-10pm daily. **Main courses** 200-350 Kč. **No credit cards.**
With regional cuisine well-done and frothy pints on tap, Restaurace U Kapucínů supplies just the basics on atmosphere, but it's good and cosy.

Resources

Tourist information

Town Hall, Horní náměstí (585 551 3385/www.olomoucko.cz). **Open** 9am-7pm daily. **No credit cards.**
The staff here can book rooms and arrange tours to Bouzov Castle just outside town. You can also pick up full listings of concerts, clubs, and food and drink in the area.

Keep watch with the Hussites in **Tábor**.

Getting there

By bus

Two or 3 buses depart Prague's Florenc station for Olomouc daily. The trip takes about 3hrs.

By car

Olomouc is 280km (51 miles) east of Prague. Take the E50/E65 south-east towards Jihlava and Brno, merging on to the E462 south of Brno and on to Olomouc.

By train

Trains leave hourly from Hlavní nádraží and take about 3hrs to reach Olomouc.

Trips Out of Town

Tábor

Though it's hard to imagine this friendly little town as a key military stronghold against the superior Habsburg forces, that's just what it was some 600 years ago. A band of religious radicals founded Tábor in 1420 following Jan Hus's execution. Led by the one-eyed general Jan Žižka, 15,000 Taborites battled the Catholic forces for nearly 15 years. Their policies of equal rights for men and women and common ownership of property did not endear them to the ruling classes, and the Taborites were eventually crushed by more moderate Hussite forces under George of Poděbrady. A statue of Žižka sits astride a hill overlooking Prague; Tábor honours him with a more modest sculpture in its main square.

The **Hussite Museum** (*see below*) features more, though it's almost entirely in Czech – a highlight is Žižka's unusual military innovation, a crude sort of tank consisting of cannons balanced on a wagon. The museum also runs tours of the **underground passages** (used as stores and refuges during the Hussite Wars) in much of the centre. The main square, **Žižkovo náměstí**, is the spoke from which labyrinthine streets and alleys radiate. Their confusing layout was a ploy to befuddle Tábor's enemies.

Hussite Museum

Žižkovo náměstí 1 (381 254 286). **Open** *Jan-Mar Nov, Dec* 8.30am-5pm Mon-Fri. *Apr-Oct* 8.30am-5pm daily. **Admission** *Museum* 60 Kč; 30 Kč concessions. *Tunnel tours* 40 Kč; 20Kč concessions. **No credit cards**.

Where to eat & drink

Beseda

Žižkovo náměstí (381 253 723). **Open** 10am-10pm daily. **Main courses** 150-300 Kč. **Credit** MC, V.
This central beerhall within the town hall serves the usual meat platters, warming soups and dumplings.

Where to stay

Černý leknín

Příběnická 695 (381 256 405). **Rates** (incl breakfast) 1,290 Kč single; 1,550 Kč double. **Credit** MC, V.
This cosy Gothic villa is Tábor's best accommodation.

Resources

Tourist information

Infocentrum, Žižkovo náměstí 2 (381 486 230). **Open** *Jan-Apr, Oct-Dec* 9am-4pm Mon-Fri. *May-Sept* 8.30am-7pm Mon-Fri; 9am-1pm Sat; 1-5pm Sun.

Getting there

By bus

Two or 3 buses depart Prague's Florenc station for Tábor daily (journey time 2hrs).

By car

Tábor is 82km (51 miles) south of Prague. Take the D1 south-east towards Jihlava and Brno, exiting at junction 21 to motorway 3 south.

By train

Trains to Vienna from Prague stop in Tábor. The journey is approximately 2hrs 30mins.

Telč

Lovely, deathly quiet and with an incongruous surrealist art collection in its palace, Telč is worth the trip if you're passing through the region on the way to Krumlov or Tábor. With a main square chock-full of immaculately preserved Renaissance buildings, still partly enclosed by medieval fortifications and surrounded by lakes, Telč is on UNESCO's World Heritage list. The rhomboid central square dates back to the 14th century, with a delicate colonnade along three sides. This and the photogenic gabled houses were added in the 16th century by Zacharía of Hradec. A trip to Genoa and a fortuitous marriage to Katerina of Wallenstein gave this Renaissance man the inspiration and means to rebuild the town following a devastating fire in 1530. Each of the pastel-hued buildings has a different façade adorned with frescoes, sgraffito or later baroque and rococo sculptures.

On the narrow end of the square stands the onion-domed 17th-century Jesuit church on one side and the Renaissance **castle** on the other, their exteriors the work of Italian architect Baldassare Maggi, hired by Zacharía in 1552 to spruce up his new home. The coffered ceilings of the Golden and the Blue Halls, and the monochrome trompe l'œil decorations that cover the Treasury are among the finest Renaissance interiors in Central Europe. The Marble Hall exhibits fantastic armour, while the African Hall contains a collection of hunting trophies.

The castle also houses a small municipal museum with a 19th-century mechanical nativity crib and a permanent exhibition of works by the Moravian surrealist Jan Zrzavý (1890-1977). The castle's peaceful gardens stretch down to the lake.

Telč Castle

Náměstí Zachariáše z Hradce (567 243 943). **Open** *Apr, Sept, Oct* 9-11.30am, 1-4pm (last tour 3.30pm) daily. *May, Aug* 9-11.30am, 1-5pm (last tour 4.15pm) Tue-Sun. **Admission** *Castle* 120 Kč; 60 Kč children. *Gallery* 20 Kč; 10 Kč children. **No credit cards**.

Tours are conducted in Czech but you can pick up a detailed English text at the ticket counter.

Where to eat

Šenk pod věží

Palackého 116 (567 243 889). **Open** 11am-10pm daily. **Main courses** 150 Kč. **No credit cards**.

Of the various restaurants in Telč, this is the most charming. It serves good Czech fare and has friendly staff and a terrace.

Where to stay

Hotel Celerin

Náměstí Zachariáše z Hradce 43 (567 243 477). **Rates** 350-1,100 Kč single; 1,150-1,350 Kč double. **Credit** AmEx, MC, V.

Romantic and friendly restored hotel of 12 rooms on the town's main square.

Pension Privát Nika

Náměstí Zachariáše z Hradce 45 (567 243 104). **Rates** 350 Kč single; 700 Kč double. **No credit cards**.

Comfortable and good value , this family-owned pension is unprepossessing but friendly.

Resources

Tourist information

Tourist Information Telč, Náměstí Zachariáše z Hradce 10 (567 243 145). **Open** *Jan-June, Sept-Dec* 8am-5pm Mon-Fri. *July, Aug* 8am-6pm Mon-Fri; 9am-6pm Sat, Sun. **No credit cards**.

The staff here can book accommodation, plus fishing, horse riding and hunting expeditions for around 200 Kč to 400 Kč for a day excursion.

Getting there

By bus

Buses leave 5 times daily from Florenc bus station and once every afternoon from Roztyly. The journey takes just under 4hrs.

By car

Telč is 150km (93 miles) south-east of Prague. Head out of Prague in the direction of Brno on the E50/D1 motorway. At Pávov follow signs to Jihlava; at Třešť follow signs to Telč.

Overnighters: Country

Camp, climb and hike in Czech paradise, go spelunking in cool Moravian caves or just sit back and sip the wine.

Prague is virtually empty in summer and on many fine weekends earlier in the year. That's because Czechs never miss a chance to breathe fresh air, do some hiking and drink the dregs of wine cellars in the countryside. Berry-picking, snoozing in the grass and jumping into lakes are all part of the ritual and all can be done easily in the densely forested mountains of the **Šumava** region, near **Kašperksé Hory** (*see p267*) or **Český Krumlov** (*see p259*).

The great outdoors is a favourite getaway and, though it's often basic, renting a cottage is the best form of accommodation to be had – camping is technically prohibited in the Šumava region. Alternatively, you could always pitch a tent in a spot that takes your fancy or stay at one of the campsites in **Český ráj** (*see below*), a lush area of lakes, woods, rocks and castles

The Czech-language *Šumava* by Miloslav Martan is a handy, fairly decipherable guide that contains trail maps along with pictures of regional flora and fauna, while a new agency, **Česká Pohoda** (*see below*), can arrange stays at rustic country cottages at rates significantly lower than those that even small town inns charge. So, if your head needs clearing, take the cure and hit the back roads.

Česká Pohoda

V Jámě 1, Prague 1 (224 162 581/ www.ceskapohoda.cz). Metro Můstek/tram 3, 14, 24. **Rates** (per person) 1,000-4,000 Kč/wk. **No credit cards**.

This agency can organise stays in cabins in some of the prettiest corners of Bohemia. The majority involve roughing it, but the lovely surroundings are worth the sacrifice.

Český ráj

Easier to reach than Šumava, but more crowded for that reason is Czech paradise, as Český ráj translates into English. Its lake, castles, woods and rock formations draw hundreds of fans in warm weather. As Central European wildernesses go, this picturesque region – a protected national park – is very nearly worthy of the name, even if it is concentrated in a small area. Though accessible by road, the best way to explore it is on foot; even reluctant amateurs can cross the region in two days.

The neighbouring towns of **Jičín** and **Turnov** provide a good base from which to begin your exploration, as signposted trails can be followed almost from the town centre of each. A great way to see Český ráj is to get the train to one town and hike over to the other for the return train journey.

The greatest concentration of protruding rocks is to be found around **Hrubá skála**: follow any of the marked footpaths from the village and you'll soon find yourself surrounded by these pockmarked giants. The **Hotel Zámek** (*see p267*) and **Hotel Štekl** (*see p267*) make the best bases for exploring the region. The most useful map is the *Český ráj Poděbradsko*, available at any decent Prague bookshop (*see p163*).

Supreme among ruined castles in the area is **Trosky** (the name means 'ruins'). Its two towers, built on dauntingly inaccessible basalt outcrops, form the most prominent silhouette in the region. The taller, thinner rock goes by the name of *Panna* (the Virgin), while the smaller one is *Bába* (Grandmother) – feminine appellations that are somewhat misleading given Trosky's hulking muscular mass. In the 14th century, Čeněk of Vartemberk undertook a monumental feat of medieval engineering by building a tower on top of each of the two promontories, with interconnecting ramparts between them.

The towers remained virtually impregnable, as they could only be reached by an ingenious wooden structure that could be dismantled in times of siege, leaving invaders with the choice of scaling the impossibly steep rocks or, more likely, beating a hasty retreat. In the 19th century Trosky Castle became a favourite haunt of Romantic poets, painters and patriots. Now you too can climb to the base of the tower for outstanding views of the countryside.

From 1 April until 31 October climbers can scale the sandstone pinnacles in the region. Simply pay the 40 Kč entry fee at any park attendant's booth – you'll need to bring your own climbing gear, however, as there's nowhere to rent equipment.

Trosky Castle

Troskovice-Rovensko (481 313 925). **Open** *Apr, Oct* 8.30am-4pm Sat, Sun, public hols. *May-Aug* 8.30am-6pm Tue-Sun. *Sept* 8.30am-4pm Tue-Sun. **Admission** 35 Kč; 20 Kč children. **No credit cards**.

Take a walk through Czech paradise, **Český ráj**. *See p264.*

Ready for Moravavíno, Jacques?

Czech wine just can't get no respect – or at least that's how it's been until recently, thanks largely to official neglect of bourgeoisie viniculture before 1989. It's been a slow recovery, but the rise of Czuppies with disposable incomes and increasingly demanding palates has finally resulted in some respectable Moravian vintages.

One interesting contender has even been conceived as a rival to Beaujolais Nouveau. A selection of young wines from three Moravian wine producers, Víno Mikulov, Vinné Sklepy Valtice and Znojmo Znovín, will be marketed jointly as Moravavíno Nouveau and offered in Czech wine shops in November 2004.

In the meantime, tastings of other Moravian wines are held throughout the year and make an easy day trip from **Brno** (*see p257*) via bus or a good stop-off on driving tours of the region. **Vinné Sklepy Valtice** offers tastes of its increasingly fine vintages in a castle cellar (Vinařská 1, 519 352 330, www.vsvaltice.cz, May, June 10am-6pm Sat-Sun, July, Aug 10am-6pm Tue-Sun, admission 50 Kč), which include three varieties. **Víno Mikulov** in Mikulov (pictured) hosts wine tasting at its St Urban shop (Průmyslová oblast 1220, 519 504 217, May-Sept 6pm-8pm Fri, admission 100 Kč, book two days in advance via fax or email: 519 510 815, klvacova@bohsekt.cz), which includes eight varieties of wine, bread, cheese and mineral water.

The first, limited distribution versions of Moravavíno Nouveau actually date back to 1997. Admittedly, it's named to appeal to the Beaujolais market and priced more cheaply for Czechs, but also to revive the Moravian tradition of St Martin's week, starting on the third Thursday of November.

Czech wine culture, though it dates back to Charles IV, has always been a late developer. Tastings of the annual harvest in Moravia only really started in the 19th century, when farmers gathered to show off their best, says Jaroslav Opatřil, sales director of Znojmo Znovín: 'The communists destroyed this tradition,' he moans, 'but we're working on its revival.'

Thanks be to St Martin, vintners now say; the holiday has been cannily adopted as a kind of trade show at which to promote wines from throughout southern Moravia together.

Znojmo Znovín has also persuaded restaurants in the region and in Brno to serve roasted goose with Moravavíno Nouveau in revival of another 19th-century tradition.

Each of the three Moravian producers markets two varietals as Moravavíno Nouveau every autumn, arguing in promotional literature that 'Moravavíno Nouveau is much more interesting than Beaujolais, which originates from one French region, including about 38 villages. So it's just one type of wine, whereas Moravavíno Nouveau includes at least six types.'

Whether that sways wine-savvy consumers – well aware that Moravia's *terroire* is not as suited to most reds as France's – remains to be seen. But a bottle of Moravavíno Nouveau does go for 60 Kč, about a third of the cost of imported Beaujolais Nouveau.

And, if that fails to sway, there's always the appeal to patriotism. Drinking Beaujolais is 'bad for Czechs and their near neighbours,' says Vinné Sklepy Valtice. 'People should consume only food and beverages that have been produced in the region where they were born and where generations of their ancestors have lived.'

Vive le vino!

Where to eat & stay

There are places close to every main tourist sight that offer filling, if uninspiring, traditional Czech food.

We've listed convenient hotels below, but if you want to sleep out, there are campsites – although most people just seem to pitch their tent on any appealing plot of land. Those who do prefer the convenience of a campsite should try **Autocamp Sedmihorky** (*see below*), or **Podháji** (no phone) just north-west of Hrubá skála on the Libuňka creek, which has the same rates and season as Sedmihorky.

Autocamp Sedmihorky

Turnov (481 389 162/www.campsedmihorky.cz/index_gb.html). **Open** year-round. *High season* 1 Apr-31 Oct. **Rates** *Tents* from 45 Kč/night. *Cars* from 50 Kč/night. *Trailers* from 60 Kč/night. *Additional charge* 40 Kč/adult; 35 Kč/child.
This campsite is convenient for exploring the sandstone rocks and as a starting point for hopping on the 268km-plus (167 miles) of cycling tracks. You can also rent bungalows for up to seven people from 220 Kč per night.

Hotel Štekl

Hrubá skála (481 389 684). **Open** *Restaurant* 10am-8pm daily. **Rates** (incl breakfast) 680 Kč single; 890-1,200 Kč double. **Main courses** 150 Kč. **Credit** AmEx, MC, V.
A decent dining room with views over the surrounding valleys. The hotel is well-worn and far from plush but perfectly serviceable.

Hotel Zámek

Hrubá skála castle (481 389 681). **Open** *Restaurant* 10am-10pm daily. **Rates** 1,510 Kč single; 2,240 Kč double. Discounts of up to 40% in winter. **Main courses** 250 Kč. **Credit** AmEx, MC, V.
Fabulous location, good prices and fantastic views from the ivy-covered turret rooms. The food in the restaurant here is traditonal Czech, with service that's a bit better than in Prague.

Getting there

By bus

Buses go twice a day from Černý Most metro station (Line C) to Jičín. If you opt not to walk from here (an ambitious hike), catch a bus on to Hrubá skála-Borek. Buses from Prague's Florenc station go daily to Turnov, where you change for a train to Doubravice. From there it's a 20min walk to Hrubá skála.

By car

The Český ráj area is about 90km (56 miles) north-east of Prague. Follow signs to Mladá Boleslav and join the E65 or Route 10 to Turnov. Jičín is 23km (14 miles) south-west of Turnov. Hrubá skála and Trosky are both just off Route 35, which is the Turnov–Jičín road.

By train

Eight trains a day leave Hlavní nádraží for Turnov. There are local connections from Turnov to Hrubá skála and Malá skála. A local train plies the line between Jičín and Turnov.

Kašperské Hory

Thoroughly isolated and ensconced in the **Šumava National Forest** (www.sumava-info.cz), yet only a two-hour drive from Prague, Kašperské Hory is an idyllic little town built on gold, which was guarded by the nearby fortress of **Kašperk**. With performing knights and damsels, and cold 11-degree beer, the ruins make for a worthwhile five-kilometre (three-mile) hike from the town centre.

Once part of the Sudetenland annexed by Hitler, the soothingly quiet country here is now on the edge of one of the largest forest reserves in central Europe with 685,200,000 square metres (7.4 billion square feet) on the UNESCO Biosphere Reserve list, and the source of the Otava and Vltava rivers. The woods are home to deer, eagles, otter and lynx and are filled with marked trails.

Dining on river fish and Staropramen is your reward upon your return from the mountain trials. For a second day, particularly for those with blistered feet, another option is the **Šumava Museum** (*see below*), featuring stuffed versions of any wildlife species you may have missed in the woods plus dusty historic and glass-making exhibits.

In the surrounding countryside, horseback riding is a local passion; the accommodating **Aparthotel Šumava 2000** (*see below*) can set you up for a day in the saddle.

Šumava Museum

Muzeum Šumava
Náměstí 140 (018 792 2226). **Open** *May-June, Sept-Oct* 12.45-5pm Tue-Sun. *July-Aug* 9am-noon, 12.45-5pm Tue-Sun. **Admission** 40 Kč. **No credit cards.**
Excellent collection of Bronze Age and medieval relics, plus local flora and fauna.

Where to stay

Aparthotel Šumava 2000

Náměstí 8, Kašperské Hory (376 546 910/fax 376 546 910/www.sumava2000.cz). **Rates** (per person) 580-980 Kč . **Credit** AmEx, DC, MC, V.
Modern, equipped with a sauna and happy to set you up with hiking maps, trekking gear, or horse riding.

Pension Soňa

Karlova 145, Kašperské Hory (376 582 454/728 736 777). **Rates** (per person) 380-680 Kč. **No credit cards.**
Basic but friendly family-run guesthouse near the central square.

Resources

Tourist information

Městské informační centrum, Náměstí 1, Kašperské Hory (376 503 422/736 503 412/www.sumavanet.cz/khory). **Open** *Jan-May, Sept-Dec* 7.15am-5pm Mon, Wed; 7.15am-4pm Tue, Thur. *June-Aug* 9am-4pm Sat, Sun.

Getting there

By bus

Five buses from Na Knižecí (Metro Anděl, line B) leave for Vimperk or Sušice, where you need to change for Kašperské Hory.

By car

Kašperské Hory is 100km (62 miles) from Prague. Take motorway 4 south 110km (68 miles) to Strakonice. From here, take road 22, about 18km (11 miles) west to Horažďovice, then road 169, which is another 20km (12.5 miles) south-west to Sušice. From here take road 145 and follow it 19km (12 miles) south to Kašperské Hory.

Moravský kras

The stars of the Czech Republic's many cave systems (*jeskyně*) are the ones north of the Moravian capital of **Brno** (*see p257*). Busloads of children and even pensioners (the rarefied air is touted as a cure for allergies and asthma) go on the guided tours through the chilly limestone caves – a welcome respite in the hot months, but bring a jumper. As this is a phenomenally popular summer attraction, long queues are inevitable.

The **Moravský kras** (Moravian Caves), comprising a series of 400 holes, is by far the most concentrated and accessible network of caves in the Czech Republic. Best visited as a day trip from Brno, these are limestone caves, created over 350 million years by the erosive action of acidic rainwater and underground streams. The **Kateřinská**, **Sloupsko-Šošůvské** and **Balcarka** caves are all within striking distance of Brno.

If you're looking to do all your caving in one go, your best bet is the **Punkevní jeskyně**, which is the largest cave in the country. Some three kilometres (two miles) of the cave's 12-kilometre (7.5-mile) length are open to the public. Passages of stalactites give way to the colossal **Macocha Abyss**: 140 metres (459 feet) deep, it was formed in part by the collapse of the ceiling of a cave further below. The tour then sends you down the narrow tunnels by boat. Visiting is a distinctly up-close experience: the passages are barely wide enough for the boats, and you'd likely be impaled by a stalactite if you stood up.

Arrive early in peak season as tours can sell out by mid morning. It's even better to reserve a place by phone, as queues can be long.

There are other attractions easily accessed by car. The most popular is the spectacular Gothic castle of **Pernštejn**; others include the Napoleonic battlefield of **Austerlitz** (Slavkov) and the **Alfons Mucha Museum** (515 322 789, closed Jan-May, Nov-Dec) housed in the Renaissance chateau of **Zamek Moravský Krumlov** (515 321 064, www.mkrumlov.cz).

Moravian Caves

Moravský kras
Skalní mlýn (516 413 575/www.cavemk.cz). **Open** Punkevní jeskyně *Apr-June* 8.20am-3.50pm Tue-Sun, *July-Aug* 8.20am-5pm Tue-Sun. *Oct-March* 8.40am-2pm Tue-Sun. Other caves *Apr-Aug* 8.30am-3.30pm daily. **Admission** *Punkevní jeskyně* (incl chairlift to entrance & boat ride) 100 Kč adults; 80 Kč concessions. *Other caves* 70 Kč adults; 30 Kč students; free under-6s. **No credit cards**.

Where to eat & stay

Hotel Skalní Mlýn

Skalní Mlýn (516 418 113). **Open** *Restaurant* 7am-11pm. **Main courses** 150 Kč. **Rates** (incl breakfast) 890 Kč single; 1,200 Kč double. **Credit** AmEx, MC, V.
A popular place and the best base for the caves – plus there's a reasonable restaurant.

Resources

Tourist information

Tourist Information Brno, Old Town Hall, Radnická 8, Brno (05 4221 1090). **Open** 8am-6pm Mon-Fri; 9am-5pm Sat, Sun. **No credit cards**.
The staff here can book rooms in and around the town and can also supply you with maps, brochures and other information.

Getting there

By bus

Buses run roughly every hr between Brno and Prague (journey time 2hrs 30mins).

By car

Brno is 202km (126 miles) south-east of Prague. The D1 motorway runs all the way to Brno. The caves are 22km (14 miles) north-east of Brno.

By train

Trains to Brno from Prague run hourly and take 3-4hrs. About 12 trains a day leave Brno for the nearby town of Blansko. Local buses then take you onwards to the caves. A tourist train travels between the Punkevní caves and the centre of Skalní Mlýn (every 40mins, Jan-Mar, Oct-Dec 8.20am-2pm, Apr-Sept 10am-4pm Mon, 8am-4pm Tue-Sun, 40 Kč adults, 30 Kč children), from which the other three caves are accessible.

Directory

Features

Directory

Getting Around

Arriving & departing

By air

Prague's only airport, the expanded, modernised Ruzyně, is 20 kilometres (12.5 miles) north-west of the centre and is not directly accessible by metro or tram. Some of the more expensive hotels offer a pick-up service from the airport if you book ahead, and a regular public bus service runs back and forth. For information in English on arrivals and departures call 220 113 314; for other airport information call 220 113 321.

CONNECTIONS TO THE CITY

Taxis are regulated but still often charge illegally high prices, and the firm with the current airport contract is known for particularly ruthless drivers. The ride (about 20 to 25 minutes) should cost around 370 Kč to the centre. Check at the airport information kiosk for the going rate to your destination. For a more honest taxi driver you could try taking your luggage to the customs depot (where people accept air-freighted shipments from abroad) and phoning one of the reputable taxi services to fetch you, such as AAA or Profi (*see p273*). Note that neither will pick you up at the regular Arrivals/Departures area.

EXPRESS AIRPORT BUS

Two express buses run every half hour from the airport into town, first stopping in Prague 6 at Metro Dejvická (final station on the green Line A) and then at Revoluční in Prague 1. The express bus service is quick and cheap at 15 Kč for the 20-minute ride to Dejvická and 30 Kč for the 35-minute ride to Revoluční. After hours, night bus No.510 goes from the airport to Divoká Šárka, from where you can catch night tram No.51 to the centre. Private bus service CEDAZ (220 114 296) runs transport between the airport and Metro Dejvická and Náměstí Republiky for 90 Kč (6am to 9pm daily). The white vans leave from outside the Arrivals terminal. The friendly, English-speaking Prague Airport Shuttle (602 395 421, www.prague-airport-shuttle.com) service provides door-to-door transport, as well as transport in Prague and throughout the Czech Republic.

LOCAL BUS

Four local buses run from he airport to metro stations about every 20 minutes from 5am to midnight. Bus No.119 runs from the airport to Metro Dejvická (green Line A), bus No.108 goes to Metro Hradčanská (green Line A) and bus No.179 goes to Metro Nové Butovice (yellow Line B). You can also catch bus No.100 in front of the main terminal for express service to the Zličín metro stop on the yellow Line B, which enters the city from the south. This is the cheapest, slowest and most crowded alternative. If you have lots of bags, you'll need to buy extra tickets for them. The buses depart from the stands in front of Arrivals. There you'll find orange public transport ticket machines (you'll need 12 Kč in change). There are also ticket machines and an information office in the airport lobby. For ticket details, *see p271*.

By rail

International trains arrive at the Main Station (Hlavní nádraží, sometimes called Wilson Station or Wilsonovo nádraží) and Holešovice Station (Nádraží Holešovice). Both are on the red Line C of the metro. Caution: it is easy to get off at Holešovice thinking that it is the main station. If your train stops at both, wait for the last stop.

The centrally located Main Station is a beautiful art nouveau building, with communist-period lower halls. It has several food stalls and a PIS (Prague Information Service) office in the main hall. There are also public showers and a 24-hour left luggage area in the lower hall. At night the station becomes a home for homeless people, drug addicts and hustlers, so it's not a good idea to hang around there or in the small park near the station – locals have nicknamed it Sherwood Forest as so much illegal redistribution of wealth goes on here. Enough said.

24-hour rail infoline

221 111 122

National and international timetable information. English spoken. For ticket prices, call 224 641 201 or 224 641 179 (8am-7pm daily).

Hlavní nádraží

Main Station

Wilsonova, Nové Město, Prague 2 (224 641 157). Metro Hlavní Nádraží/tram 5, 9, 11, 26.

Map p309 M5.

Masarykovo nádraží
Masaryk Station
Hybernská, Nové Město, Prague 1 (224 646 153/221 111 122). Metro Náměstí Republiky/tram 3, 5, 14, 24, 26. **Open** *International ticket office* 7.30am-6pm daily. **Map** p309 L3.

Nádraží Holešovice
Holešovice Station
Vrbenského, Holešovice, Prague 7 (224 615 865). Metro Nádraží Holešovice/tram 12, 25.
Map p312 E1.

Smíchovské nádraží
Smíchov Station
Nádražní, Prague 5 (224 617 686). Metro Smíchovské nádraží/tram 12.

By coach

Florenc coach station may be the least pleasant place in Prague. It's on two metro lines (yellow Line B and red Line C) – so you can make a quick getaway. Late arrivals can take the night tram or a taxi or stay in one of the hotels on nearby Na Poříčí. The 24hr coach infoline charges 11 Kč per minute.

Florenc station
Křižíkova 2, Prague 8 (infoline 900 119 041/www.csad.cz). Metro Florenc.

King's Court Express
Havelská 8, Staré Město, Prague 1 (224 234 583/224 233 334/ www.kce.cz). Metro Můstek. **Open** 8am-6pm Mon-Fri; 9am-1pm Sat. **Credit** MC, V. **Map** p308 J4.
Kings Court Express is one of the biggest and most reliable companies running coach services to and from the UK.

Getting around

Walking is the best way to see the relatively compact centre of Prague. Every twist of the city's ancient streets reveals some new curiosity.

If you're going further afield the city has an excellent, inexpensive and almost 24hr integrated public transport system that will get you just about anywhere you want to go. But in winter, you may have to put up with some noisome co-passengers who treat them as rolling bedrooms.

Driving in Prague takes some getting used to and it really isn't worth the bother on a short visit. Taxis are ubiquitous but unreliable – pretty cheap if you find an honest driver; ruinous if you let one rip you off.

The communists dammed the Vltava so thoroughly that there isn't any real freight or passenger traffic on the river – just pleasure cruises. An assortment of eccentric conveyances – including horse-drawn carriages, bike-taxis and a Disney-esque electric train that takes tourists up to the Castle and back – can all be found in Old Town Square.

INFORMATION

There are bus and/or tram connections and usually taxi stands at every metro station, and all of Prague's railway stations are connected to the metro network.

The Prague Public Transport company, DP, runs around the clock. Day service is from about 5am to about 10 minutes past midnight daily. Peak times are 5am to 8pm Monday to Friday. From midnight to 5am, night buses and trams take over. English-language content, downloadable maps, the latest route changes and incredibly arcane facts about public transport are on the DP website (www.dp-praha.cz).

Metro, tram and bus lines are indicated on most city maps. Timetables can be found at every tram and bus stop. The times posted apply to the stop where you are – which is highlighted on the schedule. If your destination is listed below the highlighted stop, you are in the right place.

Prague Public Transit Company (DP) Information Offices
Ruzyně Airport *(220 115 404).* **Open** 7am-10pm daily.
Muzeum metro station *Nové Město (222 623 777).* **Open** 6.30am-7pm Mon-Fri; 7am-6pm Sat, Sun. **Map** p311 L6.
Můstek metro station *Nové Město (222 646 350).* **Open** 7am-9pm daily. **Map** p308 J4/p309 K5.
Nádraží Holešovice metro station *Holešovice (296 191 817).* **Open** 7am-6pm Mon-Fri.
Černý Most metro station *Černý Most (222 647 450).* **Open** 7am-6pm Mon-Fri.
Anděl metro station *Smíchov (2264 6055).* **Open** 7am-6pm Mon-Fri.
Employees usually have at least a smattering of English and German and are unusually helpful. They provide free information booklets and sell tickets, maps, night transport booklets and individual tram and bus schedules (cash only).

FARES AND TICKETS

Tickets (*jízdenky*) are valid for any mode of transport (metro, bus, tram, even the funicular). Most locals have passes (*see p272*), probably the easiest option for visitors too as you can't buy a ticket on board trams or buses.

Ticket machines are only found in metro stations and dispense dozens of types of tickets. Only two need concern you, though. An 8 Kč ticket buys a single 15-minute ride on any transport above ground, or one ride of up to four stops on the metro. It is not valid for use on night transport, the Historical Tram or the funicular. A 12 Kč ticket lasts for 60 minutes at peak times (5am-8pm Mon-Fri) and 90 minutes at off-peak (8pm-5am Mon-Fri and all of Sat, Sun), allowing unlimited travel throughout Prague, including transfers between metros, buses and trams.

Babies in buggies, children under six, handicapped people, small bags and skis ride free. Children aged six to 15, large items of luggage and other sizeable items require a half-price ticket. Enormous bags and, quote, 'items that stink or look disgusting' aren't allowed on Prague public transport.

The orange ticket machines are marvels of Czechnology. They are covered with buttons marked with prices. Press once for the ticket you want, twice if you want two tickets (and so on) and then press the 'enter' button. Insert the total amount in coins (change is given) and wait an agonisingly long time for the machine's screeching mechanism to print out each ticket individually.

If you're here for anything other than a quick visit it's worth stocking up on tickets in advance. You can buy them at most tobacconists, DP information offices (*see p271*) and PIS offices (*see p291*), or anywhere displaying a red and yellow DP sticker.

Stamp your ticket (face up in the direction of the arrow) in the machine as you board a bus or enter the 'paid area' of the metro. There are no guards or gates, but plain-clothes inspectors (*revizoři*) carry out random ticket checks. They can sometimes be merciless and have little understanding of English. They have a reputation for choosing those public transport routes where tourists are most likely to be (such as tram No.22) hoping to come across a lot of confused foreigners who either don't know they should stamp their tickets or buy the ticket of wrong value. The penalty is 400 Kč or 800 Kč if you fail to produce the money on the spot. Always demand a receipt, otherwise the money may end up in the inspector's pocket.

Most ticket outlets also sell transit passes, which allow unlimited travel on the metro, trams and buses. The 24hr pass is also available at automatic ticket machines.

To validate a short-term pass, fill in your full name and date of birth on the reverse and then stamp it as you would an ordinary ticket. The pass is valid from the time it was stamped. A 24hr pass costs 70 Kč, a 72-hour pass is 200 Kč, a 168-hour pass (seven days) is 250 Kč and a 360-hour pass is (15 days) 280 Kč.

Residents usually have long-term passes valid for a month or longer, available at the DP windows and at the Karlovo náměstí metro station. You will need a recent passport photo and some ID. Long-term passes cost 420 Kč for one month, 1,150 Kč for three months and 3,800 Kč for the year. There's also a 'gliding' coupon validity for any 30- to 90-day period, so you needn't wait till the end of the month to start a pass.

In terms of disabled access, public transport is still difficult to use, as are Prague's ancient streets, but there are lifts at the following metro stations – at some you'll need help to operate the lift: Dejvická and Skalka (green Line A); Zličín, Stodůlky, Luka, Lužiny, Hůrka, Vysočanská, Kolbenova, Hloubětín and Rajská zahrada (yellow Line B); Nádraží Holešovice, Hlavní nádraží, Florenc, Muzeum, IP Pavlova, Vyšehrad, Pankrác, Roztyly, Chodov, Opatov and Háje (red Line C).

There are two bus routes served only by kneeling buses. Bus No.109B starts in Bryksova and runs via Černý Most, Florenc, Náměstí Republiky and IP Pavlova to Chodov. The No.118D runs from Zličín via Hradčanská, Náměstí Republiky and Nádraží Holešovice to Sídliště Ďáblice.

All of the newer, boxier trams also kneel, but there's no counting on when one is going to come along. You can find out which lines use the newer cars at DP information offices (*see p271*).

Metro

Prague's metro network, with a total length of 43.6 km (27 miles) running among 48 stations along three lines, is a scaled-down copy of the grandiose Moscow metro. The stations are well lit and clearly signposted; trains are clean and frequent. A digital clock on each platform informs you of the time elapsed since the last train came along (though the time until the next arrival would be more useful).

The metro comprises three lines: the green Line A (Skalka–Dejvická); the yellow Line B (Černý most–Zličín); and the red Line C (Nádraží Holešovice–Háje), which is currently being extended – two additional stops, Kobylisy and Ládví, north of Nádraží Holešovice should be opened by the end of 2004. A fourth line is due to open sometime in the next decade.

Transfers (*přestup*) are possible at three stations: Muzeum (between Line A and Line C), Můstek (between Line A and Line B) and Florenc (between Line B and Line C). The metro runs from 5am to midnight daily. Trains come every two minutes at peak times, and every five to ten minutes off-peak. For a metro map, *see p316*.

Trams

An electric *tramvaje* service began in Prague in 1891 and trams have been the preferred method of transport for most Praguers ever since.

Trams come every six to eight minutes at peak times and every ten to 15 minutes at other times. With the newer, boxier trams, you may find you need to press the green button to open the doors.

The best tram lines for seeing the city are the No.22, from the Castle to Národní třída and beyond, and the

Historic Tram (the No.91), from the Výstaviště in Prague 7 through Malá Strana, across to the National Theatre, through Wenceslas Square, Náměstí Republiky and back to Prague 7. The Historic Tram runs on Saturdays, Sundays and holidays from Easter to the middle of November and leaves Výstaviště every hour from 2pm to 7pm. The ride takes 40 minutes, and tickets cost 20 Kč for adults and 10 Kč for children.

Buses

Since 1925, *autobusy* in Prague have provided transport to places where no other public transport dares to go. They run from about 5am to midnight, after which time ten night bus lines take over (*see below*). Buses run every five to 18 minutes during peak times and every 15 to 30 minutes at other times.

Bus infoline

900 119 041. **Open** 6am-8pm Mon-Fri; 8am-4pm Sat, Sun. Calls cost 11 Kč per minute. The operators speak English.

Night trams/buses

Night buses and trams run about every 40 minutes, from midnight to about 4.30am. Every night tram (they all have numbers in the 50s) stops at Lazarská crossroads on Spálená. There's no central stop for night buses (Nos.501 to 512), but many stop at the top of Wenceslas Square (near Metro Muzeum) and around the corner from Metro IP Pavlova. You can buy a guide to night transport – showing all lines, times and stations – at the DP information offices (*see p271*) for about 10 Kč.

Funicular railway

The funicular (*lanovka*) runs for half a kilometre from the bottom of Petřín hill at Újezd (around the corner from the tram stop of the same name), stops midway at Nebozízek (at the restaurant of the same name) and continues to the top of Petřín hill. It runs every ten or 15 minutes between 9.15am and 8.45pm daily and costs 12 Kč for adults and 6 Kč for kids. Transport passes are valid, but beware: a recent scam by ticket sellers and inspectors netted thousands of crowns – don't get on board without buying a ticket and getting it stamped in the yellow machine, even if you have to move a clerk out of the way to do so.

Water transport

The Prague Steamship Company had a monopoly on river traffic way back in 1865 – and still provides most boat services on the river today. You'll find them, as well as other companies plying sightseeing and booze cruises, and rowing boats for hire, along the right bank of the Vltava.

Prague Steamship Company

Pražská paroplavební služba *Rašínovo nábřeží, Nové Město, Prague 2 (224 930 017/ www.paroplavba.cz). Metro Karlovo náměstí/tram 3, 16, 17.* **Map** p310 G9.

Taxis

The appalling reputation of Prague's taxi drivers has prompted City Hall to introduce strict guidelines. Even so, the odds are high that you will still get ripped off. The drivers waiting at ranks in obvious tourist locations are generally crooks, so avoid them. Hail a moving cab or call one of the services listed below. Make sure that you are using an authorised taxi – it should be clearly marked, with its registration number and fares printed on the doors and a black and white checked stripe along the side. If the driver doesn't turn on the meter, insist he does. If he won't, get out straight away or agree on a fee to your destination. Do neither, and the driver will demand a ruinous fare at the end of your journey; he may even resort to violence to collect it.

Ideally, your taxi experience should go something like this: the driver does not turn on the meter (*taxametr*) until you enter the cab. When he does, 25 or 30 Kč appears as the initial amount. While you are driving within Prague, the rate is set at '1' and should never be more than 20 or 22 Kč per kilometre. When your ride is over, the driver gives you a receipt (*účet* or *paragon*). (If he doesn't, you are theoretically not required to pay the fare.)

Few drivers will actually provide a receipt unless you ask. Honest cabbies print one out on the agonisingly slow machine; rip-off merchants will write you one out on a pad.

At press time, the maximum taxi rates allowed by a directive of the City Hall were: 30 Kč (if you hail a cab) or 25 Kč (if you call to book), plus 4 Kč per minute for waiting (because of a passenger request or traffic) and no more than 22 Kč (if hailed) or 20 Kč (if you booked by phone) per kilometre for normal rides. However, fares are scheduled for a slight increase.

Cab companies

AAA *233 113 31/14014.* If you're using a mobile (*see p290*), use the numbers below for cheaper calls: T-Mobile 603 331 133; Eurotel 602 331 133; Oskar 777 331 133.

ProfiTaxi *261 314 151/ 800 118 294.*

Halo Taxi *244 114 411.*

Taxi complaints

Živnostenský úřad *Staroměstská náměstí 4, Staré Město, Prague 1 (224 482 721/236 002 721). Metro Staroměstská/tram 17, 18.* **Map** p308 H3.

Rail services

Trains are generally useful only for travelling from town to town in the Czech Republic, not within Prague. *See p270.*

Driving

The worst days for driving are Friday and Sunday, when people who don't know the difference between the clutch and the brake pack their families into new Škodas for a weekend trip to their summer cottage. Czechs tend to stop in the middle of junctions on a red light, and traffic has become horrendous in the city centre as incomes and car ownership have risen steeply.

Unless you have a Czech residence permit you'll need an international driver's licence (ask a motoring organisation in your home country, such as the AA or AAA, how to apply).

Traffic regulations in the Czech Republic are similar to those in most European countries. However, there is zero tolerance for drinking and driving – drivers are not allowed to drink any alcohol at all; ditto for drugs. The use of seat belts is required in the front and – if the car is equipped with them – backs seat (though most Czechs will laugh at your faint-heartedness if you belt up). Children under 12 and anyone under 18 who is shorter than 150 centimetres (4.9ft) can not ride in the seat next to the driver unless they sit in approved safety seats and there's no airbag in the front seat. Small children must be in approved safety seats whether they're placed in the front or the back seat.

Trams, which follow different traffic lights to cars, always have the right of way. You must stop behind trams when passengers are getting on and off at a stop where there is no island, and you should avoid driving on tram tracks unless the road offers no alternative.

The speed limit for cars and buses is 90kph (56 miles per hour) on roads, 130kph (81 miles per hour) on motorways and 50kph (31 miles per hour) in towns and villages.

Motorcyclists, along with their passengers, must wear protective helmets and eyegear, and the speed limit for motorcycles is 90kph (56 miles per hour) on roads and motorways and 50kph (31.25 miles per hour) in villages and towns.

You are required to notify the police of any accident involving casualties or serious damage to a car.

Breakdown services

Autoklub Bohemia Assistance

Autoklub České republiky
Opletalova 29, Nové Město, Prague 1 (224 230 506/222 241 257). **Open** 8am-6pm Mon-Fri; 8am-noon Sat. **No credit cards.**
Call 1240 or 266 19 3 247 for 'ABA': 24-hour, seven-day-a-week emergency road service.

Central Automobile Club Prague

Ústřední automotoklub
Na strži 9, Michle, Prague 4 (261 104 111). **Open** 8am-4pm Mon-Fri. **No credit cards.**
Call 1230 or 261 220 220 (Renault Assistance) for the'Yellow Angel' 24-hour emergency road service.

Fuel stations

Leaded fuel (octane 90) is called Special, leaded fuel (octane 96) is known as Super and unleaded fuel (95D) is called Natural. Super Plus 98 and diesel fuel are also widely available. A booklet listing all the petrol and service stations (and some car parks) in Prague is available from PIS offices (*see p291*). Many service stations stay open 24 hours a day.

Insurance

If you are driving your own car, you will need to have international proof of insurance (known as a Green Card; contact your motoring organisation) and pay an annual toll for using the Czech roads. If you hire a car, insurance and toll should be taken care of for you. Otherwise, the toll sticker – which should be displayed on the windscreen – is 100 Kč for 10 days, 200 Kč for a month or 800 Kč for a year. It can be bought at post offices, most border-crossing points and petrol stations.

Parking

Parking can be a nightmare. Watch out for special zones reserved for area residents and businesses. If you park illegally, your car can be towed away (call 158 to get it back) or clamped and cost you around 1,000 Kč to retrieve – more if there's a delay. If you're new in town, the best option is to use a car park, ideally one that has 24-hour security.

Parking meters

Coin-operated parking meters dispense tickets. Display them face up on the dashboard, visible through the windscreen.

Streets in Prague 1 are separated into three types of parking. Blue zones are reserved for local residents and companies. Orange zones are for stops of up to two hours and cost a minimum of 10 Kč for 15 minutes and 40 Kč for one hour; and green zones are for stays of up to six hours and cost cost 15 Kč for 30 minutes, 30 Kč for an hour and 120 Kč for six hours. Ignore the restrictions at your peril.

Rideshare

A great way to cut the stress, while riding a lot more directly and comfortably than in a bus, sharing rides is a well-organised process at Prague's main rideshare centre.

Town to Town Agency

Národní třída 9, Prague 1 (tel/fax 222 075 407/www.spolujizda.cz). Metro Národní třída/tram 6, 9, 17, 18, 22, 23. **Open** 9am-6pm Mon-Fri; 10am-4pm Sat. **No credit cards. Map** p308 G6.

Pay a nominal deposit and you're set, with complete online listings of rides offered and passengers seeking rides, organised by destination, with times and prices.

Vehicle hire

Renting a car can be pretty expensive in Prague, with many Western firms charging higher rates than they would back home. It is definitely worth shopping around, as many small local firms charge far less than the big boys. When renting a car, be sure to bring your international driver's licence, passport and credit card with you. The agency should provide you with a green insurance card, which you will be asked to show if you are stopped by police or drive across the border. Arrange your rental a few days in advance to be sure that you get the car you want.

In addition to the places listed below, American Express (*see p286*), Čedok (*see p291*) and Student Agency (*see p289*) arrange car rental.

A Rent Car

Washingtonova 9, Nové Město, Prague 1 (224 211 581). Metro Muzeum/tram 11. **Open** 7am-7pm daily. **Rates** 1,200 Kč-4,400 Kč per day. **Credit** AmEx, DC, MC, V. **Map** p309 L5. **Other locations**: Ruzyně Airport, Prague 6 (224 281 053/220 140 370); Milevská 2, Prague 4 (241 731 618).

Avis

Klimentská 46, Staré Město, Prague 1 (221 851 225-6/fax 221 851 229/www.avis.cz). Metro Florenc/tram 3, 8. **Open** 8am-4.30pm Mon-Fri; 8am-2pm Sat, 10am-2pm Sun. **Rates** from 1,630 Kč per day. **Credit** AmEx, DC, MC, V. **Map** p309 M1. **Other locations**: Ruzyně Airport, Prague 6 (235 362 420).

Alimex

Na Petynce 22, Střešovice, Prague 6, (233 350 001/www.alimexcr.cz). Metro Malostranská/22, 23 tram to Malovanka stop. **Open** 8am-6pm Mon-Fri; 8am-5pm Sat, Sun. **Rates** from 450 Kč per day for a Škoda Fabia covered with company ads or from 800 Kč per day for an unmarked one. **Credit** AmEx, DC, MC, V. **Other locations**: Ruzyně Airport, Prague 6 (220 114 860)

Budget

Čistovická 100, Řepy, Prague 6 (235 325 713/235 301 181/www.budget.cz). Tram 22, 25. **Open** 8am-4.30pm Mon-Fri. **Rates** from 900 Kč per day. **Credit** AmEx, DC, MC, V. **Other locations**: Ruzyně Airport, Prague 6 (220 560 443); Hotel Intercontinental, Staré Město, Prague 1 (222 319 595).

Central Rent a Car

Černá růže, Na příkopě 12, Staré Město, Prague 1 (221 014 630/222 245 905/602 618 177/www.rentcentral.cz). Metro Můstek/tram 3, 9, 14, 24. **Open** 8am-8pm daily. **Rates** from 950 Kč per day. **Credit** AmEx, DC, MC, V. **Map** p309 K4.

European Inter Rent/ Europe Car Rental

Pařížská 28, Staré Město, Prague 1 (224 810 515/224 811 290/www.eurocar.cz; only in Czech). Metro Staroměstská/tram 17, 18. **Open** 8am-8pm daily. **Rates** from 2,012 Kč per day; 3,333per two days. Reduced price on longer the rental periods. **Credit** AmEx, DC, MC, V. **Map** p308 H2. **Other locations**: in most of the major cities in the Czech Republic.

Hertz

Karlovo náměstí 28, Nové Město, Prague 2 (222 231 010/www.hertz.cz). Metro Karlovo náměstí/tram 3, 4, 6, 14, 16, 18, 22, 23, 24, 34. **Open** 8am-8pm daily. **Rates** from 2,113 Kč per day; 3,499 Kč for 2 days. **Credit** AmEx, DC, MC, V. **Map** p310 H7. **Other locations**: Ruzyně Airport, Prague 6 (233 326 714); Hotel Diplomat, Evropská 15, Prague 6 (224 394 174).

Cycling

Frankly put, pedalling in Prague is hellish. There are no cycle lanes, drivers are oblivious to your presence and pedestrians yell at you if you ride on the pavement. Mountain bikes are best, as the wide wheels shouldn't get stuck in the tram tracks. Prague does, however, have plenty of parkland inside and outside the city. On public transport, bikes are allowed in the last carriage of metro trains – you are have to purchase and stamp a 6 Kč ticket for your bike.

Bicycle hire

City Bike

Královdvorská 5, Staré Město, Prague 1 (mobile 776 180 284). Metro Náměstí Republiky/5, 8, 14 tram. **Open** *Apr-Oct* 9am-7pm daily. **No credit cards. Map** p309 K3.

Cycle tours of the city, three times a day: 10am, 2pm and sunset. Reasonable rental fees.

Walking

By far the best way to get around Prague's compact centre is on foot. The excellent pocket-sized map *Praha do kapsy* is available at most newsstands. It is generally safe to walk anywhere at any time – using common sense and appropriate caution in the wee hours, of course. Prague does not (yet) have any 'bad' areas that you should avoid. Beware of bad drivers, though – they've only begrudgingly begun to stop for pedestrians at crossings because a recent law compels them to.

Resources A-Z

Addresses

Buildings have two numbers posted on them; one in red, used in city records, and one in blue, denoting the address used for letters and callers (the one used in this guide). The street name comes first, then the house number, then a district code and district number, followed by the country, thus:
Jan Novák
Kaprova 10
11 000 Praha 1
Czech Republic

Age restrictions

The legal age for driving in the Czech Republic is 18, as it is for drinking and smoking, though it's virtually unheard of for clubs, bars and shops to ask for proof of age. The age of sexual consent for all is 15.

Attitude & etiquette

Praguers sometimes seem standoffish at first. But Czechs will quickly warm to you if you attempt to speak just a word of their language. Generally there's a culture of shyness and of avoiding confrontation at all costs, and Czechs are understated about expressing happiness. They also tend to melt at the sight of children and dogs, are sexually liberal, reverent about Czech beer and their country and fiscally and gastronomically conservative.

Business

Accounting firms

Deloitte & Touche

Týn 4, Staré Město, Prague 1 (224 895 500/www.deloitteCE.com). Metro Náměstí Republiky/tram 5, 8, 14, 26. **Open** 8am-8pm Mon-Fri. **Map** p308 J3.

KPMG

Jana Masaryka 12, Vinohrady, Prague 2 (222 123 111/www.kpmg.cz). Metro Náměstí Míru/tram 4, 16, 22, 23, 34. **Open** 9am-5pm Mon-Fri. **Map** p311 M10.

PriceWaterhouse Coopers

Kateřinská 40, Nové Město, Prague 2 (251 151 111/www.pwcglobal.com). Metro IP Pavlova/tram 4, 6, 10, 11, 16, 22, 23. **Open** 9am-5pm Mon-Fri. **Map** p311 K8.

Banking

Anyone can open a bank account in the Czech Republic. Banks generally charge high fees and current accounts do not pay interest. Service is improving, but still expect long queues, short opening hours and lots of paperwork. Czech banks usually cater to individual account holders, while international banks are largely geared to corporate accounts. The five main Czech banks are Česká spořitelna (ČS), Československá obchodní banka (ČSOB), Komerční banka (KB), HVB Bank and Živnostenská banka.

Česká spořitelna

Rytířská 29, Staré Město, Prague 1, (224 101 111/freephone 800 207 207/www.csas.cz). Metro Můstek/tram 3, 9, 14, 24. **Open** 9am-5pm Mon-Thur; 9am-4pm Fri. **Map** p308 J4.
This savings bank operates a large cashpoint (ATM) network. **Otherlocations**: Václavské náměstí 16, Prague 1 (224 401 111).

Citibank

Evropská 178, Dejvice, Prague 6 (233 061 111/www.citibank.cz). Metro Dejvická/tram 20, 26. **Open** 8.30am-5pm Mon-Fri.

HVB Banka

Naměstí Republiky 3, Nové Město, Prague 1 (221 112 111/www.ba-ca.cz). Metro Náměstí Republiky/tram 5, 8, 14. **Open** 9am-4.30pm Mon-Thur; 9am-3.30pm Fri. **Map** p309 K3.

Computers

For repairs/supplies, *see p164*.

MacSource/ CompuSource

Bělehradská 68, Nové Město, Prague 2 (222 515 455/fax 222 515 456/www.macsource.cz). Metro IP Pavlova/tram 6, 11. **Open** 9am-5pm Mon-Fri. **Credit** AmEx, MC, V. **Map** p311 L10.
Both PC and Macintosh equipment are available for lease and rental.

Couriers/messengers

DHL

Aviatická 1048/12, Ruzyně Airport, Prague 6 (toll-free 800 103 000/220 300 111/www.dhl.cz). **Telephone bookings** 24 hrs daily. **Credit** AmEx, MC, V.
Daily pick-up service until 6pm on weekdays, 3pm on Saturdays.

FedEx

Olbrachtova 1, Prague 4 (244 002 200/fax 241 440 024/www.fedex.com). Metro Budějovická. **Telephone bookings** 8am-5.30pm Mon-Fri; 8am-1pm Sat. **Credit** AmEx, MC, V.

Messenger Service

Patočkova 3, Dejvice, Prague 6 (220 400 000/fax 220 400 040/www.messenger.cz). Metro Hradčanská/tram 1, 2, 18. **Telephone bookings** 24hrs daily. **Credit** AmEx, MC, V.
Local cycle couriers. Also delivers outside Prague.

Estate agents

Finding reasonably priced and adequate office space can be challenging. Make sure that any space has cable internet access lines and isn't due for disruptive repairs. Parking is better away from the centre.

Apollo

Senovážné náměstí 8, Nové Město, Prague 1 (224 222 587/fax 224 222 641/www.apollosro.cz). Metro Můstek/tram 5, 9, 24. **Open** 9am-5.30pm Mon-Fri. **Map** p309 L4.

Praha-Nexus Europe
Mezibranská 4, Nové Město, Prague 1 (224 941 283/fax 224 941 285/www.nexus-e.cz). Metro Muzeum. **Open** 9am-5.30pm Mon-Fri. **Map** p311 L6.

Interpreting & translating

Prague's many translation companies offer services in all the major European languages, plus many other languages. Rates are usually by the page.

Artlingua
Myslíkova 6, Nové Město, Prague 2 (224 922 359/fax 224 921 715/ www.artlingua.cz). Metro Karlovo Náměstí/tram 17. **Map** p310 H7.

TaP Servis
Perlova 1, Staré Město, Prague 1 (224 226 629/fax 224 211 443). Metro Můstek. **Map** p308 J5.

Law firms

Of the dozens of law firms in Prague, local firms have a better grasp of the more arcane elements of Czech law, while international firms offer better linguistic skills and more polish.

Cameron McKenna
Karolíny Světlé 25, Staré Město, Prague 1 (221 098 888/fax 221 098 000/www.law-now.com). Metro Národní třída or Můstek/tram 6, 9, 17, 18, 22, 23. **Open** 9.30am-6pm Mon-Fri. **Map** p308 G5.
The largest network of law offices in Central Europe.

Čermák, Hořejš & Myslil
Národní třída 32, Nové Město, Prague 1 (296 167 111/fax 224 946 724/www.cermakhorejsmyslil.cz). Metro Národní třída/tram 6, 9, 17, 18, 22, 23. **Open** 9am-5pm Mon-Fri. **Map** p308 H5.
Specialises in commercial law.

Czech Chamber of Commercial Lawyers
Senovážné náměstí 23, Nové Město, Prague 1 (224 142 457/ www.cak.cz). Metro Náměstí Republiky/tram 5, 8, 14. **Open** 8am-4pm Mon-Thur; 8am-3pm Fri. **Map** p309 L4.

Haarmann Hemmelrath
Ovocný Trh 8, Staré Město, Prague 1 (224 490 000/fax 224 490 033/www.haarmann hemmelrath.com). Metro Můstek/tram 3, 9, 14, 24. **Open** 8am-7pm Mon-Fri. **Map** p308 J4.
Offers advice on privatisation, acquisitions and other issues.

Office hire

Business Centrum Chronos
Václavské náměstí 66, Nové Město, Prague 1 (296 348 111 /fax 222 211 327/www.chronos.pha.cz). Metro Muzeum/tram 11. **Open** 8am-6pm Mon-Fri. **Map** p311 K6.
Offers temporary office space.

Regus
Vyskočilova 1A/1422, Kačerov, Prague 4 (244 026 111/fax 244 026 200/www.regus.com). Metro Budějovická. **Open** 9am-6pm Mon-Fri.
Offices and conference rooms.

Photocopying

See p179.

Recruitment agencies

Adecco
Spalená 10, Nové Město, Prague 1 (224 948 084/fax 224 946 500/ www.adecco.cz). Metro Národní Třída/tram 6, 9, 18, 22, 23. **Open** 9am-6pm Mon-Fri. **Map** p310 H6.

AYS
Krakovská 7, Nové Město, Prague 1 (222 210 013/www.ays.cz). Metro Muzeum/tram 11. **Open** 8am-6pm Mon-Fri. **Map** p311 K7.

Helmut Neumann International
Národní třída 10, Nové Město, Prague 1 (224 951 530/www. Neumann-inter.com). Metro Národní třída/tram 6, 9, 17, 18, 22, 23. **Open** 8am-6pm Mon-Thurs; 8am-4pm Fri. **Map** p308 H5.

Useful organisations

British Embassy Commercial Section
Na příkopě 21, Nové Město, Prague 1 (222 240 021/fax 222 243 622/ www.britain.cz). Metro Můstek/tram 3, 9, 14, 24. **Open** 9am-noon, 2-5pm Mon-Fri. **Map** p309 K4.

Economic Chamber of the Czech Republic
Hospodářská komora ČR
Freyova 27, Vysočany, Prague 9 (224 096 111/fax 224 096 221/www.komora.cz). Metro Hlavní nádraží, then tram 5, 9, 26. **Open** 8am-4pm Mon-Fri.

US Embassy Foreign Commercial Service
Tržiště 15, Malá Strana, Prague 1 (257 530 663/fax 257 531 165). Metro Malostranská/tram 12, 22, 23. **Open** 9am-midnight daily. **Map** p307 D3.

Travel advice

For up-to-date information on travelling to a specific country – including the latest news on safety and security, health issues, local laws and customs – contact your home country government's department of foreign affairs. Most have websites packed with useful advice for would-be travellers.

Australia
www.dfat.gov.au/travel

Republic of Ireland
www.irlgov.ie/iveagh

Canada
www.voyage.gc.ca

UK
www.fco.gov.uk/travel

New Zealand
www.mft.govt.nz/travel

USA
www.state.gov/travel

Consumer

There is a Czech Office of Consumer Protection, but it doesn't have English-speaking services and has been largely ineffective. It's best to adopt a philosophy of Buyer Beware. Shops sometimes exchange faulty goods, but generally don't give refunds.

Customs

There are no restrictions on the import and export of Czech currency, but if you're carrying more than 350,000 Kč out of the country, you must declare it at customs. The allowances for importing goods are:

- 200 cigarettes or 100 cigars at max. 3g each or 250g of tobacco;
- One litre of liquor or spirits and two litres of wine;
- Medicine in any amount for your own needs.

If you want to export an antique, you must have a certificate stating that it is not important to Czech cultural heritage: ask when you buy.

Customs Office

Celní ředitelství pro Prahu a Středočeský kraj
Washingtonova 11, Nové Město, Prague 1 (261 334 201/ www.cs.mfcr.cz). Metro Muzeum/tram 11. **Open** 7am-3.30pm Mon, Wed; 7am-3pm Tue, Thur, Fri. **Map** p311 L6.
Other locations: Ruzyně Airport, Prague 6 (220 114 380).

Disabled access

According to the law, all buildings constructed after 1994 must be wheelchair-friendly. Reconstructed buildings, however, need not provide wheelchair access, though many do voluntarily. Even so, it is no picnic to be in Prague in a wheelchair. There are few ramps. Most hotels provide no wheelchair access and only five railway stations in the entire country are wheelchair-friendly. The guidebook *Accessible Prague* (*Přístupná Praha*), available from the Prague Wheelchair Association (*see below*), contains maps of hotels, toilets, restaurants, galleries and theatres that are wheelchair-friendly. For travel info for the disabled, *see p272.*

Prague Wheelchair Association

Pražská organizace vozíčkářů
Centre for Independent Living (Centrum samostatného života), Benediktská 6, Staré Město, Prague 1 (224 827 210/ www.pov.cz). Metro Náměstí Republiky/tram 5, 8, 14. **Open** 9am-4pm Mon-Fri. **Map** p309 K2.
Run by the disabled for the disabled. Provides helpers, a taxi service and an airport pick-up service for the disabled. Service should be ordered as far in advance as possible. Also hires out wheelchairs.

Electricity

Electricity is 220 volts with two-pin plugs almost everywhere. Bring continental adaptors or converters with you, as they are expensive here when they are available at all.

Embassies

All embassies and consulates close on Czech holidays (*see p292*) and on their own national holidays. For other embassies, consult the *Zlaté stránky* (*Yellow Pages*) under 'Zastupitelské úřady'.

American Embassy

Tržiště 15, Malá Strana, Prague 1 (257 530 663/emergencies 257 532 716/www.usembassy.cz). Metro Malostranská/tram 12, 22, 23. **Open** 8am-noon Mon-Fri. **Map** p307 D3.

Australian Trade Commission & Consulate

Klimentská 10, Nové Město, Prague 1 (251 018 350). Metro Náměstí Republiky/tram 5, 8, 14. **Open** 9am-1pm, 2-5pm Mon-Fri. **Map** p309 M1.

British Embassy

Thunovská 14, Malá Strana, Prague 1 (257 530 278/ duty officer 602 217 700). Metro Malostranská/tram 12, 22. **Open** 8.30am-noon Mon-Fri. *Telephone enquiries* 9am-9pm Mon-Fri. **Map** p307 D3.

Canadian Embassy

Mickiewiczova 6, Dejvice, Prague 6 (272 101 800/ fax 272 101 890). Metro Hradčanská/tram 18, 22. **Open** 8.30am-12.30pm Mon-Fri.

Emergencies

All numbers listed below are free of charge.

First aid	155
Czech police	158
Fire	150

See also Health (*p279*), Helplines (*p281*) and Police (*p286*).

Gay & lesbian

Prague is a generally tolerant city and an increasingly popular destination for gay and lesbian travellers, though the proximity of Germany's major sex tourism market has led to a boomtown aspect to the commercial scene.

Help & information

The extensive online resource *Gay Guide* (prague.gayguide.net) boasts the most complete and up-to-date information available in English on the scene, where to stay, legalities and practicalities. For info on health, safe sex and other helpful organisations, *see below.*

Health

Prague isn't the healthiest place on earth. The Czech diet is pork-laden and low on fresh vegetables. Czechs top world beer-consumption charts and are unrepentant smokers. The city also has serious smog and an archaic public sanitation system to contend with. All of which makes Prague a great place for hypochondriacs.

The damp climate creates a haven for various moulds that can be hell for anyone with allergies. Salmonella thrives in a favourite Czech lunch item, mayonnaise meat salads which sit out for hours.

But if you do get ill, the chronically underfunded health-care system will soon have you feeling worse. If you have health insurance, the doctors will try to rack up points for the care they give, which they redeem for money from the health insurance companies. In general, though, if you pay cash (which is universally accepted), you'll get far better treatment than the locals who must rely on the state system.

Medical facilities are usually open 7.15am to 6pm weekdays only. If you're settling in Prague, it's best to find a GP (*rodinný* or *praktický lékař*), dentist (*zubní lékař*) and pediatrician (*dětský lékař*) close to your home or workplace. Many Czech doctors speak English or German, especially at hospitals (*nemocnice*) and medical centres (*poliklinika*).

Accident & emergency

Canadian Medical Care

Veleslavínská 30, Dejvice, Prague 6 (235 360 133/emergencies 724 300 301/www.cmc.praha.cz). Metro Dejvická/tram 20, 25, 26. **Open** 8am-6pm Mon, Wed, Fri; 8am-8pm Tue, Thur. **Credit** MC, V, DC.

Established general practice clinic with pediatrics, gynecaology, cardiology and other specialists.

Medicover Clinic

Tylovo náměstí 3/15, Nové Město, Prague 2 (234 630 111/ emergencies 603 555 006/call centre 1221/www.medicover.cz). Metro IP Pavlova/tram 4, 6, 16, 22, 34. **Credit** AmEx, MC, V. **Open** 7am-7pm Mon-Fri; 9am-noon Sat. **Map** p311 L8.

With a professional international staff, Medicover honours Central Health Insurance Office temporary insurance (*see p281*).

Motol Hospital

Fakultní nemocnice v Motole

V Úvalu 84, Smíchov, Prague 5 (224 433 681/emergencies 224 436 107-8/free phone 224 436155). Metro Hradčanská, then bus 108, 174. **Open** 24hrs daily. **Credit** AmEx, MC, V.

Emergency treatment, plus a hospital department dedicated to care of foreigners.

Na Homolce Hospital

Nemocnice Na Homolce

Roentgenova 2, Smíchov, Prague 5 (257 271 111/emergencies 257 272 191/paediatrics 257 272 025/emergencies 257 272 043/ www.homolka.cz). Tram 4, 7, 9/bus 167. **Open** *Emergency* 24hrs daily. *Paediatric department* 8am-4pm daily. **Credit** AmEx, MC, V.

English-speaking doctors and 24-hour emergency service. Care can be excellent, but given the state of the Czech public healthcare system, a private clinic is advisable. Home visits can be arranged.

Complementary medicine

Czechs have a long history of herbal cures and have embraced many Eastern medical practices. The average pharmacy (*lekárna*) stocks teas for everything from menstrual cramps to bronchitis, but you will need the help of a Czech friend. Check the *Zlaté stránky*, or *Yellow Pages* (English index at the back) for 'Health Care – Alternative Medicine'.

Contraception & abortion

Condoms are widely available in Prague and are stocked at many grocers. Abortion is safe and legal and can be arranged through most clinics.

Dentists

Dental emergencies

Palackého 5, Nové Město, Prague 1 (224 946 981). Metro Můstek/tram 3, 9, 14, 24. **Open** 7am-6.30pm Mon-Fri. **No credit cards. Map** p310 J6.

European Dental Center

Václavské náměstí 33, Nové Město, Prague 1 (224 228 984/www. edcdental.cz).Metro Můstek/tram 3, 9, 14, 24. **Open** 8.30am-8pm Mon-Fri; 9am-1pm Sat. **Credit** MC, V. **Map** p309 K5.

Medicover Clinic

Tylovo náměstí 3/15, Nové Město, Prague 2 (234 630 111/emergencies 603 555 006/ call centre 1221/www.medicover. cz). Metro IP Pavlova/tram 4, 6, 16, 22, 34. **Open** 7am-7pm Mon-Fri; 9am-midnight Sat. **Credit** AmEx, MC, V. **Map** p311 L8.

Motol Hospital

Fakultní nemocnice v Motole

V úvalu 84, Smíchov, Prague 5 (224 433 681/224 431 111/ emergencies 224 436 107-8/free phone 224 436 155/www.fnmotol. cz). Metro Hradčanská, then bus 108, 174. **Open** 24hrs daily. **Credit** AmEx, MC, V.

Opticians

Most Western clinics (*see above*) have referral services for opticians, although glasses shops, such as Eiffel Optic (*see p178*) have licensed opticians on site, who can determine your prescription.

Pharmacies

Many central pharmacies (*lékárna* or *apothéka*) have been doing business in the same place for centuries and have gorgeous period interiors that are worth seeking out even if you're super healthy.

Over-the-counter medicines are only available from pharmacies, which are usually open 7.30am to 6pm weekdays, though some operate extended hours. Pharmacies display directions to the nearest 24-hour pharmacy in their window, though this info will be in Czech. Ring the bell for after-hours service, for which there's usually be a surcharge of approximately 30 Kč.

24-hour pharmacies

Belgická 37, Vinohrady, Prague 2 (222 519 731). Metro Náměstí Míru/tram 4, 6, 16, 22, 23. **No credit cards. Map** p311 M9.
Palackeho 5, Nové Město, Prague 1 (224 946 982). Metro Můstek. **No credit cards. Map** p311 K6

STDs, HIV & AIDS

ČSAP (Česká Společnost AIDS Pomoc)/Lighthouse (Dům Světla)

Malého 3, Karlin, Prague 8 (224 810 702/web.telecom.cz/AIDS-pomoc). Metro Florenc/tram 8, 24. **Volunteers available** 9am-4pm Mon-Fri.
ČSAP is the Czech organisation for AIDS prevention and for the support of people with HIV or AIDS. In addition to a 24hr hotline, it runs the Lighthouse, a hospice for those with HIV who would otherwise have nowhere else to go.

Women's health

Bulovka Hospital

Budínova 2, Libeň, Prague 8 (266 083 239/266 083 240). Metro Palmovka/tram 12, 14. **Open** 24hrs daily.
Housed within a huge state hospital complex, the privately run MEDA Clinic here is favoured by British and American women. Prices are reasonable, the gynaecologists speak English along with some other languages and the facilities are clean and professional. Contraception and HIV testing are available.

Dr Kateřina Bittmanová

Mánesova 64, Vinohrady, Prague 2 (office 222 724 592/603 551 393/home 272 936 895). Metro Jířího z Poděbrad/tram 11. **Open** 7am-4pm Mon-Fri. **Map** p313 B3.
Dr Bittmanová speaks fluent English. She runs a friendly private practice and is on call 24 hours a day. Her fee for a general examination is 900 Kč; a smear test costs an extra 450 Kč.

Podolí Hospital

Podolské nábřeží 157, Podolí, Prague 4 (296 511 111). Tram 3, 16, 17. **Open** 24hrs daily.
The Podolí Hospital has obstetricians and gynaecologists who speak English. With modern facilities and neonatal care, it handles most births to expats.

RMA Centrum

Dukelských hrdinů 17, Holešovice, Prague 7 (233 378 809). Tram 4, 12, 14, 17, 26. **Open** 7am-5pm daily. **Map** p312 D2.
This alternative medicine centre offers homeopathy, acupuncture and acupressure, traditional Chinese medicine and massage, as well as gynaecology and mammography.

Helplines & crisis centres

Helplines generally run around the clock, but you have a better chance of catching an English speaker if you call during regular office hours. For AIDS crisis helplines, *see above*.

Alcoholics Anonymous (AA)

Na Poříčí 16, Nové Město, Prague 1 (224 818 247/736 458 870). Metro Florenc or Náměstí Republiky/tram 5, 8, 14, 26. **Meetings** 5.30pm daily. **Map** p309 M2.
Twelve-step programmes. Anyone with alcohol problems is welcome to call or attend. English spoken.

Crisis Intervention Centre

Centrum krizové intervence – Psychiatrická léčebna Bohnice. *Ústavní 91, Bohnice, Prague 8 (284 016 666). Metro Nádraží Holešovice, then bus 102, 177, 200.* **Open** 24hrs daily.
The biggest and best-equipped mental health facility in Prague, with lots of outreach programmes.

Drop In

Karolíny Světlé 18, Staré Město, Prague 1 (tel/fax 222 221 431/www.dropin.cz). Metro Staroměstská or Národní třída/ tram 6, 9, 17, 18, 22, 23. **Open** 9am-5.30pm Mon-Thur; 9am-4pm Fri. **Map** p308 G5.
Focusing on problems related to drug addiction, this informals clinic also offers HIV testing and counselling. You can call or drop 24 hours a day.

ID

Spot checks of foreigners' documents are not unheard of. A photocopy of your passport is usually sufficient. Bars and clubs virtually never ask for ID, but you may be asked to show a passport if changing money.

Insurance

Health

Foreigners are technically required to present evidence of health insurance to enter the Czech Republic, although in practice it is rarely asked for. Nationals of a country with which the Czech Republic has a reciprocal emergency health-care agreement are exempt. These countries are the United Kingdom, Greece and most of the republic's former allies in the ex-Warsaw Pact countries. However, visitors requiring a visa will have to provide proof of insurance with their application. The relevant bodies will issue visas to foreigners only for as long as they have valid health insurance.

Všeobecná zdravotní pojišťovna (Central Health Insurance), the main health insurance provider in the Czech Republic (*see below*), provides affordable policies to foreigners for urgent care coverage for up to a year. But, because of its massive debts and delayed payments, it isn't favoured by some doctors.

Most state clinics and hospitals, and a few private ones, accept VZP.

If you have travel insurance, make sure it covers central and eastern Europe.

Central Health Insurance Office

Všeobecná zdravotní pojišťovna *Tyršova 7, Nové Město, Prague 2 (221 972 111/www.vzp.cz). Metro IP Pavlova/tram 4, 16, 22.* **Open** 8am-6pm Mon-Thur; 8am-4pm Fri. **Map** p311 L9.

VZP is the main provider of health insurance in the Czech Republic, offering reasonable rates for short-term (30-day) periods.
Other locations: Na Perštýně 6, Staré Město, Prague 1 (221 668 111/fax 221 668 167); Orlická 4, Žižkov, Prague 3 (221 752 121/fax 221 752 177).

Property insurance

Insuring personal belongings is always wise and should be arranged before leaving home.

Internet

Most of the upper end hotels provide dataports these days, and there are internet cafés all over Prague. Try Jáma (*see p152*) or the Globe Bookstore & Coffeehouse (*see p144*).

If you have access to a modem line and a laptop, ask your ISP whether it has a Prague dial-in or a reciprocal arrangement with a local provider. Alternatively, if you are a frequent traveller or plan on a long stay, you could set up an account with a local ISP. The number of companies offering internet access here is growing and services are improving all the time. The standard rate for individual accounts, usually including unlimited browsing time and email, but not call charges, starts at about 900 Kč a month.

The main ISP in Prague is listed below. A list of Czech providers is also held at the Czech-language search engine Seznam (www.seznam.cz).

Telenor/Nextra

V Celnici 10, Nové Město, Prague 1 (221 181 211/www.nextra.cz/freephone 800 138 417). Metro Náměstí Republiky/tram 5, 8, 14. **Open** 8am-5am Mon-Fri. **No credit cards. Map** p309 L3.

Language

The Czech language was exiled from Bohemian officialdom and literature in favour of German until the national revival in the 19th century. Today Czech is spoken throughout Prague, though most places of business should have some English-speaking staff. German may help you in speaking to older Czechs, and many middle-aged ones speak Russian, which was a compulsory subject in schools before the Velvet Revolution.

Czech is a difficult but rewarding language to learn in that it helps penetrate the wall put up by rather shy Czechs. They light up upon hearing even an attempt at their mother tongue by a foreigner. For essential vocabulary, *see p293*.

Left luggage

There are left luggage areas/lockers at Hlavní nádraží (*see p270*) and Nádraží Holešovice (*see p271*), and at Florenc coach station (*see p271*).

Legal help

See law firms listed under Business (*see p276*) or contact your embassy (*see p279*).

Libraries

For a full list of Prague's libraries, ask at the National Library or look in the *Zlaté stránky* (*Yellow Pages*) under '*knihovny*'. Generally, you don't need to register to use reading rooms, but you do to borrow books – for this you'll need your passport and sometimes a document stating that you are a student, teacher, researcher or Prague resident. Libraries often have restricted opening hours and close in July and August.

British Council

Politických Vězňů 13, Nové Město, Prague 1 (221 991 111/www.britishcoucil.cz). Metro Muzeum/tram 11. **Open** 9am-7pm Mon-Fri. **Map** p311 K/L5.
The interior of the British Council's new location, Bredovský dvůr, was designed by the celebrated Czech architect Eva Jiřičná. The new classrooms at Bredovský dvůr are fitted with the latest technology. The reading room is stocked with all the major British newspapers and magazines, plus free internet terminals. The library is packed with materials and aids for TEFL and TESL teachers, but most of the literature in their collection is now at the Městská knihovna, or City Library (*see below*). The video library is eclectic; free screenings can be excellent.

City Library

Městská knihovna v Praze
Mariánské náměstí 1, Staré Město, Prague 1 (222 113 338/222 328 208/www.mlp.cz). Metro Staroměstská/tram 17, 18. **Open** *July, Aug* 9am-7pm Tue-Fri. *Sept-June* 9am-8pm Tue-Fri; 10am-5pm Sat. **Map** p308 H3.
The City Library is spacious, calm and state of the art. There's an excellent English-language literature section bolstered by 8,000 books and magazines from the British Council. The music and audio collections are also impressive. To borrow books (if you are staying in the Czech Republic less than six months) take your passport and a 1,000 Kč cash deposit.

National Library

Národní knihovna v Praze
Klementinum, Křižovnické náměstí 4, Staré Město, Prague 1 (221 663 331/fax 221 663 261/www.nkp.cz). Metro Staroměstská/tram 17, 18. **Open** 9am-7pm Mon-Sat. *Main reading room* 9am-10pm Mon-Sat. **Map** p308 G4.
A comprehensive collection of almost everything ever published in Czech and a reasonable international selection. This state-funded library has an ancient system of ordering books based on filling in little slips and throwing them in a box, which is emptied every two hours. The orders are brought after another hour (or a day if not stored on-site). Foreigners may only take books as far as one of the reading rooms.

Lost property

Most railway stations have a lost property office (*Ztráty a nálezy*). If you lose your passport, contact your embassy (*see p279*).

Central Lost Property Office

Karoliny Světlé 5, Staré Město, Prague 1 (224 235 085). Metro Národní třída/tram 6, 9, 17, 18, 22. **Open** 8am-5.30pm Mon, Wed; 8am-4pm Tue, Thur; 8am-2pm Fri. **Map** p308 G5.

Media

Business/news publications (English)

Business Central Europe
A monthly economics and business magazine from the *Economist.*

Central European Business Weekly
Prague-based business weekly.

Central European Economic Review
A monthly regional overview published by the *Wall Street Journal.*

The Fleet Sheet
www.fleet.cz
A daily one-page digest of the Czech press. Good coverage of major political and financial events. Faxed out each morning.

NewslineRadio Free Europe
www.rferl.org
Dry but informative daily overview of events in Eastern Europe and the former Soviet Union.

The Prague Tribune
www.prague-tribune.cz
Glossy, bilingual Czech-English monthly mag with an emphasis on business and social issues.

Radio Prague E-News
www.radio.cz
Czech state radio offers free daily news bulletins in English, Czech and other languages by email. Informative website.

General interest (English)

New Presence
English-language version of *Nová přitomnost*, a journal dating back to interwar Bohemia that offers a liberal and stimulating selection of opinion writing by both local and international writers. Not easy to find, but worth seeking out for an in-depth look at the Czech Republic. Try the Globe Bookstore & Coffeehouse (*see p144*).

The Prague Post
www.praguepost.com
The principal English-language weekly in the Czech Republic has come a long way in recent years, with cultural coverage that betters that of many papers in larger cities of the former East Bloc.

Think Again
www.thinkagain.cz
The most recent attempt at a free alt magazine has fairly thorough party listings, 'almost bi-lingual' content and lots of rants.

Transitions online
www.tol.cz
A Prague-based Czech magazine dedicated to strengthening independent journalism, *Transitions Online* is based in Prague and uses a network of locally based correspondents to provide unique, cross-regional analysis.

Czech newspapers

Blesk
The extremely popular *Blesk* ('Lightning') is a daily tabloid packed full of sensationalised news and celebrity scandals.

Hospodářské noviny
The Czech equivalent of the *Financial Times*; required reading for Czech movers and shakers.

Lidové noviny
An underground dissident paper in the communist days, *Lidové noviny*'s finest hour came in the early 1990s. Today, the paper is still respected in some right-wing and intellectual circles, but commercialism has taken a toll.

Mladá fronta Dnes
A former communist paper, *Dnes* has been the country's leading serious newspaper for years.

Právo
The former Communist Party newspaper (the name means 'Justice'; it used to be *Rudé Právo* – 'Red Justice') has become a respectable, left-leaning daily with an equally respectable circulation.

Respekt
A scrappy weekly paper, *Respekt* takes a close look at the good, the bad and the ugly effects of the Czech Republic's transformation to a market economy.

Sport
Daily sports paper with scores that are just about decipherable to non-Czech speakers.

Czech periodicals

Cosmopolitan/Elle
The local *Cosmo* fails to stand up against its Western counterparts, but *Czech Elle* successfully appeals to both teens and middle-aged women, with flashy fashion spreads and interviews.

Reflex
Reflex is a popular, low-rent style weekly with glossy format and some interesting editorial.

Živel
A cyber-punk mag with a slick design and a sub-culture slant – like a cross between *The Face* and *Wired*. It is more likely to be found in bookshops than at newsagents, and is published irregularly.

Listings

Annonce
A classifieds sheet into which bargain-hunting Czechs delve to find good deals on second-hand washing machines, TVs, cars, etc. *Annonce* is also a good flat-hunting tool. Place your ad for free, then wait by the phone – it works.

Culture in Prague
An exhaustive monthly calendar of all categories of events held throughout Prague and the republic. Published mainly in Czech, it's also available in English at Wenceslas Square bookshops. The film listings are notoriously unreliable, though.

Do města
'Downtown' is a tall-format free entertainment sheet in Czech with English translations. It's good for weekly listings of galleries, cinemas, theatres and clubs. It comes out every Thursday in bars, cafés and clubs all around town.

Kulturní přehled
A thorough monthly listing of cultural events in Prague. It's in Czech only, but asking for help deciphering it can be a great café conversation starter. Schedules for theatres, operas, museums, clubs and exhibitions.

Literary magazines

Though many have folded over the past few years, a whole pile of literary magaziness is still published in Prague, in both Czech and English. Track them down at the Globe Bookstore & Coffeehouse (*see p144*) or Big Ben Bookshop (*see p163*). The Czech-language *Revolver Review*, supposedly published quarterly (but distinctly irregular), is a hefty periodical with *samizdat* (underground) roots. The *RR* presents new works by well-known authors, along with lesser-known pieces by favourites such as Kafka. *Labyrint Revue*, a monthly magazine, and the weekly *Literární noviny* are the other two main Czech publications that offer both original writing and reviews of new work.

English publications tend to come and go. The best and most widely known is *Trafika*, a 'quarterly' – tending to lapse to an 'occasional' – showcase for international writers. Although it has recently been out of action, *Trafika*'s editors may yet revive this early and respected pioneer.

The *Prague Review*, formerly the *Jáma Review*, is a slim quarterly of plays, prose and poetry from Czechs and expats. Editors have included such literary heavyweights as Bohumil Hrabal, Ivan Klíma and Miroslav Holub.

Optimism is a monthly literary mag that's a forum for Prague's English-speaking expat community; its content ranges from the intriguing to the hopelessly trite, but it is genuinely open to young, unproven writers.

Foreign press

Foreign newspapers are available at stalls on and around Wenceslas Square and at major hotels. The *International Guardian*, *International Herald Tribune* and the international *USA Today* are available on the day of publication. Other papers arrive 24 hours later.

Television

ČT1/ČT2

There are two national public channels. ČT1 tries to compete with TV Nova, but is out of its depth financially. ČT2 serves up serious music, theatre and documentaries to the small percentage of the population that tunes in. ČT2 sometimes broadcasts English-language movies with Czech subtitles on Monday evenings. It also airs Euronews, an English-language pan-European programme, on weekdays (usually at noon) and on weekends at 7.30am.

Prima TV

A Prague-based regional broadcaster that has been lamely following the lead of TV Nova, but is slowly being revamped by new foreign partners from the West.

TV Nova

One of the first private television stations in Eastern Europe, TV Nova was initially funded by Ronald Lauder, son of Estée. It looks like US television, with old Hollywood films and recycled sitcoms dubbed into Czech.

Radio

BBC World Service (101.1 FM)

English-language news on the hour, plus regular BBC programming. For 30 minutes a day at around teatime, it transmits local Czech news in English.

Expres Radio (90.3)

A recently established station winning increasing audience with fresh programming and alt pop.

Radio 1 (91.9)

An excellent alternative music station. The Friday evening calendar show with Tim Otis (*see p227* **Bad Bohemia: DJ Tim Otis**) has everything the hip party-goer needs to know.

Radio Free Europe

Prague is now the world headquarters for RFE. It still beams the same old faintly propagandist stuff, mainly to the Middle East now, from its HQ at the former Czechoslovak Federal Assembly building.

Radio Kiss (98.0 FM); Radio Bonton (99.7 FM); Evropa 2 (88.2 FM)

Pop music, pop music and more pop music – Prague's top three mainstream music stations.

Radio Prague (92.6 FM & 102.7 FM)

Daily news in English, plus interviews, weather and traffic. Nothing too inspired, but this is a well-established station with some history behind it.

Money

Currency

The currency of the Czech Republic is the *koruna česká* or Czech crown (abbreviated to Kč). One crown equals 100 hellers (*haléřů*). Hellers come as small, light coins in denominations of 50 – after that it's 1 Kč. There are 1, 2, 5, 10, 20 and 50 Kč coins in circulation. Notes come in denominations of 20, 50, 100, 200, 500, 1,000, 2,000, and 5,000 Kč. At the time of going to press, the exchange rate was running at about 46.3 Kč to the British pound, or around 25.4 Kč to the US dollar. It's impossible to predict exchange rates, but recently they have been fluctuating upwards, so convert only as much as you need in the short-term.

The crown was the first fully convertible currency in the former East Bloc. A bizarre indicator of its viability is the number of convincing counterfeit Czech banknotes in circulation. If someone stops you in the street asking if you want to change money, it's a fair bet he'll be trying to offload dodgy notes.

Cash economy

The Czech Republic has long been a cash economy, and such conveniences as cash machines (ATMs), credit cards and cheques – travellers' cheques included – are not nearly as ubiquitous here as they are in European Union countries or the US. However, this is changing rapidly

Girls' war

Even if feminism hadn't been made a dirty word by the pre-1989 regime, visiting women might find Prague challenging at times.

Having doors opened for you and drinks paid for is nice, but other old-fashioned customs may be harder to bear. When out for a drink, for instance, if a man gets a bit grabby, he's rarely admonished. A waiter will almost invariably ask the man what wine to bring, and, even if a woman orders, it's likely to be offered to the man for tasting.

Men certainly help perpetuate the traditional roles, but is it daring to suggest that some of the differences are reinforced by the sylph-like Czech woman herself? Afterall, the *žena* manages to be sexy even when – or perhaps especially when – she's cleaning the house. A Londoner might rave about his new girlfriend's taste in film. His counterpart in Prague is more likely to be overheard saying 'You should see what she's done to the bathroom. I can see myself in the sink!'

Most of the local women of dating age – they're often home with babies by their mid-20s – are dressed to kill, in mini skirts and big shoes, whether working at a sausage stand, in the office, or on the streets in freezing winter. Sex is all around: couples have little compunction about making out enthusiastically in public – especially if it's dark or leafy. Advertisements too use sex in remarkably unsubtle ways and a popular weather forecast on national television hankered for ratings for years with its male and female strippers. Even in the literary world, whether it's Kundera, Klíma or a Jiří Menzel adaptation of Hrabal's works, Czech female characters often get the roles of maternal figures or sexpots. Ideally both.

Still, Czech men, in their unique way, certainly take pride in Slavic womanhood. They can often be heard muttering: 'There are over 10,000 American men here, married to our women. Why do you think that is?' Indeed, it is impressive to see *modelky* outdrinking anybody, at any time, anywhere (without gaining any weight). And few grown Czech men would have the temerity to disobey their mothers.

Perhaps this a legacy of ancient times? An important figure in pre-Christian mythology in Czech lands is Šárka, the cunning and brutal leader of the 'Girls' War'.

Admittedly, though, the status of Czech women seems to have fallen a bit since then. One can think of several historic reasons for the entrenched gender roles in the former East Bloc. Feminism as an ideology was badly undermined when the Soviets used the notion of women's equality as a justification for adding factory work to a full-time mother's schedule. Most intelligent, liberal Czech women still shy away from identifying themselves as 'feminists' if they want to be taken seriously. The media doesn't help either, often equating feminists with 'bra-burning loonies'. Even today, as Czech women push their way slowly into positions of power, they still have to shoulder most of the responsibility for chores and kids. As in many countries further west, having it all is doing it all.

There's hope yet that the spirit of Šárka will revive. But in the meantime, women in Prague may have to take comfort in one of the most valued courtesies men are still expected to show: when walking into a pub a male companion is expected to enter first – just in case there are any flying beer glasses.

and, in Prague, it's not difficult to find ATMs that will pay out cash on the major credit and charge card networks such as Maestro, Cirrus and Delta. Many classier shops, and restaurants, especially around Wenceslas Square and Staré Město (Old Town), accept credit cards and travellers' cheques in major currencies.

Loss/theft

The Komerční banka (*see p286*) acts as a local agent for MasterCard and Visa; in case of loss or theft call the telephone numbers given below. For lost or stolen AmEx cards, call 222 800 222, and for Diners Club call 267 314 485. To report missing travellers' cheques, call 222 800 237 for American Express or 221 105 371 for Travelex.

Banks & currency exchange

You'll find that exchange rates are usually the same all over Prague, but banks take a lower commission. However, they are only open during business hours (usually 8am to 5pm Monday to Friday).

Bureaux de change usually charge a higher commission for changing cash or travellers' cheques, although some (like those at the Charles Bridge end of Karlova street) may only take one per cent – though this can mean you're getting a poor exchange rate.

Opening an account

At some banks, such as ČSOB, there is no minimum requirement to open an account and foreign currency accounts are available without the high fees once charged.

Money transfer

To get money fast, try the American Express office or, in an emergency, your embassy. The Na příkopě branch of ČSOB processes transfers the fastest.

American Express

Václavské náměstí 56, Nové Město, Prague 1 (224 219 992). Metro Můstek or Muzeum/tram 3, 9, 11, 14, 24. **Open** 9am-7pm daily. **Map** p311 L6.

Cardholders can receive their mail and faxes here and have personal cheques cashed, but not third-party cheques.

Československá obchodní banka (ČSOB)

Na příkopě 14, Nové Město, Prague 1 (224 111 111). Metro Můstek or Náměstí Republiky/tram 3, 5, 9, 14, 24. **Open** 8am-5pm Tue-Thur; 8am-4pm Fri. **Map** p309 K4.

Specialises in international currency transactions and offers professional service, if long waits for transfers from abroad.

Komerční banka

Na příkopě 33, Nové Město, Prague 1 (222 432 111/ emergencies 224 248 110). Metro Můstek or Náměstí Republiky/tram 3, 5, 9, 14, 24. **Open** 9am-6pm Mon, Wed; 8am-5pm Tue, Thur, Fri. **Map** p309 K4.

The country's largest full-service bank, with a large network of branches throughout the country. The ATMs accept international credit cards and the bank is a MasterCard and Visa agent.

Živnostenská banka

Na příkopě 20, Nové Město, Prague 1 (224 121 111). Metro Můstek/tram 3, 5, 9, 14, 24. **Open** 8.30am-5pm Mon-Fri. **Map** p309 K4.

This old trading bank, housed in one of the most beautiful buildings in Prague, has long experience in working with foreign clients. Most staff speak a reasonable level of English.

Natural hazards

Deer ticks are known to transmit encephalitis in Central and Eastern Europe, for which a vaccine is available at many clinics. Ticks found should be smothered in soap or Vaseline, then removed by twisting in an anti-clockwise direction.

Lightning strikes are most prevalent in summer in Bohemia but pose little hazard unless you are on open ground at high elevations.

Air quality in Prague has improved, but pollution regulation is poorly enforced and the incidence of cancer is well above Western Europe's.

Numbers

Dates are written in the standard order of day, month, year. When writing figures, Czechs put commas where Americans and Britons would put decimal points and vice versa, thus ten thousand Czech crowns is written as 10.000 Kč.

Opening hours

Standard opening hours for most shops and banks are from 8am or 9am to 5pm or 6pm, Monday to Friday. Many shops are open a bit longer and from 9am to noon or 1pm on Saturday. Shops with extended hours are called *večerka* (open until 10pm or midnight) and 'non-stop' (open 24 hours daily). Outside the centre, most shops are closed on Sundays and holidays. Shops frequently close for a day or two for no apparent reason; some shops close for an hour or two at lunch; and some shops and many theatres close for a month's holiday in August. Most places have shorter opening hours in winter (starting September or October) and extended hours in summer (starting April or May). Castles and some other attractions are only open in summer.

Police & security

Police in the Czech Republic are not regarded as serious crime fighters and are just barely considered keepers of law and order. Their past as pawns for the regime combined with a present reputation for corruption, racism and incompetence has prevented them from gaining much in the way of respect. If you are the victim of crime while in Prague, then don't expect much help from the local constabulary.

For emergencies, telephone 158. The main police station, at Na Perštýně and Bartolomějská, is open 24 hours daily. In theory, an English-speaker should be on call to assist crime victims with making a report, but in practice any encounter with the Czech police is likely to unpleasant and ineffective.

Legalities

You are expected to carry your passport or residence card at all times. If you have to deal with the police, they are supposed to provide an interpreter for you. Buying or selling street drugs is illegal and a Czech drug law outlaws the possession of even small quantities. The legal drinking age is 18, but little attention is paid to this.

Postal services

Stamps are available from post offices, newsagents, tobacconists and most places where postcards are sold. Postcards and standard letters (up to 20 grams) cost 9 Kč within Europe and 14 Kč for airmail outside Europe. Always use black or blue ink – never red or green – or a snippy clerk will refuse to accept your mail.

Post offices are scattered all over Prague. Though they are being thoroughly modernised, many have different opening hours and offer varying degrees of service. All are confusing, even for Czechs. The Main Post Office (*see below*) offers the most services, some available 24 hours a day. Fax, telegram and international phone services are in the annex at Politických vězňů 4. Some services, such as *poste restante* (general delivery) and EMS express mail are theoretically available at all post offices but are much easier to use at the main office on Jindřišská.

You can send mail overnight within the Czech Republic and within a few days to Europe and the rest of the world via EMS – a cheaper but less reliable service than commercial couriers.

PACKAGES

To send or collect restricted packages or items subject to tax or duty, go to the Customs Post Office (*see below*). Bring your passport. For incoming packages, you will also need to pay duty and tax.

Wrap outgoing packages in plain white or brown paper. Packages that weigh more than 2kg (4.4 pounds), are valued upwards of 30,000 Kč or contain 'unusual contents' such as medicine or clothing must officially be cleared through the Customs Post Office, but in practice this is not usually necessary.

Uninsured packages of up to 2kg don't need to be declared and can be sent from any post office (250 Kč to the UK; 593 Kč to the US), and you don't need your passport. Up to 4kg (8.8 pounds) the consignment is treated as a package, but if you don't want to insure it, it doesn't usually need to be declared and can be sent from a post office (457-505 Kč to the UK; 715-881 Kč to the US). If the package is heavier or you would like to insure it, take it to the Customs Post Office. Take your passport along with you.

USEFUL VOCABULARY

letters *příjem – výdej listovin*
packages *příjem – výdej balíčků* or *balíků*
stamps *známky* – at the window marked *Kolky a ceniny*
special issue stamps *filatelistický servis*
registered mail *doporučeně*

Customs Post Office

Celní Pošta
Plzeňská 139, Smíchov, Prague 5, (257 019 111). Metro Anděl, then tram 4, 7, 9. **Open** 8am-3pm Mon, Tue, Thur, Fri; 8am-6pm Wed. **No credit cards.**

Main Post Office

Hlavní pošta
Jindřišská 14, Nové Město, Prague 1 (221 131 445/221 131 111). Metro Můstek/tram 3, 9, 14, 24. **Open** 2am-midnight daily. **No credit cards. Map** p309 K5.

Masarykovo nádraží

Hybernská 15, Nové Město, Prague 1 (222 240 271). Metro Náměstí Republiky/tram 5, 8, 14. **Open** 8am-8pm Mon-Fri; 8am-midnight Sat. **Map** p309 L3.

Religion

Services in English are held at these churches:

Anglican Church of Prague

Klimentská, Nové Město, Prague 1 (222 310 094). Metro Náměstí Republiky/5, 8, 14 tram. **Services** 11am Sun. **Map** p309 K2.

Church of St Thomas

Josefská, Malá Strana, Prague 1 (257 532 675). Metro Náměstí Republiky. **Services** 6pm Sat; 11am Sun (in English). **Map** p307 E3. Catholic services.

Christian Fellowship

Ječná 19 (entry at back of house), Nové Město, Prague 2 (257 530 020/224 315 613). Metro Karlovo Náměstí. **Services** 6.30pm Sun. **Map** p310 H7.

International Baptist Church of Prague

Vinohradská 68, Žižkov, Prague 3 (224 254 646). Metro Jiřího z Poděbrad/tram 11. **Services** 11am Sun. **Map** p313 B3.

International Church of Prague

Peroutkova 57, Smíchov, Prague 5 (251 566 635/www.volny.cz/jx-studio). Metro Anděl, then bus 137 or 508. **Services** 10.30am Sun.

Safety

Prague has historically been a crossroads between Europe and Asia and a major transit point for goods both legal and otherwise, and the people who purvey them. Penalties for even minor drug possession are severe, so don't take chances.

Street crime consists mainly of pickpocketing, not violent crime, though many practitioners are experts. Prague's pickpockets tend to concentrate in tourist areas like Wenceslas Square, Old Town Square and the Charles Bridge and are particularly fond of the Slavia and tram No.22 from Malostranské náměstí to Prague Castle.

It's always a good idea to use your room safe, if you have one, carry with you only the cash that you need and keep a separate record of the numbers of any travellers' cheques and credit cards, along with contact information for reporting their loss.

Seedier parts of Prague include some of Žižkov, parts of Smíchov, the park in front of

Hlavní nádraží (the main train station), and the lower end of Wenceslas Square and upper end of Národní třída.

Smoking

Smoking is not allowed on public transport in Prague, but that's about the only place people don't light up. One or two restaurants now have non-smoking areas, but generally people around you will freely light up, even if they are sharing the table with you at a pub and you are eating a meal.

Study

Founded in 1348 by King Charles IV, Charles University (Universita Karlova; *see below*) is the oldest university in central Europe and the hub of Prague's student activity. Its heart is the Carolinum, a Gothic building on Ovocný trh near the Estates Theatre. Other university buildings are scattered all over the city.

Several cash-hungry faculties now run special courses for foreigners. Contact the relevant dean or the International Relations Office during the university year (October to May) for info on courses and admissions procedures. It's best to enquire in person at the university; staff can be difficult to reach by telephone.

Below is a selection of popular offerings. For courses outside Prague, contact the British Council (*see p282*).

Charles University

International Relations Office, Universita Karlova, Rektorát, Ovocný trh 3-5, Staré Město, Prague 1 (224 491 310/fax 224 229 487/www.cuni.cz). Metro Staroměstská or Můstek/tram 3, 9, 14, 17, 18, 24. **Open** 9am-5pm Mon-Fri. **Map** p308 J4.

FAMU

Smetanovo nábřeží 2, Staré Město, Prague 1 (224 220 955/fax 224 230 285). Metro Staroměstská or Národní třída/tram 6, 9, 17, 18, 22, 23. **Open** 9am-3pm Mon-Fri. **No credit cards. Map** p308 G4.

Famous for turning out such Oscar-winning directors as Miloš Forman, Prague's foremost school of film, TV and photography runs several English courses under its Film For Foreigners (3F) programme and Cinema Studies, including summer workshops (in co-operation with New York University, Washington, Miami and Boston).

The Institute of Language & Professional Training

Ústav jazykové a odborné přípravy *Universita Karlova, Vratislavova 10, Nové Město, Prague 2 (224 990 420/fax 224 990 440/www.cuni.czi/cuni/ujop). Metro Karlovo náměstí/tram 3, 16, 17, 21.* **Open** 10am-2pm Tue-Thur. **Fees** 530-120,000 Kč. **No credit cards.**

Aimed at preparing foreign nationals who want to embark on degree courses at Czech universities, this branch of Charles University offers various Czech-language training options.

School of Czech Studies

Filosofická fakulta, Universita Karlova, náměstí Jana Palacha 2, Staré Město, Prague 1 (221 619 280/www.ff.cuni.cz). Metro Staroměstská/tram 17, 18. **Open** 9-11am, 1-3pm Mon-Wed; 11am-3pm Thur; 9-11am, noon-2pm Fri. **Fees** 28,000-68,000 Kč. **No credit cards. Map** p308 G3.

Runs year-long courses during the school year, offering a mix of language instruction and lectures in Czech history and culture (Czech Studies programme).

Summer School of Slavonic Studies

Filosofická fakulta, Universita Karlova, náměstí Jana Palacha 2, Staré Město, Prague 1 (221 619 111/221 619 262/lsss.ff.cuni.cz/lssse.html). Metro Staroměstská/tram 17, 18. **Open** by appointment. **Fees** 15,000-33,000 Kč. **No credit cards. Map** p308 G3.

This one-month summer course, which is held every year in August, is designed for professors and advanced students in Slavonic studies.

Other courses

Anglo-American College

Lázeňská 4, Malá Strana, Prague 1 (257 530 202/www.aac.edu/www.aavs.cz). Metro Malostranská/tram 12, 18, 22, 23. **Open** 9am-5pm Mon-Fri. **Fees** 9,000-41,300 Kč. **No credit cards. Map** p307 E3/4.

A Western-accredited private college offering Western-style degree courses in business, economics, the humanities and law. Limited course offerings during the summer session.

Prague Center for Further Education

Šeříkova 10, Malá Strana, Prague 1 (257 534 013/www.prague-center.cz). Metro Malostranská, then tram 6, 9, 12, 22, 23. **Open** 9.30am-6pm Mon-Fri. **Fees** 2,600-5,600 Kč. **No credit cards. Map** p307 E5.

Dynamic and interactive courses in everything from Czech film to wine tasting.

Language courses

Many schools offer Czech-language instruction. If you prefer to take a more informal approach, place a notice on one of the boards at the Charles University Faculty, the Globe Bookstore (*see p163*), Radost FX (*see p222*) or anywhere else where young Czechs and foreigners meet. Since Czech grammar is difficult, most serious learners are advised to take some systematic, professional instruction to master the basics.

Akcent International House Prague

Bítovská 3, Kačerov, Prague 4 (261 261 638/fax 261 261 688/www.akcent.cz). Metro Budějovická. **Fees** *3wk intensive (20 lessons per wk)* 7,800 Kč; *standard (2 lessons per wk over a period of 20wks)* 5,500 Kč. **No credit cards.**

A co-op run and owned by the senior teachers, this school has a good reputation for standards and quality. All classes have a maximum size of six students.

ARS Linguarum

Legerova 39, Nove Město, Prague 2 (224 266 744/fax 224 266 740/www.arslinguarum.cz). Metro IP Pavlova. **Open** 9am-4.30pm. **Fees** 350-370 Kč per lesson. **No credit cards. Map** p311 L8.
Courses of Czech are run for English, German, French, Russian, Spanish and Italian speakers and are scheduled individually, beginning and ending any time during the year. The staff includes both Czech and foreign instuctors.

LBS

Vinohradská 184, Flora, Prague 3 (267 132 127/267 132 125/www.lbspraha.cz). Metro Flora/tram 10, 16. **Open** 8am-5pm. **Fees** 440 Kč/45min lesson.
This medium-sized language school, with reasonable prices and a very professional staff comes is recommended.

Lingua Viva

Spálená 57 & 21, Nové Město, Prague 1 (222 922 292/fax 224 921 142/www.linguaviva.cz). Metro Národní třída/tram 6, 9, 18, 21, 22, 23. **Open** 9am-7pm Mon-Thur; 9am-noon Fri. **Fees** 405-5,650 Kč. **No credit cards. Map** p310 H6.
This small independent school is an upstart, with better rates and more informal instruction than most.

State Language School

Státní jazyková Škola
Školská 15, Nové Město, Prague 1 (222 232 238/fax 222 232 236/www.sjs.cz). Metro Můstek/tram 3, 6, 9, 14, 17, 18, 22, 23, 24. **Open** 12.30-3.30pm Tue; 12.30-6.30pm Wed; 12.30-3.30pm Thur, Fri. **Fees** 4,065-14,760 Kč. **No credit cards. Map** p310 J6.
The largest and cheapest language school in Prague is state run and teaches just about every language under the sun.

Ulrych Language Studio

Benešovská 21, Vršovice, Prague 10 (267 311 300/fax 271 733 551/www.ulrych.cz). Metro Náměstí Míru/tram 10, 16. **Open** 8.30am-5pm. **Fees** 670 Kč/60min lesson; 1,000 Kč/90min lesson.
Ideal for company courses; the price includes overall testing every six months. The client can choose between intensive courses (20 hours a week) or standard courses running twice a week.

Student travel

CKM

Mánesova 77, Vinohrady, Prague 2 (222 721 595/fax 222 726 370). Metro Jiřího z Poděbrad/tram 11. **Open** 10am-6pm Mon-Thur; 10am-4pm Fri. **No credit cards. Map** p311 H6.
Specialises in cheap flights, and can issue Euro 26 discount cards.

GTS

Ve Smečkách 33, Nové Město, Prague 1 (222 211 204/296 157 777/call centre 844 140 140 or 257 187 100/www.gtsint.cz). Metro Muzeum/tram 3, 9, 14, 24. **Open** 8am-8pm Mon-Fri; 10am-4pm Sat. **Credit** AmEx, DC, MC, V. **Map** p311 K6.
The best place for ISIC card-holders to find cheap student fares. Especially good international flight bargains, as well as occasional deals on bus and train travel.
Other locations: BechyÀova 3, Dejvice, Prague 6 (224 325 235/fax 224 325 237).

Student Agency

Ječná 37, Prague 2, (224 999 666/fax 224 999 660/www.studentagency.cz). Metro IP Pavlova/tram 4, 6, 11, 16, 22, 23, 34. **Open** 9am-6pm Mon-Fri, 9am-1pm Sat. **Credit** MC, V. **Map** p311 K8.
This agency sells cheap flights, buses and trains for destinations outside the Czech Republic. As well as providing travel insurance, it can also issue ISIC cards, visas and working permits for programmes abroad.
Other locations: Ruzyně Airport, departure hall, plane tickets only (222 111 909/fax 222 111 902).

Telephones

The public payphones that still take 2 Kč coins are perpetually broken; the rest run on telephone cards, which come in denominations of 50 to 150 units and can be bought at newsstands, post offices and anywhere you see the blue and yellow ČeskýTelecom sticker. Local calls cost 3,80 Kč plus 22 per cent VAT for one unit (lasting two minutes from 7am to 7pm weekdays, and four and a half minutes from 7pm to 7am weekdays, all day weekends and public holidays). International calls, which are horrendously expensive unless you use a Trick Card (*see p290*), can be made from any phone box or more easily at a private booth at the Main Post Office (*see p287*).

The international dialling code for the Czech Republic is 420. To call abroad from Prague, dial the prefix 00, followed by the country and the area codes (for UK area codes, omit the initial 0) and then the number. The country code for the United Kingdom is 44, for America and Canada it's 1 and for Australia 61. If you use the prefix 952 00, then the country code, then the number, you will be connected on a digital line at a significant discount.

Since September 2002 all telephone numbers in Prague have been on digital switchboards. All fixed lines were amended, and phone numbers always have nine digits. If you come across an old Prague fixed line number starting with 02 followed by eight digits, omit the 0 and you should be able to get through. If 02 is only followed by seven digits you may have to phone the Information on 1180, tell the operator the old number and they'll give you the current one. Most operators speak some English. The *Zlaté stránky*, or *Yellow Pages*, also has an English-language index at the back.

Český Telecom

Czech Telecom
Olšanská 3, Žižkov, Prague 3 (freephone 800 123 456/www.telecom.cz). Metro Želivského/tram 5, 9, 16, 19. **Open** 8am-4pm Mon-Fri. **Map** p313 D2.

TRICK CARDS

Trick Cards, pre-paid long distance cards, are sold at newsagents for 175 Kč to 320 Kč. One unit is worth 3.60 Kč. The rate depends on the time and destination of the phone call. During peak times on a weekday between 7am and 7pm one unit lasts 40 seconds; at weekends and on public holidays it lasts 95 seconds. You can access the lines from any public or private phone via a code number.

Faxes

You can send faxes from the Main Post Office (*see p287*) from 7am to 8pm daily (counter No.2, look for *post fax*). Faxes to Great Britain as well as the US cost 63 Kč for the first page plus 28 Kč for each additional page. You can also receive a fax marked clearly with your name at the Main Post Office (fax 221 131 402). You will be charged 16 Kč for up to 5 pages, plus 2 Kč for each additional page.

Mobile phones

Competition has led to improved services and lower rates in the Czech Republic, but since January 2004 22 per cent VAT has been imposed on telecommunication services. Nevertheless, the Czechs are somewhat obsessed with mobile phones – 70 per cent of the population, from toddlers to grannies, own one. The three main companies that are listed below offer different payment schemes and coverage areas, so it's best to get details before deciding. They are also the only companies in town who rent out phones short-term – for exorbitant sums. If you are here for a short time, pick up a combination SIM and pre-paid card for your phone.

All three companies use both the 1,800 MHz and 900 MHz wavebands, which means that owners of all standard UK mobiles can use them if they have a roaming facility (which may need to be pre-arranged, check with your network provider before you go). Newer model US cell phones on the dual system now function in the Czech Republic as in the rest of Europe.

Eurotel

Vyskočilova 1442/1b, Michle, Prague 4 (800 330 011/www.eurotel.cz). Metro Českomoravská/tram 8. **Open** 8am-6pm Mon-Fri; 9am-1pm Sat. **No credit cards.**

Leading provider of mobile phone services and subsidiary of monopoly Český Telecom.

Český Mobil

Vinohradská 167, Vršovice, Prague 10 (freephone 800 777 777/www.oskarmobil.cz). Metro Strašnická/tram 17, 18. **Open** 9am-8pm Mon-Fri; 9am-2pm Sat. **No credit cards.**

Providers of the newest mobile phone service Oskar, Český Mobil has cheaper rates under some packages, but spotty coverage.

Radiomobil

Evropská 178, Dejvice, Prague 6 (24hr service 603 603 603/603 604 604/www.t-mobile.cz). Metro Dejvická/tram 2, 20, 26. **Open** 8am-6pm Mon-Fri. **No credit cards.**

Providers of T-Mobile, the main rival to Eurotel. English-language help and loads of different service packages are available at T-Mobil shops all over the city.

Time

The Czech Republic is on Central European Time (CET), one hour ahead of the UK, six hours ahead of New York and nine hours ahead of Los Angeles, and uses the 24-hour clock. The Czechs are very prompt; never be more than 15 minutes late for a meeting.

Tipping & VAT

Czechs tend to round up their restaurant bills, though often only by a few crowns, but foreigners are usually expected to leave a ten per cent tip. If service is bad, however, you shouldn't feel obliged to leave anything. You'll find that service is often added on automatically for large groups. Taxi drivers expect you to round the fare up, but, if you've just been ripped off, don't give a heller.

A value-added tax of 22 per cent has been slapped on to retail purchases for years in the Czech Republic but only as recently as 2000 was a system set up to reimburse non-resident foreigners' VAT payments. You can claim a refund at the border or at the Ruzyně airport in the departure hall at the Customs desk on the left. You'll need your shop receipt, passport and a VAT refund form, which staff can supply. Purchases of over 1,000 Kč are eligible if taken out of the country within 30 days of sale.

Toilets

Usually called a 'WC' (pronounce it 'veh-tseh'), the word for toilet is *záchod* and there is sometimes a charge of about 5 Kč for using one. Calls of nature can be answered in all metro stations from at least 8am to 8pm, and at many fast-food joints and department stores. 'Ladies' is *Dámy* or *Ženy*, 'Gents' *Páni* or *Muži*. Czech public loos, located primarily in metro or train stations, are often locked and are generally insalubrious.

Tourist information

The English-language weekly, *The Prague Post* (www.praguepost.com) carries entertainment sections along with survival hints. Monthly entertainment listings can be found in *Kulturní přehled* (in Czech), *Kultura v Praze* and its shorter English equivalent *Culture in Prague*. (*See also p283.*) The Prague Information

Service (PIS; *see below*) also publishes a free monthly entertainment listings programme in English.

The use of the international blue and white 'i' information sign is not regulated, so the places carrying it are not necessarily official.

The best map for public transport or driving is the widely available *Kartografie Praha Plán města* (a book with a yellow cover), costing about 100 Kč, though for central areas the co-ordinates are sometimes too vague. Check you've got the latest edition.

Čedok

Na příkopě 18, Nové Město, Prague 1 (224 197 642/224 197 615/fax 224 216 324/ www.cedok.cz). Metro Můstek/ tram 3, 5, 8, 9, 14, 24. **Open** 9am-7pm Mon-Fri; 9.30am-2.30pm Sat, Sun. **Map** p309 K4.
The former state travel agency is still the biggest in the Czech Republic.

PIS (Prague Information Service)

Pražská informační služba
Na příkopě 20, Nové Město, Prague 1 (general info 12444/ www.pis.cz). Metro Můstek/tram 3, 4, 8, 9, 14, 24. **Open** *Jan-Mar, Nov-Dec* 9am-6pm Mon-Fri; 9am-3pm Sat. *Apr-Oct* 9am-7pm Mon-Fri; 9am-5pm Sat, Sun.
Map p309 K4.
PIS provides incredibly wide-ranging, free tourist information, maps and help – all with a friendly smile.
Other locations: Hlavní nádraží (main train station), Wilsonova, Nové Město, Prague 1 (224 239 258); Old Town Hall, Staroměstské náměstí, Staré Město, Prague 1 (224 482 202/224 482 018); Na Příkopě 20, Nové Město, Prague 1 (224 226 090); Charles Bridge Tower on Malá Strana-side (summer only).

Visas

Requirements can change frequently, but at press time citizens of the US, UK and other EU countries and most other European countries did not need a visa to enter the Czech Republic for stays of up to 90 days – just a valid passport with at least six months to run by the end of their visit. Under a recent law aimed at preventing illegal residence by foreigners, however, border crossings can get complicated if you don't prepare. Foreigners who do require a visa to enter the Czech Republic, including, at press time, Canadians, Australians, New Zealanders and South Africans, can no longer get theirs at the border but must apply at a Czech embassy outside the Czech Republic (but not necessarily in their home country). The process may take weeks, so early planning is critical.

Even visitors who don't require a visa may now be asked for proof that they have sufficient finances, pre-arranged accommodation and international health insurance.

Automated, extremely confusing visa information is available in English at the Foreigners' Police in Prague (*see p292*) or at the Ministry of Foreign Affairs (224 182 125, www.mzv.cz). You are technically required to register at the local police station within 30 days of arriving (if you are staying at a hotel this will be done for you). If you are from one of the countries whose residents are allowed only 30 days in the Czech Republic, you must obtain an extended visa (confusingly called an exit visa, or *výjezdní vízum*) from the Foreigners' Police office to allow you up to 90 days in total.

Longer stays

The other option, if you want to stay longer, is a residence permit (*občanský průkaz*), which isn't easy to get and must be obtained from a Czech embassy abroad.

The Czech police tend to conduct periodic crackdowns on illegal aliens. These are usually aimed at Romanians, Ukrainians, Vietnamese and other nationals considered undesirable, though a few Brits and US citizens get caught. Even so, many expats reside here illegally.

Weather report

Average daytime temperatures, rainfall and hours of sunshine in Prague.

	Temp (°C/°F)	Rainfall (mm/in)	Sunshine (hrs/day)
Jan	0-5/32-41	62/2.5	2
Feb	1-4/34-40	73/2.9	3
Mar	0-7/32-45	65/2.6	5
Apr	3-12/37-5	78/3.1	6
May	8-17/46-63	63/2.5	8
June	12-21/54-70	50/2.0	9
July	13-23/55-73	25/1.0	9
Aug	14-22/57-72	50/2.0	8
Sept	10-17/50-63	55/2.2	6
Oct	5-14/41-57	100/3.9	4
Nov	1-5/34-41	110/4.3	2
Dec	0-2/32-36	76/3.0	1

Some avoid dealing with the above requirements by leaving and re-entering the country. Border police are getting wise to the trick, however, and it can't be relied on. If you try it, be sure to get the required stamp in your passport as you leave and re-enter by saying *'razítko prosím'* ('stamp please').

Foreigners' Police

Cizinecká policie
Sdružení 1, Pankrác, Prague 4 (974 820 935) Metro Pankrác.
Open 7.30-11.30am, 12.15-3pm Mon, Tue, Thur; 8am-12.15pm, 1-5pm Wed; 7.30am-11.30pm Fri.
Other locations: Olšanská 2, Žižkov, Prague 3.

Weights & measures

Czechs use the metric system, even selling eggs in batches of five or ten. Things are usually measured out in decagrams or '*deka*' (ten grams) or deciliters or '*deci*' (ten centilitres). So a regular glass of wine is usually two *deci* (abbreviated dcl), and ham enough for a few sandwiches is 20 *deka* (dkg).

When to go

Spring

Hotel prices rise, but Prague's most awaited season, sees the city shaking off the hibernation of a long, cold and cloudy winter. While it's not unheard of for snow to linger as late as early May, temperatures are often perfect for strolling at this time of the year.

Summer

Praguers usually leave for their country cottages (*chatas*) and abandon the city to the tourist hordes, leaving surprising hotel bargains in July and Aug but many closed venues. Summers are pleasant, warm (rarely hot) and prone to thundery showers. The days are long, and it stays light until 10pm.

Autumn

This can be the prettiest time of year, with crisp cool air and sharp blue skies, but it can also be the wettest. September is a good month to visit the city, with hotel prices falling but castles still open. The streets are once again jammed with cars, the parks full of children and the restaurants busy. The days grow shorter alarmingly quickly. By the end of October, the sun sets at around 5.30pm.

Winter

Street-side carp sellers and Christmas markets help break the monotony of the long, cold, grey winter. Rooms are at their most affordable (except during the holidays) and snow makes Prague so beautiful that you forget the gloom that blankets the city. Sadly, bright, white snow is rarely poetically accompanied by a clear blue sky. Many Prague residents still burn coal for heating, which doesn't help.

Public holidays

New Year's Day, 1 Jan; Easter Monday; Labour Day, 1 May; Liberation Day, 8 May; Sts Cyril & Methodius Day, 5 July; Jan Hus Day, 6 July; Statehood Day, 28 Sept; Czech Founding Day, 28 Oct; Struggle for Freedom Day, 17 Nov; Christmas holidays, 24-26 Dec

Women

Visitors to Prague will discover that traditional gender roles are entrenched in the Czech Republic and it's often conservative way of life. Indeed, feminism is still not taken very seriously (*see p285* **Girls' War**), although some women's organisations do exist. Most of these organisations emphasise women's rights as an integral part of human rights, rather than entering into any debate about that tricky word 'feminism'.

Ženské Centrum in Prague 2 (Gorazdova 20, 224 917 224) consists of two organisations: the first, proFem, focuses on protecting women from violence; and the other, the Centre for Gender Studies, deals with women's rights in general, organising seminars and educational campaigns. The Gender Studies Library (224 915 666) also has some materials in English.

Working in Prague

To work legally in Prague you will need to obtain a work permit along with the necessary residency permit (which is confusingly termed a 'Temporary Visa for over 90 Days'). Unless you already have the residency permit, which is only available from Czech embassies and consulates outside the republic (usually after a long wait) there's little hope of you being able to find legal work.

Work permits

If you do have the residency permit and are going to be employed by a Czech company, the company itself needs to obtain a work permit on your behalf. You'll need to provide evidence of your qualifications and, in some cases, proof of any relevant work experience as well, all of which should be accompanied by official notarised translations.

Resources

The *Prague Post's* web page (www.praguepost.com) contains a mini-guide to the Kafka-esque experience of living and working in the city, and its classifieds often feature ads from service agencies willing to help for a fee. *See also p291.*

Vocabulary

For Czech food and drink vocabulary, *see p134* **What's on the menu?**

Pronunciation

a	as in gap
á	as in father
e	as in let
é	as in air
i, y	as in lit
í, ý	as in seed
o	as in lot
ó	as in lore
u	as in book
ú, ů	as in loom
c	as in its
č	as in chin
ch	as in loch
ď	as in duty
ň	as in onion
ř	as a standard r, but flatten the tip of the tongue making a short forceful buzz like ž
š	as in shin
ť	as in stew
ž	as in pleasure
dž	as in George

The basics

Czech words are always stressed on the first syllable.

hello/good day *dobrý den*
good evening *dobrý večer*
good night *dobrou noc*
goodbye *nashledanou*
yes *ano* (often *o* or just *jo*)
no *ne*
please *prosím*
thank you *děkuji*
excuse me *promiňte*
sorry *pardon*
help! *pomóc!*
attention! *pozor!*
I don't speak Czech *nemluvím česky*
I don't understand *nerozumím*
Do you speak English? *Mluvíte anglicky?*
sir *pán*
madam *paní*
open *otevřeno*
closed *zavřeno*
I would like... *Chtěl bych...*
How much is it? *kolik to stojí?*
May I have a receipt, please? *účet, prosím*
Can we pay, please? *zaplatíme, prosím*
where is... *kde je...*
go left *doleva*
go right *doprava*
straight *rovně*
far *daleko*
near *blízko*
good *dobrý*
bad *špatný*
big *velký*
small *malý*
no problem *to je v pořádku*
Do you have any light food here? *Máte nějaké lehké jídlo?*
Cool piercing! *dobrej piercing!*
It's a rip-off *to je zlodějina*
I'm absolutely knackered *jsem uplně vyfluslý*
The lift is stuck *výtah zůstal viset*
Could I speak to Václav? *mohl bych mluvit s Václavem?*

Street names, etc

In conversation most Prague streets are referred to by their name only, leaving off *ulice*, *třída* and so on.

avenue *třída*
bridge *most*
church *kostel*
gardens *sady* or *zahrada*
island *ostrov*
lane *ulička*
monastery, convent *klášter*
park *park*
square *náměstí* or *nám*
station *nádraží* or *nádr*
steps *schody*
street *ulice* or *ul*
tunnel *tunel*

Numbers

0	*nula*
1	*jeden*
2	*dva*
3	*tři*
4	*čtyři*
5	*pět*
6	*šest*
7	*sedm*
8	*osm*
9	*devět*
10	*deset*
11	*jedenáct*
12	*dvanáct*
13	*třináct*
14	*čtrnáct*
15	*patnáct*
16	*šestnáct*
17	*sedmnáct*
18	*osmnáct*
19	*devatenáct*
20	*dvacet*
30	*třicet*
40	*čtyřicet*
50	*padesát*
60	*šedesát*
70	*sedmdesát*
80	*osmdesát*
90	*devadesát*
100	*sto*
1,000	*tisíc*

Days & months

Monday	*pondělí*
Tuesday	*úterý*
Wednesday	*středa*
Thursday	*čtvrtek*
Friday	*pátek*
Saturday	*sobota*
Sunday	*neděle*

January	*leden*
February	*únor*
March	*březen*
April	*duben*
May	*květen*
June	*červen*
July	*červenec*
August	*srpen*
September	*září*
October	*říjen*
November	*listopad*
December	*prosinec*

Spring	*jaro*
Summer	*léto*
Autumn	*podzim*
Winter	*zima*

Pick-up lines

What a babe! *To je kost!*
What a stud! *Dobrej frajer!*
Can I walk you to the pig slaughter? *Můžu tě doprovodit na zabijačku?*
Do you want to try my goulash? *Chceš ochutnat můj guláš?*
I love you *Miluju Tě*
Another drink? *Ještě jedno?*

Put-down lines

What are you staring at? *Na co čumiš?*
Shit your eye out! *Vyser si oko!*
That pisses me off! *To mě sere!*
You jerk! *Ty vole!*
You bitch! *Ty děvko!*

Further Reference

Books

Literature & fiction

Brierley, David
On Leaving a Prague Window
Readable but dated thriller set in post-communist Prague.

Chatwin, Bruce *Utz*
Luminous tale of a Josefov porcelain collector.

Hašek, Jaroslav
The Good Soldier Švejk
Rambling comic masterpiece set in World War I, by Bohemia's most bohemian writer.

Havel, Václav
The Memorandum; *Three Vaněk Plays*; *Temptation*
The President's work as playwright.

Hrabal, Bohumil
I Served The King of England; Total Fears
The living legend's most Prague-ish novel, *I Served the King of England* tracks its anti-hero through a decade of fascism, war and communism. *Total Fears* is a lush new translation by the respected Twisted Spoon Press.

Kundera, Milan *The Joke*; *The Book of Laughter and Forgetting*; *The Unbearable Lightness of Being*
Milan Kundera's tragi-comic romances are still the runaway bestselling sketches of Prague.

Leppin, Paul
Others' Paradise/Severin's Journey into the Dark
Recently translated work from pre-War Prague German writer.

Meyrink, Gustav *The Golem*
The classic version of the tale of Rabbi Loew's monster, set in Prague's Jewish Quarter.

Neruda, Jan *Prague Tales*
Wry and bittersweet stories of life in 19th-century Malá Strana, from Prague's answer to Dickens.

Škvorecký, Josef *The Engineer of Human Souls*
The magnum opus of the chronicler of Czech jazz.

Topol, Jáchym
Sister City Silver
A long-awaited translation of three noir novellas by one of the city's leading young writers.

Wilson, Paul (ed) *Prague: A Traveller's Literary Companion*
Excellent collection organised to evoke Prague's sense of place.

Kafka

Kafka, Franz *The Castle*; *The Transformation & Other Stories*; *The Trial*
Kafka classics.

Anderson, Mark M
Kafka's Clothes
Erudite and unconventional book encompassing Kafka, dandyism and the Habsburg culture.

Brod, Max
Franz Kafka: A Biography
The only biography by someone who actually knew the man.

Hayman, Ronald
K: A Biography of Kafka
Widely available, dependable.

Karl, Frederick *Franz Kafka: Representative Man*
A thorough and thoughtful account of the man and his work.

History, memoir & travel

Demetz, Peter
Prague in Black and Gold
Thoughtful exploration of prehistoric to First Republic life.

Garton Ash, Timothy *The Magic Lantern: The Revolution of 1989 Witnessed in Warsaw, Budapest, Berlin and Prague*; *History of the Present*
Oxford academic's on-the-spot 1989 history and his look back a decade later, painfully explore the morality of the Velvet Revolution.

Rimmer, Dave
Once Upon a Time in the East
Communism seen stoned and from ground level.

Ripellino, Angelo Maria
Magic Prague
Mad masterpiece of literary and cultural history, which celebrates the city's sorcerous soul.

Sayer, Derek
Coasts of Bohemia
Phenomenally well-researched and witty account of the millennium-long Czech search for identity.

Shawcross, William *Dubček*
Biography of the Prague Spring figurehead, updated to assess his role in the 1989 Velvet Revolution.

Essays & argument

Čapek, Karel
Towards the Radical Centre
Selected essays from the man who coined the word 'robot'.

Havel, Václav
Living in Truth; *Letters to Olga*; *Disturbing the Peace*
His most important political writing, his prison letters to his wife, and his reflections.

Miscellaneous

Holub, Miroslav
Supposed to Fly
This collecion of poetry by this former dissident was inspired by his youth in war-torn Plzeň.

Iggers, Wilma
A Women of Prague
Fascinating – lives of 12 women, across 200 years.

Sís, Petr *Three Golden Keys*
Children's tale set in Prague, with wonderful drawings.

Various eds *Prague: 11 Centuries of Architecture*
Solid and substantial.

Film

Many of the following films can be viewed on video at, or rented from, Virus Video (*see p180*) or found periodically at film festivals or video shops.

Ecstasy (Extáze)
Gustav Machatý (1932)
Known primarily for its groundbreaking nude scene with the nubile actress who would later be known as Hedy Lamarr, this imagistic film depicts a girl frustrated with her relationship with an older man.

The Long Journey (Daleká cesta) *Alfred Radok (1949)*
Banned by the communists for 20 years, this film depicts the deportation of Jews to concentration camps.

The Great Solitude (Velká samota) *Ladislav Helge (1959)*
The Great Solitude is one of the few pre-new wave movies that goes deeper than farm-tool worship, this film focuses on how tough it is to be a rural party official.

The Shop on Main Street (Obchod na korze) *Ján Kadár & Elmar Klos (1964)*
Set during World War II in the Nazi puppet state of Slovakia, it's about an honest carpenter who must act as the person 'Aryanising' a button shop run by an old Jewish woman. Winner of the 1966 Oscar for Best Foreign Film.

Intimate Lighting (Intimní osvětlení) *Ivan Passer (1965)*
Possibly the most delightful film of the Czech New Wave, which tells of the reunion of two old friends after many years.

Larks on a String (Skřivánci na niti) *Jiří Menzel (1969)*
This tale of forced labour in the steel mills of industrial Kladno deals with politics a bit, but love – and libido – somehow always triumph. Banned soon after its release, the film was not shown again until 1989 – when it won the Berlin Film Festival's Golden Bear.

The Ear (Ucho) *Karel Kachyňa (written by Jan Procházka) (1970)*
The full force of surveillance terror and paranoia is exposed in this chilling film, whose origins go further back than the communists to Kafka. The film was banned instantly.

Otesánek *Jan Švankmajer (2000)*
Švankmajer updates a classic Czech myth about a childless couple who adopt an insatiable baby made from tree roots.

Divided We Fall (Musíme si pomáhat) *Jan Hřebejk (2001)*
The Oscar-nominated tale of a small Czech village in wartime and its residents' confrontations with moral decisions.

Želary *Ondřej Trojan (2004)*
This World War II melodrama nominated for Best Foreign Film Oscar tells the story of a nurse hiding out in a village.

Music

Dan Bárta: Entropicture (Sony)
Dan Bárta, the soulful reigning prince of Czech pop rock takes a thoughtful turn with some respected jazz men about town.

Ecstasy of St Theresa: In Dust 3 (EMI)
Jan P Muchow creates a textured digital background for the provocative vocals of Kateřina Winterová.

Rok Ďábla (Sony Music/Bonton)
This soundtrack from the hit film of the same name presents the songs of beloved Czech folk balladeer Jarek Nohavica in a completely new light.

Various: Future Sound of Prague (Intellygent)
Reliable series of the best of house and ambient sounds heard around the city's most plugged-in clubs.

Homegrown classics

Czech Serenade *Antonín Dvořák, Josef Suk, Vítězslav Novák, Zdeněk Fibich, Leoš Janáček (Supraphon)*
The pantheon of great Czech composers, in performances by a range of artists including the Czech Philharmonic and a gallery of top-class chamber players, mostly digitally recorded. The works incorporate old Czech and Moravian folk influences.

Jan Ladislav Dusík: Piano Concerto, Sonatas *Jan Novotný, Prague Chamber Philharmonic, conducted by Leoš Svárovský (Panton)*
The Prague Chamber Philharmonic delivers the energy that has set it apart from the city's larger orchestras in these excellent recordings of Dusík's 'Concert Concerto for Piano and Orchestra' in E flat major, 'Op 70' and two of his more lyrical sonatas, the F Sharp minor 'Op 61' and the A flat major 'Op 64'. Novotný's playing is particularly expressive.

Martinů, Bohuslav: Double Concerto *Orchestre National de France (Teldec/Erato)*
This lyrical composition, performed with sensitivity by soloists Jean-François Heisser and Jean Camosi, and conducted by James Conlon, provides a toothsome taste of the rarely heard modernist Czech composer at his best.

Pavel Šporcl *Pavel Šporcl (Supraphon)*
This unorthodox Czech violin virtuoso has won over audiences with his deft treatment of Smetana, Dvořák, Janáček and Martinů. This is his star debut.

Zdeněk Fibich: Symphony No 1 in F major, Symphony No 2 in E flat major, Symphony No 3 in E minor
This is a set of symphonies by the little-known romantic Czech composer now receiving a well-deserved revival. Performed by the Czech Philharmonic Orchestra under Karel Šejna, it includes two excellent shorter works.

Websites

Czech-English Dictionary
www.slovnik.cz
Millions of words translated from English, German, Italian, French and Spanish to Czech and back.

Czech Techno
www.techno.cz
The party-list link contains the original, authoritative list of what's on in the dance clubs all over town.

www.idos.cz
Searchable online train and bus timetables for every city and town in the Czech Republic.

Expats.cz
www.expats.cz
Online bulletin board with handy classifieds, tips on residency, apartment hunting and jobs.

Prague TV
prague.tv
Tune in for outlandish columns, food and drink tips, links to maps and the beer counter.

The Prague Post
www.praguepost.com
Prague's main English-language weekly reports on the issues, trends and culture with useful tourist information pages.

Prague Information Service
www.pis.cz
Comprehensive source for city events with well-organised pages of general tourist information.

Radio Free Europe/Radio Liberty
www.praguemonitor.cz
A witty daily roundup of all the latest links to English-language news and features related to the Golden City.

Time Out Prague Guide
www.timeout.com
Shameless self-promotion it may be, but here's where you'll find the best of what's new in Prague.

Index

Note: Page numbers in **bold** indicate chapters and main references; page numbers in *italics* indicate photographs.

Accommodation

Restaurants

Cafés, pubs & bars

Advertisers' Index

Please refer to the relevant sections for addresses/telephone numbers

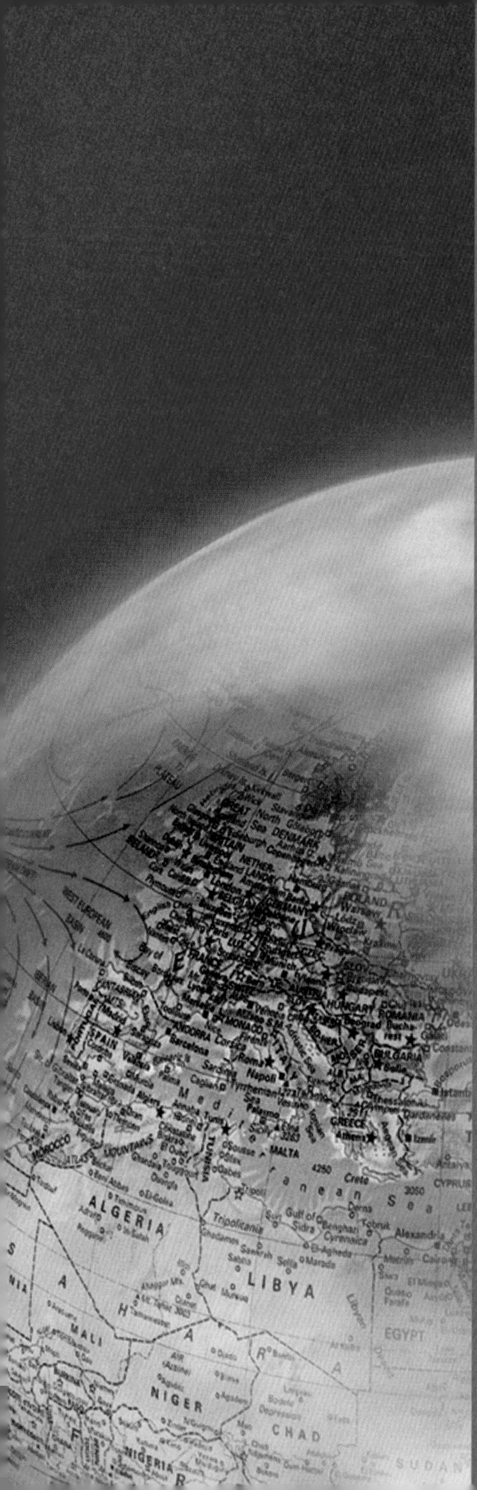

Place of interest and/or entertainment	
Railway stations	
Metro stations	Ⓜ
Parks	
Pedestrian zones	
Churches	✚
Steps	
Area name	JOSEFOV

Maps

Trips Out of Town

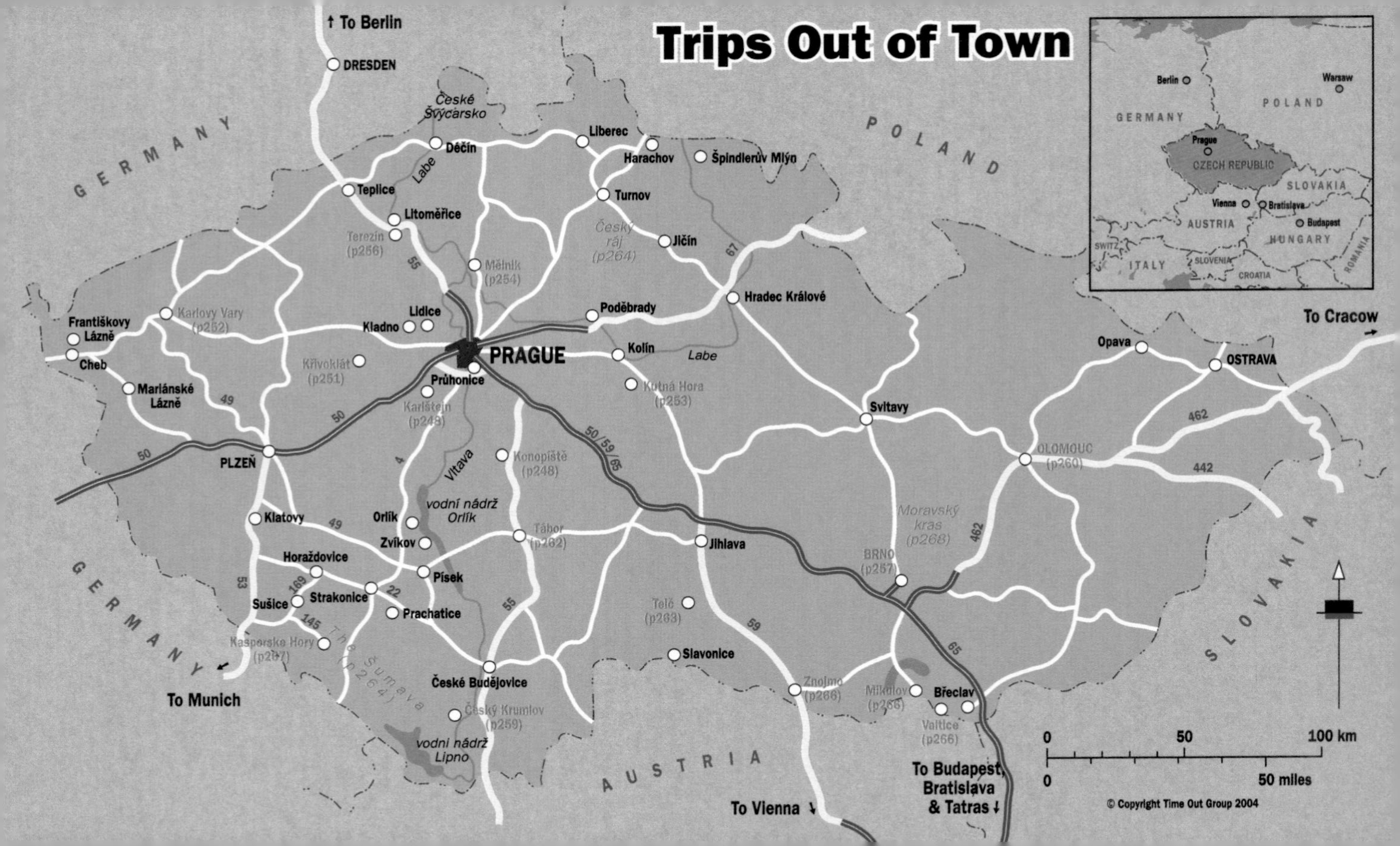

Prague Overview

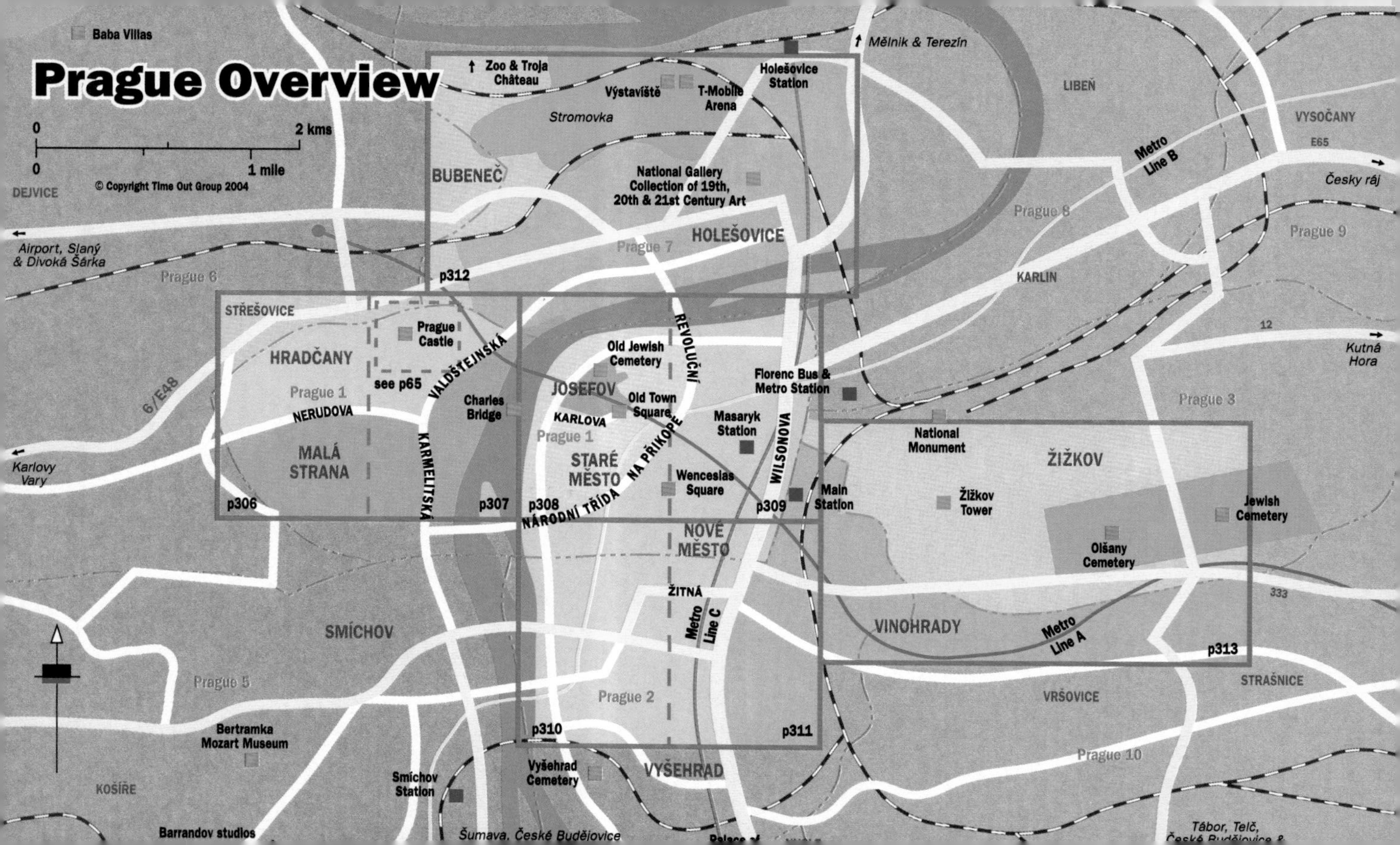

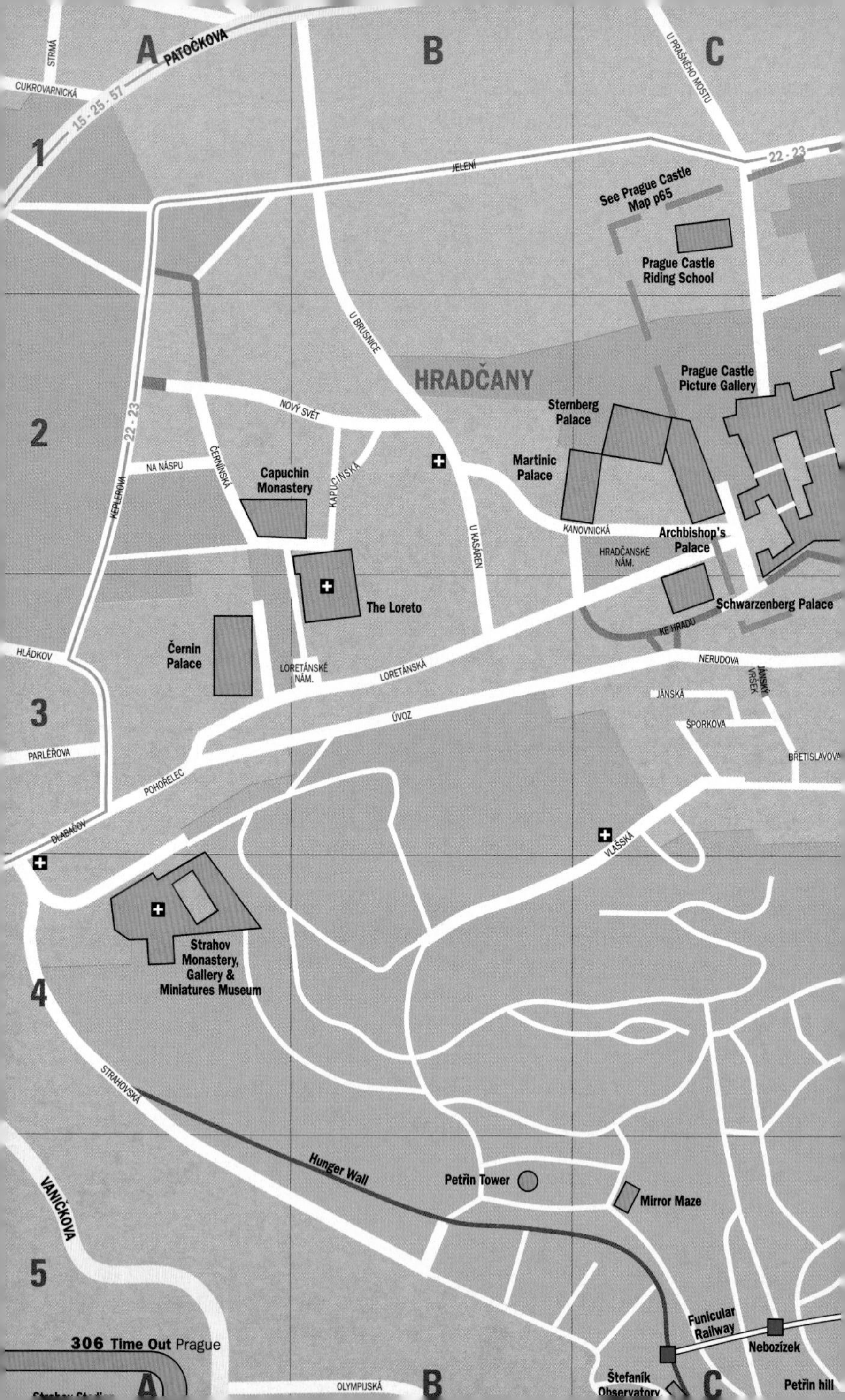
A
B
C
1
2
3
4
5
PATOČKOVA
STRMÁ
CUKROVARNICKÁ
15 - 25 - 57
U PRAŠNÉHO MOSTU
22 - 23
JELENÍ
See Prague Castle Map p65
Prague Castle Riding School
U BRUSNICE
HRADČANY
Prague Castle Picture Gallery
Sternberg Palace
NOVÝ SVĚT
Martinic Palace
22 - 23
KEPLEROVA
NA NÁSPU
ČERNÍNSKÁ
Capuchin Monastery
KAPUCÍNSKÁ
U KASÁREN
KANOVNICKÁ
Archbishop's Palace
HRADČANSKÉ NÁM.
The Loreto
Schwarzenberg Palace
KE HRADU
Černín Palace
HLÁDKOV
LORETÁNSKÉ NÁM.
LORETÁNSKÁ
NERUDOVA
JÁNSKÝ VRŠEK
JÁNSKÁ
ÚVOZ
ŠPORKOVA
PARLÉŘOVA
BŘETISLAVOVA
POHOŘELEC
DLABAČOV
VLAŠSKÁ
Strahov Monastery, Gallery & Miniatures Museum
STRAHOVSKÁ
Hunger Wall
Petřín Tower
Mirror Maze
VANIČKOVA
Funicular Railway
Nebozízek
OLYMPIJSKÁ
Štefaník Observatory
Petřín hill

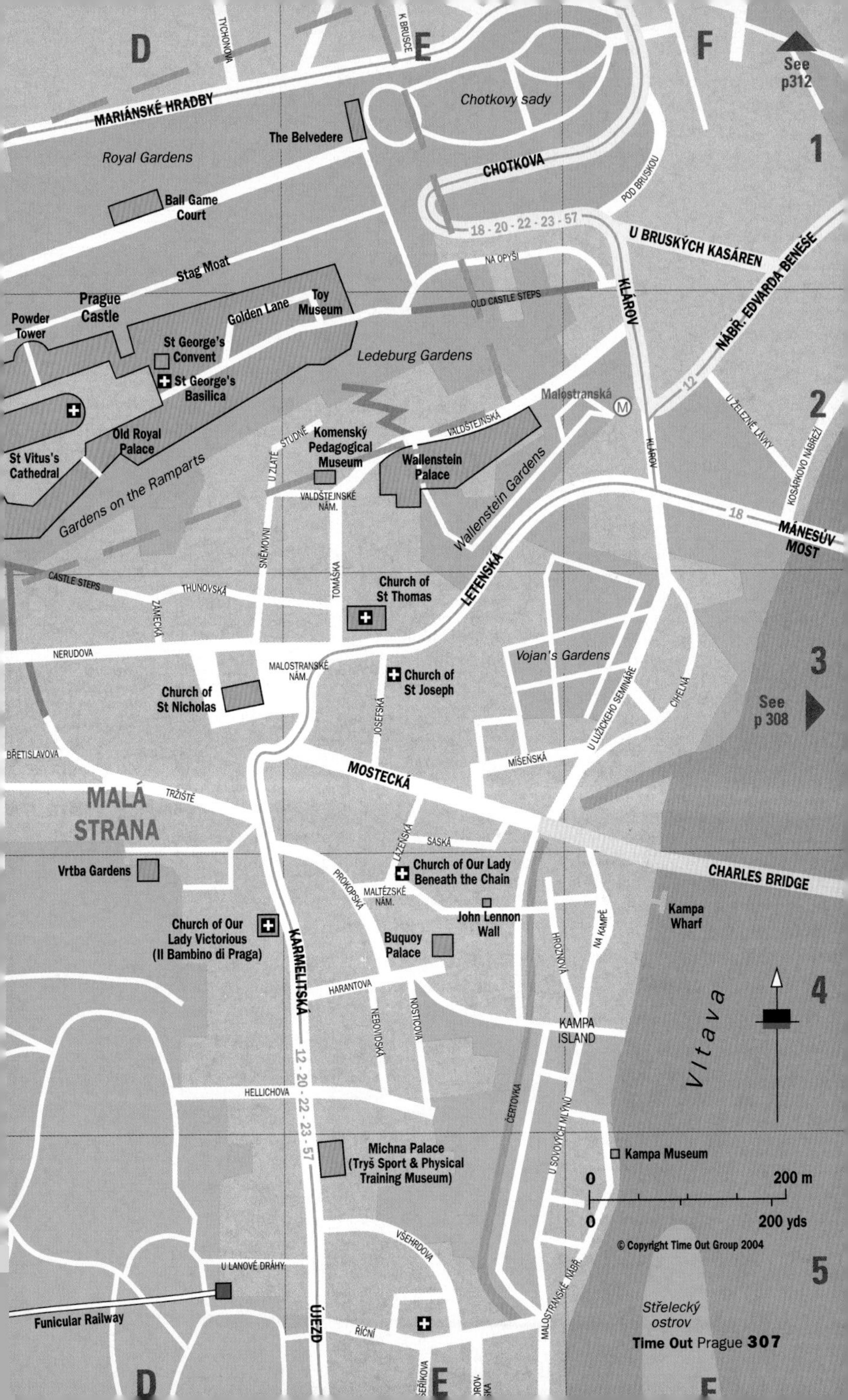
D
E
F
See p312
TYCHONOVA
K BRUSCE
MARIÁNSKÉ HRADBY
Chotkovy sady
The Belvedere
Royal Gardens
1
CHOTKOVA
POD BRUSKOU
Ball Game Court
18 - 20 - 22 - 23 - 57
U BRUSKÝCH KASÁREN
NÁBŘ. EDVARDA BENEŠE
NA OPYŠI
Stag Moat
KLÁROV
Prague Castle
Toy Museum
OLD CASTLE STEPS
Powder Tower
Golden Lane
St George's Convent
Ledeburg Gardens
St George's Basilica
12
Malostranská
M
2
U ŽELEZNÉ LÁVKY
KOSÁRKOVO NÁBŘEŽÍ
Old Royal Palace
VALDŠTEJNSKÁ
U ZLATÉ STUDNĚ
Komenský Pedagogical Museum
Wallenstein Palace
St Vitus's Cathedral
Gardens on the Ramparts
Wallenstein Gardens
VALDŠTEJNSKÉ NÁM.
18
MÁNESŮV MOST
SNĚMOVNÍ
TOMÁŠKA
CASTLE STEPS
THUNOVSKÁ
ZÁMECKÁ
Church of St Thomas
LETENSKÁ
NERUDOVA
MALOSTRANSKÉ NÁM.
Vojan's Gardens
3
Church of St Joseph
Church of St Nicholas
JOSEFSKÁ
U LUŽICKÉHO SEMINÁŘE
CIHELNÁ
See p 308
BŘETISLAVOVA
MÍŠEŇSKÁ
MOSTECKÁ
TRŽIŠTĚ
MALÁ STRANA
LÁZEŇSKÁ
SASKÁ
Vrtba Gardens
Church of Our Lady Beneath the Chain
CHARLES BRIDGE
PROKOPSKÁ
MALTÉZSKÉ NÁM.
Kampa Wharf
John Lennon Wall
Church of Our Lady Victorious (Il Bambino di Praga)
KARMELITSKÁ
Buquoy Palace
HROZNOVÁ
NA KAMPĚ
HARANTOVA
4
NEBOVIDSKÁ
NOSTICOVA
KAMPA ISLAND
Vltava
HELLICHOVA
12 - 20 - 22 - 23 - 57
ČERTOVKA
U SOVOVÝCH MLÝNŮ
Michna Palace (Tryš Sport & Physical Training Museum)
Kampa Museum
0
200 m
0
200 yds
© Copyright Time Out Group 2004
VŠEHRDOVA
U LANOVÉ DRÁHY
MALOSTRANSKÉ NÁBŘ.
5
Funicular Railway
Střelecký ostrov
ÚJEZD
ŘÍČNÍ
D
E
F

Metronome
G
Letná park
H
12 - 17 - 53
J
See p312
Hanavský Pavilion
NÁBŘ. EDVARDA BENEŠE
Vltava
1
12
U PLOVÁRNY
ČECHŮV MOST
ČECHŮV WHARF
NA FRANTIŠKU
KLÁŠTERSKÁ
KOZÍ
St Agnes's Convent
NÁM. CURIEOVÝCH
DUŠNÍ
U MILOSRDNÝCH
RÁSNOVKA
KOSÁRKOVO NÁBŘEŽÍ
DVOŘÁKOVO NÁBŘ.
PAŘÍŽSKÁ
17 - 53
U OBECNÍHO DVORA
HAŠTALSKÉ NÁM.
BŘEHOVÁ
EL. KRÁSNOHORSKÉ
BÍLKOVA
JOSEFOV
2
U STARÉ ŠKOLY
Spanish Synagogue
HAŠTALSKÁ
RÁMOVÁ
Old Jewish Cemetery
Kafka Statue
VĚZEŇSKÁ
Old-New Synagogue
Rudolfinum
17. LISTOPADU
Klausen Synagogue
V KOLKOVNĚ
DLOUHÁ
KOZÍ
MÁNESŮV MOST
18
Museum of Decorative Arts
ŠIROKÁ
Pinkas Synagogue
MASNÁ
NÁM. J. PALACHA
KOSTEČNÁ
SALVÁTORSKÁ
DUŠNÍ
MALÁ ŠTUPARTSKÁ
ALŠOVO NÁBŘ.
KAPROVA
MAISELOVA
PAŘÍŽSKÁ
DLOUHÁ
TÝNSKÁ ULIČKA
TÝNSKÁ
JÁCHYMOVA
Staroměstská
3
See p307
VALENTINSKÁ
ŽATECKÁ
Kinský Palace
House of the Gold Ring
Church of St James
Jan Hus Monument
Týn (Ungelt)
Church of St Nicholas
House at the Stone Bell
VELESLAVÍNOVÁ
MIKULÁŠSKÁ
ŠTUPARTSKÁ
OLD TOWN SQUARE
PLATNÉŘSKÁ
Church of Our Lady before Týn
KŘIŽOVNICKÁ
PLATNÉŘSKÁ
MARIÁNSKÉ NÁM.
U RADNICE
Old Town Hall
CELETNÁ
LINHARTSKÁ
Astronomical Clock
Church of St Francis
Clementinum
Clam-Gallas Palace
HUSOVA
MALÉ NÁM.
ŽELEZNÁ
Carolinum
OVOCNÝ TRH
CHARLES BRIDGE
KŘIŽOVNICKÉ NÁM.
SEMINÁŘSKÁ
KOŽNÁ
KARLOVA
KARLOVA
MELANTRICHOVA
STARÉ MĚSTO
Estates Theatre
House of the Lords of Kunštát & Poděbrady
LILIOVÁ
JALOVCOVÁ
4
ANENSKÉ NÁM.
ANENSKÁ
ŘETĚZOVÁ
Church of St Gall
HAVÍŘSKÁ
NOVOTNÉHO LÁVKA
MICHALSKÁ
NA ZÁBRADLÍ
17 - 18 - 53
HUSOVA
JILSKÁ
HAVELSKÁ
PROVAZNICKÁ
NA MŮSTKU
Bethlehem Chapel
Museum of Communism
NÁPRSTKOVA
VEJVODOVA
V KOTCÍCH
RYTÍŘSKÁ
Můstek
SMETANOVO NÁBŘ.
BETLÉMSKÉ NÁM.
BORŠOV
UHELNÝ TRH
KAROLINY
Náprstek Museum
SKOŘEPKA
28. ŘÍJNA
WENCESLAS SQUARE
BETLÉMSKÁ
PERLOVA
DIVADELNÍ
Rotunda of the Holy Cross
KONVIKTSKÁ
NA PERŠTÝNĚ
MARTINSKÁ
Church of Our Lady of the Snows
0
200 m
5
0
200 yds
BARTOLOMĚJSKÁ
JUNGMANNOVO NÁM.
SVĚTLÉ
NÁRODNÍ TŘÍDA
© Copyright Time Out Group 2004
JUNGMANNOVA
Franciscan Gardens
KROCÍNOVA
See p310
18 - 21 - 22 - 23 - 53 - 57 - 58
G
H
Národní
CHARVÁTOVA
J

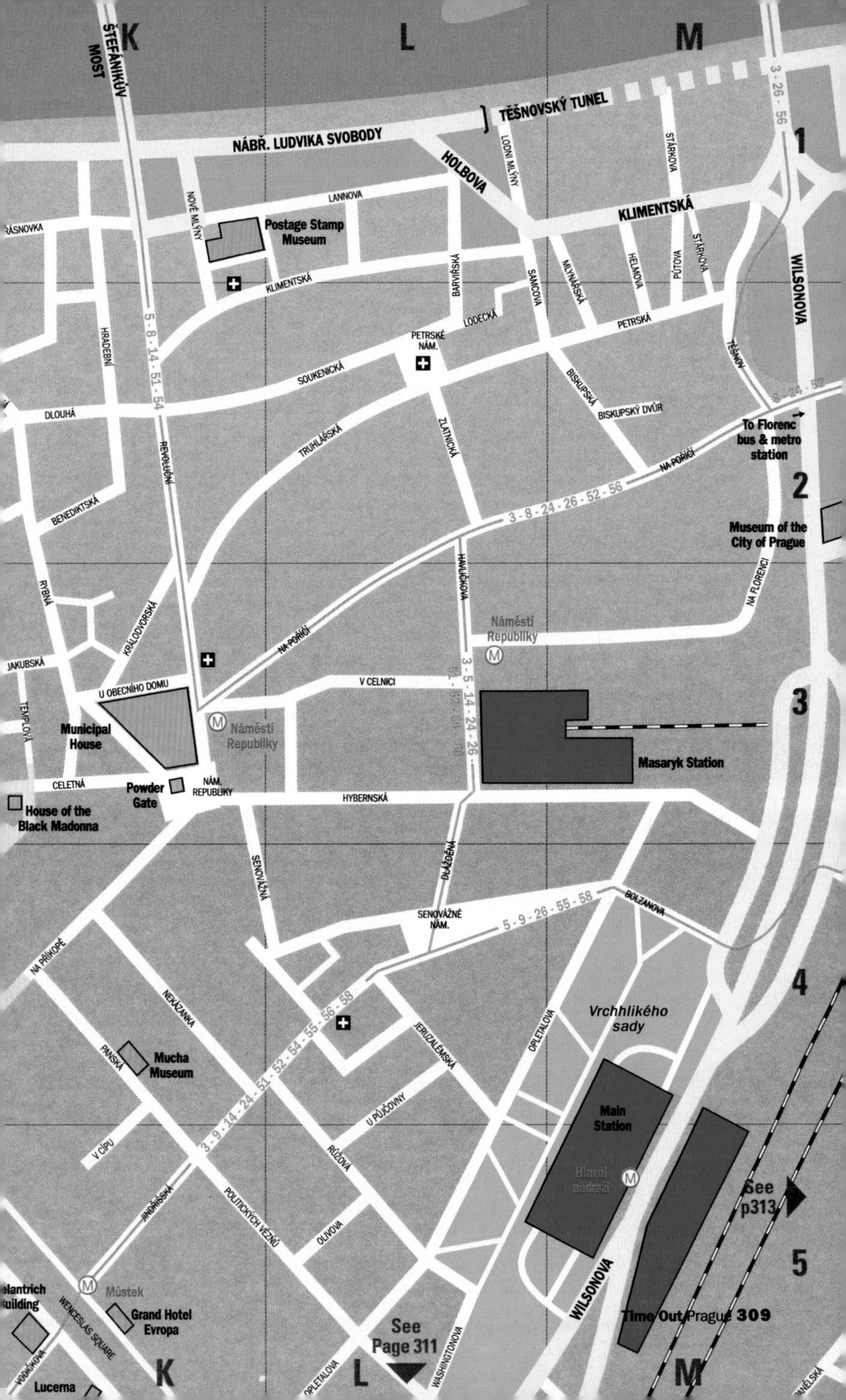
K
L
M
1
2
3
4
5
ŠTEFÁNIKŮV MOST
TĚŠNOVSKÝ TUNEL
NÁBŘ. LUDVIKA SVOBODY
HOLBOVA
LODNÍ MLÝNY
STÁRKOVA
KLIMENTSKÁ
LANNOVA
NOVÉ MLÝNY
Postage Stamp Museum
KLIMENTSKÁ
BARVÍŘSKÁ
SAMCOVA
MLYNÁŘSKÁ
HELMOVA
PŮTOVA
STÁRKOVA
WILSONOVA
LODECKÁ
PETRSKÁ
TĚŠNOV
PETRSKÉ NÁM.
HRADEBNÍ
SOUKENICKÁ
BISKUPSKÁ
BISKUPSKÝ DVŮR
DLOUHÁ
5 - 8 - 14 - 51 - 54
8 - 24 - 52
To Florenc bus & metro station
TRUHLÁŘSKÁ
ZLATNICKÁ
REVOLUČNÍ
NA POŘÍČÍ
BENEDIKTSKÁ
3 - 8 - 24 - 26 - 52 - 56
3 - 26 - 56
Museum of the City of Prague
HAVLÍČKOVA
NA FLORENCI
RYBNÁ
KRÁLODVORSKÁ
Náměstí Republiky
NA POŘÍČÍ
JAKUBSKÁ
V CELNICI
3 - 5 - 14 - 24 - 26
U OBECNÍHO DOMU
Náměstí Republiky
TEMPLOVÁ
Municipal House
Masaryk Station
CELETNÁ
Powder Gate
NÁM. REPUBLIKY
HYBERNSKÁ
House of the Black Madonna
SENOVÁŽNÁ
DLÁŽDĚNÁ
BOLZANOVA
SENOVÁŽNÉ NÁM.
5 - 9 - 26 - 55 - 58
NA PŘÍKOPĚ
NEKÁZANKA
OPLETALOVA
Vrchlického sady
JERUZALÉMSKÁ
PANSKÁ
Mucha Museum
3 - 9 - 14 - 24 - 51 - 52 - 54 - 55 - 56 - 58
U PŮJČOVNY
Main Station
V CÍPU
RŮŽOVA
Hlavní nádraží
See p313
JINDŘIŠSKÁ
POLITICKÝCH VĚZŇŮ
OLIVOVA
WILSONOVA
Můstek
Grand Hotel Evropa
WENCESLAS SQUARE
VODIČKOVA
Lucerna
See Page 311
WASHINGTONOVA
OPLETALOVA

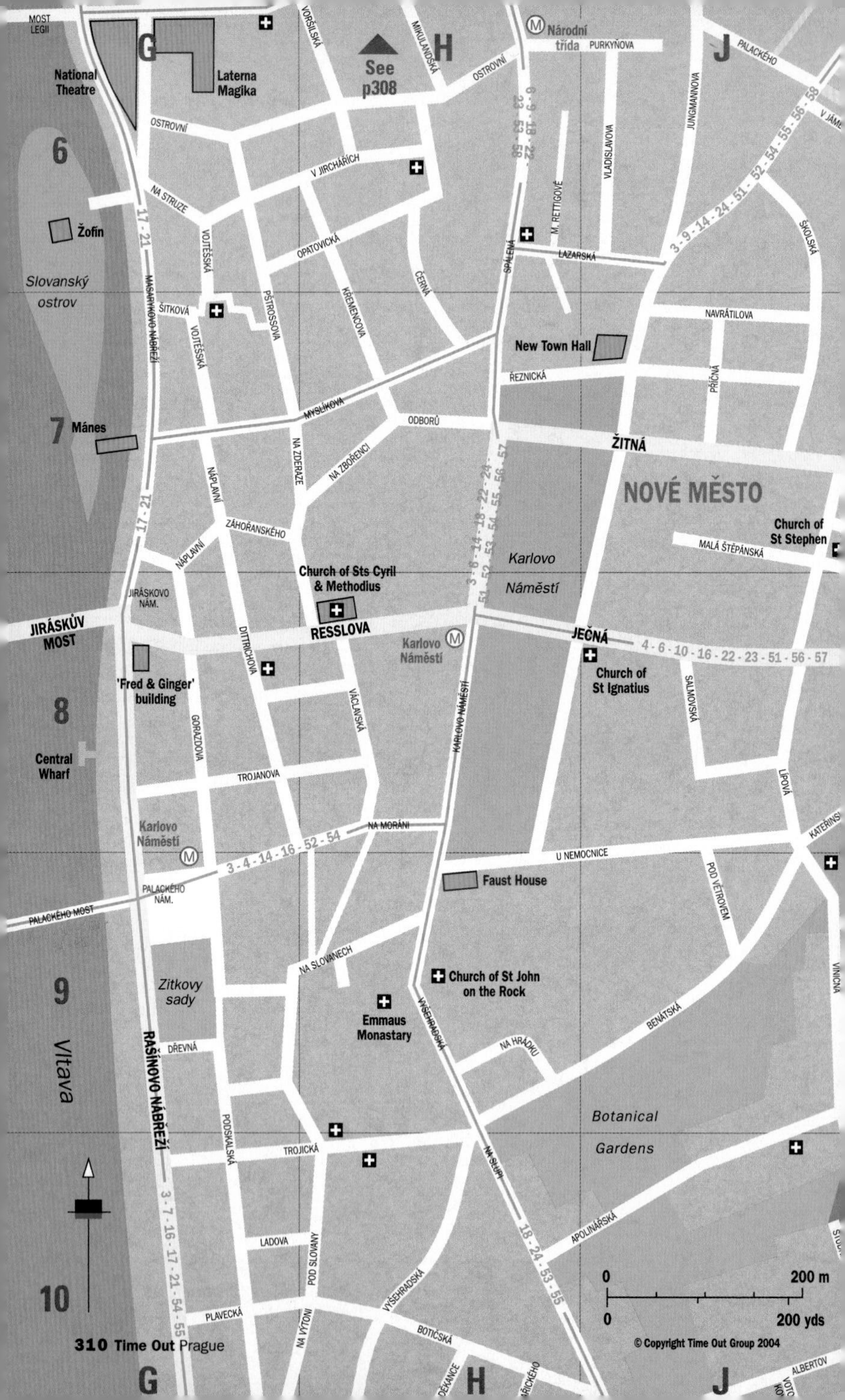
MOST LEGII
G
H
J
See p308
National Theatre
Laterna Magika
Národní třída
PURKYŇOVA
PALACKÉHO
VORŠILSKÁ
MIKULANDSKÁ
OSTROVNÍ
6 · 9 · 18 · 22 · 23 · 53 · 58
JUNGMANNOVA
V JÁME
3 · 9 · 14 · 24 · 51 · 52 · 54 · 55 · 56 · 58
6
V JIRCHÁŘÍCH
VLADISLAVOVA
M. RETTIGOVÉ
NA STRUZE
Žofín
17 · 21
OPATOVICKÁ
ČERNÁ
LAZARSKÁ
ŠKOLSKÁ
SPÁLENÁ
VOJTĚŠSKÁ
Slovanský ostrov
MASARYKOVO NÁBŘEŽÍ
ŠITKOVÁ
PŠTROSSOVA
KŘEMENCOVA
NAVRÁTILOVA
New Town Hall
ŘEZNICKÁ
PŘÍČNÁ
MYSLÍKOVA
7
Mánes
ODBORŮ
ŽITNÁ
NA ZDERAZE
NA ZBOŘENCI
NÁPLAVNÍ
3 · 6 · 14 · 18 · 22 · 24 · 51 · 52 · 53 · 54 · 55 · 56 · 57
NOVÉ MĚSTO
Church of St Stephen
ZÁHOŘANSKÉHO
MALÁ ŠTĚPÁNSKÁ
Karlovo Náměstí
Church of Sts Cyril & Methodius
JIRÁSKOVO NÁM.
JIRÁSKŮV MOST
RESSLOVA
Karlovo Náměstí
JEČNÁ
4 · 6 · 10 · 16 · 22 · 23 · 51 · 56 · 57
DITTRICHOVA
Church of St Ignatius
'Fred & Ginger' building
VÁCLAVSKÁ
KARLOVO NÁMĚSTÍ
SALMOVSKÁ
8
GORAZDOVA
Central Wharf
TROJANOVA
LÍPOVÁ
Karlovo Náměstí
NA MORÁNI
KATEŘINSKÁ
3 · 4 · 14 · 16 · 52 · 54
U NEMOCNICE
PALACKÉHO NÁM.
PALACKÉHO MOST
Faust House
POD VĚTROVEM
NA SLOVANECH
9
Zitkovy sady
Church of St John on the Rock
VINIČNÁ
Emmaus Monastary
Vltava
VYŠEHRADSKÁ
BENÁTSKÁ
DŘEVNÁ
NA HRÁDKU
RAŠÍNOVO NÁBŘEŽÍ
PODSKALSKÁ
Botanical Gardens
TROJICKÁ
NA SLUPI
3 · 7 · 16 · 17 · 21 · 54 · 55
18 · 24 · 53 · 55
APOLINÁŘSKÁ
LADOVA
POD SLOVANY
10
VYŠEHRADSKÁ
0
200 m
0
200 yds
PLAVECKÁ
NA VÝTONI
BOTIČSKÁ
ALBERTOV
© Copyright Time Out Group 2004

K
L
M
Lucerna
WENCESLAS SQUARE
OPLETALOVA
See p309
WASHINGTONOVA
WILSONOVA
State Opera
LEGEROVA
ŠPANĚLSKÁ
HELÉNSKÁ
6
NA SMETANCE
St Wenceslas Statue
Muzeum
MÁNESOVA
National Museum
VINOHRADSKÁ
11
ŠTĚPÁNSKÁ
VE SMEČKÁCH
KRAKOVSKÁ
MEZIBRANSKÁ
Čelokovského sady
VINOHRADY
See p313
ŘÍMSKÁ
ŠKRÉTOVA
RUBEŠOVA
BALBÍNOVA
ITALSKÁ
7
ŽITNÁ
ANGLICKÁ
Rotunda of St Longinus
ŘÍMSKÁ
IBSENOVA
ŠUBERTOVA
NA RYBNÍČKU
V TŮNÍCH
HÁLKOVA
SOKOLSKÁ
MIKOVCOVA
BĚLEHRADSKÁ
LONDÝNSKÁ
VOCELOVA
NÁMĚSTÍ MÍRU
Church of St Ludmila
JEČNÁ
I P Pavlova
JUGOSLÁVSKÁ
4 - 10 - 16 - 22 - 23 - 51 - 57
LEGEROVA
LUBLAŇSKÁ
TYLOVO NÁM.
Náměstí Míru
8
KATEŘINSKÁ
AMERICKÁ
RUMUNSKÁ
KE KARLOVU
Dvořák Museum
BĚLEHRADSKÁ
NA BOJIŠTI
URUGUAYSKÁ
TYRŠOVA
BRUSELSKÁ
BELGICKÁ
9
LONDÝNSKÁ
KOUBKOVA
ZÁHŘEBSKÁ
FŮGNEROVO NÁM.
LEGEROVA
SOKOLSKÁ
APOLINÁŘSKÁ
KE KARLOVU
6 - 11 - 56
JANA MASARYKA
ŠAFAŘÍKOVA
WENZIGOVA
U ZVONAŘKY
LUBLAŇSKÁ
POD NUSELSKÝMI SCHODY
10
Folimanka park
Police Museum
Na Karlově
K
L
M

A
B
C
D
E
1
2
3
Troja Château & the Zoo
Holešovice Station
Nádraží Holešovice
VRBENSKÉHO
PLYNÁRNÍ
JANKOVCOVA
ŽELEZNIČÁŘŮ
HOLEŠOVICE
Lunapark
Stromovka
Křižík Fountain
Výstaviště
T-Mobile Arena
Lapidárium
Planetarium
Šlechtovka
BUBENEČ
PARTYZÁNSKÁ
U VÝSTAVIŠTĚ
STROJNICKÁ
žel st. Praha-Bubny
ARGENTINSKÁ
DĚLNICKÁ
ZA VIADUKTEM
BUBENSKÁ
National Gallery Collection of 19th, 20th & 21st Century Art
DUKELSKÝCH HRDINŮ
VELETRŽNÍ
MILADY HORÁKOVÉ
KORUNOVAČNÍ
POD KAŠTANY
Stadion Sparta Praha
ANTONÍNSKÁ
Vltavská
BUBENSKÉ NÁBŘEŽÍ
NÁBŘ KPT. JAROŠE
Vltava
Ostrov Štvanice
HLÁVKŮV MOST
LETENSKÝ TUNEL
National Technical Museum
Letná park (Letenské sady)
Metronome
ŠTEFÁNIKŮV MOST
NÁBŘ. EDVARDA BENEŠE
BADENIHO
CHOTKOVA
Bílek Villa
Chotkovy sady
ROHANSKÉ NÁBŘEŽÍ
See p307
See pp308-309
0
400 m
400 yds
© Copyright Time Out Group 2004

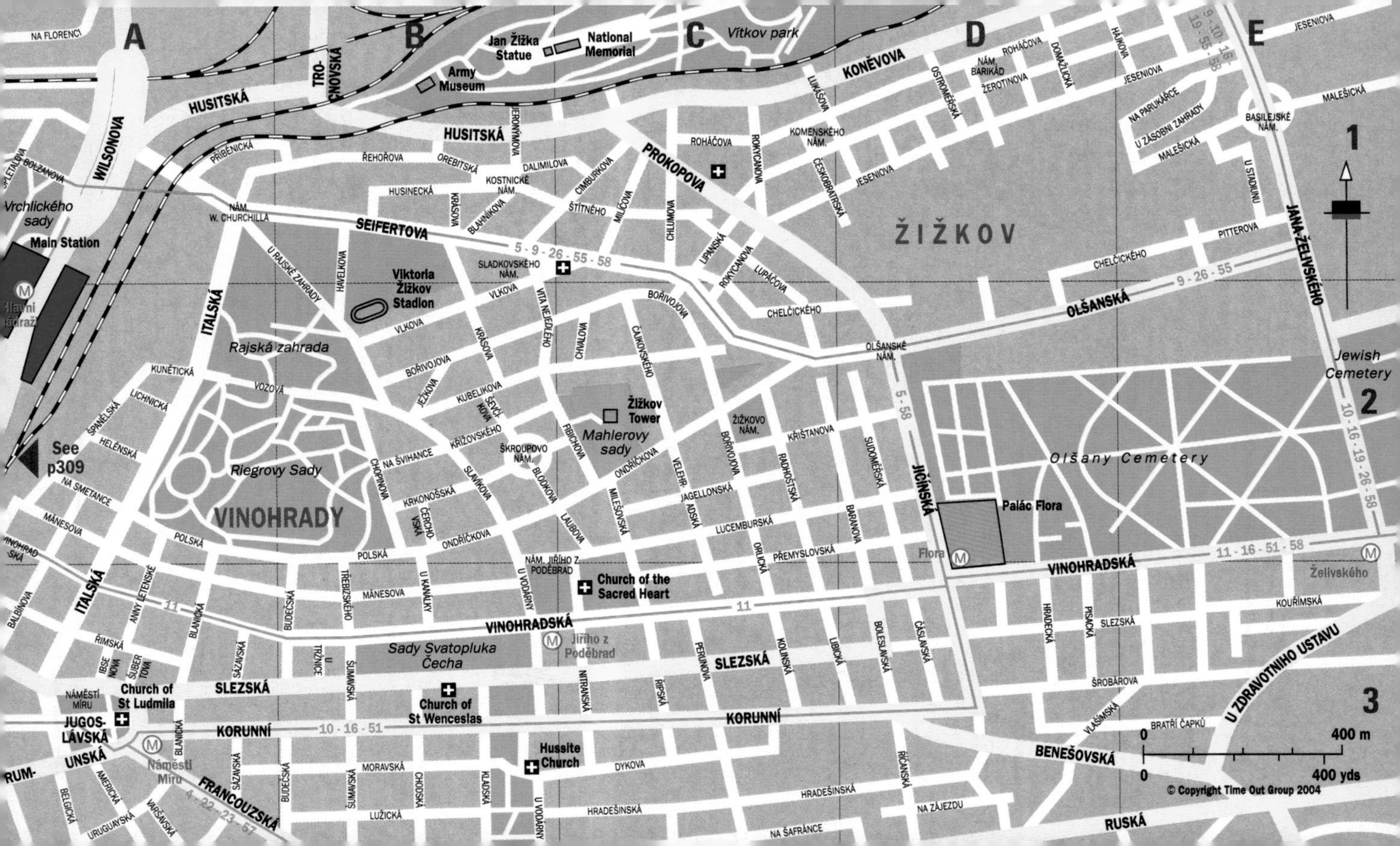

A
B
C
D
E
1
2
3
Vítkov park
Jan Žižka Statue
National Memorial
Army Museum
KOŇEVOVA
HUSITSKÁ
WILSONOVA
TRO-CNOVSKÁ
PROKOPOVA
SEIFERTOVA
NÁM. W. CHURCHILLA
Vrchlického sady
Main Station
Hlavní nádraží
ŽIŽKOV
JANA-ŽELIVSKÉHO
OLŠANSKÁ
OLŠANSKÉ NÁM.
Jewish Cemetery
Olšany Cemetery
Palác Flora
Flora
JIČÍNSKÁ
VINOHRADSKÁ
Želivského
Viktoria Žižkov Stadion
Žižkov Tower
Mahlerovy sady
Rajská zahrada
Riegrovy Sady
VINOHRADY
ITALSKÁ
NÁM. JIŘÍHO Z PODĚBRAD
Church of the Sacred Heart
Jiřího z Poděbrad
Sady Svatopluka Čecha
SLEZSKÁ
KORUNNÍ
Church of St Ludmila
Church of St Wenceslas
Hussite Church
Náměstí Míru
NÁMĚSTÍ MÍRU
JUGOSLÁVSKÁ
FRANCOUZSKÁ
BENEŠOVSKÁ
U ZDRAVOTNIHO USTAVU
RUSKÁ
0
400 m
400 yds
© Copyright Time Out Group 2004

See p309

Street Index

Prague Metro

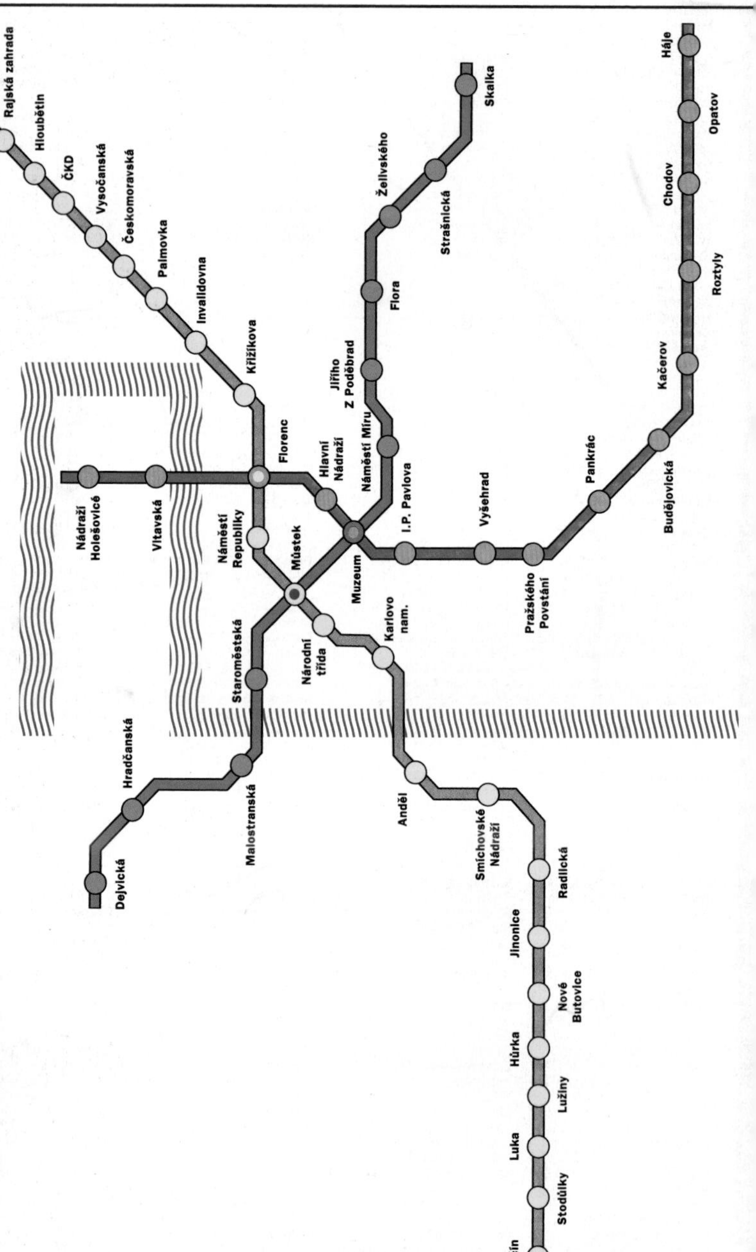